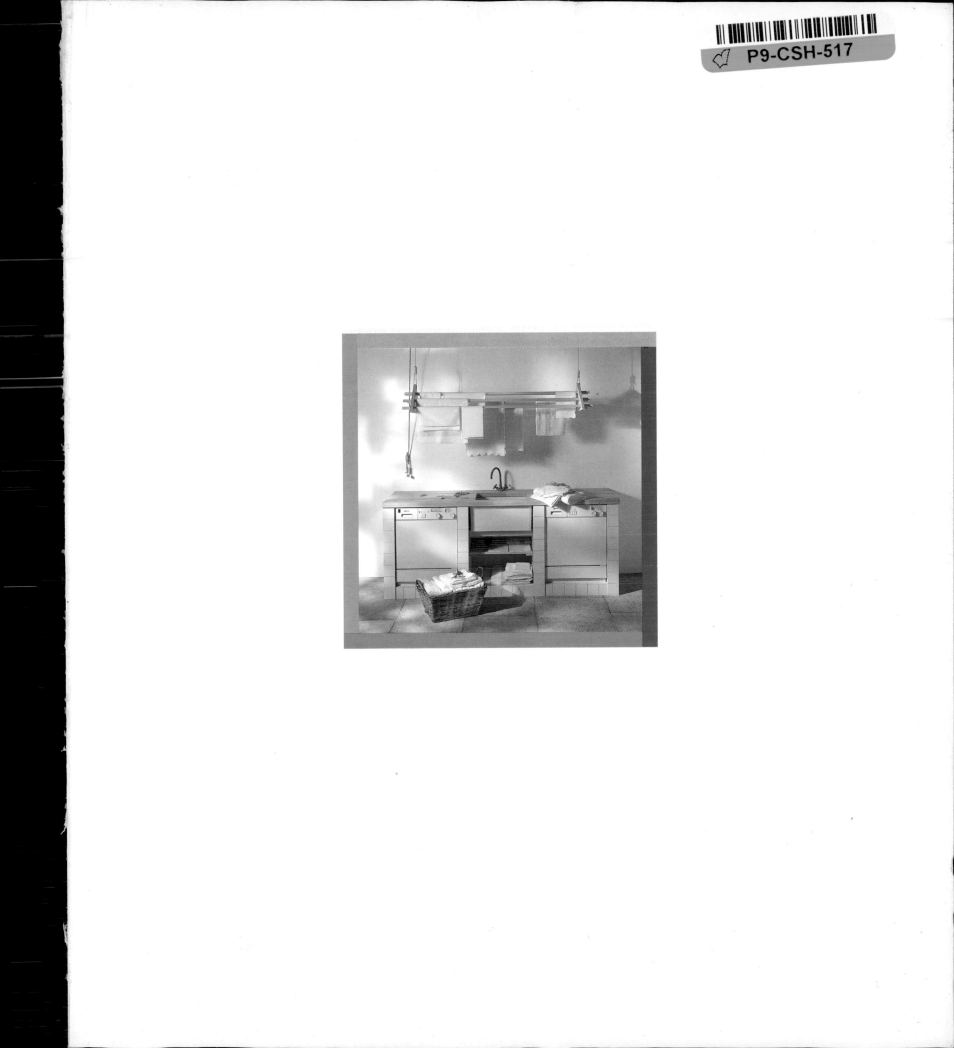

TERENCE CONRAN'S

HOUSE & GARDEN DESIGN PROJECTS

Over 45 projects and
hundreds of ideas for
making the most of your
home — inside and out

CONSULTANT EDITORS
**JOHN McGOWAN
& ROGER DuBERN**

PROJECT PHOTOGRAPHY
**HUGH JOHNSON
& NADIA MacKENZIE**

conran
OCTOPUS

First published as two separate titles; *Terence Conran's DIY by Design* and *Terence Conran's Garden DIY*, 1989 and 1991
by Conran Octopus Limited
a part of Octopus Publishing Group Ltd
2–4 Heron Quays
London E14 4JP

This new formatted edition published 2000 by Conran Octopus Ltd

Reprinted in 2002

British Library Cataloguing in Publication Data

A catalogue record for this book is available from the British Library

ISBN 1 84091 272 3

Typset by Servis Filmsetting Limited
Printed and bound in China

Consultant Editors JOHN MCGOWAN and ROGER DUBERN
Project Editor JOANNA BRADSHAW
Editors RICHARD DAWES and SIMON WILLIS
Editorial Assistant ROD MACKENZIE
Contributor ELIZABETH WILHIDE

Art Editors HELEN LEWIS and MERYL LLOYD
Design Assistant ALISON SHACKLETON
Illustrator PAUL BRYANT
Visualiser JEAN MORLEY

Photographers HUGH JOHNSON and NADIA MACKENZIE
Photographic Stylist CLAIRE LLOYD
Photographic Assistants SIMON ANDERS, SIMON LEE and PETER WILLETT

Picture Research NADINE BAZAR
Production SHANE LASK and SONYA SIBBONS

PLEASE NOTE
Before embarking on any major building work on your home, you should also check the law concerning building regulations and planning. It is also important to obtain specialist advice on plumbing, gas and electricity, before attempting any alterations to these services yourself.

While every effort has been made to ensure that all the information contained in this book is correct, the publishers cannot be held responsible for any loss, damage or injury caused by reliance upon the accuracy of such information.

DIMENSIONS
Exact dimensions are given in metric followed by an approximate conversion to imperial. Do not mix metric and imperial dimensions when you are making a calculation.

CONTENTS

CONTENTS

Contents

INTRODUCTION
TO HOUSE PROJECTS

There is a growing passion for improving houses and apartments as people young and old, rich and poor, take satisfaction in making their homes comfortable and stylish. People everywhere restore, revamp, repair and revitalize their homes, and in doing so many have discovered the pleasure of doing-it-themselves.

This is a book that encourages the use of the talents of a designer as well as the traditional DIY crafts and skills of carpentry, decorating, plastering and so forth. I have taken the simple, practical, everyday things around the house – the things for which we most often turn to DIY, such as a set of shelves for books or a more congenial bathroom arrangement – and

have shown how they can be designed and constructed to give you a stylish solution. For every room there are complete projects which will benefit any home. The way you finish them is entirely up to you and your choice of finish will personalize your work and make it *your* home.

Take, for example, the kitchen projects. These show how to create a completely new kitchen to fit any size room, or how to improve an existing one. As with all of the projects, the basic structures can be adapted and used in many different ways around the house. The appearance of the finished work will differ markedly by your choice of tiles,

laminate or wood surfaces, paint and stain colours, and by what goes into the kitchen when it is in use.

In addition to the projects, I have given ideas and inspiration to assist you with your DIY. The work of architects and designers, as well as amateurs and enthusiasts around the world, illustrates the opportunities that exist for dedicated home improvers to enhance the function and appearance of their homes, with style and by design.

I have started the book with a workbench and tool cupboard. Get them right and they will provide the example and temptation to encourage you to continue the good work elsewhere in the house.

Terence Conran.

TOOLS, MATERIALS AND TECHNIQUES

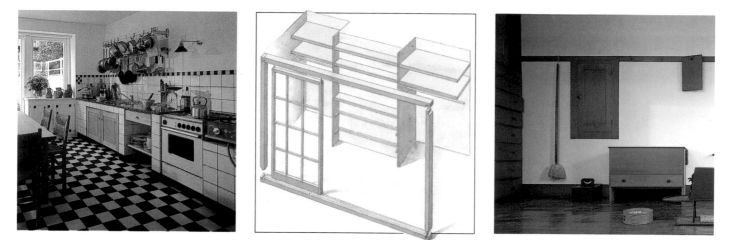

Part 1 contains all the technical information you need to build the projects in this book. Essential tools, materials and techniques are described in full, and are accompanied, where relevant, by explanatory diagrams. To help you locate the techniques, cross references are printed in bold throughout the project text, and at the top of every page.

Parts 2, 3 and 4 of the book are divided into the three main areas of the home: Kitchens and Dining Areas, Living Rooms, Workrooms and Halls, and Bathrooms and Bedrooms. Each section contains a lengthy introduction with detailed guidance and inspirational photographs for each room, followed by DIY projects. These consist of comprehensive tools and materials lists, a photograph of the finished project, an assembly illustration and step-by-step diagrams.

Before starting work, plan each project carefully so that it can be tailored to your personal requirements. In particular, think about plumbing and electricity, so that pipe and cable runs can be modified if appropriate, so avoiding unnecessary upheaval once work has commenced.

Tools

Tools for Preparation

Adhesive spreader These are palm-size pieces of semi-flexible plastic with serrated or notched edges which are used to spread adhesives over wide surfaces, evenly, and at the correct rate. Because the size of the serrations or notches affects the spreading rate, adhesive manufacturers usually supply a spreader with their adhesives for brands where a spreader is required: mainly contact-types and tiling and flooring adhesives.

Bench stop and vice A woodwork vice is fitted to the underside of a bench, with the jaws level with the bench top. The jaws are lined and topped with hardwood to protect the work and any tools being used. Some vices also incorporate a small steel peg (a 'dog') that can be raised above the main jaw level. This allows awkward or long pieces of wood to be cramped in position when used with a bench stop which is fixed at the opposite end of the bench.

Sliding bevel (1) This is a type of square used to mark out timber at any required angle. The sliding blade can be locked against the stock by means of a locking lever and the blade can form any angle with the stock.

Marking gauge (2) Essential for setting out woodworking joints, this is used to mark both widths and thicknesses with only a light scratch. The gauge comprises a handle, on which slides a stock bearing a steel marking pin. This movable stock can be locked in any position with a thumb screw so the steel pin is fixed at a precise point.

Mortise gauge (3) Similar to a marking gauge, it has two pins, one fixed, one adjustable, to mark out both sides of a mortise at the same time. Some types have an additional pin fixed below the beam so that the tool can be used as a marking gauge.

Profile gauge This is also called a shape tracer or a scribing gauge. It comprises a row of steel pins or plastic fingers held in a central bar. When pressed against an object, like a skirting board, the pins follow the shape of the object.

Marking knife Used to score a thin line for a saw or chisel to follow, ensuring a precise cut. The flat face of the knife can be run against the blade of a try square or straight-edge.

Mitre box A simple open-topped wooden box which is used to guide saws into materials at a fixed 45° or 90° angle, to ensure a square cut.

Plumb bob and chalk A plumb line is used to check verticals and mark accurate vertical lines, in chalk, on walls. A plumb bob is simply a pointed weight attached to a long length of string. Before use, the string can be rubbed with a stick of coloured chalk. Hold the string in the required position at the top, wait for the plumb bob to stop swinging, then carefully press the string against the wall at the bottom and then pluck the string to leave a line on the wall. More expensive models of plumb bobs incorporate line winders and powdered chalk containers which automatically dust the line with chalk as it is withdrawn.

Portable workbench A collapsible, portable workbench is vital for woodworking. A large, fixed workbench in a garage or shed is important, but the major advantage of the portable type is that it is lightweight and can be carried to the job, where it provides sturdy support when final adjustments have to be made.

A portable bench is like a giant vice – the worksurface comprises two sections which can be opened wide or closed tightly according to the dimensions of the work and the nature of the task. It can hold large and awkward objects.

Scribing block To fit an item neatly against a wall (which is very unlikely to be completely flat),

the item has to be 'scribed' flat to the wall using a small block of wood and a pencil (see **Techniques, page 31**). A scribing block is simply an offcut of wood measuring about 25 × 25 × 25mm (1 × 1 × 1in). The block is held against the wall, a sharp pencil is held against the opposite end of the block, and the block and the pencil are moved in a unit along the wall to mark a line on the item to be fitted. If you cut to this line, the item will then fit tightly against the wall.

Spirit level (9) Used for checking that surfaces are horizontal or vertical. A 100cm (36in) long level is the most useful all-round size. An aluminium or steel level will withstand knocks and it can be either I-girder or box-shaped in section. Ideally, a 250mm (10in) 'torpedo' spirit level is also useful to have, for working in confined spaces such as alcoves and inside cupboards. It may be used with a straight-edge over longer surfaces.

Steel measuring tape A 3m (3yd) or 5m (5yd) long, lockable tape (metal or plastic) is best, and one with a top window in the casing makes it easier to read measurements.

Steel rule Since the rule is made of steel, the graduations are indelible and very precise. A rule graduated on both sides in metric and imperial is the most useful. The rule also serves as a precise straight-edge for marking cutting lines.

Straight-edge Can be made from a length of 50 × 25mm (2 × 1in) scrap wood. It is used to tell whether a surface is flat and also for checking whether two points are aligned with each other.

Trimming knife A razor-sharp blade which is used to mark extremely accurate cutting lines and for a wide range of trimming jobs. The type with a retractable blade is the safest to use.

Try square (4) An L-shaped precision tool comprising a steel blade and stock (or handle)

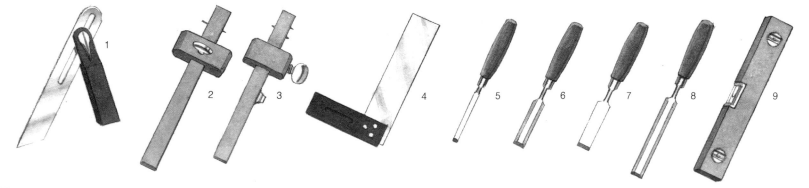

set at a perfect right-angle to each other on both the inside and outside edges. Used for marking right-angles and for checking a square.

SUPPLEMENTARY TOOLS

Drill stand Enables a power drill to be used with extreme accuracy when, for example, joining dowelling (*see* **Techniques, page 30**). The hole will be perpendicular to the surface and its depth can be carefully controlled. The drill is lowered on to the work with a spring-loaded lever which gives good control and accuracy.

Metal detector Pinpoints metal objects such as electric cables and water and gas pipes hidden in walls, ceilings and floors. Electronically operated, it buzzes or flashes when metal is found.

TOOLS FOR SHARPENING AND CUTTING

Chisels Used to cut slots in wood or to pare off thin slivers. Some chisels may be used with a mallet when cutting slots. When new, a chisel's cutting edge is ground and must be honed with an oilstone to sharpen it.

Mortise chisel (5) Used with a mallet for cutting deep slots.

Firmer chisel (7) For general DIY use around the home.

Bevel-edge chisel (6) Used for undercutting in confined spaces, such as when making dovetail joints.

Paring chisel (8) Has a long blade for cutting deep joints or long housings.

Dowelling jig A simple dowelling jig cramps on to a piece of work, ensuring that the drill is aligned accurately over the centre of the dowel hole to be drilled. It also guides the drill vertically.

DRILLS

Hand drill (10) For drilling holes for screws or for making large holes, particularly in wood. It will make holes in metal and is useful where there is no power source. A handle attached to a toothed wheel is used to turn the drill in its chuck.

Power drill (11) These range from a simple, single-speed model (which will drill holes only in soft materials) to a multi-speed drill with electric control. Most jobs call for something in between the two, such as a two-speed drill with hammer action. The two speeds enable most hard materials to be drilled and the hammer action means that you can also drill into the hardest walls.

DRILL BITS

You will need a selection of twist bits in various sizes and of different types for wood and metal, for use with a drill.

Auger bit (17) Has a tapered, square shank that fits into a carpenter's brace. It is used to make deep holes in wood, the usual lengths being up to 250mm (10in). Diameters range from 6mm ($\frac{1}{4}$in) to 38mm ($1\frac{1}{2}$in). The tip has a screw thread to draw the bit into the wood.

Flat bit (16) Is used with an electric drill. It has a point at the end of the shank and its flat shank end allows it to slot into the drill chuck. Diameters are from 19mm ($\frac{3}{4}$in) to 38mm ($1\frac{1}{2}$in). For maximum efficiency the bit must be turned at high speed from about 1000 to 2000 r.p.m. It can be used to drill into cross grain, end grain and also man-made boards.

Countersink bit (15) After a hole is drilled in wood, a countersink bit is used to cut a recess for the screwhead to sit in, so ensuring that it lies below the surface. Different types are available for use with a carpenter's brace and an electric drill. Head diameters are 9mm ($\frac{3}{8}$in), 12mm ($\frac{1}{2}$in) and 15mm ($\frac{9}{16}$in). Carbon-steel bits are used on wood, but high-speed steel bits can be used for wood, plastic or metal.

Twist drill bit (13) Used with an electric drill for drilling small holes in wood and metal. Carbon-steel drills are for wood, drilling into metal requires a high-speed steel drill.

Dowel bit (12) Used to make dowel holes in wood. The tip has two cutting spurs on the side and a centre point to prevent the bit from wandering off centre. Diameters range from 3mm ($\frac{1}{8}$in) to 12mm ($\frac{1}{2}$in).

Masonry bit (14) Has a specially hardened tungsten-carbide tip for drilling into masonry to the exact size required for a wallplug. Special percussion drill bits are available for use with a hammer drill when boring into concrete.

End-mill/Hinge-sinker bit (18) Primarily used for boring 35mm ($1\frac{3}{8}$in) or 25mm (1in) diameter flat bottomed holes in cabinet and wardrobe doors to accept the hinge bosses on concealed hinges. End mills are used in electric drills, ideally fitted in drill stands, and should be set to drill no deeper than 12mm ($\frac{1}{2}$in) (fig 7 below).

Oilstone and honing guide The first sharpens and the second maintains the correct angle for sharpening chisel and plane blades. An oilstone is a rectangular block of stone with grit on both sides. Oil is used as a lubricant while the blade is being sharpened on the stone, so you will need a can of fine oil to hand.

The honing guide is an inexpensive tool which makes sharpening easier and more efficient. The blade of the tool to be sharpened is inserted at an angle and cramped in place, then the guide is repeatedly rolled back and forth on the surface of the oilstone.

Power router (19) This portable electric tool is used to cut grooves, recesses, and many types of joints in timber, as well as to shape the edge of long timber battens to form decorative mouldings. A whole range of cutting bits in different shapes and sizes is available and when fitted into the router the bits revolve at very high speed (about 25,000 r.p.m.) to cut the wood smoothly and cleanly (20). Although hand routers (which look like small planes) are available, whenever routers are referred to in this book, it is the power router to which the remarks are directed.

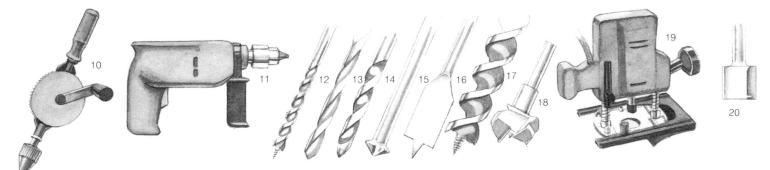

Tools

Saws

Circular saw (1) Invaluable for cutting large pieces of timber or sheets of board. It will also cut grooves and angles. The most popular size has a diameter of 187mm (7¼in). Circular saws can be extremely dangerous and must be used carefully. The piece of work must be held securely and the blade depth set so that it will not cut into anything below the work. The tool should be fitted with an upper and a lower blade guard. Support your work on scrap battens to avoid cutting into workbenches or floors.

Coping saw (2) Used to make curved or circular cuts. It has a narrow blade, which can be swivelled. When cutting, the blade can be angled as necessary so that the frame clears the edge of the work. Drill a hole close to the edge of the piece to be cut out, and thread the coping saw blade through the hole before reconnecting it to the handle and starting to cut.

Dovetail saw (3) Also called a gent's saw, this fine-tooth form of tenon saw with a stiffened back is ideal for making delicate and precise saw cuts. It is particularly useful for making dovetail joints.

Panel saws (4) Are hand saws used for rough cutting rather than fine carpentry. They have a flexible blade of 510–660mm (20–26in), and are useful for general-purpose cutting of wood and fibre boards.

Jigsaw (7) Will cut a variety of materials, and is much more versatile than a circular saw, although not as quick or powerful. It also cuts curves, intricate shapes, angles and holes in the middle of panels. The best models offer variable speeds – slow for hard materials and fast for soft. The latest models have either a reciprocating or a pendulum action. In the latter case the blade goes backwards and forwards as well as up and down, which allows for much faster cutting on straight lines.

Padsaw (5) Designed to cut holes and shapes in wood. It has a narrow, tapered blade which will cut keyholes, for example. A hole is first drilled and the saw blade is inserted to make the cut. Padsaws are useful for cutting holes for inset sinks where a power jigsaw is not available

Tenon saw (6) For cutting the tenon part of a mortise and tenon joint (see **Techniques, page 28**), and also useful for other delicate and accurate work. It has a stiffened back and the blade is about 250–300mm (10–12in) long.

Surforms Available in a range of lengths from approximately 150–250mm (6–10in), these rasps are useful for the initial shaping of wood. However, further fine finishing by hand is needed to obtain a smooth surface. The steel blade has a pattern of alternating small teeth and holes through which waste wood passes, so that the teeth do not get clogged up. When blunt, the blade is simply replaced.

Supplementary Tools

Hacksaw For cutting metal. A traditional hacksaw has a wooden handle and a solid metal frame. The blade is tensioned by a wing-nut. Modern hacksaws have a tubular frame which is adjustable for different lengths of blade. A 'junior' hacksaw is ideal for sawing small items or for working in confined spaces.

Hand Tools

Abrasive paper see **Sanding block**

Cramps

For securing glued pieces of work while they are setting. There are many types of cramp, but the G-cramp is the most commonly used and is available in a wide range of jaw sizes.

Wooden wedges are sometimes useful for securing an object while it is being glued. You can make two by cutting diagonally through a block

of wood. For instructions on how to make and use folding wedges, see page 21.

Sash cramps. These employ a long metal bar, and are indispensable for holding together large frameworks, although you can improvise in some cases by making a rope tourniquet. This consists of a piece of rope which is tied around the object, and a length of stick to twist the rope and so cramp the frame tightly.

Webbing cramp A nylon webbing cramp applies even pressure around frames when they are being assembled. The webbing, like narrow seat-belt type material, is looped around the frame, pulled as tight as possible by hand, and then finally tightened by means of a screw mechanism or ratchet winder. Webbing cramps are cheaper alternatives to sash cramps.

G-cramp (8) Also called a C-cramp or fast-action cramp, it is important for our projects that the jaws of the cramp open at least 200mm (8in). The timber to be held in the cramp is placed between the jaws which are then tightened by turning a thumb-screw, tommy bar or other type of handle. In the case of the fast action cramp, one jaw is free to slide on a bar, and after sliding this jaw up to the workpiece, final tightening is achieved by turning the handle. In all cases, to prevent damage to the piece of work, scraps of wood are placed between it and the jaws of the cramp.

Gimlet Used to make a small pilot hole in wood to take a screw. It is twisted into the wood with a continuous circular movement.

Hammers

Cross-pein hammer (10) The pein is the tapered section opposite the flat hammer head, and it is used for starting off small pins and tacks held in the fingers.

Pin hammer A smaller version of the cross-pein; this is useful for light work.

Claw hammer (9) The claw side of the head of the hammer is used to extract nails from a piece of work, quickly and cleanly.

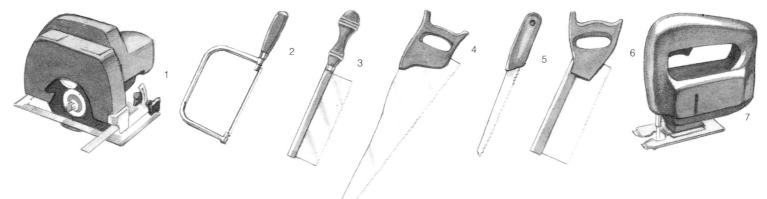

Mallet Most commonly used to strike mortise chisels, although if a chisel has an impact-resistant handle then a hammer may also be used. The tapered wooden head ensures square contact with the object being struck.

Nail and pin punches Used with a hammer to drive nails and pins below the surface so that they are hidden and can then be filled. The pointed end is 'cupped' to fit neatly over a nail or pin head.

Orbital sander Otherwise known as a finishing sander, this gives a fine, smooth surface finish to wood. A gritted sanding sheet is fitted to the sander's base plate. Sheets are graded from coarse to fine, and the grade used depends on the roughness of the surface to be sanded. Orbital sanders produce a great deal of dust, so always wear a mask when using one.

Pincers Used to remove nails and tacks from wood. The bevel-edged jaws grip the nail close to the surface of the wood, and the pincers are rocked back and forth to extract it.

PLANES

Smoothing plane (11) A general-purpose, hand-held plane for smoothing and straightening surfaces and edges. The plane is about 250mm (10in) long and its blade 50–60mm (2–2$\frac{1}{2}$in) wide. The wider the blade the better the finish on wide timber. There is a fine adjustment for depth of cut and a lever for lateral adjustment.
Power plane (14) Finishes timber to precise dimensions. A one-hand model is lightweight and can be used anywhere, whereas the heavier two-hander is intended for workbench use. A power plane will also cut bevels and rebates.
Jack plane (13) Longer than a smoothing plane, it is used for straightening long edges and is a good all-purpose plane.
Block plane (12) Held in the palm of the hand, it is easy to use for small work and chamfering edges. Also useful for planing end grain.

Rasp A rasp is a type of coarse file for wood, available with flat or half-round surfaces. It is used to shape wood, often when scribing an edge to fit against a wall.

Sanding block and abrasive paper A sanding block is used with abrasive paper to finish and smooth flat surfaces. The block is made of cork, rubber or softwood and the abrasive paper is wrapped around it. Make sure in doing so that the paper is not wrinkled. Abrasive paper used without a block tends to produce an uneven surface. Sheets of abrasive paper are graded from coarse to fine and are selected according to the roughness of the surface to be sanded. Coarse paper is used for a very rough surface and fine paper for finishing.

Screwdrivers There is no single type of screwdriver that is better than the rest; personal preference is what matters. They come in many shapes and sizes, and the main differences are the type of tip (for slotted or cross-point screws), the length, and the shape of the handle, which varies from straight or fluted to bulb-shaped. Cross-point screwdrivers can be used on most cross-point screws but the 'Supadriv' recess screw requires a purpose-made screwdriver.

Ideally, you should have a range of screwdrivers for dealing with all sizes of screws. Ratchet models, which return the handle to its starting point, are easy to operate since your hand grip does not need to change. The spiral action screwdriver is very effective (though very expensive) and it works like a bicycle pump rather than by turning the handle.
Cordless screwdriver A fairly new tool, it is quite expensive but can save much time and effort. Mainly used for cross-point screws.

SUPPLEMENTARY TOOLS

Metal file Gives a metal edge the required shape and finish. Most files are supplied with a removable handle which can be transferred to a

file of a different size. Flat or half-round files (one side flat, the other curved) are good general-purpose tools.

Hand staple gun A trigger-operated tool which fires a staple straight into a surface, usually fabric, fibreboard or thin wood over a wooden batten. Its advantage over conventional pinning with a hammer is that, as it is used one-handed, the other hand is free to hold the work.

Power staple gun Easier to fire. Fires heavy-duty staples into thicker surfaces, such as ceilings. It is preferable to buy the same brand of gun and staples to prevent jamming.

Paintbrushes A set of paintbrushes for painting and varnishing should ideally comprise three sizes – 25mm (1in), 50mm (2in) and 75mm (3in). A better finish is always achieved by matching the size of the brush to the surface – a small brush for narrow surfaces, a large brush for wide areas.

Electric paint sprayer Can produce a very smooth finish once its use is mastered. It may be preferable to hire rather than buy one – initially at least – since compressed air spray guns and compressors are expensive. Always work parallel to the surface you are spraying, applying two thin coats of paint rather than one thick coat.

Spanner A spanner is required for tightening coach-bolts, and any type that fits the head of the bolt is suitable. If the correct-size open-ended or ring spanner is not available, any type of adjustable spanner may be used.

Mastic applicator gun Also called a caulking gun, is used to eject a bead of mastic-type waterproofing sealants into gaps where water might penetrate, such as around shower trays. A cartridge of mastic or sealant is held in a frame, and a plunger pushes the mastic out of a nozzle at the end of the cartridge.

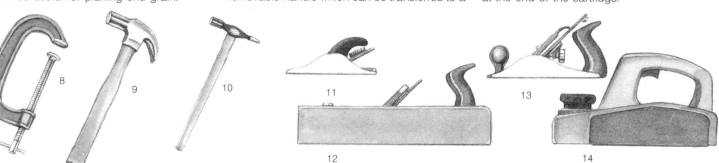

8   9   10   11   12   13   14

MATERIALS

TIMBER

Timber is classified into two groups – softwoods and hardwoods. Softwoods come from evergreen trees and hardwoods from deciduous trees. Check your timber for defects before buying it. Avoid wood which is badly cracked or split, although you need not be concerned about fine, surface cracks since these can be planed, sanded or filled. Do not buy warped wood, as it will be impossible to work with. Check for warping by looking along the length of a board to see if there is any bowing or twisting.

When you get your wood home, condition it for about ten days. As the wood will have been stored in the open air at the yard, it will be 'wet'. Once indoors, it dries, shrinks slightly and will warp unless stored flat on the ground. If you build with wood as soon as you get it home, your structure could run into problems later as the wood dries out. To avoid warping and aid drying, boards should be stacked in a pile, with offcuts of wood placed between each board to allow air to circulate. This will lower the moisture content to about 10 per cent and condition the wood, ready for use.

Softwood Although softwood is usually referred to as 'deal' or 'pine', it comes from many different sources. Softwood is much less expensive than hardwood and is used in general building work. Softwood is sold in a range of standard sizes. After 1.8m (6ft), lengths rise in 300mm (12in) increments up to 6.3m (20ft 8in). Standard thicknesses are from 12mm ($\frac{1}{2}$in) up to 75mm (3in) and widths range from 25mm (1in) to 225mm (9in).

It is important to remember that standard softwood sizes refer to sawn sizes – that is, how it is sawn at a mill. When bought this way, softwood is suitable only for rough constructional work such as floor joists and basic frames. However, the smooth wood used for the projects in this book, for which appearance and accuracy are

important, will need to have been planed. Such wood is referred to as PAR (planed all round), and, since planing takes a little off each face, planed softwood is approximately 5mm ($\frac{3}{16}$in) smaller in width and thickness than its stated size. Standard sizes should, therefore, be thought of as rough guides rather than exact measurements, although it is increasingly common for DIY stores to sell PAR softwood by its actual size rather than its nominal size.

Hardwood Expensive and not as easy to obtain as softwoods, hardwoods often have to be ordered or bought from a specialist timber merchant. Many joinery shops and timber yards will machine hardwood to your exact specification. In home woodwork, hardwood is usually confined to mouldings and beadings, which are used to give exposed sawn edges a neat finish. Today most hardwood mouldings are made from ramin, a pale wood; or from redwood.

BOARDS

Boards Boards are mechanically made from wood and other fibres. They are versatile, relatively inexpensive, and made to uniform quality. They differ from natural wood, in that they are available in large sheets. You need to know the advantages of each type of board before making your choice. All boards are made in sheets of 2440 × 1220mm (8 × 4ft), and most stockists will saw them to the size you require.

Hardboard The best known of all fibreboards. Common thicknesses are 3mm, 5mm and 6mm ($\frac{1}{8}$in, $\frac{3}{16}$in and $\frac{1}{4}$in). As hardboard is weak and has to be supported on a framework, it is essentially a material for panelling. Denser types of hardboard can be used for cladding partitions; softer types for pinboards.

Medium board As it is softer and weaker than hardboard, medium board is often, therefore, used in thicker sheets – usually 12mm ($\frac{1}{2}$in).

MDF (medium-density fibreboard) A good, general-purpose building board. It is highly compressed, does not flake or splinter when cut, and leaves a clean, hard-sawn edge which does not need to be disguised as do other fibreboards. It also takes a very good paint finish, even on its edges. Thicknesses range from around 6mm to 35mm ($\frac{1}{4}$in to 1$\frac{3}{8}$in).

Chipboard Made by binding wood chips together under pressure, it is rigid, dense and fairly heavy. Chipboard is strong when reasonably well supported, but sawing it can leave an unstable edge and can blunt a saw. Ordinary screws do not hold well in chipboard and it is best to use twin thread screws (see **Screws, page 18**). Most grades of chipboard are not moisture-resistant and will swell up when wet. Thicknesses range from 6mm to 40mm ($\frac{1}{4}$in to 1$\frac{1}{2}$in), but 12mm, 19mm and 25mm ($\frac{1}{2}$in, $\frac{3}{4}$in and 1in) are common.

Chipboard is widely available with the faces and edges veneered with natural wood, PVC, melamine, or plastic laminates. The latter are often in coloured finishes and imitation wood-grain effects.

If used for shelving, chipboard must be well supported on closely-spaced brackets or bearers. The better-quality laminated boards are far stronger than plain chipboard.

Plywood Made by gluing thin wood veneers together in plies (layers) with the grain in each ply running at right-angles to that of its neighbours. This gives the board strength and helps prevent warping. The most common boards have three, five or seven plies. Plywood is graded for quality, taking into account the amount of knots and surface markings present: A is perfect; B is average; and BB is for rough work only.

MR (moisture-resistant) board is suitable for *internal* jobs where damp conditions prevail, such as in a bathroom. Plywood is available with a range of surface veneers such as teak, oak or mahogany, or with a decorative plastic finish. The

MOULDINGS (See page 18)

Square

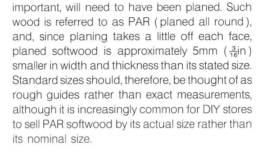
Rectangular

Scotia

Quadrant

Corner

usual thicknesses of plywood are 3mm, 6mm, 12mm and 19mm ($\frac{1}{8}$in, $\frac{1}{4}$in, $\frac{1}{2}$in and $\frac{3}{4}$in).

Blockboard Made by sandwiching natural timber strips betweeen wood veneers, the latter usually of Far Eastern redwood or plain birch. Although plain birch is a little more expensive than redwood it is of a much better quality. Other expensive varieties have a double veneer of plywood and an exotic wood. Blockboard is very strong, but can leave an ugly edge when sawn (gaps often appear between the core strips), making edge fixings difficult. Blockboard is graded in the same way as plywood and common thicknesses are 12mm, 19mm and 25mm ($\frac{1}{2}$in, $\frac{3}{4}$in and 1in). It is a very rigid board and is therefore ideal for a long span of shelving.

Laminboard A high-quality blockboard with no gaps between the core strips. It is expensive and is best used only where the quality required justifies the cost.

Tongued-and-grooved boarding Also called match boarding, or matching, this tongued-and-grooved boarding is widely used for cladding frameworks and walls. The boarding has a tongue on one side and a slot on the other side. The tongue fits into the slot of the adjacent board to form an area of cladding; this expands and contracts according to temperature and humidity without cracks opening up between boards.

Ordinary tongued-and-grooved boarding fits together like floorboards, but tongued-and-grooved boarding for cladding has some form of decoration; this can be a beaded joint, or, more commonly, a chamfered edge, which forms the attractive V-joint of tongued, grooved, and V-jointed (TVG) boarding.

ADHESIVES AND FILLERS

Adhesives Modern types are strong and efficient. If they fail, it is because the wrong adhesive

is being used or the manufacturer's instructions are not followed carefully. For all general indoor woodworking, use a PVA (polyvinyl acetate) woodworker's glue – all glue manufacturers produce their own brand. Use a waterproof PVA in areas where there may be water splashing or condensation. If joints do not meet perfectly, a gap-filling adhesive can be used.

Ceramic tiles require their own special adhesive (of a thick, buttery consistency) which is supplied, ready mixed, in tubs. If tiles are likely to be regularly splashed – around sinks for example – you should use a waterproof tile adhesive. Some brands of adhesive can also double as grouting cement for filling the gaps between tiles.

Fillers If the wood is to be painted over, use a standard cellulose filler – the type used for repairing cracks in walls. This filler dries white and will be evident if used under any other kind of finish. When a clear finish is needed, fill cracks and holes with a proprietary wood filler or stopping. These are thick pastes and come in a range of wood colours. You can even mix them together or add a wood stain if the colour you want is not available. It is best to choose a colour slightly paler than the surrounding wood, since fillers tend to darken when the finish is applied. Some experimentation may be needed, using a waste piece of matching wood.

In fine work, a grain filler is used to stop the final finish sinking into the wood. This is a paste, thinned with white spirit, and then rubbed into the surface. It is supplied in a range of wood shades.

FINISHES

The choice of finish is determined by whether the wood or board is to be hidden, painted or enhanced by a protective clear finish.

LACQUER

Quick-drying cellulose lacquer is the best finishing treatment to apply to wood furniture. It is resistant

to heat, scratches and solvents, and, when sprayed on, produces a superb finish.

POLISHES

French polish Refers to a particular polish, but it is also the collective term for all polishes made with shellac and alcohol. French polish is ideal where a light to medium brown tone is required. The finish itself is not highly protective.

Button polish Will give a more golden or orange tone than standard French polish.

White French polish or **transparent polish** Produces a clear finish, allowing the natural colour of the wood to show through. French polishing demands patience if it is to be mastered and many people prefer to apply a clear polyurethane varnish with a conventional wax polish covering it.

PAINT

A liquid gloss (oil-based) paint is suitable for wood, and is applied after a suitable undercoat. Generally, two thin coats of gloss are better than one thick coat. Non-drip gloss is an alternative. It has a jelly-like consistency and does not require an undercoat, although a second coat may be needed for a quality finish. If you intend to spray on the paint, then you must use a liquid gloss.

VARNISH

Normally applied by brush, varnish can also be sprayed on. It is available as a gloss, satin or matt finish, all clear. However, varnish also comes in a range of colours, so that you can change the colour of the wood and protect it simultaneously. The colour does not sink into the wood, so if the surface of the wood becomes scratched or marked then its original colour will show through. For this reason, a wood stain or dye is sometimes used to change the colour of wood. It sinks into the wood, but offers no protection, so a varnish or clear lacquer also needs to be applied.

Half-round

Twice-rounded

Hockey-stick

Reeded

Astragal

Mouldings, Battens and Dowels

Mouldings Are used as ornamentation and to cover gaps or fixings in a wooden construction. The term 'moulding' encompasses everything from a simple, thin bead edging to architraves and skirting boards. A variety of shaped cutters produce many different shapes and sizes. In the unlikely event of your being unable to buy the shape of moulding you want, you could make your own using a router.

Mouldings are cut from hardwood – usually redwood (which is dense and hard) or ramin (a paler wood). You can buy more exotic hardwood mouldings, mahogany for example, from a specialist timber merchant. These are expensive and you may well prefer to stain or varnish a cheaper moulding to obtain the colour you want.

Decorative mouldings are available in standard lengths of 2m or 3m (6ft 6in or 10ft). The following types are among those which are ideal for edging man-made boards and are available in a variety of sizes: half-round; twice-rounded; hockey-stick; reeded; and astragal. Square or rectangular mouldings range from 6 × 6mm ($\frac{1}{4} \times \frac{1}{4}$in) to 12 × 38mm ($\frac{1}{2} \times 1\frac{1}{2}$in) in size.

Other types of moulding include scotia and quadrant, which cover gaps between the meeting parts of a structure. Corner mouldings are a plain version of the scotia, and can be used inside or outside a joint.

When buying mouldings, check each one to make sure that the length is straight and free from large or dead knots, which are likely to fall out and leave holes. Fungal staining is something else to watch for, especially if you intend to use a clear finish. If you need several lengths of mouldings for the same job, check that you get a good match. Have a close look at the edges and colour and grain of each length, as mismatching can leave surface ripples or uneven edges.

Battens A general term used to describe a narrow strip of wood. The usual sizes are 25 × 25mm (1 × 1in) or 50 × 25mm (2 × 1in).

Battens serve one of two main functions. They can be screwed to a wall to serve as bearers for shelves. Alternatively, they can be fixed in a framework on a wall, with sheet material or boards mounted over them to form a new 'wall'.

Dowels Used to make framework joints or to join boards edge-to-edge or edge-to-face.

Hardwood dowels are sold in diameters ranging from 6–10mm ($\frac{1}{4}$–$\frac{3}{8}$in). You can buy packs of dowels cut to length (either 25mm or 38mm [1in or 1$\frac{1}{2}$in]), or you can buy long lengths and cut them to size. Generally speaking, dowel lengths should be about one-and-a-half times the thickness of the boards being joined.

Dowels are used in conjunction with adhesive and, when the joint is complete, it is important to let excess adhesive escape from the joint. Dowels with fluted (finely grooved) sides and chamfered ends will help this process. If you have plain rather than shaped dowels, make fine sawcuts along the length and chamfer the ends yourself.

Nails

For general-purpose framework construction.

Round wire nails With large, flat, circular heads, these are used for strong joins where frames will be covered, so that the ugly appearance of the nails does not matter.

Annular ring-shank nails Use where really strong fixings are required.

Round lost-head nails or **oval brads** (*oval wire nails*) Use when the finished appearance is important. The heads of these nails are driven in flush with the wood's surface and they are unobtrusive. They should be used when nailing a thin piece of wood to a thicker piece and there is a risk of splitting the wood. This danger is greatest when nailing close to the end of the wood, or when the nail is too large.

Panel pins For fixing thin panels, these fine, round wire nails will be required. These have tiny, unobtrusive heads that can be driven in flush with the wood's surface or punched below it.

Hardboard pins Copper-plated and with a square cross-section. They have deep-drive diamond-shaped heads that sink into the surface – ideal for fixing hardboard and other boards to timber in areas subject to condensation, where steel pins could cause black staining.

Masonry nails For fixing timber battens to walls as an alternative to screwing and wallplugging. Where a quick and permanent fixing is required, use the hardened-steel type.

Screws

All types of screws are available with either conventional slotted heads or cross-point heads. The latter look neat and are the best type to use if you are inserting screws with an electric screwdriver.

For most purposes, screws with countersunk heads are ideal as the head lies flush with the surface after insertion. Round-head screws are used for fixing metal fittings such as shelf brackets and door bolts, which have punched-out rather than countersunk screw holes. Raised-countersunk head screws are often used alone or with metal screw cups where a neat appearance is important.

Wood screws These have a length of smooth shank just below the head. When joining two pieces of wood, this produces a strong clamping effect as the screw is tightened, but there is also a possibility of the unthreaded shank splitting the wood so extra care is required.

Twin-thread screws Quicker to insert than ordinary wood screws and less likely to split wood. Except for larger sizes, they are threaded along

Nails and Screws

1 *Screw cup;* 2 *Wall anchor bolt;* 3 and 4 *Frame fixing (nylon plug and plated screw);* 5 *Veneer pin;* 6 *Hardboard pin;* 7 *Panel pin;* 8 *Oval brad;* 9 *Round wire nail;* 10 *Annular ring-shank nail;* 11 *Masonry nail;* 12 *Countersunk screw with slotted head;* 13 *Countersunk screw with cross-point head;* 14 *Round-head screw;* 15 *Raised countersunk head screw;* 16 *Dome-head screw;* 17 *Twin-thread screw.*

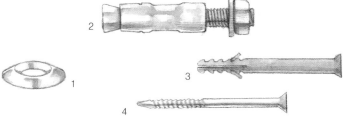

their entire length, giving an excellent grip in wood, and also in fibreboard, chipboard, blockboard and plywood. The best types are zinc-plated (rust-resistant) and hardened (stronger and less prone to head damage when inserted with an ill-fitting screwdriver).

WALL FIXINGS AND BOLTS

The choice of wall fixing depends on the type of wall and the size and weight of the object that is being fixed to it.

Wallplugs Use a masonry drill bit to drill a hole which matches the size of screw being used (a No 10 bit with a No 10 screw, for example). Insert the plug in the hole, then insert the screw through the object being fixed and into the plug. Tighten the screw for a secure fixing.

Solid wall fixings The method of fixing to a solid brick or block wall is to use a wallplug. Traditional fibre wallplugs have been superseded by plastic versions which will accept a range of screw sizes, typically from No 8 to No 12.

Stud wall fixings To guarantee a secure fixing for stud walls, you should locate the timber uprights which form the framework of the wall and drive screws into them. If you want to attach something heavy and the timber uprights are not in the required position, then you must fix horizontal battens to the timber uprights, otherwise the fixing will be unsafe.

Hollow-wall fixings Used on hollow walls, which are constructed from plasterboard partition or lath and plaster and are found in modern and old houses, respectively. There are many types of these fixings including spring toggle, gravity toggle and nylon toggle, and nearly all of them work on the same principle: expanding wings open up to grip the back of the plasterboard or lath and plaster, securing the fixing.

Wall anchor bolt For heavier objects, such as a kitchen unit which will be heavily loaded, a more robust fixing using a wall anchor bolt is advisable. It is similar to a wallplug in principle, but has its own heavy-duty machine screw. You need to make a much larger hole in the wall, typically 10mm ($\frac{3}{8}$in) in diameter. The sleeve of the anchor expands in the hole as the bolt is tightened and grips the wall firmly.

LATCHES

Magnetic catches Most useful on smaller doors which are unlikely to distort. There must be perfect contact between the magnet fixed to the cabinet frame and the striker plate which is fixed to the door. The other important factor is the pulling power of the magnet – on small cabinet doors a 'pull' of 2–3kg ($4\frac{1}{2}$–$6\frac{1}{2}$lb) is sufficient. On wardrobe doors a 5–6kg (11–13lb) 'pull' is needed to keep the door closed.

Magnetic push latches are also useful. Push on the door inwards and it springs open just enough to be grasped and fully opened by the fingers.

Mechanical latches Common types are the spring-loaded ball catch and the roller catch. Again, alignment is vital to success, which is why adjustable types are favoured. A mechanical push latch is activated by pressure on the door itself, so a door handle is not necessary.

Peglock catches Particularly suitable for kitchen and bathroom cabinets, where atmospheric conditions can cause doors to distort.

HINGES

The easiest types of hinge to fix are those which do not have to be recessed into the door or door frame – flush, decorative flush (for lightweight doors) or cranked (for cupboard doors). For fixing flaps, piano hinges are used. They are sold in 1.8m (6ft) lengths, and are cut to the required size with a hacksaw. For fixing heavy doors or for

a very neat finish, butt hinges, which are recessed, are a good alternative.

Adjustable concealed hinges are used for chipboard and MDF doors. A special drill bit is required to cut cylindrical holes in the door, but the hinges are adjustable once fitted.

SLIDING DOOR TRACKS

Doors can either be suspended from above or supported from below. The track for glass or panel doors is made from PVC, and comes in a variety of colours. The door simply slides along the channel in the track.

Top-hung track Small tongued sliders or adjustable wheel hangers fixed to the top edge of the door sit in the track. Small guides keep the bottom edges of the door aligned.

Bottom-roller track The door slides on small rollers located in the track. Guides fitted at the top of the door keep it aligned in the track.

TILES

Ceramic tiles Ceramic tiles offer a functional and highly practical form of wallcovering. They are popular for kitchens and bathrooms, where durable and waterproof surfaces are essential. There is an enormous range of tiles available, and prices vary according to size, shape and design. The most common sizes are 108 × 108mm ($4\frac{1}{4}$ × $4\frac{1}{4}$in) and 150 × 150mm (6 × 6in), but rectangular shapes are also widely available.

'Universal' tiles have angled edges which ensure that uniform joint spacing is left when the tiles are butted up against each other.

Tiles are sold in boxes of 25 or 50, which will cover one half or one square metre (yard). After deciding on the number of tiles required, allow a few extra to cover breakages. Unless you are using only one box, do not use the tiles straight from the box – mix them up with tiles from other boxes to disguise any slight colour variations.

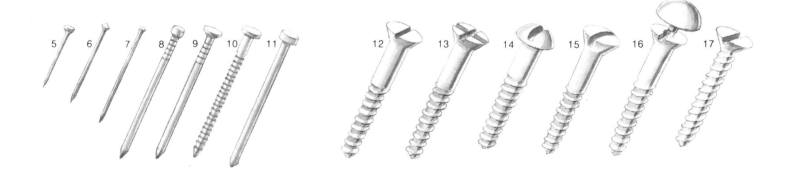

TECHNIQUES: SAWING AND CUTTING

WOOD

Wood is available either sawn or planed. Sawn wood is rough in appearance, but is close in width and thickness to the dimensions you specify when ordering. Planed wood is smoothed on all sides, but planing removes about 5mm ($\frac{3}{16}$in) from both the nominal width and the thickness. Sawn wood is ideal for building frameworks, but choose planed wood where a smooth finish is important. Wood should be straight and relatively knot-free. The surface should also be undamaged.

When building a framework of critical thickness (such as the basic kitchen unit modules on page 86) you may find it difficult to obtain wood of exactly the required thickness. If so, buy wood that is slightly oversized and plane it down.

After building, a fine surface can be obtained by sanding, either by hand with **abrasive paper** wrapped around a **sanding block**, or by using an electric **orbital sander**. In both cases, start with medium-grade abrasive paper and finish with fine; only sand in line with the grain, rather than across it, as this can cause scratching.

Wood finishes If a varnish, wax polish or paint finish is required, it can be applied easily with a brush (or rag). An alternative, often used by professional furniture makers, is to finish woodwork with a quick-drying cellulose lacquer (see **Materials, page 17**), which can be applied with a **paint sprayer**. Before spraying, make sure that any holes are filled with stainable wood filler, and stain the surface, if required, before sanding it smooth. The first coat of lacquer is applied as a sealer. Leave it to dry for 30–60 minutes, then rub down the surface with fine abrasive paper. Next, apply a second, finishing, coat of lacquer.

MEASURING AND MARKING SQUARE

Mark cutting lines lightly with a hard pencil first, then use a **trimming knife**, **straight-edge** or **try square** along a rule to create a sharp, splinter-free line.

To mark timber square, use a try square with the stock (handle) pressed against a flat side of the timber, called the face side or face edge. Mark a line along the square, using a knife in preference to a pencil, then use the square to mark lines down the edges from the face mark. Finally square the other face side, checking that the lines join up right around the timber.

Check a try square for accuracy by pressing it against a straight edge. Mark along the blade, then turn the handle over to see if it aligns with the line from the other side.

If you are measuring and marking a number of pieces of the same length, then cramp them together and mark across several of them at the same time.

SPACING BATTEN

This is simply an offcut of wood, about 19mm or 25mm square ($\frac{3}{4}$in or 1in square), which is used to ensure that any slats to be fixed across a frame are spaced an equal distance apart. To ascertain the length to cut the spacing batten, simply bunch all the slats at one end of the frame. Measure to the other end of the frame and divide by the number of spaces (which you can count while you have the slats laid side by side). The resulting measure is the length to cut the spacing batten, which is used to set each slat into its exact position.

BRACING

When making a door or any similar frame, it is vital that it should be square, with corners at perfect right-angles. You can ensure this by using one of two bracing methods.

3-4-5-method Measure three units along one rail, four units down the adjacent rail, then nail a bracing batten accurately to one of the unit marks. Pull into square so that the bracing batten measures five units at the other unit mark, forming the long side of a triangle. Saw off the batten ends flush with the frame, but do not remove the batten until frame is fitted in place. For large doors such as those on wardrobes, fix two braces on opposing corners.

---

① Marking Timber to Length and Square All Round
Mark across the face of the timber with a trimming knife held against a try square blade. Move knife around corners and mark sides, and finally mark other side to join up the lines.

② Using Spacing Battens to Space Out Slats Evenly
Bunch the battens together at one end of the frame, then measure to the other end of the frame. Divide this number by the number of spaces required; cut spacing batten to this length.

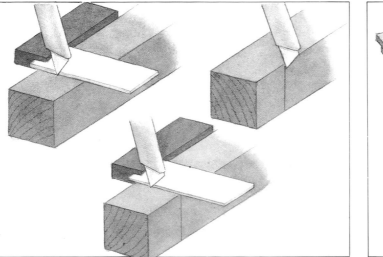

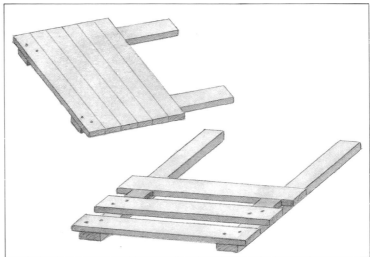

Try square method Nail a batten into one rail, pull into square by using a try square, and then nail the batten into the adjacent rail.

MAKING FOLDING WEDGES

Folding wedges are very useful for cramping large frames on a bench top during assembly. The wedges are always used in pairs, but more than one pair may be used to hold a large framework.

Make each pair of wedges from a piece of timber (hardwood is an ideal material for this) measuring $38 \times 38 \times 330$mm ($1\frac{1}{2} \times 1\frac{1}{2} \times 13$in). Make the wedges by sawing the timber diagonally into two pieces.

To use the wedges, a wooden batten is first nailed to the bench and the item to be cramped is placed against the batten. Another batten is nailed to the bench, parallel with the first, and about 45mm ($1\frac{3}{4}$in) away from the item. The wedges are now placed between the item and the second batten. Next, the ends of the wedges are knocked inwards with two hammers, thereby cramping the frame.

SAWING AND CUTTING

Cross-cutting to length by hand Hold the timber firmly with the cutting line (*see* **Measuring and Marking Square, page 20**) overhanging the right-hand side of the bench (if you are right-handed). With the saw blade vertical and the teeth on the waste side of the line, draw the handle back to start the cut. To prevent the saw from jumping out of place, hold the thumb joint of the other hand against the side of the saw blade.

Rip-cutting by hand With the timber or board supported at about knee height, start the cut as described above, then saw down the waste side of the line, exerting pressure on the down cut only. If the saw blade wanders from the line, cramp the edge of a timber batten exactly above the cutting line on the side to be retained, and saw along it.

Using a portable power saw If the cutting line is only a short distance from a straight edge, adjust the saw's fence so that when it is run along the edge of the timber, the blade will cut on the waste side of the cutting line. If the timber is wide, or the edge is not straight, cramp a batten to the surface so that the saw blade will cut on the waste side of the line when it is run along the batten.

Ensuring a straight cut When cutting panels or boards using a **power circular saw** or **jigsaw**, the best way to ensure a straight cut is to cramp a guide batten to the surface of the work, parallel with the cutting line, so that the edge of the saw sole plate can be run along the batten. Obviously, the batten position is carefully adjusted so that the saw blade cuts on the waste side of the cutting line. Depending on which side of the cutting line the batten is cramped, when using a circular saw, it is possible that the motor housing will foul the batten or the G-cramps used to hold it in place. In this case, replace the batten with a wide strip of straight-edged plywood cramped to the work far enough back for the motor to clear the cramps.

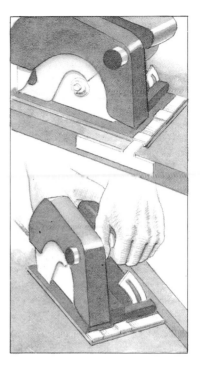

6 **Straight Power-Saw Cutting**
Top **Use the rip fence of the saw if cutting near the edge.** *Above* **cutting alongside the batten.**

3 **Bracing a Frame Square**
Nail a batten across a corner of the frame so that a 3-4-5 shape triangle is formed.

4 **Making Folding Wedges**
Saw wood diagonally. Nail batten to bench; wedges fit between batten and item being cramped.

5 **Cross-cutting to Length**
Hold the timber firmly. Steady the saw blade with the thumb joint as you start to saw.

7 **Cutting with a Tenon Saw**
Start the cut as for a hand saw. As the cut progresses keep the blade horizontal.

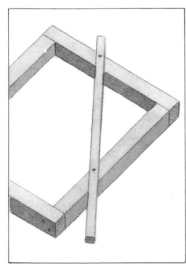

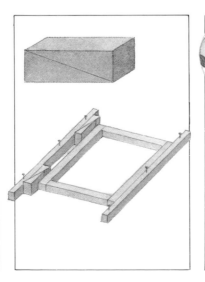

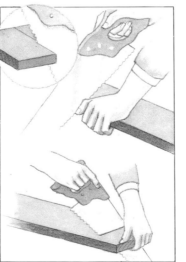

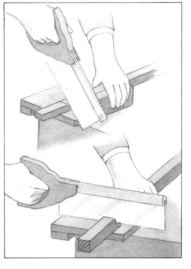

TECHNIQUES: CUTTING AND PLANING

CUTTING A CIRCLE

With a jigsaw Mark the circle on the face of the panel. If you do not have a compass, a good makeshift alternative can be made with a loop of string pivoted on a drawing pin at the centre of the circle. Hold a pencil vertically in the loop at the perimeter to draw the circle.

In order to have a neat, splinter-free edge, carefully score around the cutting line with a trimming knife.

To start the cut, drill a hole about 10mm ($\frac{3}{8}$in) in diameter just on the inside of the circle. Insert the jigsaw blade through this hole and start the cut from this point, sawing carefully just on the waste side of the cutting line. By scoring the cutting line it will be easier to follow the line and get a smooth edge.

With a coping saw Mark out the circle, score the cutting line, and drill a hole just inside the circle as described above. Disconnect the blade from one end of the frame, pass the blade through the hole, and re-connect it to the frame. It will

be best to cramp the piece of work vertically when cutting the circle. The blade can be turned in the frame as necessary to help the frame clear the piece of work, but even so, with a coping saw you will be restricted in exactly how far you are able to reach away from the piece of work. If the circle is some way from the edge, use either a power jigsaw or a hand padsaw to cut it.

With a padsaw A padsaw, also called a keyhole saw, has a stiff, triangular pointed saw blade attached to a simple handle. A very useful padsaw blade is available for fitting in a regular knife handle.

Because this saw has no frame, it is ideal for cutting circles and other apertures, like keyholes, anywhere in a panel.

Preparation of the circle for cutting, such as marking out, scoring, and drilling for the blade, is the same as for the other methods. When cutting with a padsaw, keep the blade vertical and make a series of rapid, short strokes without exerting too much pressure.

CUTTING CURVES

The technique is basically the same as for cutting a circle, except that there will be no need to drill a hole in order to start the cut. You can use a jigsaw, coping saw, or padsaw to make the cut. A coping saw is ideal for making this type of cut because most of the waste can be removed with an ordinary hand saw, you will be cutting close to the edge of the wood, so the saw frame will not get in the way.

CUTTING GROOVES AND HOUSINGS

The easiest way to cut grooves (or housings) is to use a router fitted with a bit set to the depth required for the groove. Use a straight-sided router bit. Ideally, the router bit should be the exact width of the groove or housing, so that it can be cut from one setting. If this is not possible, then use a smaller router bit and cut the groove or housing in two or more goes. Make the first cut along the waste side of the line with a batten clamped in line with the

housing to guide the base of the router. If a deep groove is required, it may be necessary to make a shallow cut first, then a deeper one.

To cut housings by hand, start by marking out the groove with a trimming knife which will ensure a neat finish. Hold the piece of work on a bench and, with a tenon saw, make vertical cuts just inside the marked lines to the depth of the groove. If the groove is wide, make a series of other vertical cuts in the waste wood. Now chisel out the waste, working from each side to the middle. Finally, with the flat side of the chisel downwards, pare the bottom of the housing so that it is perfectly flat.

CUTTING REBATES

A rebate is an L-shaped step in the edge of a piece of timber.

To cut a rebate by hand, use a marking gauge to mark the rebate width across the top face of the piece of work and down both sides. Mark the depth of the rebate across the end and sides.

Hold the timber flat and saw down on the waste side of the marked line

---

① Straight Rip-cutting
Cramp a straight batten alongside the cutting line and saw beside the batten. A wedge holds the cut open.

② Using a Power Jigsaw
For a straight cut clamp a batten alongside line. Cut a circle by following line.

③ Cutting Circles by Hand
***1** drill a small hole and cut circle using a padsaw; **2** making cut with a coping saw.*

④ Chiselling a Groove
After making saw cuts at side, chisel out waste from each side. Finally pare base flat.

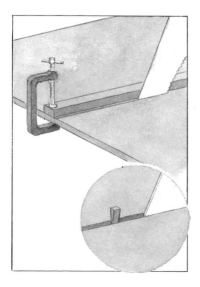

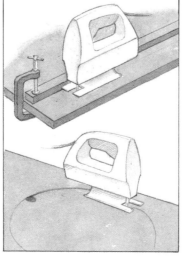

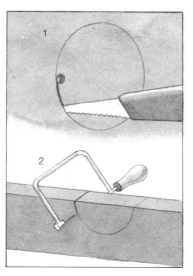

to the depth of the rebate. Then use a chisel to cut out the waste one bit at a time along the end grain.

It is very easy to cut a rebate using a router, and in this case it is not necessary to mark out the rebate unless you want a guide to work to. However, do practise on scrap wood to be sure of setting the router to cut to the correct depth and width.

If using a straight cutter, adjust the guide fence on the router so that the correct width is cut, then plunge and adjust the cutting depth so that the router will cut to the correct depth. When the router is correctly set up, simply hold it flat on the piece of work and move it against the direction of the cutter's rotation.

If you are using a cutter with a guide pin, simply adjust the depth of cut and then run the cutter along the edge of the wood to form the rebate. The cutter will follow irregularities in the wood, so make sure your wood is perfectly straight.

MAKING A V-BLOCK

A V-block is useful for holding circular items steady while they are being worked on. Make the block from a length of 75 × 50mm (3 × 2in) PAR timber – the actual length should be a little longer than the item to be held. The V is made to a depth of about 25mm (1in) in the 75mm (3in) side of the timber. Cut the V using a circular saw with the blade tilted to 45°. Cramp the block firmly and fit the saw with a guide fence to keep the cut straight. Cut up one side and down the other. Practise on scrap wood while adjusting the depth and width of cut to give the correct size V-shape. Alternatively you can use a V-cutter bit in a router. It may take two or three passes with the router to make the V to the full depth and width of the cutter.

PLANING

By hand   Make sure that the plane blade is sharp and properly adjusted. Stand to one side of the work with feet slightly apart so you are facing the work and feeling comfortable. Plane from one end of the piece of work to the other, starting the cut with firm pressure on the leading hand, transferring it to both hands, and finally to the rear hand as the cut is almost complete. Holding the plane at a slight angle to the direction of the grain can sometimes improve the cutting action.

With a power plane   Remove ties and loose clothing; overalls are ideal. Wear goggles and a dust mask. Start the plane and turn the adjuster knob to set the depth to cut. Start with a shallow cut and increase the cutting depth if necessary. Make sure the work is cramped in place.

Stand comfortably to one side of the work and, holding the plane with two hands, set it into the work at one end and pass it over the surface to the other end. Push the plane forwards steadily; not too fast or you will get a wavy surface finish. When you have completed the work, switch off and make sure that the blades stop spinning before resting the plane down with the cutting depth set at zero.

DRILLING

To ensure that screwheads lie level with the surface of plywood, chipboard and hardwood use a **countersink drill bit**.

To minimize the risk of splitting timber, drill pilot and clearance holes for screws. For small screws, pilot holes can be made with a **gimlet**.

The **clearance hole** in the timber should be fractionally smaller in diameter than the screw shank.

The **pilot hole** in the timber to receive the screw should be about half the diameter of the clearance hole. The depth of the pilot hole should be slightly less than the length of the screw.

Drilling vertical holes   To ensure vertical holes mount the drill in a stand. If this is not possible, stand a try square on edge so that its stock is resting on the work alongside the drilling position, and the blade is pointing up in the air. Use this as a siting guide and line up the drill as close as possible with the square to ensure the drill is vertical. It is also helpful if an assistant can stand back and sight along the drill and square from two sides to ensure the drill is straight.

⑤ Making a V-block
Cut out a V in a block of 75 × 50mm (3 × 2in) timber using a circular power saw tilted to cut at 45°.

⑥ Drilling Vertical Holes
With a drill stand, not only will the drill bit be held vertical, but depth is controlled.

⑦ Freehand Drilling Guide
When drilling it can be helpful to stand a try square alongside the drill to ensure accuracy.

⑧ Drilling Depth Guide
There are various guides to control drilling depths, such as rings for drills, and sticky tape.

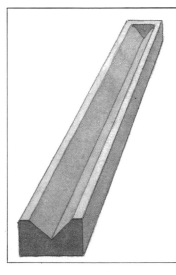

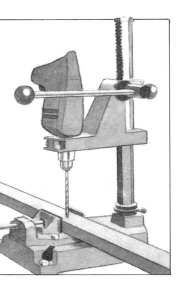

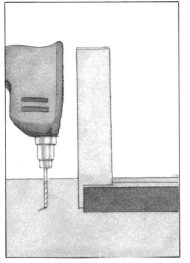

TECHNIQUES: WALL FIXINGS

SCREWING

When screwing one piece of wood to another ensure that half of the screw penetrates through the bottom piece of wood. Its thickness should not exceed one-tenth of the width of the wood into which it has to be inserted. Keep screws at a distance of five times their shank diameter from the side edge of the wood, and ten times the shank diameter from its end.

NAILING

The correct length of nail to use is two-and-a-half to three times the thickness of the timber being fixed. However, check that the nail will not pierce right through two pieces being fixed. Wherever possible nail through the thinner piece of wood into the thicker piece.

Nails grip best if driven in at an angle ('skew nailing'). A row of nails should be driven in at opposing angles to each other. Framework joints are usually held in by skew nailing. Cramp or nail a block of wood temporarily against one side

of the vertical piece to stop it sliding as the first nail is started.

To prevent wood from splitting, particularly if nailing near an edge, blunt the points of the nails by hitting them with a hammer before driving them home. Blunt nails will cut through timber fibres neatly, while pointed nails are more likely to push the fibres apart like a wedge, leading to splitting.

WALL FIXINGS

Solid wall The normal fixing for a solid wall is a woodscrew and plastic or fibre wallplug. Before drilling the fixing hole, check with a metal detector that there are no pipes or cables hidden below the surface. Drill the holes for the wallplug with a **masonry drill bit** in an electric drill. The wallplug packing will indicate the drill size to use. Switch to hammer action if the wall is hard. The screw should be long enough to go through the fitting and into the wall by about 25mm (1in) if the masonry is exposed, and by about 35mm (1⅜in) if fixing into a plastered wall.

If the wall crumbles when you drill

into it, mix up a cement-based plugging compound (available from DIY stores). Turn back the screw by about half a turn before the compound sets (in about five minutes). When it is hard (in about one hour) the screw can be removed and a heavy fixing can be made.

If your drill sinks easily into the wall once it has penetrated the plaster layer, and a light grey dust is produced from the hole, you are fixing into lightweight building blocks. In this case, special winged wallplugs should be used for soft blocks.

To make a quick, light-to-medium weight fixing in a solid wall, a masonry nail can be used. Choose a length that will penetrate the material to be fixed, and pierce an exposed masonry wall by 15mm (⅝in) and a plastered wall by about 25mm (1in). Wear goggles in case the hardened nail snaps when you strike it, and hammer it gently through the material to be fixed and into the wall.

Lath and plaster For a strong fixing, screw directly into the main

vertical studding timbers to which the laths are nailed. You can find these studs with a **metal detector** (see **Stud wall,** below).

For a lightweight fixing you can screw into the wood laths. These can be located by probing with a pointed implement such as a gimlet. Then insert a twin-thread woodscrew. For medium-to-heavyweight fixings into lath and plaster, drill between the laths and use a cavity-wall fixing suitable for lath and plaster, such as a spring toggle, gravity toggle or nylon toggle.

Stud wall For a strong fixing into a plasterboard-covered stud wall, make a screw fixing directly into the vertical timber studs. You can find these by tapping the wall to check where it sounds most dense, and then probing these areas with a pointed implement until a firm background is found. Alternatively, you can make a small hole in the wall, and push a stiff wire into it horizontally until an obstruction is felt, which will be the stud. Withdraw the wire and hold it on the surface of the wall

❶ Drilling Holes for Screws in Timber
Drill a clearance hole in the thinner place. Countersink this hole, then drill a pilot hole to slightly less than screw length. *Inset* To counterbore, drill to the diameter of the screw head, to required depth then as above.

❷ Techniques for Joining Wood by Nailing
Nail should be two-and-a-half to three times the thickness of the timber being fixed. Assemble frames on bench by nailing against batten. *Inset* Blunt nail points to avoid splitting timber.

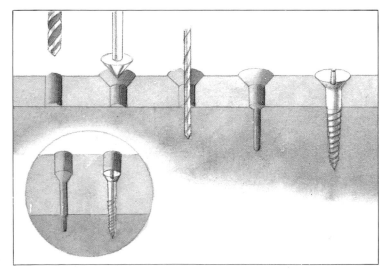

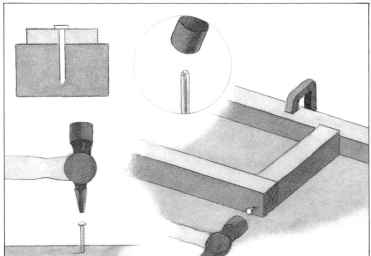

so that the edge of the stud can be marked. By drilling about 25mm (1in) to the farther side of this mark, the centre of the stud will be found and a screw can be inserted.

To avoid making holes in the surface of a wall, a **metal detector** can be used. Move it over the wall to locate a pattern of nail fixings and mark this on the surface. Vertical rows of nails indicate a stud. Alternatively, use one of the newer electronic stud and joist detectors. This is moved over the surface to detect a change in density between the different construction materials. A change indicates a stud.

If a fixing cannot be made into a stud, a lighter fixing can be made into plasterboard by using a fitting designed for that material. Follow the manufacturer's instructions for the size of hole required, which can be made in plasterboard with an ordinary twist drill bit.

Cavity wall Cavity walls comprise a solid inner leaf of bricks or building blocks surfaced with plaster and separated from the outer leaf of bricks or stone blocks by a cavity about 50mm (2in) wide.

When tapped, a cavity wall sounds solid. For fixings, treat it as a solid wall (*see page 24*).

BEVELLED BATTENS

These provide a very secure method of holding heavy objects on to a wall. The battens are formed by sawing a strip of wood lengthways with the saw blade set at 45° This results in two interlocking pieces of wood. One piece, with the sloping face pointing upwards and the narrower face facing the wall, is screwed to the wall. The other piece, with the sloping face pointing downwards and the narrower side facing the item to be hung, is screwed to the item to be fixed. When the item is lifted into place, the battens interlock for a very secure fixing.

For security, the battens should be formed by sawing a 100 × 25mm (4 × 1in) strip of timber lengthways. Screw fixings, applied to the wall and into the item to be hung, should be at about 200mm (8in) intervals. Use No 10 woodscrews, 38mm (1½in)

long, into the item to be hung, and 65mm (2½in) long into the wall. Wallplugs will also be required.

FIXING RIGHT-ANGLE BRACKETS

These are right-angle steel strips pre-drilled for screw fixing and are useful for fixing timber frames to walls and ceilings, as long as brackets are positioned out of sight (*see Fixing down worktops, page 00*).

Decide where you want the bracket, hold it in place on the frame and use a pencil to mark the centre of one screw fixing position. Drill a pilot hole and fix the bracket with one screw. Repeat for the other brackets. Position the frame and check that it is vertical. Mark centre points of the bracket fixing holes on the wall or ceiling. Remove the frame and use a masonry drill to make plug holes at the required positions. Press plugs into holes. Before replacing the frame and screwing brackets in place, check that brackets are still accurately positioned on the frame. Drill pilot holes for remaining screw fixings, and insert screws.

③ Skew Nailing for Strength
Assemble frames by skew nailing (driving nails at an angle). The joint will not then pull apart.

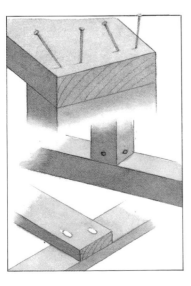

④ Using a Nail Punch
For a neat finish, use a nail punch to drive nail heads below the surface, then fill indentation.

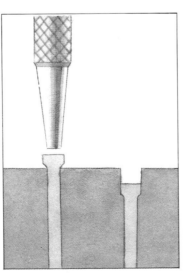

⑤ Using Bevelled Battens
For a secure fixing on a wall use bevelled battens made by sawing a batten lengthwise at 45°.

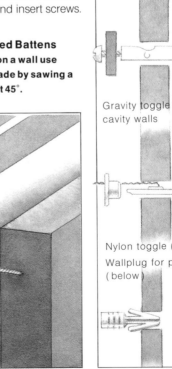

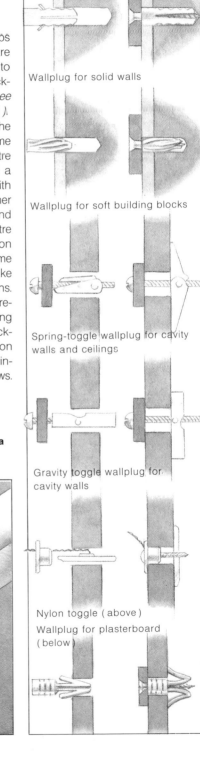

TYPES OF WALL FIXINGS

Wallplug for solid walls

Wallplug for soft building blocks

Spring-toggle wallplug for cavity walls and ceilings

Gravity toggle wallplug for cavity walls

Nylon toggle (above)

Wallplug for plasterboard (below)

TECHNIQUES: WOOD JOINTS

WOOD JOINTS

Butt joint This is the simplest frame joint of all. The ends of the timbers to be joined must be cut square so that they butt together neatly. Corner and T joints can be formed, which are glued and nailed for strength. Corrugated fasteners can also be used to hold these joints, especially where the sides of the frames will be covered to hide the fasteners. When T joints are being formed from inside a frame, they can be **skew nailed**.

Corner joint These are simple 'knock down' fittings fixed with screws; they are used to fix boards together at right-angles. They are described as 'knock down' because some are in two parts for easy disassembly, and even the simple fittings can be unscrewed. They do not look very attractive, but are useful where they will be hidden – by a fascia, for example.

Mitre joint Popular for making picture frames, but suitable for other

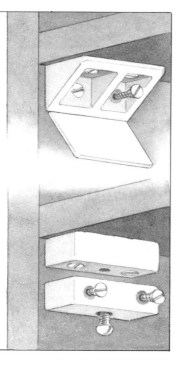

right-angle corner joints. Cut the joints at 45° using a mitre box as a guide. A simple mitre joint is glued and pinned, but a stronger joint can be made using dowels, or by making oblique saw cuts into which wood veneers are glued.

Halving joint Also known as a half-lap joint these may be used to join wood of similar thickness at corners or to T or X joints. The joint is formed by cutting each piece to half its thickness. Use a **try square** to mark the width of the cut-outs and a **marking gauge** set to half the thickness of the wood to mark their depth. Be sure to cross-hatch the waste wood with a pencil so that the correct side is removed. To form a corner half-lap, saw down as for making a tenon joint (*see below*). To form a 'T' or 'X' half-lap, saw down on each side of the 'T' cut-out to the depth of the central gauge line, then chisel out the waste.

Housing joint Used mainly for shelving, this is basically a slot into which a shelf fits. The 'through'

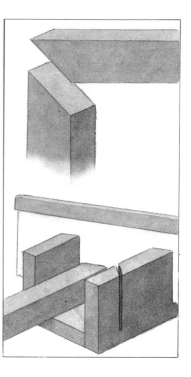

② Corner Fitting Joints
Ideal for joining woods and boards at right angles. *Top* A one-piece fitting; *Bottom* A two-part type. Both are easily fitted using screws.

⑤ Cutting Mitre Joints
Mitres make right-angle corner joints. Using a mitre box as a guide for ensuring a 45° angle cut out the joint with a tenon saw.

① Simple Butt Joints
Top **Corner and** *Below* **T joints can be formed by skew nailing or by using corrugated fasteners.**

③ Types of Halving Joints
Top **A corner halving joint.** *Bottom left* **A T-halving joint.** *Bottom right* **A cross halving joint.**

④ Forming a Halving Joint in Timber Battens
Mark width of the cut-out. Mark half the thickness of the wood with a marking gauge. Cross hatch area to be removed. Saw down sides with a tenon saw, then chisel out the waste.

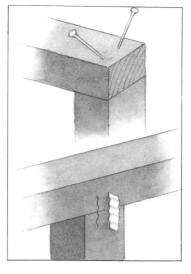

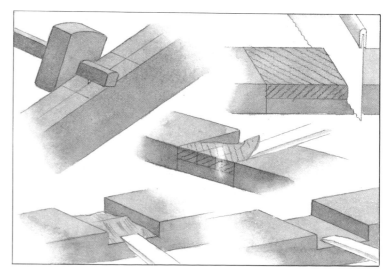

housing joint goes to the full width of the shelf, while a 'stopped' housing joint is taken only part of the way across the board. Chisel the waste away from each side. In the case of a stopped housing, chisel the waste from the stopped end first. If you have a router, it is easier to cut a housing joint by running the router across the board against a batten which is cramped at right-angles to the board.

A rebate joint is similar to a housing joint at the top of a board, and can be cut in a similar way.

BARE-FACED HOUSING JOINT

This type of housing joint, used at the corners of a frame, is a much stronger joint than the common butt joint or lapped joint because the tongue of one piece is held in a housing cut in the other piece. The joint will be held firm with good woodworking adhesive and by nailing or screwing down through the top into the upright. However, because of the short grain on the outside of the groove, this piece is left overlong while the joint is made, and then the 'horn' (the excess timber) is cut off neatly, flush with the side of the joint. The tongue should be no thicker than half the width of the timber being joined.

Carefully mark out the joint with a trimming knife, a try square and a marking gauge. The depth of the housing should be about one-third to a half the thickness of the upright. Cut the sides of the housing to the required depth using a tenon saw held vertical, or a carefully set circular saw. Cramping a batten alongside the housing will help to keep the cut straight. Remove the waste with a chisel, working from both sides to the middle, and holding the chisel with the flat side downwards. Alternatively, cut the housing with a router (*see* **Cutting grooves and housings, page 22**).

Mark out the vertical piece so that the tongue will fit exactly in the housing. Use a marking gauge to mark out the tongue. Cut the rebate with a router or with a tenon saw to form the tongue (*see* **Cutting grooves and housings, page 22.**).

6 **Forming Mitre Joints**
Top **Glue and pin together a simple mitre joint.** *Bottom* **Reinforce the joint with a corner block, dowels or wood veneer.**

8 **Types of Housing Joints**
Top **A through housing joint;** *Middle* **Through housing joints on the side of a central support;** *Bottom* **A corner housing joint.**

7 **Stages in Forming a Through Housing Joint**
Mark width of the housing according to thickness of wood being joined. Use a trimming knife. Mark depth with marking gauge. Cut down sides with tenon saw. Chisel out the waste, working from both sides to the middle.

9 **Stages in Making a Bare-faced Housing joint**
Leave a 'horn' of surplus timber to support the short grain which will be on outside of the groove. Mark width of piece being joined. Mark and cut housing as before. Saw off horn.

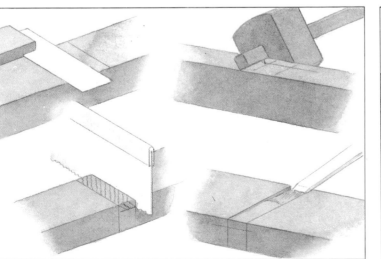

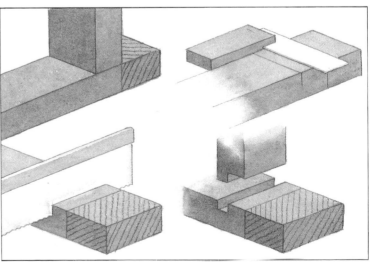

TECHNIQUES: WOOD JOINTS

Mortise and tenon joint   A mortise and tenon joint can be marked out with a **mortise gauge**. Mark out the tenon (the tongue) so that it is one-third of the thickness of the piece of wood. The mortise (the slot) is marked at the same width in the other piece. The length of the mortise should match the width of the tenon being fitted. Drill out most of the waste with a series of holes using a bit slightly smaller than the mortise width. Working from the centre, chop out the mortise with a chisel to the depth required. If making a through joint (in which the end of the tenon is visible), turn the wood over and complete the mortise from the other side.

Hold the tenon piece upright, but sloping away from yourself, secure in a vice, and use a tenon saw carefully to cut down to the shoulder. Then swivel the wood around to point the other way, and saw down to the other side of the shoulder. Next, position the wood vertically and cut down to the shoulder. Finally, place the wood flat and saw across the shoulder to remove the

2   **Marking and Cutting a Mortise and Tenon Joint**
Mark the length of the mortise slot to match the size of the rail being joined. Set the mortise gauge to the width of the chisel being used to cut out the mortise slot. (Chisel should be about one-third the width of wood being joined.) Use the mortise gauge to mark the mortise, and also the tenon, on the rail. Drill out the mortise and complete the cut with a chisel. Use a tenon saw to cut out the tenon.

1   **Mortise and Tenon Joints**
Top **A common or stopped mortise and tenon joint.** *Below* **Through mortise and tenon joint.**

3   **Making a Haunched Mortise and Tenon Joint**
Leave rail over-long. Mark out as before but allow for shoulder at top. Cut mortise slot, then saw down sides of shoulder which is completed with a chisel. Cut tenon as shown.

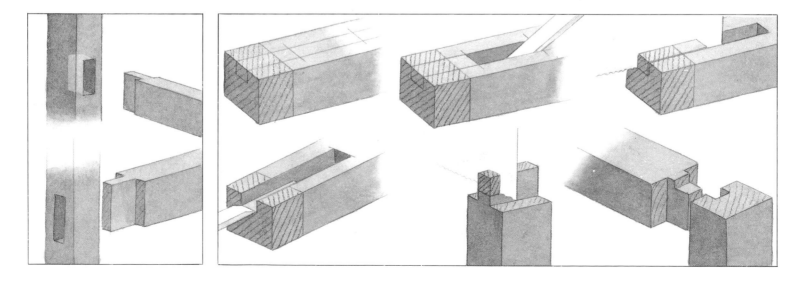

waste. Repeat for the waste on the other side of the tongue. Check that the two pieces fit well before gluing and assembling the joint. For added strength and a better appearance, cut small additional shoulders at each end of the tenon. These joints are the type used in the wardrobe with hinged doors project (*see page 212 for instructions.*)

Haunched mortise and tenon joint For joints at the corner of a large frame, such as the doors in the Japanese wardrobe project on page 238, a square haunch or shoulder can be left in the tenon to increase its effective width and considerably strengthen the joint.

The joint is marked out with a try square, marking knife, and marking gauge as for an ordinary mortise and tenon, but allowance is made for a square shoulder at the top as shown in the diagram.

To prevent the small amount of cross-grain timber above the mortise from being pushed out when the mortise slot is cut, the rail is left overlong at this stage to create a 'horn'

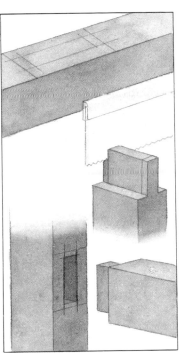

⑤ Shouldered Tenon Joint
For enhanced strength and appearance, cut small additional shoulders at each end of the tenon. Do this by sawing down.

which is cut off after the joint has been made and assembled.

Bare-faced mortise and tenon joint If the tongue of a tenon joint is offset to one side, this produces a bare-faced tenon as shown in the diagram. This produces a strong joint where narrow rails, such as the trellis rails in the Japanese wardrobe doors (page 238), meet the thicker frame rails. The mortise slots in the frame rails can be cut farther back from the front edge for extra strength, and the bare-faced tenons of the trellis rails allow the front faces of these rails to lie flush with the front face of the door.

A bare-faced tenon is cut in the same way as a **halving joint** (or **half-lap joint**).

Dovetail joint A dovetail joint is made so that the 'pins', which are the protruding fingers, interlock in both parts of the joint, giving it a great pull-out strength. The joint can only come apart in the same way as it is assembled.

A sliding bevel is used to mark out the dovetail pins on one rail, and the dovetail shape is cut out using a dovetail saw or fine-toothed tenon saw to leave a central pin.

The thickness and shape of the pin are marked on the other piece, called the 'post', and the marks are taken round on to the ends using a try square. The post is held upright and the waste inside the two outer tails is cut out using a dovetail saw, while a coping saw is used to cut across the bottom of the waste and then pared to the bottom line.

④ Making a Bare-Faced Mortise and Tenon Joint
Tenon is offset to one side. Mark and cut as shown here.

⑥ Marking Out and Cutting a Dovetail Joint
Mark a line the thickness of the matching piece. Using a mortise gauge, mark top of the pin. Mark sides of pin with sliding bevel set at slope of 1 in 6. Cut pin with tenon saw. Hold pin on other piece. Mark dovetail and cut out waste with tenon and coping saws. Pare base accurately with chisel to achieve good fit.

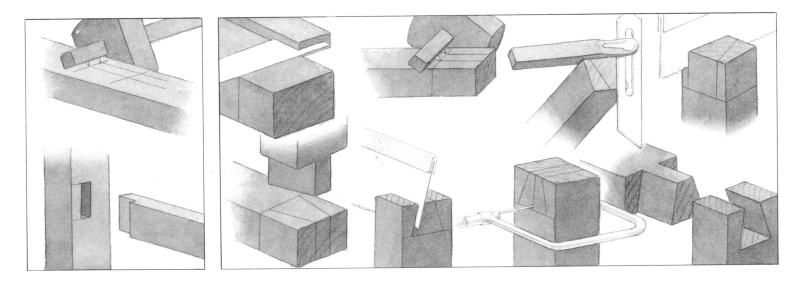

TECHNIQUES: WOOD JOINTS AND SCRIBING

Dowel joint Dowels are a strong, simple and hidden means of joining wood together.

Use pre-cut grooved dowels with bevelled ends (*see* **Materials, page 18**). These range from 6mm ($\frac{1}{4}$in) diameter by 25mm (1in) long to 10mm ($\frac{3}{8}$in) by 50mm (2in). The dowel length should be about one and-a-half times the thickness of the wood being jointed. If you need to use dowelling of a larger diameter (as used in the cupboard door frames in the kitchen and for alcoves shelves and cupboards), cut your own from lengths of dowel. Cut grooves down the length of dowel to allow glue and air to escape, and chamfer the ends. When making your own dowels, their length can be twice the thickness of the wood.

On both pieces of wood, use a **marking gauge** to find the centre line, and mark with a pencil. Drill the dowel holes to half the dowel length with the drill held in a **drill stand**, or aligned with a **try square** stood on end. Drill the dowel holes in one of the pieces to be joined, insert centre points in the holes, then bring the

two pieces of the joint together so they are carefully aligned. The centre points will make marks in the second piece of wood where the dowel holes should be drilled. Drill the holes to half of the length of the dowels, plus a little extra for glue. Where dowels are used for location rather than strength, such as for joining worktops, set the dowels three-quarters into one edge and a quarter into the other.

Put adhesive in the hole and tap dowels into the holes in the first piece with a mallet. Apply adhesive to both parts of the joint; bring the pieces together and cramp them in position until the adhesive has set.

GLUING

All joints are stronger if glued. Make sure that surfaces to be joined are clean and well-fitting. Cramp surfaces together while the glue is setting, but not so tightly that all the glue is squeezed from the joint. Use waterproof glue for joints that may be subject to dampness. If the parts do not fit tightly, use a two-part gap-filling glue, not PVA adhesive.

① Types of Dowel Joint
Dowels can join panels edge to edge and join frames at corners. They can be hidden or have ends exposed.

② Dowels to Join Panels
Right Mark dowel positions. Drill holes, insert centre points. Mark second piece.

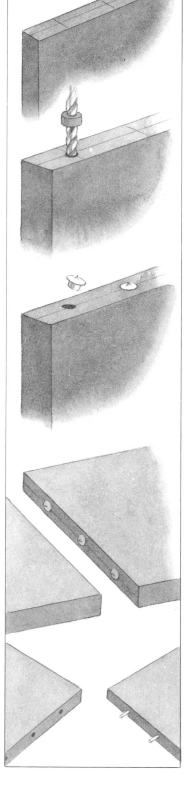

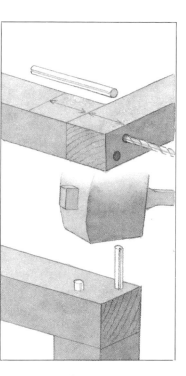

③ Making a Dowelled Frame
If edge of frame will not be seen, drill holes for dowels after making frame. Hammer dowels home; cut ends flush after glue dries.

④ Using a Dowelling Jig
If dowels are to be hidden, a dowelling jig makes it easy to drill holes that align in both pieces.

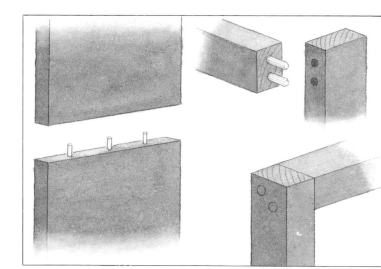

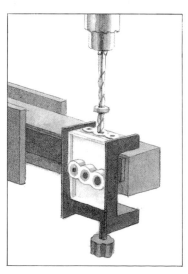

SCRIBING AND LEVELLING

Scribing long lengths When you are fitting a worktop, horizontal panel, shelf, or vertical panel to a wall, you are likely to find that it will not touch the wall at every point since it is extremely unlikely that the wall will be flat and square. To avoid such gaps, it is necessary to scribe the item to the wall.

Hold the item in place and as close to its final position as possible. If it is a worktop, make sure that it is level and at right-angles to whatever is next to it. If it is an upright, make sure that the front edge is held vertical. Where the gap is at its widest, pull the panel forward so that the gap is 25mm (1 in). Take a block of wood 25mm (1 in) long and place it on the panel, against the wall, at one end. Hold a pencil against the other end of the block, and draw the pencil and block along the wall so that the pencil makes a line, which reproduces the contours of the wall.

With an electric jigsaw or a padsaw, cut along the line. Where the line is too close to the edge to saw,

shape the panel to the line using a shaping tool, such as a **Surform** or a wood rasp. Press the panel against the wall and check that it fits neatly all the way along.

Scribing in alcoves It is more difficult to scribe in an alcove because a horizontal panel will usually fit neatly only *after* it has been scribed to a wall.

Using a large wooden square (you can make one from timber battens following the 3-4-5 principle of producing a right-angled triangle, see page 20), find out if one, or both, of the side walls are square and flat. If they are, you can carefully measure between them at the required height of the worktop. Then saw off the ends of the worktop to this length and position it, before finally scribing it to the rear wall as described above.

If the side walls of the alcove are not square, you can mark out the worktop using a cardboard template *(see* **Using templates** *)* of each side wall and part of the rear wall which you then scribe to fit.

Using a profile gauge This device *(see* **Tools, page 12** *)* is used for reproducing a complicated shape and is useful if you have to fit, for example, a worktop around something such as a decorative timber moulding. It comprises a row of movable pins or narrow plastic strips held in place by a central bar. When pressed against a shape, the pins follow the outline of the shape. The profile gauge is then held on the item to be fitted and the shape transferred to it by drawing around the profile gauge with a pencil. After use, realign the pins.

Using templates When cutting around an awkward-shaped object, such as a pipe, it is a good idea to make a template of the obstruction. Make the template from cardboard or thick paper. Cut and fold the template to make it as accurate as you can. When you are satisfied that you have a good fit, place the template on the item to be fitted, and mark around it to produce a cutting line. Alternatively, glue the template in position and cut around it.

Levelling battens When fixing battens to a wall with **masonry nails**, first lay the battens on the floor and drive the nails almost all the way through them. On the wall, use a **spirit level** to position the batten horizontally and draw a pencil line along the top edge of the batten. Hold the batten in position and drive one of the end masonry nails part of the way into the wall. Check that the top of the batten aligns with the guide line, then rest the spirit level on the batten and, with the bubble central, drive the nail at the other end of the batten into the wall. Check again that the batten is level before driving in all the nails.

If fixing the batten with screws, drill **clearance holes** in the batten as above and, with a pointed tool, mark the wall through a screw hole at one end of the batten. Drill and plug the wall at this point *(see* **Wall fixings, page 24** *)* then screw the batten to the wall. Level the batten as above, mark the other screw positions, then remove the batten and drill and plug the wall in preparation. Finally, screw the wall batten in to place.

⑤ Scribing Long Lengths to Fit Against a Wall
Where gap is widest pull panel forward so gap is 25mm (1 in). Hold pencil against 25mm (1 in) wide block; move block and pencil along wall to draw cutting line. Cut along this line.

⑥ Fixing Levelling Battens to a Wall
If fixing with masonry nails drive these into battens first. Hold batten in place and mark wall. Holding batten on marked line, insert nail at end. Recheck level; drive in other nails.

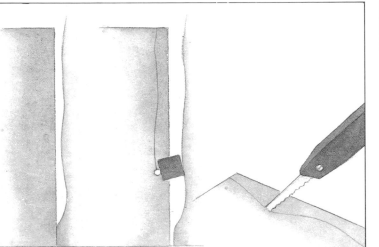

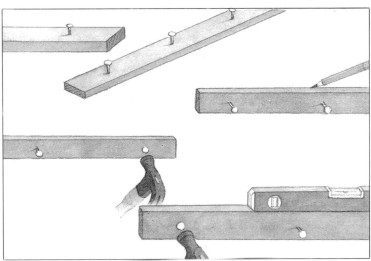

TECHNIQUES: FITTING DOORS AND HINGES

Levelling kitchen units Floors are rarely level, so that when installing kitchen units you must work from the highest spot in the room. Assemble the units and temporarily place them in position. Take a long, straight wooden batten and place this on the top of the units. Place a spirit level on the horizontal batten, to find the highest unit. Work from this unit and bring all the other units up to this level by placing pieces of plywood or hardboard underneath them. After this is done, the worktops can be installed, and the inset sink fitted and connected.

Alternatively, if you have yet to construct the units, you can build each one to the exact height required to compensate for differences in floor level. This levelling technique is very useful for old properties where floors are invariably uneven. First, lay straight battens around the floor where the units will be positioned – one batten at the front edge and one at the back. Work from the high point and pack up the battens so that they are level. Mark on them the positions of the

units and at each point measure the gap to the floor. Increase the height of each unit by this amount.

Finding verticals Use a plumb line to mark a vertical line on a wall. Tap a nail into the wall where you want the vertical to be, and tie the plumb line to it. When the line is steady, hold a scrap of wood on the wall so it just touches the string and mark the wall at this point. Repeat the procedure at a couple of other places. Alternatively, rub the plumb line with chalk. When it stops swinging, press it against the wall, then pluck the string to leave a vertical chalk line on the wall.

HANGING DOORS

Hinged cupboard or wardrobe doors There are two ways to fit hinged doors; they can be **inset** to fit between side frames, or they can be **lay-on** where the doors cover the side frames.

Inset doors look attractive, but they are harder to fit than lay-on doors because they must be very accurately made to achieve a uni-

form gap all round the opening. Lay-on doors cover the frame and hide any uneven gaps. Also, the concealed hinges that are normally used to hang a lay-on door are adjustable, making it easy to alter the door so that it opens and closes smoothly and accurately.

Sliding cupboard and wardrobe doors Small doors slide in double U-channel tracks made from timber or plastic. Shallow U-channel track is fitted along the bottom front edge of the opening and a deeper track is fitted at the top, to the underside of the front edge. The grooves in the track should match the door thickness and it is important to fit the top track exactly vertically above the bottom track. Make sliding doors so that they overlap each other by about 45–50mm (1¾–2in). Their height should be the distance from the bottom of the groove in the top track, plus 6mm (¼in). After assembly of the unit, the door can be fitted by lifting it up and into the top track, and then slotting it into the bottom track for a neat fit.

Heavier doors must be hung using a top- or bottom-track roller system. Fitting is usually straightforward if you follow the manufacturer's instructions. Even if the track has been fixed so that it is not exactly horizontal, there is usually a way of adjusting the doors so that they move and close smoothly.

FITTING HINGES

Inset doors Flush hinges are the easiest to fit. They are simply screwed to the edge of the door and the frame, and require no recessing. However, they cannot be adjusted after fitting. The inner flap of the hinge is screwed to the edge of the door, while the outer flap is screwed to the inner face of the frame.

Fix the hinges at equal distances from the top and bottom of the door. With a tall or very heavy door, fit a third hinge centrally between the other two. Mark the hinge positions on the edge of the door with the hinge knuckle (joint) in line with the door front. Drill **pilot holes** and screw on the inner flap. Hold the door in place or rest it on something

① Using a Profile Gauge
To reproduce complicated shapes, press the gauge against object; use it as a pattern.

② A Method of Levelling Kitchen Units
Temporarily position the units or the partition frames. Place spirit level on a straight batten to find the highest unit. Pack plywood or hardwood pieces under other units to bring them to this level.

③ Fitting Sliding Door Track
Heavy doors are best hung on bottom track. Track screws to floor and rollers are inset in door bottoms.

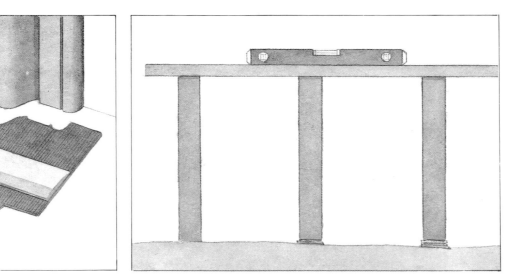

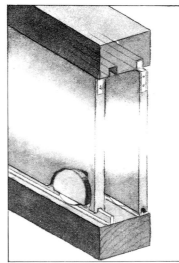

to raise it the correct height, making sure that it is accurately aligned top and bottom, and mark the positions of the hinges on the frame. Remove the door and extend these lines using a try square. Hold the door against the frame so it is in an open position, and screw the outer hinge flaps in place, so that they match up with the guide lines.

Butt hinges are conventional flapped hinges and are available in steel (commonly) or in brass, which is better for high-quality work. They are fitted in the same way as flush hinges, except that the hinge flaps have to be recessed into the timber using a chisel or router.

Mark out the hinge positions as for flush hinges, making sure that the hinges are not positioned so that the fixing screws will go into the end grain of cross members and be likely to pull out.

The length of the hinges is marked out first, using a marking knife, then the width of the hinge and the thickness of the flap are marked using a marking gauge. With a chisel held vertical, and a mallet, cut

down around the waste side of the recess, then make a series of vertical cuts across the full width of the recess. Remove the waste by careful chiselling, then finally pare the bottom of the recess flat using the chisel held flat side downwards.

If you are careful, you can remove the bulk of the waste from a hinge recess using a straight bit in a router. The bit is set to cut to the depth of the recess, and afterwards the corners can be finished off using a chisel.

Lay-on doors Modern, adjustable concealed hinges are the most commonly used. There are many types available, and they come with full fitting instructions. Some types are face-fixed and simply screw in place on the inside face of the door, but usually a special end mill hinge-sinker bit is used to drill a wide, flat-bottomed hole for the hinge body in the rear surface of the door. Next, the base plate is screwed to the side frame. Finally, the hinge is attached to the base plate and the adjusting screws are turned until the door fits perfectly in place.

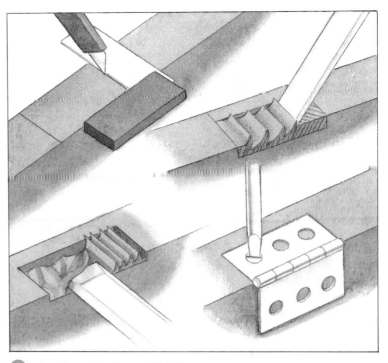

6 **The Stages in Fitting a Butt Hinge**
Using a try square and a trimming knife, mark out the length of hinge. With a marking gauge mark width and thickness of hinge flap. With chisel vertical, cut round outline of hinge. Make series of cuts across width of recess. Pare out the waste then check that the flap lies flush. Once this is done, screw the butt hinge in place.

4 **Fitting a Flush Hinge**
Flush hinges are very easy to fit. Screw the outer flap to the frame and the inner flap to the door.

5 **Fitting a Butt Hinge**
Butt hinges must be recessed into the door and frame so that hinge flaps are flush with surface.

7 **Fitting Face-Fixed Concealed Hinges**
This hinge is simply screwed to the inside face of the door and frame.

8 **Fitting Recessed Concealed Hinges**
Blind hole is drilled for hinge body. The base plate arm is adjustable.

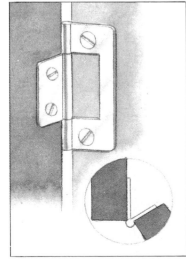

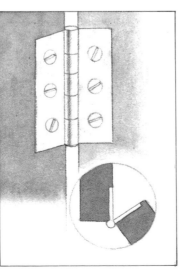

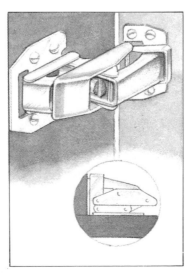

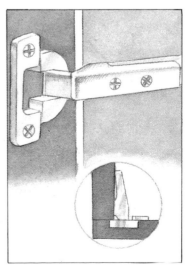

TECHNIQUES: FITTING CATCHES AND LOCKS

FITTING CATCHES

Many types of concealed hinges have built-in closers, so catches are not required. With conventional hinges, magnetic catches are popular. The magnet is fitted to the side of the cabinet and the catch plate is then positioned on the magnet. The door is closed on to the catch and pressed hard so that the catch plate marks the door. The door is opened and the catch plate is then simply screwed to the door.

Ball catches are very neat devices. On the central edge of the door a hole is drilled to accept the body of the ball catch, which is pressed into place. The door is closed and the ball marks the edge of the cupboard. The door is opened and the striker plate carefully positioned to coincide with the centre of the ball. If you are recessing the striker plate, its outline should be drawn around, using a trimming knife. The striker plate is then recessed into the cabinet so that it lies flush with the surface enabling the catch to operate smoothly.

1 Magnetic Cupboard Catch
A magnetic catch is screwed to the inside face of a cabinet and the catch plate is screwed to the frame.

FITTING DOOR LIFT MECHANISMS

Actual fitting instructions vary with the type of mechanism, but basically all screw inside the cupboard on the side of the carcass, close to the top. Two lift mechanisms are required per door, and they are designed to throw the door upwards and outwards, and clear of the ceiling.

With the type we use in the Wardrobe with Hinged Doors project (page 212), the mechanism is screwed to the side face of the frame just below the top of the wardrobe, and just inside the front edge. It is held with three screws. The lift-up flap is screwed to the opening part of the mechanism with two screws, the top screw being fixed the thickness of the wardrobe top plus 28mm ($1\frac{1}{8}$in), down from the top edge of the door flap to be sure that the flap opens without disturbing the wardrobe front or the ceiling.

FITTING LOCKS

The neatest lock is a cabinet mortise lock. To fit, mark the centre line in the

2 Fitting a Ball Catch
Drill door edge centrally for ball catch body which is pressed in place. Striker plate fixes to frame.

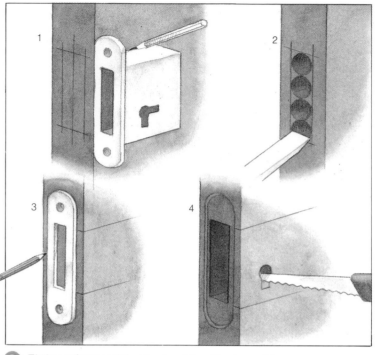

3 Fitting a Cabinet Mortise Lock to a Cupboard Door
1 Mark the centre line on the door edge and measure and mark the width and thickness of the lock on door edge. 2 Use a dowel bit to clear out the mortise and clear out the slot with a chisel. 3 Push lock into the mortise slot and mark around cover plate. 4 Cut a recess for the plate, then form a keyhole using a padsaw (also known as a keyhole saw).

4 Fitting Top-Hinged Door Lift Mechanism
Two types of door lift mechanisms are shown below. On the left is a combined hinge and stay as used in the Wardrobe with Hinged Doors project. Also shown is a conventional stay.

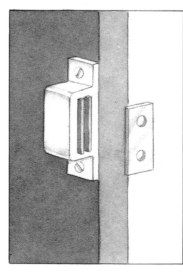

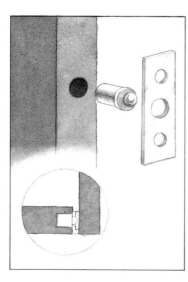

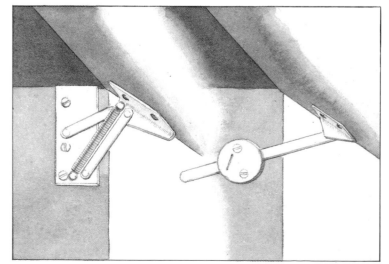

edge of the door and measure and mark the width and thickness of the lock body. Using a dowel drill bit of the same thickness as the lock body, drill out a series of overlapping holes to remove the bulk of the waste, and clear out the slot with a chisel. Push the lock into the mortise slot, mark around the cover plate and cut a recess. Measure the lock for the keyhole position, mark this on the front face of the door, drill the hole and saw a slot for the key. Close the door, turn out the lock bolt to mark the cabinet side, and fit the lock keep-plate there.

A straight cupboard lock, as used on the Tool Cupboard project (see page 45), is very easy to fit and operate. It simply screws to the back of the door after the keyhole has been cut out with a padsaw.

Start by making a thick paper template of the outline of the lock with a cut-out for the keyhole accurately positioned. Hold the template on the face of the door and mark the keyhole. Drill a hole at the top to the correct size, and below this drill a line of smaller holes which can be en-

larged into a slot for the keyhole. You can use a padsaw (which is also known as a keyhole saw) for this purpose.

Hold the lock in place behind the door, and fit the key to position the lock accurately. Mark and drill the fixing lock positions. Screw the lock in place. A brass keyhole escutcheon fitting may be supplied, and this is simply tapped into place into the keyhole flush with the face of the cabinet front.

In the case of the Tool Cupboard project (see page 47 for full instructions), it will be necessary to cut away part of the door side rail to allow the lock to fit flush with the edge of the door. To do this, hold the lock against the edge of the door and on the inside, mark the outline of the lock. Drill through the side rail, within this outline, and carefully chisel away the waste so that the lock fits snugly when it is slipped into place behind the door front.

Once the lock has been fitted, the door should be closed and the key operated so that the lock bolt marks the edge of the other door. With a

chisel, cut a rebate in this position for the lock bolt, and then cover the recess with a striking plate (also supplied with the lock). This is held in position, and its outline is marked with a knife. A shallow recess is then cut with a chisel so that the plate can be placed flush with the surface.

A cut cupboard lock, or drawer lock, is harder to fit because a recess has to be cut behind the cupboard or drawer front. A double recess is required – one for the lock mechanism, and the other for the back plate which is also recessed into the edge of the door or drawer for a neat fit and a smooth finish.

Hold the lock in position and mark the outline of the back plate on to the back and the edge of the door. Also mark where the mechanism rebate is required. First cut out the mechanism rebate using a chisel, then make the shallower rebate for the back plate. When the lock fits accurately, cut out the keyhole, then screw the lock in position. Fit the keyhole escutcheon and the striking plate as described above and finally check the lock.

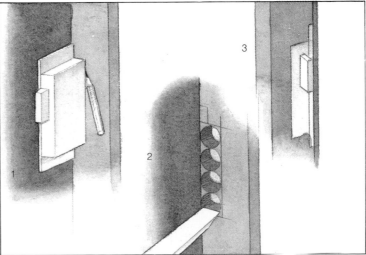

❼ Fitting Cut Cupboard Lock
1 **First chisel out the recess for the mechanism, then make a shallower rebate for the lock backplate.** *2* **When lock fits neatly, cut out keyhole.**

❺ Fitting a Surface-Mounted Cupboard Door Lock
Make a template of lock outline. *1* **Hold template on the door at lock position.** *2* **Drill hole and saw a slot.** *3* **Position the lock with the key in place.** *4* **Screw lock to door.**

❻ Fitting a Cupboard Lock on a Framed Door
1 **Hold the lock in position behind the frame and mark its outline.** *2* **Drill within the outline and chisel out waste.** *3* **Slide the lock through the aperture and fit as on left.**

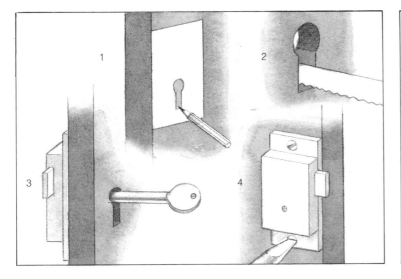

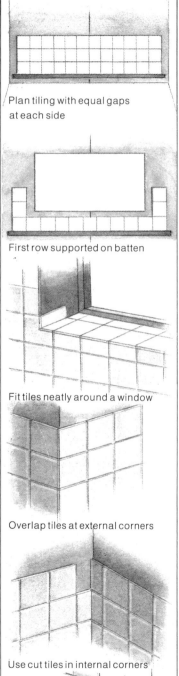

Plan tiling with equal gaps at each side

First row supported on batten

Fit tiles neatly around a window

Overlap tiles at external corners

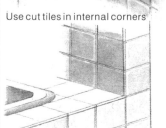

Use cut tiles in internal corners

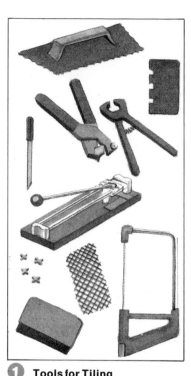

❶ Tools for Tiling
Top to bottom **Adhesive spreaders – metal and plastic; scoring tool; cutting pliers; tile nippers; heavy-duty cutter; spacers; file; saw; grout spreader.**

Planning When tiling, accurate setting out is essential. The tiles must be applied absolutely level and, after tiling, no cut edges should show. Only factory-glazed edges, or half-round edge tiles which are made to be seen, should be visible. With the modular frames of the basic kitchen units (*see page 86*) note that the frame width is designed so that the front face tiles exactly cover the ends of the frames and the edges of the tiles fixed to each side of the frames. Tiles on the side panels are arranged so that cut tiles are right at the back of the units. Similarly, if any tiles have to be reduced in height, these cut tiles should be at floor-level where they will be less noticeable.

When tiling a plain wall, centralize the tiles on it, using cut tiles of equal width in each corner. If the wall has a prominent window, arrange the tiles to give it a neat border. In both cases, adjust the height of the tiles by having cut tiles at floor or skirting-board level. Plan your tiling scheme so that part-tiled walls and low vertical surfaces, such as the side of a bath, have whole tiles on the top

row. You may have to compromise on the best overall arrangement for the room. To deal with window reveals (recesses), have glazed edges visible around the front of the reveal, and have cut tiles butting up to the window frame.

Setting out Start by making a gauging rod. This is simply a length of straight timber, about 38×12mm ($1\frac{1}{2} \times \frac{1}{2}$in), on which pencil lines are drawn to indicate tile widths, including spacers. To mark the lines, lay out a row of tiles along the gauging rod, with spacers between them – unless tiles incorporating spacers are being used. Draw a line across the gauging rod to coincide with the centre of each joint. If rectangular tiles are used, a second gauging rod is needed for tile heights.

Use the gauging rod(s) to set out accurately the tile positions. When you are satisfied with the arrangement, fix a perfectly straight batten of timber (about 38×12mm [$1\frac{1}{2} \times \frac{1}{2}$in]) horizontally across the full width of the area to be tiled to support the first row of complete tiles. Next, fix vertical battens at each side to support the

❷ Making a Gauging Rod
Lay out a correctly spaced row of tiles and on a batten accurately mark tile widths including spacers.

❸ Setting out the Wall
Centralize tiles on a dominant feature like a window, and fix batten one tile height above floor.

❹ Starting to Fix Tiles
Also fix vertical battens at each side. Spread adhesive in corner and press tiles firmly into place.

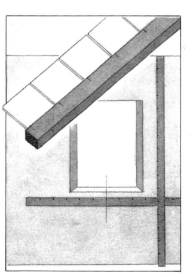

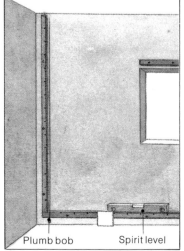

Plumb bob   Spirit level

last row of complete tiles at the sides and to keep the tiling square. Use the gauging rods to mark off on the wall battens the exact tile widths and heights, as this will help you to keep the tiling square. If you are tiling a plastered wall, temporarily fix the tiling battens with partly driven-in masonry nails. If tiling on wood or plywood, use ordinary wire nails.

TILING TOOLS

Adhesive spreader A simple evenly notched plastic tool which spreads a bed of tile adhesive.

Tile cutter There are various types of tile cutters available. Some resemble a pencil and have a tungsten-carbide tip which is drawn across the tile to score the surface where the break is required. A better type is a cutter resembling a pair of pincers. This has a cutting wheel to score a cut line, as well as jaws between which the tile is placed before the cutter handles are squeezed, pincer-like, to make the cut. A heavy-duty cutter for thick, large tiles consists of a jig with a cutting-lever arm.

Tile saw Consists of a tungsten-carbide rod-saw blade fitted into a frame. It will cut tiles to any shape: L-shaped, curved, etc. The tile to be sawn is cramped in a vice.

Tile spacers Nowadays it is common for tiles to be supplied with plain edges, rather than with built-in spacer lugs moulded on the edges of the tiles. Spacer lug tiles are simply butted together and are automatically evenly spaced as they are positioned. However, with plain-edge tiles it is important to place spacers between the tiles as they are positioned. This creates even gaps between the tiles for grouting.

Tile nippers A pincer-like device for removing narrow strips which are too small to be handled by a conventional cutter. It will also cut shaped tiles.

Tile-file Useful for cleaning up sharp and uneven edges of a cut tile.

Grout spreader Flexible rubber blade for spreading grout.

Sponge Used for cleaning away adhesive and grout from the surface of a fixed tile.

Tiling process Start in a bottom corner and spread adhesive over about 1 square metre (1 square yard). Rake it out evenly using the notched spreader which is usually supplied with the adhesive. Working from a corner, press the tiles into the adhesive with a slight twisting motion. If tiles without spacers are used, hold them evenly apart with plastic wall-tile spacers. These can either be pressed well into the joints and left in place, or they can protrude from the surface, in which case they can be pulled out after an hour or so and re-used elsewhere. At this stage, fit whole tiles only. Tiles that have to be cut to fit around obstacles can be fitted later.

Cutting edge tiles Wait for 12 hours after the main area of tiling has been completed, before removing the setting-out battens. Tiles can then be cut to fill the gaps around the perimeter. Measure the space into which the tile is to fit, remembering to allow for the spacers between tiles. Use a tile cutter to cut a straight line across the surface of the tile. Use the notched spreader to apply adhesive direct to the back of the tile,

and press it into place. If necessary, smooth rough edges with tile file.

Cutting around difficult shapes To cut around a pipe, snap the tile along the centre line of the pipe, then score the pipe's outline on the surface. For a neat finish, saw around the pipe outline using a **tungsten-carbide rod-saw** held in a conventional **hacksaw** frame. Alternatively, nip away the pipe cut out by snapping off small pieces of the tile, using tile nippers or a pair of pincers. Tiles to be fitted around basins and window openings can also be scored along the cutting line and then nipped. Alternatively, the cut-out can be sawn to avoid breakages if the part to be cut out runs close to the edge of the tile.

Finishing off Once the tiles are firm they should be grouted with a waterproof grout applied with a rubber spreader. When the grout is just beginning to set, use a small rounded stick to press the grout into the joint lines, then wipe off the excess grout with a damp sponge. When the grouting has dried, polish the surface with a dry duster.

---

5 **Cutting Tiles to Size**
Score along glazed side, then break tile along line using a cutting tool. Saw awkward shapes.

6 **Cutting Around Pipes**
Mark position of hole on face of tile. Snap tile along centre line. Score outline, then nip out waste.

7 **Grouting Tiles to Finish**
Use rubber blade squeegee to press grout into joints. As grout sets press rounded stick along joints.

8 **Drilling a Hole in Tiles**
Stick masking tape on drill point. Use masonry drill bit. Switch to hammer action when tile drilled through.

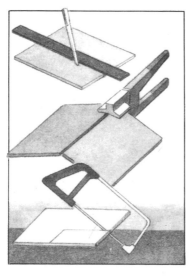

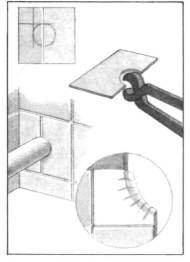

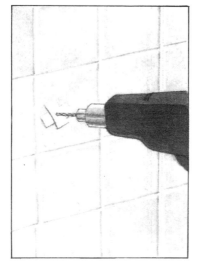

WORKBENCH AND TOOL CUPBOARD

This is the starting point for all serious DIY enthusiasts. If you make this well it will lead you to undertake many other projects around the home. You will also have a solid bench to work on and practical, safe storage for your tools – two ingredients that will make your DIY enjoyable, comfortable and efficient.

The workbench should be made first. For simplicity, I have used a ply-skinned fire door with a solid timber core; this is just as tough as the conventional solid beech top used for most professional benches, but is much cheaper. The frame is made from pine, and houses a plywood shelf for large pieces of equipment. A woodworker's vice and retractable stop for planing have been fitted to the bench.

The tool cupboard is fitted to the wall with bevelled battens and its two wings, which double as doors, are fitted with locks and fold back against the wall when the cupboard is in use. It is essential to incorporate lockable doors on a tool cupboard, especially in a household such as mine, where tools vanish with unfailing regularity. All your tools, fittings, nails and screws have their own storage area and are easily visible, so there is no excuse not to return them to their rightful place when your work is finished; searching around for missing tools never fails to upset the enjoyment of DIY work.

Work lamps are clamped to the top of the cupboard to provide sufficient light where it is most needed, and the gap behind the cupboard allows wiring to be installed for electrical sockets.

Several coats of clear, shiny varnish were applied to the cupboard to give it a thoroughly professional look. Enjoy it and use it well.

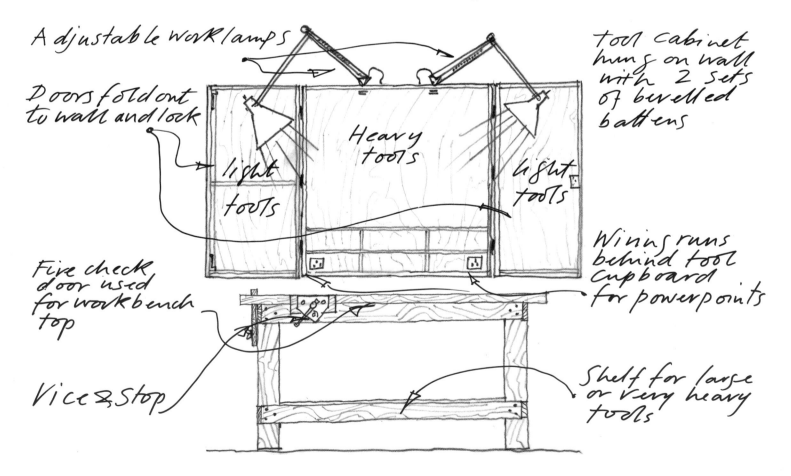

Adjustable work lamps

Doors fold out to wall and lock

tool cabinet hung on wall with 2 sets of bevelled battens

Heavy tools

light tools

light tools

Fire check door used for workbench top

Wiring runs behind tool cupboard for power points

Vice & Stop

Shelf for large or very heavy tools

WORKBENCH

A sturdy woodworking bench helps you to achieve good results, and constructing your own will provide valuable woodworking experience.

For neatness and a solid construction, the top and bottom rails are rebated into the bench legs. To speed up and simplify the job, you could omit the rebates and simply glue and screw the rails to the sides of the legs with a PVA adhesive.

The top of the workbench is a solid-core, fire-check flush door blank measuring 1980 × 610mm (6ft 6in × 24in). The top should overhang the frame – by 100mm (4in) at each end, by 12mm ($\frac{1}{2}$in) at the back and by at least 25mm (1in) at the front. The overhang allows enough space for G-cramps to hold items to the bench top. The overall height of the bench is 940mm (37in), which is a comfortable working height for a person about 1.8m (6ft) tall. Decide at an early stage what is a comfortable working height for you, and adjust the leg lengths accordingly.

The rail lengths are dependent on the size of the door blank used, to give the overhangs mentioned above. Whether or not you rebate the rails into the legs will also affect the length of the rails. The long rails fit inside the shorter end ones. If you rebate the rails, note that the top rails are thicker than the bottom ones. So the top rails will be shorter than the bottom rail lengths by the difference in thickness between the two rails.

MATERIALS

Part	Quantity	Material	Length
LEGS	4	150 × 150mm (6 × 6in) PAR softwood	902mm (35$\frac{1}{2}$in)
TOP RAILS	2 long 2 short	133 × 32mm (5$\frac{1}{4}$ × 1$\frac{1}{4}$in) PAR softwood	to suit door size
BOTTOM RAILS	2 long 2 short	150 × 25mm (6 × 1in) PAR softwood cut down to 133 mm (5$\frac{1}{4}$in) wide for neatness to match top rails	to suit door size
BENCH TOP	1	solid core, fire-check flush door blank	1980 × 610mm (6ft 6in × 24in)
BENCH TOP BATTENS	2	50 × 38mm (2 × 1$\frac{1}{2}$in) PAR softwood	length of the sides between the legs
SHELF	1	12mm ($\frac{1}{2}$in) plywood	as above
BENCH VICE	1		
HANGING BARS	2	25mm (1in) dowel	to suit bench width

TOOLS

FOLDING PORTABLE WORKBENCH/VICE

TRIMMING KNIFE

STEEL RULE

TRY SQUARE

PANEL SAW

TENON SAW

CHISEL about 19mm ($\frac{3}{4}$in) wide bevel-edge type

CHISEL about 25mm (1in) wide firmer type

MALLET

DRILL (hand or power)

TWIST DRILL BITS

COUNTERSINK BIT

MARKING GAUGE

WEBBING CRAMP (or rope and scrap of wood to make tourniquet)

SCREWDRIVER (cross-point or slotted, depending on screw type)

SMOOTHING PLANE

SANDING BLOCK AND ABRASIVE PAPER

ROUTER (an alternative to a chisel for cutting rail rebates)

JIGSAW (or padsaw or coping saw) – to make cut-out for vice

SPANNER to fit coach screws used to fix vice

FLAT DRILL BIT to make cut-out for bench stop, and holes for hanging bars

TWIST DRILL BIT to make holes for bench-stop bolt

MARKING OUT THE LEGS

Mark the legs to length, squaring the cutting line on all faces, and then cut the legs. Check they are of identical length by standing them together and comparing their height.

If the rails are to be rebated into the legs, mark out the rebates (see **Techniques, page 22**).

MARKING-UP FOR TOP RAIL

Line up one of the short rails flush with the top of the leg to mark off the depth of the rebate. Line up a try square underneath to mark off the line squarely. Score a line on to the leg with a trimming knife. Mark all four faces of the leg (see **Techniques, page 20**).

① Marking and Making the Leg Rebates for Rails
Left Mark rebates for the top and bottom rails. *Centre* Cut top rebates with a tenon saw; bottom rebates with a tenon saw and chisel. *Right* The leg rail after rebating has been done.

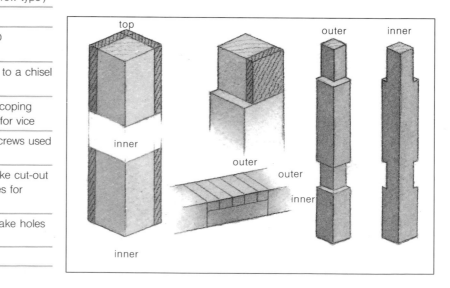

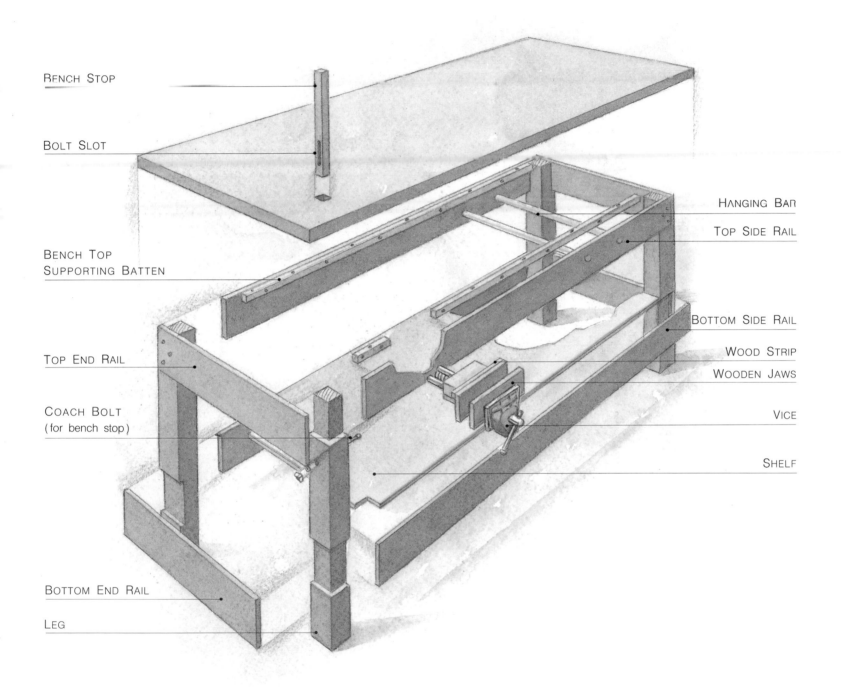

BENCH STOP

BOLT SLOT

BENCH TOP
SUPPORTING BATTEN

TOP END RAIL

COACH BOLT
(for bench stop)

BOTTOM END RAIL

LEG

HANGING BAR

TOP SIDE RAIL

BOTTOM SIDE RAIL

WOOD STRIP

WOODEN JAWS

VICE

SHELF

WORKBENCH

Set the marking gauge to the thickness of the top rail and mark this off on to the top, inner and outer faces of the leg, as shown (fig1, page 40). Repeat the whole procedure for the other three legs.

MARKING-UP LEG FOR BOTTOM RAIL

For the top of this rail to finish 350mm (14in) from the ground, measure this distance up the leg and mark with a pencil. Put the rail in place underneath and line up your try square underneath. Remove the rail and score a line with a trimming knife for the position of the bottom of the rail. Replace the rail against the try square, then move the square to the top of the rail. Remove the rail again and score a line with a trimming knife for the position of the top of the rail. Lining up in this way ensures greater accuracy. Continue lines round to the other three faces.

Re-set the marking gauge to the thickness of the lower rail and mark this thickness off on to the inner and outer faces of the legs as shown (see fig 1, page 40).

CUTTING FOR TOP RAIL

Hold the leg in a portable workbench or cramp it to a solid table or trestle and, cutting on the waste side of the line, make the horizontal cuts first, using a tenon saw to the marked depths. Then make the vertical cuts, using a tenon or panel saw, on both the outer faces. Remove any waste with a chisel. Alternatively, use a router, with the depth set to the thickness of the rails.

Repeat this procedure for the other three legs.

CUTTING OUT FOR BOTTOM RAIL

Make horizontal cuts with a tenon saw on the outer faces of one leg at the top and bottom of the rail position, to your marked depths. To cut out the rebate, make a series of cuts with a tenon saw down to the marked depths, about 12mm ($\frac{1}{2}$in) apart; then pare out the waste with a bevel-edge chisel and a mallet (see **Techniques, page 22**).

Repeat for the other three legs until the surface is flat.

END FRAME ASSEMBLY

The rails must fit tightly. If necessary, make the rebates so that they are fractionally undersize and plane down the rails slightly until they fit tightly in the rebates.

Apply glue to the leg rebates and position the bottom rail, so that it is flush with the sides. Drill and countersink through the rail into the legs and screw them together with 50mm (2in) No 10 screws – three on each leg. Repeat at the top for the top rail, gluing and screwing as before, using 65mm (2$\frac{1}{2}$in) No 10 screws.

Repeat the whole procedure for the second end frame. If you want to simplify construction by not using rebates, simply glue and screw the rails to the face of the legs. However, make sure that the frames are assembled square, and that the rails overhang the legs by the thickness of the rail.

Clean up, plane, and chamfer all the outer edges, then remove any excess glue and sand down all the surfaces for a smooth finish.

ADDING THE LONG RAILS

Stand the two end frames upright and fit the bottom long rails in place, gluing the leg rebates as before. Remember that the tighter the legs fit, the stronger the frame will be. For a sturdy frame, the shoulders must be pulled up tightly before screwing them together. To do this, use either a webbing cramp or a rope tourniquet around the frame at the joints. If using rope, loop a thin piece of wood in the rope each side and twist the wood round and round to make the frame secure.

Glue and fit the top rails and then tighten them together with a cramp or a rope tourniquet.

Pilot-drill and screw through the rails into the legs in three places, as for the end frames. Once the rails have been screwed, the cramp can be removed.

Clean up, and chamfer the top and bottom edges of the bottom rails and the bottom edges of the top rails. Sand down the framework and plane the top of the framework and the top rail flush.

① Assembling the Workbench End Frame
Lay the legs on a flat surface and check that bottom rail fits tightly into the rebate. Glue and screw in place. Fit the top rail in a similar way then repeat for the legs at the other end.

② Adding the Side Rails and Supporting Battens
Glue and nail the bottom side rails into the leg rebates first, then repeat for the top rails. In each case hold the frame tightly together with a rope tourniquet to keep it square. *Inset* Corner detail.

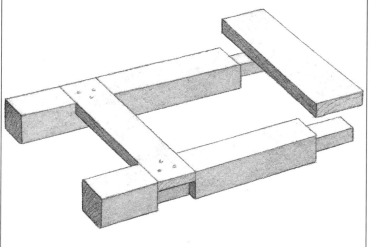

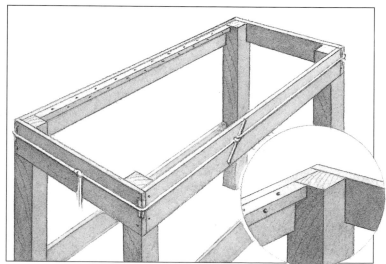

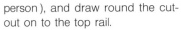
FITTING THE BENCH TOP

Take two battens of 50 × 38mm (2 × 1½in) DAR, cut to the length of the sides between the legs. Drill and countersink the battens on two adjacent faces for screws to fix to the side and top (ours had five along the side and six along the top). Choose the best side of the frame as the front. Then, at the back, cramp one of the battens in place to the inside of the frame, flush with the top of the top rail, and screw through the side into the rail. The front batten will be fixed after fitting the vice.

Put the top in place, equalizing the overhang each end and allowing 12mm (½in) overhang at the back, and the remainder at the front (enough to take a cramp). Do not screw the top down yet.

FITTING A VICE

You will need a vice that fits into the top rail. There is a wide range of woodworking vices to choose from. All have wide-opening jaws and are designed to fit to the underside of the bench top, on the front edge close to a leg, so that the top edge of the jaws (after the lining has been fitted – see below) is level with the bench top. Some smaller vices simply cramp on to the underside of the workbench, but it is best to use one that is designed to be bolted in place. A square body seating will ensure easy fitting to the bench top.

Choose the largest vice you can afford – a jaw opening of about 330m (13in) is ideal, but maximum openings range from 115mm (4½in) up to about 380mm (15in). The larger vices often have a useful quick-release mechanism which allows you to pull the jaw out and in without having to wind the handle as normal. Make sure that the body of the vice and the sliding jaw have holes to take the plywood liners which protect the work, the vice and the working tools.

The method of fitting varies slightly according to the make of vice chosen, but this is how we fitted ours. Remember that the top of the steel jaws must finish a little way down from the worktop, say 12mm (½in), to allow for a wooden strip, which is part of the jaw liners, to be fitted easily.

Measure the depth of the vice. Subtract from this the thickness of the worktop, minus 12mm (½in) (see fig 3). You will need a packing piece of the same thickness to go under the bench top and to fit between it and the vice.

MAKING THE CUT-OUT FOR THE VICE IN THE SIDE RAIL

You will first need to make a template of the vice. Put the vice on end with its packing piece in place, and draw round it on to a piece of thick paper or card. Simplify the lines to make cutting the side rail easier. Cut out the template and hold it to the underside of the bench top, about 300mm (12in) in from the front left hand for a right-handed person (or from the right for a left-handed

person), and draw round the cut-out on to the top rail.

To make the cut-out, remove the bench top, and cut round the line with an electric jigsaw or by hand with a padsaw or coping saw

Cramp the second bench-top supporting batten in place to the front top rail as before (see **Fitting the Bench Top, left**) and screw it in place, cutting out the section where the gap has been left for the vice with a padsaw or a coping saw. Glue and screw the bench top back in place through the battens.

Slide the vice into position, with the packing piece in place. Drill pilot holes up through the fixing holes in the bottom of the vice, through the packing piece, and into the worktop. Fix the vice securely in place using coach screws and washers.

MAKING THE WOODEN JAW LINERS

The liners are wooden pieces fitted inside the jaws of the vice so as to finish flush with the top of the bench. They serve to protect work while it is being held in the vice.

From 12mm (½in) plywood, cut two pieces slightly longer than the steel jaws of the vice. The width of the plywood should equal the distance between the top of the bench and the runner of the vice.

Cut a piece of scrap hardwood to the same thickness as the distance between the top of the steel jaws and the top of the worktop, and to the same length as that of the wooden jaw liners. Glue in place to the front edge of the bench, flush with the worktop, so that it rests on the vice.

FITTING THE REAR WOODEN JAW

Mark through the holes in the front of the vice on to one of the wooden jaw liners. Transfer the marks to the other liner. Drill and countersink the liners at these marks and screw through these holes and the holes in the back into the worktop.

FITTING THE FRONT WOODEN JAW

Close the vice with the front wooden jaw cramped in place, and screw through the front holes into the jaw.

3 Fitting the Bench Vice
Thickness of packing piece is depth of vice, less thickness of worktop minus the wooden strip.

packing piece

4 Fitting the Wooden Jaw Liners to the Vice
Jaw liners (made from 12mm [½in] plywood) finish flush with the bench top. The rear jaw liner is fixed by screwing it into worktop. Screw through the front of the vice to fix the front liner.

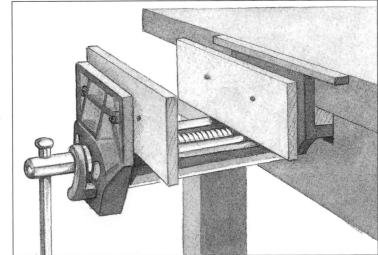

WORKBENCH

THE BENCH STOP

A bench stop which can be raised above the bench top when required is useful, for example, for pushing against while large pieces of work are planed or chiselled.

The bench stop fits just outside the front leg at the vice end. To mark the position of the bench stop on the bench top, square round from the outer edge of the leg using a pencil and try square. The line should be continued from the underneath, up the front edge, and on to the top of the workbench. Measure back from the front edge to coincide with the leg. Square off the line from the side.

Take a piece of hardwood batten about 25 × 38mm (1 × 1½in) and cut to about 250–300mm (10–12in) long. Mark round the end of the batten in position behind the pencil marks on the worktop as shown: that is, to the *outside* of them. Check that the lines will allow the bench stop to fit alongside the leg. Go over the pencil marks with a trimming knife.

Using a flat drill bit as near as possible in size to the bench-top cut-out, drill right through the worktop. Cramp a piece of packing underneath the hole, so that you can then pare out the edges down on to the packing, to avoid breaking the wood underneath. Take care to pare out fractionally *within* the line. Check occasionally with a try square that you are cutting down square. Keep paring out until the batten slots into the hole and can be moved up and down, but stop while the fit is still fairly tight.

TO FIX THE BENCH STOP

We used a 150mm (6in) long, 9.5mm (⅜in) diameter coach bolt with a washer and a butterfly nut. Mark where the bolt is to be on the leg. (This must be far enough down to clear the top rail.) Fit the stop in place flush with the top. Transfer the bolt mark on to the bench stop – this will be the top of the slot. Move the stop up to the highest position required, that is, about 75–100mm (3–4in), and mark off the bolt position for the bottom of the slot.

Take the bench stop out. Mark off the centre line and drill a line of holes 9.5mm (⅜in) in diameter along the length of the slot, with a packing piece held underneath. Pare out the slot with a chisel until the bolt slides freely inside. Alternatively, use a router to make the slot.

At the marked line on the leg, mark a vertical line in the exact centre of the bench-stop position, to make sure that the bolt fits in the middle of it. Use a 9.5mm (⅜in) drill bit to drill right through the leg at this point. Slide the stop into place and push the bolt through from the inside of the leg and through the slot. Fix the screw in place with a washer and a butterfly nut.

FITTING THE SHELF

Measure the outside dimensions of the frame and cut a piece of 12mm (½in) thick plywood to this size. Make notches in each corner for the legs by measuring and cutting with a power jigsaw or a panel saw. Clean up and chamfer the top edges of the shelf and then slot it in place on the bottom rails.

FITTING THE HANGING BARS

These hanging bars are fitted beween the long rails at the opposite end to the vice, and are very useful for hooking things on, such as G-cramps, a dustpan and brush, a paint kettle and other essential items that you may need to hand.

Cut two lengths of 25mm (1in) dowel to the width of the underframe, plus a little extra for planing off afterwards. Mark dowel positions about 300mm (12in) and 600mm (24in) in from each of the rail ends, in the centre of both the back and front top rails of the bench.

Using a flat drill bit of the same diameter as the dowel, drill holes at the marks, through the rails, back and front. Put dowels through the holes, hammering them in after smearing the ends with PVA glue. Plane off the ends flush with the rails for a smooth and neat finish.

THE VICE AND BENCH STOP

Often the vice can be used in conjunction with the stop to hold large items.

1 **Fitting the Bench Stop**
Enlarge the line of holes in the stop to form a slot. Slot in bench is formed in the same way.

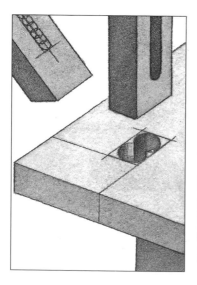

TOOL CUPBOARD

It is important to store tools in a safe and secure place where they are also readily accessible when required. Properly stored tools stay sharp and rust-free, and with each tool in its correct place you will not waste time looking for tools.

This cupboard provides an ideal place to store tools. It is fixed on to the wall of the workshop or garage where you would normally do DIY. When the cupboard is in use, the doors open out flat to the wall on each side for easy access to the tools. You can fit it out to suit your requirements and to leave space for new tools as you buy them.

The rack incorporates sockets for power tools, and adjustable lamps to give excellent illumination of the worksurface below. When not in use, the lamps can be pushed out of the way, and the doors closed. For safety, the cupboard is permanently screwed to the wall through bevelled battens and the doors have a lock for security and to keep the tools out of the way of children.

MAIN CUPBOARD SECTION

Cut the back panel by sawing the full sheet of 12mm ($\frac{1}{2}$in) plywood in half to form a 1220 × 1220mm (48 × 48in) sheet. Use a circular saw (or panel saw), running the sole plate of the saw against a straight batten cramped to the surface of the plywood sheet to ensure a straight cut (see **Techniques, page 21**).

Measure the exact length of the back panel and cut two pieces of 100 × 25mm (4 × 1in) timber to this length to form the side rails. Glue and screw these rails edge-on to the back panel with screws about every 230mm (9in), through from the back. Use 25mm (1in) No 8 screws.

Cut two pieces of 100 × 25mm (4 × 1in) timber about 1220mm (48in) long for the top and bottom rails. Offer up the pieces and mark off the internal lengths. Cut them squarely to fit between the side rails. Glue and screw these pieces in place on to the back panel, as for the side rails. Using 50mm (2in) No 8 screws, fix the sides to the top and bottom rails by inserting two screws into each corner joint.

Finish by removing excess glue and planing any protruding edges. Sand smooth.

DOOR SECTIONS

The door front panels are formed by cutting the remaining 1220 × 1220mm (48in × 48in) wood panel in half in order to form two 610 × 1220mm (24 × 48in) panels.

Cut two pieces of 75 × 25mm (3 × 1in) timber to length for the side rails. Glue and screw these in place as for the main cupboard section.

Again using 75 × 25mm (3 × 1in) timber, measure for the top and bottom rails as above, and glue in place between the side rails, screwing through the door front. Insert two screws in each corner to secure the sides to the top and bottom.

FITTING OUT THE INSIDE

The inside of the tool cupboard can be fitted out to your individual requirements. However, for safety, heavy equipment *must* be in the main cupboard, while light things are best stored in the doors.

MATERIALS

Part	Quantity	Material	Length*
SIDE RAILS	2	100 × 25mm (4 × 1in) PAR timber	1220mm (48in)
TOP & BOTTOM RAILS	2	100 × 25mm (4 × 1in) PAR timber	1220mm (48in)
CUPBOARD SHELVES	3	100 × 25mm (4 × 1in) PAR timber	1220mm (48in)
MOUNTING BATTENS	2	100 × 25mm (4 × 1in) PAR timber	1220mm (48in)
SHELF DIVIDERS	4	100 × 25mm (4 × 1in) PAR timber	100mm (4in)
DOOR SIDE RAILS	4	75 × 25mm (3 × 1in) PAR timber	1220mm (48in)
DOOR TOP & BOTTOM RAILS	4	75 × 25mm (3 × 1in) PAR timber	610mm (24in)
BOLT MOUNTING BATTEN	1	75 × 25mm (3 × 1in) PAR timber	1220mm (48in)
SLOTTED SHELVES	2	75 × 25mm (3 × 1in) PAR timber	610mm (24in)
SHELF EDGING STRIPS	3	12 × 12mm ($\frac{1}{2}$ × $\frac{1}{2}$in) PAR timber	1220mm (48in)
CHISEL MOUNTING SLOTS	1	50 × 50mm (2 × 2in) PAR timber	1220mm (48in)

From 1 sheet of 12mm ($\frac{1}{2}$in) plywood 2.44 × 1.22m (8 × 4ft)

BACK PANEL	1		1220 × 1220mm (48 × 48in)
DOOR PANELS	2		610 × 1220mm (24 × 48in)

Also required: Offcuts of planed timber and plywood to make tool-mounting blocks

*Approximate lengths only

TOOLS

STEEL RULE

TRIMMING KNIFE

TRY SQUARE

CIRCULAR SAW (or panel saw or power jigsaw)

TWO G-CRAMPS

SCREWDRIVER (cross-point or slotted, depending on type of screws being used)

SMOOTHING PLANE

SANDING BLOCK AND ABRASIVE PAPER

DRILL (hand or power)

TWIST DRILL BIT

MASONRY DRILL BIT

FLAT BIT

COUNTERSINK BIT

COPING SAW or POWER JIGSAW to cut blocks, to fit tool handles

TENON SAW

TOOL CUPBOARD

The other safety note concerns electric sockets. If you put these in as we have, they will be at a convenient working height and the cables serving them can be run neatly in conduit in the gap created behind the cupboard by the bevelled battens on which it is mounted. It is most important to ensure that the cupboard is screwed firmly to the wall, and to keep a note of the positions of the cable runs if you drill the back panel to mount tools in the future. The same caution must be applied to the wiring of lamps if these are fixed to the top of the cupboard.

SHELVES FOR THE MAIN CUPBOARD

Cut these from 100 × 25mm (4 × 1in) timber to the same length as the top and bottom rails. Work out the position of the shelves by laying the cupboard down and trying the equipment in place.

When the shelves are correctly positioned, mark the centre line on to the sides, and continue the line on to the back to give a line for the screw positions. Glue the shelves in place and screw through from the back and through the sides.

Decide, according to your requirements, how you want to partition the shelves. For the dividing pieces, measure up and cut them to size from the same size of timber as for the shelves. Put the dividers in place and mark around them on the inside of the cupboard. Take the dividers away, and drill through the back panel from the front so that you can see where to screw from the back. Replace the dividers, countersink the fixing holes in the back panel, and then screw through from the back.

Pin 12 × 12mm ($\frac{1}{2}$ × $\frac{1}{2}$in) battens in place at the front of the shelves to prevent things from falling off. Fit small strips across the shelves where planes will be positioned so that the plane blades do not rest on them and get damaged.

MOUNTING TOOLS

Some tools, such as power drills and mallets, can be mounted on solid blocks of wood.

Roughly draw around the shape of the handle on to a piece of thick paper, and cut wood to this shape with a jigsaw or coping saw.

To fit the handles in place, screw through from the back using the method for fitting shelf dividers.

For the chisel slots use a piece of 50 × 50mm (2 × 2in) timber with a row of holes drilled to a diameter smaller than the chisel handles.

Using a flat bit, drill a row of holes through the middle of the block. With a tenon saw, cut slots in the front as shown to allow the chisel blade to turn in through the slot.

Various spring clips and hooks can be used to hold other tools.

SHELVES FOR THE DOORS

These shelves have slots cut in them to a variety of sizes, providing a useful way to store screwdrivers, marking gauges, and other tools that are longer than they are wide.

1 Forming the Chisel Slots
Holes are drilled in 50 × 50mm (2 × 2in) timber with chamfered edge, and slots are cut out.

Drill holes in the middle of the shelves and cut through them from the front to form slots in the same way as for the chisels. Fit the shelves as for the main cupboard.

Try squares are held in place by pieces of 75 × 25mm (3 × 1in) timber rebated with a tenon saw.

2 Making a Saw Holder
A block of wood shaped to fit inside a saw handle is fitted with a turnbuckle made from plywood.

FITTING THE TOOL MOUNTS

An advantage of this tool cupboard is its versatility. You can fit it out to suit your precise requirements, but leave enough space for more tools to be added later.

3 Fitting the Door Hinges
Doors carry a lot of weight so hinges must be substantial and secured with long screws.

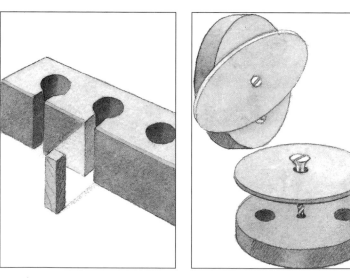

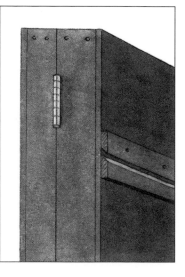

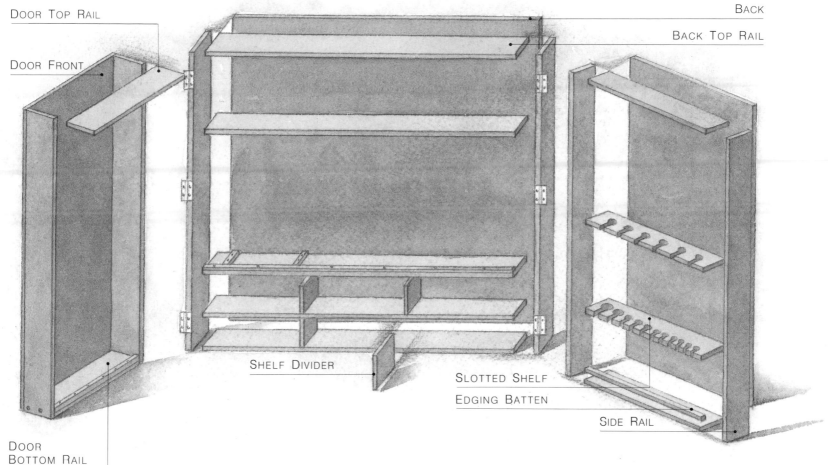

DOOR TOP RAIL

DOOR FRONT

DOOR BOTTOM RAIL

BACK

BACK TOP RAIL

SHELF DIVIDER

SLOTTED SHELF

EDGING BATTEN

SIDE RAIL

TOOL CUPBOARD ASSEMBLY

MOUNTING SAWS

Tools with open handles, such as saws, can be mounted on shaped blocks of wood fitted with turnbuckles that fit inside the handles.

Use a piece of wood slightly thicker than the handle and draw around the inner shape of the handle on to this wood. Cut out the wood to this shape with a jigsaw or coping saw and then cut a piece of 6mm ($\frac{1}{4}$in) plywood or MDF.

Screw the block to the door with two screws. Screw the turnbuckle to the block with one central screw which is secure but will allow the turnbuckle to turn.

Screw hooks can be placed as necessary in the front doors.

HANGING THE DOORS

Hang the doors on the main cupboard using three butt hinges for each (see **Techniques, page 33**).

The left-hand door is secured with two swan-neck bolts which fit into catch plates fitted to the bottom rail and to the underside of the top shelf (the top rail is not easy to reach). To make it possible to fit the bolts, screw a strip of 75 × 25mm (3 × 1in) timber to the inside edge of the door's side rail. Fit a cupboard lock (see **Techniques, page 35**) and door handles as required.

FIXING TO THE WALL

For security, the cupboard is hung on bevelled battens (see **Techniques, page 25**). Cut two lengths of 100 × 25mm (4 × 1in) timber to the width of the cupboard. To bevel the battens, cut each piece lengthwise through half of its thickness with the saw blade angled at 45°. Screw the top batten to cupboard back; lower part to the wall.

Screw the top-section battens to the back of the cupboard about 180mm (7in) down from the top, and about 250mm (10in) up from the bottom, using about seven 38mm (1$\frac{1}{2}$in) No 10 screws in each.

Put the lower-section battens in place under the top-section battens and measure down from the top to the bottom edge of the lower batten. Decide where the cupboard is to sit on the wall, then measure this distance down and fix the lower batten to the wall at this height with 65mm (2$\frac{1}{2}$in) No 10 screws and wallplugs.

Measure down and fix the upper batten in the same way, or sit the cupboard on the first batten and mark the wall for the other batten.

Secure the cupboard firmly to the wall by screwing through the back into the lower-section battens. This is most important if electrical sockets are to be fitted inside the cupboard.

PART 2

KITCHENS AND DINING AREAS

By designing and building your own kitchen which is very often the most important room in the house, you will derive deeper satisfaction from it than any off-the-peg kitchen can ever give. The final result will be a kitchen that is tailored exactly to your own requirements in terms of style and practicality.

As you plan your kitchen, consider as many alternatives as you can, until you know precisely what you want to achieve. On the following pages are many inspirational ideas and suggestions for kitchens and dining areas; these can be adapted to your own design. In addition, there is a complete kitchen, and utility room units to build yourself, as well as many original and classic designs for kitchen fittings, from plate racks to display shelves. Begin with a minor project if you lack confidence and skill, and gradually build up your hand-made kitchen.

Whether you are creating a whole kitchen from scratch, improving an existing one or merely adding a wooden knife rack, building it yourself gives your kitchen a truly personal quality. It also provides an opportunity to have kitchen fittings you know are well designed and well built.

ASSESSING THE WORKLOAD

The level of change you wish to make to a kitchen will depend upon a number of factors. If you want to completely re-design the kitchen, you must consider just how far you can go. Building and fitting new units, worksurfaces and shelves is well within the skills of most DIY enthu-siasts. However, if you are intending to redesign the layout and move services – plumbing pipework, electrical cables, socket outlets, light fittings and gas pipes – then the undertaking is considerable. In addition, you must consider any legal restrictions imposed upon work involv-ing gas, water and electricity. The golden rule is to call in expert help where there are legal restrictions, or if you have any doubts at all about your ability.

Always remember that any alterations to services later on could involve consid-erable disruption, since moving units may mean disturbing existing flooring, tiling and plasterwork.

Budget for professional help as neces-sary and get estimates before you start work so that you do not begin with a grand plan and run out of money half way through the operation.

If you are relatively happy with the position and capacity of existing units but are unable to live with the style, then consider revamping with replacement doors and a new worksurface.

There are often small changes that can be made completely transform an existing kitchen. A new set of shelves for display-

ASSESSING AND PLANNING

Building a complete, co-ordinated and fully fitted kitchen such as this one in natural wood (above) requires careful planning. Moving fixtures and fittings can involve new plumbing and rewiring, both of which will require professional assistance and costly upheaval. The time, effort, cost and skills required to create such a kitchen must be honestly assessed before work begins, to avoid problems later on.

There are plenty of smaller projects to undertake in the kitchen. Perhaps the most simple, functional, visually effective and easily assembled is a stainless steel hanging bar (previous page). Pots, pans and other cooking utensils hang from butcher's hooks. The bar can be attached between two kitchen units or two walls, or be suspended from the ceiling.

ing kitchen utensils or a plate rack in natural wood for example. Another simple device is a steel hanging bar for storing everything from fish slices to saucepans, making the kitchen more attractive and more practical to cook in.

Once you have decided precisely what you want to undertake, map out a schedule and a budget. You may find that you cannot afford the time or the money to do all the work immediately, in which case decide on priorities. Include in your budget an amount in excess of the cost of materials and professional help as a contingency against possible problems – say ten per cent on top of your basic estimate.

Consider well in advance the amount of disruption that will be caused to what is a major room in your home. Will you be able to continue to use the kitchen while it is being built? Other arrangements may have to be made for cooking. Prepare your family for the mess that will result from the work. Above all consider safety, particularly if children are likely to use the area while work is in progress.

You will enjoy the work and be pleased with the results if you have not undertaken more than you can handle. Make sure that you have purchased all the materials necessary for each stage of the process before you get started and that you have the right tools for the job. Finishing, detailing and decorating can take more time, effort and expense than actual construction but are important.

FORM AND FUNCTION

As you plan your new kitchen, or when making alterations to an existing one, always consider how you want it to look and to function when finished. The beauty of this kitchen is the quality of the materials used – natural wood, mosaic tiles and marble – combined with a simple yet elegant design. It is effective because it has been made with faultless precision and a great deal of attention to detail. There are no brackets to break the graphic line of the shelves, no decorative detail to detract from its minimal style and nothing is placed on show unless it is as attractive as the kitchen itself.

MATERIAL EFFECTS

More than anything else, it is the materials which you choose for your kitchen fittings that will influence the overall feel and appearance of the room. Consider two basic styles of kitchen and the materials which fashion them.

In recent years, kitchens used on an industrial scale – in restaurants, hotels and other places where cooking is quite literally an industry – have become a powerful influence on domestic kitchens.

An industrial-looking kitchen tends to have a formal, high-tech atmosphere, streamlined and sleek in appearance, with an emphasis on efficiency and hygiene. The two qualities valued most by professional chefs are durability and ease of cleaning. It is not easy to turn the industrial kitchen into part of the living room, nor to make it cosy. This is a style for a separate kitchen – a serious cooking centre, so rustic ideas are not suited to this approach. This does not mean, however, that an industrial influence will make your kitchen look like the inside of a laboratory or chemical plant. It does mean using high-quality, tough materials with a minimum of decorative detailing. Walls can be faced with white ceramic tiles, either extending to the ceiling with a painted wall area above, or broken up with bands of coloured tiles.

Stainless steel is indisputably the first choice for professional-looking worktops. Very easy to clean and thus hygienic, stainless steel wears gracefully and looks attractive even when it has been scratched and lost its gleam. Stainless steel is quite expensive, however, so if there are financial constraints, it can be substituted by laminates or a worksurface of white ceramic tiles, marble or granite.

PROFESSIONAL POLISH

Borrow ideas from professional kitchens when planning which materials to use. In this large and luxurious arrangement, created for some very serious cooking indeed (above right), the style is strictly professional and incorporates an enormous extractor hood, double swing doors and an open charcoal grill. The materials are functional, durable and attractive, not homely and decorative.

In a smaller domestic kitchen, similarly strong materials can be equally effective (above left). Stainless steel has been used for professional-looking fittings, and marble slips provide a hardwearing floor.

Many domestic kitchens these days double up as eating rooms and living rooms, and it is common for members of a household to spend a great deal of time there. For this purpose, the kitchen area needs to be comfortable and habitable, with a more homely atmosphere.

Natural materials are marvellous for this type of kitchen. They look and feel welcoming as well as elegant, and the great popularity of the country-style kitchen bears this out. Wood, stone, terrazzo, granite and slate are generally more tolerant of all the knocks, scratches and dirt stains which occur naturally in a kitchen than are man-made materials which scar and deteriorate rather than age gracefully. Even though marble stains if oil or alcohol touches its surface, it retains a pleasing patina of age; but if a white laminate suffers a deep scratch, it remains on the surface as an unsightly scar. Wood that is chipped, scratched or stained will wear well and age in a graceful manner, while old plastic will start to break up, chip and disintegrate after a lot of wear. Wooden worksurfaces will last longer if a tough hardwood such as beech or maple is used. Synthetics have their advantages though; they can be used effectively and a lot less expensively than natural materials in a kitchen/living room. Tiled and vitreous-enamelled surfaces are other options which age well and are durable. Most people will use some laminate surfaces in their kitchen and it is worthwhile considering juxtaposing them with, for instance, an old wooden kitchen table, or a weathered butcher's block. Such a contrast of old with new, natural with synthetic, is highly effective and invariably creates interesting visual effects.

SURFACE CO-ORDINATION

The gleaming appeal of polished stainless steel has been enhanced in this kitchen (above left) by choosing only steel utensils and then storing them on a stainless steel hanging bar. The colours in the kitchen are muted and the design is plain so that the room has a studied co-ordination about it.

Another kitchen (above right) shares this overall approach of co-ordination but has been achieved using different materials. Simple bricks, painted white, form the basis of the kitchen. The storage units are finished in white laminate and the floor is warm terracotta quarry tiles. These elements blend well with the high wooden shelf and the large basket above the oven.

MATERIAL EFFECTS

UNDERSTATED ELEGANCE

Gleaming terrazzo (stone and marble chips set in concrete) on the worksurface, the palest wood for units, doors and floor and muted shades on other surfaces and objects, give this kitchen its understated elegance (right). A small open-plan kitchen shows a truly original design, which could be achieved using DIY (below left). Warm, natural, polished wood has been used for the plate rack, worksurface and floor. The doors and units are painted in a pale finish. In a separate, small galley kitchen (below right), the paint on the walls and doors is again pale. It offsets the rich finish of the terrazzo worksurface which incorporates a section of wood to act as a built-in chopping board – easily achieved and highly practical.

HAND FINISHED

Doing-it-yourself means implementing original ideas using unusual materials and finishes. One-room living in an open-plan warehouse (opposite above) dictates that only a corner is available for a kitchen. This design could be equally effective in an office, workshop or studio. Breeze blocks form the base of the island unit which is topped with a laminate worksurface. The blocks echo the rough-cast concrete of the walls. All the materials here are strong and basic like the building they are placed in.

In a small space, such as this attic kitchen (opposite below left), contrasting surfaces could be unattractive, so the wood panelling on the sloping walls has been bleached to match and blend with the wooden worksurface.

A useful hatch from kitchen to dining room (opposite below centre) incorporates an attractive cupboard. The kitchen is beautifully finished in wood panelling which has been painted a clear, bright eau de nil, a colour which continues through the hatch to the dining room. The white cupboard door panels stand out in strong, geometric relief.

When the kitchen is on show (opposite below right), the appearance is very important. Anyone would be happy to eat and relax next to this line of white units with their marble worktop, and a wall of marble slips (tiles).

KITCHEN LAYOUT

Finalizing the exact location of every unit and fitting in your kitchen involves careful planning at an early stage to avoid problems later on. A kitchen is first a working area, so you should make sure that it will be easy to use. You should check the location of your doors, plumbing and lights, then calculate how best to arrange the areas intended for food preparation, cooking and eating. Bear in mind that you will want to have your cooking utensils to hand.

If there are children about, make certain that any electrical sockets and open shelves will be safely out of reach. Storage should also be considered before you set to work; think about how much space you will need for cleaning and laundry equipment, cutlery, crockery, laundry products and food..

As you make your plans, give a thought also to what external doors can let in – muddy boots and draughts for example. Weigh up these disadvantages with the positive reasons for having an external door in the kitchen – easy access to a garden or rubbish disposal area, fresh air, and somewhere to bring in the shopping. How these elements affect your kitchen design depends on how you want to use your kitchen. Some people prefer to be on their own whilst working in the kitchen; others love having people wandering in and out, making the kitchen the social centre of their home.

If you own a lot of attractive kitchen equipment, think about building a special shelving system to display it to advantage. As with a row of cups hanging on hooks, great aesthetic pleasure can be derived from allowing a kitchen's function to determine its form or shape. Do also consider though that anything displayed in a kitchen accumulates grease and dust, so remember to think about cleaning chores too as you finalize the plans.

While kitchens should be designed to encourage easy cooking and mobility, the particular plan you choose will depend on your own preferences.

There are five basic floor plans. One is the linear or single-line kitchen, with everything lined up against one wall – excellent if the wall is long enough or if the kitchen is basically a passage. The galley or corridor kitchen, arranged along two facing walls, should have the sink and the cooker on the same side of the kitchen and give enough room for bending down – at least 1200mm (48in) between the facing units. It is generally not recommended unless built against a dead end or a window. The L-shaped kitchen is very popular – deservedly, for it combines well with a living area in the kitchen and makes good use of limited wall space. A U-shaped kitchen is ideal for a small area, like an alcove, and offers one of the most convenient and adaptable arrangements of space for preparation and cooking; usually the worktops here run round in an unbroken sequence, one leg of the U can often act as a room divider, with the eating area beyond it. Lastly, there is the island kitchen, a favourite with professional or very confident cooks who appreciate its adaptability and the way it can display their culinary prowess; an island unit can also act as a room divider.

The sink should be positioned at the centre of a kitchen, beneath a window if possible (for natural light), not in a corner where it is difficult to get at, but with food preparation areas on either side. As moving a sink may require expensive plumbing alterations, you may wish to leave it where it is.

The strong, geometric architectural lines of a modern building have been reflected in this kitchen. Gleaming white units and shelves in big, chunky shapes house only black, white, chrome and yellow objects.

KITCHEN LAYOUT

We have mentioned the five commonly used kitchen layouts, but there is no need to stick rigidly to any of these plans. In nearly all kitchens there is a vast potential for flexible space management, using the varying heights of base units, shelving and oven housings.

Central islands, in particular, provide opportunities both to divide a kitchen and to focus attention on the cooking going on there – if so wished. Breakfast bars can serve this function just as effectively as island cooking centres but in a different way – by clearly marking out the cooking from the eating areas. If there is room in your kitchen, it is always best to make some clear distinction between the two.

The sink, cooker and preparation areas, along with the fridge, should form a 'work triangle' whose sides, when combined, should not exceed 6–7m (20–23ft) in length. This works out at no two centres being more than a double arm-span apart, economizing on movement. Neither should they be uncomfortably close. A cramped kitchen can cause accidents, so plan the layout in order to allow more than one person at a time to move around the room safely.

Cookers should *not* be placed under windows – someone could get burned trying to open the window. Neither should a hob or cooker come at the end of a run of cupboards – it is best to have a worktop on either side of it, although it could be placed across a corner.

You should also consider the washing machine, if this is going to be in the kitchen. Washing machines, wherever they are located, do have a tendency to leak or flood at least once in their lifetime, so bear this in mind when planning drainage and choosing a floor covering. For plumbing reasons, it is easier to keep a dishwasher and a washing machine close together and near the sink.

AROUND THE KITCHEN TABLE

A niche has been carved in a storage unit for slotting a round table into neat and secure alignment with the open display storage of this small kitchen (opposite above).

Purposefully combining old and new can be very attractive as in this standard, modern, white kitchen (opposite below). The polished wood floor complements a rustic wooden table. It has been placed at an interesting angle for practical reasons as well as for visual interest. If the table is to be used for more formal occasions, it is best separated from the working kitchen. A screen (above) has been built-in as part of the kitchen. The table is a neat extension of that screen, so is linked to, but effectively separated from, the kitchen itself.

CORNER KITCHEN

In a tight narrow corner, precise planning and a design with an eye for detail are required to make the best use of what small space there is (left). Here, there are neatly arranged fittings and a maximum amount of storage space.

KITCHEN LIGHTING

In kitchens even more than in other rooms, intelligent lighting is essential, so plan it from the start. Natural light sources should be considered first: think carefully about what will be placed near a window or glazed door and whether it will benefit from sunshine and a view. The sink may or may not require this privilege. A table could be more deserving of natural light if you intend to sit there regularly. General electric lighting for kitchens should aim to give the maximum adaptability – and lights should be able to be directed differently for different activities. Avoid a single central ceiling light, because of the shadows it will throw on worksurfaces as well as its marked lack of aesthetic appeal.

Worksurfaces must be highlighted for safe and efficient food preparation – tungsten strip lights built into wall-mounted cabinets avoid the problem of the cook working in his or her own shadow. Check that the light bulbs will be hidden from eye-level at both sitting and standing heights.

Systems of track holding a number of lights with independent switches are useful in kitchens, as are pivoting hinged fittings mounted under kitchen wall cabinets to provide downward illumination onto worksurfaces. If you also eat in the kitchen in the evening, put in a dimmer control to fade out all the kitchen clutter by the sink and worksurfaces while you are eating.

There are many different types of light fitting and bulb. Fluorescent bulbs use less electricity, burn cooler and last far longer than standard tungsten. They not only give an attractive light but have the disadvantage of flickering slightly which many find unpleasant. They also emit a hum which can be irritating.

Tungsten bulbs, also available as strip lights, are preferable except where it is vital to avoid the heat they give off or where long life is essential. They range usually from 40 to 150 watts in lighting power. Tungsten lamps can shatter from thermal shock if splashed with cold water and so need a completely enclosed fitting near wet or steamy places.

Low-voltage tungsten halogen is excellent in kitchens, particularly in the form of small spots. It gives a clear, white light and makes glass, china, ceramics and chrome gleam.

Tungsten strips fitted below shelves prevent a large handsome hood from casting a shadow over the hob (above left).

Knocking out the walls of a kitchen has allowed natural light into an otherwise dark corner (above right), and downlights have been installed at strategic points.

A small kitchen in a corridor has the benefit of French doors that lead to the garden and provide natural light (opposite). Below cupboards, strip lights illuminate the worksurface and elsewhere downlights provide extra light.

ESSENTIAL SERVICES

Getting essential services correctly installed, moved or altered is not an optional extra and should be budgeted for from the start, particularly as there are no real money-saving short cuts to good plumbing, gas and electrical installations.

When planning a kitchen, work out the maximum number of machines you are likely to need in it. It is more convenient to install all the supply and waste pipes in one go than merely to deal with your present demands. Later, you may have to call in someone to put in further pipes and wires, disrupting the established system.

All appliances and heating should be installed by experts – the utility company or one of their approved contractors. Most modern appliances have built-in safety devices however.

Gas, whether it is natural, propane or butane, although not in itself poisonous when burnt, can give off noxious fumes and water vapour. Rooms with gas appliances therefore need good ventilation. Take care both to avoid gas flames being affected by draughts and to keep gas cylinders safely outside.

Fatal accidents in the home are seldom caused by electrocution but fires from overloading electrical outlets, faulty wiring, inadequate insulation or overheating are a very real danger. Only qualified electricians can be relied upon to install electrical systems to legal requirements. Cookers, hobs and ovens must be connected directly to the distribution box.

These three kitchens were custom-designed for particular spaces using distinctive ideas to suit the specific style, cooking, storage and display requirements of the owners. All the essential services – wiring, plumbing, lighting – were planned in minute detail before work began; no rearrangement could now be achieved without major and costly disruption to the layout and finish of each kitchen.

SCREENING AND SEPARATING

Today, modern kitchens are at the heart of family life, and modern cooks do not want to be locked away surrounded by pots while the rest of the family and/or guests are talking elsewhere. Yet some division between cooking and eating areas is desirable. To mark this division without isolating the cook, several approaches have been evolved.

Island units, sometimes containing a cooker, are an obvious way of dividing the cooking and eating/living areas, as are units jutting out in peninsular forms. Such plans guard the work triangle from interruption while allowing the cook to take part in any conversation. Often, a peninsular unit can double as a breakfast bar, which makes it easier for food to be served hot from the cooker. Most breakfast bars are at worktop height (900mm/33in), so bar stools are required. Clearly these are not very safe for young children, or comfortable for the elderly.

The simplest screen is a purpose-built partition made with wood stud and finished to match your kitchen decoration. It can be of any height to suit your kitchen design. You can incorporate storage and display into the structure with a high shelf for display, shelves on one or both sides, or attach hooks or a wire mesh for hanging utensils and pans.

Other forms of screening can be devised, utilizing whatever appeals to you and what you happen to have, such as pots and pans, or bottles of preserved fruits and vegetables. If, however, you plan on having, and often using, a separate dining room, think about installing a hatch between the kitchen and dining room. When shut, this will leave the dining room as a quiet area and keep especially pungent smells inside the kitchen. When open, the cook can talk fairly easily to the rest of the household and pass out dishes with the minimum delay.

COUNTER DIVIDERS

In two spacious open-plan areas (above), the kitchen is separated from the main room by a breakfast bar. This has been simply achieved by installing a worktop which overlaps a basic unit on the side facing into the main room, so creating a space beneath it for sitting and for storing stools. By adding a sink to this worksurface, plates can be cleared easily from the main room to this counter which has a dishwasher below it on the kitchen side.

COOK'S HATCH

In this unusual arrangement (opposite), a hatch between the kitchen and dining room runs directly behind the cooker hob. Designed for a virtuoso cook rather than a busy family, it allows direct delivery of sizzling hot dishes. Behind the hob, a simple island unit, consisting of a stack of drawers, has an extended wooden worktop which effectively divides the kitchen and provides practical chopping and preparation space close to the cooker.

STYLING DETAILS

As these three kitchens show, what you choose to display in a kitchen, and how you display it, is as important to its style as the basic design. By planning, building, finishing and then equipping your kitchen yourself, you can ensure a harmonious result. Detail is a crucial element in the overall visual impact of the room.

COUNTRY KITCHEN

If you want to evoke an informal, colourful, country atmosphere, abundant and pretty in appearance (above left), display lots of your favourite decorative china intermingled with fresh food in baskets and dried food in glass storage jars. This approach will work only if you are prepared to clean the china regularly, since it will attract grease and dirt if on display. Also, ensure that your basic kitchen provides a sympathetic background to this gentle jumble. A traditional dresser is an ideal background for your display, but here a very simple and inexpensive kitchen of melamine-covered fibreboard has been given a dresser effect by hanging mugs from the top shelf on butcher's hooks and using the worktop under the shelves as part of the display. Nothing overtly modern or hard in appearance has been allowed to intrude and spoil the effect.

METALLIC EFFECTS

By contrast, another cook prefers to display stainless steel utensils with chrome and glass kitchenware (below left). The result is equally effective and harmonious because here all that is soft and pretty has been expelled. The hanging bar and the shelf are also metallic and the speckled background enhances the gleaming, utilitarian display.

In another tiny kitchen this approach has been taken to its stylistic conclusion (opposite). The whole kitchen is sharp and metallic: everything is either stainless steel or chrome, with one white wall providing definition for a professional hanging bar and its polished pans. A single pretty plant in a terracotta pot provides a strong point of contrast in an otherwise hard and potentially clinical environment.

A Place For Everything

If you like a generally informal, cosy approach to your kitchen style, remember that the general clutter this may well entail requires a largish space. If you have only a small kitchen, perhaps of the galley type, you will have to impose a certain discipline to make controlled use of a space in which only one person can cook. In such a case, a more high-tech and practical design may be appropriate.

When you do have a spacious kitchen, you can afford to be less practical and spread out expansively, but this should not mean chaotically or unattractively. An informal arrangement can create in effect a still-life of fruits, vegetables, pots, crockery and attractive kitchen utensils.

A Welsh dresser, although very popular, is by no means the only way of displaying objects of interest, charm or beauty. Think about building pigeon holes to store and display spice or herb jars, interesting old bottles – or interesting new ones for that matter. Despite the potential that space gives you for disorder, try to arrange objects neatly and in a manner that is appealing to the eye. If uncertain about what to display, work on the principle that if you have got it and it is good, show it!

Deep shelf lipping adds support which can be especially useful for long shelves to stop them bowing. Used in conjunction with back battens, lipping is essential if you are intending to store heavy objects, such as cassoulet dishes or any other large vessel. Place on the topmost shelves those things you use infrequently. Always incorporate an extra-thick lipping to prevent objects falling down.

Although it may seem obvious, it is difficult to overstress the importance of really strong and secure fixings for all wall cupboards and shelves, especially when heavy crockery or pots and pans are going to be stored on them.

AN ORDERLY DISPLAY

Where space for storage is limited, a kitchen has been allowed to extend into a hallway (opposite above). Here an entire wall has been given over to open shelves. Cleverly but very simply designed and constructed, this unit echoes the open shelves in the kitchen beyond, and fills the wall, framing an existing window. The arrangement works well because of the order the shelves impose. They are narrow and placed at varying depths to neatly accommodate certain items, so clutter cannot accumulate and everything is clearly accessible and easily found. The supports form partitions which ensure that the storage is grouped so that a wide range of objects can be placed together, without looking cluttered or randomly arranged.

IN A STRAIGHT LINE

Shelves placed so that they follow the contours of a room, and are regularly spaced, provide a strong geometric grid for neat open displays. A pigeon-hole effect allows for a formal display of china and glass (opposite below left). Each square is self-contained and highlights the objects it houses.

Another simple but highly effective design (opposite below right), with fibreboard and melamine shelves on battens across an alcove, contains a more relaxed display of everyday crockery and glass.

SMART JARS

Dried foods, when stored in large glass storage jars in neat rows, look extremely attractive, and give a kitchen a traditional atmosphere. Storage jars remind us of old-fashioned shops and wholesome home cooking. Here (left), they are displayed to great effect on a custom-made unit which blends perfectly with its surroundings. It is made from simple wood or fibreboard and covered in white tiles so that it appears to be part of the wall it stands on. The depths of the three shelves match precisely the height of the jars. Antique salt containers and old olive oil bottles standing on polished wood add to the traditional effect.

FLOORING

Bear in mind when choosing the particular type of floor covering for your kitchen that it should reflect and enhance the style of the rest of the kitchen – starkly modern white tiles could be out of place in a farmhouse style kitchen, for example. A floor is a crucial influence on a kitchen. The type of flooring you decide on will be partly dictated to you by the sort of sub-floor you have underneath. Although there are ways around the problem you may not be able to put terracotta or ceramic tiles on top of wooden joists, as timber bends and moves, potentially causing cracking of the tile joints or even of the actual tiles. Equally, if you choose

vinyl or vinyl tiles – both common floor coverings – cold, potentially damp concrete or stone underneath will require chipboard, hardboard or latex screeding beneath it. You may be restricted by not being on solid foundations or by needing to insulate sound from the level below.

Be careful that the floor of a kitchen in an older building is not too uneven and that it relates properly to the levels of adjoining rooms. Any abrupt change of level could be dangerous as well as unsightly so calculate beforehand exact levels, re-hanging doors if necessary.

Vinyl is probably the most common and least expensive form of kitchen floor

covering and comes in a huge variety of different colours and patterns. Many of these can give pleasing imitations of ceramic or even polished wooden floors. Vinyl lasts well, can be cleaned easily, is waterproof and resistant to oils, fat and most chemicals – though not to heat. It can be laid on hardboard, over tightly fitting, even floorboards and can be cushioned underneath for greater warmth and comfort. Vinyl asbestos, which is even cheaper than vinyl, comes in the form of brittle tiles. Remember that a textured finish on vinyl shows fewer stains.

Although vinyl flooring is extremely popular and practical, cork tiling is also

TERRACOTTA TILES

In the homely kitchen of an old country house, the furniture is freestanding and old fashioned (below left) and the materials are natural. A floor of terracotta quarry tiles is the natural and traditional choice for such a room. Quarry tiles age beautifully, are durable and highly attractive. However, traditional tiles of this kind are best used at ground-floor level and the sub-floor must be carefully considered before you start work.

CHEQUERBOARD CERAMIC

Elegant chequerboard squares, traditionally in ceramic tiles or stone, look good in most kitchens. Here (below right), the chequerboard design on the floor echoes the square tiles below the worksurface and on the walls. If a floor is not suitable for ceramic tiles, a similar effect can be easily achieved by using patterned vinyl flooring instead. This is relatively cheap and easy to maintain.

worth considering. It is an excellent insulator, for both sound and heat, and is pleasantly warm to walk on. Cork tiles are easy to clean, but may chip and dent.

Ceramic tiles look splendid, are long-lasting and easy to clean. They can feel cold underfoot however, (this will depend in part on your heating arrangements), are expensive and, as mentioned, are not suitable for all types of floor. Terracotta tiles can often add a visual warmth underfoot.

Heavy-duty quarry tiles are extremely hard-wearing; they are non-slip and extremely tough, but the weight of them makes them impractical for a floor above ground level, and upper floor kitchens are better off with good quality linoleum or vinyl flooring. Terracotta, granite and marble are also tough and durable, as are wooden floors, as long as they are heavily sealed in areas of constant use.

Linoleum, for many years regarded as old-fashioned and unattractive, is now enjoying a revival, with some extremely good designs available. Sheet linoleum is very hardwearing, to industrial standards, and not difficult to lay, but usually requires a sub-floor of hardboard.

Wood is also worth considering for the kitchen, although it does absorb grease stains and requires regular scrubbing in order to keep it clean. Painted floors are not practical, and neither is carpet or coir.

Whichever floor covering you choose, do not attempt to lay it yourself without getting advice either from the retailer or manufacturer. Always check that the surface or sub-floor on which it is to be laid is correctly prepared and treated.

Make absolutely sure you are using the right adhesive, the correct edging, that there is no problem damp below the floor and that you are equipped with precisely the right tools for trimming the flooring. If you are not confident, get in experts to do the laying. It will be less expensive than re-doing it yourself.

DURABLE RUBBER

Synthetic rubber stud flooring is available in sheets or large tiles. Its appeal lies partly in its smart, contemporary appearance and partly in its excellent durability and ease of maintenance. The range of colours available makes it suitable for a wide variety of modern kitchen styles. Here (below left), bright red has been used to provide a splash of colour in an otherwise completely white kitchen.

NATURAL CORK

Cork is a warm surface for a kitchen floor; it has the advantage of being a natural material which is easy on the eye, and is a relatively inexpensive alternative to wood. It is not as durable as vinyl or rubber, but ages pleasantly and, if properly sealed and polished, is not difficult to maintain. In this neat and functional kitchen (below right), wall-to-wall cork tiling provides a perfect complement to the wooden table and chairs.

UTILITY ROOMS

A utility room should be functional, practical and labour-saving, but does not need to be a large room. It should have enough space for a washing machine and drier, a generous sink and drainer, storage cupboards and an airing rack.

In a self-contained utility room, clothes can be soaked, washed, dried and ironed, and household cleaning equipment stored (dangerous materials such as bleach and cleaning fluids should always be kept out of reach of children). Essential chores can also be carried out in a utility room: cleaning shoes, mending clothes, polishing silver and brass are among them.

Utility rooms need to be carefully planned and fitted, so consider first your sink and laundry machinery; this should be positioned to allow easy access for repairs, servicing and ventilation. A double sink with a generous draining board is particularly useful in a utility room, where clothes can be soaked, bleached and washed by hand. Decide whether your existing plumbing system is adequate for your equipment. If not, call in professional help to make any necessary alterations. Remember that laundry equipment can leak occasionally, so the floor should be floodproof.

An airing rack can be suspended from the ceiling and, if necessary, an ironing board can fold down from the wall.

An open utility area is hidden when not in use by a large Venetian blind (above). The ironing board folds out from a cupboard when needed.

A changing area for a baby, below a port-hole window onto the garden has been incorporated into this attractive utility room, created in a lean-to extension (below left).

Utility rooms can often be fitted into narrow spaces (opposite and below right) where a line of units houses the machines and a sink. Use the space above for useful cupboards or shelves where dangerous cleaning materials can be safely stored away out of reach.

DINING ROOMS

Today, eating rooms are frequently incorporated into the living room or kitchen. The short leg of an L-shaped living room or one corner, or a wall of a kitchen often acts as the eating room. The kitchen table itself is where a family frequently gathers to eat; a separate dining room – with all the suggestions of formality that dining conveys – has now become something of an anachronism, as well as being a rarity and a luxury. Like most luxuries, a totally separate dining room is therefore something worth cherishing.

Traditionally, the formal dining-room was a place of ostentatious and magnificent display. Carefully segregated from the kitchen, which was frequently a food-chilling distance away, it boasted suites of matching furniture in mahogany or walnut, on which gleamed the family silver. Above these, the walls were crowded with family portraits. Meals were served with a matching formality.

Recently, the reaction to such formality, plus the fact that many homes do not have the space for a dining-room proper, has obscured the real potential of dining rooms. An elegant but welcoming and attractive eating room is the perfect setting for relaxed, leisurely, sociable meals.

Comfortable chairs and soft lighting encourage guests to linger, talking, over their food and wine; eating together is a supremely social act.

But a dining room can serve other functions besides just eating and entertaining, important though these two are. A desk in one corner can make it an extra room for quiet study, a comfortable armchair another place for reading.

The dining room is also a place for display; it can offer somewhere to exhibit collections of treasured or 'best' objects such as crockery, glasses, candlesticks and other paraphernalia – even racks of wine.

If you prefer, and can afford, antique or reproduction formal furniture such as mahogany sideboards, then your dining room style is set and you can enhance it best with beautifully finished shelves and a flattering lighting system. However, as an alternative, consider building a display unit or a fitted sideboard. Display crystal glasses on glass shelves, a china collection on open plate racks or open a hatch between the kitchen and dining room and make it a decorative feature.

Far from being outdated, an imaginatively planned dining room greatly enhances a home and your lifestyle.

DECORATIVE DISPLAYS

In a cool, sleek room the modern dining table and chairs are placed beside a wall of display shelving (opposite above). Here, books and music equipment are on show, but such a structure could be equally effective for storing china or glass.

A collection of ceramic pots is magnificently displayed in a dining room (below right) on shelves built into a false alcove. The pots are perfectly lit from a spotlight (not shown) placed above them.

An attractive unit (opposite below left) has been designed like a traditional dresser top. A larger unit (opposite below right) creates a fitted dresser, with a backing of wood panelling and drawers incorporated below a wide central shelf. With its gently mottled paint finish, it is the perfect setting for a display of 1930s china.

DINING AREAS

An antique table and chairs are placed in a section of an open-plan layout (below left) to provide a formal dining room atmosphere. Note the attractive display shelves which are part of the adjoining kitchen, and act as a screen.

In an old house, a creative modern design (opposite below centre) incorporates a fitted metal table with window shelves.

THE KITCHEN SYSTEM

The problem faced by many people when trying to install a fitted kitchen is that most walls are out of true and uneven, and are often not at right angles to the floor. The entire procedure of fitting your immaculate factory-made cupboards can easily become a nightmare, which is made worse when walls are covered with pipes and electrical wiring.

This system is designed to make the installation and scribing of kitchen fittings as simple as possible; it allows existing pipework to run behind the fittings and, most importantly, allows you to decide for yourself what sort of finish is most suited to your personal style.

This is a kitchen system that enables you to plan your space in the best possible way, allowing you to put all your cooking equipment on display or, if you prefer, shut away behind closed doors. You can fit in gleaming new modern equipment, or use existing cookers and fridges. The dimensions are flexible and the permutations are innumerable.

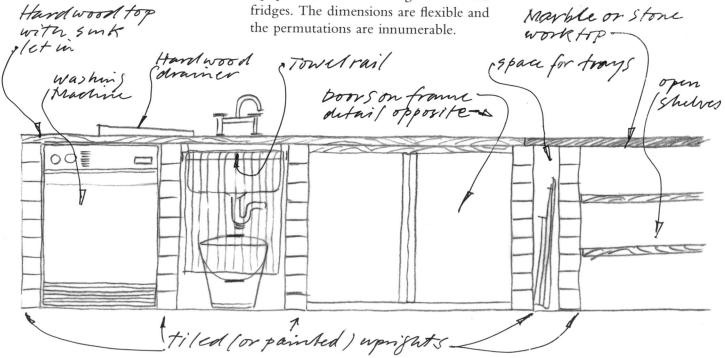

Hardwood top with sink let in

washing Machine

Hardwood drainer

Towel rail

Doors on frame detail opposite →

Marble or stone work top

space for trays

open shelves

tiled (or painted) uprights

FRONT ELEVATION

High level oven or Microwave with refrigerator below built into floor-to-ceiling partition

open shelves

open shelves

drawer

cooktop recessed into work surface

doors detail below

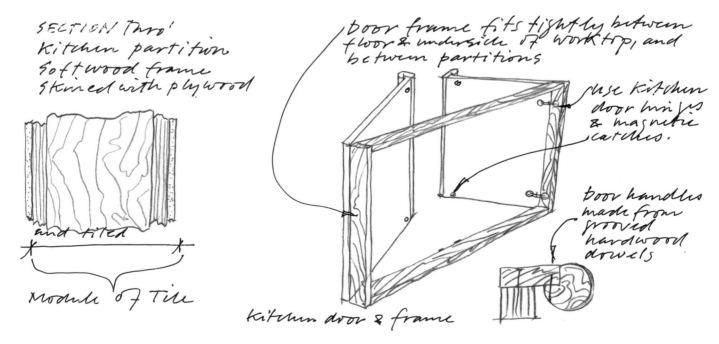

SECTION Thro' Kitchen partition Softwood frame Skined with plywood

and tiled

Module of Tile

door frame fits tightly between floor & underside of work top, and between partitions

use kitchen door hinges & magnetic catches.

door handles made from grooved hardwood dowels

kitchen door & frame

PAINTED KITCHEN

THE KITCHEN SYSTEM: PAINTED KITCHEN

In this rustic kitchen, the basic partition units have been painted rather than tiled. Open shelves have been incorporated in between the partitions and a rail for storing hanging towels and tea-cloths has been built-in under the sink. A wood-lipped tiled worktop lies over the partition units and provides a workspace that is both practical and easy to clean.

To complete the country atmosphere, traditional slatted shelves, a hanging bar for kitchen utensils, and a knife rack have been mounted on the wall. These provide extra storage, are easy to construct, and make stylish additions to the basic kitchen system.

LAUNDRY ROOM

Using essentially the same basic system as the kitchen, the sturdy uprights of the laundry unit support a traditional deep-glazed ceramic Belfast sink which is set beneath a solid maple 'butcher block' worktop. A washing machine and tumble dryer can be placed on floor plinths and are housed on either side of the sink, underneath the worktop, to give a neat, symmetrical appearance.

A slatted shelf is built-in under the sink and between the two partition units to provide storage for washing powder and other essential cleaning materials. Below the shelf there is room for a large laundry basket to store dirty clothes.

A clothes horse on a pulley can be built and positioned over the unit for airing clothes, sheets and large items such as duvets. With a laundry like this, doing the washing could almost become a pleasure.

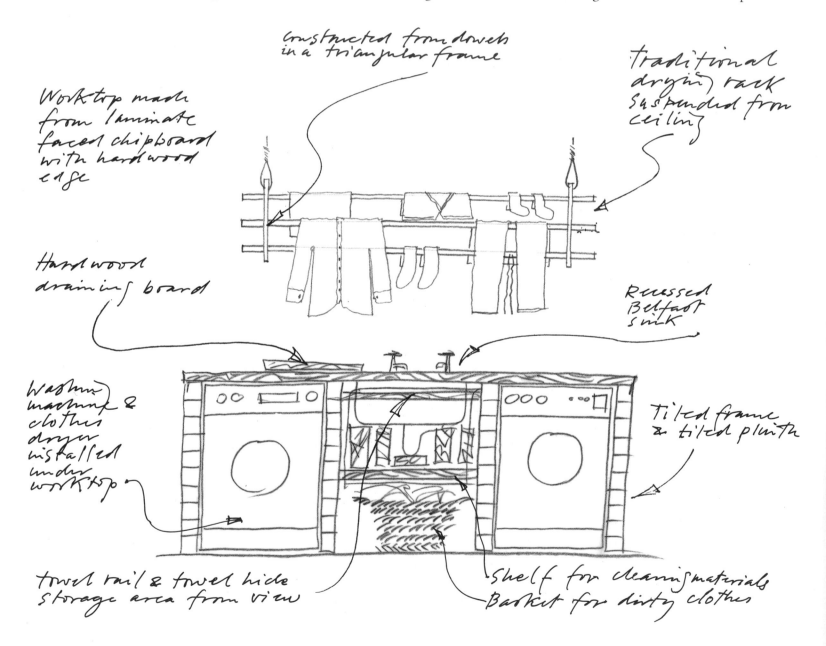

constructed from dowels in a triangular frame

traditional drying rack suspended from ceiling

Worktop made from laminate faced chipboard with hardwood edge

Hardwood draining board

Recessed Belfast sink

Washing machine & clothes dryer installed under worktop

Tiled frame & tiled plinth

towel rail & towel hide storage area from view

Shelf for cleaning materials
Basket for dirty clothes

THE KITCHEN SYSTEM

The basic element of this kitchen is the upright partition, which is tiled. Alternatively, it could be painted, clad in tongued, grooved and V-jointed timber, or covered with melamine laminate.

The width of the partition units is adjusted to match the width of the tiles being used so that they exactly cover the edges of the tiles that are fixed to the side panels. The spacing between the partitions is adjusted to suit the width of the appliances, shelves and cupboards to be fitted. A worktop covers the tops of the panels, and overhangs them by 20mm ($\frac{3}{4}$in). As the overall width of the worktop affects the front-to-back depth of the partition panels, it is important to decide on the worktop depth right at the beginning (see **Worktops, page 92**).

The upright partition units are assembled, clad (skinned), tiled, grouted and battened ready for fixing the shelves, before the partitions are fitted in place.

BASE UNITS

When building base units of a critical thickness, you may find it difficult to obtain wood of exactly the required thickness. In this case, buy wood that is slightly oversized and plane it to the correct thickness.

Height You may have to modify slightly the height of the panels to suit the tiles you are using and the equipment to be fitted into the kitchen. The working height used in this project is 930mm (36$\frac{1}{2}$in), which allows for a worktop thickness of 40mm (1$\frac{1}{2}$in), while the overall height of the basic element – the upright partition panel – is 890mm (35in). This height is based on using whole tiles to cover the partition panel (eight tiles high).

Depth The front-to-back depth of the partition panel is 630mm (24$\frac{3}{4}$in), which allows a worktop of 650mm

(25$\frac{1}{2}$in) in depth to overlap the panel by 20mm ($\frac{3}{4}$in). If you buy a standard 600mm (23$\frac{1}{2}$in) deep worktop you should reduce the partition panel depth to 580mm (22$\frac{3}{4}$in).

At the back of the panel, the rear stud is inset by 50mm (2in) to allow for scribing, if required, for pipe and conduit runs. This space can also be used to provide ventilation for cookers and refrigerators. Gas appliances must have a separate flue. Allowance has been made in the design for a back panel and/or a door to be fitted, if required.

Spacing You can adjust the spacing between partition panels to suit appliances, your preferences for cupboard widths, and so on. Our panels are 600mm (23$\frac{1}{2}$in) apart.

Shelves The design allows for the top shelf to rest one tile's depth down from the top of the partition panel to line up with the tiled fascias. When the hardwood lipping is added to the shelf, it finishes flush with the front edge of the partition.

Intermediate shelves also line up with the fascia tiles, but are set half-a-tile in from the front edge. This looks neat and allows doors to be fitted on the front if desired. (The top shelf is not fitted in this case.) All shelves rest on timber battens, which are then hidden by the front lipping on the shelves.

Floor Plinths These are optional, but they give a neat finishing touch, and are useful if the floor is very uneven. The underside of the plinths can be packed up as necessary if the floor is uneven, and the front edge scribed to the floor before tiling (see **Techniques, page 36**). The plinths are made one tile high.

The kitchen system has been designed to be adapted easily. Full instructions for building the kitchens illustrated on pages 78–9, 80–1 and 83 are given on the following pages.

If you decide to build the complete system, the order of work checklists (below), will help you to compile your own construction schedule.

The elements of each kitchen are listed below for ease of reference:

TILED KITCHEN

Basic Partition Units and Shelves
Worktop

Optional extras:
Back panel
Floor plinth
Built-in slatted shelf
Doors and door handles

Tall Partition Unit
Wall-Mounted Shelf Unit

Additional Projects:
Built-in plate rack and drip tray
Hanging bar for kitchen utensils
Airing rack

PAINTED KITCHEN

Basic Partition Units and Shelves
Knife Rack
Wall-Mounted Slatted Shelves
Removable Towel Rail

ORDER OF WORK CHECKLIST

TILED KITCHEN

Tiled base units incorporating shelves, back panels and floor plinths, and a worktop.

1 Decide depth of worktop.
2 Decide height of worktop (to match tile height and equipment).
3 Decide on thickness of partition units (thickness of the partition must match tile width).
4 Decide on spacing of units, and whether you will incorporate shelves or built-in appliances such as a dishwasher.
5 Construct the basic frame including tall partitions if required.

6 Decide on quantity and position of shelves.
7 Mark out position of shelf-support battens.
8 Attach intermediate cross rails.
9 Clad the frames in 12mm ($\frac{1}{2}$in) plywood, using round wire nails.
10 Fit the back panel support battens.
11 Tile the sides of the partition units except for the back and bottom rows of tiles (to allow room for scribing the partition unit to fit).
12 Make and fix the shelf-support battens.
13 Put partitions in place, adding any remaining tiles; scribe to fit if necessary, and fix to the wall battens and floor with angle brackets.
14 Cut the back panel and slot it into place.
15 Make up and fit the shelves.
16 Make, tile and fit the floor plinth.
17 Tile the front faces of the partition units.
18 Fit worktop and any lipping.
19 Fit door frame if required.
20 Construct wall-mounted shelf units (with shelves if required).

PAINTED KITCHEN

Painted partition units with shelves, and a tiled worktop.

1 Decide depth of worktop.
2 Decide height of worktop.
3 Decide thickness of partition units.
4, 5, 6, 7, 8 as tiled kitchen.
9 Clad the frame in 12mm ($\frac{1}{2}$in) MDF, using oval nails punched in 2mm ($\frac{1}{16}$in) below the surface.
10 Make and fit the shelf-support battens.
11 Fit MDF fascia panel to front edge of each partition.
12 Fix the partition units in place. Attach to wall with angle brackets, and paint as required.
13 Make up and fit the shelves.
14 Fit and tile worktop.

TOOLS

TRIMMING KNIFE

STEEL RULE

TRY SQUARE

HAMMER

NAIL PUNCH

PANEL SAW (or circular power saw)

TENON SAW

SCREWDRIVER (cross-point or slotted, depending on type of screw used)

SANDING BLOCK and ABRASIVE PAPER (or power finishing sander)

DRILL (hand or power)

COUNTERSINK DRILL BIT

MASONRY DRILL BIT

PAINTBRUSH – 38mm ($1\frac{1}{2}$in)

TILING TOOLS

TILE-SCORING TOOL

TILE CUTTER

ADHESIVE SPREADER

TILE SPACERS

GROUT SPREADER

BUILDER'S SPIRIT LEVEL

TWO G-CRAMPS

ADDITIONAL TOOLS

POWER JIGSAW for cutting panels and fitting inset sinks and hobs

ROUTER (or circular power saw) for making cupboard handles

DOWELLING JIG for jointing worktops

V-BLOCK to hold dowelling for door handles

MATERIALS

Note: All dimensions are finished sizes – either sawn or planed.
Materials listed are for constructing one base unit with shelves, and a floor plinth.

BASE UNITS – BASIC FRAME

Part	Quantity	Material	Length
FRONT STUD	1	75 × 50mm (3 × 2in) sawn softwood	890mm (35in)
BACK STUD	1	As above	790mm (31in)
TOP RAIL	1	As above	575mm (22$\frac{3}{4}$in)
BOTTOM RAIL	1	As above	575mm (22$\frac{3}{4}$in)
INTERMEDIATE RAILS	As required	As above	480mm (19in)

CLADDING (covering for frame and floor)

SIDES	2	12mm ($\frac{1}{2}$in) shuttering grade plywood	890 × 630mm (35 × 24$\frac{3}{4}$in)
FLOOR	1	12mm ($\frac{1}{2}$in) shuttering grade plywood	600 × 630mm (23$\frac{1}{2}$ × 24$\frac{3}{4}$in)

SHELVES

TOP SHELF	1	15mm ($\frac{5}{8}$in) melamine-faced chipboard	600mm (23$\frac{1}{2}$in) wide × 618mm (24$\frac{1}{2}$in) deep
INTERMEDIATE SHELF	1	15mm ($\frac{5}{8}$in) melamine-faced chipboard	600mm (23$\frac{1}{2}$in) wide × 575mm (22$\frac{3}{4}$in) deep
TOP AND INTERMEDIATE SHELF LIPPING		38 × 12mm (1$\frac{1}{2}$ × $\frac{1}{2}$in) planed hardwood	600mm (23$\frac{1}{2}$in)

SHELF-SUPPORT BATTENS

TOP SHELF	1	19 × 19mm ($\frac{3}{4}$ × $\frac{3}{4}$in) planed softwood	618mm (24$\frac{1}{2}$in)
INTERMEDIATE SHELF	1	As above	575mm (22$\frac{3}{4}$in)

FLOOR PLINTH

FRONT SUPPORT JOIST	1	100 × 25mm (4 × 1in) sawn softwood	600mm (23$\frac{1}{2}$in)
MIDDLE SUPPORT JOIST	1	As above	As above
REAR SUPPORT JOIST	1	As above	As above

TILES

TILES	As required	108 × 108mm (4$\frac{1}{4}$ × 4$\frac{1}{4}$in) white ceramic wall and floor tiles	

CONSTRUCTING THE BASIC PARTITION PANEL

BASIC FRAME

Nail the front stud to the top rail using 75mm (3in) round wire nails. Make the job easier by nailing against a spare batten cramped to a bench, nailed to the floor, or fixed to a wall, so that there is something solid to nail against. The parts should rest on a flat surface while being nailed; this will help to hold them flush and stable.

Turn the assembly over and nail the front stud to the bottom rail.

Fix the back stud between the top and bottom rails, 50mm (2in) in from the ends, and nail it in place. This will make it easier to fit the unit to the rear wall later on.

In the case of the partition panel of the laundry area, the back stud should be inset by 100mm (4in), which will allow for a ducting pipe from the tumble dryer.

POSITIONING INTERMEDIATE RAILS

Intermediate cross rails coincide with the centre line of the shelf support positions, so these must be decided upon at this stage. The finished project will look better if the shelves align with joins between whole tiles. In our basic unit, one shelf is positioned one tile down from the top, and the other is midway between this shelf and the surface of the floor plinth.

On the front and back studs, measure down and mark the shelf top at the required height. Next, mark off the shelf thickness of 15mm ($\frac{5}{8}$in) and then the thickness of the shelf support batten, 19mm ($\frac{3}{4}$in). The middle of the batten position will be the centre line of the internal cross rail. Repeat the procedure for the second shelf.

With the basic square frame resting on edge (support the back stud with an offcut of 50mm [2in] wood), nail all the intermediate rails, correctly positioned, firmly in place.

CLADDING THE FRAME

On the outside edges of the front and back studs, mark the centre lines of the cross rails. The sides (which will be nailed to these cross rails) will conceal these rail positions. It is best to mark the centre lines of the rails accurately, although the heads of the fixing nails give a rough guide to the positions of the cross rails. Also mark the centre line of the back stud on the faces of the top and bottom rails of the frame.

Lay the frame flat, place a side panel cut from 12mm ($\frac{1}{2}$in) shuttering plywood on top, and align the front edge of the panel with the front edge of the front stud. If you are going to tile the panel, nail it in place *along the front edge only* using 38mm (1$\frac{1}{2}$in) round wire nails, about 150mm (6in) apart. If you are going to paint the panel, then use MDF and oval nails.

You will have made sure that the side panels are cut square, so use these as a guide to getting the basic frame square. Having nailed the front only, pull the rest of the frame into square, if necessary, to align with the edges of the panel, then nail through the panel into the frame, spacing the nails 150mm (6in) apart. To ensure that the nails go into the frame, transfer the centre-line marks of the intermediate and back rails on to each side panel.

Turn the partition over and repeat for the other side panel.

TILING

It is best to tile the basic partition panels before they are fitted, unless you are fitting a back panel, (see **Fitting a Back Panel, page 88**). Lay the panel flat, mark guide lines to ensure accurate tile spacing, spread tile adhesive, and press the tiles in place, working on a small area at a time (see **Techniques, pages 36**). Tile from front to back and top to bottom.

If the floor or wall is uneven where the units are to stand (or if there are pipe runs to cover), leave off the back and bottom rows of tiles and shelf-support battens until the units have been scribed to fit (see **Techniques, page 31**). Do not tile the front edge at this stage. When the tiles are dry, grout them. Turn over the units and repeat the process. Make up as many partition panels as are required to build your own kitchen system.

❶ The Basic Frame
The back stud is inset by 50mm (2in) between the top and bottom rails to make fitting to the wall easier.

❷ Intermediate Rail
Shelf batten position is one tile-space down from the top. Rail should coincide with shelf position.

❸ Positioning Intermediate Rail for Lower Shelf
After the first intermediate rail has been nailed in place, the second one should be positioned accurately to coincide with the centre line of the shelf-support batten.

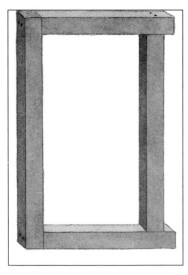

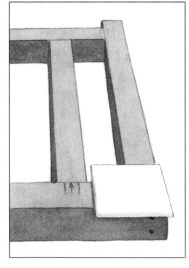

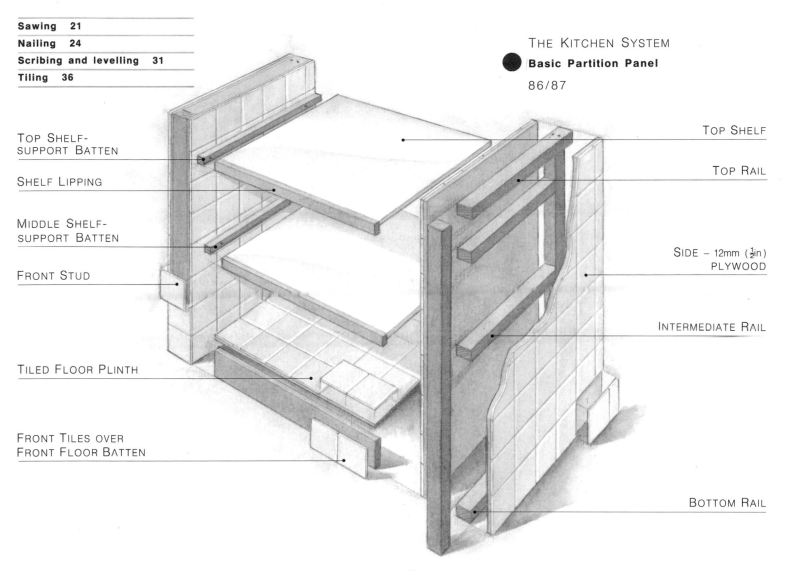

TOP SHELF-
SUPPORT BATTEN

SHELF LIPPING

MIDDLE SHELF-
SUPPORT BATTEN

FRONT STUD

TILED FLOOR PLINTH

FRONT TILES OVER
FRONT FLOOR BATTEN

TOP SHELF

TOP RAIL

SIDE – 12mm ($\frac{1}{2}$in)
PLYWOOD

INTERMEDIATE RAIL

BOTTOM RAIL

❹ Cladding the Sides of the Basic Frame
Mark the centre lines of the cross rails on the outside of the frames and carefully join up these marks on the 12mm ($\frac{1}{2}$in) plywood as a guide for nailing the sides on to the frame.

❺ Nailing Down the Sides
Nail the front edges at 150mm (6in) intervals. Pull the frame square, then nail along the guide lines.

❻ Tiling the Basic Partition
Tile from front to back and from top to bottom to keep cut tiles out of sight at the back or at floor level.

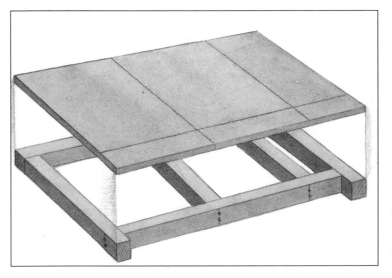

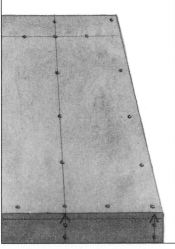

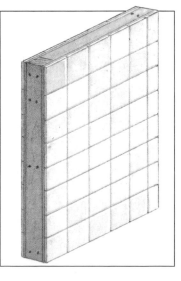

MAKING UP PARTITION UNITS

PAINTED PARTITION UNITS

Painted, as opposed to tiled partition units are shown in the photograph of the kitchen on page 80 and illustrate the versatility of the basic unit design.

The building techniques are the same as before, except that the frames are clad in 12mm ($\frac{1}{2}$in) MDF (medium-density fibreboard) instead of 12mm ($\frac{1}{2}$in) plywood. For a smooth finish, carefully punch the oval nail heads about 2mm ($\frac{1}{16}$in) below the surface of the board, then fill the holes with a proprietary wood filler. The frame should be sanded down once it is dry with a sanding block and abrasive paper.

Finish the front edge of each partition unit by applying a strip of MDF as a fascia panel, nailed in place and smoothed in the same way as the side panels. Chamfer the front edges of the fascia panels with a sanding block, then add the shelf battens. Fix the panels in place (*see opposite page*) and paint them.

TALL PARTITION UNITS

Tall partition units are required to house eye-level wall ovens, microwave ovens, refrigerators, and so on. Construction is as for low partition units, fixing all the cross rails at the levels required to coincide with the supports. Remember to fix a rail where the worktop meets the partition as this will take a lot of weight.

As the maximum standard length of plywood is 2440mm (8ft) there will be a join if the units are taller than this. The join must be at a cross rail so that the cut edges can be nailed down. If there is not a convenient cross rail, then put in an extra one for this purpose.

SHELVES SUPPORTING COOKERS

These shelves must be substantial to support the weight of the appliance. Use 50 × 25mm (2 × 1in) battens for the shelf supports and 25mm (1in) chipboard or MDF for the shelves. The front fascia is cut from the same material as the shelves, to the width of the shelf and to the depth required – in this case, one tile deep. Either screw or glue and nail the front piece to the front edge of the shelf, and tile the front face.

FITTING A BACK PANEL

If a back panel is to be fitted on a basic unit (perhaps to hide pipes where there is to be an open shelf), this must be done before fitting the shelves and floor plinth, and also before tiling the sides. The front-to-back measurements of the shelves and plinth should be reduced to make them fit. If the partition panel unit is to be fitted over pipes, scribe the partition around these now to ensure a good fit (*see* **Techniques, page 31**).

Once all the partitions are sitting in place, correctly scribed, take the first partition and mark a line 50mm (2in) in from the back. Cut two lengths of 19 × 19mm ($\frac{3}{4}$ × $\frac{3}{4}$in) batten to the height of the partition and fix a batten just in front of the marked line. Glue and nail it in position. Repeat for the second partition. Tile the surface (*see* **Techniques, page 36**), but only up to the batten. Repeat as necessary.

Make and fix the shelf-support battens (*see opposite page*) allowing a 6mm ($\frac{1}{4}$in) gap for the thickness of the back. Put partitions back in place and fix to the floor (*see opposite page*).

Cut the back panel from 6mm ($\frac{1}{4}$in) MDF or plywood. The height is the same as the partitions, and the width is as the floor and shelf widths. Slot the panel in place from the top and screw through to the battens, using four screws on each side. You may need to undo the shelf-support battens temporarily for an easy fit.

Make up the shelves (*see opposite page*), adjusting the front-to-back dimension accordingly. Replace the support battens and fit the shelves.

FLOOR PLINTHS

Each floor plinth is constructed from 12mm ($\frac{1}{2}$in) shuttering plywood with 100 × 25mm (4 × 1in) sawn timber battens supporting it, assuming you

---

❶ Cladding Painted Partition Units with MDF
Use 12mm ($\frac{1}{2}$in) MDF to clad units.
Punch nail heads below surface.

❷ Construction of Tall Partition Units
The basic construction method is the same as for the low partition units.
Intermediate rails should be included wherever shelves are required or fixings are to be made.

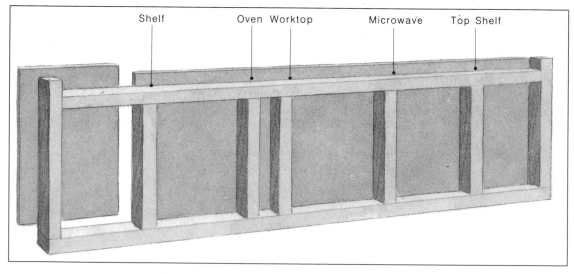

Shelf   Oven Worktop   Microwave   Top Shelf

are using 108×108mm ($4\frac{1}{4} \times 4\frac{1}{4}$in) tiles. The front-to-back dimensions are again adjusted accordingly.

Cut the 12mm ($\frac{1}{2}$in) plywood plinth panel to size and nail the battens to it at the front, back and middle. Inset the back one slightly to make scribing easier.

In a laundry room or kitchen it is normal to set the washing machine and tumble dryer on the floor, but 'built-in' models of washing machines are available also, and these look better set on tiled floor plinths as shown in the photograph. If you intend to do this, put in two extra support battens to take the weight of the machines. Pack glassfibre loft insulation between the battens to reduce noise.

Tile the top from front to back and from the middle outwards, so that any cut tiles are equal at either side (see **Tiling Techniques, pages 36**). Grout the tiles to finish. If an appliance is to be placed on a floor plinth, make sure that tiles suitable for floors and walls are chosen as thin wall tiles will crack under the weight and vibration.

SHELVES

We chose easy-to-clean melamine-laminated chipboard for our shelves, but you may prefer to use another type of man-made board, such as blockboard or plywood (see **Materials, timber and boards, page 16**). All shelves are edged at the front with a wooden lip and this thickness has to be allowed for when fixing the shelf-support battens in position.

FIXING SHELF-SUPPORT BATTENS

The positions of the shelf supports are already marked on the front and back studs (see **Positioning Intermediate Rails, page 86**). With a pencil, link up the lines on the tiles.

Use 19×19mm ($\frac{3}{4} \times \frac{3}{4}$in) planed timber for the shelf supports, and cut them to the length required. The top one is the depth of the partition unit, minus the thickness of the lipping. The middle one is the depth of the partition, less half a tile width and the thickness of the lipping.

Hold each batten in position on the panel and mark two fixing-screw positions, approximately 50mm (2in) from the ends of each batten, but adjusted so that the screws will not be too near the edges of the tiles once in place.

Using a 4.5mm ($\frac{3}{16}$in) drill bit, drill two clearance holes in each batten (see **Techniques, page 23**). Hold each batten in place again and mark the screw positions on the tiles. Drill the tiles with a 7mm ($\frac{9}{32}$in) masonry drill to ensure that the batten-fixing screws will not crack the tiles when they are driven home.

Drill a 3mm ($\frac{1}{8}$in) hole through the centre of each clearance hole in the partition panel side. Countersink holes in the face of each batten and screw the battens into place using 50mm (2in) No 8 screws. Hide the battens by painting them with a suitable colour to blend with the tiles you have chosen.

MAKING THE SHELVES

Hold the shelf piece in a vice with the front edge, which is non-laminated, facing upwards.

Glue and nail 38×12mm ($1\frac{1}{2} \times \frac{1}{2}$in) planed wood lipping to this edge so that the top edge is flush. The lipping must underhang the shelf enough to hide the battens, that is by 19mm ($\frac{3}{4}$in). Use 25mm (1in) round wire nails, blunting the points first so as not to split the wood. Nail carefully, making sure that the lipping is flush with the surface as you proceed. Wipe off surplus glue. Punch the nail heads below the surface, then fill the holes and sand down.

Paint, or stain and varnish, the lipping. Ours is stained with white oil to match the worktop.

Where a shelf has to fit into a corner, cut off the underhang of the lipping where the front of the shelf meets a partition, and screw a batten to the wall, level with the side battens on the partition unit, to support the shelf at the back.

FIXING PARTITION UNITS IN PLACE

The partition units are neatly fixed to the rear wall with metal angle brackets at positions where they will be

---

3 **Fitting a Back Panel**
Scribe partition units around pipes and cut slots. Fit a panel-support batten to the face of the unit.

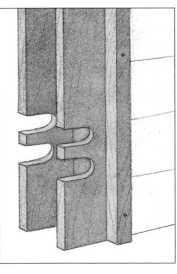

4 **Construction of a Tiled Floor Plinth**
Floor plinth comprises 12mm ($\frac{1}{2}$in) plywood on 100×25mm (4×1in) sawn timber battens. The back batten is inset by about 50mm (2in). Front tiles overlap the edges of the top tiles.

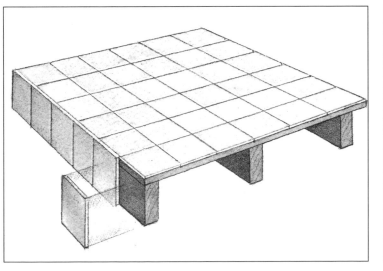

5 **Fixing Shelves In Place**
Hardwood lipping fixed to the front edge of a shelf (inset) hides support battens screwed to units.

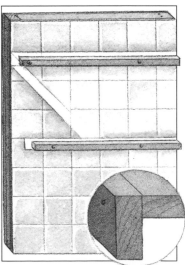

hidden at the very top and at shelf height. Brackets are also used to fix the units down into the floor where they will be hidden by the floor plinth units when in place.

Position the partition units according to the plans. It is important to have a partition unit where you have to turn a corner, to support the two edges of the worktop.

Do any scribing necessary to fit the partitions to the wall or floor *(see* **Techniques, page 31** *)*.

Fix any remaining tiles that have been left off to allow for scribing. In order to do this you will have to unscrew the shelf-support batten and re-attach it after tiling. Fit in the shelves and then the floor plinth.

Fix the partition down to the floor using angle brackets *(see* **page 25** *)*. Do this by removing the floor plinth and fitting the brackets where they will avoid the joists supporting the floor plinth. Slide the floor plinth back into position.

Fix high partitions to the wall batten, and also fix them to the floor and ceiling, if necessary, using angle brackets where they cannot be seen, such as behind the cooker, just underneath the back shelf, or on top of the shelf above eye-level.

When all the partition units are fixed, tile and grout their front faces to finish the unit.

Doors

The doors are hinged in pairs and inset within a timber frame as a neat addition to the basic unit.

Making the Frame

Measure the opening where the doors are to fit and make a frame to these external dimensions.

Dowel joint the horizontal rails between the uprights with two 12mm ($\frac{1}{2}$in) dowels at each frame corner *(see* **Techniques, page 30** *)*. While the glue is setting, the frame should be held square on a flat surface with sash cramps. Alternatively, improvise by resting the frame against a batten temporarily nailed to the bench top. Another batten is nailed to the bench a short distance from the other side of the frame, and the cramp is tightened by driving two folding wedges from opposing sides *(see* **Techniques, page 21** *)* between the edge of the second batten and the frame side.

From 12mm ($\frac{1}{2}$in) hardwood dowelling cut eight dowels, the length of which should be twice the thickness of the wood it is going through, plus 12mm ($\frac{1}{2}$in). Use a tenon saw to cut two grooves 1– 2mm ($\frac{1}{32}$–$\frac{1}{16}$in) deep, along the dowel length. This will allow the glue and air to escape as the dowel is driven in. With abrasive paper, round off one end of each dowel.

With a 12mm ($\frac{1}{2}$in) drill bit, drill two holes through each corner joint to a depth of twice the thickness of the wood being fixed. Wrap a band of adhesive tape around the drill bit to indicate the correct depth.

Apply glue to each hole and wipe it around the inside with a small stick. Insert the dowels and hammer them almost home, leaving the ends protruding for the time being. Leave the frames cramped square.

When the glue has set, remove the cramps and saw off the dowel ends flush with the surface.

Fixing the Frame

Before fixing the frame, it must be held square by nailing a batten temporarily across the top and one side of the frame *(see* **Techniques, 3-4-5 method of bracing, page 20** *)* and fig 2 below. *)* After fixing the bracing batten, saw off the ends of the batten flush with the frame to make a neat edge.

Drill and countersink the uprights of the frame and the bottom rails. Fit the frame in position and screw it to the partition units and to the floor. After fixing, remove the bracing batten from the frame.

Making the Doors

For a painted finish, cut the doors from 19mm ($\frac{3}{4}$in) MDF so that they fit the frame with a 2mm ($\frac{1}{16}$in) gap all round. There are many different types of door handles which can be fitted to finished doors. Opposite you will find instructions for making and fitting the handles shown in the illustration. Hinges and catches must also be fitted to the doors *(see* **Techniques, page 33** *)*.

❶ Jointing of Frame Corners
Two 12mm ($\frac{1}{2}$in) dowel holes in the ends of the rails are the same length as the thickness of the uprights.

❷ Making the Door Frame Square
Before fitting the frame, hold it square temporarily by nailing a batten across the top and one side using the 3-4-5 method of ensuring a right-angled corner. See Techniques, page 20, for further details.

❸ Fitting the Door Handles
A right-angled rebate is cut in 25mm (1in) dowel which is fitted to hardwood lipping on the door edge.

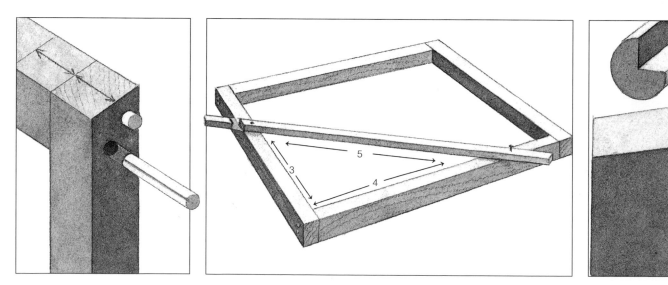

MAKING THE HANDLES

To make our handles, you will need a router, and a V-block to hold the dowelling from which the handles are made *(see **Techniques, Making a V-block, page 23**)*. The dowelling is placed in the V-block and rebated with the router. (You can use a circular saw for this, but it is much more difficult to achieve a good finish.) Cut the doors so that they are narrower by the thickness of the lipping, that is, 12mm ($\frac{1}{2}$in).

Cut two lengths of 25mm (1in) diameter dowelling to the length of the door plus 50mm (2in) extra to allow the dowelling to be nailed in the V-block. The V-block should be a 1m (39in) length of 75 × 50mm (3 × 2in) timber with a 25mm (1in) deep V cut in one face. Nail each end of the dowel in the V-block and mark off the finished length. Hold the V-block firmly in a vice.

Working from one end to the other, rout to the depth of the lipping (12mm [$\frac{1}{2}$in]) between the marks. Cut the dowel to its final length. Cut two lengths of 32 × 12mm (1$\frac{1}{4}$ × $\frac{1}{2}$in) hardwood lipping to the length of the dowels. Glue and pin the lipping to the dowel, then sand smooth. Glue and pin the lipping on to the door edges and finish as required.

SLATTED SHELF

Slatted shelves are easy to build and are particularly useful in airing cupboards. In the laundry room *(see **page 83**)*, a slatted shelf has been built-in under the Belfast sink. A number of cross slats are nailed to side rails which rest alongside the same type of shelf-support battens as those used in the basic partition unit in the main kitchens.

Cut two pieces of 50 × 25mm (2 × 1in) planed timber for the side rails to the required front-to-back depth of the shelf. Our shelf is set back about 100mm (4in). Cut the support battens to the same length

HINGED DOOR ASSEMBLY
Doors are hinged within a simple frame assembly which is screwed in place between partition units

and fix in place *(see **Shelf-Support Battens, page 89**)*.

Cut the required number of slats (we used seven) from the 50 × 25mm (2 × 1in) planed timber. The length of these should be the width between partitions, less 2mm ($\frac{1}{16}$in) to fit exactly.

Set the side rails in from the ends of the slats by the thickness of the supporting battens. Use offcuts or scrap wood of the same thickness as the support battens. Lay them next to the side rails before laying the front slat across them, so that the battens are at the very ends. Nail the slats in place.

Cut a spacing batten *(see **Techniques, page 20**)* to ensure that the remaining slats are spaced evenly, then nail them in place. Finish off the shelf by painting, staining or varnishing it as required.

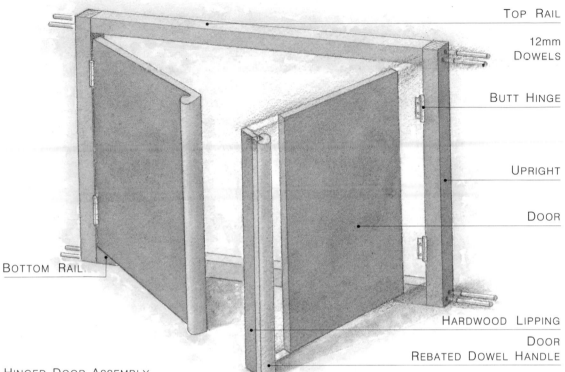

TOP RAIL

12mm DOWELS

BUTT HINGE

UPRIGHT

DOOR

HARDWOOD LIPPING

DOOR
REBATED DOWEL HANDLE

BOTTOM RAIL

❹ Making a Slatted Under-Sink Storage Shelf
A number of cross slats are nailed to side rails; these rails rest on 19 × 19mm ($\frac{3}{4}$ × $\frac{3}{4}$in) shelf-support battens which are then fixed at each side to the tiled partition units.

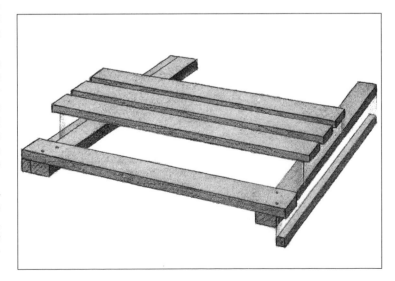

WORKTOPS

There is a wide range of worktops from which to choose. In the main kitchen we used a 38mm (1½in) solid wood top, finished with white oil. The worktop in the small kitchen is 25mm (1in) chipboard which is tiled, and lipped at the front with hardwood. A wide selection of melamine laminate worktops is available. The front edges are often rounded (post-formed), or they can be square-edged and lipped with hardwood. Most standard worktops are 32mm (1¼in) thick.

If a material like marble or granite is chosen, it will look better if it is made to look thicker at the front edge by bonding a strip of similar material under the front edge. At the back, the worktop's edge will probably be covered by the wall tiles.

Alternatively, the worktop can be fitted to the wall by scribing, or by cutting into the wall, although it is easier to cover the gap at the back with a narrow hardwood strip fixed to the wall. If the wall is very uneven, a hardwood strip can be fixed horizontally to the back of the worktop. This strip can be scribed to the wall.

JOINING WORKTOPS

You will probably not need to join worktops end-to-end unless you have a very long run, but you will almost certainly need to turn a corner. Remember that all joins must coincide with a partition for support.

Joins should be dowelled (see **Techniques, page 30**) using a dowelling jig to ensure that the surfaces are absolutely flush. You then rout out or drill the surfaces for jointing connector bolts on the underside; there are several types available and they all come with fitting instructions. Alternatively, for corner jointing post-formed worktops, specially shaped metal strips are available to cover the joints neatly.

FIXING DOWN WORKTOPS

Fix the worktop to the partitions with angle plates – two per side of each partition – and screw up through any door frames into the worktop. If you are fixing a solid-wood worktop, allow for expansion and shrinkage in the wood by using specially slotted angle plates. Where a worktop

meets a high partition, screw a 50 × 50mm (2 × 2in) batten to the partition for the worktop to rest on. Screw up into the worktop from the underside of the batten (if it is a solid wood worktop, use a screw slot). Angle the front edge of the support batten backwards so that it will not be seen and set it back from the front edge. Another method of fixing down a worktop is to use a flat metal plate screwed down into the pillar before the worktop is laid over it, and then up into the worktop, see fig 2.

If the worktop is to be tiled, do this after fitting, then add a hardwood lipping. Seal the gap at the back of the worktop to finish..

SINKS AND HOBS

These are supplied with templates for the required cut-outs. Hold the templates in position and draw around them. Drill 12mm (½in) diameter holes in each corner, inside the line. Put the blade of the jigsaw through one of the holes, and saw around the line (see **Techniques, Cutting a circle, page 22**).

FRONT CONTROL PANEL FOR HOB

Screw a small length of 19 × 19mm (¾ × ¾in) batten into the partitions at a depth and distance back to suit your control panel. Screw through into the battens following the appliance manufacturer's instructions.

BELFAST SINK

This type of sink sits on a support under a cut-out in the worktop. Make a template of the inside shape of the sink and use this to make the cut-out as for sinks and hobs (above). Because the worktop should overhang the sink, the cutout must therefore be smaller than the inside of the sink. With a router, form a shallow groove on the underside of the worktop, all around the cut-out, about 6mm (¼in) from the edge. This is a drip groove which will help to prevent water from running under the worktop. Seal around the rim of the sink and the underside of the worktop using a silicone-rubber sealant. Make a circular cut-out in the shelf support to allow the waste

---

① How to Join Worktops
When joining worktops, reinforce the under-surface by fitting jointing connector bolts.

② Fixing Down Worktops
Angle plates (brackets), top, and corner plates, bottom, are used for fixing worktops in place.

③ Fitting an Inset Sink or Cooker Hob
Templates are supplied for marking the top so that a cut-out can be made with a jigsaw. Clips on the underside of the sink or cooker hob hold the appliance in place once a hole has been cut.

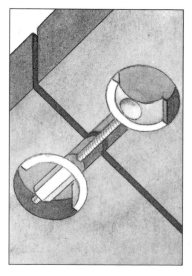

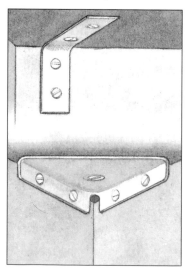

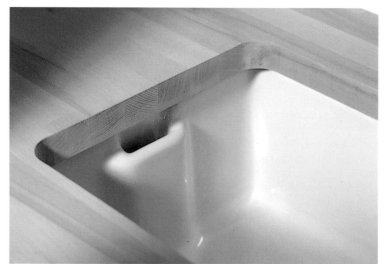

trap to be fitted into the sink. Stiffen the front edge of the shelf support with 50 × 25mm (2 × 1in) timber lipping. Cut a hole, or holes, in the worktop behind the sink to allow the taps to be fitted. Belfast sinks are generally very heavy, so it may be wise to consult a plumber before attempting to fit such a sink yourself.

TILING A WORKTOP

Tiling a worktop provides a very hard-wearing, hygienic surface which is easy to clean and therefore ideal for a kitchen. However, a tiled surface is not suitable for all purposes – for food preparation you need a smooth, wipe-clean surface, such as melamine-laminate. For chopping vegetables and meat you need a surface of solid hardwood, such as maple, which is what butchers' blocks are made from. So in a kitchen there is a good case for having a choice of worksurfaces.

When buying tiles for a worktop, be sure to tell your supplier what you will be using them for. Some thin wall tiles crack when used to work on, so thicker tiles suitable for both walls and floors are preferable. Some outdoor-type tiles, particularly those with a metallic glaze, are not suitable for preparing food on.

If possible, avoid white grout as it is very difficult to keep clean, although the latest two-part epoxy type is better in this respect. A good choice is a dark-coloured waterproof grout. A wide range of coloured grouts is available, and colouring powders can be mixed with white grout to your own requirements. If tiles without spacers are used, keep them close together to minimize the width of grouting.

It is essential that the worksurface to be tiled is stable and securely fixed before you begin tiling. We recommend 25mm (1in) chipboard. Plywood of the same thickness is also suitable, although more expensive. Try to avoid tiling over solid wood as the wood tends to expand and shrink too much, loosening the tiles.

Before starting to tile, tack a batten temporarily to the outer edge of the worktop to give a surface to tile against. Then lay out the tiles in a dry run to see whether any cutting will be required. This will almost certainly be the case, so keep the cut tiles to the back. If the tiles have to be cut at each end of the worksurface, make sure that the cut ones will be at least half a tile's width. If the initial setting-out reveals only thin strips at each end, move all of the tiles sideways by half a tile's width so as to make the end tiles wider.

On the temporary edging batten, mark where the middle tile falls and start tiling from there. Spread tile adhesive over the worktop to cover about 1m square (1 yd square) using a notched tile adhesive spreader to ensure an even bed of adhesive. Press the middle tile into the adhesive with a slight twisting motion, then add other tiles to the front edge on each side of this tile. Make sure that they butt against the temporary edging batten. Next, fit whole tiles, working back from the front middle tile towards the back wall. Use a try square and a straight-edge to ensure that this row is straight. Now, working from front to back again, fill in with tiles on each side of this row to complete the main area of tiling. (After this, cut and fit the edge tiles, *see* **Tiling Techniques, page 36**).

Complete the job by removing the temporary edging batten and replacing it with hardwood lipping, the top edge of which should be level with the surface of the tiles. The lipping should be deep enough to cover the entire thickness of the worktop. Grout the joints between the tiles and the space between the tiles and the lipping. Finally, seal the tile-to-wall joint with silicone-rubber sealant to make it waterproof.

④ Working out Tile Positions
Tack a batten temporarily to the front edge of the worktop. Set out tiles in a 'dummy run'.

⑤ Order for Laying Tiles
Lay front tiles from the middle, then work to the back and fill in at each side of the worktop.

⑥ Tiled Worktop
In the painted kitchen project shown on page 80, our tiled worktop is finished off with a neat wooden lipping to create a functional but attractive surface to work on when cooking.

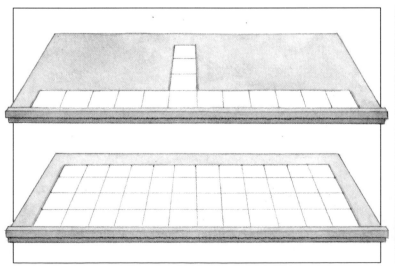

WALL-MOUNTED SHELF UNIT

The wall-mounted shelf units are built in a similar way to the floor units. They are neatly mounted to wall battens, so there is no visible means of support. When the units are mounted on a stud wall, extra support is required, so horizontal battens are fixed to the wall to support the vertical wall battens. Therefore, the top and bottom rails are thinner in these units, and the sides have cut-outs at the back to slot over the battens on the wall.

MAKING THE PARTITION

Remember that each shelf unit needs a partition panel at each end. Some partitions will support shelving at each side.

Mark out on the walls where you want the shelf runs to be. For the best visual effect, keep the wall shelf partitions above the centre lines of the base partitions. Work out what you want to incorporate within the shelves – for example, a cooker hood, a plate rack and a hanging bar for utensils. Decide on the overall height of the shelving. In our case, the partitions are 600mm (23½in) high by 350mm (13¾in) deep.

The basic frame is made from 50 × 50mm (2 × 2in) PAR (planed all round) timber clad with 6mm (¼in) MDF (medium-density fibreboard) panels. Two panels are required for each partition unit.

Cut two rails (for top and bottom) 350mm (13¾in) long, and three uprights 510mm (20in) long. Note that for fixing to a stud (hollow) wall, the top and bottom rails will be 50 × 25mm (2 × 1in) and 325mm (12¾in) long.

Nail together the basic frame so that the back stud is set one stud's thickness in. Glue and nail on the side panels, fixing one edge first, before pulling the frame into square so that the other sides line up with the panel. Check that the wall batten slides into the back space.

TOOLS

TRIMMING KNIFE

STEEL RULE

TRY SQUARE

HAMMER

NAIL PUNCH

PANEL SAW (or circular power saw)

TENON SAW

SCREWDRIVER

SANDING BLOCK AND ABRASIVE PAPER (or power finishing sander)

DRILL (hand or power)

DRILL BITS

COUNTERSINK BIT

MASONRY DRILL BIT

PLANE

SPIRIT LEVEL

PAINTBRUSH – 38mm (1½in)

ADDITIONAL TOOLS

METAL OR STUD DETECTOR

FLAT BIT (diameter of utensil bar) – for drilling partition panels for bar

MATERIALS

Part	Quantity	Material	Length
PARTITION UNIT (two required per shelf unit)			
SIDE PANEL	2	6mm (¼in) MDF	350 × 600mm (13¾ × 23½in)
FRONT FASCIA PANEL	1	6mm (¼in) MDF	As above
TOP RAIL*	1	50 × 50mm (2 × 2in) PAR timber	350mm (13¾in)
BOTTOM RAIL*	1	As above	As above
FRONT STUD	1	As above	510mm (20in)
BACK STUD	1	As above	As above
WALL BATTEN	1	As above	As above
SHELVES			
TOP SHELF	1	15mm (⅝in) melamine-faced chipboard	325 × 600mm (12¾ × 23½in), or as required
BOTTOM SHELF	1	As above	As above
MIDDLE SHELF	1	15mm (⅝in) melamine-faced chipboard	250 × 600mm (10 × 23½in), or as required
SHELF LIPPING	3	12 × 38mm (½ × 1½in) hardwood	As above
TOP AND BOTTOM SHELF-SUPPORT BATTENS	4	15 × 25mm (⅝ × 1in) PAR timber (Buy 19 × 25mm [¾ × 1in] timber and plane down	325mm (12¾in)
MIDDLE SHELF SUPPORTS	2	As above	250mm (10in)
*TOP RAIL (for stud wall fixing)	1	50 × 25mm (2 × 1in) PAR timber	325mm (12¾in)
*BOTTOM RAIL (for stud wall)	1	As above	As above

TOP SHELF-SUPPORT
BATTEN

SHELF EDGE-BANDING

MIDDLE SHELF-SUPPORT
BATTEN

MIDDLE SHELF

BOTTOM SHELF-SUPPORT
BATTEN

BOTTOM SHELF

FRONT FASCIA PANEL

TOP SHELF

WALL BATTEN

BACK STUD

FRONT STUD

BOTTOM RAIL

❶ **The Partition Basic Frame**
Note that the back stud is inset by the
thickness of the wall batten for a neat
fit and to make scribing easier.

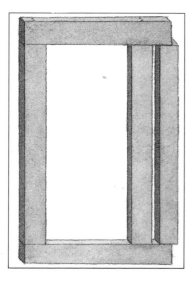

❷ **Cladding the Frame Unit**
6mm ($\frac{1}{4}$in) MDF is nailed to the sides,
and front fascia is nailed on to cover
the edges of the frame unit.

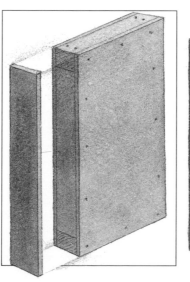

❸ **Fixing the Shelf Battens**
Battens are fixed at the top, middle
and bottom. *Inset* fixing a batten to
make the top flush.

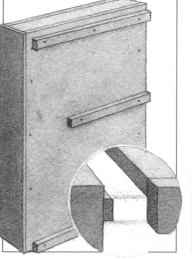

❹ **Solid Wall Fixing Method**
Batten is securely plugged and
screwed to the wall; the partition
(cut-away) slots over the batten.

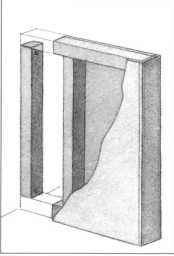

WALL-MOUNTED SHELF UNIT

Measure the total thickness of the partition and cut front fascia strips from 6mm ($\frac{1}{4}$in) MDF to that width and 600mm ($23\frac{1}{2}$in) high.

Nail on the front fascia and punch the nail heads below the surface (see **Techniques, Nailing, page 24**). Chamfer the edges with a plane and sand them down. If the panels are to be a different colour from the wall, it is a good idea to paint them before you fix them to the wall.

SHELF-SUPPORT BATTENS

Plane the timber down to 15 × 25mm ($\frac{5}{8}$ × 1in) to make shelf-support battens, and fit these to the partitions before fixing the partitions to the wall. The shelves will look better if they are set back slightly from the front of the partitions. The middle shelf has to be set back even farther – about 100mm (4in).

Decide how many shelves you need and where you want them according to your own storage requirements. Ours are flush with the top and bottom of the partitions, and a middle shelf is fixed midway between the top and bottom shelves.

① Stud Wall Fixing Method
The wall batten is screwed to horizontal battens that are nailed to wall studs.

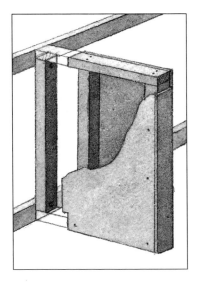

Cut the support battens to length, allowing for the lipping which is fixed to the front edge of the shelf (that is, the battens should be cut to the shelf's depth). Glue, then screw or nail the battens in place.

SHELVES

The shelves are made from 15mm ($\frac{5}{8}$in) melamine-faced chipboard with 12mm ($\frac{1}{2}$in) thick hardwood lipping. Glue and nail the lipping to the front edge. Fill the nail holes, sand smooth when dry, and finish as required, according to your chosen decorative scheme.

PLATE RACK

If you are incorporating a plate rack (see opposite page for assembly instructions), it is important to make this up before fixing in place the supporting partitions which sit on either side of it.

FIXING UP THE PARTITIONS

Solid walls In most cases the partitions will be fixed above a worktop. This should have been fitted level, so measure up from it when marking the positions of the wall battens. Use a spirit level to double check that these marks are level. Then, using masonry nails, temporarily fix a straight horizontal batten to the wall for the wall battens to rest on while they are fixed. Drill the wall for wallplugs and screw the wall battens securely to the wall.

Slot the partition unit over the wall battens and glue and screw through the sides into the wall battens with 25mm (1in) No 8 woodscrews, using four either side.

Stud walls Locate the wall studs (see **Techniques, Wall Fixings, page 24**) and nail a 50 × 50mm (2 × 2in) batten horizontally at the top and bottom of where the partition units will be placed. Screw the 50 × 50mm (2 × 2in) upright wall battens to the horizontal battens on the wall for support.

Nail up the frame as before, but use 50 × 25mm (2 × 1in) timber for the top and bottom rails which will be shorter by the thickness of the horizontal battens. Cut out 50 × 25mm (2 × 1in) slots on the back corners of the inside panels using a 50 × 25mm (2 × 1in) timber off-cut as a template. Nail the panels down, then slot the partitions over the wall battens, screwing through the sides into the wall battens as before. Do not include cut-outs at the ends of the shelf units.

COOKER HOOD

The hood can be a simple recirculating type, which needs only to be fixed between two partition panels and connected to a power supply, or it can be a more efficient extractor type. With the latter type,

USE SHELVES FOR DISPLAY
The wall-mounted shelf unit is ideal for display as well as for practical storage.

you will need to cut an outlet in a convenient external wall for fumes to escape through. The hood is then either connected directly to the outlet or linked to it with slot-together plastic ducting if they are some distance apart. The manufacturer's instructions will have full details.

It will probably be necessary to fit mounting battens to both the wall and the partition units. Fit a narrow shelf at the top to line up with the top of the partition units, but do not fit lipping at the front as the cooker hood's front panel will conceal this. Fit battens at an angle on each inside face of the partition units to hold the front panel. This can be a sheet of stainless steel or painted MDF. If you use MDF, secure the panel by screwing through into the battens. But if the panel is stainless steel, it is neater to glue it in place with epoxy resin

You can adapt the fitting of the cooker hood according to its design and how it fits into the rest of your kitchen system.

HANGING BAR FOR UTENSILS

This is simply a chrome-steel or wooden rod which fits at each end into a wall partition panel. S-shaped meat hooks are hung on the bar to take utensils.

To fix the bar, drill holes of its diameter into the sides of the appropriate partition unit so that the bar will clear the bottom rail but rest *on* it. Use an off-cut of bottom rail as a spacer to mark off the lowest part of the hole on the bottom edge of the partition panel.

Cut the rod to a length equivalent to the distance between two partition panels, plus 100mm (4in).

② Positioning the Hanging Bar
Use an offcut of the bottom rail to mark a position on the partition for the hanging bar.

BUILT-IN PLATE RACK AND DRIP TRAY

This is a simply designed storage unit which is intended to be built-in between two wall-mounted shelf units (see overleaf for instructions and page 78 for a photograph of the unit in position). For a perfect result, great accuracy and attention to detail as well as a helping pair of hands, is called for, but the finished unit is solid, secure and stylish. Wooden dowels are inserted at regular intervals into three wooden rails which are angled to suit the size of your crockery. Instructions for a drip tray made from melamine-faced chipboard are also included. The drip tray allows you to leave crockery on the plate rack to dry by itself.

SAVE TIME IN THE KITCHEN
Dishes can be neatly stacked and left to dry on this stylish plate rack.

TOOLS

TRIMMING KNIFE

STEEL MEASURING TAPE

TRY SQUARE

TENON SAW

HAMMER

MORTISE GAUGE

POWER DRILL

DRILL BITS

HOLE SAW 38–50mm ($1\frac{1}{2}$–2in) to suit frame diameter (or use a router)

POWER JIGSAW

MALLET

ADDITIONAL TOOLS

V-BLOCK

DRILL STAND (or home-made drill guide) – for accurate vertical drilling

MATERIALS

PLATE RACK

Part	Quantity	Material	Length
FRAME	3	38–50mm ($1\frac{1}{2}$in–2in) diameter softwood dowel	As required
RACK SPACERS	As required	12mm ($\frac{1}{2}$in) softwood dowel	137mm ($5\frac{1}{2}$in)
RACK SPACERS	As required	12mm ($\frac{1}{2}$in) softwood dowel	250mm (10in)

DRIP TRAY

Part	Quantity	Material	Length
TRAY BASE	1	15mm ($\frac{5}{8}$in) melamine-faced chipboard	As required
EDGE FRAME	4	38 × 12mm ($1\frac{1}{2}$ × $\frac{1}{2}$in) hardwood lipping	As required
SUPPORT BATTENS	2	10 × 6mm ($\frac{3}{8}$ × $\frac{1}{4}$in) softwood	As required

BUILT-IN PLATE RACK AND DRIP TRAY

Cut the three large frame dowels to length. To calculate the length of each dowel, add the distances between the partitions, plus 100mm (4in). The 100mm (4in) allows for 25mm (1in) either end to slot into the partitions, and 25mm (1in) excess either end. A nail can be driven in to this excess to secure the dowel to the V-block while the holes are being drilled in it (see **Techniques, Making a V-block, page 23**). The excess will be sawn off later.

Position one dowel in the V-block. Draw a straight line along its length using a steel straight-edge resting against one side of the block (fig 1). Starting 62mm (2½in) in from one end, mark off 35mm (1⅜in) centres along it. Use a pencil or mortise gauge to do this.

Using the first dowel as a guide, transfer the 35mm (1⅜in) centres to a second dowel. For the third dowel, mark a line down its length as described above, and continue the line across the end section to the centre. Draw a second line, at 96° to the first. Continue the second line along the length of the dowel.

Use the first dowel to transfer the 35mm (1⅜in) centres to the third dowel, making the marks between the two lines. Put the first dowel in the V-block with the marked hole-centres vertical. Nail it down at either end to secure it.

DRILLING THE HOLES

Start to drill the vertical holes, (see **Techniques, page 23**).

Each hole should be drilled to a depth of 12mm (½in). Use a drill stand, a drill guide set at 90°, or make your own drill guide.

MAKING A DRILL GUIDE

You will need a block of wood 100 × 50mm (4 × 2in). Make a V-shaped cut-out in it so that it will fit neatly over the dowel resting in the V-block. Drill a hole through it vertically (see above).

Thread the drill bit through the hole in the drill guide and place the tip of the bit on the first hole. Pull the guide into position, resting on the V-block, then drill a 12mm (½in) deep hole. Drill all the required holes in the same way.

ASSEMBLY

Cut 25mm (1in) from each end of each of the three frame dowels. (This is the excess used when nailing the dowel to the V-block.)

By tapping gently with a mallet, fit all the 137mm (5¼in) dowels into one of the frame dowels (one with a single row of holes) and all the 250mm (10in) dowels into the other frame dowel.

Join the two sections together to complete the assembly. You will need help when aligning the dowels. If the fit is very tight, it will be easier to cramp it together in a woodworker's vice. An extra-tight fit may be achieved by cramping the rack in a vice. If the fit is loose, put a little waterproof glue in the holes to fill any gaps.

Look down the length of the rack to check that it is perfectly aligned. If it is not, twist the rack into alignment by getting one person at each end of the rack to adjust it.

FIXING IN POSITION

The plate rack must be fixed in position before the supporting partitions are finally fixed in place.

Offer up the rack to one partition. Tilt it back until an angle is found in which plates will sit comfortably. Mark the dowel positions on the partition sides.

Position the wall batten in its correct position at the back of the partition so that this can be drilled at the same time.

Cut out the holes to a depth of 25mm (1in) with an electric drill and hole saw or with a router.

Fit one partition in place and carefully slot the rack into it. Meanwhile, ask someone to hold the partition against the other end of the rack for you so that the position for the three holes can be marked and the holes drilled. The partition can then be tapped into the rack to secure it in position. Finally, attach the second partition to the wall batten. For further ideas and instructions for a variety of wall-mounted plate racks and shelves, hanging bars and suspended shelves see **pages 66–69 and 114 and 116**.

❶ Marking-Up Plate Rack Dowel Hole Centres
Rest dowel in a V-block and mark off centres at 35mm (1⅜in) intervals. Transfer all the marks on to the second dowel. On the third dowel draw a second line at exactly 96° to the first

❷ Using a Drill Guide
With dowel nailed in to a V-block, line up on first hole. Use scrap wood as a drill guide.

❸ Drilling the Dowel Holes
A drill guide, which you can make yourself, helps to keep the drill bit vertical. Drill 12mm (½in) holes.

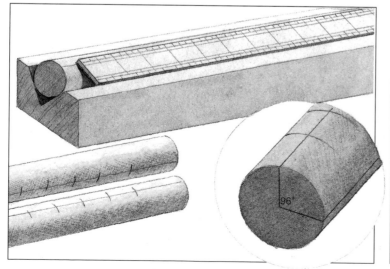

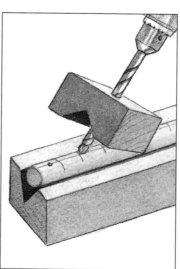

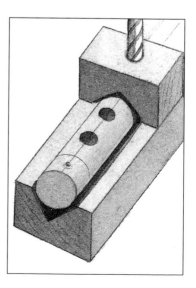

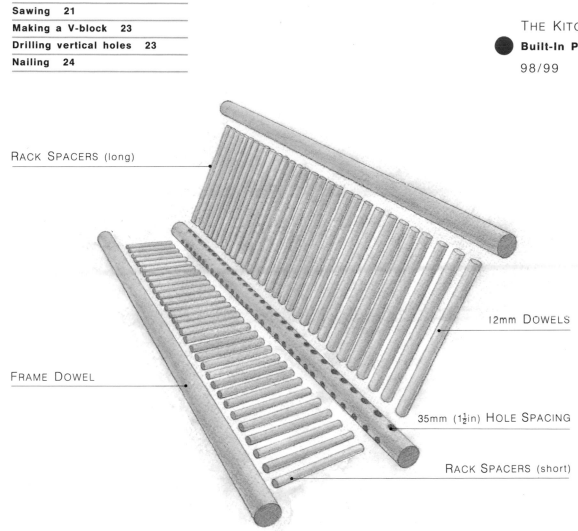

RACK SPACERS (long)

FRAME DOWEL

12mm DOWELS

35mm (1½in) HOLE SPACING

RACK SPACERS (short)

DRIP TRAY

This is removable for easy drying or cleaning. Cut the tray-support battens to the same length as the shelf-support battens, and pin and glue them to the bottom of the partitions.

Make a tray base from 15mm (⅝in) melamine-faced chipboard. Cut two pieces of lipping to the depth of the tray. Saw 10mm (⅜in) from each to leave them 25mm (1in) high. Glue and pin the pieces of lipping to the tray base ends so that they are flush with the underside (fig 5). Cut the front and back lippings to cover the length of the tray plus the end lippings. Pin and glue them in place, leaving a 10mm (⅜in) underhang at front and back. Make small cut-outs at the back to allow tray to slide over support battens.

Waterproof the interior edges of the tray with a silicone bath sealant. When using a mastic applicator gun, it is easier to push the nozzle away from you to provide an even flow of sealant rather than pulling the nozzle towards you.

❹ Positioning the Plate Rack Between Partitions
The assembled plate rack is fitted between two wall-mounted shelf partition units and slips neatly into the three holes that are drilled into each partition side panel for a safe and secure fixing.

❺ Making the Drip Tray
The melamine-faced chipboard tray, edged with hardboard lipping, rests on two support battens. End lipping strips are fixed first (top), then front and back lippings.

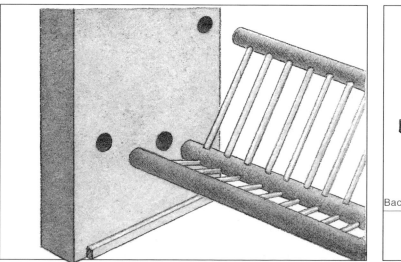

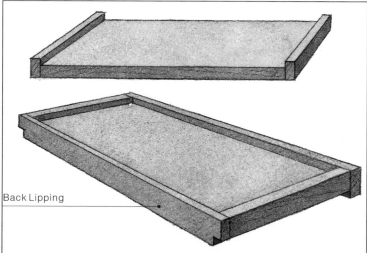

Back Lipping

WALL-MOUNTED SLATTED SHELVES

STEEL MEASURING TAPE

STEEL RULE

TRIMMING KNIFE

TRY SQUARE

TENON SAW

MITRE BOX

SCREWDRIVER

DRILL (hand or electric)

COUNTERSINK DRILL BIT

MASONRY DRILL BIT

FLAT DRILL BIT for hanging bar

SPACING BATTEN (made from an offcut)

Cut a 45° mitre at each end of the 38mm (1½in) diagonal. Glue and screw together the two 75 × 25mm (3 × 1in) pieces. Use two 25mm (1in) No 8 screws.

Lay the L-shaped piece on the workbench and place the diagonal in position. Mark off the diagonal's internal shoulder on to the L-shape at both ends (fig 1). Continue the lines around edges and on to backs.

Mark the position for each screw hole, 19mm (¾in) from the pencil line and centrally on the wood. Drill and countersink pilot holes. Lay the L-shaped section on the bench and place a 12mm (½in) thick offcut of wood in position (fig 2). This is so the diagonal lies centrally in the 75 × 25mm (3 × 1in) L bracket. The diagonal can now be repositioned, and glued and screwed in place.

Make up extra brackets as required. Allow one bracket for each 1200mm (48in) of shelf. If the shelves are likely to be heavily laden, fix brackets every 900mm (36in).

FIXING BRACKETS TO A WALL

The leg of the bracket that is over-lapped by the other piece at the top is the one that is fixed to the wall (fig 3). Drill countersunk pilot holes and fix the brackets to the wall by means of a temporary batten, to ensure that they are level.

MATERIALS

Part	Quantity	Material	Length
L-SHAPE BRACKETS	2	75 × 25mm (3 × 1in) softwood	350mm (14in)
DIAGONAL BRACKET	1	50 × 38mm (2 × 1½in) softwood	410mm (16½in)
SLATS	5	50 × 19mm (2 × ¾in) softwood	As required

Optional: hanging bar of 19mm (¾in) wood dowel or metal rod

HANGING BAR

Drill holes for the bar in the brackets before fixing them to the wall. Decide the distance between the brackets and cut the bar to this length plus 38mm (1½in).

Mark on the diagonals the positions for the bar holes according to the size of the objects you intend to hang from it. Drill the holes to the same diameter as the bar and 19mm (¾in) deep. Fix the first bracket to the wall, slot in the hanging bar, then fit the second bracket on the other end and fix it to the wall.

FIXING SLATS

Cut the slats to the required length, allowing an overlap of 75mm (3in) at each end. Fix the front slat flush with the front of the brackets. Use a single 12mm (½in) No 6 screw in each bracket. Space the remaining slats at equal centres, with the edge of the back slat butted up against the wall for a neat finish.

1 **Marking-Up Brackets for Positioning the Diagonals**
Screw the flat pieces of wood together at right-angles. Temporarily fit the diagonal strut. Mark off the internal shoulders and continue the lines on to the back faces of the brackets.

2 **Fixing the Diagonal Strut**
Use a suitable offcut of wood to give support to the diagonal strut when fixing it in place.

3 **Finished Shelf Bracket**
The top rail sits on top of the wall rail and the brackets are braced by the diagonal strut.

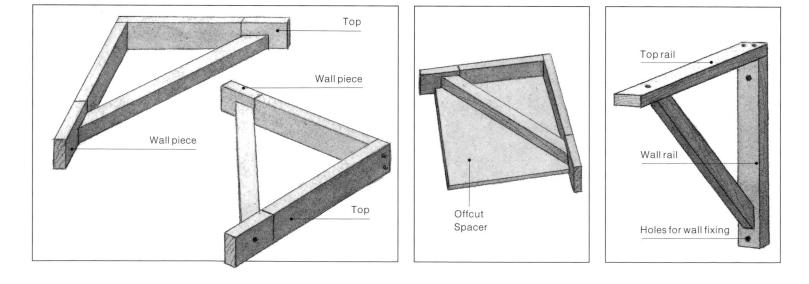

Top

Wall piece

Wall piece

Top

Offcut Spacer

Top rail

Wall rail

Holes for wall fixing

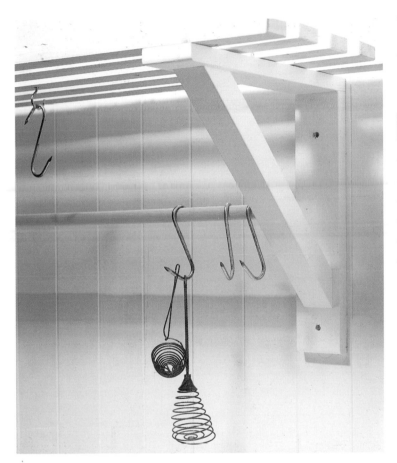

REMOVABLE TOWEL RAIL

Made from 38–50mm (1½–2in) diameter dowel, available from timber and builders' merchants.

TOOLS

STEEL MEASURING TAPE
TRY SQUARE
TENON SAW
DRILL (hand or power)
DRILL BITS
HACKSAW
SCREWDRIVER
METAL FILE/EMERY CLOTH
PARING CHISEL OR ROUTER

Measure the distance between the base partitions. Cut the dowel to this length. Mark 25mm (1in) in from each end and cut off a disc from each end. Mark the centre of each disc and the dowel at either end.

Drill a pilot hole in one end of the dowel, then insert a 38mm (1½in) No 8 wood screw, leaving just the shank protruding by 12mm (½in). Repeat at other end. Use a hacksaw to cut off the screw heads. File off any burr from the shank ends so about 8–10mm ($\frac{5}{16}$–$\frac{3}{8}$in) of shank will be protruding. For the discs, drill a series of 4mm (⅛in) diameter holes from the centre of each disc to the edge to form a slot. The holes should be drilled to the same depth as the protruding screw shanks. To ensure this, stick tape to the drill bit at the correct distance from the tip. Use a chisel to clean out the slot. A much easier method of forming a slot is to use a router with a 4mm (⅛in) diameter cutter if you have one.

Drill 4mm (⅛in) diameter screw holes through each disc on either side of the centre line. Hold the dowel horizontally in place and mark off the positions of the discs. Then hold each disc in position to mark off screw hole positions. They should be about 75mm (3in) below the work surface and set back about 50mm (2in) from the front. Screw to partition and slot rail in place.

4 Fixing Brackets to the Wall and Adding the Slats
Drill holes for hanging bar and slot it in place before fixing the second bracket to the wall. Nail a batten to the wall temporarily to keep the brackets level. Screw down slats.

5 Cutting and Shaping Ends
Use a screw shank to form the rail pivot. For the slot, drill a series of holes in an offcut.

6 Fixing the Rail in Place
Use a narrow chisel to form a slot in the disc for the rail pivot. Screw the disc to the partition sides.

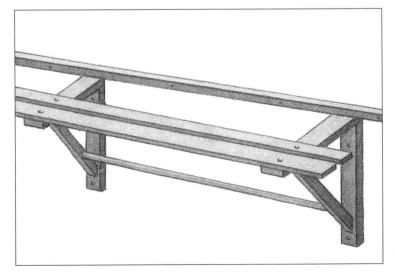

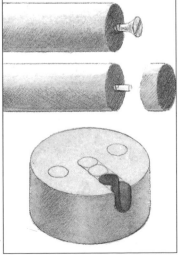

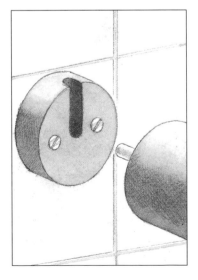

Knife Rack

A knife rack is a useful addition to the kitchen system, and this is a quick and easy project to build.

Working from the back, glue and nail both verticals on to the first slat. Allow each end of the slat to protrude 75mm (3in) beyond the verticals (fig 1).

Fix the remaining slats at 38mm (1½in) centres. Use a spacing batten (*see* **Techniques, page 20**) to ensure accurate spacing between the slats. Leave a space for the knife slot. Glue the 25 × 6mm (1 × ¼in) spacers to the spare slat. There should be a spacer at each end and one in the middle of the slat (fig 2).

Glue the facing piece of the knife slot over the spacers. Secure with G-cramps, allow the glue to set and then sand it down.

Fix the knife-slot section to the verticals in the centre of the space left, again working from the back.

Drill countersunk holes through the front of the rails into the wall at the desired spot. As the load is light, it is not necessary to fix the rack to the studs in a lath-and-plaster wall or a hollow wall.

Materials

Part	Quantity	Material	Length
SLATS	7	25 × 19mm (1 × ¾in) softwood	850mm (34in)
BACK OF KNIFE SLOT	1	25 × 25mm (1 × 1in) softwood	850mm (34in)
FRONT OF KNIFE SLOT	1	25 × 6mm (1 × ¼in) softwood	850mm (34in)
SPACERS	3	25 × 6mm (1 × ¼in) softwood	50mm (2in)
VERTICALS	2	25 × 19mm (1 × ¾in) softwood	450mm (18in)

1 **Nailing the Verticals to the Horizontal Slats**

Work from the back and nail the vertical rails to the horizontal slats leaving a space for the knife slot to be fitted. Use a spacing batten to ensure that slats are evenly spaced.

2 **Forming the Knife Slot from Timber Battens**

The knife slot batten is thicker than the others to accommodate knife handles. The slot is formed from a thin slat laid over three offcuts which act as spacers for the knives.

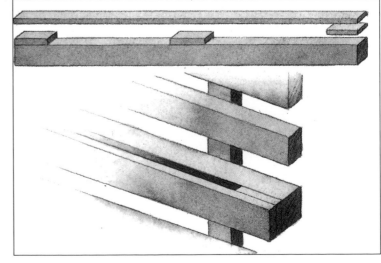

AIRING RACK

TOOLS

STEEL MEASURING TAPE

STEEL RULE

TRY SQUARE

SANDING BLOCK coarse and fine sand paper

JIGSAW OR PANEL SAW

ELECTRIC DRILL

FLAT BIT

TRIMMING KNIFE

Cut the square piece of wood in half diagonally. Round off all the corners with coarse, then fine sandpaper. Paint the wood if required.

Mark the centres for the holes in one end piece. Mark the holes at 100mm (4in) centres and 45mm (1¾in) in from the edge. Drill the six (dowel) holes to 25mm (1in) diameter and the small (rope) holes to 6mm (¼in) diameter. Cramp both end pieces together, then use the first piece as a template to mark the hole positions on the second piece. Drill the holes in the second piece. Locate the dowels in the two end pieces, leaving about 75mm (3in) protruding either end.

Find the positions of the ceiling joists. If they run at right-angles to the rack, then, after fixing the pulleys, adjust the position of each end piece to align with the pulley above it. If the ceiling joists run parallel with the rack, choose the most convenient one to fix the pulleys to. Align the end pieces with pulleys. Fix double pulleys at the side from which you want to operate the rack.

Screw the cleat to a convenient place on the wall. Tie the rope to the rope hole in the end piece. Feed the rope through the single pulley, across to the double pulley, down to the cleat, up through the double pulley again, and then down to the other triangle. Tie this end in place to form a loop. Take up the slack rope and wind it around the cleat.

Check that the rack will move easily then apply wood glue into dowel holes to fix them.

MATERIALS

Part	Quantity	Material	Length
ENDS	1	25mm (1in) plywood (or MDF)	400mm sq (16in sq)
RAILS	6	25mm (1in) diameter hardwood dowel	2m (6ft 6in) long

ONE SINGLE PULLEY, ONE DOUBLE PULLEY (screw-in or screw-on type)

A HANK OF SASH CORD AND ONE CLEAT

❸ Marking-Up Airing Rack End Pieces for Rails
Two triangular end pieces are cut from a 400mm (16in) square of 25mm (1in) plywood. Mark holes at 100mm (4in) intervals on a line 45mm (1¾in) in from the side edges.

❹ Hanging the Airing Rack
A double and a single pulley should be securely fixed into ceiling joists. Fix a cleat firmly to a nearby wall and arrange cords as shown so that the airing rack can be raised and lowered easily.

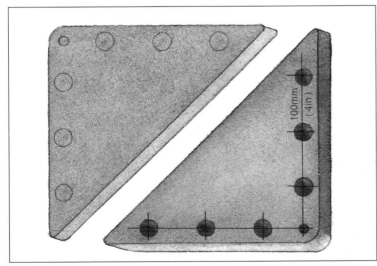

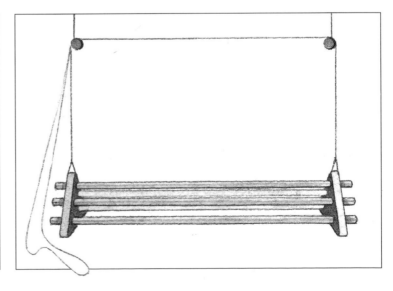

SERVING AND DISPLAY UNIT WITH MIRRORS

I built shelving similar to this a few years ago in my house in Provence; as it has been so successful there it seemed an ideal project for this book. It works on the principle that everybody likes to display their favourite china, bowls, platters and pans, as these objects create an appetizing backdrop for any kitchen or dining room. The shelving is based on an idea that I first saw in a restaurant in Positano, Italy. The most important aspect of the design is the panels of mirror that are slightly angled to reflect the components of the bowls and platters which sit on the shelf. In Positano, wonderful bowls of antipasto were displayed and the effect was mouth-watering and demonstrated that, with a little ingenuity, less can be more. The mirror provides an entrancing double vision of a rich arrangement of food and wine, to be enjoyed while sitting at the dining table or working in the kitchen.

The design also incorporates a waist-high wide shelf which can be used as a serving surface in a dining area. The finish you choose for the shelving unit can be varied to suit your particular decorative scheme. The wide shelf shown here is marble, which, while very effective as a display background for bowls of fruit, vegetables and seafood, may be substituted for a more economical material if your finances are limited. But don't dispense with the mirrors!

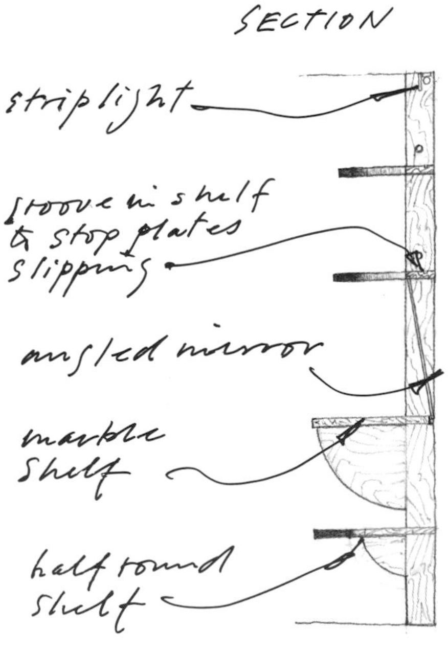

SECTION

striplight

groove in shelf to stop plates slipping

angled mirror

marble shelf

half round shelf

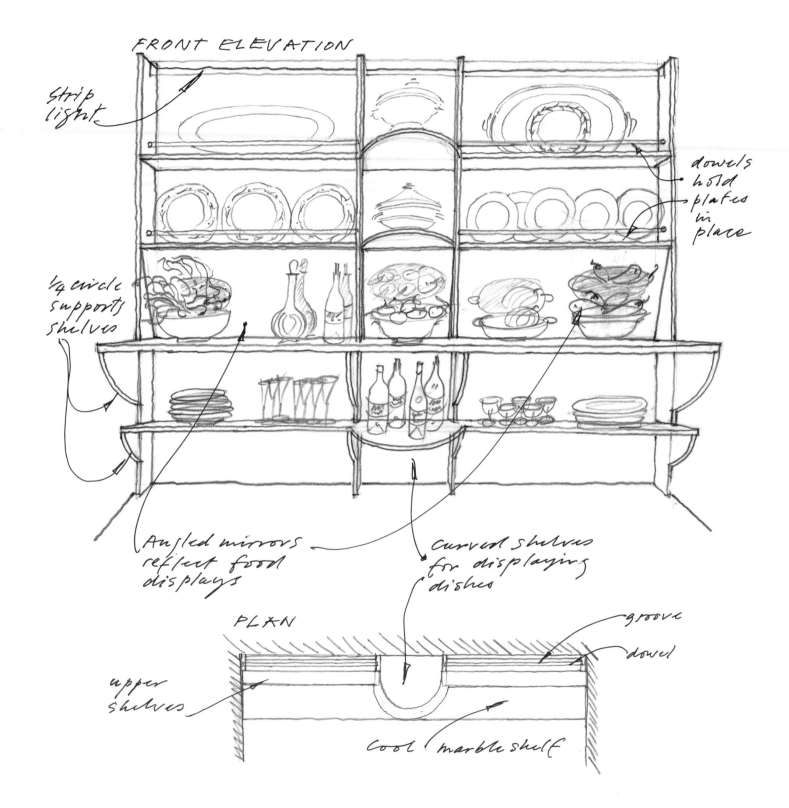

FRONT ELEVATION

Strip light

dowels hold plates in place

¼ circle supports shelves

Angled mirrors reflect food displays

curved shelves for displaying dishes

PLAN

groove

dowel

upper shelves

cool marble shelf

SERVING AND DISPLAY UNIT WITH MIRRORS

This dining room shelf unit has been designed to be both decorative and practical. The wide serving shelf provides plenty of space from which food can be served and displayed, while the angled mirrors behind reflect the food and flowers, to create a pleasing interplay of colour and shape. Above, there are grooved shelves on which to display plates, and there is a shelf below the serving shelf for jugs, bowls, cutlery and so on. A concealed light behind the pelmet provides subtle mood lighting at meal times. To maximize impact and storage space, the unit reaches to the ceiling.

The unit can butt up against a wall at one end or fill an alcove, be free standing or run from wall to wall. The serving shelf can be marble (as here), slate, solid wood, or painted MDF or blockboard. If marble is used, any join *must* be made to lie over an upright so that it is fully supported.

For the main structure, the vertical partitions are 25mm (1in) MDF; the straight shelves are 19mm ($\frac{3}{4}$in) blockboard (for stiffness); and the curved shelves are 19mm ($\frac{3}{4}$in) MDF, which is easier to cut into curves than the thicker fibreboard.

The unit is built in two sections. The lower section up to the serving shelf is constructed and fixed in place, and then the top section, above the shelf, is added. The whole unit is fixed to the wall with angle brackets located in the shelf rebates, and the shelves are then slotted in to conceal the brackets.

The overall dimensions of the unit are based on the depth of the serving shelf. This one is 460mm (18in) deep, which is ideal. If you prefer a different size, you will have to adjust all the dimensions accordingly. Remember that the depth of the serving shelf should always be equal to the depth of the curved shelves for neatness.

Precise vertical dimensions up to the top of the mirror section are given, together with all the shelf depths, so that the angle of the mirror will be exact.

To allow the overall height and width to be varied, the top section above the mirror can be whatever height is required to reach your ceiling. The outer shelf sections can be whatever width is required, but for a balanced appearance make sure that they are of equal measurements either side of the central curved section.

If the unit does not have to fit into a specific width, then just make each outer section twice the width of the central section. This gives the unit attractive proportions.

MATERIALS

Part	Quantity	Material	Length
UPPER VERTICAL PARTITIONS	4	25mm (1in) MDF	As required × 150mm (6in)
UPPER STRAIGHT SHELVES	4	19mm ($\frac{3}{4}$in) blockboard	As required × 150mm (6in)
HALF-ROUND SHELVES	2	19mm ($\frac{3}{4}$in) MDF	487 × 393.5mm (19$\frac{1}{4}$ × 15$\frac{1}{2}$in)
PELMETS	3	19mm ($\frac{3}{4}$in) MDF	As required
PLATE-RETAINING RAILS	3	25mm (1in) diameter dowel	As required
SERVING SHELF	1	Optional thickness – minimum 25mm (1in) MDF	As required
SHELF SUPPORT BATTENS	3	50 × 25mm (2 × 1in) softwood	As required
LOWER VERTICAL PARTITIONS	4	25mm (1in) MDF	770 × 150mm (30 × 6in)
LOWER STRAIGHT SHELVES	2	19mm ($\frac{3}{4}$in) blockboard	As required × 280mm (11in)
CENTRE CURVED SHELF	1	19mm ($\frac{3}{4}$in) MDF	500 × 460mm (19$\frac{1}{2}$ × 18in)
LARGE QUADRANTS	4	25mm (1in) MDF	from 1250 × 300mm (49 × 12in)
SMALL QUADRANTS	4	25mm (1in) MDF	from 130 × 570mm (5 × 22$\frac{1}{2}$in)

ALSO: 3 mirrors, strip lights, 3mm ($\frac{1}{8}$in) lipping, 40 angle brackets, 65mm × 65mm × 16mm (2$\frac{1}{2}$in × 2$\frac{1}{2}$in × $\frac{5}{8}$in)

TOOLS

PANEL SAW

JIGSAW (or padsaw)

DOWELLING JIG

CRAMPS

STEEL MEASURING TAPE

TRY SQUARE

TRIMMING KNIFE

ROUTER

HAMMER

SPIRIT LEVEL

POWER DRILL

SCREWDRIVER

HACKSAW

PLANE

SANDING BLOCK

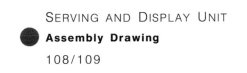
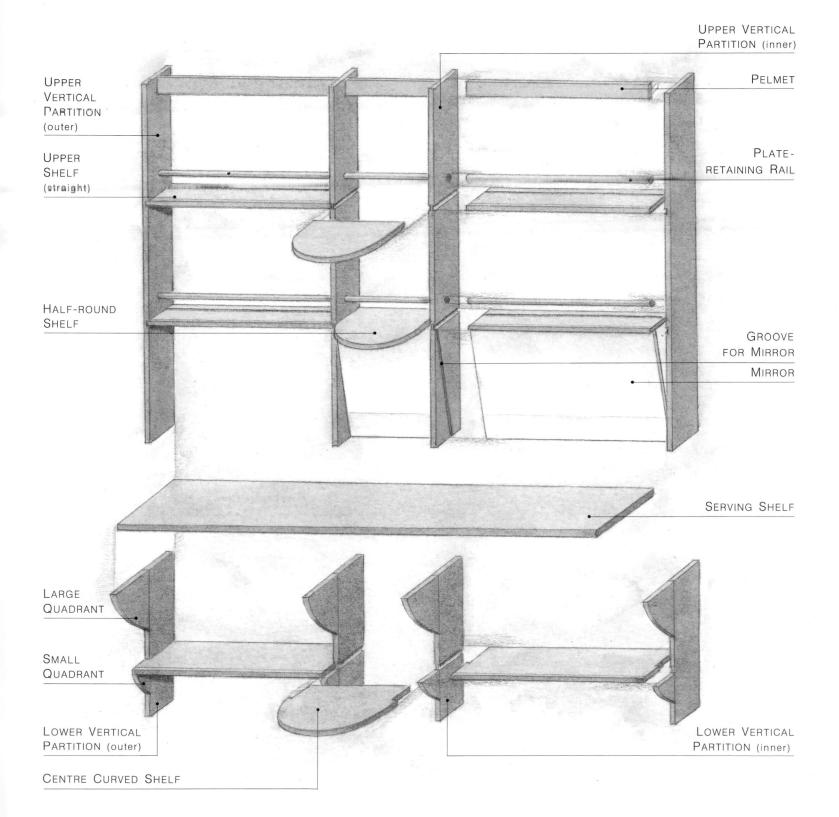

UPPER VERTICAL
PARTITION (inner)

PELMET

PLATE-
RETAINING RAIL

UPPER
VERTICAL
PARTITION
(outer)

UPPER
SHELF
(straight)

HALF-ROUND
SHELF

GROOVE
FOR MIRROR

MIRROR

SERVING SHELF

LARGE
QUADRANT

SMALL
QUADRANT

LOWER VERTICAL
PARTITION (outer)

LOWER VERTICAL
PARTITION (inner)

CENTRE CURVED SHELF

SERVING AND DISPLAY UNIT WITH MIRRORS

LOWER SHELF SECTION

Using 25mm (1in) MDF, cut four verticals 770mm (30in) – the height of the underside of the serving shelf – by 150mm (6in). For the serving shelf supports, cut out four quadrants from a strip of MDF 300mm (12in) wide and at least 1250mm (49in) long, so that the radius of each can be 300mm (12in). Draw the shape of one quadrant before cutting it out with a jigsaw or padsaw and sanding this to a smooth curve. Use this quadrant as a pattern for marking out the remaining three quadrants. For the lower shelf supports, cut out four smaller quadrants from a strip 130mm (5in) wide by 570mm (22½in) long, so that the radius of each can be 130mm (5in). Again, cut out one quadrant and use this as a pattern for the remainder.

FIXING QUADRANTS

Using 10mm (⅜in) dowels, 50mm (2in) long, glue and fix the large quadrants to the front edges of the uprights. Use a dowelling jig or dowel points to align the holes, ensuring that the top edges of the quadrants and uprights are flush.

Cramp each assembly and allow sufficient time for the glue to set. This will be easier if you leave square notches on the quadrants to cramp against, sawing them off later to complete the curve.

Measure 300mm (12in) up from the bottom edge of each vertical for the position of the top of the smaller quadrants. Fix all four in place as for the large quadrants.

ROUTING FOR SHELVES

The top edge of each lower quadrant aligns with and supports the bottom of each lower shelf. Use a try square and a pencil or trimming knife to mark the top of the quadrant on to all vertical pieces where a shelf will be supported. Using a router with a 19mm (¾in) bit, cut out a housing to the top of the line at a depth of 6mm (¼in). Carry out this procedure on the inner faces of the end vertical pieces and then repeat the process on both faces of the inner vertical pieces.

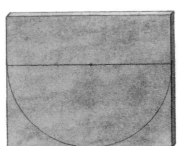

Upper Half-Round Shelf

Cut from a rectangle of 19mm (¾in) MDF measuring 487 × 393.5mm (19 × 15½in). Measure 150mm (5in) in from the back edge and draw a line across. At centre point of this line draw a semi-circle as indicated.

Centre Curved Shelf

Cut from a rectangle of 19mm (¾in) MDF measuring 460 × 500mm (18 × 19½in). Mark 280mm (11in) in from the back edge. From this line draw a curve to meet front edge in the centre. Saw rebates as shown.

Lower Straight Shelf

The span of the shelves is flexible, but they must be of equal length on each side. Shelf width is 280mm (11in). Both rebates are 150mm (6in) long. The outer rebate is 19mm (¾in) wide, the inner 6.5mm (¼in).

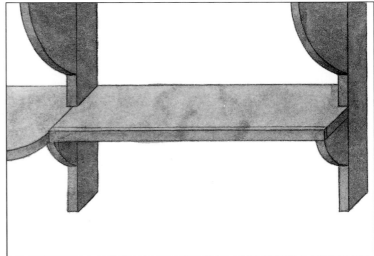

① Assembly of Lower Vertical Partition Panel
Cut lower vertical from 25mm (1in) thick MDF. Serving shelf support is quadrant of MDF with radius of 300mm (12in). Small quadrant has 130mm (5in) radius. Fix quadrants using dowels.

② Fitting a Lower Straight Shelf Between Partitions
Make sure that the shelves at each side are of equal length. The depth of each one should be 280mm (11¼in) including edge lipping. Shelf ends are rebated to cover the verticals.

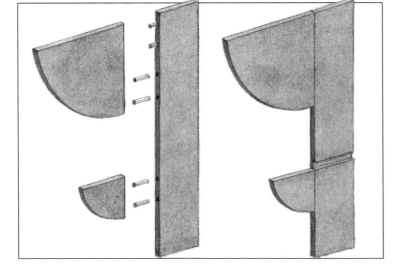

CENTRE CURVED LOWER SHELF

For the centre curved lower shelf, cut out a rectangle from 19mm ($\frac{3}{4}$in) MDF, 460 × 500mm (18 × 19$\frac{1}{2}$in). The 500mm (19$\frac{1}{2}$in) will be the width. Mark 280mm (11in) in from, and parallel to, the back edge – this will be the depth of the straight shelf. From this line, draw and cut a curve to meet the front edge in the centre. Mark 150mm (6in) in from and parallel to the back edge. Saw out rebates from both sides, 6.5mm ($\frac{1}{4}$in) wide and 150mm (6in) long; these locate in the housings cut in the vertical partitions.

LOWER STRAIGHT SHELVES

Calculate how long you want your 19mm ($\frac{3}{4}$in) blockboard shelves to be each side of the curved shelf, making sure that they are of equal length. The depth of each one should be 280mm (11in) including a 3mm ($\frac{1}{8}$in) lipping, glued and pinned to the front edge. Cut out the two shelves, then cut rebates from each end – 150mm (6in) long, and 6.5mm ($\frac{1}{4}$in) wide on the inner edge; 19mm ($\frac{3}{4}$in) wide on the outer edge. This will ensure that they meet at the centre line of the inner verticals with the curved centre shelf. The outer edges of the straight shelves should cross the outer verticals and finish flush with the outside of the unit.

FIXING IN PLACE

Position one of the uprights against the wall as a guide to marking on the wall the position of the serving shelf. Mark an accurate line for the underside of the shelf along the back wall and any side wall. Using a spirit level, ensure that the line is horizontal throughout its length.

Fix softwood battens measuring 50 × 25mm (2 × 1in) along the back wall on the underside of the line to give extra support to the serving shelf. Three battens are needed, cut to fit the distance between the verti-

cal sections. If an end vertical is being fixed directly into a return wall, screw directly through the upright and quadrant into the wall. Drill and generously countersink the holes – one near the top edge, one near the bottom of the vertical, and two in each quadrant. Put the upright in place and mark off the positions of the screws on the wall. Remove the vertical and drill holes for 50mm (2in) No 8 screws in the wall. Insert wallplugs, replace the vertical and screw into the wall.

If the end vertical is away from a return wall then it must be fixed to the back wall with 65mm × 65mm × 16mm (2$\frac{1}{2}$in × 2$\frac{1}{2}$in × $\frac{5}{8}$in) angle brackets – one at the top and one set into the shelf rebate.

The shelf rebate bracket will be concealed by the shelf when this is in position. The shelf will have to be trimmed to allow for this bracket. To conceal the top bracket, fix it vertically to the wall so that the top 'arm', which protrudes from the wall at a right-angle, will rest in a slot cut in the top edge of the vertical partition. The back arm of the bracket should be set into a slot chased into the wall so that it allows the rear edge of the vertical to be held firmly.

The bottom of the vertical can be fixed by using a 'dowel' of 3mm ($\frac{1}{8}$in) diameter steel rod or screw bolt cut to a length of 25mm (1in) with a hacksaw. Half of the 'dowel' should be sunk into the floor and the remainder into the underside of the vertical partition. The difficult part is locating the hole in the vertical partition directly over the 'dowel' protruding from the floor. To do this, first fix the 'dowel' in the vertical partition, then offer up the vertical in its exact position against, and at 90° to, the wall. Tap the top edge sharply with a hammer so that an impression of the 'dowel' will be left in the floor. This indicates the drilling position. The 'dowel' can be an easy fit since its function is simply to hold the base of the partition in place. Protect

the top edge of the vertical partition with a block of scrap wood before striking it with a hammer.

Screw the protruding arm of the bracket to the top edge and fix the second bracket into the shelf rebate and the wall.

Fit the supporting batten in place against the underside of the line, fixing it to the wall with 50mm (2in) No 8 screws at 300mm (12in) centres. Offer up the next vertical and fix it to the wall using the same method as the first. Repeat this process for the remaining two verticals, gluing in the shelves as you work along the wall. The floor 'dowel' can be left out of the two middle vertical partitions.

SERVING SHELF

The serving shelf sits on the battens and verticals. If you are using marble or slate, no fixing will be necessary as its weight will be enough. For a timber shelf, use dowels to fix it to the top edges of the uprights and quadrants. If the shelf is to be painted, simply screw down into the uprights.

UPPER SHELF SECTION

Measure the distance from the top of the serving shelf to the ceiling. Measure it in three places – both ends and the middle. Take the smallest dimension, if they differ, and cut four verticals to this length from 25mm (1in) MDF. Each vertical must be 150mm (6in) wide. Measure up 655mm (25in) from the bottom

Side Section of Display Unit
This section shows how the shelves are spaced, and the positioning of the quadrant supports of the lower shelves. Note that the mirror slopes forward to display items placed on the serving shelf.

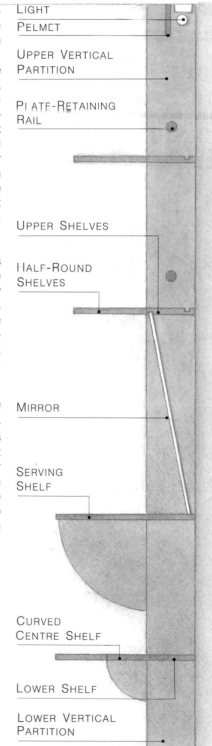

LIGHT

PELMET

UPPER VERTICAL PARTITION

PLATE-RETAINING RAIL

UPPER SHELVES

HALF-ROUND SHELVES

MIRROR

SERVING SHELF

CURVED CENTRE SHELF

LOWER SHELF

LOWER VERTICAL PARTITION

SERVING AND DISPLAY UNIT WITH MIRRORS

DOUBLE THE IMPACT WITH ANGLED MIRRORS

The angled mirrors behind the serving shelf reflect its contents and create a lush and dramatic display of colour and shape. The curved shelves and quadrants add further interest to the composition.

edge. This gives a good size and enables the mirror to rest at a good angle. Divide the remainder of each vertical by the number of shelves required and space them equally.

ROUTING FOR SHELVES

Using a 19mm ($\frac{3}{4}$in) cutter as before, rout out housings to a depth of 6mm ($\frac{1}{4}$in) for the shelves on all the inner faces. (Again, do not cut on the outside of the end sections.)

MIRROR SECTION

Use the router with a 6mm ($\frac{1}{4}$in) cutter to make the grooves for the mirror. Cut 2mm ($\frac{1}{12}$in) in from the front and rear edges, to make a

6mm ($\frac{1}{4}$in) deep diagonal groove, as shown (far right). Do this on the inner faces of all four verticals.

PLATE-RETAINING RAILS

Mark the centres of the holes to hold the rails, on the inner faces of the verticals, 100mm (4in) up from the shelf rebates and 75mm (3in) in from the front edges. Bore 25mm (1in) diameter holes, 12mm ($\frac{1}{2}$in) deep, using a router or a drill fitted with a flat bit.

UPPER STRAIGHT SHELVES

These are all lipped at the front in the same way as the lower shelves, to a total depth of 150mm (6in), includ-

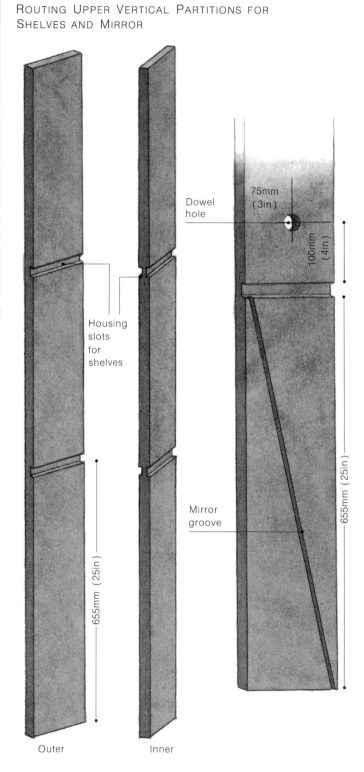

ROUTING UPPER VERTICAL PARTITIONS FOR SHELVES AND MIRROR

Dowel hole

75mm (3in)

100mm (4in)

Housing slots for shelves

655mm (25in)

655mm (25in)

Mirror groove

655mm (25in)

Outer   Inner

ing lipping. Cut the required number to length, then glue and pin lipping to the front edges.

HALF-ROUND SHELVES

Using 19mm ($\frac{3}{4}$in) MDF, cut out a rectangle for each shelf required, 487 × 393.5mm (19$\frac{1}{4}$ × 15$\frac{1}{2}$in).

Draw a line across the sheet 150mm (6in) in from the back edge. The centre point of this line will be the centre point for the circle. Draw and cut out the half circle at the front on each shelf (see page 110).

CUTTING GROOVES

With a router, cut a groove for each mirror in the underside of two of the straight shelves; the groove should be 2mm ($\frac{1}{12}$in) back from the front edge. It should be 6mm ($\frac{1}{4}$in) deep and the same thickness as the mirror plus a little extra to allow the mirror to slot in. Cut a corresponding groove in the underside of one of the half-round shelves. Measure off from the grooves the exact dimensions for each mirror, making sure you allow for the amount slotted in the top and sides.

The bottom edges of the mirror should be polished to avoid damage to the serving shelf.

Again with a router, cut plate grooves in the upper faces of all upper straight shelves, 6mm ($\frac{1}{4}$in) deep and wide, and forward from back edge to accommodate plates.

PLATE-RETAINING RAILS

Calculate the lengths for the plate-retaining rails to fit into the straight shelf sections, adding 10mm ($\frac{3}{8}$in) at each end so they slot into the uprights. Cut the required number from 25mm (1in) diameter dowel.

ASSEMBLY

Put one of the uprights in position (one against a wall first if you have one) resting on the serving shelf, directly above the lower vertical. This upright is fixed either to a side wall with screws or fixed to the back wall with angle brackets set into the shelf rebates as for the lower section. Fix an additional bracket in the mirror section, as low as possible behind the groove. This will then be hidden when the mirror is in place.

① Mirror and Partition Fixing
Top edge of mirror is housed in a groove in the underside of the shelf. Angle brackets fix vertical panels.

② Fixing of Pelmets
Pelmets are cut from 19mm ($\frac{3}{4}$in) MDF. They shield strip lights and are fixed with angle brackets.

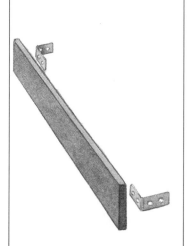

USING THE UPPER DISPLAY SHELVES TO BEST ADVANTAGE
The upper shelves reach to the ceiling for maximum visual impact and to give plenty of storage space. The half-round shelves bring objects on view forward in a dramatic way.

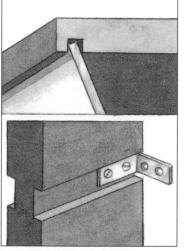

For the next part of the assembly you will need an extra pair of hands. Slot the mirror and rails into place, gluing as you go. You will need to sand the ends of the dowels to fit.

Offer up the next upright in position. Secure it with angle brackets fitted in the shelf rebates and at the very top, on both sides. You can fix an extra bracket on one side, before the mirror is installed.

Plane or sand the shelves, slot over the brackets, then glue the edges and slot into place.

Offer up the central mirror, rails and the next upright, and secure as before. Fit the shelves, then repeat the procedure for the last section.

PELMET

Measure the internal dimensions between the verticals for the three pelmets. Cut the three pieces to length from 19mm ($\frac{3}{4}$in) MDF. These must be deep enough to shield the strip lights. Fix angle brackets to each end of each pelmet section, then screw them into the uprights.

Before securing the pelmet in place, you can fit extra brackets from the back of the wall to the top of the verticals to give extra rigidity, but ensure that the pelmet will conceal these. Fit the tungsten strip lights. Finally, fill over all of the screw heads prior to decoration.

DIVIDED SHELVES

CONSTRUCTION

These kitchen shelves are ideal for storing crockery and utensils neatly and safely. The basic shelves and dividers can be made from either 19mm ($\frac{3}{4}$in) melamine-faced plywood or from 15mm ($\frac{5}{8}$in) melamine-faced particleboard. The lower shelf has a 25mm (1in) deep lip on the front which is glued and pinned flush with the underside.

The upper and lower shelves run to the full width of the unit. Main vertical dividers are fitted between them at 1140mm (45in) intervals and at the ends. The centre shelves are fitted between the main dividers. If you are storing plates, glassware and pans, you can fit 10mm ($\frac{3}{8}$in) additional dividing leaves between the main dividers.

Dowel joints are used to join all the components in this unit. First, the intermediate shelf units are assembled on the main upright dividers using 8×40mm ($\frac{5}{16} \times 1\frac{1}{2}$in) beech dowels, to pass right through the inner dividers. Then the top and bottom shelves are fitted over dowels of the same size in the top and bottom edges of the main dividers.

Smaller dowels (6×30mm [$\frac{1}{4} \times 1\frac{1}{4}$in]) are used to fit the plywood dividers to the underside of the top shelf. The unit is covered at the back with a panel of 4mm ($\frac{1}{8}$in) plywood or painted hardboard. The panel is pinned to the edges of the main dividers and shelves, and also to the thin plywood dividers.

To prevent items rolling off the intermediate shelf, you can fit either a deep lip (second bay from left in the main photograph), or a narrow hardwood beading of approximately 6×6mm ($\frac{1}{4} \times \frac{1}{4}$in) to the shelf surface about 50mm (2in) back from the front edge (as in the bay with the dinner-plate rack).

Mount the unit by screwing into the walls at each end, through the end dividers and by fixing the main dividers in the rear wall with the brackets used to hang kitchen cupboards. Whichever method is chosen, it is essential to use a strong, secure fixing because these shelves are *very* heavy when loaded.

1 The Critical Dimensions
In this exploded view, only two bays are shown, but the unit can be extended to room width. Between the main dividers, plywood dividing leaves can be fitted to the underside of the top and intermediate shelves.

2 Joints to Use
Dowel joints are recommended, although housing joints can be used if greater strength is required.

3 Plywood Dividers
These are fitted to shelf undersides using dowels or housing slots, then glued and pinned to the back panel.

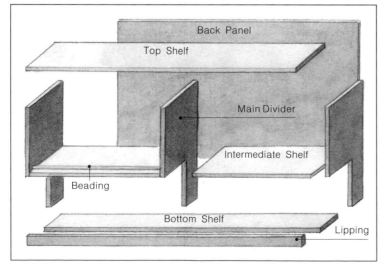

Back Panel
Top Shelf
Main Divider
Intermediate Shelf
Beading
Bottom Shelf
Lipping

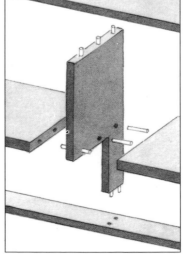

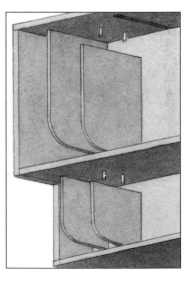

HANGING BARS

CONSTRUCTION

Hanging bars for storage make a feature of the rafters in this attic room. The rafters hold the bars a short distance from the sloping ceiling, allowing the space behind to be used for storage. A decorative dado rail above the cupboard front stops anything from slipping down.

If your attic room has a flat, sloping ceiling, then fit false rafters to the ceiling by nailing through the plaster into the real rafters beneath. Alternatively, mount the hanging bars on timber blocks, or in wardrobe brackets. The hanging bars can be steel tubing, such as black-painted electrical conduit, or the hollow rod sold for hanging rails in wardrobes. This is available with a chrome, nickel or brassed finish, or with a white plastic coating. Alternatively, you can use copper tubing. In all cases, a 19mm ($\frac{3}{4}$in) diameter is recommended.

To support the bars, use saddle-type pipe clips screwed directly into the undersides of the rafters. Mount the lowest bars first, about 100mm (4in) above the dado rail. With a long, straight batten, pencil and spirit level, mark the clip positions on the rafters. Mount the clips at each end first. Tie a string line between these to double check that they are level, then start fixing the intermediate clips, loosely at this stage working towards the middle and using the string line as a guide. Fit the tubing into the clips, then fit the remaining screws. Use particleboard screws for fixing the clips, as these grip strongly. Fit the second and third rails in the same way, spacing each 100mm (4in) away from the rail below. If you have a flat, sloping ceiling and you intend to mount the hanging bars in wardrobe-rail support brackets, first snap a chalked string line on the surface of the ceiling to leave a horizontal line as a guide for positioning the brackets. Next, locate the rafter positions using a small metal detector (ceiling fixing nails will be driven into the rafters). Fix the support brackets against the marked line using particleboard screws.

❶ Fixing the Bars
Support the bars, 100mm (4in) apart, with pipe clips. Align with a spirit level. Old-fashioned saddle pipe clips (shown) look most effective, but modern equivalents are suitable. Fit chamfered wood plugs in the pipe ends.

❷ Using Hidden Rafters
Where rafters are hidden, mount the bars in wardrobe-rail support brackets fixed to the rafters. Alternatively, fix false rafters to the ceiling, or fix hanging bars to mounting blocks, which are fixed to the rafters.

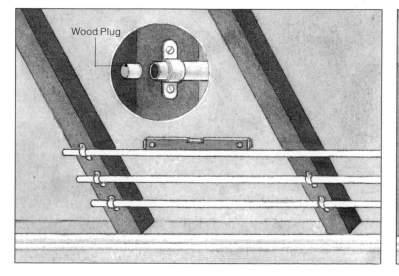

Wood Plug

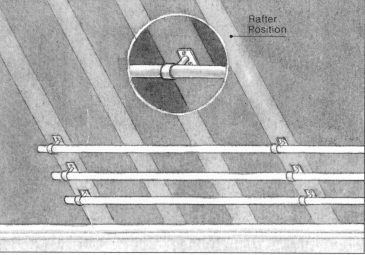

Rafter Position

SUSPENDED SHELVES

These shelves suspended over a breakfast bar make excellent use of space which would otherwise be wasted, as well as providing a light and airy divider between the kitchen and the dining area.

The shelves must be suspended securely using steel tubing fixed firmly to the ceiling joists. You may be able to get chrome-steel tubing in the required lengths and threaded for fixing into screw-fixed securing plates. Metal fabricators and ship's chandlers are likely sources. An alternative is to use lengths of studding (threaded steel rods). These are covered by the steel tubing which is used for wardrobe hanging rails and which is ideal for spacing the suspended shelves on the studding. Wardrobe rail is readily available with a chrome, nickel (matt) or brassed finish, or covered with a white plastic coating.

The shelves can be solid hardwood to match the worktop, although it is perfectly acceptable to make them from a hollow timber frame skinned with plywood. This skin can have a hardwood veneer to match the worktop. The technique for making the shelves is as for the Wall of Display Shelving project (see page 156).

The upper shelf can be made up and hardwood lipping applied around it to hide the edges of the plywood facing panels and to give the appearance of solid wood.

With the lower shelf, it is best to fit the underside facing panel *after* the shelf is in place and the nuts on the suspension rods have been tightened with a spanner.

With the hollow method of shelf building, allow for cut-outs in one edge if you wish to hang glasses by their stems. In this case, the hardwood lipping on that edge will have to be increased to at least the depth of the cut-outs.

To hold the shelves in their required positions, they are suspended on lengths of steel studding inside steel tubes which act as spacers. The studding to use is M10 size (about 10mm [$\frac{3}{8}$in] diameter) which is available in lengths up to 1m (39in). Studding can be shortened by sawing, or, where the ceiling

❶ The Basic Construction
The shelves can be a simple timber frame skinned with sheets of plywood and lipped with hardwood.

❷ Support Batten
Lengths of steel studding hang from a 75 × 50mm (3 × 2in) batten bolted between convenient ceiling joists.

❸ Drilled Upper Shelf
Holes are drilled through cross rails to take studding. Decorative steel tubing spaces the shelves.

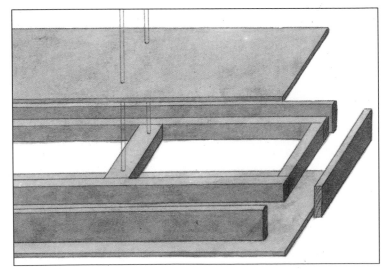

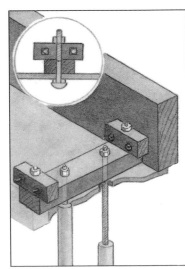

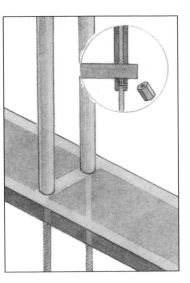

DOOR FRONTS

is high, it can be extended by joining lengths with extension nuts.

At the top, the studding is bolted through holes drilled in 75 × 50mm (3 × 2in) timber which itself is bolted with fixing pieces between ceiling joists above the shelving position. When making the shelf frames, work out where the hangers will be and make sure that there are frame cross rails at these positions to give additional, strong support.

The 19mm ($\frac{3}{4}$in) steel tubing is passed over the protruding studding before the upper shelf is fitted and held with a nut on the studding (use an extension nut if you need to extend the studding). Shorter tubes are slipped over the studding before you fit the lower shelf, which is also bolted in place on the underside. The securing nuts can be recessed into the frame cross rails before the bottom panel is fitted. With a solid wood shelf, the nuts can be fitted in pre-drilled recesses which are filled with matching wood plugs glued in place. The plugs are then planed and sanded down so that they lie flush with the surface.

④ Concealed Fixings for Nuts
Drill recesses in underside of the lower shelf. If solid, plug the recesses. If hollow, fit a fascia panel.

It is easy to greatly improve the appearance of a kitchen by replacing solid cupboard doors with glazed doors. In this way the contents of the cupboards become a focal point.

It will be virtually impossible to convert the old doors, so remove them, but before throwing them away, note down their dimensions, and the positions of the hinges and handles. Remove both and use again.

Make new doors from 75 × 19mm (3 × $\frac{3}{4}$in) PAR timber (the old doors were probably 19mm [$\frac{3}{4}$in] thick).

Cut the side rails slightly longer than required – they can be cut back to the correct length later. Cut the top and bottom rails to length to allow for the type of corner joint to be used. For the strongest job, use haunched mortise and tenon joints (see **Techniques, page 28**). After the joints have been made and the doors assembled, the lengths of waste on the side rails can be cut off flush with the top and bottom rails. You will need a router to cut a rebate along one edge at the back to take the glass. Turn over the frame and round over the front inner edge if required using a router fitted with a rounding-over cutter.

If you do not feel confident to tackle a haunched mortise and tenon joint, you can make the door frames using dowel joints (see **Techniques, page 30**). These, if properly glued, will be strong enough to secure the frames.

The glass is fitted into the rebate from the back of the door. It is bedded on putty and held with wooden glass beading, secured by pins. These must be driven in very carefully. Various styles of beading are available. If you do not have a router, use a moulding to create a rebate. Glue and pin it to the inner edge of the frame at the front, creating a rebate behind for the glass to be fixed, as above. Mitre the corners. Replace hinges, apply a finish and add handles.

① Fitting Frame and Glass
Use a haunched mortise and tenon joint (below). Rebate frame; round front inner edge; insert glass.

② Alternative Method
Form rebate by pinning moulding to frame's inner edges. Secure glass with putty or beading.

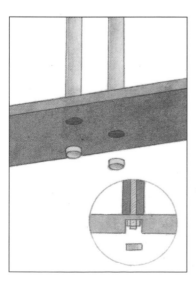

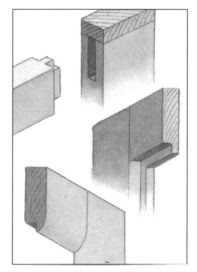

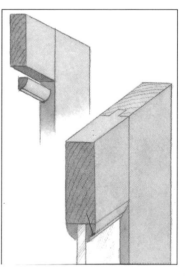

PART 3

LIVING ROOMS, WORKROOMS AND HALLS

More than any other room, a living room should reflect your personal taste and way of life. It is here that your own ideas of comfort, elegance, style and decoration can be put into practice. You can use DIY to dramatically enhance the personality of the room by restoring existing features or introducing character by adding architraves, mouldings and other architectural devices. Shelves in living rooms are normally used for displaying treasures and collections, and exert a strong influence on the room. Using DIY, shelves can be custom-made to suit the room and your possessions. In addition, an ugly fireplace can be revamped, and wooden floors can be made good by stripping and waxing, staining or painting, while the installation of a new lighting system can transform a room.

Workrooms and studies must be both practical and comfortable, so DIY can be used to convert a small room, or even a corner of a room or hall, into a purpose-built home office or workroom. With specially designed shelving, lighting and display you can make your work area both a delightful place to be in and a truly functional space.

DESIGN FOR LIVING

The living room is a place where any DIY work you do should be of the highest quality that you are capable of, having taken into account time and money constraints.

The shelving system in the comfortable living room (previous page) is well finished and has been ingeniously designed to fit wall-to-wall. It also runs around the room at picture-rail height, above the door. The top shelf provides a decorative display area for an attractive and imposing collection of wooden horses. Accent lighting is provided by ceiling downlighters.

DISTINCTIVE DISPLAY

Designing a display unit involves careful consideration of many factors. A fitted unit for storage and display must respond to the shape, character and decorative scheme of the room as well as to the objects it will house. In a luxurious modern house (right) a designer has created a room of strong, clean lines in which the materials are important. The display unit for contemporary ceramics, books, a television and a video recorder, with useful drawers beneath for hidden storage, has used this theme. Natural wood has been used for the wide shelf and as edging for the upper shelves providing controlled graphic lines. The positioning of the ceramic pots was important to the design but equally well thought-out was the position of the television. The grey shelves and drawer fronts match the sofa and blend beautifully with the colour-washed wall and its modern painting.

In a more conventional setting (below left) low cupboards fill an alcove. The space above has been used creatively and lends character to the room. To provide a large area for plants and bulky objects, there is a gap above the cupboards and then small pigeon holes for individual items, and a separate section for storing books and magazines.

The equal squares formed by a simple white display unit (below right) echo the design of a glazed door. Such a design suits a collection of treasured objects which require prominent display and which are linked to one another by texture and colour.

AROUND THE CORNER

The owner of this room clearly likes to work close to a collection of books. The polished floor and antique furniture ensure that the room retains the atmosphere of a study rather than a home office (left). In keeping with this character, the custom-made black shelves fit neatly into two corners of the room and are strong and distinctive. Shelves finished in cream or white, and designed to fill rather than edge a wall, would 'disappear' into the structure of the room. With this design, the shelves, and the books they contain, are given prominence. Black used so extensively can be very effective, but it has to be linked to the decorative scheme – hence the black chair and black lamp shade.

SMALL SPACES

In an open-plan studio, the kitchen is part of the living room but cleverly separated from it by a simple island unit (below left). An upright radiator has been installed to save further space. Because space is limited, there is very little display in the room and the design is utterly plain and easy to DIY.

In a small awkward corner of a living room, an inventive design for shelves, an alcove and low cupboards works on many levels (below right). It uses space effectively, providing neat hidden storage behind plain doors as well as open shelves for books. The alcove also provides an enhancing framed display for a plaster bust, which demands pride of place in the room. By painting the structure white to match the walls and avoiding decorative detailing, the unit merges into the room.

ASSESSING THE WORKLOAD

Nothing can rival hand-made, custom-designed, original fixtures and fittings in a living-room. However, this is not a room for learning from, and experimenting with, DIY: the standard of your work must be as high as you can make it, the quality of the materials you use as good as you can afford, and the detailing and finishing as perfect as your skills allow.

If, for example, you want a fully fitted cupboard which is going to add character to the room as well as useful storage space, try building a similar structure as a trial run in a less exposed area of the house. If you want some fitted shelves for displaying a treasured collection, think carefully about the design, and, if you are not particularly confident, choose the design which is easiest to construct.

Some of the most effective DIY tasks to undertake in the living room will, if they are done properly, 'disappear' when completed. Wire management is one of them.

Remove skirting and floorboards so that you can channel wires from lights, the television, music equipment and so on, to an area that will be hidden when you replace the woodwork. If this is not possible, box-in wires and any water pipes as necessary. Flat speaker wires can always be run under carpet.

Another effective DIY task can be to dispense with superfluous fixtures. Unwanted shelves tend to attract clutter, so do not think that you must always add fixtures and fittings to a room; sometimes taking away unnecessary elements can be equally important.

The architectural details of a room have a subtle but important impact. By revamping or replacing woodwork such as architraves, dados, pelmets, panelling, skirting and so on, you greatly improve the appearance of the room.

All of these tasks are relatively simple but enormously effective.

INSPIRING WORK

The three rooms illustrated here have each benefited from both good design, and the work of highly skilled professional craftspeople, who have created well-conceived and superbly finished fittings.

A broad display shelf (above left) has distinctive and strongly decorative metal supports designed to define the structure and give it, and the objects it carries, handsome prominence in the room.

In a beautifully mellow, welcoming and elegant room (above right), the distinctive oak skirting and the fireplace's wooden frame are absolutely made-to-measure.

Magnificent woodwork (opposite) in a Shaker room results from the skills of generations of craftsmen. The simple structures are stunning in their practical beauty. The detailing on joints, handles and hinges has a human quality which declares the great pleasure and care with which these fittings were conceived and constructed.

Structural Shelving

Shelving that is designed specifically for the space that it fills and the objects which it displays, is likely to be far better than any that you buy ready-made or in kit form. The crucial point to remember is that shelves should always blend in well with the dimensions and architecture of a room rather than stand out from them.

If you are installing shelves in an alcove, fill the alcove from top to bottom and from side to side. Never run a line of shelves down the centre of an alcove, because you will create ugly gaps around it. If you are building a wall of shelves, make sure that they cover the entire wall. If the wall is interrupted by a door, why not try and frame the door with the shelving structure.

When a room contains awkward spaces, such as a low or sloping attic wall, a DIY shelving system can make excellent use of otherwise wasted space by providing an extra storage area.

Framing shelves by lining the area to be shelved with wood at the top, bottom and sides will give them a professional finish and a neat definition. Scribing the frame and securing it to the wall is no more difficult than fitting kitchen units; the shelves themselves will then be fitted to the wooden frame rather than to the wall, and brackets or supports can be incorporated into the frame. Dividers and shelves can then be made to the same specification as the frame, and act as supports for the shelves as well as giving a pigeon-hole effect.

As a general rule, it is a good idea to use a shelving system that allows brackets to be completely invisible. One of the most effective ways of achieving this is to make the shelves from hollow oblong pieces of wood rather than from single planks, so that brackets can be fixed inside the structure. This method of fixing also gives the shelves a strong, sculptural line, so

that, when painted, they blend in with the painted walls of the room.

Glass shelves that slot into the two side walls of an alcove look very neat, although achieving this effect is not always possible. Constructing a wooden frame onto which glass shelves can be fitted is a suitable alternative and also allows you to incorporate electrical wiring for concealed lighting underneath and behind the wooden frame. Glass shelves when lit from above or below look especially attractive.

Sometimes battens or brackets can be used to decorative effect. Specially-made iron brackets can make a very strong feature of shelving in a room.

Made to Measure

You cannot have the sort of shelving shown on these pages unless they are built specifically for the space into which they fit. Fitted shelves are an important asset in a living room. They provide open storage which is unique to that room and lend an individual character to it. Bought shelves can never complement the shape and dimensions of a room in the same way as tailor-made designs.

In two of the rooms, whole walls have been shelved to great effect. A large collection of books (opposite) stretches from floor to ceiling and frames an existing window and a radiator. A more problematic space has been filled (centre) allowing the sloping ceiling to dictate the dimensions of the shelving structure, ensuring a strong architectural quality.

Alcove Shelves

In two modern interiors, alcoves have been specifically created to carry display shelves. These can be easily incorporated into a DIY scheme using a false wall or building out an existing wall to form an alcove.

In a large expanse of wall (top) the alcove of shelves breaks up an otherwise flat area and is filled with an informal arrangement of books and objects. Because of the defined shelf area, the effect remains neat and contained.

A half-wall screens two sections of a room (below) and has been grooved to support the edges of inset glass shelves.

STORAGE SOLUTIONS

Space is perhaps the greatest luxury a home can offer these days. If you live in a limited space then it is important to stow away as many as possible of life's essentials. Objects and clutter can make even a generous room seem smaller, so make sure that anything you do store out in the open is worthy of the visual attention that it will receive.

If you enjoy being surrounded by personal treasures, private mementoes, ethnic artefacts picked up on travels abroad and collections of everything from tin toys to African masks, then provide yourself with the shelf space to carry these objects. Fill alcoves, whole walls, spare corners in halls, free space under stairs and on landings with shelves. The shelves themselves should be simple and not prominent, so as to impose order on treasured clutter.

A carefully constructed collection of one type of object calls for a quite different approach. If, for instance, you have a liking for 1930s china, rare books, antique bronzes or model cars discovered over the years then you will want to display your collection as a coherent group. For this purpose, neat, symmetrical shelving placed in a prominent position is the ideal solution.

If you confine yourself to a few very special objects, then give them space and frame them in an alcove of shelves lit from above, or place one object on a handmade plinth. The area around them should be kept empty.

In the living room, there are items other than personal treasures to consider. Books, music equipment, records, tapes and compact discs, clocks, plants and many other objects may require shelving; try to design it so that the objects fit the shelving by spacing and dividing the shelves appropriately. Doing-it-yourself gives you the opportunity to ensure that shelving units are custom designed.

If you are creating a special display area, consider incorporating lighting to highlight the objects. Make the shelves themselves as stylish as possible by using good quality materials and a clean, strong design that suits both the room's decorative scheme and the objects on display.

Well-designed shop fittings, as well as ideas from magazines and the inspiration from these pages, should provide an interesting source of ideas.

Finally, be absolutely sure that the shelving you build is strong enough to take the weight you intend to place on it. There is nothing so sad as a sagging shelf.

SYMMETRICAL BALANCE

Simple alcove shelves on either side of a chimney breast (opposite above) carry a large collection of colourful china and objects.

Double doors are completely framed by a shelving structure which fills an entire wall (opposite below left).

On either side of a window (opposite below right) a collection of fine glass vases is well displayed on shelves which form alcoves. For added character, an attractive old radiator has been restored and painted, rather than hidden.

STRONG SUPPORT

To add interest in a modern room (below left), a wall has been given an alcove to carry shelves which are lit internally. Such a structure can be built out from any wall and provides a good alternative to a fireplace.

An asymmetrical wall under sloping eaves has created uneven alcoves (below centre) but these have been used effectively to carry strong, broad shelves.

In a home office (below right) a table slots neatly between the natural wood supports of two equal shelving units. Note the use of strong carrier bags for storage on lower shelves; a neat and cheap solution.

TAILOR-MADE DISPLAY

GLORIOUS GLASS

Glass shelves are particularly effective for displays because they are narrow, unobtrusive and transparent. They can be supported by various means: simple studs support smoked glass (opposite above left) which beautifully displays a collection of fossils. It is easier to use glass in an alcove such as this, or in a sloping recess (opposite below right) formed above a low cupboard. The glass is not vulnerable to damage by protruding into the room, so it can safely hold delicate objects such as these antique glasses.

Where a glass shelf is not contained within a framework, the supports must be very strong. Metal bars (opposite above right) hold thick glass shelves which are also being secured by the back wall into which they have been indented for support.

Tough steel wire (available from ships' chandlers) partially obscured by a hanging ornament (opposite below centre), runs through holes in the glass to suspend these shelves. Give glass shelves a light source from above so that diffused light filters through to illuminate the objects below.

COLOUR FOR CONTRAST

The understatement of glass is one way of enhancing a display. A colourful setting can offer another. In an emerald green room (opposite below left), the vivid wall colour has been carried on to the shelves to blend them with the room and to provide a stunning background for books and objects. The thick, hollow shelves, conceal their supports to give an architectural unity.

PERCHED ON THE WALL

Individual perches have been created for a collection of decoy ducks and carved birds (left) to form a truly original grouping on one wall. A perfect example of an ingenious display, tailor-made for a special collection.

FIREPLACES AND HEARTHS

Fireplaces should be considered in two ways. The first is as a source of heat. If that source of heat is a real wood- or coal-burning fire with all the associated warm glow, comfort and well-being, then your living room has a great natural asset. It may be dirty, wasteful of energy, hard work and highly impractical, but you can only curl up and feel very cosy in front of a *real* fire. Radiators, under-floor heating, electric and gas fires (with the exception of some very effective coal-effect gas fires) hardly compensate.

You may want to re-open an existing fireplace that has been blocked off. Tampering with electricity or gas in any way involves checking legal restrictions. It is often safer, and sometimes essential, to leave the removal of gas or electric heaters to professionals. You must also check that the chimney is unblocked satisfactorily, that the flue is not cracked or damaged (this could lead to the escape of noxious fumes), and that the grate you install is both suitable and efficient for the situation. It is wise to get a professional to check the fireplace before you make any changes yourself.

The second consideration of the fireplace is as a visual focal point for the room and its decorative scheme. A fully-fledged fire surround and mantel form a dominating feature in a room. Removing and replacing a surround is often simpler than you may imagine, but the task is a building, rather than a decorating one. The work will probably involve some brick and plaster work and woodwork. Seek professional guidance and do not undertake the tasks unless you feel confident in your ability to do the work well. When installing a grate and the surrounding fireproof bricks or metal shield, your work should be checked very carefully, since any work which is less than perfect could lead to serious cracks or even an

FOCAL POINTS

A number of inventive design ideas are combined in an outstanding open fireplace (above). The chimney is flanked by windows which give added prominence to the fireplace; a magnificent slab of stone forms the raised hearth. The fireplace is a simple square framed in polished steel, perfectly suited to the style of the room. Above the fireplace is a clever variation on the traditional mantel shelf. A small shelf has been built into the chimney breast and a pretty arched alcove curves above it.

A more traditional approach (centre) is seen in this wooden fire surround and mantel, designed to match the adjoining dado and panelling details. The wood is finished with a subtle paint technique that highlights the decorative detailing, while a warm glow from the flames is reflected from the metal fire backing.

PURE AND SIMPLE

A simple but effective design (below) reduces the fireplace to an opening framed in brick and wood. It can be just as important to remove a decorative fireplace from a room as to add one to it, especially if you want the room to have a modern atmosphere. Again, the wooden frame matches adjoining woodwork – here, it is the wood skirting. The hearth has been reduced in size. It is merely a row of heat resistant stones that abut with the wooden floor.

outbreak of fire. Never underestimate the disruption and mess which this whole process will involve.

The style of your fireplace should depend on the style of the room. A grand installation will add distinction to a period room. The most important consideration is to match the period of the fireplace to that of the room. Removing an ugly recent design in a Victorian building and replacing it with an original Victorian fireplace will undoubtedly improve the room, particularly if your overall scheme involves restoring period architectural details throughout.

Alternatively, you may wish to reduce rather than enhance the impact of the fireplace. Taking out an overbearing monstrosity and leaving a neat opening, edged, perhaps, with a rim of polished steel or with plain white heat-resistant tiles, will suit a more clean-cut and minimal room. You do not have to replace a mantel if you want a plain surround and it may suit your scheme to do away with the fireplace altogether and present a flat-fronted chimney breast. In this case, a smoke-deflecting ledge is advisable. Another option would be to use the hollow chimney breast for built-in shelving and display.

There is an enormous range of period, reproduction and modern grates available, as well as fireplace surrounds, so it may be interesting to design and build your own fireplace. Your work must be of high quality since a fireplace is such a focal point in a room. You can use exposed or plastered brickwork, or wood to great effect. Marble slabs for a grate and slips for a surround are also a possibility. You can buy period tiles, reproductions of traditional designs or contemporary tiles. Whatever approach you decide to take, do not begin until you have a clear design to follow or an example to copy.

A PERFECT SETTING

An old fireplace serves as a reminder of the original architectural character in an otherwise sweeping redesign of the Arts and Crafts villa (above). The chimney has had its adjoining walls removed to open up the ground floor and it now acts as an impressive screen between living and dining areas. This delightful iron and tile fireplace with its decorative wood mantel could be an inspiration for a hand-made DIY fireplace. Alternatively, a period fireplace can be bought from a specialist and installed in a living room. Take care to choose a fireplace that suits the age, architecture and overall decorative scheme of the living room.

Another fireplace which perfectly combines with the style of the room is this one in natural brick (centre). In a relaxed living room, the warm, mellow tones of the brick match the furnishings and objects. A brick fireplace is not beyond the building capabilities of a good amateur bricklayer.

MODERN AND MINIMAL

A striking design in a minimal modern room (below). The fireplace surround is made from high quality heat-resistant ceramic tiles which carry over from the floor. The energy source is provided by gas, not a real fire, and allows for the use of these exotic, indestructible volcanic rocks as 'fuel'. The grate is formed by a basket of galvanised steel, and a panel of specially heat-resistant glass is used as a material for the reflective backing.

FLOORING

In many houses the living room has a variety of roles to play. It is not just somewhere to sit, relax and entertain, as it often has to double as a playroom, a study, a library, a television room, and maybe even as a dining area.

All these functions have to be taken into account when choosing the flooring. One thing is certain, the room will be in constant use, so the flooring must be capable of withstanding a lot of wear.

Although the flooring will run from wall-to-wall in most cases, it can be combined with other floor-coverings. For example, a varnished wooden floor with a central carpet square or rugs laid on it can be most effective.

If you prefer a hard floor, then tiles, whether ceramic, quarry, marble, slate or stone, can all be used in living rooms if the setting is right. They can be softened by the addition of rag rugs and dhurries.

Wood, of course, is an excellent flooring material. You can lay a new wood-strip or wood-block surface over an existing floor, or you can use the existing wooden floorboards, as long as they are in good condition.

RESTORING A WOODEN FLOOR

Take a good look at the floor to make sure it is suitable for restoration. If it is very badly worn, it may need to be completely renovated, or covered with an entirely new wooden floor.

If there are wide gaps between the floorboards, fill them with wooden strips. These should be planed along their length to form a slight taper. Apply PVA (polyvinyl acetate) adhesive to the sides, and then tap the strips into place in the gaps. Allow the glue to set, then plane the strips level with the surface of the floor.

If the floorboards are uneven because of heavy wear that is no more than about 3mm ($\frac{1}{8}$in) deep, it may be possible to resurface the floor by sanding it smooth. If the floorboards have worn more deeply, either replace them or turn the affected boards upside down and re-lay them. Alternatively, cover the floor with plywood and lay on new wood-strip or block floor over the top.

If your floorboards are old, try to replace the worn ones with matching old boards from a secondhand timber merchant or an architectural salvage yard. New boards, even when they are stained to match the old ones, will tend to stand out.

RE-LAYING FLOORBOARDS

If there are damaged boards, or many wide gaps between them, it will be best to lift the old boards by prising them up, so that the best boards can be re-laid without gaps, and replacement boards fitted to fill the empty spaces.

After removing the old boards, pull out the old fixing nails. Re-lay the boards, ensuring that they are tightly pressed together, by using folding wedges (see **Techniques, page 21**) between each block of four or five boards and a scrap of wood temporarily nailed to the joists. Nail boards in place before removing wedges and laying another four or five boards.

BLEACHED WOOD
This impressive wooden floor has been bleached, given a pale paint wash and then varnished for durability. It will not resist heavy wear but can be easily restored, and provides a beautiful background for the room.

LUXURIOUS MARBLE
Marble slips have a splendid impact on a room and can be used effectively in bathrooms and halls as well as living rooms. Marble is a cold and hard substance, however, it is also undeniably luxurious.

PAINTED WOOD
In a large loft space, a wooden floor has been painted pure white. If you are prepared to retouch it regularly, and use existing boards which are less than perfect, this is a simple solution for a broad expanse of floor.

RESURFACING A FLOOR BY SANDING

Make sure all floorboards are securely nailed down. Any that are split or badly damaged should be replaced. Pull out protruding carpet tacks, and with a hammer and nail punch, drive down the heads of the board-fixing nails so they are about 3mm ($\frac{1}{8}$in) below the surface.

You should hire an industrial floor sander for treating the main part of the floor, with a smaller hand disc sander or belt sander for finishing off the edges against the skirting.

The floor sander looks like a giant vacuum cleaner with a revolving drum around which abrasive sheets are fixed.

Although floor sanders have dust extraction bags, these are not entirely effective, so wear a dust mask and old clothes. Before starting work, open the windows in the room and use masking tape to seal around doors leading to adjacent rooms.

The sander should be used along the length of the floorboards, never across them, as this can cause scratches.

Tilt the sander back before switching on, then gradually lower it to the floor and allow it to move forward under its own power, restraining it slightly so that it does not travel too fast. Work forwards and backwards in a line with the boards, overlapping each pass by 50mm (2in).

After the main area has been sanded, sand the edges with the hand machine. Finish corners with a scraper and hand sanding block. Finally, vacuum the floor and wipe over it with white spirit.

FINISHING TREATMENTS

Staining   Any replacement boards that are lighter in colour than the rest should be stained darker. With a rag, apply the stain and rub it evenly into the wood to bring out the desired colour. Remember that most clear finish deepens the colour of the wood, so test it first in a corner.

Sealing   Floorboards can be sealed with several coats of one- or two-part polyure-thane-based varnish/sealer which dries to a clear gloss, satin, or matt coat on the surface. Alternatively, use an oleo-resinous seal, which will soak into the surface to give a scratch-resistant sheen. To darken the colour of the floor, use a varnish stain, or polish with floor wax.

Liming   This technique involves rubbing a white pigment into the grain of the wood before sealing it. It is easiest to use white paint thinned with white spirit since these materials are usually to hand, but you can use limed wax, or gesso, which is plaster of Paris. Paint the liming mixture along the boards, covering a small area at a time, and wipe the mixture off with rags, leaving a white stain in the cracks. Finally, seal the floor with varnish.

Painting   If there are many new floorboards, painting will avoid a patchy appearance. Apply undercoat and two coats of a hard-wearing oil-based gloss paint, or a satin finish paint.

COIR MATTING

The natural quality of coir matting has a similar decorative effect to wood and is often a good alternative. In its own right, it is also very popular as a muted, warm background for many styles of rooms, ancient and modern.

NEW WOOD

Wooden floors are available today in a vast range, and many of them are easily installed by an amateur. They are usually sold in sections. This broad-planked floor in pale wood is especially suitable for a light and airy studio.

OLD WOOD

Old wooden floors, provided that not too many planks have been replaced and are in a reasonable condition, can be beautifully restored by stripping and finishing. They can be stained or oiled to deepen the tone of the wood.

ROOMS TO WORK IN

If you work from home, fitting out a personal workspace will be a major priority when it comes to designing your home. Equally, you may need a private den or study, a well-equipped workshop, a sewing room or a darkroom. Whatever your requirements, if you have a limited budget, you will achieve something far more comfortable, efficient and practical by designing and building it yourself than by installing ready-made fittings.

Few DIY tasks are more satisfying than creating a room, or a section of a room,

which is a pleasure to work in. Unlike the rest of your home, you will not be sharing a work room or using it for tasks other than those for which it is specifically designed, so you are free to indulge yourself and create your ideal personal working space.

By adapting the projects in this book, you will find that you can create precisely what you need for a tailor-made work-room, whether it is a wall-mounted unit of pigeon-hole shelving, a simple desk top made from a door, or a pinboard.

DOWN TO WORK

The ultimate Modernist environment for a designer – a pure white minimal room (above) – has a work area separated from the main room by the raised back of a desk unit; a simple but highly effective device.

An ingenious use of space on one side of a bedroom (opposite) where high storage shelves are reached by a sliding ladder. A drawing board is fitted into a high level worksurface partly supported by an attractive stack of drawers. The window is left intact.

HOME OFFICE

Whether you work from home, or merely want a private area for paperwork and home management, for your children to study in, or for your own reading and contemplation, then you must first allocate the amount of space that can be given over to a home office.

A small room is ideal, but if this is not possible or practical, there are many ways to screen-off a section or corner of a living room or bedroom, part of a hallway or landing, or even a part of the garage. Work areas should be neither too enclosed nor over exposed, so a movable screen may be the answer, so that the room or landing can be easily restored to its original dimensions. Build one in wood, create a Japanese version using stretched paper or fabric, or buy a ready-made one, budget permitting.

Of course an effective work area can be made without a partition or screen but you must define the workspace or be prepared for it to spread across the room.

Once the area is defined, then plan the office with care and work out what you need to build in terms of a desk or writing surface, shelving, display boards and storage. Keep it simple and remember the practical limitations of wire management, lighting and comfort.

The desktop can be made from an old door, a panel of melamine-faced chipboard or wood placed on a bought trestle or dark pedestal. Position it close to a natural light source and ensure that all storage areas are within easy reach when you are sitting at the desk.

We live in the age of the computer. Storing paperwork, files and notes is no longer any more important than wiring-in the electrical equipment, calculators, personal computer, printer and keyboard. The development of new technology in the business office has spread across to the home office and the study. Children now use computers to help them study as well as to play computer games for entertainment. These activities are as much a part of their lives as reading or playing with toys.

If you want to build a safe, comfortable workstation, incorporating a computer system, then consider the following factors: a surface to carry a keyboard should be at a comfortable working height; lighting should not interfere with the screen, but should play on to paperwork and the desk or writing surface. Invest in a really good office chair rather than risk back injury, and make sure that the room is well-ventilated and adequately heated.

OFFICE STORAGE

The sparse and functional office of a fashion designer has simple adjustable shelving on a standard system of brackets (opposite above). On one wall, the shelves are backed with felt to form a pinboard.

A unit of storage cupboards, with some sliding and some hinged doors (below left), provides ample hidden storage behind a modern desk for office clutter.

A storage unit doubles as a screen to separate a work area (below right) and has access to drawers and cupboards on one side; a fitted desk forms the other side.

To display her work, a sculptor has suspended glass shelves from strong steel wires (opposite below right) in her home workroom. Hidden storage is cleverly provided by shelves obscured by a Venetian blind.

A PLACE FOR A DESK

In an alcove, a desk is simply a laminated board (opposite below centre) offset by two beautiful classic folding chairs.

In a small area adjoining a living room (below centre) a wooden structure supports a wide worksurface and extends to form a fitted sofa.

A mezzanine floor has been built-in to a house to create a wonderful open office area (opposite below left).

MAKING AN ENTRANCE

There is great potential for DIY improvements in entrances, hallways, passages and landings. The front door itself and the area immediately outside it should be welcoming and attractive, perhaps providing shelter and certainly making the transition from outside to indoors as comfortable and convenient as possible.

The entrance hall to any building is important. It sets the scene for what is to come and allows an area for hellos and goodbyes. An entrance that leads directly into a room is rarely ideal, so preserve your hallway at all costs, even if it may appear to be a waste of precious living space initially.

Passages, stairways and landing are not only the spaces between rooms but are also areas that can be utilized for storage and display, work areas or places to sit.

They should be decorated, planned and restored with almost as much care and attention as the living room.

In period homes, the architectural details in the hallways and on the stairs are often neglected or allowed to deteriorate, so concentrate on restoring them to their former glory. In modern buildings, make the entrance as atmospheric as possible and ensure that the lighting is subtle but functional. A common problem, especially for entrance halls, is the clutter that naturally accumulates there – everything from muddy boots, umbrellas and overcoats, to bicycles, push-chairs and unwanted furniture. Create a proper storage area for essential items and discard unwanted objects. Don't forget to install a large doormat. Mud, grit and moisture can quickly ruin hall carpets.

FLOOR TO CEILING

An open hall has durable, white ceramic tiles (above left) which reflect the natural light. A fitted cupboard provides storage.

The hall is defined by a large area of fitted matting (above right). Where walls have been removed in a conversion, a curved wall is a useful and attractive form of transition from hall to living area. Downlights are suitable for halls and passages as lights which hang or protrude from the ceiling break up a narrow space and are easily knocked when furniture is being moved around.

A wall given over to fitted cupboards in a passage way (opposite) provides spacious storage in a compact area. Two types of flooring add to the style of this hall and stairway, with slate used at the entrance and pale wood on the stairs and landing.

HALLS, PASSAGES AND STAIRS

BELOW STAIRS

A neat office has been created in an otherwise dead space below stairs in a hallway (above). Simple shelves on battens form open storage for books and files. A false back hides wires for lamps and for the personal computer while a broad shelf forms the desk top.

OPEN CLOAKROOM

In a corner of a hall (right) an open cloakroom, which is reminiscent of a locker room, has been created. Across an alcove, the stylish but practical grid of poles provides a useful hanging space and a shoe storage area. Great care has been taken in choosing and mixing pale colours and natural textures to open up and lighten the area. Bleached and white-washed wooden panelling is used on some walls and on the ceiling, while other walls have exposed brickwork, painted white. The area is given an added sense of space by an expanse of mirror.

What you decide to do in the way of DIY in your halls and passageways is dependent on several factors. You may want to restore mouldings, panelling, dado rails, doors, architraves and the floor in a period hallway. Ugly gas and electricity meters, wires coming from outside the house and door bells and alarms may have intruded and require boxing-in.

You can improve the appearance and ambience of a dark, tunnel-like hall by replacing a solid door that leads from it with a glazed one, or even by installing an interior window to allow light to enter from another room.

Apart from good restoration and decoration, the most important way to improve your entrance and passageways is to take a long hard look at the lighting. Such areas often have only an overhead pendant light or two, or unflattering fluorescent strips. Consider installing wall-lights or spotlights on dimmer switches so that a low level of light can be maintained through the night for safety and security reasons. Taking into account the fact that furniture will be moved through the passages and could damage protruding or hanging fittings, downlights can be very practical and they produce a flattering light. Decide on your lighting solutions before you undertake restoration or deco-

TRADITIONAL DISPLAY

The colour, style and impact of a beautifully crafted display unit in a hallway (left) perfectly suits the collection of decorative old tins it holds and the architecture of the house. The design, which has been carried up beside the stairs, uses tongued-and-grooved panelling, and architraves to form separate compartments for the display. In eighteenth- and nineteenth-century houses, pine was often painted over with deep colour tones.

A HALL OF BOOKS

Beneath the stairs in an ample hallway (above) is a perfect place for extra bookshelves, provided they are created and shaped to precisely fit the wall they are placed on.

ration so that you can organize the wiring without disrupting the clean state of newly decorated surfaces.

If space is limited elsewhere in your home, take a look around your hall, passageways and landings to see how you can free up extra space for storage and display. All sorts of dead space, empty walls and under-utilized corners are to be found there. If you follow the guidelines on structural shelving and fitted storage in this book, then rows of book shelves or fitted cupboards can be built in passages without destroying the dimensions. Designers often integrate floor-to-ceiling cupboards into halls, with flush doors to give the appearance of a blank wall, behind which all manner of clutter can be conveniently tidied away.

Neat coat hooks can be made into a feature in an entrance hall and a shoe rack can be an attractive addition. Somewhere to place mail, newspapers, circulars and the many other small items that can congregate near the front door, is also an advantage. A hall table may be the solution but you could consider that a unit combines shelves, hooks and a shoe rack.

If you are desperately in need of a home office space or work area, then do not rule out a corner of the hall or the area under the stairs as a possible solution.

ALCOVE SHELVES AND CUPBOARDS

Many rooms have a chimney breast with an alcove on either side. This design allows you to integrate storage space into an alcove without disturbing the unity of the wall. This is achieved by repeating a triangular moulding from the face of the alcove cupboard doors on a decorative panel placed over the fireplace. Larger mouldings of the same shape also form the wall supports for the alcove shelves in the recesses, and for the angled pelmet which conceals the tungsten strip lights. The repetition of this decorative device provides a unifying element to the design and detailing of the whole wall.

How you decorate the shelves, doors and panels is dependent on your scheme for the rest of the room. This project is an example of my philosophy that tries to ensure that fittings which are built-in to the structure of a room blend into the existing architecture and features rather than argue with them.

SECTION OF
CUPBOARD DOOR

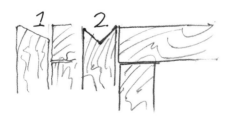

top edge of doors
can be bevelled
in 2 ways to
provide a finger
grip

PLAN OF CUPBOARD
& WALL DECORATION

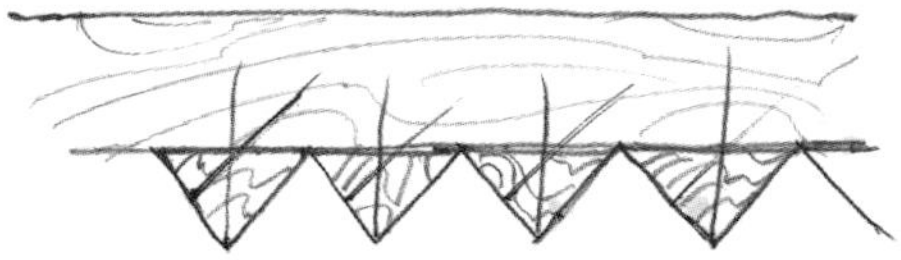

triangular slats
glued & pinned
to door panels —
then filled &
painted.

FRONT ELEVATION:

Triangular shelf support battens echo the shape of the door & wall decoration.

Wall decoration echos door panels.

Concealed lighting at back of shelves.

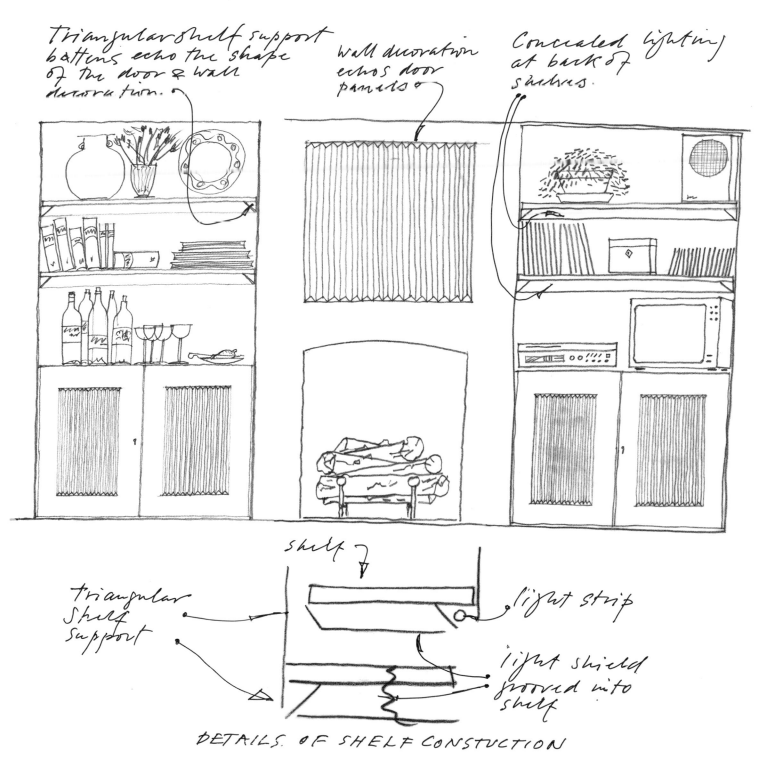

shelf

triangular shelf support

light strip

light shield grooved into shelf

DETAILS OF SHELF CONSTUCTION

Alcove Shelves and Cupboards

Living rooms always call for a reasonable amount of storage and display space; one way of creating it is to make use of the wasted space on each side of a chimney breast, or in a corner, by fitting shelves and a cupboard. A basic design is described below, but the project is easy to adapt to suit your own requirements. You may want alcove cupboards and shelves to house a television, music equipment, books, drinks and glasses, or favourite objects. The function will probably determine the height of your cupboards and shelves, so think about your specific storage needs before you start work. For example, you may want to construct just one cupboard for use as a drinks cabinet. Alternatively, you may like to vary the number of shelves above a cupboard, according to the size and type of objects you wish to store or display on them.

The linenfold decoration which has been added to the cupboard doors here is echoed on the wall with a panel of the same design, adding an individual and interesting detailing. By varying the kind of moulding you use on the cupboards and on the wall, you will be able to adapt the overall design to suit your own decorative scheme. Another way of adding a personal touch to the design is to vary the cupboard door fittings, by using different door handles or knobs.

Whatever the design, it is most important to ensure that all gaps are filled and edges are smoothed so that the cupboards and shelves appear to be part of the structure of the room, even if they are not painted the same colour. The shelf battens should be disguised as much as possible to blend in with the wall. In this project we show how a shelf batten can incorporate a light above a shelf, lending muted tones to the colour scheme of the walls.

TOOLS

- STEEL RULE
- TRIMMING KNIFE
- TRY SQUARE
- PANEL SAW (or circular saw)
- TENON SAW
- HAMMER
- SCRIBING BLOCK
- CHISEL bevel-edge type
- MALLET
- DRILL (hand or power)
- DRILL BIT
- MASONRY DRILL BIT
- COUNTERSINK BIT
- END MILL for fitting concealed hinges
- POWER JIGSAW
- SANDING BLOCK AND ABRASIVE PAPER (or finishing sander)
- HAND PLANE (or power plane)
- SPIRIT LEVEL
- NAIL PUNCH

MATERIALS   For one alcove:

Part	Quantity	Material	Length*
UPRIGHTS	2	50 × 50mm (2 × 2in) PAR timber	As required – ours 838mm (33in)
HORIZONTAL RAILS	2	50 × 50mm (2 × 2in) PAR timber	Width of alcove, less 100mm (4in)*
BACK SUPPORT BATTENS	2	50 × 25mm (2 × 1in) PAR timber	Width of alcove
SIDE SUPPORT BATTENS	4	50 × 25mm (2 × 1in) PAR timber	Depth of alcove, less 100mm (4in)*
BASE FRONT AND BACK SUPPORT BATTENS	2	25 × 25mm (1 × 1in) PAR timber	Width of alcove
BASE SIDE SUPPORT BATTENS	2	25 × 25mm (1 × 1in) PAR timber	Depth of alcove
ALCOVE SHELF-SUPPORT BACK BATTENS	2	38mm (1½in) triangular section	Width of alcove
ALCOVE SHELF-SUPPORT SIDE BATTENS	4	38mm (1½in) triangular section	Depth of alcove, less 38mm (1½in)
LINENFOLD-WALL PANEL DECORATION	As required	38mm (1½in) triangular section	Height of wall panel
LINENFOLD DOOR DECORATION	12 per door	25mm (1in) triangular section	Door height, less 200mm (8in)
DOWELS	1	Approximately 1.8m (6ft) hardwood dowelling	As required
BASE PANEL	1	4mm or 6mm (⅛in or ¼in) plywood	Alcove width × depth, less thickness of skirtings & front frame
TOP PANEL	1	25mm (1in) MDF or blockboard	Alcove width × depth
CUPBOARD SHELF	1	19mm (¾in) MDF, chipboard, or blockboard	Alcove width × depth of alcove, less 75mm (3in)*
DOORS	2	19mm (¾in) MDF	½ alcove width, less 8mm (⅜in) × front frame height less 25mm (1in)
ALCOVE SHELVES	2	25mm (1in) MDF	Alcove width × alcove depth, less 25mm (1in)
CENTRE WALL PANEL	1	6mm (¼in) MDF or plywood	Chimney breast width × height required

*Approximate lengths only – refer to copy for actual size.

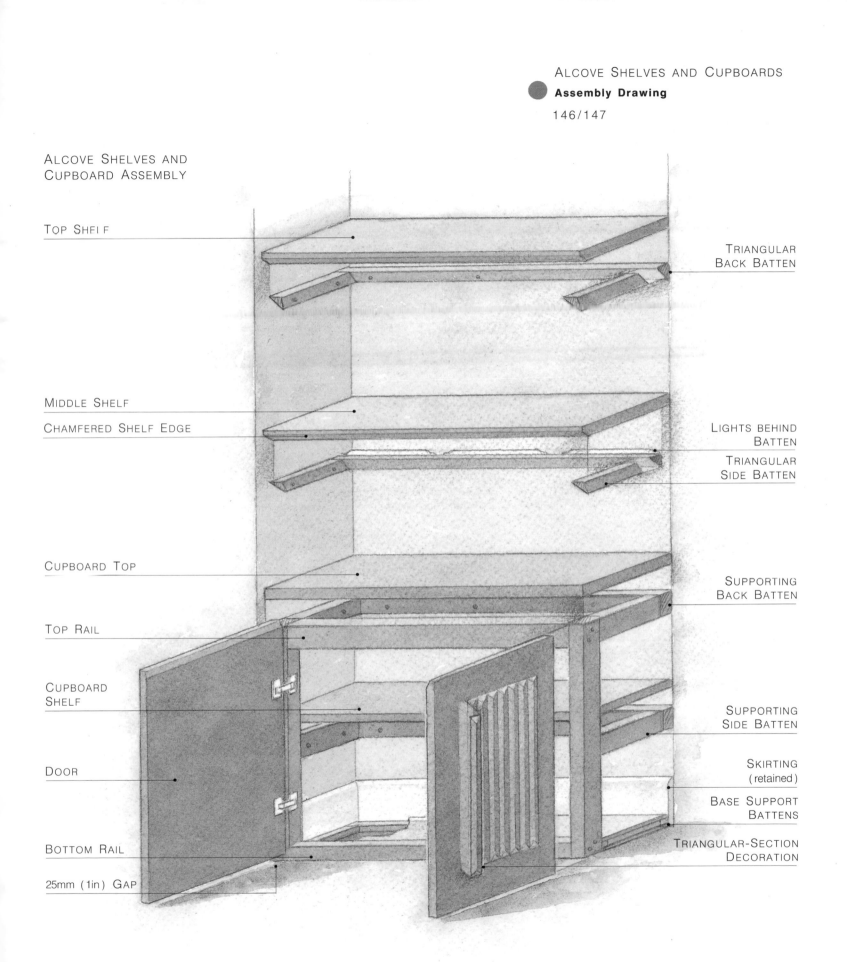

ALCOVE SHELVES AND
CUPBOARD ASSEMBLY

TOP SHELF

MIDDLE SHELF

CHAMFERED SHELF EDGE

CUPBOARD TOP

TOP RAIL

CUPBOARD
SHELF

DOOR

BOTTOM RAIL

25mm (1in) GAP

TRIANGULAR
BACK BATTEN

LIGHTS BEHIND
BATTEN

TRIANGULAR
SIDE BATTEN

SUPPORTING
BACK BATTEN

SUPPORTING
SIDE BATTEN

SKIRTING
(retained)

BASE SUPPORT
BATTENS

TRIANGULAR-SECTION
DECORATION

THE CUPBOARDS

MAKING THE FRAME

Using 50 × 50mm (2 × 2in) PAR (planed all round) timber, cut two uprights to the desired height, allowing for the thickness of the top. The height of our cupboards, including the top, is 865mm (34in).

Measure for two horizontal rails so that they fit inside the uprights, and cut these from the same size of timber as used for the uprights. Dowel joint the horizontal rails between the uprights with two 12mm ($\frac{1}{2}$in) dowels at each corner (*see* **Techniques, Dowel Joints, page 30**). Before fixing the frame it must be held square with a bracing batten (*see* **Techniques, page 20**). For a more detailed description and illustrations of making door frames, see The Kitchen System, Doors, page 90.

FITTING THE FRAME

To fit the frame into the alcove it will be necessary to scribe the uprights to the wall (*see* **Techniques, page 31**). If there is skirting around the walls of the alcove, the side rails should be scribed around it. Alternatively, remove small sections of skirting, using a tenon saw and a chisel, where the side rails will fit. Another option is to remove the skirting entirely, although this rarely looks satisfactory.

Set the frame about 25mm (1in) back into the alcove, fixing it in place with two screws and wallplugs on each side (*see* **Techniques, page 24**). Countersink the screwheads so that the holes can be filled and painted over.

FIXING THE SUPPORTING BATTENS

The supporting battens for the cupboard top and for the cupboard shelf are made from 50 × 25mm (2 × 1in) PAR timber.

Using a spirit level, mark a line all the way around the alcove from the top of the frame. Cut the back batten to the full width of the alcove and fix it to the wall, under the line at the back, using screws and wallplugs to secure it in position.

Cut two side battens to fit between the back batten and the front frame.

Fix the battens to the wall at the marked lines as before.

Decide on the height of the cupboard shelf or shelves, and cut and fit the supporting battens at the appropriate height, making sure that they are level.

FIXING THE BASE

The cupboard base panel is made from 4mm ($\frac{1}{8}$in) or 6mm ($\frac{1}{4}$in) plywood and is supported at the edges on 25 × 25mm (1 × 1in) battens.

At the front, glue and nail a supporting batten to the inner face of the bottom rail of the front frame. Fix it 4mm ($\frac{1}{8}$in) or 6mm ($\frac{1}{4}$in) down from the top (depending on the thickness of the plywood you are using), so that the base panel sits flush with the frame.

At the back, glue and pin a similar batten to the skirting. Use a spirit level resting on the bottom rail of the front frame to mark the height of the base panel at the back, and measure down 4mm ($\frac{1}{8}$in) or 6mm ($\frac{1}{4}$in) to mark the height of the rear base supporting batten so it can be fitted easily and accurately.

Using timber of the same size, cut side supporting battens to fit between the front and rear battens, and glue and pin these battens to the skirting at each side.

Cut the plywood base to size, and use panel pins to fix it to the supporting battens at the front, back and sides of the frame. Use a cellulose filler to fill the join between the base and the frame, and sand it smooth when dry.

FIXING THE TOP

Measure the width of the alcove and the depth from the back wall to the front edge of the frame. If the wall is very uneven, increase these measurements to allow the top to be scribed to the wall.

Cut out the top from 25mm (1in) medium-density fibreboard (MDF), blockboard or chipboard. If using blockboard or chipboard, it will need to have a lipped front edge for protection and neatness.

Scribe and fit the top in place and fix at the front by screwing up through the frame. At the back, screw down through the top, and do

① Assembly of the Cupboard Framework Using Dowels
The cupboard frame is made simply by butt-jointing top and side rails. Joints are reinforced with dowels; two per joint. Protruding ends are cut off flush once glue has hardened.

② Fitting the Cupboard Base
Battens are placed at the front, rear, and sides (not shown). The base is pinned to the top.

③ Fixing the Top Section
The frame is set back 25mm (1in) from front of alcove. Screw up into top panel.

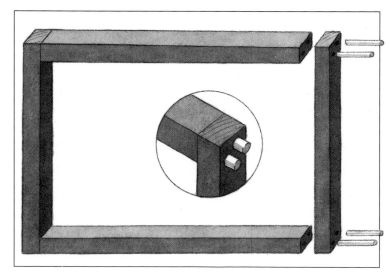

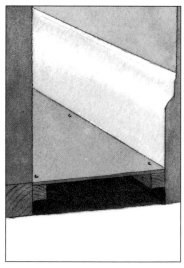

the same at each corner, countersinking the screwheads so that the holes can be filled and painted over afterwards.

Plane and sand the front edge flush with the frame if you have used MDF. Fill and sand this join flush.

FITTING THE CUPBOARD SHELF

Cut the cupboard shelf from 19mm ($\frac{3}{4}$in) MDF, blockboard or chipboard (with a lipped front edge). Check that it fits well and rest it on the supporting battens.

MAKING AND FITTING THE DOORS

Using 19mm ($\frac{3}{4}$in) MDF, cut two panels to fit the front, flush with the top, but leaving a 25mm (1in) gap at the bottom. The size of the gap at the sides of the doors is determined by the hinges used – consult the manufacturer's instructions. We have used concealed self-closing hinges, and the doors overhang the inner edges of the frame by an amount specified in the manufacturer's instructions, usually about 15mm ($\frac{5}{8}$in) so that the hinges will operate correctly (*see* **Techniques, page 32**).

To create a finger-grip, chamfer the top edge of each door to 45° through two-thirds of its thickness, leaving about 5mm ($\frac{3}{16}$in) flat on top.

The 'linenfold' front detail is created with 25mm (1in) triangular-section ramin or pine (fig 4). Measure and mark a square on each door for the 'linenfold', leaving a suitable border around the edge (ours is 100mm (4in) at top and bottom, and about 90mm (3$\frac{1}{2}$in) at each side). Cut sections to length and chamfer the ends to 45° (fig 4).

Mark a centre line vertically down the door, and working outwards from this, glue each length on to the surface, pinning through the side faces in about three places. Continue in each direction until the required number of triangular-shaped sections are fixed with an equal border at each side.

Fit the doors using the concealed hinges according to the manufacturer's instructions (*see* **Techniques, page 33**).

DETAIL OF LINENFOLD DOORS
This photograph shows the full effect of the linenfold door decoration, together with the neatly chamfered fingergrip. You can vary the kind of decoration you use on the door front according to your personal taste.

4 **Making and Decorating Cupboard Doors**
Left Top edges of doors are chamfered to provide a fingergrip. *Inset* Fixing of linenfold. *Centre* First linenfold fitted. *Right* Cut a triangular section and chamfer the ends to 45°.

ALCOVE SHELVES AND CUPBOARDS

THE SHELVES

The shelves are made from 25mm (1in) MDF boards that are supported by 38mm (1½in) triangular battens which are fixed to the walls of the alcoves.

CUTTING THE TRIANGULAR BATTENS

If you cannot find suitable triangular timber mouldings at your local timber suppliers, you can cut them yourself from 50 × 50mm (2 × 2in) PAR timber with a circular saw.

Tilt your circular saw blade to 45° and cut the timber diagonally along its length so that it is split into two equal triangular sections. If your saw blade is not large enough to cut right through in one pass, cut partway through and complete the cut with a panel saw. Finally, clean up the sawn faces with a smoothing plane for a neat finish.

If you do not have a suitable circular saw, your timber supplier should easily be able to make this cut for you.

FIXING THE TOP SHELF

Decide on the height of the top shelf. From the triangular battening, cut a back batten to span the width of the alcove and fix to the wall.

Cut the side battens to length, which should be the distance from the back of the alcove to 38mm (1½in) in from the front edge. Use triangular battens, and cut a 45° chamfer on the front end so that the batten will tail away from the front edge of the shelf. Chamfer the back end of the batten in the same direction so that it fits snugly into the corner against the back batten. Fix side battens in place.

Cut out the shelf from 25mm (1in) MDF to the width of the alcove and to a depth whereby it is set back into the alcove by 25mm (1in). Chamfer the front edge of the shelf through half its thickness to allow the front edge of the bevelled side batten to run into the chamfer and create an unobtrusive support for the shelf. Screw shelf down on to back and side battens. Fill joins and gaps, and when the filler is hard, sand smooth.

❶ Cutting the Triangular Battens Yourself
Tilt your circular saw blade to 45° and cut down length of timber to split it.

❷ Fixing the Shelves
Top and middle shelves fix onto triangular battens that are screwed to the walls. One batten hides a light.

ALCOVE SHELVES IN PLACE
The shelves (above) are 25mm (1in) thick MDF boards which are screwed down on to the battens.

SHELVES AND BATTENS
The chamfered support battens blend neatly with the chamfered front alcove shelves (below).

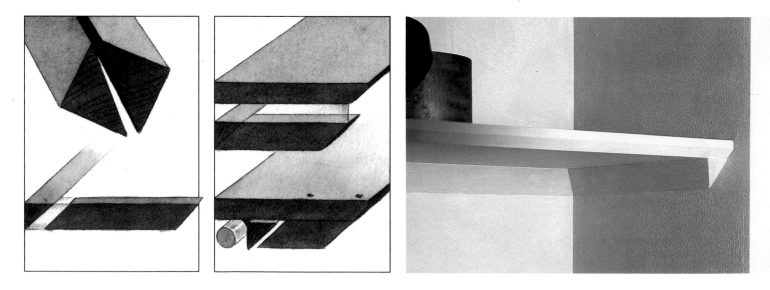

FIXING THE MIDDLE SHELF

Decide on the height of the shelf and cut the back batten to fit into the alcove. In this case the back batten is fixed about 75mm (3in) out from the wall so that a light can be fitted behind it. Do not fit the batten securely in place at this stage.

Cut the side battens so that when chamfered at front and rear they will be 75mm (3in) away from the wall at the back, and 38mm (1½in) in from the front. Fix the side battens in place, screwing and plugging them tightly to the alcove wall so that they are both level.

Cut the shelf to size from 25mm (1in) MDF and fit it on the side battens, chamfering the front as before. Screw it down on to the side battens, countersinking and refilling the screwheads.

The back batten, which is cut square at the ends, is positioned under the shelf behind the ends of the side battens. It is fixed in place by screwing down through the shelf. This provides a cover for the light fittings and also acts as a beam to support the shelf and prevent it from sagging. Countersink the screw holes and fill them after inserting the screws into the holes.

LIGHTING

For the concealed lighting under the middle shelf we used three 300mm (12in) long tungsten tube lamps secured behind the back batten.

THE CENTRE WALL PANEL

Although not essential to the project, we fitted a centre panel on the chimney breast to give a unified look by continuing the theme of the door decoration. The panel is 6mm (¼in) MDF or plywood on which 38mm (1½in) triangular-section timber is glued and pinned. The panel is simply screwed to the chimney-breast wall, filled, smoothed, and painted to match the walls, cupboards and shelving.

SOFT LIGHTING IN ALCOVES

When lighting is needed, built-in tungsten strips (above), offer a good alternative to a more commonly used fluorescent version.

CONCEALED LIGHTING

The concealed lighting under the middle shelf throws a muted shadow into the alcove and creates a softer atmosphere in the room. Taken from below, this photograph (left) shows the positioning of the concealed tungsten strip lighting. When viewed from straight on, the lighting is hidden behind the back shelf batten.

WALL OF DISPLAY SHELVING

The simplicity, style and sheer practicality of a whole wall of shelves without any visible means of support is what I wanted to achieve with this design.

I realized that if steel brackets were inserted into the wall and fixed firmly, I could then construct hollow-core shelves to slide over the brackets and hide them.

A great advantage of this construction method is that all of the wiring for audio-visual equipment, telephones and lighting can be contained in the cavity of the shelf rather than trailing around on the surface in an untidy, spaghetti-like mess.

They also give the room a horizontal emphasis as there are no uprights dividing the shelves, which are necessary with conventional shelving to stop the shelves sagging in their lengths.

To complete the shelves I painted them the same colour as the wall so that they had a sculptural quality and became part of the fabric of the room.

METAL SUPPORTS

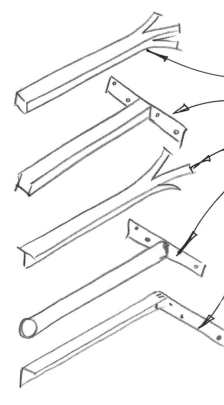

Various metal supports for shelves either grouted into a brick wall or screwed to the surface.

When you secure the metal supports to the wall, see that they are perfectly aligned to fit the shelf by tying them firmly to a pre-notched length of timber.

LONGITUDINAL SECTION

ply skin

metal support inserted into shelf frame

ALIGN YOUR SUPPORTS

metal support

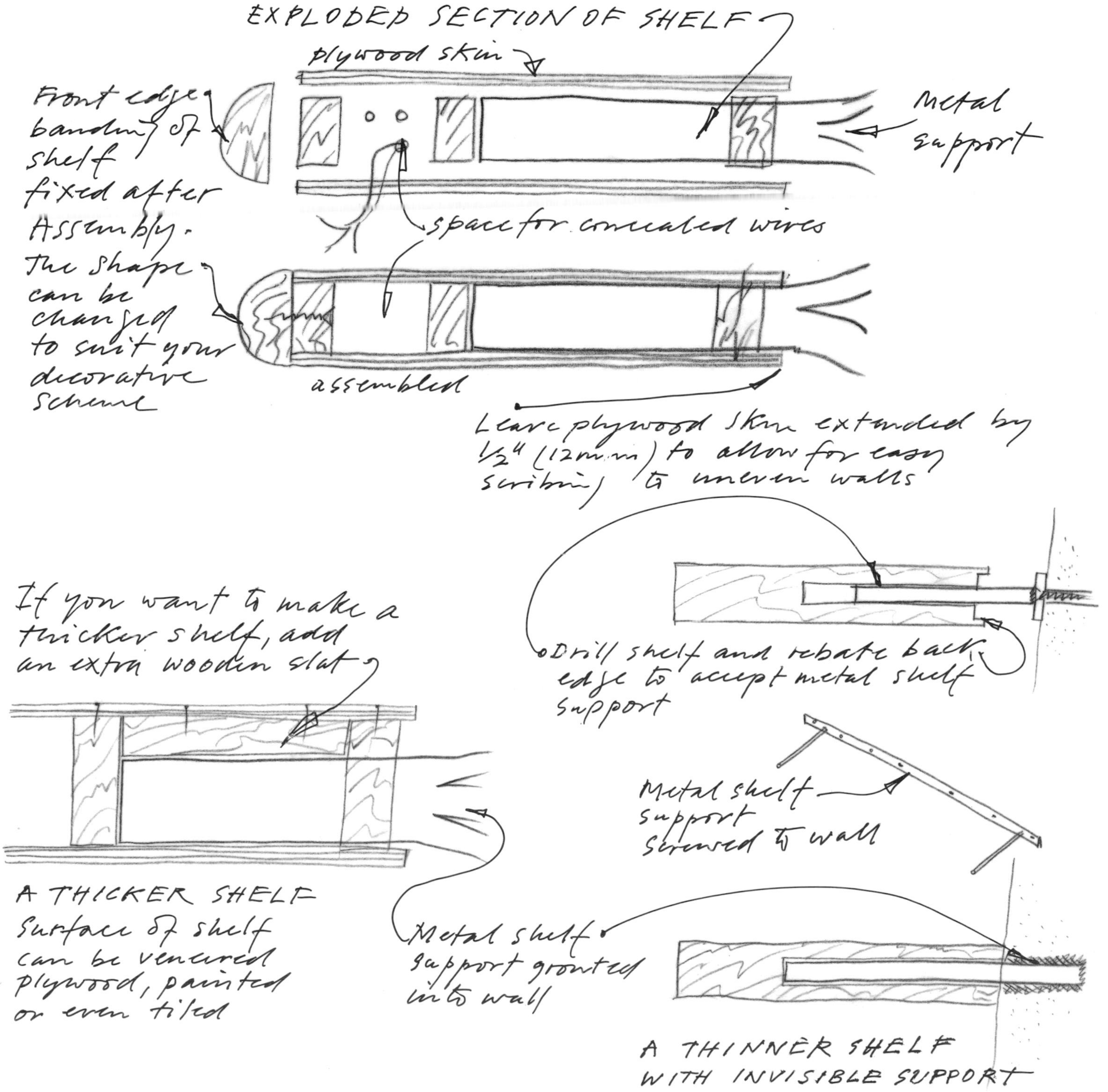

EXPLODED SECTION OF SHELF

plywood skin

Front edge banding of shelf fixed after Assembly. The shape can be changed to suit your decorative scheme

Metal support

space for concealed wires

assembled

Leave plywood skin extended by 1/2" (12mm) to allow for easy scribing to uneven walls

If you want to make a thicker shelf, add an extra wooden slat

Drill shelf and rebate back edge to accept metal shelf support

Metal shelf support screwed to wall

A THICKER SHELF
Surface of shelf can be veneered plywood, painted or even tiled

Metal shelf support grouted into wall

A THINNER SHELF WITH INVISIBLE SUPPORT

WALL OF DISPLAY SHELVING

This project features shelving without any visible means of support, giving clean lines without any ugly brackets. It is all done by making a hollow box-section shelf unit comprising top and bottom plywood-skin panels over a sturdy timber framework, creating the appearance of a thick, solid shelf. For added strength on long shelf runs, protruding steel rods are drilled into the rear wall. They slide into the box frame of the shelf. Battens-only fixing can be used for a run of shelving up to 2440mm (8ft) long and 450mm (18in) wide. It is important to note that steel rods should only be driven 75mm (3in) into walls, whether they are solid or hollow. For cavity walls, the rods should not bridge the cavity. If the walls are plasterboard or plywood, stud walls or lath and plaster, then the steel rods should be inserted directly into the main vertical timber studs within the wall.

CONSTRUCTION

Decide on the height of your shelves and, using a spirit level, mark their position on the wall; continue these lines on to the end walls. Measure up for length and the required depth and for each shelf cut two pieces of 9mm ($\frac{3}{8}$in) thick plywood, or 12mm ($\frac{1}{2}$in) MDF or chipboard. If the shelves are to be longer than 2440mm (8ft), you will have to butt-join the lengths. In this case there must be a batten positioned inside the shelving to support the cut ends.

From 50 × 25mm (2 × 1in) PAR battening, cut one piece to the length of the shelf for the front batten. Cut two end wall battens to the width of the shelf, less the thickness of the front batten. Cut two back battens to the length of the shelf less twice the thickness of the end battens so that they will fit between the latter. Cut further battens to the shelf width, less three

batten thicknesses, to fit between the front and back shelf battens at each end and at about 610mm (24in) intervals along its length.

Lay out all the pieces in place on the top skin of the shelf to make sure that they fit together.

Fix some scrap pieces of wood to the underside of the top skin panel for the steel rods to rest on. These pieces should be of a suitable thickness (about 19mm [$\frac{3}{4}$in]) to allow the rods to fit roughly midway in the edges of the back battens. Cut the pieces, if necessary, to fit in between the cross battens inside the shelf, and use wood adhesive to glue them to the top skin. They will need to be at intervals of about 610mm (24in) to coincide with the steel rod positions.

Draw a guide line the thickness of the scrap wood on to the back batten to help positioning when you are drilling steel rod back battens.

The rods should be spaced about

every 610mm (24in) roughly midway between the cross battens. They should run the width of the shelf from front to back, butting up against the inner side of the front batten and going into the wall about 75mm (3in), beyond the thickness of the plaster. Cut the required number of rods from 12mm ($\frac{1}{2}$in) steel rod.

Cramp the two back battens together, and using a drill bit which is slightly larger in diameter than the steel rod (a 13mm [approx. $\frac{1}{2}$in] drill bit and 12mm [$\frac{1}{2}$in] diameter steel rod), drill through the two battens together in the appropriate places. Use a pencil to number the battens.

Nail up the internal frame of the shelf, marking the side which is to be fixed to the upper skin. Spread glue on the top side of the frame and lay the top skin panel in place. Draw a line around the edges of the frame and the skin panel to mark a centre line of the inset battens to give you a

TOOLS

STEEL MEASURING TAPE

SPIRIT LEVEL

TRY SQUARE

PANEL SAW (or power circular saw or jigsaw)

SCREWDRIVER (cross-point or slotted, according to screws used)

HACKSAW

TWO G-CRAMPS

POWER DRILL or HAND BRACE

TWIST DRILL BIT, FLAT BIT or AUGER BIT

MASONRY DRILL BIT

HAMMER

NAIL PUNCH

SMOOTHING PLANE

POWER FINISHING SANDER (or hand-sanding block)

METAL FILE

MATERIALS

Part	Quantity	Material	Length
SHELF PANEL	2	9mm ($\frac{3}{8}$in) plywood or 12mm ($\frac{1}{2}$in) MDF or chipboard – width as required	As required
FRONT BATTEN	1	50 × 25mm (2 × 1in) PAR timber	As shelf length
END WALL BATTENS	2	50 × 25mm (2 × 1in) PAR timber	As width of shelf, less thickness of front batten
BACK BATTENS	2	50 × 25mm (2 × 1in) PAR timber	Length of shelf, less twice thickness of end battens
INTERMEDIATE BATTENS	As required to fit at 610mm (24in) intervals along shelf length	50 × 25mm (2 × 1in) PAR timber	Shelf width, less three batten thicknesses
ROD SUPPORT BLOCKS	As above	50 × 25mm (2 × 1in) approximately PAR timber	About 300mm (12in)
STEEL ROD SHELF SUPPORTS	One per 610mm (24in) length of shelf run	12mm ($\frac{1}{2}$in) diameter mild steel rod	Distance from inner side of front batten to back of shelf, plus plaster thickness, plus 75mm (3in)
SHELF FRONT EDGE (rounded)	1	75 × 50mm (3 × 2in) PAR timber	As shelf length

BASIC ASSEMBLY

BACK BATTEN (shelf)   BACK BATTEN (wall)

SHELF PANEL
(upper)

STEEL ROD

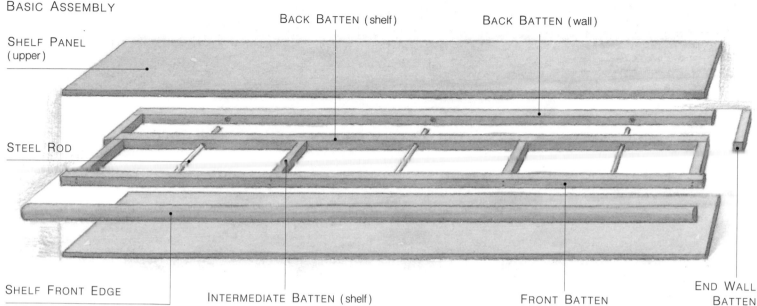

SHELF FRONT EDGE

INTERMEDIATE BATTEN (shelf)   FRONT BATTEN

END WALL
BATTEN

nailing line. Nail the skin in place, punch in nail heads and fill the indentations.

Repeat for the other skin panel.

To make a rounded edge at the front, cut a piece of 75 × 50mm (3 × 2in) timber to the length of the shelf. Glue and pin it (along the centre line) to the front edge and punch the nail heads well below the surface. Mark a half-round curve on the ends using a suitable plastic cup or carton. Continue rough guide lines on to the top face so that you can use a circular saw to take off the corner edges, before planing.

FIXING THE SHELF

Fix the rear-wall batten in place with screws and wallplugs. Then, using a 12mm ($\frac{1}{2}$in) masonry drill bit, drill through the pre-drilled holes in the wall batten, making the holes in the bricks or blocks about 75mm (3in) deep. Screw the end battens in place against the rear-wall batten.

Bevel both ends of the steel rods with a metal file, then push the rods into the holes in the wall. Slot the shelf on to the protruding rods and slide it over the end battens and on to the rear-wall batten.

❶ Stages in Assembling the Box-section Shelf Unit
Basic framework nailed up; holes for steel rods between battens.

❷ The rear-wall and side battens fit neatly into the recess created by insetting the side and back shelf battens. Holes for rods match up.

❸ The lower shelf panel is fixed and upper shelf panel exploded away to show how the softwood frame is neatly recessed.

❹ Front edge is fixed to front batten and rounded off. Through-section (5) shows steel rod resting between support blocks.

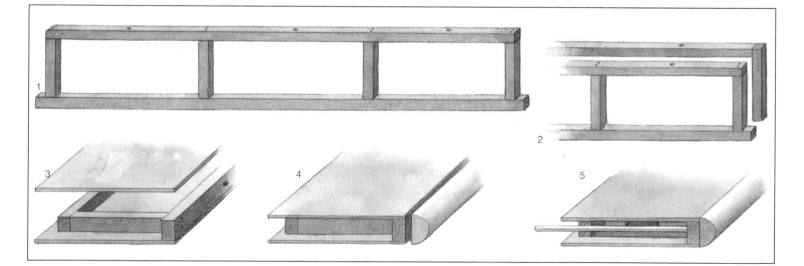

HOME OFFICE

Whether you need a place in which to do your household accounts and other domestic paperwork or whether you earn your living from home (a growing trend in this age of computerization), you will need a quiet, well-organized space that encourages you to get down to work. This design for a home office provides everything for the essential work area, although it cannot, unfortunately, guarantee the necessary peace and quiet.

I have used conventional steel filing cabinets as pedestals for the desk. The cabinets are well engineered to allow the heavy drawers to run smoothly and to lock securely. The wall unit is pigeon-holed with adjustable shelves on 'magic wires' so all your files, ledgers and office equipment can be neatly stacked away.

Because the unit is fixed away from the wall with bevelled battens, there is enough space behind it for wiring-in power points; these allow for the increasing amount of electronic equipment that modern life deems necessary.

It is important to have light on the worksurface: it allows you to see what you are doing and also acts as an invitation to industry and concentration. The light here is provided by a concealed tungsten strip across the full width of the worksurface, illuminating the pinboard and its memory-jogging messages.

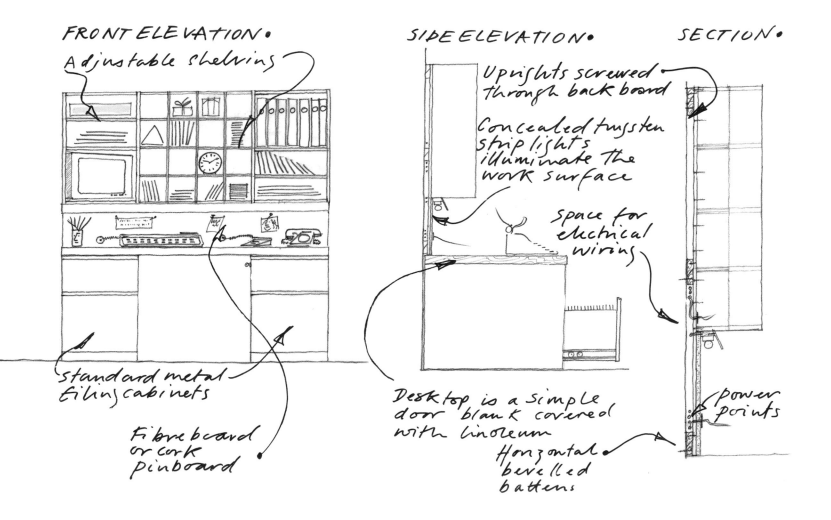

FRONT ELEVATION•
Adjustable shelving

standard metal filing cabinets

Fibreboard or cork pinboard

SIDE ELEVATION•
Uprights screwed through back board

Concealed tungsten strip lights illuminate the work surface

space for electrical wiring

Desktop is a simple door blank covered with linoleum

Horizontal bevelled battens

SECTION•

power points

HOME OFFICE

This project offers an easy way to create office space in the home. The desk could not be simpler – it is just a door blank laid across a couple of two-drawer filing cabinets. At the back of the desk a pinboard is fixed to the wall, and above it is a boxed unit of adjustable pigeon-hole shelves. These are very adaptable as they are supported by 'magic wires'. This means that their heights can be altered easily and sections can be removed or interchanged to accommodate office equipment, materials, books, and so on.

To give a good, general-purpose working light, strip lights are concealed behind a pelmet fixed to the bottom of the shelf unit. Electrical sockets and a telephone point can be installed in the pinboard section to allow a desk lamp, word processor or typewriter, telephone, and other equipment to be connected. Also incorporated in the design, are two conduit covers, drilled through the centre of the pinboard, to take cables serving the keyboard and printer through to the back of the unit where they will be hidden.

There is quite a bit of wiring behind this unit. Therefore, both the wall unit and the pinboard are mounted on bevelled battens, which not only give a strong fixing, but also form a gap for the wiring.

If you do not want to hide the wires behind the unit, and the backing wall is solid, with sound plaster, then you can mount the wall unit and the pinboard directly on the wall by screwing through the back panel into wallplugs. In this case, the screw-heads will show, so for neatness either fit screw cups under the screw-heads or alternatively fit screw covers over them.

The main benefit of this wall unit is that it can be attached to any wall to create an instant study or office, whether it be in the corner of a living room or in a spare bedroom.

TOOLS

STEEL MEASURING TAPE

STEEL RULE or STRAIGHT-EDGE

TRY SQUARE

ADHESIVE SPREADER

TRIMMING KNIFE

POWER CIRCULAR SAW (or power jigsaw)

DRILL (hand or power)

MASONRY DRILL BIT to suit size of wallplugs used

TWIST DRILL BIT for clearance holes

TWIST DRILL BIT for pilot holes and magic wire location

COUNTERSINK BIT

PADSAW (if jigsaw not available) for cutting recesses for electrical sockets

ROUTER and ROUTER BIT

SCREWDRIVER (cross-point or slotted, depending on screws used)

ORBITAL SANDER (or hand-sanding block)

PAINTBRUSH

MATERIALS

Part	Quantity	Material	Length
DESK UNIT			
BASES	2	Two-drawer filing cabinets	
DESK TOP	1	Plywood-faced interior door blank	As required
PINBOARD			
BACKING BOARD	1	12mm ($\frac{1}{2}$in) plywood or blockboard, 300mm (12in) wide	As desk top
FACING BOARD	1	12mm ($\frac{1}{2}$in) medium fibreboard, 300mm (12in) wide	As desk top
MOUNTING BATTENS	2	75 × 25mm (3 × 1in) PAR timber	As desk top
WALL UNIT			
BACK PANEL	1	12mm ($\frac{1}{2}$in) plywood or blockboard, 870mm (34$\frac{1}{2}$in) wide	As desk top
SIDE PANELS	2	19mm ($\frac{3}{4}$in) plywood or blockboard, 330mm (13in) wide	870mm (31$\frac{1}{2}$in)
MAIN DIVIDERS	2	19mm ($\frac{3}{4}$in) plywood or blockboard, 330mm (13in) wide*	Distance between top and bottom panels
TOP AND BOTTOM PANELS	2	19mm ($\frac{3}{4}$in) plywood or blockboard, 330mm (13in) wide*	Distance between side panels
MIDDLE DIVIDERS	3	12mm ($\frac{1}{2}$in) plywood, 330mm (13in) wide*	Distance between top and bottom panels
CENTRAL SHELVES	12	12mm ($\frac{1}{2}$in) plywood, 330mm (13in) wide	200mm (8in)
SIDE SHELVES	6	12mm ($\frac{1}{2}$in) plywood, 330mm (13in) wide	Distance between main divider and side
MOUNTING BATTENS	2	100 × 25mm (4 × 1in) PAR timber	As desk top
PELMET			
FRONT PANEL	1	12mm ($\frac{1}{2}$in) plywood, 75mm (3in) wide	As desk top
SIDE PANEL	2	12mm ($\frac{1}{2}$in) plywood, 75mm (3in) wide	150mm (6in)
CORNER BLOCK	2	25 × 25mm (1 × 1in) PAR timber	75mm (3in)

*Approximate lengths only – refer to copy for actual size

BASIC ASSEMBLY

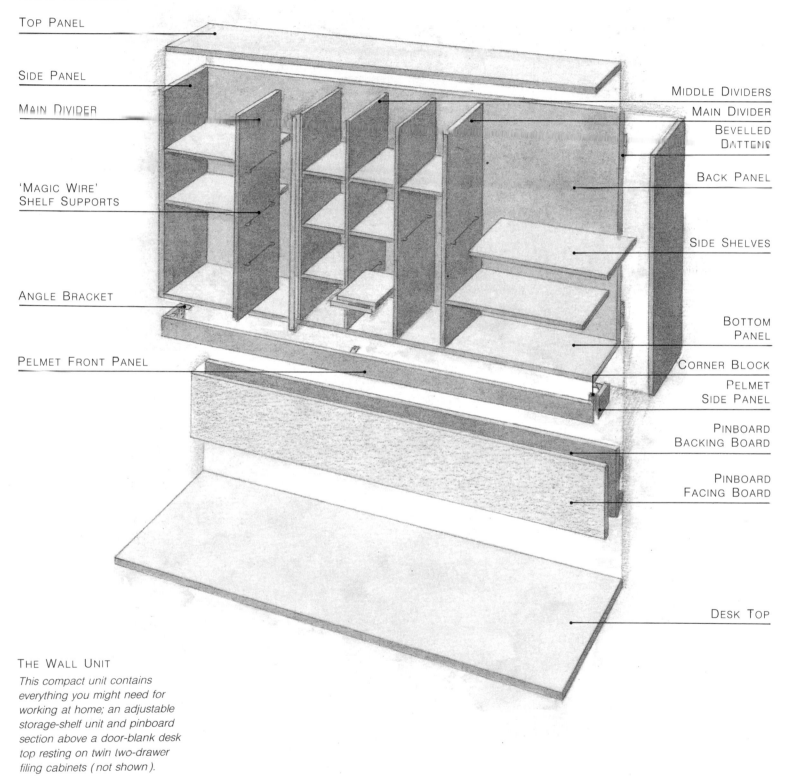

TOP PANEL

SIDE PANEL

MAIN DIVIDER

'MAGIC WIRE'
SHELF SUPPORTS

ANGLE BRACKET

PELMET FRONT PANEL

MIDDLE DIVIDERS

MAIN DIVIDER

BEVELLED
BATTENS

BACK PANEL

SIDE SHELVES

BOTTOM
PANEL

CORNER BLOCK

PELMET
SIDE PANEL

PINBOARD
BACKING BOARD

PINBOARD
FACING BOARD

DESK TOP

THE WALL UNIT

*This compact unit contains
everything you might need for
working at home; an adjustable
storage-shelf unit and pinboard
section above a door-blank desk
top resting on twin two-drawer
filing cabinets (not shown).*

HOME OFFICE: DESK AND WALL UNIT

DESK

Position the filing cabinets about a metre (3ft) apart. Place the desk top across them. This can be a plywood-faced interior flush-door blank, finished as required (*see* **Techniques, hanging doors, page 32**). We covered our door with a sheet of thick linoleum which makes a good writing surface. To stick it in place, use a contact adhesive applied to the upper surface of the door with a serrated spreader. Cut the linoleum slightly oversize, position it carefully, then weight it down overnight to allow the adhesive to harden. Finally, with a knife, trim off the surplus linoleum at a slight angle to leave a neatly bevelled edge.

PINBOARD

Cut the backing board for the pinboard from 12mm ($\frac{1}{2}$in) plywood or blockboard to the length of the desk top. Our board is 300mm (12in) high, but this measurement can be adjusted to suit your personal storage requirements.

Cut out the pinboard itself to the same size. We have used Sundeala medium fibreboard, but you can use any material that will take pins, such as cork or felt-covered fibreboard. In the latter case, the felt covers the board, front and sides, and is stapled or glued at the back.

Screw the pinboard to the backing board using countersunk-head screws fitted into screw cups for neatness. About four screws at both the top and bottom will be sufficient.

FIXING THE PINBOARD TO THE WALL

The pinboard on its backing board is mounted on two pairs of bevelled battens. Each pair of battens is made from 75 × 25mm (3 × 1in) PAR (planed all round) timber cut to the full length of the pinboard. Cut centrally through each length with a circular-saw blade set at 45° to make a pair of bevelled battens (*see* **Techniques, page 25**) or buy ready-made ones. Bevelled battens allow the pinboard to fit snugly against the wall but to leave enough space to conceal electrical wiring for lamps, a telephone and a word processor or typewriter which sit on top of the desk.

Place the pairs of bevelled battens on the back of the pinboard to position them and screw the upper ones, the correct way round, to the back of the pinboard.

To fix the pinboard to the wall, first rest it in place at the back of the desk top. This is important as the desk gives extra support for the things above. Hold the lower battens in place under the two fixed ones, and with a pencil mark their positions on the wall.

Take the pinboard away and, using wallplugs, screw the lower battens to the wall. Hang the pinboard on the battens, making sure that the two sets of battens interlock neatly.

WALL UNIT

The unit shown here is made from 12mm ($\frac{1}{2}$in) blockboard, with a lip applied to the front edge. Alternatively, used black-painted veneered chipboard, which is available lipped and ready to use or ordinary veneered chipboard, with either a wood or a plastic finish, left natural or painted black.

Using 12mm ($\frac{1}{2}$in) plywood, blockboard or veneered chipboard, cut out the back panel to the same length as the desk top and to the desired height; ours is 870mm (34$\frac{1}{2}$in) high, which allows for four shelves in the centre with a depth of 200mm (8in) each.

Using 18mm ($\frac{3}{4}$in) plywood or blockboard, cut out the side panels, the top and bottom panels and the two main dividers. The side panels should be the height of the back panel, the top and bottom panels fit between them, and the two main dividers fit between the top and the bottom panels. The depth of all these panels is as required – in our case it is 330mm (13in). Lip all the front edges of these panels with a hardwood moulding.

Lay the back panel on a flat surface, and place the top, bottom and side panels in their positions on top of it. Mark these positions on the front of the back panel.

1 **Securing the Pinboard**
Pinboard is medium fibreboard screwed to plywood or blockboard, and hooked over bevelled battens.

2 **Spacing Out the Middle and Main Vertical Dividers**
Put centremost divider in place, exactly in centre. Use two shelf panels to position next the dividers on each side of the central one. Position all of the dividers in this way.

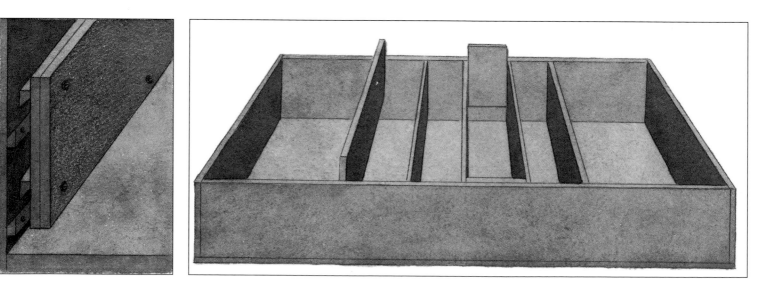

POSITIONING THE DIVIDERS

Your starting point for positioning the dividers will be the position of major items, such as a word processor, that need to be fitted in. Otherwise, you can start with the pigeon-hole section in the middle. This has been planned to provide up to 16 pigeon-holes 200mm (8in) square – four across by four high.

Cut three middle dividers to the same dimensions as the main dividers, but from 12mm ($\frac{1}{2}$in) plywood, blockboard or veneered chipboard. From the same material, cut 12 shelves, in our case measuring 330 × 200mm (13 × 8in). Lip the front edges of all the shelves and dividers with hardwood.

Put the central divider in place, exactly in the centre, and mark its position on the back panel. Use two of the shelves to position the next divider on either side of the central one. Then repeat the procedure to position the main dividers. When you have done this, the positions of all the dividers will be marked on the back panel.

SHELVES

Measure the space between the main divider and the side of the wall unit on each side. Using 12mm ($\frac{1}{2}$in) plywood, cut shelves to these dimensions and lip the front edges. You will need three shelves on each side of the main divider.

Position all the shelves with equal spacing between them. Even if some of the shelves are to be left out to accommodate tall books and office equipment, it is still worth making all the shelves and their fixings in case extra shelf space is needed later. When the shelves are correctly positioned, mark their positions on to the sides of the panels and then on to the dividers.

DRILLING THE BACK PANEL

Remove all the panels and shelves, and pilot-drill the back panel through from the front, along the centre of the lines marked for the top, bottom and side panels, and for all the dividers. Turn the panel over and countersink the holes from the back of the panel.

❸ Fixing the Dividers in the Wall Unit Framework
Mark the centre line of each divider to ensure accurate positioning. Drill, countersink and then screw the divider in place, fixing it securely through the top and bottom panels.

DETAIL OF HOME OFFICE

The pinboard includes a power socket and a metal disc to house electrical wiring for office equipment. The position of the pigeon-hole shelves can be adjusted to accommodate large items such as a word processor.

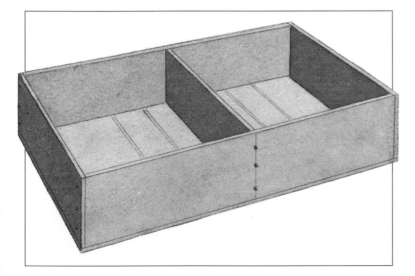

HOME OFFICE: WALL UNIT

DRILLING SIDE PANELS AND DIVIDERS

Allowing two per shelf, buy the required number of 'magic wire' supports of the appropriate length. Pre-drill the side panels and dividers to take the shelf supports. Positioning the drill on the *centre* of the lines marked for the shelves, use a 3mm ($\frac{1}{8}$in) twist drill bit to drill through the dividers, but drill only 9mm ($\frac{3}{8}$in) into the side panels. Make sure that the holes at the front of the unit are set back a little from the edge so that the front of the shelf will conceal the wires. The holes at the back are spaced according to the length of the 'magic wires'. This will allow the wires to be pushed fully into the holes.

ASSEMBLING THE OUTER FRAME

Fix one side panel by gluing and screwing it from the back.

Drill and countersink holes in the end of the side panel to fix one of the long panels (top or bottom). Glue and screw this panel in place. Pull the back panel over the edge of the workbench, then screw up from the back into the long panel. Repeat the procedure for the other side panel of the outer frame.

After gluing the ends and rear edge of the other long panel, fit it in position and screw through the side panels into the ends. Do not insert screws at the back until you have fitted the dividers, so that small adjustments can be made if necessary when the dividers are positioned.

FIXING THE DIVIDERS

Apply glue to the ends of the central divider and put it in place, checking with a try square that it is square to the frame and vertical. To ensure accurate positioning of the screws in the ends of the divider, draw a line from the centre line of the divider, over the front edges of the long panels, and then across them. Drill, countersink and screw the divider in place through the long panels. As one panel is not yet fixed, it is possible to make adjustments, if necessary, to ensure that the front edges are flush. Repeat the procedure with the other dividers, working from the centre outwards until they are complete.

Turn the unit over and, working from the back, screw the remaining long panel in place, and then all the dividers.

FITTING SHELVES

Position the 'magic wires' in the dividers. Using a router, make 3mm ($\frac{1}{8}$in) grooves 9mm ($\frac{3}{8}$in) deep in the edges of the shelves, so that the shelves will be able to be slotted over the 'magic wires'. Make sure that the grooves stop short of the front edges of the shelves, so that the grooves and the wire supports will not be seen from face on.

FINISHING OFF

Fill the screw holes, rub down the filler when dry, and apply your chosen finish (*see* **Techniques, page 20**). The finish should be selected so that it suits the style of the home office and blends in with decorative scheme you have planned for the room.

FIXING THE UNIT TO THE WALL

The unit is hung using two pairs of bevelled battens, in the same way as the pinboard, but with 100 × 25mm (4 × 1in) battens (*see* **Techniques, page 25**). Place the two pairs of battens on the back of the unit to position them, and fix the *top* battens to the back of the unit. It is important to ensure that the fixing screws go through into each upright panel and divider, to give sufficient strength to hold the unit.

To fix the unit to the wall, hold it in place on top of the pinboard and mark off the position of the lower battens on the wall, as for the pinboard. Take the unit away and screw the lower parts of the battens to the wall using wallplugs. Hang the unit in place, making sure that the battens interlock to give a snug and secure fixing.

PIGEON-HOLE SHELF UNIT

The shelves offer ample storage space and are secured firmly to the wall with bevelled battens.

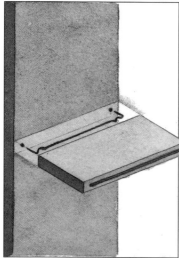

1 Hidden Shelf Fixing
'Magic wire' shelf supports 'plug' into holes drilled in wall unit dividers; shelf slots over wires.

PELMET

Using 12mm ($\frac{1}{2}$in) plywood or blockboard, cut out the pelmet front from a piece the length of the unit and about 75mm (3in) wide. Cut two side pieces to the same width and about 150mm (6in) long.

Mitre the front corners and fit a 25 × 25mm (1 × 1in) batten, cut to the depth of the pelmet, to the inside of each corner. Glue and screw it in place to the front and side pieces.

Fit the pelmet in place to the underside of the unit using steel angle brackets behind the pelmet – one at each end and one in the middle of the unit.

Fit lights behind the pelmet. We used four tungsten-tube strip lights. The wiring for the lights can be run down the space behind the units created by the bevel of the battens.

It is easy to cut recesses in the pinboard with a jigsaw or a padsaw to take electrical sockets and a telephone point. Conduit covers with the centres drilled out can be fitted to take the cables for office equipment and table lamps.

❷ The Pelmet Fixing Method
Pelmet panels are neatly mitred and screwed to corner blocks. Brackets fix pelmet to unit.

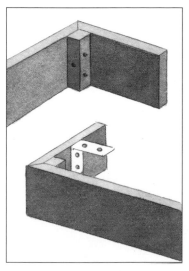

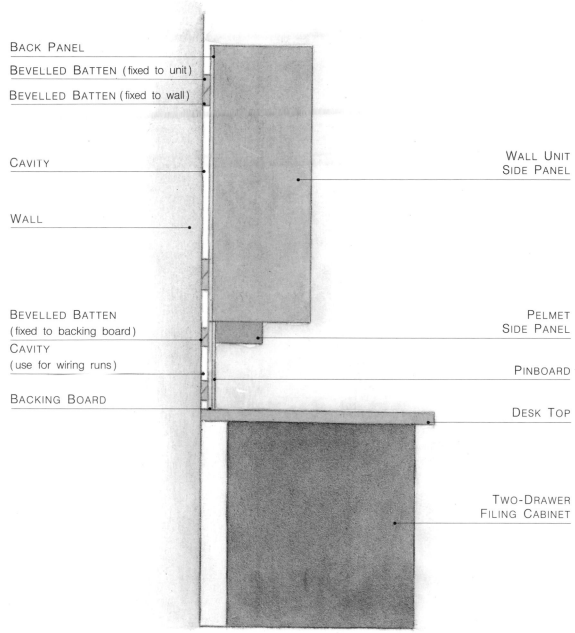

BACK PANEL

BEVELLED BATTEN (fixed to unit)

BEVELLED BATTEN (fixed to wall)

CAVITY

WALL

BEVELLED BATTEN
(fixed to backing board)

CAVITY
(use for wiring runs)

BACKING BOARD

WALL UNIT
SIDE PANEL

PELMET
SIDE PANEL

PINBOARD

DESK TOP

TWO-DRAWER
FILING CABINET

SIDE VIEW OF HOME
OFFICE

RADIATOR COVER

Radiators are often an eye-sore, particularly modern ones. This design offers a solution that screens a radiator from view but still allows a free passage of air and heat; it will look good in a modern or a traditional interior in any room in the house. The design is adaptable for any size of radiator. The front panel, which lifts off easily for maintenance or adjustment, can be made from vertical or horizontal timber slats. The wooden cover may be left as natural wood or finished in any colour or texture to fit in with your chosen decorative scheme.

If the radiator is a low one, then an excellent alternative design is to make the frame deep enough so that a cushion can be added on top, thereby transforming the radiator cover into a seat. This is particularly effective where your radiator is underneath a bay window.

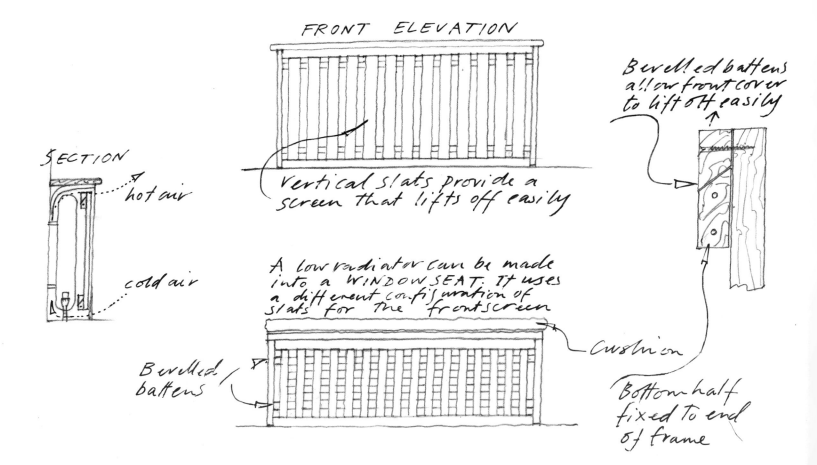

FRONT ELEVATION

Vertical slats provide a screen that lifts off easily

SECTION

hot air

cold air

Bevelled battens allow front cover to lift off easily

A low radiator can be made into a WINDOW SEAT. It uses a different configuration of slats for the front screen

Bevelled battens

cushion

Bottom half fixed to end of frame

RADIATOR COVER

The radiator cover can be adapted in size to suit any shape of radiator. With low radiators in an alcove or bay, the shelf and sides can be widened to form an attractive seat. In all cases the front panel is easily removable for decorating, bleeding air from the radiator, or adjusting the valves. Heat-reflecting foil should be fixed to the wall behind the radiator with double-sided adhesive tabs.

The advantage of a radiator cover is that it can hide an ugly feature of a room. Think about small children when building this project; if there are children in the home, make sure that the front panel of the radiator does not contain gaps that are wide enough for young arms and legs to get caught in.

MAKING THE FRAMEWORK

To calculate the overall dimensions of the cover, measure the width of the radiator to just beyond the valves and the height, allowing an extra 50mm (2in) clearance between the top of the radiator and the shelf. Mark these positions accurately on the wall with a pencil.

TOOLS

STEEL MEASURING TAPE
SPIRIT LEVEL
HEAT-RESISTANT ADHESIVE
SCRIBING GAUGE
PANEL SAW
CIRCULAR SAW
POWER DRILL and SUITABLE DRILL BITS
JIGSAW
SANDING BLOCK and ABRASIVE PAPER
SURFORM
SCREWDRIVERS

MATERIALS

Part	Quantity	Material	Length
SHELF	1	25mm (1in) chipboard or MDF	As required
SIDES	2	25mm (1in) chipboard or MDF	As required
BACK HORIZONTAL BATTEN	1	75 × 25mm (3 × 1in) softwood	Distance between side battens
BACK VERTICAL BATTENS	2	25 × 25mm (1 × 1in) softwood	As required
BEVELLED BATTENS	4	From 100 × 25mm (4 × 1in) softwood	Distance between side panels
WICKETS	As required	75 × 25mm (3 × 1in) softwood	As required
DOWELS	4	6mm ($\frac{1}{4}$mm) dowel	30mm ($1\frac{1}{4}$in)

The side panels should be cut so that they protrude by 50 to 75mm (2 to 3in) in front of the radiator. The top should overhang the sides lengthwise by about 50mm (2in) and protrude 25mm (1in) at the front. Use 25mm (1in) chipboard or MDF (Medium-density fibreboard) for the sides and the top.

FIXING THE SIDES

Cut two 25 × 25mm (1 × 1in) wooden battens to the same height as the sides. If there is a skirting board, the sides of the radiator can be scribed to fit neatly over the skirting, so that they blend in well with the walls (see **Techniques, page 31**). Similarly make sure that the battens are cut so that they stop above the skirting for a neat finish.

1 **Marking Top Shelf Batten**
Batten is centralized on underside edge of shelf panel, and fixing screw depth is marked.

2 **Counterboring Screw Hole**
Mark drill bit with tape to depth required and drill hole larger than screw head.

3 **Fixing Sides and Top**
Side panels are screwed and plugged to walls. Top shelf fixes to sides on dowels.

4 **Bevelled Battens**
Using 100 × 25mm (4 × 1in) timber cut to internal width, saw lengthways at 45° in ratio of $\frac{2}{3}$ to $\frac{1}{3}$.

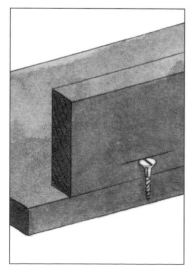

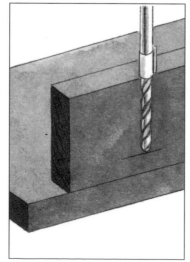

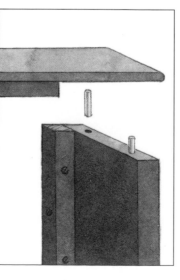

Sawing 21	**Bevelled battens 25**
Drilling 23	**Dowel joint 30**
Screwing 24	**Scribing long lengths 31**

BASIC ASSEMBLY

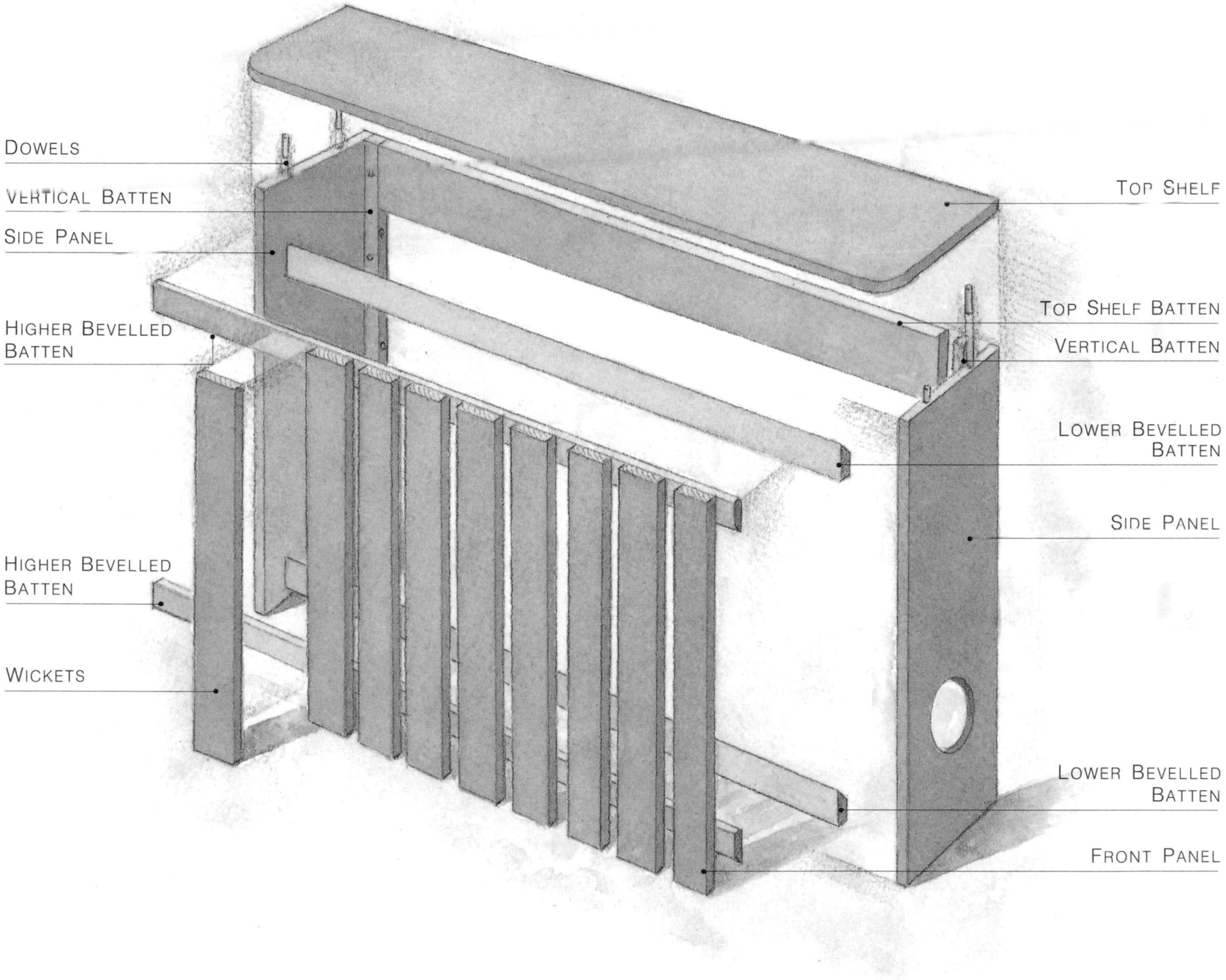

DOWELS
VERTICAL BATTEN
SIDE PANEL
HIGHER BEVELLED BATTEN
HIGHER BEVELLED BATTEN
WICKETS
TOP SHELF
TOP SHELF BATTEN
VERTICAL BATTEN
LOWER BEVELLED BATTEN
SIDE PANEL
LOWER BEVELLED BATTEN
FRONT PANEL

RADIATOR COVER

Drill and countersink the battens on two adjacent faces. Glue and screw them to the inside faces of the sides, flush with the back edges.

For easier access when adjusting the radiator valve, cut a 125mm (5in) diameter hole at a required place in the circle, then cut around it with a jigsaw (*see* **Techniques, cutting a circle, page 22**). Smooth the edges.

Fix the sides to the wall by screwing through the battens. Check that the sides are vertical.

MAKING THE TOP SHELF

To round off the corners, use a suitable object – a saucer, for example – to mark arcs on them. Cut away the waste with a jigsaw or coping saw. Finish with a sanding block. To finish the edges, round off and shape the corners with a plane or a Surform, and then sandpaper the edge of the shelf for a neat finish.

Alternatively, use a router with a 12mm ($\frac{1}{2}$in) rounding-over cutter attached to cut the top of the edge and then the bottom of it. Smooth by sanding down with a block and

sandpaper. You may prefer to leave the corners square and to glue a half-round moulding to the front of the radiator cover. In this case tape the moulding in place temporarily until the glue has set.

Cut a 75 × 25mm (3 × 1in) horizontal batten to fit between the vertical side battens. Lay the shelf upside down on the bench and place the horizontal batten on it so that its ends are equidistant from the ends of the top.

Offer up a screw to the side of the batten and the back edge of the top shelf, holding it so that the tip is about 6mm ($\frac{1}{4}$in) short of the top surface of the shelf. This is to ensure that the screw will not break through to the shelf's surface. Mark off the position of the screwhead on the batten (fig 1, page 168).

Find a drill bit slightly larger than the screwhead. Hold this against the batten with its tip against the position of the screwhead. Fix a piece of tape around the drill bit to indicate the depth to which you should drill. Drill downwards until the tape is at the top edge of the batten (see fig 2

on page 168). Glue and screw the batten using three equally spaced screws.

FIXING THE TOP SHELF

The shelf is dowelled to the sides using 30mm (1$\frac{1}{4}$in) dowels (fig 3, page 168). Drill two 6mm ($\frac{1}{4}$in) diameter holes in each top edge of the sides. The holes should be half the length of the dowels. Transfer the hole positions exactly to the underside of the shelf and again drill 6mm ($\frac{1}{4}$in) holes to half the dowel length.

Glue the dowels and the top edges of the sides and fix the shelf in position.

THE FRONT PANEL

Measure the width between the sides. Calculate how many 75 × 25mm (3 × 1in) equally spaced vertical wickets are required. The width of the spacing is optional, but it is very important that the spaces are not wide enough for children to get their hands, feet or head accidentally stuck between the front panel slats of the cover.

Measure for the height of the wickets, allowing for a 50mm (2in) gap at both top and bottom. Cut the wickets to this dimension.

Battens should be cut to the width between the side panels. Cut two from 100 × 25mm (4 × 1in) timber. To bevel them, use a circular saw set to 45°, cutting lengthwise through each batten to divide it into two portions, one twice the size of the other (fig 4, page 168). The wider portions will be fixed between the sides of the cover. The narrower portions will be fixed to the wickets.

FRONT PANEL ASSEMBLY

Lay out the wickets on the bench using a spacing batten between them (*see* **Techniques, page 20**). Lay the pairs of bevelled battens in place across the wickets so that they are flush with the top and bottom. Make sure that the battens are the right way round – that is, the narrower one is at the top in each case and lying at the correct angle (fig 1).

Remove the wider battens. Mark the top edge of the bevel round on to the back face (fig 2), so you will not screw over this line.

Screw the batten to the first wicket, using two screws at each end. Continue to screw down to the remaining wickets using the spacing batten for accurate distribution.

Mark·off on the wider battens where they are to be screwed to the side panels. Either measure down from the top or offer up the gate to its correct position.

Drill clearance holes through the sides, then countersink and screw the battens in place.

1 Assembling Wickets and Bevelled Battens of Front Panel
Use a spacing batten to place the wickets an equal distance apart with the same space at each end. The battens line up neatly with the top and bottom edges of the wickets.

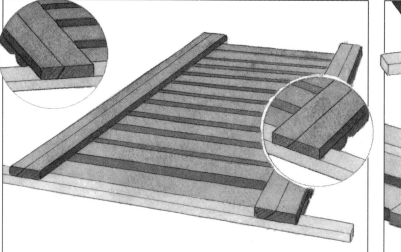

2 Fixing the Wickets
Screw top (narrow) batten to each wicket using two screws. Line on back of wicket is screw guide.

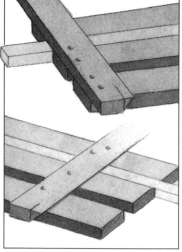

MERGING A RADIATOR COVER WITH ITS SURROUNDINGS

Cool, luxurious stone has been used wall-to-wall in this Mediterranean-style setting (left) to box-in and cleverly disguise a radiator cover. The result is a stylish low-level storage or seating area which enhances the painting on the wall above it.

INCORPORATING A RADIATOR IN A DIVIDING WALL

Here two radiators have been built-in to a wall of windows which divides a porch and a hall (below left). Building-in a radiator cover in this way complements the clean lines of the walls.

SMALL-SPACE LIVING

Many radiators are situated under windows (below centre). Here, where space is limited, a shelf has been added above the radiator cover for an extra storage and display area. The cover wickets echo the design of the wooden platforms that support the sofa beds.

HIGH CEILINGS AND TALL WINDOWS

This light and spacious living room (below right) contains two radiator covers which, with the addition of cushions, are adapted to form comfortable window seats.

WORKROOM IDEAS

ADJUSTABLE SHELVING

To be efficient when working at home you need to be well-organized and comfortable, and that requires careful planning. In both the examples shown here the pinboard, shelving and furniture harmonize well with the decorative treatment of walls and floor.

Adequate storage is essential – there is nothing more frustrating than being swamped by paper and unable to find anything. Drawer storage will probably be required and is ideally provided by a deep filing-cabinet-type drawer. You will also need cupboards and lots of shelves, as shown on the right. Here, a sturdy, adjustable shelf system has been combined with pinboards for messages and memos.

The shelves are ordinary 15mm ($\frac{5}{8}$in) melamine-faced chipboard on adjustable steel shelf supports spaced about 610mm (24in) apart to ensure that the shelves do not sag when heavily loaded.

At the bottom of the adjustable

tracks, wide shelf supports are fitted to carry a melamine-faced worktop which provides extra space for storage and working. This standard 600mm (23$\frac{1}{2}$in) wide and 30mm (1$\frac{1}{4}$in) thick worktop is lipped with hardwood and rests on 470mm (18$\frac{1}{2}$in) wide shelf supports to which it is screwed from the underside.

Pinboards are constructed from 9.5mm ($\frac{3}{8}$in) medium fibreboard panels cut to fit between the adjustable shelf uprights. The panels are covered in felt which is stapled into place at the back.

PLAN STORAGE

Another simple storage idea is shown in the photograph of the drawing office on the opposite page. Neat U-shaped brackets support half-round gutters which store plans and drawings.

Temporarily fix a vertical batten to the wall to align the brackets, and use a spirit level to mark horizontal lines for their heights. Space them all equally, marking screw holes on the wall. Drill and plug the wall, screwing the brackets in place.

1 **Marking Height of Shelving**
Cut uprights to equal length. Hold upright against the wall and mark the position of the base.

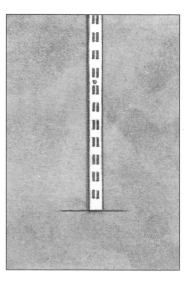

2 **Fixing Batten to Wall**
Temporarily nail a batten to the wall to align with marked line. Check that it is horizontal.

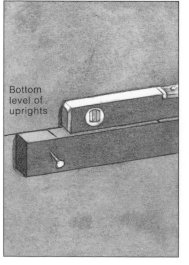

3 **Mark Screw Fixing Holes**
Rest upright on temporary batten, check it is vertical, then mark screw hole positions on wall.

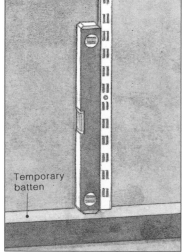

4 **Cut Pinboard to Shape**
Fit two uprights and double-check they are level. Measure between them; cut pinboard to fit.

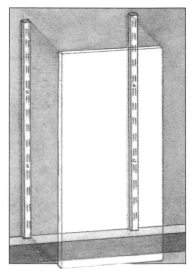

HOW TO FIX ADJUSTABLE SHELVING

When fixing the shelving to a solid wall, measure the wall and decide how many uprights are required. You will need one at each end and intermediate uprights spaced a maximum of 610mm (24in) apart.

Allowing for wider brackets to be fixed at the base of each upright to support the worktop adequately, decide how high you need the shelving supports and, using a hacksaw, cut all the uprights to this length at the same point between slots. Using a hacksaw, cut through at a solid part of the uprights between two pairs of slots.

Hold an upright against the wall at one side and decide at what height it should be. Mark the bottom of the upright on the wall and remove it. Use a straight batten and spirit level, or a chalked string line, to draw or snap a straight horizontal line on the wall at this height.

Tack a straight batten temporarily to the wall with the batten's top edge level with the marked line. Mark along the batten where the uprights will be fixed. Use a metal detector to check that there are no electric cables or water pipes in the wall at these points.

Rest one of the slotted uprights on the end batten and, while holding a spirit level against the upright to ensure that it is vertical, use a pencil to mark screw holes.

Drill the wall at the marked points, insert wallplugs, and screw the upright in place. Repeat for each of the other uprights. Make sure that the slots are in line with each other.

Measure the spaces between the uprights and cut the pinboard panels to fit. Cover them with felt and fit the panels by screwing them to the wall, using screwcups under the heads for neatness. For an invisible fixing, glue the panels in place with panel adhesive, use double-sided sticky pads, or hang them using keyhole plates fixed to the backs of the panels and hooked over woodscrews inserted in wallplugs.

Finally, slot the brackets into place, fit the shelves, and screw them to the brackets from the underside.

5 **Fitting the Pinboard Panels**
Fit pinboards by screwing through using screw cups or by hanging-on concealed keyhole plates.

6 **Fitting Bracket and Shelf**
Slot brackets into place and fix shelves to the brackets by screwing through from the underside.

7 **Fixing to Hollow Walls**
On hollow walls screw on three horizontal battens, fixing them through into the main wall studs.

8 **Fixing-up Plan Brackets**
Temporarily fix a vertical batten to the wall to align brackets. Drill, plug, and screw them to wall.

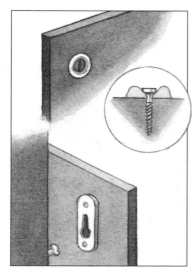

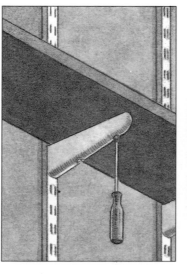

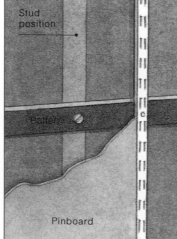

Stud position

Pattern

Pinboard

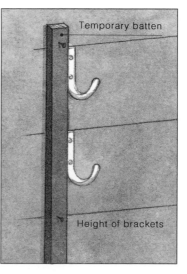

Temporary batten

Height of brackets

REPLACING SKIRTING

It is attention to detail that adds the finishing touch to a room. In this minimal hallway (left) the traditional handrail and balusters of a half-turn staircase have been boxed-in to give a clean, appealing line to this previously dominant feature. A staircase feature like this can be made simply by cladding a sawn timber frame with 12mm ($\frac{1}{2}$in) MDF. The technique is similar to that used for making the basic kitchen partition units *(see page 86)*.

The basis of the timber framework should be the newel posts. They are an integral part of the staircase construction and should be retained.

BUYING AND MAKING SKIRTING

In the examples shown here, the skirting boards provide elegant finishing touches.

The type of skirting shown may be available ready-made from a good timber merchant. The size normally available is 25 × 225mm (1 × 9in). Made from softwood, it can be stained with wood dye, if required.

If you cannot find a ready-made skirting, try a specialist timber supplier who may have a milling machine capable of producing the exact moulding you require.

There are two DIY ways to produce an elaborate moulding. The easiest is to build one up as shown in fig 2 by combining plain planks with suitable ready-made mouldings or bearings. This may not produce exactly what is required, but will provide an acceptable match.

For an exact match you need a router and one or two cutters from a specialist router bit manufacturer. First, draw the outline of the moulding on to lined tracing paper. If you are copying a moulding, a profile gauge makes this an easy task. By studying the outline you will be able to break it down into its various shapes, which you can match up to router bits from the range available. You can then build up the moulding by making several passes with the router, changing router bits and/or the angle of wood as necessary.

---

① Modernizing a Staircase by Boxing it in
A staircase can be boxed-in by means of MDF sheets simply nailed to a timber frame. The MDF panels will then appear to be an extension to the existing surrounding walls.

② Making Skirting
To match an existing skirting yourself, build one up with suitable planks and mouldings.

③ Fixing to Plastered Wall
Nail the skirting board to wood blocks and a batten which is screwed and plugged to the wall.

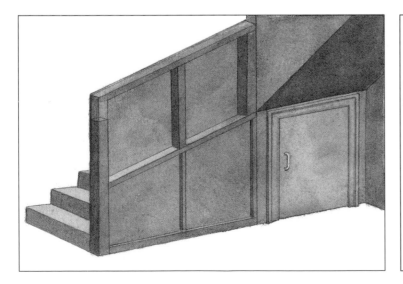

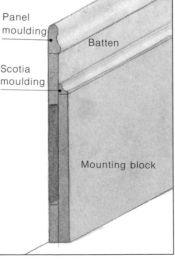

Panel moulding

Batten

Scotia moulding

Mounting block

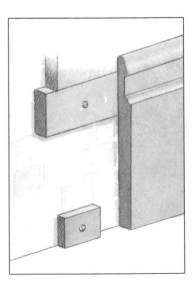

GLASS SHELVES

FITTING SKIRTING AND ARCHITRAVES

When fixing skirting boards to a firm, flat base of MDF, the moulding can be nailed in place using oval nails. Punch the nail heads below the surface and fill the indentations, rubbing down the filler before painting it over.

When fixing a skirting board to a plastered wall, nail it to wood blocks of the same thickness as the plaster layer. The blocks are screwed and plugged to the wall.

At external corners, the edges of the skirting should be mitred. At internal corners, one skirting board is cut square and is fixed into the corner. The end of the adjacent skirting is scribed to the profile of the first and simply butts against it.

Architraves, the mouldings around door frames, are mitred at 45° at the top corners, and at the bottom are cut square with the floor. They are held securely in place on the surface of the plaster around the door by nailing through them into the frame of the door.

④ Dealing with Corners
Skirting and architraves at external corners can be mitred. At internal corners butt-join and scribe them.

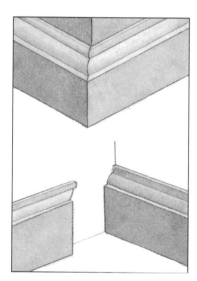

Glass shelves are excellent for display, but the glass must be sufficiently thick to take the load to be placed on it and the supports must be securely fixed.

Ideally, use toughened glass or laminated safety glass, although ordinary float glass can also be used. The important requirements are, firstly, that the glass is thick enough for its intended purpose and, secondly, that shelf supports are spaced with this in mind. Ask your glass merchant's advice.

The minimum thickness of glass that can be used for shelving is 6mm ($\frac{1}{4}$in). This is suitable for light loads only and brackets should be spaced no further than 400mm (16in) apart. For normal loading, increase the thickness of the glass to 9mm ($\frac{3}{8}$in) and space the brackets up to 700mm (27$\frac{1}{2}$in) apart. If the shelves are likely to be heavily loaded – with books, for example – use 9mm ($\frac{3}{8}$in) glass, but reduce the bracket spacing to a maximum of 500mm (19$\frac{1}{2}$in). For safety, ask the supplier to polish the edges of the glass.

In the photograph here, the glass shelves rest on shelf-support brackets fixed to the side walls of an alcove. There is a wide range available of these neat brackets in metal and plastic. Sometimes the brackets simply screw to the sides of the alcove, but more commonly the brackets are pushed into pre-drilled holes, allowing the position of the shelves to be altered if a series of holes is drilled. Another way of installing adjustable glass shelves is to fit an adjustable shelving system for which special glass-shelf holding brackets or adaptors are available.

For an 'invisible' method of fixing, there are cantilever supports, where a narrow bracket that extends to the full width of the shelf is fixed to the rear wall, and the glass shelf is slotted into the bracket.

For bathrooms, there is a wide range of glass shelf-support brackets, usually with a chrome finish.

⑤ A Selection of Supports
A selection of support brackets for glass shelves: fixed and adjustable bracket types are available.

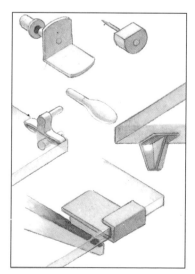

⑥ Invisible Cantilever Glass Shelf Support
For an 'invisible' fixing a cantilever bracket is fixed to the rear wall.

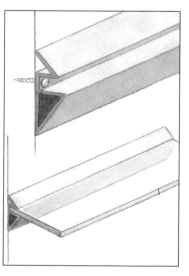

PART 4

BATHROOMS AND BEDROOMS

The bathroom is not a simple room to renovate, restore or redecorate. Often, a new bathroom seems to be an expensive luxury when compared with other home improvements which seem more urgent. Besides, any undertaking in the bathroom can turn into a major task if new plumbing is involved. However, as the hand-built bathroom and other projects featured later in this chapter show, DIY in the bathroom can be as easy and satisfying to carry out as in any other room. Leaving the bath, basin, shower and lavatory in place, you can completely transform your bathroom by tiling walls, by laying a new floor and by adding shelves and cabinets, towel rails and mirrors to existing decorative schemes.

In the bedroom, DIY gives you the opportunity to create clothes storage to match your exact requirements. You can make the room more comfortable and practical by producing your own built-in wardrobes, constructing a bed or even creating a work area. By using a folding screen, a spare room that is used as a study or for storage can be quickly and efficiently modified to be a guest bedroom.

People are often put off doing DIY in the bathroom because they feel that it inevitably involves complex plumbing tasks. However, there is an enormous amount that can be done which is simple and effective. With today's easy-to-use, flexible plumbing and piping accessories, much plumbing can be undertaken by the amateur. But always check that it is legal for you to tamper with plumbing and that you are insured for resulting leaks and damage. Never undertake this kind of work unless you are fully confident of your ability.

Also, before you plan your new bathroom, or revamp an existing one, make sure that you plan the workload carefully in advance. Moving bathroom fittings is not always possible given existing water pipes, and moving the main drain which serves the lavatory can be particularly difficult. There are always important legal restrictions on this for obvious reasons. Remember too that wiring must comply with the regulations and that only pull-cord switches and approved shaver sockets can be placed in the bathroom. Overflows and drainage in floors are also important, given the likelihood of water spillage on the occasions when taps are accidentally left to run, or when baths or showers overflow.

Below the Surface

A false wall hides plumbing and wiring, and provides an alcove for recessing a radiator (previous page). Getting the 'workings' of the bathroom out of the way so that the surface materials are uninterrupted is the most important aspect of a successful bathroom. Here the material is magnificent marble used in the form of slips (solid marble tiles) which cover almost every surface including the floor.

In a small house or apartment where space is limited, the bathroom is often the ideal place to plumb-in a washing machine; again, there may be restrictions on this, so make sure you are within the law and the safety regulations and get some expert advice before you start.

Using wooden stud partitions, or brick or breeze-block surrounds, it is not difficult to build your own housings for baths and basins, perhaps incorporating storage space and a vanity unit. Finishing can be with tiles, wood panelling, marble slips or laminates. A fitted cupboard, perhaps a variation on your bedroom clothes storage, can be installed for storing towels,

household linen, and bulk purchases of toilet rolls, as well as soaps and lotions.

It is a good idea to make a feature of interesting jars and bottles, bowls of small soaps, shaving equipment, and other bathroom accessories. They are often appealing enough to display on open shelves. Fitting mirrors, towel rails, new taps and other features can enhance the style as well as the practicality of your bathroom. By changing these small features, it is sometimes possible to transform the look of a bathroom economically and without a complete reworking of the plumbing system, so think carefully about what kind of DIY is necessary.

MIRRORS AND TILES

A sophisticated white bathroom is apparent simplicity itself (opposite) with its perfect grid of tiles. The floor to ceiling mirror gives a sense of space and reflects light. Chrome taps and shower fittings together with a long chrome rail for towels, unify the decorative scheme.

A DIY bathroom (above), finished with ceramic tiles and a white linoleum floor, has mirror on two facing walls to add light and space, with glass shelves neatly fitted into a recess. Brightly coloured accessories lend a cheerful air.

LIGHTING AND HEATING

Safety first is essential when considering how to heat, ventilate and light your bathroom. Any electrical installation in a bathroom should be carried out by a qualified electrician and checked by the electricity board before use.

Lighting a bathroom is a challenge but with the range of fixtures and types of bulbs available today, you can achieve excellent results. If your bathroom has no window, invest in good lighting to compensate for the lack of natural light.

Avoid fluorescent strips. The effect this light gives is too dull and even, and does nothing to flatter either the attractive surfaces in a bathroom, or the person using it. An overhead, central pendant is rarely necessary or useful in a bathroom and once again will limit the attractiveness of the whole room. Consider the many other possibilities. Hidden strips of tungsten can give a warm glow to an alcove or a shelving system. Tungsten strips or bulbs can also be used around a mirror for a Hollywood effect. Low-voltage fittings with tungsten halogen bulbs will make your bathroom sparkle – especially if it is modern and features chrome and ceramics. Remember to incorporate lights so that they reflect off mirrors but do not produce glare.

If your bathroom is to be styled as a comfortable and relaxing room, perhaps with easy chairs, warm natural woods and softer decoration, then the lighting should enhance this. You cannot install side lamps or pretty wall lights, but ensure that what lighting you do incorporate is easily adjusted with dimmer switches (placed outside the bathroom) and is subtle, rather than glaring, light. Candles can be used if you really want to indulge yourself in romantic lighting.

You may want to read while soaking in the bath, so ensure that a light is suitably placed to make this possible, and that you have incorporated space to place your book out of water's reach while you are washing yourself.

Showers can present lighting problems. Closing the shower curtain could make it very dark. Avoid this by strategically placing light fittings or consider fitting an outdoor bulkhead in the shower. It is essential to plan your lighting before you undertake any tiling.

Daylight is always an added pleasure in a bathroom. Blinds can lend privacy to the room; if you are not overlooked, the window can easily remain undressed. A skylight will be very pleasing in a bathroom and is often a good addition if the room is without a window.

Undue condensation in a bathroom is unpleasant and can damage the decoration or fabric of the room. Both heating and ventilation are important if condensation is to be avoided. It is usually illegal to have an internal bathroom without a window, unless you have adequate air extraction and circulation; this should remain switched on for a certain time whenever the room is used. Seek professional advice on this.

The heating will depend upon the system in your house or apartment but try to incorporate heated towel rails. Radiators are now available which are shaped as towel rails and are specially designed for bathrooms; alternatively, you can install electrically heated rails with a safe bathroom switch.

WARM ILLUMINATION

Reflected in a wall of mirror above the bath in this warm and elegant bathroom (opposite above) is a false wall which hides pipes and wiring. It also provides a recess into which a basin, mirror and shelf as well as a discreet cupboard have been fitted. Tungsten strip lighting has been incorporated into the wood cornice of the room, providing a general soft illumination. The radiator is stylish and contemporary, and fits neatly beneath the window. Wooden blinds and a chrome bar stretching the width of the room for hanging towels, are excellent accessories.

STRONG ACCESSORIES

In a small bathroom (opposite below left) a grid provides a durable radiator cover to keep it flush with the line of the wall.

A heavy-duty, waterproof, industrial-type light fixture hangs above a basin (opposite below centre) to great effect. Its grid design is reflected in the vertical radiator which heats the room.

Another method of waterproof lighting is to install bulk-head outdoor lights in the bathroom, shown here (opposite below right) giving strong, concentrated light above a basin.

Bathroom Materials

The bathroom should be, of necessity, a room of resistant, durable surfaces. Marble, mirror, slate, laminate, chrome, plastic, vitreous china, treated wood and water-resistant paint are the tough, elegant materials that bathrooms are made of. Softness can be provided by towels, bathrobes, comfortable easy chairs, cotton shower curtains and bath mats.

You can soften a bathroom considerably with accessories, or turn it into a stark interior – the level of sleek functionalism is up to you. For example, if you decide to tile the room, the type of tiles you choose can have dramatically different effects. Brick-shaped tiles in white ceramic with a border of a contrasting dark colour produce an old-fashioned and traditional appeal. Expensive marble slips are a pure luxury; decorated tiles will have their own impact, while plain white squares will provide a simple harmony.

The materials you choose will depend largely on your budget. Marble or granite is not easily affordable or simple to install without professional help. Tiles are also a relatively expensive way to decorate large areas, although not difficult to apply if a wall surface is flat. Wooden panelling can be highly effective and tiles should be used for areas where water will often be splashed, and other wall surfaces can be painted with water-resistant paint.

Floor coverings must be practical, resilient and preferably water resistant. The drawback to using ceramic or marble tiles, or other hard surfaces for flooring is that they are cold; whereas sealed cork and cushioned vinyl provide warmth. Carpet is best avoided, but rugs, especially if made from washable cotton, are a good alternative. Any bathroom floor should be able to withstand damp; vinyl tiles and wood block will rise easily if water penetrates the surface so consider carefully your choice of flooring.

Mixing Materials

Small white tiles, a clear plastic shower curtain and a pretty porthole window (above) create a bright, airy bathroom in a small space.

Exposed brick forms a partition wall between bedroom and bathroom (centre). The strong texture of the brick is offset against the clean and smooth white tiles.

Glass bricks are an excellent choice for a bathroom (below) as they are easily wiped clean and allow light to shine through them. Here they have been effectively combined with a steel sink with exposed pipes and a dramatic black Venetian blind.

Decorative Finishes

A showerhead has been recessed into marble slips above a bath (opposite left) and a deep alcove allows for generous shelves. The elements of the bathroom are unified by the pale grey marble to stylish effect.

Black and white tiles form a decorative chequerboard frieze (opposite right above) in this lively bathroom. The black slats on the white blinds continue the duotone theme. Other strong features include the chrome supports for the double basins and the 'dressing-room' lights around the mirror.

Unusual finishes give this bathroom originality (opposite right centre). The basin unit is in wood stained black and is topped with marble-chip terrazzo to produce a dramatic and luxurious effect.

The rolled top of an old-fashioned bath tub (opposite right below) and the traditional contrasting strip of tiles at picture rail height set the scene for a bathroom styled in the past. A basin has been set into an old wood cabinet and the mirror has a wooden frame.

BATHS AND SHOWERS

Deciding upon the type of bath or the brand of shower unit to use is perhaps the most daunting aspect of planning a bathroom, since there is such a wide range available nowadays. Your own DIY skill lies in placing the bath and shower in an attractive, practical and water-tight unit.

A bath is best placed in a niche or alcove and if one is not ready-made in the room, you can create one with a hand-built partition made from wooden panelling, brick or breeze blocks, or, alternatively, glass bricks. A separate shower unit can be placed against this panel. The whole area is finished in the same material for unity.

Shower units can be placed above a bath if space is limited, and a screen or curtain hung around the bath to avoid water spillage and provide privacy. Consider using a cotton curtain, if it can drip dry, as an alternative to plastic. A glass screen is also an attractive option and can be hinged so that it is turned away when not in use.

Ready-made shower units that come as a separate shell to fit into your bathroom can be effective but will not harmonize nearly as well as a unit built yourself. The shower head, tap and water temperature gauge should be all that protrudes from the wall but make sure you have access to the mechanism and pipework if necessary, in case of problems. Using a stud partition makes this a lot simpler. Similarly, with a casing for the bath, make sure you can gain easy access to the area behind and beneath the taps.

You can give the effect of a sunken bath in a reasonable-sized bathroom by building a generous frame around the bath in wood, which is then tiled.

When building a partition for a bath, consider including a small alcove or niche in the wall as a decorative feature, and remember that you can vary the width of the shelf surrounding the bath.

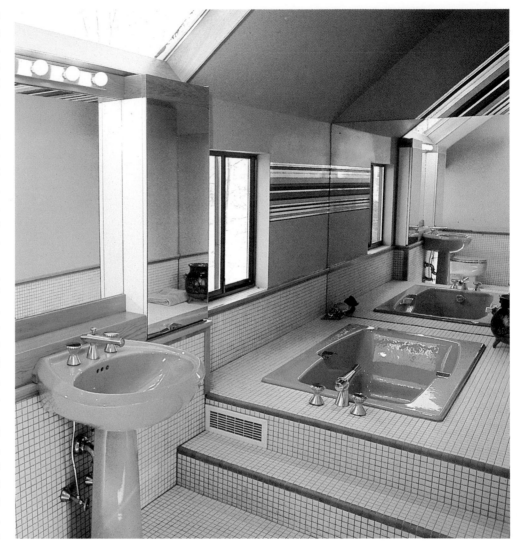

LOW-LEVEL TILING

A false step raised above the floor creates the impression of a sunken bath (above). The luxury of this is heightened by the use of soft grey mosaic tiles, an edging of beech wood, and a wall of mirror. Heating is situated below the raised step and escapes through a vent.

TWO-TONE CHEQUERBOARD

The most effective shower unit is built-in to a bathroom (opposite) with a raised shower tray and is part of the overall design rather than an added extra. Link all elements with the facing material – here a dramatic use of black and white tiles produces a pleasing effect.

BASINS AND VANITY UNITS

There are two basic alternatives for basins: freestanding designs, often on a pedestal; or basins fitted into a framework, commonly known as a vanity unit. What you build around your basin will to some extent depend upon this choice.

A vanity unit can be a very simple but highly effective DIY project. It consists of a broad shelf or top into which is set a basin; the unit is supported by open shelves or cupboards. By building it yourself you can ensure that the unit fits the dimensions of your bathroom precisely, is integrated into the decorative scheme, and contains storage space according to your needs.

If you are reconstructing or building a completely new bathroom, then your decision on how to construct the vanity unit will be decided as part of the overall bathroom design. Vanity units can, of course, also be installed as part of a revamp of an existing bathroom.

The frame, in wood or brick, can be tiled or painted, with melamine-laminate shelves underneath, and doors placed over them if required. Any material that is hard and waterproof – such as solid marble, melamine, ceramic tiles, or natural but treated wood – can be used for the top surface of the unit.

Another example of a false wall creating an attractive recess for a basin (above) beautifully finished in sleek, cool terrazzo tiles.

An interesting idea for double basins in a spacious bathroom (below left) has them either side of a central column faced in mirror.

A 30s-style bathroom (below right) with traditional decorative elements has a vanity unit with a marble top and an elegant mirror.

You can embellish both fitted and freestanding basins with all manner of bathroom accessories. A vast range of ready-made accessories is available – shelves, toothbrush mugs and holders, mirrors and cabinets – which can coordinate with toilet-paper holders, towel rails, soap dishes and clothes hooks. Alternatively, you can combine hand-made shelves and accessories with bought items. For an original approach, especially in a period house, you could fit antique or second-hand pieces such as a hanging shelf unit with fitted mirrors from the Victorian era, a mirror with an attractive frame, or old shop fittings could serve as wall cupboards.

Make sure that you have ample room over the basin to bend over and wash your hair without banging your head or splashing water around. A basin that is too small is often a major problem in a bathroom. You could consider using an old-fashioned kitchen stone sink if you want a more generous basin.

Changing or installing new taps has a dramatic effect in the bathroom. For the hand basin it is far more practical to fit a mixer tap which combines hot and cold water so that you can rinse your hands comfortably and quickly.

This stylish modern bathroom takes the design for its vanity unit from a fitted kitchen (above). A white melamine top has an inset basin with a range of drawers and cupboards below.

A stone 'Butler' sink, usually the preserve of the country kitchen, has here been incorporated into a bathroom (below left). The unit which surrounds it has deep open shelves for towels and forms a screen to hide the lavatory.

In a tiny cloakroom (below right), the black rim of the small sink is continued in the window-sills. A curved, laminate front hides plumbing.

BATHROOM STORAGE

What you keep in the bathroom apart from essential items depends upon the size of the room. A large bathroom can accommodate a spacious cupboard, which you can build yourself, for storing linen, towels, bulk supplies of toilet paper and anything else you want out of the way. A tiny bathroom should be more minimal with only fittings and essential toiletries in evidence. Towels and bulk supplies can be stored elsewhere.

Closed cupboards and open shelves are the ideal combination for bathroom storage. Open shelves can carry jars, flowers, towels and other objects, but remember that whatever you display in a bathroom has to be regularly washed and dusted. It is easy to be seduced into displaying rows of jars, soaps, pretty bottles and lotions as seen in endless magazine articles, but sometimes a relatively bare bathroom can be more practical. The area above the basin and the shelf around the bath is the favourite place for such displays. When planning yours, take into account which items you need to hand and which would look better behind closed doors; build your units accordingly.

On open shelves, store items neatly in containers. Large wicker baskets can add an attractive and softening dimension to a white-tiled bathroom.

Shelves can be tiled if they are built as chunky hollow constructions rather than made of single planks of wood. Glass shelves are always well-suited to bathrooms. You can create a unit incorporating glass shelves in the design so that they rest within a frame of wood. Cabinets are also reasonably easy to construct and can have mirrored or painted doors.

Design the whole area above the basin with care, taking into account the amount of display space you want and how much hidden storage you need there. If you have children, you should store razors and medicines in a lockable cabinet, that is out of reach of tiny hands.

A built-in cupboard can be extremely useful. In a limited space, cupboards can be fitted as part of a vanity unit, but in a larger bathroom design a cupboard to fill an entire wall. Doors can be made of wooden louvre slats or painted MDF and laminated or glazed. Either of the cupboard designs in the bedrooms section (see photographs on pages 214 and 232) can be adapted for the bathroom.

If kitchen space is limited, washing machines and dryers can be housed behind cupboard fronts, but ensure that the doors are ventilated and that the machines can be easily reached for maintenance. In some cases, however, it is illegal to install washing machines in the bathroom, so make sure you are within the law.

The cistern and the area of waste pipes behind a lavatory can be concealed behind a wooden housing which will also provide a useful shelf along the top. If you have a bidet, this can be fitted in a similar way for a neat appearance. Whenever you box-in pipes, always consider turning the wooden box itself into something useful, such as a shelf or even a seat.

If you are building your own bath surround, consider incorporating a hinged shelf if there is room at the end of the bath, so that the otherwise dead space beneath can be used for storage.

Soiled clothes and linen are often kept in an overflowing and rather untidy basket or plastic container which does nothing to enhance a bathroom. If you are creating your own bathroom, consider building in a box for dirty linen. In an existing bathroom, one could be incorporated into a cupboard. A broad shelf could have a boxed-in support and be hinged along its length, or in part, to act as a lid; in addition, you could turn the lid into a seat with a loose cushion.

BATHROOM STORAGE

This vanity unit is designed for storage (top) with its practical drawers and cupboards.

In a high but narrow Edwardian bathroom (above) the dead space near the ceiling has been used for pine storage cupboards, housed in a false wall.

A glossy stylized bathroom (opposite) has ceramic-tiled, steel-faced partitions to hold glass shelves. Further storage is provided on metal trolleys which are pushed in to the recesses when not in constant use.

Given adequate space, the bathroom is an excellent location for a spacious, fully fitted cupboard when you require extra storage. This elegant fitted unit (top) is given a graphic and stylish black trim.

The area around the basin is easily utilized for extra storage (above). Here the cupboards are situated above and below the basin to hide all bathroom clutter.

BEDROOM POTENTIAL

The bedroom is a private haven for relaxation and sleep and it is here that you can concentrate on building projects which will heighten your enjoyment of the room and enhance it.

There are still many practical considerations to think about before starting work: clothes storage, lighting, and comfort are all important factors – but what you put in your bedroom, and the style you create there, is completely up to you. There is enormous potential here and DIY can make all the difference between an untidy, uncomfortable and unrelaxing room and a well-appointed, stylish and appealing one.

Wardrobes are an obvious project to undertake, since good fitted storage will add enormously to the tidiness and convenience of the room and increase the value of your home. They can also vastly improve its appearance. By designing and building them yourself you can ensure that they fit the dimensions of the room precisely and are in keeping with its decorative scheme and architectural detailing.

Window seats are a delightful addition if you want somewhere to read and relax, have a room with a view and need some extra storage, since the area below the seat provides space for bedding, linen and additional clothes.

Of course, you can also build a bed. There is a spectacular bed project with built-in spacious storage later in this chapter, but a simpler model could be created instead. A base for a mattress is all you need. It could be at a high level in order to make the best use of limited space. Below it you can create a storage area, a desk or a second bunk bed. The possibilities are numerous.

You can embellish a hand-made or shop-bought bed in many ways. Add a headboard as something to rest against, as a decorative feature and as protection for the wall behind. A simple frame with four posts, one at each corner of the bed, connected at the top, will transform any simple divan into a magnificent and luxurious four poster.

The materials you use in the bedroom are not going to have to endure too much wear and tear, so it is here that you can splash out on more luxurious materials; they will not need to be replaced as often as those used elsewhere. Expensive wood or painted cheaper wood is always effective. In small spaces, mirror can be used for door fronts and in recesses for forming a dressing-table area.

SEATING SOLUTIONS

The broad sweep of a bay window (opposite above) has been turned into a sunny place to sit with an easily-constructed wooden window seat. Low level radiators fit below the centre seat. In a smaller bedroom (opposite below right) a padded window seat has filled the gentle curve of a bay window.

In the narrow corner of a bedroom (below centre), a television has been placed on an angled bracket above a built-in storage box. Plump cushions on top turn it into a seat.

INSPIRING IDEAS

Romantic muslin drapes (below left) are hung above a bed from wooden poles bound together and suspended from the ceiling by chains.

A flat-fronted, wall-to-wall fitted wardrobe has been given glamorous mirror doors (below right). The wall of glass reflects and doubles any light source in the room, adds depth and space, and is stunning in a room which is dedicated as much to dressing as to sleeping.

Dramatic decorative detailing has been added to a bedroom (opposite below left) by uplights placed on columns. These highlight a curved architrave which frames a door. On either side are fitted cupboards.

Providing practical bedside shelves, a unit in mellow wood (opposite below centre) has been built at the head of a bed, situated beneath an attractive sloping window. The wide shelf which sits on top of the unit offers display space and the lower shelves can carry books, radio, lights and other essentials.

BEDROOM STORAGE

Clothes are the major items for storage in bedrooms. You may also want rows of bookshelves, a linen chest, a vanity unit for make-up and toiletries, a display area for a treasured collection, or a corner fitted as a home office. These are, however, added extras. We all have to store clothes; a dressing room is undoubtedly the best solution but is only possible with adequate space.

DIY not only allows you the freedom to design and build a fine cupboard in keeping with the room but also to fit out that cupboard, or dressing room, to meet your individual needs. You can decide the length of shoe rails, the depth and number of drawers for underwear, accessories, socks and scarves, the length of hanging rail for all the bulkier garments, and the number of shelves and how they should be divided for sweaters and jeans.

There are many ready-made storage accessories for fitting out cupboards, and some of the most effective are made from wire mesh and plastic; they include drawers and containers. Alternatively you can construct all your fittings from wood. Fit mirrors to the inside doors of cupboards so that you can check your appearance. Visit a few shops which you consider to be well-designed, see how they display their

Linking a bedroom with a bathroom (above) is a passage which has been transformed into a walk-in wardrobe with ingenious wooden fittings.

A false wall has created a deep and beautifully detailed recess for a window and allowed for low subtle cupboards to be added on either side (centre).

clothes, and use this as inspiration to fit out your own hanging space.

A dressing room or dressing area can be made even in quite limited space by building a partition in the bedroom, utilizing a passage or using a box room. Line it from top to bottom with pigeon-holes, rails, shelves and drawers to create a neat, orderly area of storage.

You can incorporate lighting into a cupboard or as part of the dressing room by installing it under shelves. In addition, make sure you have adequate light in front of the mirror.

Low cupboards or high shelves can be equally effective in a bedroom – as discreet storage or display areas for any kind of item from linen and towels to personal mementoes.

In a very small bedroom, a studio room for living in, or a box room for guests, built-in storage is particularly important. Use every spare inch of space to the best possible advantage, filling whole walls with shelves and cupboards, building units rather than using freestanding wardrobes or tables. Make the bed into a storage area by choosing a mattress or divan that can be placed on a storage platform. Place shelves above the bed instead of bedside tables.

A magnificent built-in wardrobe, everybody's dream (below and opposite) is fitted with superb clothes storage – a rail, suspended open drawers and neat shelves. The folding doors are faced with mirror.

TILED BATHROOM

Traditionally, bathrooms tend to be rather badly organized rooms, in which a collection of pipework and bathroom equipment is arranged, so it seems, to suit the convenience of the plumber rather than the bather.

This design tries to organize the various elements of a bathroom so that plumbing work, which can often look rather brutal and unappealing, is hidden from view. The bathroom is uncluttered and easy to clean; requirements which I think are essential, given that the whole point of a bathroom is hygiene.

The bathroom system is remarkably easy to construct once you have mastered the simple art of cutting, laying and grouting wall tiles. The cavity behind the bath, shower and washbasin allows for pipework and drainage to be hidden from view. The large mirror behind the bath, whilst not essential, gives a sense of scale to a small space.

Tile colours and pattern can obviously be selected to suit your own particular preferences. I think that plain white tiles combined with white baths, basins, bidets and showers are particularly pleasant in bathrooms; they have light, reflective qualities, that induce an atmosphere of cleanliness and hygiene.

Tiled frame for a simple vanity unit

Mirror

light under tiled shelf

Recessed Basin in tiled top with wood shelf & towel rail

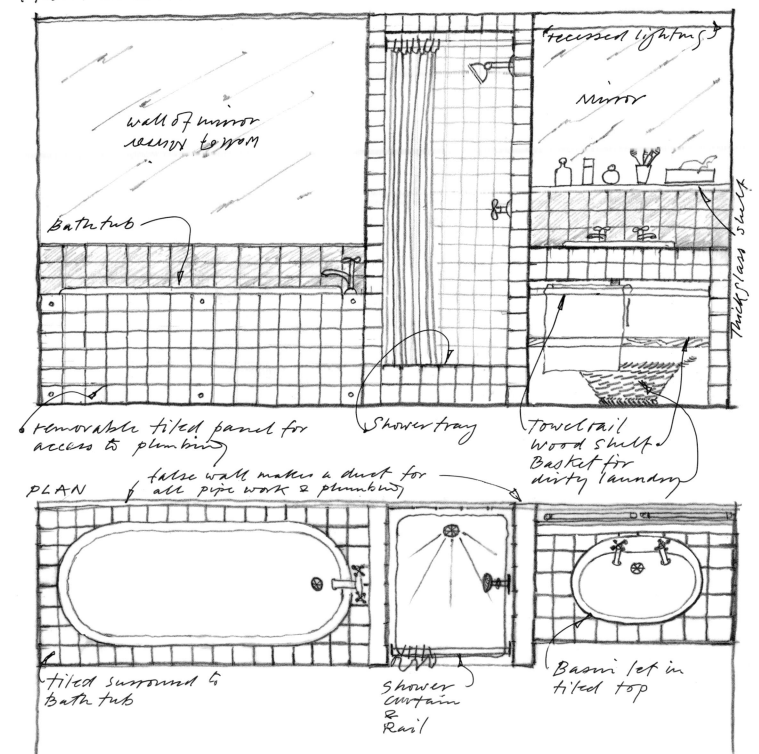

FRONT ELEVATION.

wall of mirror

mirror

recessed lighting

Bath tub

Thick glass shelf

removable tiled panel for
access to plumbing

Shower tray

Towel rail
Wood shelf
Basket for
dirty laundry

PLAN

false wall makes a duct for
all pipe work & plumbing

tiled surround to
Bath tub

Shower
curtain
&
Rail

Basin let in
tiled top

TILED BATHROOM: BATH UNIT

This project shows how to make a tiled bathroom with the fitments set into hollow panel frames so that all the pipework is kept out of sight. The dimensions of the frames are based on those of your bathroom suite and your wall tiles. Obviously, the layout will have to be adapted to suit your particular bathroom.

It is strongly advised that you make a sketch of the proposed bathroom and discuss it with your plumber and electrician so that they can suggest the exact positioning of pipes and wiring, where access will be needed, and the sequence in which the work will be carried out. Coordinating your tasks with the installation of the plumbing and wiring will have to be carefully worked out between the three of you, since it is easier to put in the pipes and cables as the elements of the bathroom are built. Of course, this is not a problem if you are doing your own plumbing. This is now feasible, thanks to the availability of a wide range of easy-to-fit modern plumbing components, such as plastic supply and waste pipes, and push-fit joints. However, by building the frames and fitting some of the panels temporarily, it should be possible to do all the plumbing in one session.

Before starting, it is important to spend some time working out the dimensions carefully so that the minimum of tiles will need to be cut, and so that any cut tiles can be positioned where they will be least noticeable. Try to use only whole tiles. Where horizontal tiles meet vertical tiles at a corner, the horizontal ones should always overlap the vertical ones. This will occur at the top of the shower tray and where the bath and wall tiles come on to the bath. Always think about how water will run off the tiles. Wherever possible it should not run down into a joint, but off one tile and onto another to avoid unnecessary water penetration.

TOOLS

STEEL MEASURING TAPE

SPIRIT LEVEL

TRY SQUARE

METAL DETECTOR

TRIMMING KNIFE and MARKING GAUGE (useful but not essential)

CIRCULAR POWER SAW (or panel saw)

TENON SAW

POWER JIGSAW (or pad saw)

DRILL (hand or power)

TWIST DRILL BITS for pilot and clearance holes

MASONRY DRILL BIT to suit wallplugs being used

COUNTERSINK BIT

COLD CHISEL

SMOOTHING PLANE

ROUTER and ROUTER BIT

PLUMB BOB and CHALK

SCREWDRIVER

HAMMER

NAIL PUNCH

POWER FINISHING SANDER (or hand-sanding block)

TILING TOOLS

SILICONE-RUBBER SEALANT APPLICATOR (if required)

MATERIALS

Part	Quantity	Material	Length
BATH FRAME			
TOP AND BOTTOM RAILS	4	75 × 50mm (3 × 2in) PAR timber	Bath length, plus width of two tiles
UPRIGHT RAILS	8	75 × 50mm (3 × 2in) PAR timber	Height to bath rim, less 100mm (4in)*
END FRAME TOP AND BOTTOM RAILS	4	75 × 50mm (3 × 2in) PAR timber	Distance between inside faces of front and back panels
END FRAME UPRIGHT RAILS	4	75 × 50mm (3 × 2in) PAR timber	Height to bath rim, less 100mm (4in)*
END SHELVING STRIPS	2	12mm ($\frac{1}{2}$in) shuttering plywood; cut to tile width	Distance from back wall to front face of bath panel
BACK SHELVING STRIP	1	Plywood as above; width as above	Length of bath
FRONT SHELVING STRIP	1	Plywood as above; cut to tile width, less a tile thickness to allow shelf tiles to overlap edge of facing tiles on bath panel	Length of bath
BATH PANEL	1	Plywood as above; width as height of front frame	Length: as front frame and to overlap end panels (if fitted)

*Approximate lengths only – refer to copy for actual size

The entire framework is made from 75 × 50mm (3 × 2in) PAR softwood, skinned with 12mm ($\frac{1}{2}$in) shuttering plywood, which is strongly water-resistant. Our tiles are 108mm ($4\frac{1}{4}$in) square, a size which is readily available and works well with this framework.

BATH

Measure up for the frames to fit each side of the bath, allowing for 12mm ($\frac{1}{2}$in) plywood to be fixed on top. This will be exactly level with the rim of the bath and will allow the tiles to rest on the bath rim for an easily sealed joint.

Using 75 × 50mm (3 × 2in) timber, nail up the frames so that the top and bottom rails run the full length of the bath recess and the uprights fit between them – one at each end and two spaced inside them at equal distances.

The bath will either rest in a cradle or will be supplied with adjustable legs. The manufacturer's assembly instructions should be carefully followed. To spread the load across several floor joists, the bath feet should be rested on 75 × 50mm (3 × 2in) battens laid on their sides on the floor, and allowance should be made for these when measuring the height of bath. The bath should be carefully positioned lengthwise and widthwise to ensure that water drains properly to the waste outlet.

BATH FRAME ASSEMBLY

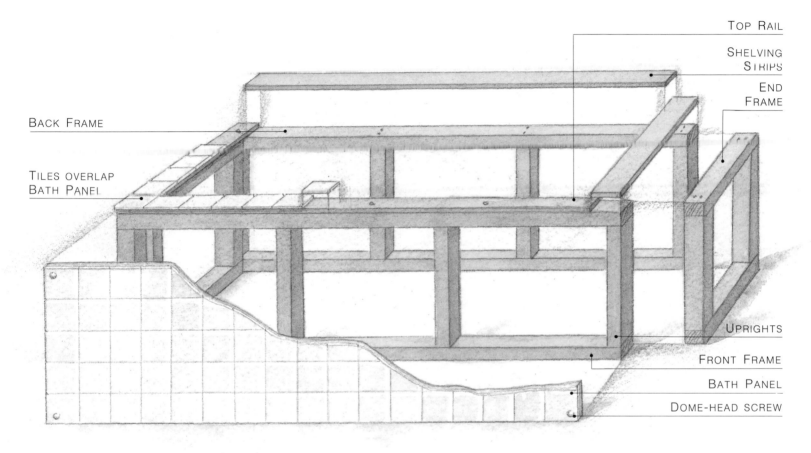

TOP RAIL

SHELVING STRIPS

END FRAME

BACK FRAME

TILES OVERLAP BATH PANEL

UPRIGHTS

FRONT FRAME

BATH PANEL

DOME-HEAD SCREW

End frames are made up in the same way as the front and back frames. They are fitted between them and allowance is made for the thickness of the front panel (12mm [½in] plywood). If you are fitting the bath tight to the wall or partitions at the foot or head, these end frames can be dispensed with, although you will need to cut top rails at the ends to support the shelving strips.

FIXING FRAMES

Screw the back frame to the wall, packing underneath it if necessary to ensure that it is level. Screw through the end frames into the back frame uprights and into the wall or partition at each end if there is one there. Put the bath in place and level it for correct drainage.

Position the front frame, screwing it into the end frames and the side walls or partitions where appropriate.

FITTING THE PLYWOOD SHELVING STRIPS

Measure up for these strips using 108mm (4¼in) wide (or tile width if different) 12mm (½in) shuttering plywood to the width of the frame to the outer edges of the front frame, so that they fit across the bath at the head and foot, overhanging on the inside edges of the top rail.

Measure the spaces along the sides of the frame between the end shelves and cut two more lengths of plywood to fit between them. Note that the front shelf will be slightly narrower than the others as the tiles on this shelf will overlap the edges of the tiles used to cover the front panel of the bath unit.

Apply clear silicone-rubber sealant to the inside edges of all of the shelves and screw them down into the frame all round so that the plywood butts against the bath exactly level with the rim. The join between the bath and the shelves must be sealed with silicone-rubber to prevent water getting under the edging tiles. These strips make a good surface for tiling.

FITTING THE FRONT PANEL

Cut out the front panel from 12mm (½in) shuttering plywood and fit it over the frame and any end panels, if these are required. The front panel must be removable to make access easy in case you need to adjust or repair the internal plumbing. The panel is fixed with dome-head mirror screws inserted through the tiles once these have been fixed.

TILED BATHROOM: SHOWER UNIT

MATERIALS

SHOWER PARTITION

Part	Quantity	Material	Length
FRONT STUD	1	75 × 50mm (3 × 2in) PAR timber	Floor to ceiling height
TOP AND BOTTOM RAILS	2 per side	75 × 50mm (3 × 2in) PAR timber	Back of front stud to back wall
BACK STUD	1	75 × 50mm (3 × 2in) PAR timber	As front stud, less 100mm (4in)*
MIDDLE RAILS	As required	75 × 50mm (3 × 2in) PAR timber	Internal distance between front and back studs
SIDE PANELS	2 per side	12mm ($\frac{1}{2}$in) shuttering plywood	Length and width as overall dimensions of partition frame

SHOWER BASE

Part	Quantity	Material	Length
TOP AND BOTTOM RAILS	4	50 × 50mm (2 × 2in) PAR timber	Width between side partitions
SIDE STUDS	4	50 × 50mm (2 × 2in) PAR timber	Height of shower tray, less 112mm ($4\frac{1}{2}$in)*
FRONT PANEL	1	12mm ($\frac{1}{2}$in) shuttering plywood; width as distance between side panels	Height of base frame
TOP PANEL	1	As above; width as above	Distance from front of base panel to shower tray

SHOWER ROOF

Part	Quantity	Material	Length
ROOF PANEL	1	12mm ($\frac{1}{2}$in) shuttering plywood; width of recess	Depth of shower recess
FRONT PANEL	1	As above; width as shower base panel	Height of tiles, less 12mm ($\frac{1}{2}$in)
FRONT PANEL SUPPORT RAIL	1	50 × 50mm (2 × 2in) sawn timber	As width of roof panel
ROOF FIXING BATTENS	2	50 × 50mm (2 × 2in) PAR timber	As depth of roof panel, less 62mm ($2\frac{1}{2}$in)*

*Approximate lengths only – refer to copy for actual size

SHOWER PARTITIONS

Measure the floor-to-ceiling height for the front stud in exactly the place where it will be positioned. Then measure for the top and bottom rails to be positioned behind the front stud, having previously worked out the front-to-back depth of your shower recess. Cut them to length from the 75 × 50mm (3 × 2in) PAR timber. Next, cut the back stud to fit between the top and bottom rails, that is, the length of the front stud, less 100mm (4in) which is the thickness of the top and bottom rails (but measure these because 100mm [4in] is only their nominal rather than actual thickness).

BASIC FRAME

Nail the front stud to the top rail with 75mm (3in) round wire nails, driving them in with a support behind (see **Techniques, page 23**). Nail the bottom stud in place at the bottom, then insert the back stud 12mm ($\frac{1}{2}$in) in from the ends, to make scribing easier when the partitions are fitted to the wall. (If pipes have to be run along the back, this back stud can be positioned even farther in.) Nail the back stud in place. Repeat the process for a second side partition, if required.

MIDDLE RAILS

These brace the basic frame to make it sturdier, and are also used to make fixings from any adjacent support battens and fittings. They should therefore be placed at levels which coincide with the fixtures for these fittings.

In our case, a rail is needed where the basin and shelf supports meet the side. You may also need some additional support for the shower mixer or spray head, depending on the type of shower used (see fig 2, page 202). Another position for a cross rail would be where you have to make any joins in the plywood skin to make up the full height of your room. Space out other cross-rails at intervals of approximately 610–900mm (24–36in).

It is a good idea to fit a small removable access panel opposite the shower fitments in case there is

① Assembly of the Shower Partition Basic Frame
Assemble basic framework from PAR timber as shown, using round wire nails. Nail front stud on top rail, then bottom rail, and add the back stud, insetting it by 12mm ($\frac{1}{2}$in) to aid scribing.

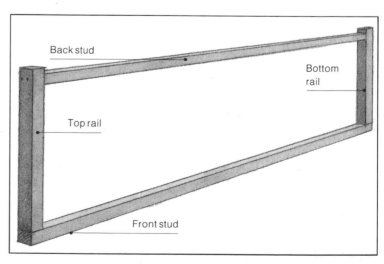

Back stud

Bottom rail

Top rail

Front stud

Sawing 21

Skew nailing 24

SHOWER UNIT ASSEMBLY

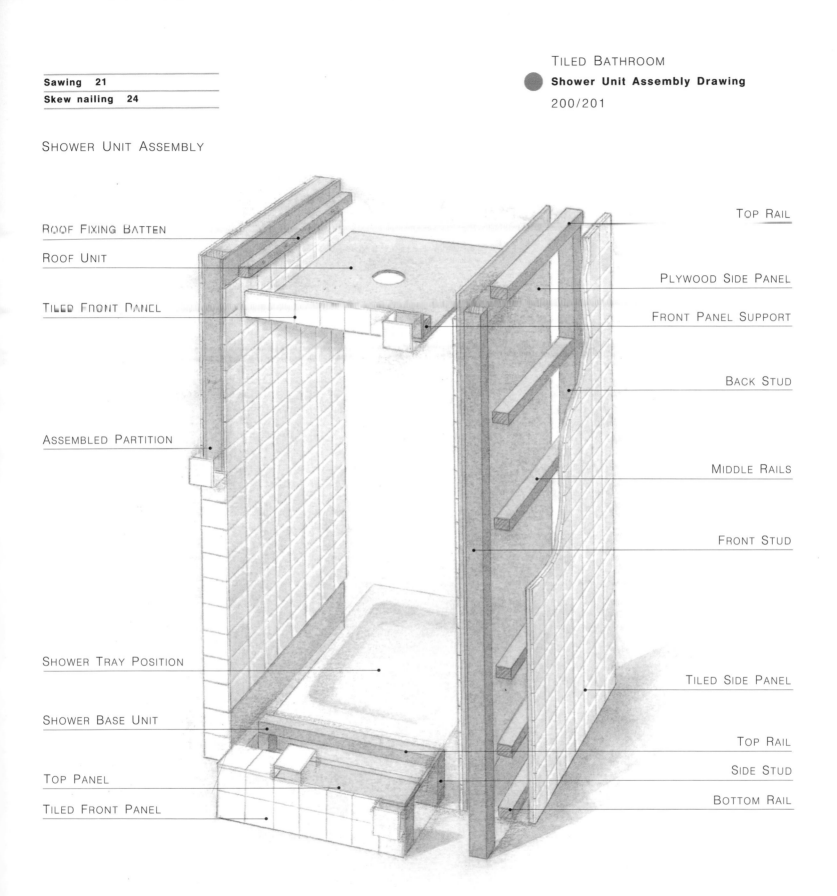

ROOF FIXING BATTEN

ROOF UNIT

TILED FRONT PANEL

ASSEMBLED PARTITION

SHOWER TRAY POSITION

SHOWER BASE UNIT

TOP PANEL

TILED FRONT PANEL

TOP RAIL

PLYWOOD SIDE PANEL

FRONT PANEL SUPPORT

BACK STUD

MIDDLE RAILS

FRONT STUD

TILED SIDE PANEL

TOP RAIL

SIDE STUD

BOTTOM RAIL

ever a problem with the plumbing. This is done by making a panel to coincide with whole tiles (fig 2). The panel is fixed into additional rails inside the frame. You may prefer to make one large panel to give access to the shower mixer control and the spray head. If you are using a plumber, ask his advice.

ADDING THE SIDES

When both frames are nailed up, measure for the side panels to finish flush with all the edges. Then cut out the required number of panels from 12mm ($\frac{1}{2}$in) shuttering plywood, making sure that you cut them all square. Mark the centre lines of all the studs on the edges of the frames as a guide for accurate nailing down of the side panels.

Lay the frame flat and lay the *inner* plywood panel on top. Line up the edge of the panel accurately with the *front* stud. Glue together, and then nail down into the stud about every 150mm (6in), using 38mm ($1\frac{1}{2}$in) round wire nails. Use the centre marks on the edges of the frame as a guide to the nail posi-

tions, to ensure that they are driven centrally into the rails.

Having nailed the front stud, pull the rest of the frame into square to align with the other edges of the plywood. Mark off on to the face of the plywood the centre lines of the rails and back stud so that you have guide lines for nailing.

Continue nailing down along the top and bottom rails, the back stud and the middle rails, checking as you do so that the frame is still square. Do not fix the other side panel at this stage.

Repeat for the other partition.

FIXING PARTITIONS

Put the partitions in place, spacing them by the width of the shower tray. Use a spirit level and plumb bob to check that the partitions are standing vertically. Do any scribing necessary to fit the partitions to the wall (*see* **Techniques, page 31**). This does not have to be very accurate as the finish to the wall will be achieved with the wall tiles. Fix the partitions in place by screwing through the back stud and packing any gaps be-

tween the back stud and the wall where the screws are positioned.

Screw through the top rail into the ceiling. If possible, screw into the ceiling joists. (You can find these by using a metal detector to locate the ceiling fixing nails *see* **Techniques, Wall fixings, page 24**). If the partitions fall between two joists (as is likely where the partitions run parallel with them), secure a length of 75 × 50mm (3 × 2in) timber between the joists and fix into this. Depending on the location of your bathroom, you may have to go into the loft to do this, or it may be necessary to lift a few floorboards in the room above the shower position. In this case, it is a good idea to get an electrician to install a ceiling light at the same time.

Finally, screw the bottom rail into the floor, packing under it if necessary to ensure that it sits square.

Temporarily fix the other plywood panel with a few nails only, not fully driven home. This will allow easy removal later, during plumbing, and will allow you to finish your framework first.

SHOWER BASE

Put the shower tray in place temporarily and adjust its legs so that the top of the tray is the height of the whole tiles. Make a frame from 50 × 50mm (2 × 2in) PAR timber to the width of the recess, by the height of the shower tray, but allowing for the thickness of the plywood panel which will rest on top. The rails should run to the full width between the partitions with the uprights between them. Butt the frame to the front of the shower tray and screw through the uprights into the plywood sides of the partitions.

Make up an identical frame to the front, to be positioned in from the front edge by the thickness of the plywood. Glue and screw through the upright into the side partitions as before. If, as in our case, the total width of the step is only one tile, the two frames will almost touch each other. Cut a piece of 12mm ($\frac{1}{2}$in) plywood to fit the front of this frame, flush with the top edge. Cut a top piece to rest on top of the frame, flush with the front of the frame and

① Adding Sides to Frame
Middle rails are required at fixing positions for the bath or basin unit, possibly for the shower fixture, and also where it is necessary to join plywood panels. Nail down every 150mm (6in).

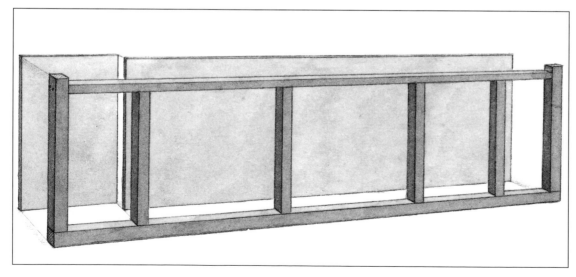

② Fitting an Access Panel
It is wise to fit an access panel opposite shower fixtures. Panel should coincide with whole tiles.

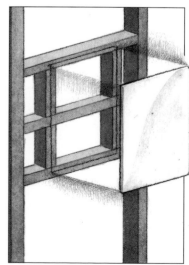

butting up to the shower tray. Do not fit these pieces yet: you will need access for fitting the shower tray and installing the waste trap and pipework (see **Plumbing and Wiring, page 206**).

Refer to the manufacturer's instructions on how to assemble and install the shower tray. Some trays have to be rested on sturdy timber battens to spread the weight of the tray when it is in use: if this is the case with yours, you may have to adjust the height of the support legs to accommodate the thickness of the support battens.

When fixing bathroom fittings into the timber frame, use an applicator to insert a generous line of clear silicone-rubber sealant between the fitting and the framework. This acts as a second line of defence should water get under the tiles owing to the breakdown of the sealant which will be used between the fitting and the tiles (see **Tiling, page 36**).

SHOWER ROOF

Measure the recess in the shower area and cut out a roof panel from 12mm (½in) shuttering plywood. Cut a front panel to rest on top of it, so that the total depth is sufficient to house a shower downlighter, while the panel lines up with a joint line in the tiled partitions and the wall. It is best to work out exactly where the tiles will fall. Alternatively, tile the partitions first only up to where you require the roof. Next, make up the roof unit and continue tiling.

Use a 50 x 50mm (2 x 2in) batten, glued and screwed in place, to join the roof panel and the front panel together at right-angles. Assuming it is safe to do so, cut a hole in the middle of the roof panel, and fit the downlighter according to the manufacturer's instructions.

Cut two lengths of 50 x 50mm (2 x 2in) timber to be fixed horizontally on the inside faces of the partition panels, to allow the roof unit to be fixed to the sides. Cut these battens so that they will fit behind the front batten, but do not secure them, or the roof unit, at this stage as the plumbing must be completed first.

Buy a shower rail the width of the shower recess and fix in place.

③ Making Shower Base to Height of Shower Tray
The base comprises two frames, covered by a front panel and joined by a top panel which is cut to the width of one tile. If shower tray is only one tile high, top and bottom rails of frame will almost touch.

④ Shower Roof Assembly
Cut roof panel to fit between partitions. Front panel must be deep enough to hide shower downlighter.

GLASS SHELF
A sleek glass shelf sits above the basin unit, see page 207 for instructions.

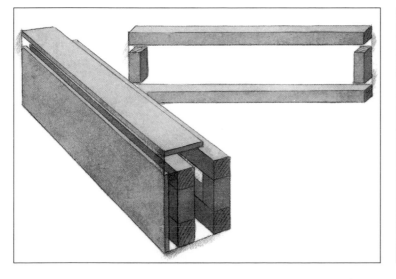

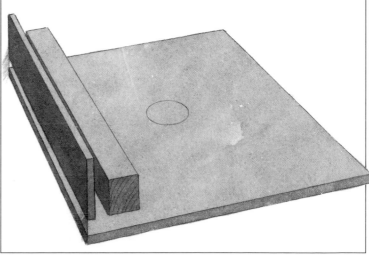

TILED BATHROOM: BASIN UNIT

MATERIALS

Part	Quantity	Material	Length
BASIN UNIT			
PARTITION FRAME FRONT STUD	1	75 × 50mm (3 × 2in) PAR timber	Height of basin, less 12mm ($\frac{1}{2}$in)
TOP AND BOTTOM RAILS	2	75 × 50mm (3 × 2in) PAR timber	Distance from inside face of front stud to back wall
BACK STUD	1	75 × 50mm (3 × 2in) PAR timber	Height of basin, less 12mm ($\frac{1}{2}$in) less 100m (4in)*
MIDDLE RAIL	1	75 × 50mm (3 × 2in) PAR timber	Distance between inside faces of front and back studs
SIDE PANELS	1 or 2	12mm ($\frac{1}{2}$in) shuttering plywood; width as overall width of frame	Height of frame
FRONT PANEL	1	Plywood as above; to give sufficient depth to hide underside of basin	Distance between partition panel and side of shower partition
TOP PANEL	1	19mm ($\frac{3}{4}$in) shuttering plywood; width as depth of recess	Width of alcove
FRONT PANEL SUPPORT RAIL	1	75 × 50mm (3 × 2in) or 50 × 50mm (2 × 2in) PAR timber, plus scrap pieces for securing	Width of alcove
BASIN SUPPORT BATTEN	1	50 × 50mm (2 × 2in) PAR timber	As top rail of basin partition frame
UNDER-BASIN SHELF PANEL	1	12mm ($\frac{1}{2}$in) melamine-faced chipboard or plywood (if to be tiled); width as depth of recess, less about 125mm (5in)	Distance between inside faces (after tiling) of shower and basin support partitions
SHELF LIPPING	1	50 × 25mm (2 × 1in) pine	As above
SHELF-SUPPORT BATTENS	2	25 × 25mm (1 × 1in) PAR timber	As width of under-basin shelf panel
GLASS SHELF	1	Toughened glass as recommended by supplier. Width as required, plus 12mm ($\frac{1}{2}$in) to be set in rear-wall plaster	Width of basin alcove, plus 25mm (1in)
REAR-WALL GLASS SHELF-SUPPORT BATTEN	1	12 × 12mm ($\frac{1}{2} \times \frac{1}{2}$in) hardwood (or as plaster thickness)	Width of basin alcove, plus 25mm (1in)
SIDE-WALL GLASS SHELF-SUPPORT BATTEN	1	12 × 12mm ($\frac{1}{2} \times \frac{1}{2}$in) hardwood (or as plaster thickness)	Width of glass shelf, less 12mm ($\frac{1}{2}$in), or batten thickness (if different)
PELMET PANEL	1	19mm ($\frac{3}{4}$in) plywood; width as tile depth	Width of basin alcove
PELMET SUPPORT BLOCKS	2	50 × 25mm (2 × 1in) PAR timber	As pelmet depth, less 25mm (1in)

*Approximate length only – refer to copy for actual size

BASIN

The basin is set into a tiled surface with a shelf underneath. The frame is fitted between the shower partition and another low-level partition. Alternatively, you can make the fixing between two low-level ones.

BASIN PARTITION

Decide how high you want your basin, and how far out from the wall you want it to extend. Allow a generous space around the basin.

Make up the partition frame in the same way as for the shower, but only one middle rail will be required. This will be at the level you want to fit the shelf supports. Note this level as you will need to know it once the sides are in place.

Mark the centre lines of the rails and studs on the edges of the frame as a guide for nailing on the side panels. Cut these out. If the partition is to be fitted against a wall, it will need only one side panel. Do not fix it at this stage. If it is not going against a wall, fix only the outer one (farthest from the basin) by following the procedure for the shower partition on page 200 (glue and nail the front stud first, and pull it into square to complete fixing). Fix the partition panel in place as described above.

If the partition is to be fitted to a wall, stand the framework 12mm ($\frac{1}{2}$in) away from the wall, checking that it is vertical and packing the bottom rail level if necessary. Use packing pieces between the frame and the wall at the point where the screws go in. If this distance varies because the wall is uneven, make the 12mm ($\frac{1}{2}$in) gap between the frame and the wall the maximum width. This will avoid any need for scribing to fit the frame to the wall, and will still allow for whole tiles to fit the front edge of the partition. Fit inner side panel in place and temporarily nail to frame.

Sawing 21
Nailing 24
Finding verticals 32

Basin Unit Assembly

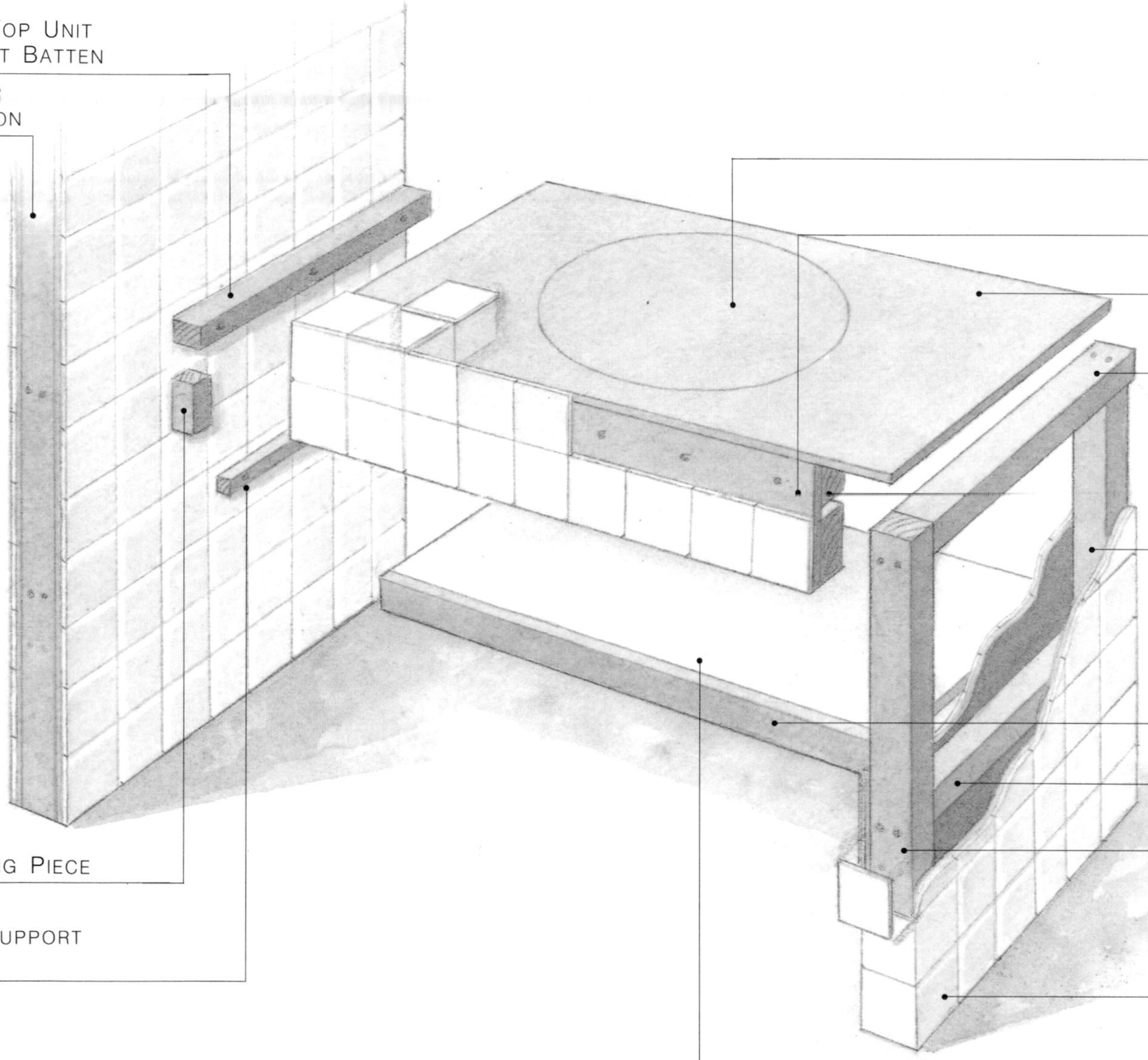
Basin Top Unit Support Batten
Shower Partition
Securing Piece
Shelf-support Batten
Basin Recess (cut to shape of template supplied with basin)
Front Panel
Top Panel
Top Rail
Front Panel Support Rail
Back Stud
Shelf Lipping
Middle Rail
Front Stud
Basin Partition
Shelf (adjust position to suit storage requirements)

TILED BATHROOM

FRONT PANEL

Measure the width of the recess from inside the basin partition to the side of the shower partition and cut a piece of 12mm or 19mm ($\frac{1}{2}$in or $\frac{3}{4}$in) shuttering plywood to fit across this width. The depth of this piece should be enough to hide the underside of the basin. Work it out so that the total depth will coincide with whole tiles, after allowing for the thickness of the top panel.

TOP PANEL

Measure up for the top panel to fit the width and depth of the alcove, and to finish flush with the front of the low partition. Cut the panel from 19mm ($\frac{3}{4}$in) shuttering plywood. Use a 75 × 50mm (3 × 2in) or a 50 × 50mm (2 × 2in) batten cut to the length of the front panel to join the top and front panels together at right-angles. Make sure that the front panel rests under the top panel, and that there is a space at the end to slot over the end partition. Glue the batten in place and screw through the panels into it.

FIXING THE BASIN FRAME ASSEMBLY

To support the basin unit at the shower partition end, cut a 50 × 50mm (2 × 2in) batten to length and screw it to the side of the shower partition, fixing into the cross-rail inside the partition. It must be fixed exactly level with the top of the low partition. Rest the unit in place, but do not secure it yet as it will need to be removed for plumbing.

Cut the aperture for the inset basin by using the template supplied by the basin manufacturer. Use a power jigsaw to cut this hole, or do it by hand with a padsaw. Check that the basin fits in the hole, but do not fit it until you have tiled the top panel.

Screw scrap pieces of 50 × 50mm (2 × 2in) timber to the back of the front panel to secure it to the partitions at each side.

PLUMBING AND WIRING

At this stage the plumber can fit the basin, shower tray and bath, and install the supply and waste pipes.

Inset showers can be fitted now, and the pipework can be put in place for surface-mounted types, although the fittings themselves, for both types of showers, are installed after tiling.

Also, have the wiring put in at this stage, with tails left protruding for lights, shaver sockets, heaters or electrical showers and so on to be fitted later.

PERMANENT FIXING OF PARTITION SIDES, BASIN AND SHOWER UNITS

Fix all the second sides to the partitions by nailing into the studs and rails. Screw the basin unit in place down through the top panel into the partition and support batten and through the scrap pieces to secure to the partitions at each side.

For the shower base, screw the front panel in place on to the front frame, and fix the top piece down on to the front and back frame. Insert silicone-rubber sealant between the frame and bathroom fittings, where appropriate.

For the roof unit, screw the 50 × 50mm (2 × 2in) battens into

the plywood sides for the roof to fit correctly, and screw through the roof panel into the battens. However, if you prefer to do most of the tiling on a flat surface, do not secure the roof panel until it has been tiled, leaving off the tiles at the edges, at the points where you will be screwing through into the battens. Fix the ceiling panel in place, then tile over the screws.

TILING

Protect the bathroom fittings while you are tiling, as they can be spoilt by adhesive and grout. If they are in wrappings, keep these on for as long as possible. Begin tiling (see **Techniques, page 36**); below are some tips relevant to this project.

Tile the sides of the partition first, but note the middle rail positions before, so you know where to fit the shelf supports. Work from the front edge to the back so that any cut tiles will be against the wall.

Apply the shower roof tiles before fixing the roof panel in place. Leave off the edging tiles so that you can screw the roof panel to its fixing

---

① **Assembly of Basin Top Unit from 19mm ($\frac{3}{4}$in) plywood**
Cut the top panel to the width and depth of the basin alcove. Glue and screw the top panel and front panel to a square batten so that they are at right-angles, the front panel resting beneath the top panel.

② **Making up the Under-basin Shelf Assembly**
The shelf is cut to inside width of recess and is set back slightly from front of the side partitions. Wooden lipping, glued and pinned to front edge of shelf, hides shelf-support battens which are screwed to partition units.

battens. If you have already fixed the shower roof, tile the partition walls up to it.

Tile the front surfaces next, that is, the front edges of the partitions, the front panels of the basin, shower tray and bath panel.

Tile the top surface, that is, around the bath, basin and shower. Around the bath, where a lot of water is likely to lie, put some extra adhesive around the outer sides of the tiles so that they slope very slightly towards the bath.

Tile the walls and remaining partitions next. If you are fitting a glass shelf, apply tiles up to one tile's width below the level of the shelf on those walls where the shelf will be fitted. Fit the glass shelf (see below) and complete the tiling afterwards.

Finally, if you previously tiled the shower roof whilst it was still flat, you can now fix the remaining tiles on the partition sides – these were initially left off in order to screw the roof unit to its fixing battens. These can be held in place with sticky tape while the tile adhesive sets. If the shower roof has already been fixed,

tile with the aid of a simple home-made timber T-support. This is lightly wedged in place between the roof and the floor to hold each row of tiles in place while the adhesive sets. The support will be needed for only about 15 minutes on each row.

After a minimum of 12 hours the joints between the tiles can be grouted with a waterproof grout, and the tiles can be polished clean.

Fix the bath panel, and any access panels, with dome-head mirror screws. You can drill clearance holes easily with a masonry drill bit. Do not press too hard, and make sure that your drill is *not* switched to hammer action. Put a piece of sticky tape on the tile where you want to drill the hole, to prevent the drill bit from skidding across the surface.

Finally, apply a silicone-rubber sealant to all joins between the bathroom fittings and the ceramic tiles and to all internal corners where partitions meet the original walls. Sealants are available in white, clear and a range of colours, and are supplied with full instructions. To eject a bead of sealant, you usually

press a plunger with your thumb, although trigger-operated aerosol packs are also becoming popular.

GLASS SHELF

Setting a glass shelf in a wall is an unorthodox method of fitting, but, if properly done, the effect of having no visible means of support is well worth the effort. However, for an easier solution, rest the glass on rubber door stops screwed into the wall – two stops at each end – after the wall or partition has been tiled.

For a concealed fixing, ask your supplier what thickness of toughened glass you need for your span. Ours is 12mm ($\frac{1}{2}$in) glass spanning 1100mm (43in). The glass must be cut to size and the edges polished.

Stop the tiles one tile's width below where you want the shelf. Cut a slot into the wall at the back and the end to the thickness of the plaster and about 25mm (1in) or so wide. Fix in place a thin batten to the thickness of the plaster, minus the thickness of the shelf.

Where the shelf meets the shower partition, you must cut a slot to the thickness of the glass in the facing panel. Do this either by drilling a row of overlapping holes with a diameter the same as the shelf's thickness, and chisel out the waste to make a straight-sided slot, or use a jigsaw or router to cut a neat slot.

Slot the shelf into place. This can be difficult and it may be necessary to cut away a little extra plaster above where the shelf has to go. Fill any gaps with wall filler or tile adhesive, then complete the tiling up to the shelf. Above the shelf you can add a mirror, or tile the wall.

UNDER-BASIN SHELF

This is made from 12mm ($\frac{1}{2}$in) melamine-faced chipboard, but you can use plywood if you are going to tile the shelf. Cut the shelf to the width of the recess and to the

required depth. It will look better if it is recessed back from the front edge a little way – 108mm ($4\frac{1}{4}$in), ie one tile's width, in our case.

Cut lipping from 50 × 25mm (2 × 1in) pine. Hold the shelf in a vice and glue and nail the lipping to the front edge of the shelf so that the top edge of the lipping is flush with the shelf surface and the bottom edge hides the support battens. Punch the nail heads below the surface, fill the holes, sand smooth and apply a finish.

SHELF-SUPPORT BATTENS

These support the shelf at each side from behind the lipping to the back wall. Cut two pieces to length from 25 × 25mm (1 × 1in) timber. Drill two clearance holes in each batten, then drill into the tiled sides at the marked levels. Countersink the holes and screw the battens in place.

MIRROR

Fit the mirror to the wall with dome-head mirror screws if it is already drilled for these. If it is not, use corner-fixing mirror plates. When using mirror screws, put a tap washer over each screw behind the mirror to keep it slightly away from the wall. Whichever type of mirror fixing you use, be careful not to over-tighten the fixing screws, as you may crack the glass; ask your glass supplier for advice.

PELMET

To conceal the overhead lighting, fix a pelmet above the mirror in the basin recess. Make the pelmet from 19mm ($\frac{3}{4}$in) plywood; cut it to the width of the recess and to the depth of one tile. Cut two support blocks from 50 × 25mm (2 × 1in) timber, about 25mm (1in) less than the pelmet depth, to fit behind the pelmet strip at each end. Screw these into the wall and the side partition in order to fit the pelmet in place securely.

③ Fitting a Glass Shelf Using Hidden Supports
The wall is channelled to the thickness of the plaster for a batten which is fixed at the back and sides of the alcove. The shelf is made of toughened glass and rests neatly on the batten. After fitting, fill any gaps then finish tiling.

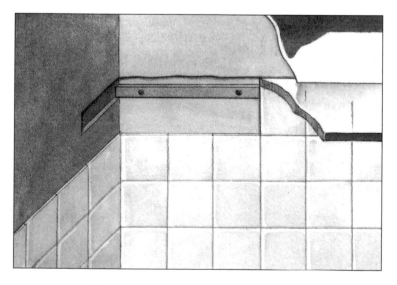

PANELLED BATHROOM

Often, the best ideas are the simple ones. Very few things in life are more unpleasant than trying to dry yourself with a damp towel, so if you install this room-width rail combined with a radiator you can remedy this forever. The rail here is made from chromed tube, but could be finished in coloured enamel or be made in timber like the spar of a yacht.

All of the pipework in this bathroom has been hidden neatly behind a false wall which is simply constructed from painted tongued-and-grooved pine boarding. This is a particularly good solution as a section of the panelling can be mounted on a batten frame to create an access panel which can be easily removed if you have any plumbing problems.

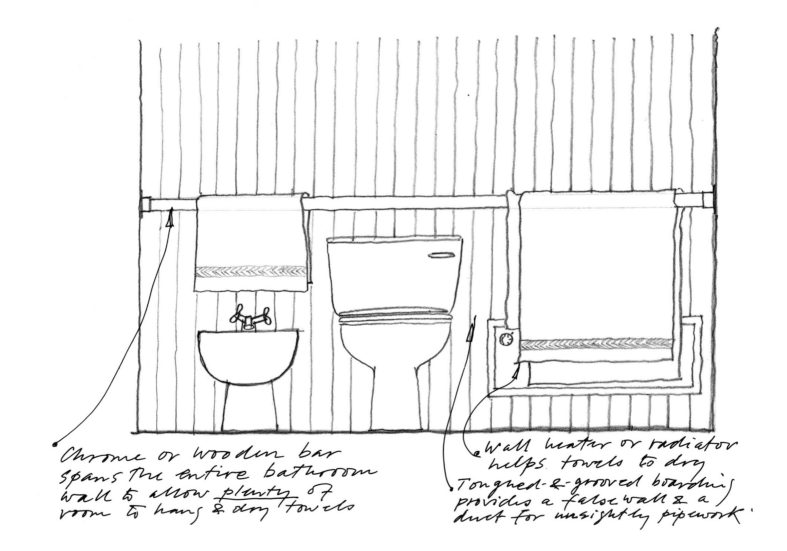

Chrome or wooden bar spans the entire bathroom wall to allow plenty of room to hang & dry towels

Wall heater or radiator helps towels to dry
Tongued-&-grooved boarding provides a false wall & a duct for unsightly pipework.

PANELLED BATHROOM

Building a false wall is a clever way of concealing ugly pipework in the bathroom. The job is relatively easy if you are fitting a new bathroom suite. However, if a suite is already installed, you may have to move one or more of the components to make space for the new wall. Check that this is possible, bearing in mind the position of waste pipes and drains.

The false wall is made by fixing battens to the existing wall and covering them with timber boards. These are normally tongued and grooved, and can range from plywood strips faced with an attractive veneer to solid timber such as pine. Normally, they are fitted vertically over horizontal battens.

The battens need only be of rough-sawn softwood, and should be at least 50 × 50mm (2 × 2in) if you intend to run pipes behind them. They should be fixed at centres of about 610mm (24in). There is no need to strip off any of the wall decoration before fixing the battens.

The spacing of the battens is determined largely by the thickness of the boards to be used, but also by the degree of rigidity required. It is important for the panelling to be more rigid in places where it may be leant against. As a general guide, 9mm ($\frac{3}{8}$in) boards would have battens at centres of 400–500mm (16–20in), while 12mm ($\frac{1}{2}$in) boards need battens set 500–610mm (20–24in) apart.

Always begin and end battens a short distance from corners or ceilings so that nails are not driven into the last few millimetres of the boards, as this can cause splitting.

In order to bring all the battens flush with each other, plywood or hardboard packing pieces may have to be used behind some of the screws. This will certainly be necessary with an undulating wall. Check the battens carefully with a long straight-edge, for unless they are completely flush, you will not be able to fix the boards on to them properly.

The 50mm (2in) battens should provide enough space to conceal most bathroom pipes. If not, use thicker battens. Screw the battens to the wall, cutting out sections to accommodate pipework where necessary. However, if the wall is perfectly flat, you can fix the battens with masonry nails, provided they are long enough to go at least 12mm ($\frac{1}{2}$in) into the masonry.

If you want to attach boards of random lengths, for effect, then additional horizontal battens will be needed, spaced to suit how you plan to cut the boards. Position the boards so that the cut ends meet in the centre of a batten and those at either end are both of a similar width.

You can fix the boards with nails or with special clips which slot on to the tongue and are then nailed to the battens. Nailing through the face of the boards is the simplest and quickest method of fixing, but the nail heads must be punched below the surface and the holes filled with a matching wood filler. It is not necessary to match the wood if the boards are to be painted.

TOOLS

STEEL MEASURING TAPE

SPIRIT LEVEL

SCREWDRIVER

NAIL PUNCH

HAMMER

PANEL SAW

TENON SAW (fine-toothed)

JIGSAW (or padsaw)

TONGUE-AND-GROOVE CLIPS

MITRE BOX

POWER DRILL

DRILL BITS FLAT BIT (or expansive bit) COUNTERSINK BIT

MASONRY BIT

MATERIALS

Part	Quantity	Material	Length
WALL BATTENS	As required	50 × 50mm (2 × 2in) (minimum) sawn softwood	Width of wall
BOARDS	As required	9 or 12mm ($\frac{3}{8}$ or $\frac{1}{2}$in) thick boards	As required
ALUMINIUM POLE (or chrome or wood)	1	37mm ($1\frac{1}{2}$in) diameter aluminium, chrome or wooden pole	As required
SUPPORT DISCS	2	18mm ($\frac{3}{4}$in) thick MDF discs	

Nailing through the tongues with very thin 'lost head' pins provides an invisible fixing. These are driven at an angle into the tongue and are hidden by the groove of the next board. You may find that the wood splits in some cases, since dry pine is rather brittle. Do not worry if this should happen. Just break off any splinters; the splits will be covered by the groove of the next board, which is slotted over the tongue.

If the boards are to be pinned, fix the first with its groove in the corner, and check with a spirit level that it is standing vertically. Adjust the board as necessary before securing it by driving pins through the grooved edge. These are the only surface pins used and should be sunk below the surface with a nail punch. The holes should be filled with a matching wood filler.

Pin the other side of the board,

① Fixing Tongued, Grooved and V-Jointed Boards with Nails
First board, left, is scribed to side wall, ensuring board is vertical. Pin to batten, driving nail through grooved edge. Tap next board, right, over tongue and pin through tongue. Repeat for all succeeding boards.

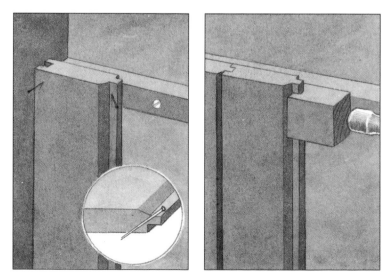

angling the pins through the tongue. Fit a pin into each wall batten.

Tap the next board over the tongue to hide the fixing nails. Protect the edge of the board from the hammer with a piece of scrap wood.

Clips are easy to use and provide a stronger fixing than pins, but are more expensive. They are designed to lock into the lower part of a groove.

The tongued edge of the first board goes into the corner you are starting from. Cut off the tongue with a fine-toothed tenon saw. Position the cut edge in the corner and pin it in place or use a special starter clip. Then secure the grooved edge with a clip. This is hidden by the next board inserted in the groove.

If boards of random length have to be butt-jointed at their ends, use a mitre box with a right-angle slot for very accurate saw cuts. Do not fill the gaps between the joints.

The boards used in our bathroom were stopped short of the floor, giving an attractive finish. The lower edge was decorated with beading. To do this, fit a temporary batten at the bottom at the required height above the floor, to serve as a finishing guide for the bottom edge of each board. When it is removed, the bottom edges of the boards will be flush with each other.

Glue and pin the beading in place along the lower edge of the boards. Also, fix the beading in the corners and along the ceiling line to hide gaps. It should be pinned to the walls or ceiling and not to the boards. Again, the heads of the pins should be sunk below the surface and the holes filled with a matching wood filler. If you prefer to avoid nail holes, fix the beading with a contact adhesive.

It is advisable to provide easy access to pipework and joints for maintenance or repair. Therefore, fix a few strategic boards with screws rather than pins, cutting off the tongues, so that the boards in question can be lifted out easily. Make a feature of the screws by using dome-head or brass screws.

Although timber boards provide an excellent way of covering up old or unsightly walls, they must never be used on damp walls. The cause of the dampness should be traced and eliminated. The only form of damp that they will cure is condensation, since the new wall surface will be warmer.

If an insulating blanket is to be applied between the battens to increase the heat retention of an outside wall, first cover the wall with vapour check sheeting (either polythene or building paper) and fix the battens over it. Although this will ensure that no damp strikes through to the wall, it is not a cure for existing damp or the structural damage that it can cause.

Finally, remember that all timber can move with changes in moisture. Therefore, all boards should be conditioned before use by keeping them in the room in which they are to be used for about a week beforehand.

TOWEL RAIL

A feature is made here of the towel rail, which runs the width of the bathroom. A 37mm (1½in) diameter anodised aluminium pole was chosen, although chrome or wood can be used. If the pole is very long, a couple of intermediate supports will prevent it sagging.

If you have to make your own support discs, use 19mm (¾in) MDF. To mark out a circle for a disc, draw around an object of a suitable size. Cut out the circle (see **Techniques, page 22**) with a jigsaw or padsaw.

Mark off the diameter of the pole in the centre of each disc and cut it out with a flat bit or expansive bit, or a jigsaw or coping saw. Repeat for the other disc.

Countersink two drill holes in each disc, fit the discs on to the pole, and get a helper to hold the pole horizontally while you mark off the screw hole positions on the wall. Remove the pole and discs and drill and plug the holes in the wall.

Replace the discs on the pole and get a helper to hold the pole while the screws are fixed. Use 50mm (2in) No 8 screws.

Fill the screw holes, sand down when dry, and apply a finish to the discs to match the pole or the wall.

② Fixing Boards with Clips
Saw off tongue. Push the board over a starter clip and secure grooved edge with clips.

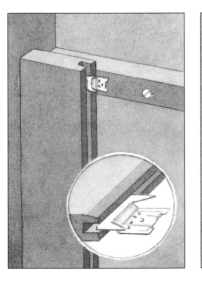

③ Finishing the False Wall with Beading at the Bottom
Boards are fixed to 50 × 50mm (2 × 2in) wall battens or whatever thickness necessary to hide pipes. For neatness stop the boards short of the floor and pin a beading here.

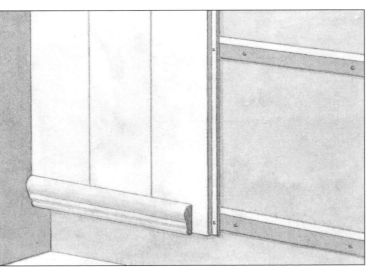

④ Towel Rail Support Discs
Make support discs from 19mm (¾in) MDF and cut hole in centre for rail using a jigsaw or a coping saw.

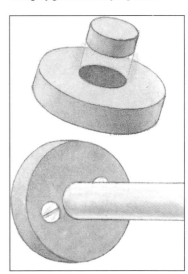

WARDROBE WITH HINGED DOORS

I suppose the dream that most people want to realize when furnishing their bedroom is to have a complete, well-fitted wall of clothes storage units. Although very expensive to buy, these fitted units are relatively easy to build yourself at home.

Wardrobes never seem large enough to allow all your clothes to hang properly without being crushed, and there is always the problem of last season's clothes, which are not being worn but still have to be stored; bulky items such as bags and suitcases must also be considered. This solid wardrobe has ample storage space for everything and will add value to your home should you wish to move in the future. Its simple wooden frame can be scribed to the wall, floor and ceiling if they are uneven or sloping.

The main doors have framed panels, and the panels could be easily replaced with mirror if you prefer a reflective wall. The upper doors are hinged and fitted with a stay so they will remain open when you stow away your luggage.

The interior can be fitted with hanging rails, shelves (either solid or slatted), and a shoe rail. A full-length mirror could also be fixed to the inside of one of the doors.

A shoe rail is fitted into the bottom of the wardrobe

Wood framework of wardrobe

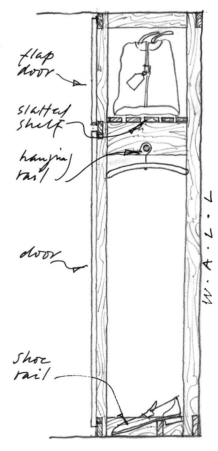

flap door

slatted shelf

hanging rail

door

shoe rail

W·A·L·L

SECTION

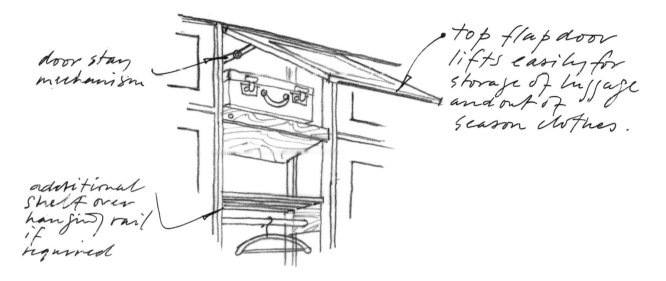

door stay mechanism

top flap door lifts easily for storage of luggage and out of season clothes.

additional shelf over hanging rail if required

front elevation of wardrobe with masses & masses of space for clothes!

WARDROBE WITH HINGED DOORS

These wardrobes comprise three independent double-wardrobe sections linked together. Each section is designed as a free-standing unit to which you fit end panels if necessary. You can build as many sections as you wish, and the design allows for a single section to be built easily should your storage needs or available space require it. You can fit one or both end frames to the wall. In either case, end panels are not needed to fit the frame at the end(s) adjoining the wall.

Buy the doors ready-made from a DIY store or timber merchant. The style is optional, but check that either a small version is available for the top cupboard, or that you can make smaller doors to match the main ones. Alternatively, cut down a standard door to make the top ones.

To make the doors, melamine-faced chipboard panels can be used, to which mouldings can be fixed to give a panelled appearance. The size of the doors governs the overall dimensions of the framework. They should extend from floor to ceiling, with an equal allowance of just over 25mm (1in) at the top and bottom, and where the main doors and the top doors meet. The doors are recessed about 10mm (⅜in) from the front edge of the frame for neatness.

The other important dimension is the depth of 610mm (24in), since this is the optimum for hanging and storing clothes.

TOOLS

STEEL MEASURING TAPE

PANEL SAW

TENON SAW

DOWELLING JIG

ADHESIVE

MALLET

POWER DRILL (with twist drill bits)

SPIRIT LEVEL

ROUTER

SASH CRAMP

SCREWDRIVER

WALLPLUGS (or cavity-wall fixings)

PIN HAMMER and PANEL PINS

CHISEL

OPTIONAL TOOLS FOR SCRIBING:

JIGSAW

PADSAW

SURFORM or RASP

MATERIALS

Per *double* wardrobe section unless otherwise stated

Part	Quantity	Material	Length
DOORS			
2 large and 2 small to fit from floor to ceiling with an allowance of 25mm (1in) at top, middle and bottom. Width of doors governs overall width of wardrobe.			
FRAMES	(Quantities given are for one frame. Three frames required per double wardrobe)		
POST	2	100 × 38mm (4 × 1½in) PAR softwood	Floor to ceiling height
CROSS RAIL	3	100 × 38mm (4 × 1½in) PAR softwood	410mm (16in), plus 50mm (2in) if using tenon joints
END PANELS	(Quantities given are for one frame. Two end frames required per free-standing double wardrobe)		
END PANELS, TOP AND BOTTOM	2	6mm (¼in) veneer-faced or plain plywood; width is distance between posts, plus 25mm (1in)	Height between top and middle rails, and middle and bottom rails, plus 25mm (1in)
BEADING		12 × 12mm (½ × ½in) PAR softwood	Sufficient length to fit around perimeter of end panel
HANGING BAR			
HANGING BAR	2	25mm (1in) dowel or broom handle	Distance between frames, plus 38mm (1½in)
SPACING RAILS			
SPACING RAILS	12	50 × 38mm (2 × 1½in) PAR softwood	Width of door, plus 4mm (5/32in), plus 38mm (1½in) if using tenon joints
SLATTED SHELF			
SHELF SLATS	7	50mm × 19mm (2 × ¾in) PAR softwood	Length of wardrobe, plus 25mm (1in)
TOP SHELF			
TOP SHELF	2	19mm (¾in) plywood; width 580mm (22¾in)	Distance between frames, plus 19mm (¾in)

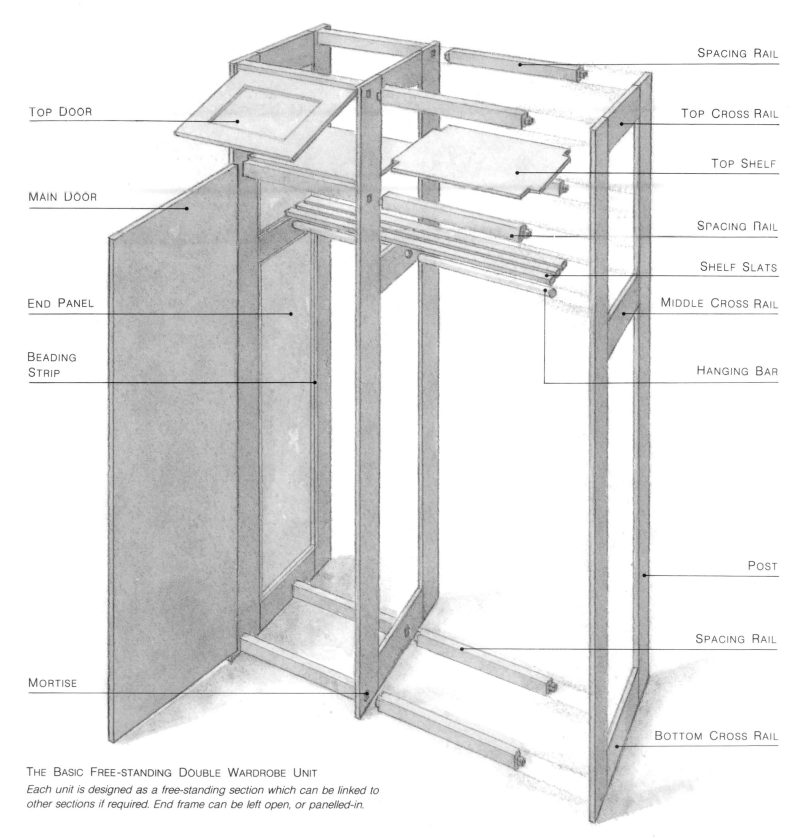

TOP DOOR

MAIN DOOR

END PANEL

BEADING
STRIP

MORTISE

SPACING RAIL

TOP CROSS RAIL

TOP SHELF

SPACING RAIL

SHELF SLATS

MIDDLE CROSS RAIL

HANGING BAR

POST

SPACING RAIL

BOTTOM CROSS RAIL

THE BASIC FREE-STANDING DOUBLE WARDROBE UNIT

*Each unit is designed as a free-standing section which can be linked to
other sections if required. End frame can be left open, or panelled-in.*

WARDROBE WITH HINGED DOORS

BASIC ASSEMBLY

FRAME ASSEMBLY

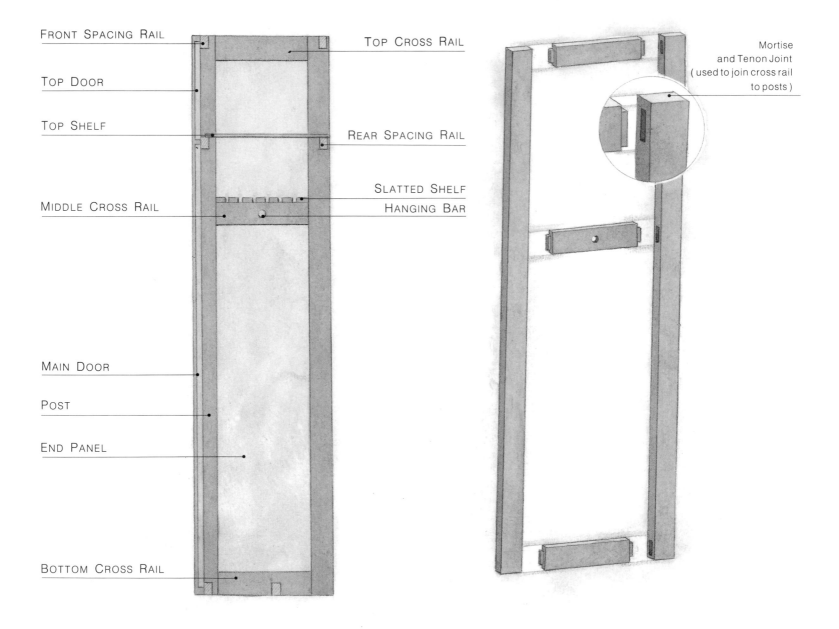

FRONT SPACING RAIL

TOP DOOR

TOP SHELF

MIDDLE CROSS RAIL

MAIN DOOR

POST

END PANEL

BOTTOM CROSS RAIL

TOP CROSS RAIL

REAR SPACING RAIL

SLATTED SHELF
HANGING BAR

Mortise and Tenon Joint (used to join cross rail to posts)

1 Components of the Wardrobe Shown in Cross-section
The depth of the wardrobe is 600mm (24in) which is the optimum for clothes storage. Note that bottom rear spacing rail is set forward to form a shoe rack.

2 Jointing of the Cross Rails to the Posts
Wardrobe frames made by fixing three cross-rails between two posts using glued mortise and tenon joints as shown, or dowel joints.

FRAMES

Measure up for the height of the frames. If your floor or ceiling is uneven, make all the frames to the largest measurement and scribe them to fit.

To make the posts, cut two lengths of 100×38mm ($4 \times 1\frac{1}{2}$in) softwood to the required measurement. Side rails are fixed between the posts at the top, bottom and at the height of the clothes rail, using glued mortise and tenon joints or dowel joints (see **Techniques, pages 28, 30**). The tenons or dowels need be only about 25mm (1in) long.

Measure for the required length of the rails to fit between the posts (add on about 50mm [2in] for the tenons, if you are using them) and cut three rails from the 100×38mm ($4 \times 1\frac{1}{2}$in) softwood. The top and bottom rails fit flush with the ends of the posts. The middle rail supports the hanging bar for your clothes.

In the centre of the middle rail drill a 25mm (1in) diameter hole for the hanging bar. This can be cut from 25mm (1in) dowel or a broom handle. Decide how high you want the bar to be as this will determine the height at which you fit the middle rail. The height of the bar is governed by the configuration of your doors, and on the length of your longest item of clothing, when on a hanger.

Make up the required number of frames but do not drill the holes right through the end frames – these should be drilled to only half the thickness of the rail. Before drilling the holes, mark out their centres very accurately to ensure that the hanging bar fits easily.

END PANELS

Measure up for the two end panels. They should be cut to the height between the top and bottom rails and to the width between the posts, plus 12mm ($\frac{1}{2}$in) all round. Cut them from either veneer-faced chipboard or plywood, for a wood finish, or from plain plywood if you want a painted finish rather than a varnished effect.

Use a router to make a rebate 12mm ($\frac{1}{2}$in) wide and 19mm ($\frac{3}{4}$in)

③ Fitting Spacing Rails into Wardrobe Frames
Mortise and tenon joints are used to join the spacing rails to the wardrobe frames. Each tenon is half the thickness of the timber that is used for making the posts and the cross rails.

④ Fitting the End Panels
End panels are fitted in rebates cut inside the frames and held with beading (below).

FRAME AND END PANEL
Detail inside the wardrobe (above) shows spacing rail shoe rack and frame scribed around skirting.

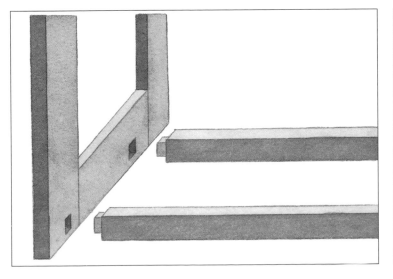

Wardrobe with Hinged Doors

deep around the inside of the frame. Do not fit the panels yet as you will need to fit a sash cramp through the frames when assembling them later. Repeat the process in order to house the other end panels if your chosen design calls for it.

Spacing Rails

The 50×38mm ($2 \times 1\frac{1}{2}$in) rails fit between each frame at the top, the bottom and between the two rows of doors. They are also fitted using either mortise and tenon or dowel joints (*see* **Techniques, pages 28, 30**). Each tenon should be half the thickness of a post so that one tenon each side will meet the other in the middle of a post.

Cut each spacing rail to the width of a door, plus 4mm ($\frac{1}{8}$in) for clearance all round the door, plus the depth of the tenons if you are using them. Cut the required number of spacing rails to length, allowing for six between each frame.

The three front rails are set back from the front face of the posts by the thickness of the doors plus 10mm ($\frac{3}{8}$in). The bottom back rail is

set forward about 225mm (9in) from the back edge to act as a shoe rail. The top and middle back rails are set forward about 12mm ($\frac{1}{2}$in) to allow for easy scribing of the frame to the wall.

Hanging Bars

Cut the required number of hanging bars to the same length as that of the spacing rails, including an allowance for tenons so that they will meet in the middle of the posts, as with the spacing rails. If you plan to fix the rails with dowels, remember to allow extra length on these bars, so that they meet fully in the middle of the posts.

Fitting the Frames

Position one frame at a time and scribe it to fit at the wall, floor and ceiling (*see* **Techniques, page 31**). Ensure that each frame is level with the next.

Either scribe around the skirting or remove it and replace it later. Mark where each frame will sit and identify each so that its position will not be interchanged. Fix the first end

---

Wardrobe Interior
Generous storage space is provided by a slatted shelf (above) and a sturdy wooden hanging bar.

① Assembly of Slatted Shelf
Slats form shelf on middle cross-rails. Cross-rails are also drilled to take the hanging bars.

② Top Door Hanging and Handle Detail
Top doors hinge on a door lift mechanism which is screwed to the tops of the side frames. Note the rebate on the bottom of the door edge to create a finger-hold for easy access.

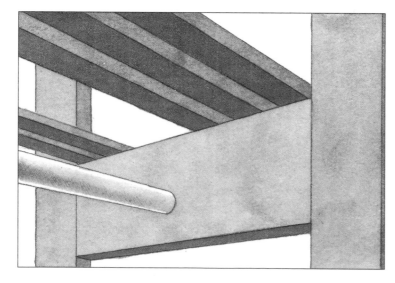

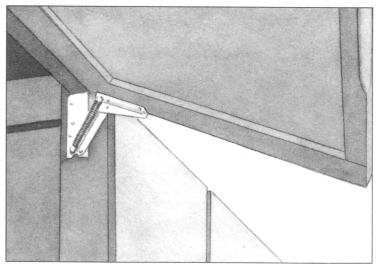

frame in place using angle brackets at the ceiling and floor on the inside (*see* **Techniques, page 25**). Ensure that the frame is plumb. If you are fitting it to the wall at the end, allow a 25mm (1in) gap. This will be covered later with a scribing fillet. Alternatively, screw into the wall, placing a 25mm (1in) spacing batten between frame and wall.

FITTING THE SPACING RAILS

Glue and fit the spacing rails and the hanging bar in position into the first end frame. Position the next frame with the joints already glued. Secure the two frames with sash cramps across the width and allow time for the glue to set. Repeat this operation for as many frames as you are using, fitting each frame as you go.

FITTING THE END PANELS

Fit each end panel into the rebate in each end frame. To secure a panel use beading pinned on the inside to finish flush with the frame.

SLATTED SHELF

The slats run the whole length of the wardrobe, resting across the middle rails of the frames. The outer ones butt against the posts and the others are spaced equally between them. If you have to join lengths, butt-join them at a frame. Pin the slats down to each rail.

TOP SHELF

Each 9mm ($\frac{3}{8}$in) plywood top shelf rests on the middle spacing rails. It is set back a little from the front edge to conceal it or, better still, rebated into the rail. Cut each shelf to meet its neighbour in the middle of the centre post. Cut out notches in the corners to fit around the posts. Pin down the shelf to the spacing rails at the back and front. Repeat for each shelf.

MAIN DOORS

Hang the main doors using 75mm (3in) brass butt hinges (*see* **Techniques, page 33**). Fit the hinges so the doors are set back 10mm ($\frac{3}{8}$in) from the front edge. This will mean that you must not pull your doors open by more than 90°, or the hinges will be weakened or even pulled out. If you feel it necessary (if children will use them, for example), fit stays to ensure that this will not happen.

Finally, fit handles of your choice and any form of panelling or applied decoration to the front of the doors.

TOP DOORS

These are hinged at the top. It is well worth buying a special hinge called a 'door lift mechanism' which acts as a combined hinge and stay (*see* **Techniques, Fitting Door Lift Mechanisms, page 34**). A spring action allows the door to be raised and remain in an open position.

Rout out a rebate or chamfer to create a finger-grip along the bottom edge of each door. Fit magnetic catches to all the doors (*see* **Techniques, page 34**).

SCRIBING FILLET

If you are fitting the frame to a wall at the end, use a scribing fillet to fill the gap between the wall and the end frame; this will ensure a neat and secure fit. Set back the fillet by the same amount as the doors. It can then be painted to match either the doors or the wall.

SKIRTING BOARD

If there is a skirting board already in position against the wall, it will be necessary to remove the skirting from between the frames. Cut a piece of skirting to length so that it fits exactly the space that exists between each frame.

❸ Hinging of Main Doors
Brass butts are used to hinge main doors which are set back from edge of frames.

WARDROBE STORAGE SPACE
With doors open, the wardrobe gives access to solid top shelf, slatted shelf and hanging bar.

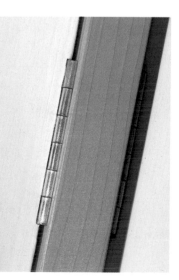

FOLDING SCREEN

Screens have many uses in the home, subdividing space both physically and visually, and defining different areas.

This screen has a second use as a clothes horse for a bedroom or hall. With the addition of a hanging rail, wooden knobs and a shelf, it can quickly become an elegant and simple wardrobe for use in a spare room, for a weekend guest, or in a student's or child's bedroom.

The geometric grid of wooden slats can be rearranged to make the particular pattern of your choice. The slats can either be painted, stained in a variety of colours, or left simply as natural wood. Alternatively, each panel of the screen can be covered on one side with a light fabric to provide a more private room divider. The traditional and ingenious webbing hinge allows the panels of the screen to be folded flat when not in use.

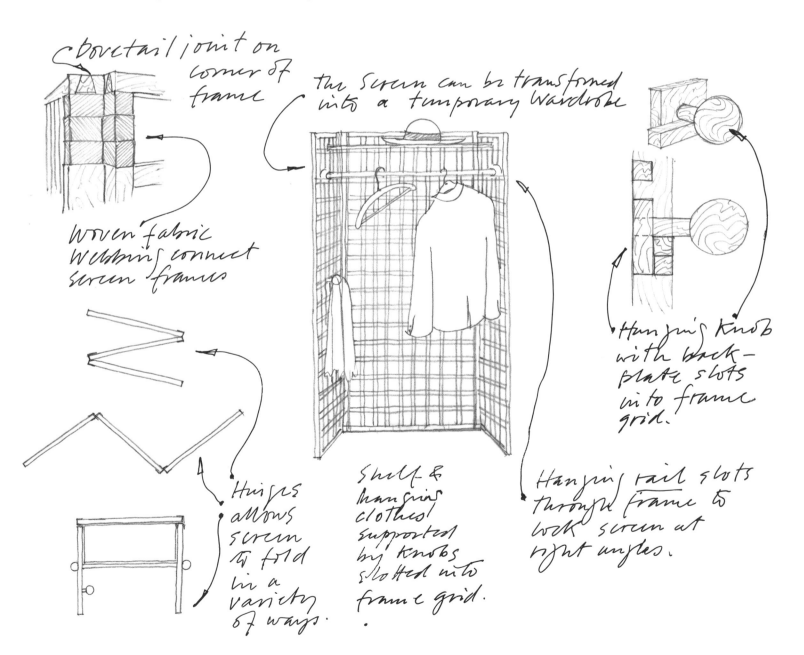

dovetail joint on corner of frame

the screen can be transformed into a temporary Wardrobe

Woven fabric webbing connect screen frames

Hinges allows screen to fold in a variety of ways.

Shelf & hanging clothes supported by knobs slotted into frame grid.

Hanging knob with back-plate slots into frame grid.

Hanging rail slots through frame to lock screen at right angles.

FOLDING SCREEN

You can use a folding screen to divide space in a room or to hide ugly corners and unsightly features in various rooms in the home. If you pin lightweight gauze to one side of an open frame, it will provide a screening effect without reducing light transmission too much. Alternatively, you can pin or staple an opaque material to one side to form a solid screen. For our screen, we created a trellis.

TOOLS

STEEL MEASURING TAPE

TRY SQUARE

MARKING GAUGE (or MORTISE GAUGE)

SLIDING BEVEL

TRIMMING KNIFE

FINE-TOOTHED DOVETAIL SAW or TENON SAW

COPING SAW

PANEL SAW, POWER CIRCULAR SAW (or POWER JIGSAW)

PARING CHISEL 12mm ($\frac{1}{2}$in)

DOWELLING JIG

DRILL (hand or power)

CENTREPOINT BIT

FLAT BIT (or auger bit if hand brace is used)

MALLET (or hammer and scrap of wood for driving in dowels)

SASH CRAMPS (or webbing cramp or folding wedges)

PIN HAMMER (or similar lightweight hammer)

FINISHING SANDER (or HAND-SANDING BLOCK)

STAPLE GUN (or pin hammer and tacks)

PAINTBRUSH 38mm (1$\frac{1}{2}$in)

MATERIALS

Note: Quantities are for one frame; three frames required

Part	Quantity	Material	Length
OUTER FRAME UPRIGHTS	2	50 × 25mm (2 × 1in) PAR timber	1730mm (5ft 8in)
OUTER FRAME TOP AND BOTTOM RAILS	2	50 × 25mm (2 × 1in) PAR timber	710mm (28in)
HORIZONTAL FRAME CROSS BATTENS	15	25 × 25mm (1 × 1in) PAR timber	Approximately 660mm (26in)
VERTICAL FRAME CROSS BATTENS	6	25 × 25mm (1 × 1in) PAR timber	Approximately 1680mm (5ft 6in)
BATTEN FIXING DOWELS	42	6mm ($\frac{1}{4}$in) dowel	30mm (1$\frac{3}{16}$in)
HANGING RAILS	As required	25mm (1in) dowel, approximately 760mm (30in) long	Distance between screen frames, plus approximately 38mm (1$\frac{1}{2}$in)
HANGING RAIL ENDS	6 (2 per rail)	75mm (3in) or 63mm (2$\frac{1}{2}$in) diameter wooden ball	
SHELF	1	12mm ($\frac{1}{2}$in) plywood, about 300mm (12in) deep	Approximately 760mm (30in)
KNOB BACK PLATE	1	25mm (1in) PAR timber, about 75mm (3in) wide	Approximately 125mm (5in)
KNOB STOPPER BATTEN	1	25 × 25mm (1 × 1in) PAR timber	Approximately 125mm (5in)
KNOB DOWEL	1	25mm (1in) dowel	75mm (3in)
KNOB END	1	50mm (2in) diameter wooden ball	

Using traditional fabric hinges which fold in both directions allows the screen to be used in either a Z-shape, or in a U-shape, so that rails can be hung across its width for a temporary wardrobe. Additionally, a detachable shelf can be added. It fits neatly above the hanging rail. Also, wooden knobs can be slotted into the screen wherever required for hanging clothes. When not in use, the screen can be simply folded flat for easy storage.

The screen can be made from as many panels as you require. Ours comprises three, each 1730mm (5ft 8in) high by 710mm (28in) wide. The cross battens within the outer frame create spaces 75mm (3in) square. Each frame is made with dovetail joints at the corners for strength. However, you may prefer to use dowel joints (see **Techniques, page 30**) at the corners. These joints are perfectly reliable if also glued securely with a modern woodworking adhesive such as a PVA-type.

MAKING THE SCREEN PANELS

The outer frame of each panel is cut from 50 × 25mm (2 × 1in) PAR (planed all round) timber. For each panel, two uprights and two rails (top and bottom) are required. Our uprights are 1730mm (5ft 8in) long and the rails are 710mm (28in) long. Ensure the ends are exactly square.

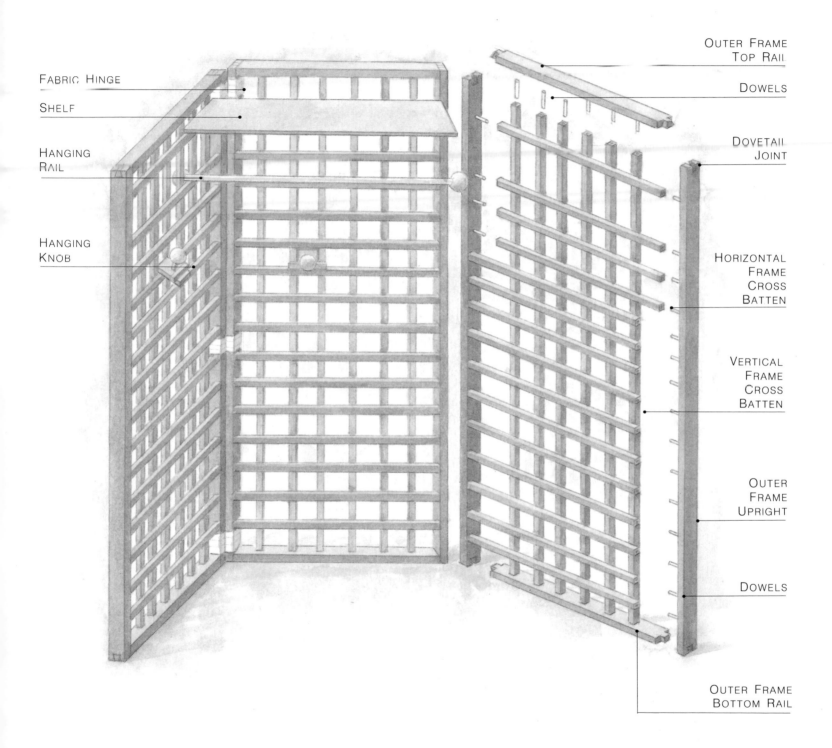

FABRIC HINGE

SHELF

HANGING RAIL

HANGING KNOB

OUTER FRAME TOP RAIL

DOWELS

DOVETAIL JOINT

HORIZONTAL FRAME CROSS BATTEN

VERTICAL FRAME CROSS BATTEN

OUTER FRAME UPRIGHT

DOWELS

OUTER FRAME BOTTOM RAIL

FOLDING SCREEN

DOVETAILING THE TOP AND BOTTOM RAILS

For a full description of how to make a basic dovetail joint (*see* **Techniques, page 29**). included here are instructions that are specific to this project. Set your marking gauge to the thickness of the rail and mark off this distance from the end of the short rail, continuing the line around both faces and edges. Repeat for each end of the top and bottom rails.

Mark off the approximate pin shape on to the end of a piece of scrap wood of the same stock size and work out the correct setting for your marking gauge (or mortise gauge if you have one).

Using the gauge, mark off the lines of the top of the pin on to the outer face of the rail. Then, using the sliding bevel, mark out the pin on to the ends of the rails using a pencil sharpened to a blade. Continue the lines of the bottom of the pin round on to the inner face, using a try square (fig 1). Repeat the procedure for each end of the top and bottom rails of each frame.

Hold the rail upright in a vice and saw down through each pencil line to the depth of your marked line, using a fine tenon saw or a dovetail saw. Then hold the rail horizontally in the vice to remove the shoulders of the tail, to leave only the pin, sawing down to the marked line of the tail. Repeat the procedure for each end of the top and bottom rails.

DOVETAILING UPRIGHTS

Using the marking gauge as before, set it to the stock thickness and mark off the ends as before, continuing the lines right around the rail. Number each joint to ease assembly later.

Lay a short rail lengthwise on top of a long one to mark off the thickness of the pin. Then stand the short rail upright at the end of the long one to mark the cut-out to house the pin on to the long rail, which will be the 'post' (fig 2).

Repeat for each joint, making sure that you number them as you go, as they will not be interchangeable. Transfer the marks round on to the ends with a try square. Mark each end of the uprights in this way.

To make the vertical cuts, the post must be held firm. It is best to place it upright in a vice, supported with long packing pieces cramped on either side, and then to stand on steps to reach it. Cutting *inside* the pencil lines (the waste side), make angled cuts to the marked line.

To remove the waste from the post, use a coping saw to cut down the centre and out to each side, being sure to stay a little way inside the marked lines. Pare down to the sides with a paring chisel. Repeat for the other ends of the uprights and fit the joints together, matching the identification numbers. Identify the face of the rails and uprights as well as their pins and tails. It is a good idea to do a practice joint first on a piece of scrap wood.

CROSS BATTENS

With the frame dry assembled, measure the internal dimensions and cut the cross battens from 25 × 25mm (1 × 1in) PAR to these measurements. In our case, there are 15 horizontals and 6 verticals per panel. Dismantle the frame.

We used 6mm (¼in) diameter hardwood dowels, 30mm (1¼in) long to fix the cross battens into the outer frame. (This is about the right size. If your dowel sizes are different, you will have to adjust the dimensions accordingly.)

Using a dowelling jig, drill the ends of all the battens in their centres to a depth of 19mm (about ¾in), using a 6mm (¼in) diameter centrepoint or dowel drill (also called a lip-and-spur drill).

MARKING DOWEL HOLES

Take the vertical battens and bunch them up together on the top and bottom rails, against the shoulders of the dovetail joints. Measure to the other shoulder and divide this figure by the number of spaces. This will give you the gap between all the battens. Measure this distance in from the shoulder, plus half the thickness of the batten. The first dowel hole centre will be on this line. From then on, mark the dowel hole centre lines according to the spacing measurements already calculated. The final distance should be

1 Dovetailing the Rails
Depth marked all round; top of pin marked. Dovetail marked on end; bottom of pin marked.

2 Marking the Frame Uprights
Depth and thickness of rail pin marked; then shape of pin marked on frame upright.

3 Completing the Outer Frame Dovetail Joints
Top rail pin is cut with a fine tenon saw or a dovetail saw. Frame upright post is cut with dovetail and coping saws. Clean up the joint with a pairing chisel for a good, secure fit.

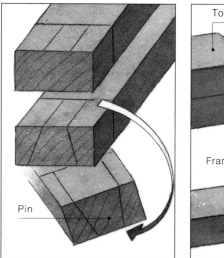

Pin

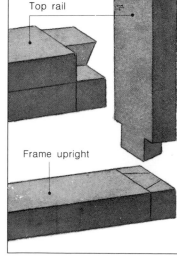

Top rail

Frame upright

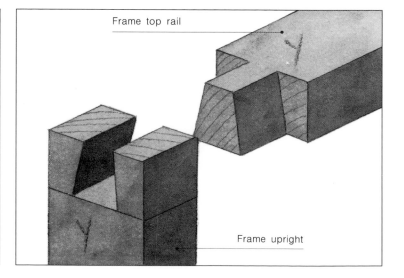

Frame top rail

Frame upright

the same as the first. Transfer the hole marks to all the other top and bottom rails.

To mark the dowel hole positions widthways, find the centre of the rail width and measure out from it exactly half the thickness of the vertical batten. (This will be less than the nominal 25mm [1in].) Draw a line down the rail. Where it crosses the dowel hole lines will be the dowel hole centre points (fig 5).

Repeat the above procedure for the horizontal battens on the upright posts, spacing them apart by the same distance as for the vertical battens. Space one of the battens down from the top, and then the rest of them up from the bottom. This will create a larger gap between the top horizontal batten and the next one down, which is where the removable shelf fits.

To mark the dowel hole positions widthways, measure exactly half the batten thickness out from the centre, but in the opposite direction to that of the vertical battens. This ensures that the horizontal battens are fitted *exactly* in front of the verticals.

Drill all the marked holes to a diameter of 6mm ($\frac{1}{4}$in) and a depth of 12mm ($\frac{1}{2}$in).

ASSEMBLING THE PANELS

To assemble a panel, put a small amount of glue in each dowel hole in the top and bottom rails. Insert the dowels. Put a small amount of glue into the hole on each end of the vertical battens and push them into all the dowels.

Take one of the posts and glue and assemble both of the dovetail joints on one side. Then glue and dowel all of the horizontal battens into the upright post. Glue and join the second post, the dovetails and the dowels simultaneously.

Use sash cramps (or a webbing cramp or folding wedges) across the panel to pull the joints together. Then, using a spacing block, check that all the spaces are equal, and pin the battens to each other where they cross, using the spacing block as you go. Repeat the procedure for the other two panels and apply the finish of your choice according to your decorative scheme.

④ Working Out Dowel Hole Spacing for Vertical Battens
Bunch the vertical battens together on top and bottom rails against shoulders of the dovetail joints. Measure gap to other shoulder and calculate spacing of battens.

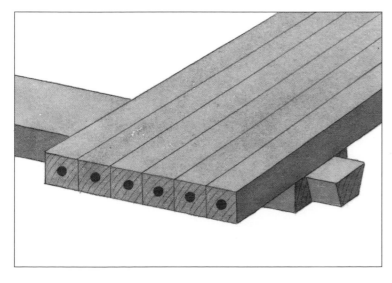

⑤ Vertical Batten Assembly
Mark and drill dowel holes in rails. Apply glue and insert dowels. Glue holes in battens and attach dowels.

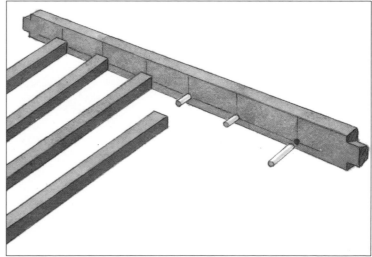

TEMPORARY WARDROBE
The screen can be easily converted to a wardrobe for hanging clothes. Useful when guests come to stay.

FOLDING SCREEN

FABRIC HINGES

The three panels are joined together with fabric hinges at the top, bottom and middle. These allow the screen to fold in either direction. Each hinge has three separate strips to it, made from 25mm (1in) wide coloured webbing to match the finish you choose for the screen.

The two outer strips are identical and are fixed first, leaving a space for the middle one, which is fitted the opposite way around. Follow the diagram to fit the first strip, by stapling or tacking it on to one panel and joining it to the next by winding

round in a figure of eight to cover the ends. Put temporary staples in to hold the webbing firm where necessary while winding round. Staple the last face to the panel and push the end through on to the next face. This should conceal the staples on both panels. Repeat for the other outer strip of webbing fabric.

Follow fig 3 to fix the middle strip. You will not be able to take this one round as far as the others, concealing only the first set of staples and not the second set. Push the end through on to the next face as before. Make three hinges between each pair of panels.

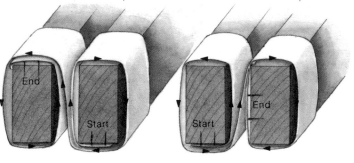

Outer strips   Middle strip

DETAIL OF SCREEN HINGE
The fabric hinge enables the screen to fold in two directions. Fabric matches screen colour.

1 **Assembling Horizontals**
Apply glue and push first upright post into dovetails of top and bottom rails. Glue and dowel.

2 **Assembling the Second Upright Post**
Glue and join dovetails and dowels. Batten left out at top at same time.

3 **Making the Hinges**
Wind webbing fabric around the panel uprights in the direction of the arrows to form a secure hinge.

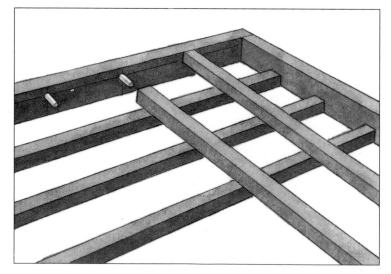

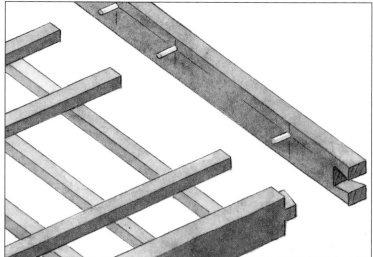

HANGING RAILS

Set the screen up in a U-shape and measure across for the hanging rails from the outside edges of the cross battens, plus 19mm ($\frac{3}{4}$in) each end to go into 75mm or 63mm (3in or 2$\frac{1}{2}$in) diameter wooden knobs. Cut the required number of hanging rails from 25mm (1in) dowel. Each rail will be about 760mm (30in) long if made to our dimensions.

Put each knob in turn into a vice and drill it to a depth of 19mm ($\frac{3}{4}$in) using a 25mm (1in) flat bit. Assemble the rails by gluing the dowel and knobs together and slot them into place where desired.

SHELF

Use 12mm ($\frac{1}{2}$in) plywood to make a shelf, if required. This rests on top of the cross battens and is easily removable when you want to fold the screen. Cut the shelf to fit (about 300mm [12in] deep). As it is intended as a temporary shelf it should not be used for heavy items, but it is perfectly adequate for shirts and other light clothes.

HANGING KNOBS

To make a back plate, use a piece of 25mm (1in) PAR softwood as high as one section of the outer dimensions of the horizontal battens and of a width to fit easily between the vertical battens.

Using a 25 × 25mm (1 × 1in) offcut, cut a piece as long as the outer dimensions of one upright batten to the next. This is the stopper. Put the back plate into position in one square and the stopper in place to the front of it, to mark where it will fit on the back plate.

Drill a 25mm (1in) diameter hole in the back plate, its centre about 25mm (1in) up from the top of the stopper position, to a depth of 12mm ($\frac{1}{2}$in). Cut a piece of 25mm (1in) dowel to a length of 75mm (3in) and glue it in the hole. Glue and pin the stopper in place to the back plate.

Drill a 25mm (1in) diameter hole to a depth of 19mm ($\frac{3}{4}$in) into a 50mm (2in) diameter wooden knob and glue it in place on top of the dowel. Hanging knobs can be slotted into any square.

④ Pinning the Battens
Cramp frame and, with an offcut to check the exact dimension of the spacings, pin battens together.

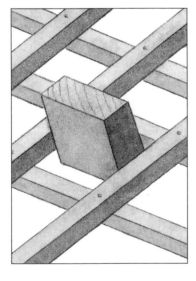

⑤ Marking the Hanging Rail and Hanging Knobs
Hanging rail is 25mm (1in) diameter dowel with wooden knobs at ends. Hanging knobs comprise batten across back plate on which wooden knob on short dowel is fixed.

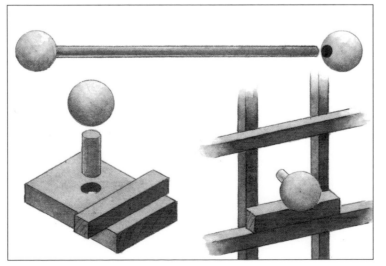

DETAIL OF WARDROBE

As a wardrobe, the screen is a stylish addition to any bedroom, hall or spare room.

JAPANESE WARDROBE

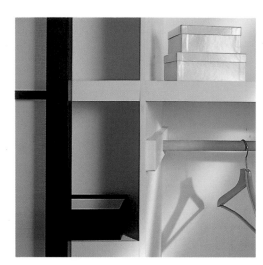

Although this particular sliding screen has been designed as a wardrobe in a bedroom, the same construction would look equally stylish in a living room. To me, there is nothing more serene than a traditional Japanese room and I have tried to echo this serenity in this project.

It is essential that the frame that holds the screens forms a rectangle, with every corner an exact right-angle. For this reason you will notice that there is a scribing fillet around the edge of the screen's frame to take up the inaccuracies of your floor, walls and ceiling.

The screens are simply constructed to a rectangular module which will vary according to the exact size of the wall you wish to screen. I have used a tough, natural, creamy cotton rather than traditional Japanese paper to back the screen, but you could alter the material to suit your own decorative scheme.

One of the great bonuses of this screen wall, apart from the benefit of hiding away clutter, is that a light inside the wardrobe will be gently diffused by the fabric and provide an elegant backdrop to your bedroom or living space.

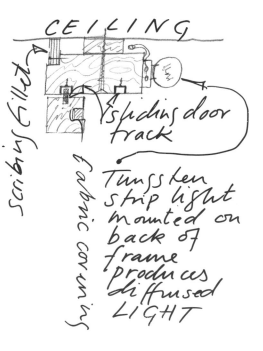

PLAN OF WALL FIXING –
Block to take up unevenness between wall ceiling & frame

WALL

Wallplug

sliding door track

sliding Door cloth backing held in place by fillet

scribing fillet painted the same colour as Wall and Ceiling

SIDE ELEVATION OF CEILING FIXING

CEILING

scribing fillet

fabric covering

sliding door track

Tungsten strip light mounted on back of frame produces diffused LIGHT

FRONT ELEVATION OF JAPANESE WARDROBE

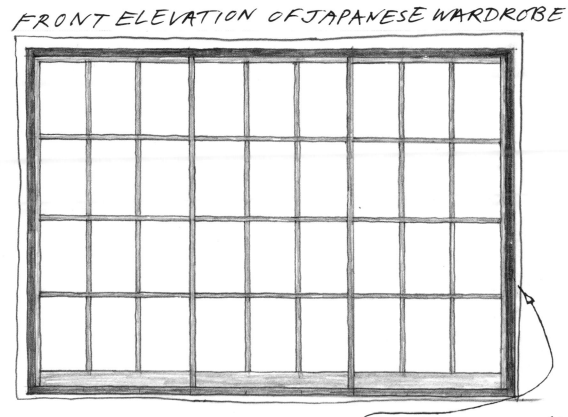

Gap between wall
and wardrobe frame
filled with scribing
fillet.

PLAN

hanging
rail

shelves

sliding doors

uprights fixed
to sides of chimney
breast to form side
of shelving unit.

Japanese Wardrobe

The lightweight sliding doors of this fitted wardrobe are divided with a narrow trellis-like framework and backed with fabric to produce a Japanese-style 'wall'. The doors are designed to fit wall-to-wall across a room with (or without) a chimney breast and alcoves. Lights are fitted behind the doors to light the inside of the wardrobe and to throw a diffused light into the room when the doors are closed – an excellent way to create a restful atmosphere in a bedroom.

In our design, the doors slide in front of the chimney breast, completely hiding it. Vertical partition panels are fitted to each side of the chimney breast, protruding a short distance in front of it and allowing narrow shelves to the width of the chimney breast to be incorporated.

If you are building this wardrobe on a flat wall, you will still need to fit two internal partition panels to support the hanging rails and the deep shelves. However, in this case all the shelves will be deep, and there will be room for three hanging rails instead of two.

For neatness, where there is no chimney breast, make the vertical partition panels as two narrow plywood-covered box sections.

MATERIALS

Part	Quantity	Material	Length
PARTITIONS	2	19mm ($\frac{3}{4}$in) plywood, blockboard or chipboard. Width as inside depth of cupboard (530mm [21in] in our case)	Room height
DEEP SHELVES	4	As above; 518mm ($20\frac{1}{2}$in) wide to allow for thickness of shelf lipping	Distance between partition panels and side walls
SHALLOW SHELVES	6	19mm ($\frac{3}{4}$in) plywood, blockboard or chipboard. Width as distance from chimney breast to front of partition panels, less 12mm ($\frac{1}{2}$in)	Distance between partition panels
SHELF LIPPING	10	38 × 12mm ($1\frac{1}{2} \times \frac{1}{2}$in) PAR pine or hardwood	As shelf lengths
DEEP SHELF REAR SUPPORT BATTENS	4	25 × 25mm (1 × 1in) PAR softwood	As shelf length
DEEP SHELF SIDE SUPPORT BATTENS	8	25 × 25mm (1 × 1in) PAR softwood	Shelf depth, less 38mm ($1\frac{1}{2}$in)
SHALLOW SHELF REAR SUPPORT BATTENS	6	25 × 25mm (1 × 1in) PAR softwood	As shelf length
SHALLOW SHELF SIDE SUPPORT BATTENS	12	25 × 25mm (1 × 1in) PAR softwood	Shelf depth, less 38mm ($1\frac{1}{2}$in)
HANGING RAIL	2	Chrome rail or 25mm (1in) diameter dowel	Alcove width
RAIL SUPPORT BATTENS	4	75 × 25mm (3 × 1in) PAR softwood	2 at 530mm (21in) 2 at 610mm (24in)

DOOR FRAMES

TOP AND BOTTOM RAILS	2	100 × 50mm (4 × 2in) PAR softwood	Room width, plus 150mm (6in)*
UPRIGHTS	2	As above	Room height*
TOP SCRIBING FILLET	1	25 × 30mm (1 × $1\frac{1}{4}$in) PAR softwood	Room width*
SIDE SCRIBING FILLET	2	As above	Room height*

DOORS (quantities are for one door. Our project uses three doors)

STILES (side rails)	2	50 × 50mm (2 × 2in) PAR softwood	Internal height of door frame, less clearance for door gear
TOP RAIL	1	50 × 50mm (2 × 2in) PAR softwood	One-third of internal width of frame
BOTTOM RAIL	1	100 × 50mm (4 × 2in) PAR softwood	As above
HORIZONTAL TRANSOMS (central bars)	3	25 × 25mm (1 × 1in) PAR softwood	Internal width of door frame, plus 25mm (1in)
VERTICAL MULLIONS (central bars)	2	25 × 25mm (1 × 1in) PAR softwood	Internal height of door frame, plus 25mm (1in)
SIDE FABRIC FASTENING BATTENS	2	9 × 9mm ($\frac{3}{8} \times \frac{3}{8}$in) PAR softwood	Internal height of door frame, plus 100mm (4in)
TOP AND BOTTOM FABRIC FASTENING BATTENS	2	9 × 9mm ($\frac{3}{8} \times \frac{3}{8}$in) PAR softwood	Internal width of door frame, plus 100mm (4in)

*Dimensions are oversize to allow for trimming later.

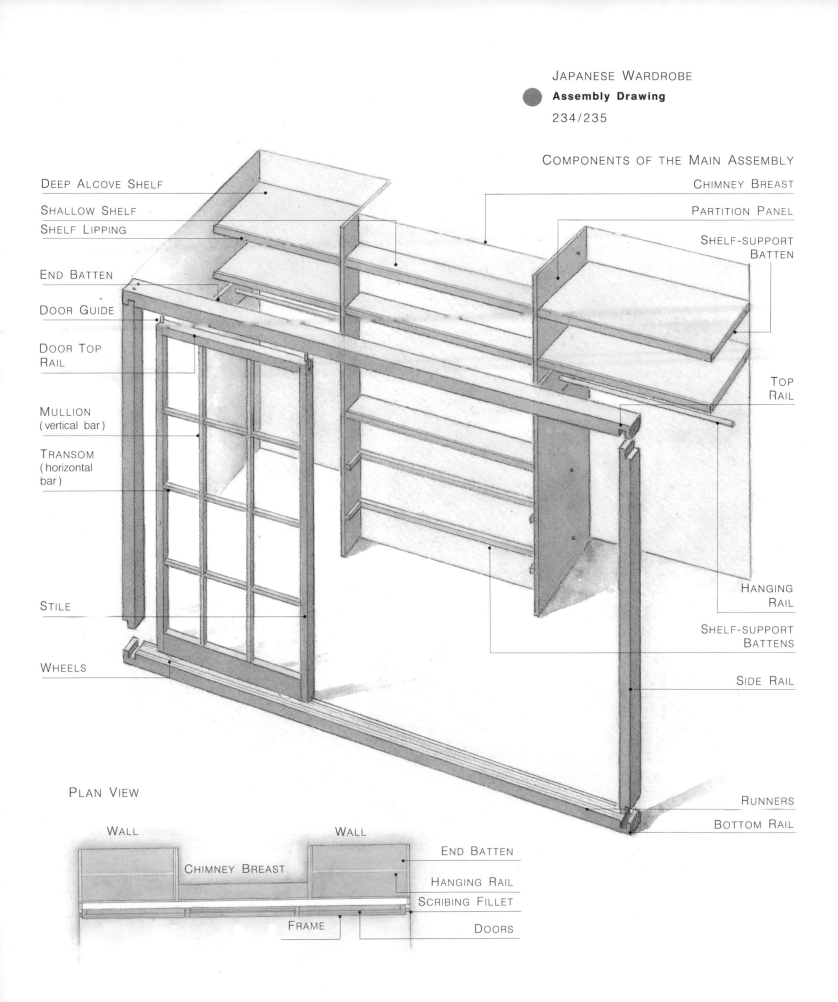

COMPONENTS OF THE MAIN ASSEMBLY

DEEP ALCOVE SHELF

SHALLOW SHELF

SHELF LIPPING

END BATTEN

DOOR GUIDE

DOOR TOP RAIL

MULLION (vertical bar)

TRANSOM (horizontal bar)

STILE

WHEELS

CHIMNEY BREAST

PARTITION PANEL

SHELF-SUPPORT BATTEN

TOP RAIL

HANGING RAIL

SHELF-SUPPORT BATTENS

SIDE RAIL

RUNNERS

BOTTOM RAIL

PLAN VIEW

WALL

WALL

CHIMNEY BREAST

END BATTEN

HANGING RAIL

SCRIBING FILLET

FRAME

DOORS

Japanese Wardrobe

Setting out

Decide on the internal layout of the wardrobe: the height of the hanging rails, the position of the shelves, etc. Our shelves are spaced at 350mm (14in) centres down the chimney breast, with hanging rails in the alcoves at either side and two deep shelves above the main hanging rail.

Mark the internal depth of the wardrobe (ours is 610mm [24in], a good width for hanging clothes). Mark all the way round: on walls, floor and ceiling. Start by marking a point 610mm (24in) out from the rear wall at each end and mark on to the side walls just above the skirting. Hang a chalked plumb line on each wall to align with these marks and snap the line to mark a vertical line. Snap a chalked line on to the ceiling to join these two lines. Repeat for the floor. This line will be the inside of the door frame.

If you are working in an old house where the room is not square, you may not be able to measure out from the end wall to fix the position of the door frame. Instead, you may have to use the 3-4-5 method (see **Techniques, page 20**) to get the frame at right-angles to one, or both, of the side walls. Mark the frame position on the floor, then snap vertical lines on the side walls and finally snap a line on the ceiling. Also, in an old house the floor, walls and ceiling may slope a lot. If this is the case, you may have to use packing pieces under the floor rail and scribe wide packing pieces between the sides and top of the door frame to fill odd-shaped gaps. It is vital that the door frame is square, regardless of how much the walls, floor and ceiling are out of true.

After marking the inside of the door frame line, measure back 75mm (3in) and snap another line around the walls, floor and ceiling parallel with the first line. This inside line marks the front edge of the shelves and partition panels.

Partitions

Cut partition panels to the height of the room from 19mm ($\frac{3}{4}$in) plywood, blockboard or chipboard. These are fixed on each side of the chimney breast and their width is the distance from the rear wall to the inside line (530mm [21in] in our case).

Position the panels, check that they are upright by packing them out if necessary, and screw and wallplug them to each side of the chimney breast.

If there is no chimney breast, make and fix two twin-skinned hollow partition panels as follows:

Each partition is made from two panels of 9mm ($\frac{3}{8}$in) plywood on a 50 × 25mm (2 × 1in) PAR timber framework. The panels should be slotted over 50 × 25mm (2 × 1in) battens fixed to the rear of the wall, floor and ceiling to give a strong, invisible fixing. Within the panels, fit cross battens to provide a strong fixing to coincide with the positions of the shelves and hanging rails.

Shelves

On the back and side walls mark the positions of the undersides of the shelves, using a pencil, spirit level and straight-edge (a straight length of planed timber batten will do).

Cut shelf-support battens from planed pine to run along the back and side walls, allowing for the thickness of the lipping on the front of the shelves. The battens are 25 × 25mm (1 × 1in) (see **Materials list, page 234**).

Drill and screw the battens to the rear walls, side walls and partition panels, ensuring that they are level with one another, and on each side of the partition panels. Wallplugs will be required where the battens are fixed to masonry walls.

Fill over the screwheads and paint the battens so that they match the wall colour.

Cut the shelves to fit from 19mm ($\frac{3}{4}$in) plywood, blockboard or chipboard, and lip the front edges with 38 × 12mm (1$\frac{1}{2}$ × $\frac{1}{2}$in) pine or hardwood so that the top edge is flush and the lipping overhangs to hide the support battens.

Hanging Rails

Use proprietary chrome rails and end supports, or 25mm (1in) diameter wooden dowels, cut to fit the widths of the alcoves. The dowels are fitted in 75 × 25mm (3 × 1in) end battens cut to fit the width of the cupboard from the frame to the back wall in the case of the end battens, and from the front edge of the partition panels to the back wall for the inside battens. To form the hanging rail, the inside battens are drilled centrally to hold the dowels and the end battens drilled to correspond. To fit the rail, screw the end batten to the wall, slot the inside batten on to the dowel, then fit the dowel in the fixed batten, and finally screw the other batten in place, checking with a spirit level that the rail is level. Make sure that the rails on each side are level with one another, and are at the desired height.

Sliding Door Frame

The frame is built to give a 30mm (1$\frac{1}{4}$in) gap at the top of the frame and at each side, to allow for scribing for a neat finish while coping with skirting and irregularities in the wall and ceiling surfaces. When you measure up, allow for these spaces and make the frame to these external dimensions.

The frame is made from 100 × 50mm (4 × 2in) PAR (planed all round) timber and is constructed with bare-faced housing joints (see **Techniques, page 27**) at the corners. This type of joint is very strong, but the short grain on the outside of the grooves is a weakness and therefore the top and bottom rails are left about 150mm (6in) overlength to form 'horns' which are trimmed off after the joint is made.

Put the top and bottom rails side by side and cramp them together. Mark off the external width of the frame on to them. Rest a frame upright across the top and bottom rails to mark off the internal dimensions and then mark this line square on the top and bottom rails using a try square and a trimming knife. Set a marking gauge to half the thickness of the uprights and mark off from the internal face, squaring across as you go with a try square and a trimming knife.

Use a router to cut out the housing (or groove) as marked, or saw along the inside (waste side) of the housing lines using a fine-toothed tenon saw and then chisel out the waste wood.

Cut the frame uprights to length. (Note that these fit into the bottom of the housings.) Using the marking gauge as set for marking out the housing, mark off for the tongues at the ends of the rails which will fit into the housings.

Cut out the waste with a tenon saw so that the tongues fit securely in the housings.

Dry assemble the frame to check that the external dimensions are accurate enough to fit the room size with approximately 30mm (1¼in) spaces at the top and at each side of the frame. These will be filled using the scribing fillets which will ensure a neat fit.

Take the frame apart and fit the sliding door gear. The method of fitting depends on the type and you must follow the manufacturer's instructions. It is very important to choose a door gear in which the wheels run along a bottom track, rather than hang from a top track, otherwise our frame will not be suitable. It is much easier to fit this bottom-running track and the guide track at the top before the frame is finally assembled.

Assemble the frame, gluing the joints and screwing through the top and bottom rails into the uprights. At this point the frame must be braced square before the glue sets. This is done by nailing two diagonal braces on opposing corners of the frame following the 3-4-5 method of bracing (see **Techniques, page 20**).

FIXING THE FRAME

Lift the frame into position, ensuring that the upright rails are centralized between the side walls, with a 30mm (1¼in) gap at each side. Use a spirit level to check that the bottom rail is absolutely level, and if necessary adjust it with packing pieces. With the diagonal braces still in position, screw the bottom rail to the floor after scanning the floor with a metal detector to ensure that the screws will not puncture pipes or wiring just beneath the floorboards. Use 75mm (3in) No 10 woodscrews, and, if possible, try to coincide the screws with the positions of the floor joists (floorboard fixing nails will indicate their location).

Check that the frame is vertical, then drill the side rails and wall at about 610mm (24in) intervals so that the frame-fixing screws complete with wallplugs (ie, Fischer Frame Fixings or equivalent) can be inserted. Before tightening the screws, insert packing pieces between the uprights and the wall at the fixing points, keeping the pack-

ing pieces 25mm (1in) back from the front edge of the frame so that the scribing fillets can later be fitted between the frame and the wall. Check that the frame is still square by measuring across the diagonals, to ensure that they are of an equal length. If necessary, adjust the packing on either side.

Drill and screw the top rail to the ceiling, using 100mm (4in) No 12 screws, and fixing into the ceiling joists where possible. As with the uprights, at the screw position insert packing pieces between the top of the rail and the ceiling before finally tightening the screws.

Check again that the frame is square, and then remove the bracing battens.

Between each side and the walls, and between the top rail and the ceiling, scribe a fillet, made from 6mm (¼in) plywood, to the wall and ceiling to fill the space. Fix the fillet by screwing into packing pieces.

Fill over the screwheads and, when dry, paint the frame the same colour as the wall so that it blends in with the rest of the room.

① Shelf Construction and Fitting of Shelf-support Battens
Shelves have lipping on front edges to hide the support battens and to stiffen the shelves to help prevent them from sagging. Remember to allow for the thickness of the lipping by setting back the side battens.

② Shelf Lipping
Plywood, blockboard or chipboard shelves have hardwood lipping glued and pinned to the front edge.

③ Housing Joints in Frame
Housing joints are used at the corners of the frame. Note the horns which are cut off later.

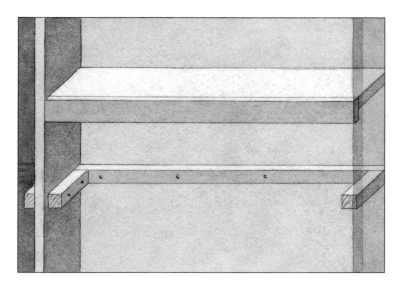

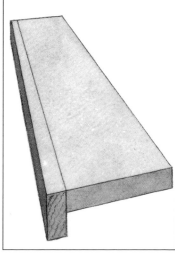

Japanese Wardrobe

Sliding Doors

Work out the external dimensions of the doors. For the door height, measure the height of the internal frame, allowing for the clearance specified in the instructions supplied with the sliding door gear. For the door width, divide the internal width of the frame by the number of doors required (we use three), allowing for the doors to overlap each other by the thickness of the door stiles.

Using timber as specified in the Materials list (page 234), cut the door stiles (side rails) slightly overlength and mark off on them the positions of the top and bottom rails. Haunched mortise and tenon joints are used to join the door components at the corners (*see* **Techniques, page 29**).

Cut the top and bottom rails to length and chop out the mortises in the stiles, then cut the tenons on the rails. The stiles are left overlength at this stage to avoid breaking out the end of the mortise while cutting it.

Dry assemble the door frame and check that the joints fit well.

Repeat the procedure for the other doors.

To make the transoms (horizontal internal bars) on each door, measure the internal width between the stiles, and cut three transoms to this length, plus 25mm (1in). (The number of bars can be varied according to the size of the doors you are making.) Measure the distance between the top and bottom rails and cut two mullions (vertical bars) to this length, plus 25mm (1in). (Again, the number of bars can be varied to suit the door size.) The bars are joined to the frame with bare-faced tenon joints and where they overlap they are joined with cross halvings.

Take the frame apart and cut the mortises for the sliding door wheels in the bottom edge of the bottom rails (see the manufacturer's instructions).

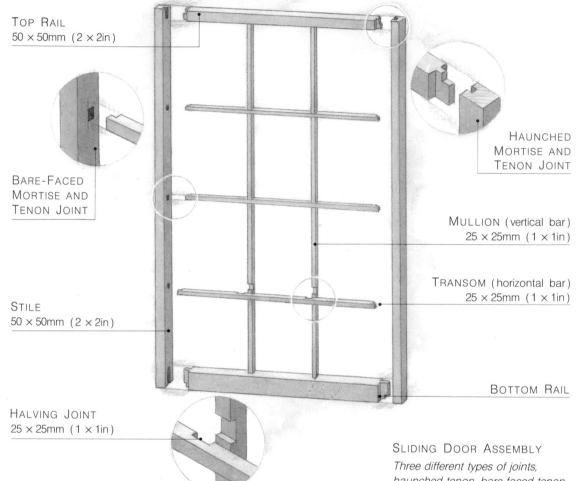

TOP RAIL
50 × 50mm (2 × 2in)

BARE-FACED MORTISE AND TENON JOINT

STILE
50 × 50mm (2 × 2in)

HALVING JOINT
25 × 25mm (1 × 1in)

HAUNCHED MORTISE AND TENON JOINT

MULLION (vertical bar)
25 × 25mm (1 × 1in)

TRANSOM (horizontal bar)
25 × 25mm (1 × 1in)

BOTTOM RAIL

SLIDING DOOR ASSEMBLY
Three different types of joints, haunched tenon, bare-faced tenon, and halving, are used in assembly.

Work out the spacing for all the internal bars and mark them on the inside faces of the frame. Set the mortise gauge to the full thickness of the 25 × 25mm (1 × 1in) bars, and gauge a line from the back of the door frame to mark the front positions of the bars.

Using a square-edge chisel (a mortise chisel is ideal, although an ordinary firmer chisel will do), or a router cutter, chop out, or rout, mortise slots to 12mm ($\frac{1}{2}$in) depth, and to half the thickness of the square bars, by their full width.

Set the marking gauge to the width of the chisel or router cutter that you have used for cutting the mortises, and using this setting, mark off the thickness of the tenon on the ends of the internal bars. Reset the gauge to 12mm ($\frac{1}{2}$in) and mark off the lengths of the tenons on both ends of each bar. Cut the (bare-faced) tenons. When fitted, the back of each bar should lie flush with the back of the door frame.

Cut halving joints at the intersections of all of the bars (*see* **Techniques, page 26**).

Start assembly by gluing the cross halving joints and assembling the bars carefully, as they are easy to break. Assemble the top and bottom rails into the mullions, gluing all the joints beforehand.

Apply glue to the mortises and shoulders on one side of the doors and assemble the stile on to this side of the tenons of the top and bottom rails and transoms simultaneously.

Repeat the procedure to fit the second stile.

Put sash cramps across the doors in line with the transoms, or put a web cramp right around the door. Check that the door is flat and square (the diagonals should be equal).

When the glue has set, remove the cramps and cut the excess timber off the door stiles. Use a sharp plane to skim the faces of the door to ensure that all the joints are flush.

JAPANESE WARDROBE

With the lights switched on, this wardrobe becomes an interesting trellis-like framework. The diffused light behind the fabric panels creates a restful backdrop in any room.

Repeat for the other doors. If you find these joints too hard to make, or too time-consuming, the door could be dowelled together *(see* **Techniques, page 30** *)*. Dowel joints are perfectly secure when glued with PVA adhesive.

To fit the fabric behind the door, a groove is formed in the back of the door frame, and the fabric is laid in the groove, where it is then held in place with a batten pressed into the groove. Use a router to make the groove, which should be 9mm (⅜in) wide and the same depth. The groove is cut in the back of the door frame with its outer edge 25mm (1in) in from the inside of the frame.

Cut a 9mm (⅜in) square batten and check that it is a tight fit when slid into the groove. If necessary, plane it to fit. Cut lengths of batten to fit the groove, mitring the corners.

Following the door gear manufacturer's instructions, fit the wheel into the mortises previously cut in the bottom of the doors, and fit the guides to the tops of the doors.

Try the doors in place and check that they run correctly. If necessary, adjust the door gear according to the manufacturer's instructions. Paint or finish the doors as required.

For the fabric we used 50% polyester/50% cotton sheeting. Cut and fit the fabric by laying the door

❶ Fitting the Fabric Behind the Door Using Battens
To fit the fabric neatly, it is held in a groove in the back of the door by a batten which fits in to the groove, holding the fabric taut. Mitre the corners of the battens for a neat effect.

frame down and draping the fabric over it. You will need a helper to keep the fabric taut. Fit one long edge, screwing the batten in place to hold the fabric down. Pull the fabric taut to fit the opposite edge in the same way. Fit one end like this, and finally fit the opposite end in the same way. Screw the battens in place rather than pin them, as this allows them to be removed neatly when the fabric is to be cleaned.

Fit the doors in place *(see* **Techniques, page 32** *).*

Wire in the internal lights. We used tungsten-tube strip lights fitted to the back of the door frame at the top and sides, to give an even light.

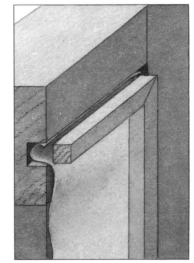

BED WITH TRUCKLE DRAWER

A lack of adequate storage space for blankets, duvets and unseasonal clothing is a perennial problem in bedrooms.

This generous bed provides storage space under the mattress, in a pull-out truckle drawer, and beneath the head-board, which is padded to make sitting up in bed and reading a book a real pleasure. The bed is designed so that it is easy to dismantle should you wish to move house, something that is quite often a problem with conventional double and king-size beds.

The loose covers of the headboard and footboard are easily removable for cleaning and can be made from fabric to coordinate with the other soft furnishings in your bedroom.

Generous storage space at the head and in the foot of the bed

pull on loose covers fit over 1" (25mm) foam glued to the foot & head-boards

Velcro fastening

Angled back provides comfortable support for reading in bed.

pull out drawer on castors slides underneath foot of bed.

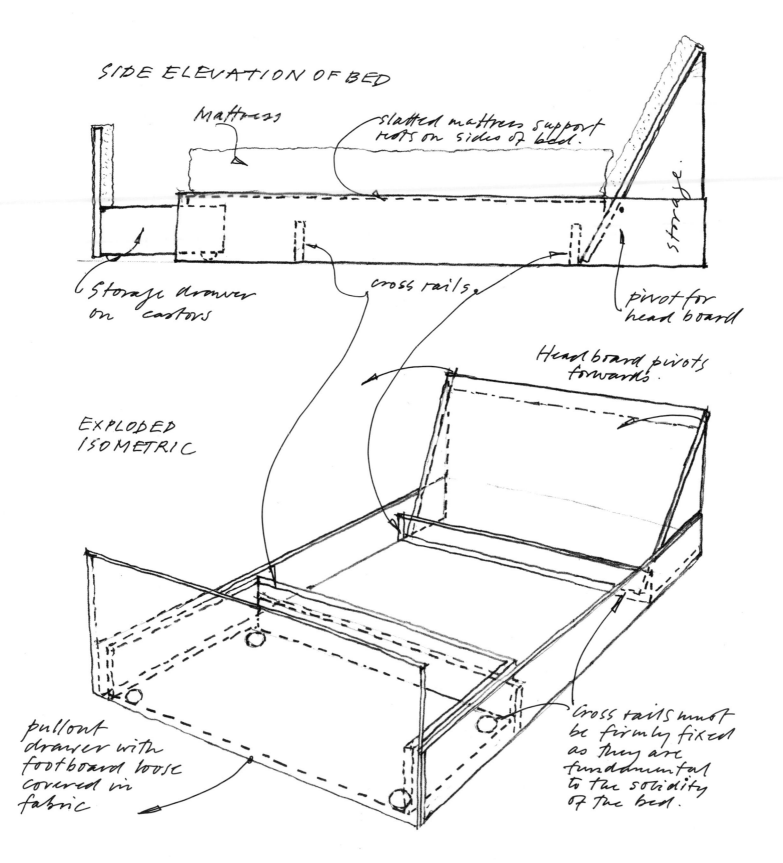

SIDE ELEVATION OF BED

Mattress

slatted mattress support rests on sides of bed.

storage.

Storage drawer on castors

cross rails.

pivot for head board

EXPLODED ISOMETRIC

Head board pivots forwards.

pullout drawer with footboard loose covered in fabric

Cross rails must be firmly fixed as they are fundamental to the solidity of the bed.

Bed with Truckle Drawer

The bed should be assembled in the room for which it is intended. However, it is designed to be taken apart and reassembled if necessary – when moving house, for example.

Firstly, decide how large the bed is to be. The length will be determined by that of the mattress – 2m (6ft 6in) is standard – plus 350mm (14in) for the headrest section. When the bed is positioned in the room, there must be sufficient space between its end and a wall or furniture for the truckle drawer to be pulled out fully by means of the footboard. The drawer shown is 610mm (24in) long.

The width of the bed is again determined by the size of the mattress. The 'king size' mattress here is 1.8m (6ft) wide, but the bed can be made for one of 1.5m (5ft) or 1.35m (4ft 6in). It can also be adapted for a single-width mattress. The bed's height is also optional. Ours is 450mm (18in), offering plenty of storage space below.

The angled headboard provides comfortable support when you are sitting up in bed, and the upholstered top panel is readily removable to give access to ample storage space in the headrest section.

Further 'long-term' storage space – for duvets and other bedding, for example – is available below the bed. This is reached by removing the mattress and the central slatted section of the mattress support.

The main components of the bed are constructed from 19mm ($\frac{3}{4}$in) plywood, MDF or chipboard. The edges of the latter will have to be lipped with hardwood, which must be allowed for when you are calculating the dimensions.

The Shaker-style pegboard shown in the photograph on page 242 is simple to construct. It consists of a timber batten fixed around the room at picture-rail height which is then fitted with wooden hanging pegs at regular intervals. The pegs are used for storage, to hang curtains or even pictures.

MATERIALS

Part	Quantity	Material	Length
THE BASE			
SIDE PANELS	2	19mm ($\frac{3}{4}$in) plywood, MDF or chipboard	Length of mattress plus 350mm (14in) × required height
CROSS DIVIDERS	2	As above	Width of mattress × height of sides less 100mm (4in)
CORNER BATTENS	4	50 × 50mm (2 × 2in) softwood	Height of cross dividers
HEADBOARD			
TRIANGULAR HEADBOARD SUPPORTS	2	19mm ($\frac{3}{4}$in) plywood, MDF or chipboard	1125 × 575mm (45 × 23in) divided diagonally
TRIANGULAR FILLERS	2	As above	As required to fit
CROSS RAIL	1	75 × 25mm (3 × 1in) softwood	Width of mattress
HEADBOARD SECTIONS	2	19mm ($\frac{3}{4}$) plywood, MDF or chipboard	Width of mattress (see text for height)
STRENGTHENING BATTEN	1	50 × 50mm (2 × 2in) softwood	Width of mattress less 37mm (1$\frac{1}{2}$in)
MATTRESS SUPPORT SECTION			
SIDE RAILS	2	75 × 50mm (3 × 2in) softwood	Length of mattress plus approximately 75mm (3in)
END RAIL	1	As above	Width of mattress
CENTRE RAIL	1	As above	Length of mattress plus approximately 75mm (3in)
SLATS	As required	75 × 25mm (3 × 1in) softwood	Width of mattress
CROSS BATTENS	4	75 × 25mm (3 × 1in) softwood	Internal distance between cross dividers
TRUCKLE DRAWER			
FOOTBOARD	1	12mm ($\frac{1}{2}$in) MDF	Width of bed less 12mm ($\frac{1}{2}$in) × height as required
DRAWER SIDES	2	As above	Height of sides of bed less 150mm (6in)
BACK	1	As above	Height of drawer sides × width of mattress less 50mm (2in)
BASE	1	As above	Internal dimensions of truckle drawer

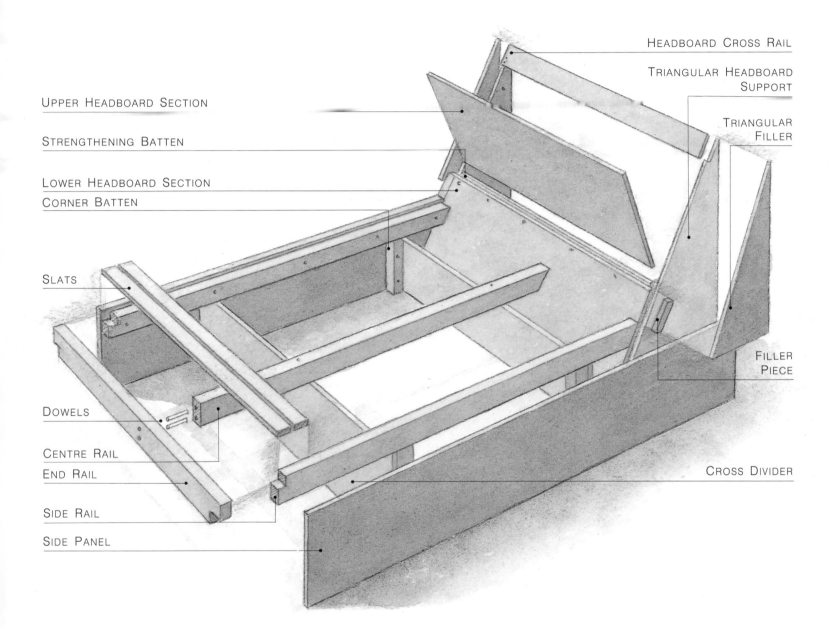

HEADBOARD CROSS RAIL

TRIANGULAR HEADBOARD SUPPORT

TRIANGULAR FILLER

UPPER HEADBOARD SECTION

STRENGTHENING BATTEN

LOWER HEADBOARD SECTION

CORNER BATTEN

SLATS

FILLER PIECE

DOWELS

CENTRE RAIL

END RAIL

CROSS DIVIDER

SIDE RAIL

SIDE PANEL

THE BASIC CONSTRUCTION OF THE BED

All the main components of the bed are shown here, except for the cross battens which fit under the slats, and the truckle drawer which fits under the bed end.

Bed with Truckle Drawer

Tools

STEEL MEASURING TAPE

ADHESIVE

TRY SQUARE

SPACING BATTEN

PANEL SAW

POWER DRILL

TENON SAW

ROUTER

SCREWDRIVER

CRAMPS

HAMMER

FILLING KNIFE

PLANE (or sanding block and abrasive paper)

The Base

Cut two side panels from 19mm (¾in) plywood, MDF or chipboard to the mattress length plus 350mm (14in) × required height. This one is 2.35mm × 450mm (7ft 8in × 18in).

You will also need two cross dividers and four corner battens. Measure 610mm (24in) in from each end of the side panels and mark the positions of the cross dividers. Drill and countersink the corner battens on one face. Check that they are square with a try square. Then, glue and screw them to the sides, inside the positions for the cross dividers and flush with the bottom edge.

Put the cross dividers in position against one of the sides, flush with the bottom edge (and outside the four corner battens), then drill, countersink and screw through the dividers into the corner battens (fig 1). Do not glue this fixing, as it can then be taken apart easily if the need arises, when moving house for example.

Put the other side panel in place and fix in the same way.

Headboard

By dividing diagonally, cut two triangular headboard supports from one rectangle measuring 1125 × 575mm (45 × 23in).

Headboard Cross Rail

A headboard cross rail supports the headrest at the top. Cut one length from 75 × 25mm (3 × 1in) timber, to the width of the mattress.

Making the Frame

Lay down one of the triangles and stand the cross rail on end, flush with the front edge of the triangle at the top, and as far to the point as it will go without overhanging the back. Mark its outline on to the end of the triangle. Repeat on the other triangle (fig 2).

Using a tenon saw or a jigsaw, cut inside the marked lines to remove the waste. This creates a notch for the headboard cross rail to sit on.

Fit the two triangular supports inside the sides, at the head end, flush with the ends of the sides. Drill and countersink the inside of the triangles in at least four places on each side, and screw one to each of the side panels (fig 3).

Put the cross rail in place. Drill and countersink the cross rail and screw it into the triangle's notches, keeping the screws low in the cross rail. Make sure that the ends of the cross rails are flush with the outside of the triangles (fig 4).

For the triangular fillers (fig 5), position a piece of MDF on the side panel. Line it up with the back edge of the triangular support and mark off the triangle on to it. Cut out this triangle and repeat for the other side. Fix the fillers in place by drilling, countersinking and screwing from the inside of the triangular supports. Use three screws each side.

The headboard consists of two pieces, one above the other, cut to the width of the mattress. For the height of the lower piece, measure up the triangular support from the floor to about three-quarters of the way up the thickness of the mattress,

① Fixing the Cross Dividers to the Side Panels
Glue and screw the corner battens to the side panels, then position the cross dividers against the battens, flush with the bottom edge, and screw in place through the dividers and into the battens.

② Headboard Cross-Rail
Hold the cross rail on end at the top of the triangular support and mark out the notch.

③ Fixing the Triangular Headboard Support
Screw headboard supports to insides of the side panels.

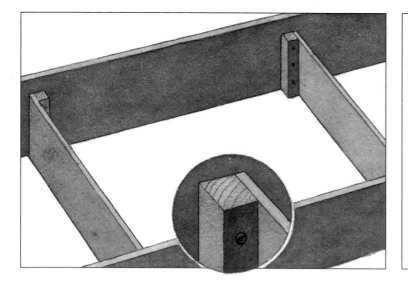

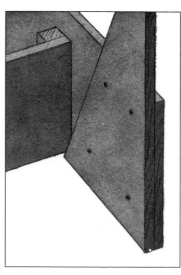

with the mattress in place. The higher piece measures the distance from that point to the top of the triangle plus 12mm ($\frac{1}{2}$in). The extra portion is a fingergrip for removing the panel when necessary for access to the space below.

STRENGTHENING BATTEN

The strengthening batten is cut from 50 × 50mm (2 × 2in) softwood to the width of the mattress minus 38mm (1$\frac{1}{2}$in), which is the thickness of the two triangular supports. Glue and screw the lower headboard section to the front edges of the triangular supports. Put the strengthening batten at the top of the lower headboard section on the underside, and cramp it in place half way up its thickness, thereby creating a 25mm (1in) rebate for the top part of the headboard to be located in. Drill, countersink and screw through the lower headboard section into the batten. Try the top headboard piece in place, then remove it for covering. The upholstery will bring it flush with the sides of the triangular fillers for a tidy finish.

Hold a piece of 25 × 25mm (1 × 1in) softwood batten against the gap between the top of the lower headboard section and the side panel. Mark off the top and bottom and cut with a tenon saw. The bottom will be at an angle to fit the side of the bed. Glue and nail or screw the batten in place to each side (fig 1, page 248). Plane, then sand off completely flush. The batten acts as a filler to give a clean line, and will be filled and painted in with the rest of the bed.

The top edge of the side panels should be rounded over either with a router and a rounding-over cutter, or by planing and sanding. Alternatively, glue and pin a half-round moulding to the top edges for a professional-looking finish.

PADDED HEADBOARD

The padded and upholstered headboard pulls forward to reveal additional storage space at the bed head.

4 Fixing Headboard Cross Rail in Place
Headboard cross rail is fixed with two screws kept low in the cross rail.

5 Fixing the Triangular Fillers at each Side
Triangular fillers made from the same material as the side panels give a flush finish at each side. Cut the fillers to fit exactly and screw through from the inside of the triangular supports.

6 Headboard and Batten
Screw lower headboard section in place. Cramp the strengthening batten to top edge and screw down.

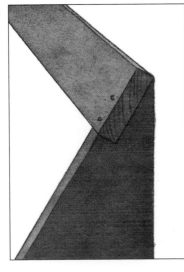

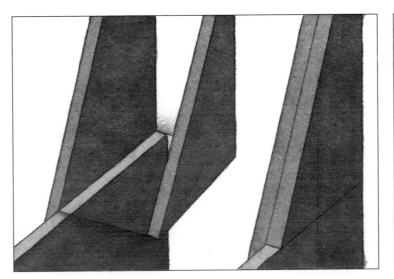

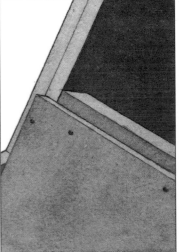

Bed with Truckle Drawer

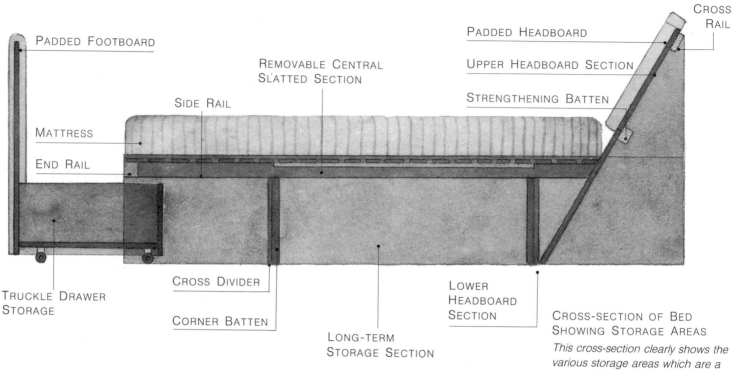

PADDED FOOTBOARD

HEADBOARD CROSS RAIL

PADDED HEADBOARD

REMOVABLE CENTRAL SLATTED SECTION

UPPER HEADBOARD SECTION

SIDE RAIL

STRENGTHENING BATTEN

MATTRESS

END RAIL

TRUCKLE DRAWER STORAGE

CROSS DIVIDER

CORNER BATTEN

LONG-TERM STORAGE SECTION

LOWER HEADBOARD SECTION

CROSS-SECTION OF BED SHOWING STORAGE AREAS

This cross-section clearly shows the various storage areas which are a feature of the design. The truckle drawer is particularly accessible.

1 **Adding the Filler Piece**
Use a piece of softwood to fill the gap between the side and lower headboard section.

2 **Fixing the Mattress-support Side Rails in Place**
Cut the headboard ends of the mattress-support side rails at an angle to fit neatly against the lower section. Note that the top edge of the side panel is rounded over to give a neat finish.

3 **Joining the End Rail**
End rail is joined to side rails using corner halving joints; end rail laps on top and is screwed to side rails.

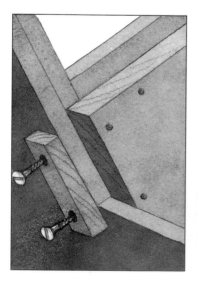

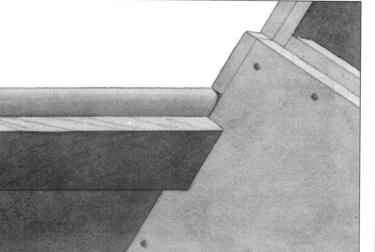

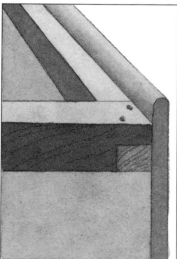

MATTRESS SUPPORT SECTION

The side rails are cut to the length of the mattress, plus a little overlength so that the angle can be cut into the headboard. Place their 50mm (2in) faces on the cross dividers alongside the sides, and scribe one end of each rail to the headboard. Cut this angle and push them up against the headboard, then mark them off flush with the ends of the side panels and cut them square.

The end rail is cut to the width of the mattress. Cut corner halving joints (see **Techniques, page 26**) to join the side and end rails (fig 3).

Glue and screw the side rails in place, screwing through the rails and into the side panels. Fix the end rail in place by inserting small screws through the halving joints.

The centre rail is cut from 75 × 50mm (3 × 2in) softwood to the length of the mattress plus a little overlength. Rest it on the cross dividers, and scribe to the angle of the headrest, as before. Cut the centre rail to length to butt tightly

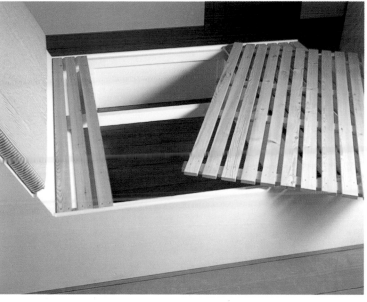

A unit of the mattress support section (above) lifts out for access to ample but unobtrusive storage space under the bed.

against the inner face of the end rail. Screw it down into the cross dividers.

Drill through the end rail into the end of the centre rail in two places, to a depth of between 75mm and 100mm (3–4in) and dry-dowel the

joint using 12mm ($\frac{1}{2}$in) dowelling (see **Techniques, page 30**).

Work out how many slats you need by dividing the length of the mattress by 100mm (4in) – the total of one slat plus a gap. Cut all the

slats to the width of the mattress. The area between the cross dividers is a slatted unit which can be lifted out to give access to storage below.

The softwood cross battens hold the slats together on the slatted unit. Measure the internal distance between the cross dividers and cut four lengths of 75 × 25mm (3 × 1in) to this dimension.

Using a spacing batten (see **Techniques, page 20**), space the slats equally and mark the position of the cross battens on to the first slat. The two outermost slats should be positioned in from the ends by the thickness of the side rails – that is, at least 50mm (2in). Screw the ends of the outer cross battens in place to the first slat. Continue along the cross battens, spacing and screwing down the rest of the slats. Then space the innermost two cross battens equally in between and screw them in place (fig 5).

Place this panel on the centre section and screw the remaining slats into the side rails, spacing them equally. Make sure that there is a slat flush with each end.

4 Joining End and Centre Rail
Centre rail butts against end rail. Drill through end rail and hammer dowels in place.

5 Making the Under-Mattress Lift-Out Slatted Unit
The slatted unit between the cross-dividers can be lifted out. Slats are screwed to four cross battens. The outer two cross battens are inset so that they clear the side rails.

6 Spacing the Fixed Slats
Place lift-out unit over the centre section and screw remaining slats, equally spaced, to side rails.

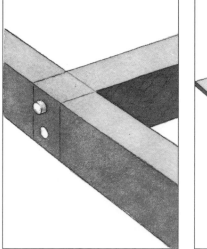

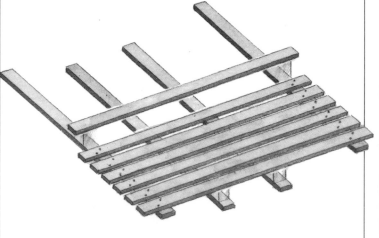

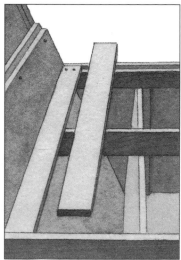

BED WITH TRUCKLE DRAWER

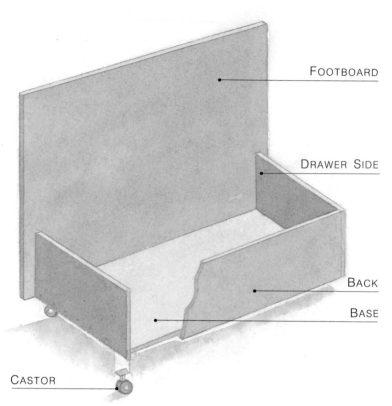

FOOTBOARD

DRAWER SIDE

BACK

BASE

CASTOR

of the base around the outside of the carcass. Finally, screw 50mm (2in) castors to the four corners of the base to allow easy movement.

UPHOLSTERY FOR THE BED

THE PADDING

The padding is expanded-polystyrene foam of three different thicknesses, covered with Dacron. The best way to cut the foam is to use an electric carving knife. Alternatively, use a bread knife, a hacksaw blade, or any blade with a serrated edge.

HEADBOARD

Cut a piece of 50mm (2in) foam to the size of the headboard's upper section. Spray one face of the headboard with latex spray adhesive and stick the foam to it, smoothing it down carefully.

Cut a piece of 50mm (2in) foam to the length of the top edge and, positioning it carefully, stick it in place with spray adhesive.

Use 25mm (1in) foam for the sides. Cut two pieces, each to the length of the headboard's side, plus the thickness of the foam covering the top, and stick one on each side.

Stick a thin layer of Dacron over all the foam with the spray adhesive and leave to dry.

FOOTBOARD

Cut one piece of 25mm (1in) foam to the width of the footboard, to run from the top of the drawer sides up and over the top of the footboard and down to the bottom edge.

Draw a line on the inside face of the footboard in line with the top of the drawer sides and spray adhesive on the wood down to this line, and on to the outside face.

Stick down the foam, starting at the line and smoothing it on to the wood. Ease it over the top and down the other side of the footboard.

Cut two pieces of 25mm (1in) foam to fit the small sections either side of the drawer, on the inside face of the footboard, and stick in place.

Cut two pieces of 12mm ($\frac{1}{2}$in)

① Truckle Drawer Assembly
Note that sides are set in from the footboard and that the back sits within the sides.

THE TRUCKLE DRAWER

The bed should be finished before you make the drawer. The footboard is cut from one piece of MDF to 12mm ($\frac{1}{2}$in) less than the overall width of the bed. Its height is as required – ours is 890mm (35in).

Preferably, the height of the two MDF drawer sides should be at least 150mm (6in) lower than the sides of the bed. This allows the drawers to run underneath the end rail and accommodates castors. Our sides are therefore 300mm (12in). The length is 610mm (24in).

For the back, cut one piece of

MDF to the height of the drawer sides. Its width should be that of the mattress minus 50mm (2in). Glue and screw through the sides into the back edges, then glue and screw through the footboard into the sides, ensuring that the footboard overlaps the sides equally.

Measure the internal dimensions of the rectangle for the size of the base, and cut it to size from MDF. The base should be spaced 25mm (1in) up from the bottom edges of the sides. To fix it firmly in place for screwing, lay the base on scrap battens 25mm (1in) thick, then place the carcass over the base. This will ensure an even 25mm (1in) spacing up from the bottom edges of the carcass.

Screw through into the edges of the base on all four sides, having marked the height of the centre line

② Padding the Headboard
Stick 50mm (2in) thick foam to upper headboard section and top edge; 25mm (1in) foam at sides.

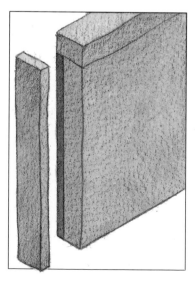

③ Padding the Footboard
One piece of 25mm (1in) foam covers front/back of footboard, plus 12mm ($\frac{1}{2}$in) foam at sides.

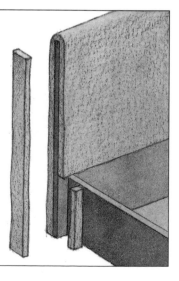

foam to the size of the side edges and stick one to each edge.

Put a layer of Dacron over the foam, stick in place and leave to dry

THE COVERS

These are welted covers with loose flaps folded under the bottom edge and joined by Velcro.

You will probably need to join widths of fabric. Joins should be made in two equally spaced seams. If you use a patterned fabric, you will also have to match from width to width, which can be quite difficult. Plain fabrics are therefore the easiest to work with. If you want to avoid joining widths, you could use a plain fabric and work with it sideways instead of lengthways.

If you do not feel capable of making a panelled border on the covers, you can achieve equally good results by using a single seam to join the front and back sections of the cover together.

HEADBOARD

Cut two panels – one for the front and one for the back of the padded headboard, allowing additional fabric all round for seams, and for joining any widths. If you have to make joins, do so first, cutting the fabric oversize and matching the seam positions of the front and back panels.

Fold the panels in half across their width and make a nip at the centre of the top edge, to match up the panels when sewing.

Next, measure for the long border to go round the top and sides and under the bottom edge by 75mm (3in) at each end. Cut out the border panel, allowing extra each side for the seams. Fold in half widthways and make nips in the centre and where the corners will be, on both edges.

Place the front section to the border panel, edge to edge and right sides together, matching the nips and corners. Pin, tack and then machine-stitch the seam, working from the centre nip outwards, first in one direction and then the other, along the top and down the other two sides as far as the corners. Machine-stitching in both directions

ensures that the two pieces of fabric are sewn evenly.

Attach the back panel to the other edge of the border, right sides together and with nips and corners matching exactly. Pin, tack and machine-stitch as before, down to each corner.

Neaten all the edges of the flaps by turning under the hems to the wrong side and machine-stitching. Cut a strip of Velcro to the length of the long flaps and machine-stitch it in place to the edges of the fabric so that one overlaps the other. Fold in the two end pieces first, and join the long flaps together with the Velcro for a neat finish.

FOOTBOARD

Measure the padded footboard from edge to edge and cut one panel for the inside face, allowing extra all round for the seams, plus about 75mm (3in) to enclose the padding at the bottom (be sure to account for joining any widths and make the joins first). Cut the panel for the outside face, allowing extra all round, plus enough to flap under

the bottom edge. Cut out material for the long panel, allowing enough extra fabric for the seams and for folding under the bottom edge.

Make up the cover as for the headboard, equalizing the seams and attaching the outside face first. On the inside face, sew down as far as the drawer sides, then attach a small piece of fabric each side to cover the narrow border either side of the drawer. Machine-stitch them on to the cover with the right sides together. Carefully cut and fit round each drawer side turning the edges under and then machine-stitching. Neaten all the bottom edges by turning under a flap and machine-stitching.

On the outside, fold in the ends and fold the long edge under. Fit to the bottom edge with Velcro, using the soft part on the fabric and the hard part on the wood. To attach Velcro to the wood, glue, tack, or staple it in place, or use self-adhesive Velcro.

On the inside face, secure the bottom edge and side flaps with Velcro as before.

---

4 Making the Cover for the Headboard
Cut the front and back panels allowing extra fabric all round for seams and joining widths, plus about 75mm (3in) to flap under the bottom edge. Pin, tack, then machine sew seams.

5 Making the Cover for the Footboard
Make up as for the headboard, carefully cutting and fitting around drawer sides. At the narrow sides of the drawer, attach thin strips of fabric. Fix down with Velcro along the bottom edge and along side flaps.

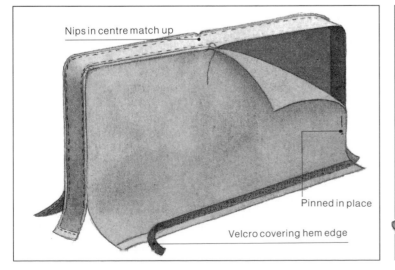

Nips in centre match up

Pinned in place

Velcro covering hem edge

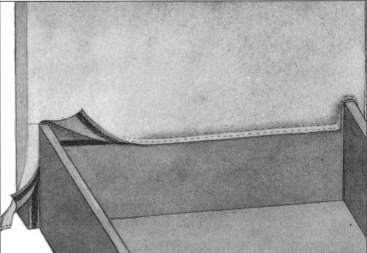

CUPBOARDS WITH ARCHITRAVES

Many old houses have plain chimney breasts which protrude into the room, forming alcoves on each side. In such cases, cupboard doors with decorative architraves can be fitted to create a stylish feature. The same effect can be achieved if there is an entrance door on one side of the chimney and an alcove on the other, as in our example.

To increase the depth of the cupboard, the doorway can be brought forward by a small amount (as with the doorway on the left of the picture) without detracting from the overall effect.

A straightforward architrave can be formed simply by fixing various boards and mouldings on to the wall surface around the door. If you want to hang the doors forward, as on the left in this example, then you need to build a column-like box section architrave.

Decorative architrave To form an architrave that fits directly on to the door surround itself, simply fix the mouldings to the wall around the door. Investigate local timber mer-chants for suitable mouldings, bearing in mind that larger mouldings can often be formed by joining together two or three smaller ones of the same type.

The edges of the boards can be rounded off, grooved, or otherwise shaped with a router that is fitted with a suitable cutter.

Fix the first (widest) moulding to the wall using screws and wallplugs, and, where possible, nail it direct to the door frame. The other pieces of moulding can then be simply glued and nailed in place.

Box-section architrave In this case a simple timber box is formed on each side of the door opening. The front piece is joined to the sides using a bare-faced housing joint, or with dowels (see **Techniques, pages 27, 30**). A pilaster effect can be achieved by cutting grooves with a flute cutter in a router on a second piece of timber fixed to the face of the front piece. Glue and screw blocks behind the box section at the top to box-in the architrave at the top of the frame.

Making a cornice The cornice is formed by gluing a batten behind the lower edge of a cornice moulding. Another, smaller, cornice moulding is glued and pinned between the larger cornice and the door architrave (fig 3, right). Form the cornice above the box section by fitting battens behind the mouldings, as before. For the moulding underneath, use coving. Add triangular fillers at ends and shape with a coping saw (fig 3, bottom).

① Fixing a Decorative Architrave
A wide decorative architrave can be built-up by fixing mouldings around a door frame.

② Built-out Box-section
A built-out architrave can be made by fixing a box-section around the door opening.

③ Finishing the Built-out Architrave at the Top
The box is completed at the head of the door and the space between the box-section and the ceiling is filled with a wooden cornice moulding. Cross-section on right shows cornice moulding fixed to architrave above a door.

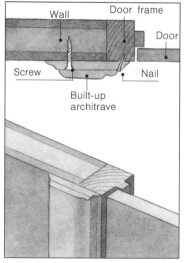

Wall — Door frame — Door — Screw — Nail — Built-up architrave

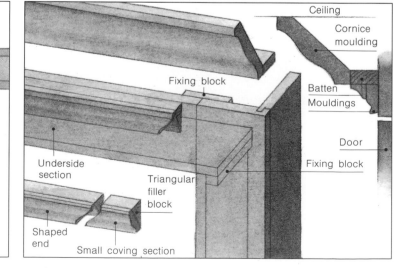

Door frame — Wall — Door stop — Wall battens — Cupboard door — Fluted grooves (if required)

Ceiling — Cornice moulding — Fixing block — Batten — Mouldings — Underside section — Triangular filler block — Door — Fixing block — Shaped end — Small coving section

PANELLED BATH

The basic bath framework is made from 50 × 25mm (2 × 1in) PAR softwood. You will need six vertical studs (including wall battens), cut to tho dictanco botwoon the floor and the underside of the bath rim.

You will also need two end rails, the same width as the bath, less about 125mm (5in); two side rails, the same length as the bath, less about 75mm (3in); and an intermediate stud which should be the distance between the side rails.

For the bath panelling, use some 12 × 100mm ($\frac{1}{2}$ × 4in) TGV (tongued, grooved and V-jointed) pine board, the same length as the vertical studs. Use as many pieces as are necessary to clad the side and end of the bath.

The removable panel section consists of two cross rails made from a 425mm (16$\frac{3}{4}$in) length of 75 × 12mm (3 × $\frac{1}{2}$in) PAR softwood.

Cut the wall battens and vertical studs to length. Mark where the wall battens will be fixed. They should be inset by about 12mm ($\frac{1}{2}$in) from the edge of the bath rim.

Cut rebatcs 75mm (3in) wide by about 12mm ($\frac{1}{2}$in) deep in the edges of two vertical studs, 150mm (6in) down from the top, and 150mm (6in) up from the bottom. These allow the cross rails of the removable panelling to be fitted. The panel provides access to pipework.

Screw and plug the wall battens to the wall. Fix a vertical stud temporarily to each wall batten. Temporarily screw two uprights together in an L-shape to form the corner studs. Wedge the studs under the bath rim at the external corner.

Measure between the studs and cut the end and side rails to length. Remove studs and assemble side and end frames by butt-jointing cross rails to vertical studs, gluing and nailing each joint. For ease, set the upper cross rails 25mm (1in) down from the top of the vertical studs. Nail an intermediate stud between side frame cross rails.

Hold the frames flat and square while the glue sets. To fit, screw them to the wall battens, and to each other at the external corner.

Cut the TGV matching to tuck under the bath rim. Cut off the

tongues from two lengths and fix these together at the external corner, either by mitring their edges, or by butting them to a quadrant moulding (fig 2, inset). Fix them to the frame by carefully screwing through from the back. Fix subsequent lengths using fixing clips (*see* **Panelled Bathroom, page 211**).

Fix the last four sections of TGV matching to the two 75 × 12mm (3 × $\frac{1}{2}$in) cross rails, leaving a short length protruding to catch behind the fixed panelling.

---

1 **Building a Timber Tongued-and-Grooved-Clad Bath Panel**
Nail together a simple frame using 50 × 25mm (2 × 1in) timber. Screw the frames together at the corner, and to wall-fixed battens at each end. Note removable panel for access to bath waste and tap connections.

2 **Bath Panel Corner Detail**
TGV matching clads frame. External corner edge is mitred or finished with quadrant moulding.

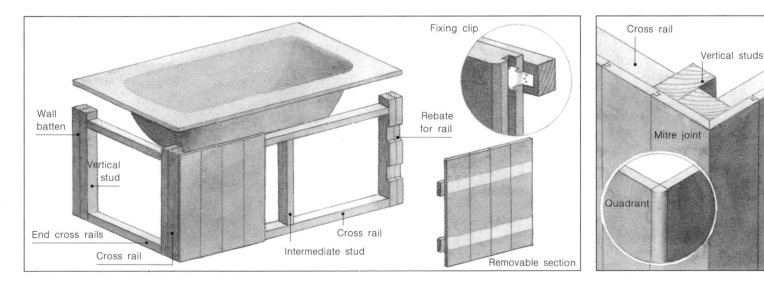

Fixing clip

Wall batten

Vertical stud

End cross rails

Cross rail

Rebate for rail

Cross rail

Intermediate stud

Removable section

Cross rail

Vertical studs

Mitre joint

Quadrant

INTRODUCTION
TO GARDEN PROJECTS

If you have a garden, the chances are that you already 'do it yourself'. Planting, seeding, mowing, turfing, fencing and paving are, for the majority of gardeners, all DIY activities, since few people today have either the space or the means to justify a full-time gardener.

This book is a logical extension of that established outdoor DIY tradition. It contains a range of projects, from the very simple to the more complicated, which shows you how to make a variety of structures, including containers, seats, trelliswork and even a summer house. All of these are important, classic garden accessories, the design of which is too often overlooked.

Achieving success in DIY is to do with confidence. Once you have completed a simple project, this will give you the confidence to move on to a more complicated piece. If you are a DIY beginner, choose the simplest item in terms both of design and tools required and progress gradually as your skills develop.

If the garden is a good place to practise and refine your DIY skills, you can also get away with a lower standard of finish: precision and perfection are not really at home in the garden, where a weathered, rustic appearance can be a positive attribute. Materials need not be expensive and what you make will usually have cost less than the retail product in the garden

centre, although this is not invariably the case. You can buy ready-made trellising, for example, for far less than the wood you would need to make it, so to economize by doing-it-yourself you must carefully examine what is commercially available from the garden centre and make the proper comparisons.

The great benefit of DIY in the garden, however, is the degree of satisfaction it affords – the pleasure of making something that has been tailored to suit your own space and needs. What you make will often be better designed than its equivalent in the garden centre; more importantly, it will reflect your own taste and sense of style more successfully.

Terence Conran.

Planning a Garden

In the words of Sir John Soane, good design should contain an element of 'hazard and surprise'. Although Soane was talking about interior design, this important principle applies equally to the disposition and arrangement of outdoor space. Nothing is less memorable than a garden which can be surveyed in a single glance: you want to be able to move through a garden and be surprised by what you discover around each corner.

Fortunately, 'hazard' in gardening is easy to create. Changes of direction, with paths leading around structures which divide and separate different areas within the garden, immediately generate interest. Forms can be created very simply with trelliswork over which climbing plants are trained, providing a sort of growing 'veil' through which to walk.

Even more important are changes in level. In this, as in so much of garden design, there is a great deal to be learned from Japan. Different levels give a sense of movement, transforming even the dullest patch of ground. And because plants like falling over edges or trailing over walls, a change in level provides endless opportunities to blend architectural form with planting, thereby softening the lines of the design.

Trellising, planters adjacent to the house, fast-growing creepers and climbers grown up the walls can all help to blend a house in with its setting, anchoring it to its environment and creating an established garden within a short space of time. One great advantage of garden DIY is that if your house has distinctive architectural details, such as decorative bargeboarding, it is easy to incorporate these features into the design of your garden structures. Something as simple as picking out a colour from a door to use on seating or containers can help to unify the overall design and visually link the house to the garden.

Because the garden is an organic place where things grow, the materials you use for structures and accessories should be natural ones as far as possible. Plastic has no affinity with plants: the two simply do not go together. Artificial materials always stand out in a garden because they do not weather in the way that natural ones do. Wood, stone, terracotta, brick and – for some reason – metal all work well in the garden, harmonizing with one another so that you can vary the textures and surfaces in an interesting way. What is particularly appealing about all of these materials is the way they age and weather, oxodizing, bleaching, staining and acquiring lichens and mosses so that they meld into the garden. Show gardens, because they have not had time to mature, always look too new and clean for my taste. You can encourage ageing if your garden is looking too new by scrubbing salt or domestic bleach into wooden decking to achieve a weathered look or by painting non-pasteurized milk, house-plant food or manure made into a slurry onto concrete or terracotta surfaces to speed up the growth of lichen.

THE OUTDOOR ROOM

Good garden design is a question of creating an outdoor space that reflects your needs, style and preferences, and is at the same time compatible with the materials, structures and details of your house. The garden should be a natural extension to the house, rather than a jarring contrast. Sources of inspiration for garden designs include the ever-popular informal look of the English country cottage, the open-plan architectural terraces of modern town gardens, and the contemplative beauty of Japanese landscape settings.

If the garden needs an element of wilderness and a certain lack of precision to be truly inviting, it is also the place for colour. Far too often, people play safe with garden accessories, sticking to the traditional shades of white or a dark green which fades into the background. Splashes of bright colour are an attractive and appealing feature of Mediterranean gardens and, contrary to popular belief, such vivid accent shades also work in countries where summer light is not as intense. Colour makes a strong positive statement, and is also extremely cheerful in the winter when the garden is least interesting. Yellow, for example, goes equally well with the fresh greens of summer and the greys of winter. Blue (either dark blue or blue-grey) is another good garden colour. If you make your own garden accessories, you can decide for yourself what colour you want to paint them, rather than having to accept the limited and uninspiring shades that are on offer commercially.

Finally, a garden, in the same way as a room, needs a focus of interest: the path must lead somewhere; the view through the pergola must reveal something at the other end; a formal layout of beds demands a centrepiece. Whatever you base your design around should look positive and well-considered, not half-hearted. A large terracotta pot tumbling with colourful plants, an inviting garden seat in a shady place, a patio under a striped awning, a garden pond full of fish or a collection of strange, disparate containers all make good focal points as long as they are properly complemented by their environment. There are many excellent ideas illustrated in this book to stimulate your imagination, but the important point is that these are merely a starting place for your own plans and ideas. Your garden is the place where you can express your own personality and idiosyncracies to create the kind of outdoor room you want to live in, whether it is formal or rustic.

PRACTICALITIES

A new garden should start with a plan which takes into account practical as well as aesthetic considerations. A camera is a useful tool in the planning process: take photographs of the views from the house to the garden (and at the upper levels, too) as well as from the garden to the house. A simple sketch of the plot annotated with rough dimensions will help you to decide on the layout of paths, beds and patio. For a formal design you may wish to work out a strong controlled grid or a symmetrical framework of beds and connecting paths. For a more informal, natural arrangement, it is still important to think about where the paths will go and what shape beds they will create: too often, paths are laid without due regard to the shape of the beds, with awkward and ill-judged results. You should also work out any changes in level required or note existing slopes or steps, as well as features such as mature trees and garden sheds.

PLANNING A GARDEN

Although the climate of your garden cannot be altered radically, it can be tempered. Exposure to strong winds can be limited to some extent by the filtering effect of boundary hedging, fencing or trellis. In a dry area, a damp microclimate can be created by the addition of a pond, around the perimeter of which moisture-loving plants can flourish. Shade can be supplied by a variety of means, both manmade and natural, including awnings, arbors, and vines or climbers trained over trellis or wire frameworks. Too little light poses another problem. You cannot, of course, reorientate a garden which faces the wrong way, nor do much about the deep shade cast by high walls. But you can clear out overgrowth, take down fencing and drastically prune overhanging branches to let in as much light as possible. Unfortunately if the sun doesn't shine, there is little you can do about it.

Many other factors will have a bearing on the eventual design:
- The siting of a compost heap, a tool shed and utility area
- Access to water
- The position of eating or sitting areas
- Barbecues
- Areas in which children can play and in which to site play equipment
- Permanent fixtures such as mature trees, existing walls and boundaries
- The presence of any eyesores which may need to be camouflaged
- The need for privacy or security
- Noise from neighbouring gardens
- Special requirements such as the extreme climate of a roof garden
- The amount of time you can spend
- Your budget

All gardens benefit from careful organization. Planting stands a greater chance of success if the basic framework is right.

DESIGN AND DETAIL

Gardens thrive on an element of surprise, hidden corners and changes of level. Decking is a harmonious outdoor surface, and can be planned in advance to provide different seating and eating levels and beds for planting (above). Strategically placed, arbors or trelliswork can act as a focal point in the garden, directing the eye to splashes of colour (above left and opposite).

COLOUR IN THE GARDEN

Colour has long been a neglected element in the garden as far as structures, accessories and garden furniture are concerned (overleaf). Containers, seats, trellis, fences and walls can all be painted to give a positive lift to the overall design of a garden.

PART 5

SEATING AND EATING

In every garden there should be a place where you can sit down, look with pleasure at what you have achieved and think about all the hard work that remains to be done. Any seating area, whether it is a bench in a shady corner or a patio equipped with table, chairs, awning and barbecue, becomes a focal point in the garden's design; its position, accordingly, is part of that initial process of architectural planning. Should it be in sun or shade? In view of the house or in a more secluded location? If you intend to eat outdoors, at least partial shade will be required. Eating outside, preferably in dappled sunlight, is one of the great pleasures of life.

You can sit in the garden to read a book, have a drink, watch the children play, eat a meal or simply take stock of your surroundings, and there are as many styles of garden seat as there are functions for them to fulfil. Which type of seat you choose should reflect the general plan and style of your garden. The quality of light and shade is a very important consideration, not only for personal comfort, but also for good growing conditions and for intrinsic interest.

SEATING AND EATING

Seats and table tops must be designed so that water does not sit on the surface and rot or rust them away. A fractional tilt to a seat or table top will ensure that water drains off; slats or drainage holes fulfil the same function and there are also new outdoor paints which protect garden furniture to a much greater degree than traditional undercoat and gloss.

Much garden furniture, particularly the cast-iron or painted metal variety, is too ornate for my taste. Tables and seats which are clean-lined, whether they are curved or rectilinear, look much more confident and suit outdoor living much better. Simple garden furniture allows the focus of attention to remain on the planting. This is not to dismiss wrought-ironwork out of hand. Benches with

wrought- or cast-iron ends, but plain slatted backs and seats, can be attractive and are more comfortable than all-metal versions which heat up in the sun.

Garden seats can also be amusing. In the nineteenth century, rough-hewn tree branches were nailed together to create whimsical Gothick benches, a kind of visual joke. In a similar vein are sections of tree trunk used as bench supports, a chimney pot filled with sand as a table base or a stone slab inset into a clipped box hedge, with the foliage making a living upholstered back. One of the most irresistible designs is the tree seat, almost a ground-level tree house, which forms a platform around the base of a tree.

In addition to semi-permanent garden furniture, there are many varieties of

ready-made garden seat which work equally well indoors. Painted wooden benches, wickerwork, rattan and basket chairs, folding canvas chairs and metal park chairs suit their location and are generally light enough to move easily.

With garden tables, there is the same choice between permanent fixtures and tables which can be set up as required. Stone, marble and ceramic tiles are excellent materials for table tops; folding

OUTDOOR LIVING
Stepped timber seating (above) provides interesting and versatile changes of level in a garden. A terrace of herringbone paving and shaded by mature plane trees (right) makes a delightful outdoor eating area.

Overleaf *A range of garden seating ideas.*

SEATING AND EATING

metal tables, traditionally associated with French parks are more economic.

Seating areas are almost always more pleasurable and useable if there is a degree of shade. If your patio is exposed to the full force of the sun, there are many ways of creating shade that look appropriate as well as stylish. In this area, the yachting world is a fruitful source of visual ideas. Sail-like canvas awnings, varnished wooden frameworks for climbing plants, and canvas in bright clear colours eyeletted and lashed to a simple metal frame all have a faintly nautical flavour. A simple metal armature or framework with a vine trained over is a particularly Mediterranean solution to the problem; narrow gauge trellis overhead breaks up sunlight into a small square grid, taking the power out of it. Shop blinds fitted with a retractable mechanism, canvas clipped on to a wood and wire frame or a large market umbrella are other effective ideas. For a more theatrical effect, a bright, patterned fabric can be knotted and tied to poles like an oversize scarf, or you can borrow ideas from tent design. Plain canvas (perhaps painted on the underside) or broad blue-and-white stripes are crisp, fresh and appealing.

Most people today want their outdoor eating area to be a cooking area as well. A barbecue area is particularly easy to build, a good project for DIY in the garden. Brick or stone are the best materials for construction and you will probably also need to pave around and beneath the barbecue to make cleaning easy. At the simplest level of design, you can buy a mass-produced cast-iron barbecue and simply set it on to a brick or stone slab. If you are building the barbecue as well as its setting, it is best to line it in firebrick as a precaution against the intense heat.

Barbecues should be sited with care. Not only do they generate a great deal of

heat, they are also smoky. Avoid positions where smoke and cooking smells will drift into the house – or worse, through your neighbour's windows. Overhanging plants are likely to be singed or even incinerated; adjacent walls will be blackened by smoke, although this is not necessarily unattractive.

You can extend the potential of outdoor eating areas by the addition of good garden lighting. Outdoor lighting calls for a degree of sensitivity, since obvious, glaring fixtures will immediately rob your garden of whatever charm it possesses; on the other hand, subtle, diffused light sources create an instantly magical atmosphere. Garden lighting should be as unobtrusive as possible, with fittings built into walls or shielded in some way.

When you furnish a garden, what you choose should be simple, so as not to compete with the planting; practical, for obvious reasons; and architectural, to contribute to your overall plan or design. You can use this opportunity to go one step further and think about the way you furnish your home indoors as well: a continuation of the same basic attitude will bring the house and garden closer together, to the benefit of both.

OUTDOOR SEATING AREAS

If you intend to use a seating area as a place for outdoor meals you will need to provide a degree of shade or shelter. Sitting in the full glare of the hot midday sun is very unpleasant for any length of time; on the other hand, you do not necessarily want to have to move indoors on account of a few drops of rain. Solutions include integrated terraces and balconies, awnings, and trellis supporting a canopy of vines or climbing plants. Perhaps the most appealing of all in fine weather is a table and chairs placed in the dappled shade under a tree, a natural shelter which filters the light to just the right degree.

GARDEN BENCH

When it comes to garden furniture, people tend to have rather conservative taste. Although they might tolerate modern and even occasionally avant-garde pieces in the home, these are less welcome for outdoor living, where the emphasis has generally been on the traditional. Wrought-iron seating typically has a Victorian flavour, and, in recent years, the designs of Sir Edwin Lutyens have been enormously influential, with their classically inspired curves.

This garden bench with its upright railed back and plain, flat seat and legs owes something to the strict functional beauty of nineteenth-century Shaker furniture. Extremely simple by comparison with much of what is commercially available for the garden, the bench is nevertheless one of the more demanding projects to make. This is partly because garden furniture must be finished to a higher standard than other garden structures, as it will receive closer inspection.

Even if you move your garden furniture indoors for the winter it will have to take some degree of weathering. Allowing water to collect on a surface is the quickest way of causing deterioration and decay. Here the seat slopes slightly so that water drains off and, similarly, where the back joins the seat a narrow gap has been left to allow water to flow down. The straight edges of the legs are bevelled so that accidental knocks by the lawnmower do not cause too much damage.

The height of the back is a critical factor in the design. Equally distinctive is the back's reeded quality. This is, perhaps, not a bench for lounging, although, supplied with a long cushion, it would work very well indoors.

Don't be afraid to let colour make a positive statement in the garden. Yellow and various tones of blue look as good in winter as they do in summer and are more eye-catching than the more sedate shades of dark green or white.

GARDEN BENCH

The garden bench is perhaps the most familiar piece of garden furniture. Building one yourself will almost certainly be cheaper than buying one, and will give you a real sense of satisfaction. If needs be, you can adapt the design shown here to suit the size and proportions of your garden and your individual requirements. Choose the site for your bench with care, positioning it to serve as a focal point that draws the eye in a certain direction; alternatively, you could place it to provide sanctuary in a tranquil, shady corner of the garden where you can retreat to sit in peace, quiet and comfort.

This garden bench could be made from hardwood, but it will be considerably cheaper and more environmentally acceptable if you make it from good-quality softwood. In the latter case, it is important that you treat the timber with good-quality wood preservative at all stages of construction to ensure that it will give you many years of service. A clear wood preservative should be applied to the timber after the component pieces have been cut, but before the joints are assembled; the strength of the joint will not be affected if you allow about 24 hours for the preservative to dry thoroughly before applying the glue.

A second coat of preservative should be applied after construction, before the application of the final finish.

Using clear preservative will allow you to keep your options open regarding whether you finish the bench by painting or by applying a water-repellent wood stain of the type used widely on timber window frames. If you finish the bench by painting it, it is a good idea to use an exterior gloss paint or microporous (satin sheen) system. Such paint often contains a penetrating preservative wood primer, and this should be used in preference to a second coat of clear wood preservative.

The ideal way to construct the bench to ensure many years of service is to use traditional mortise and tenon joints for the main frame and dowel joints for the back rest slats and the seat boards. However, if you feel that you do not possess the necessary skills to cut accurate mortise and tenon joints, then the entire bench could be made using dowel joints throughout. If you do only use dowel joints, however, it will be more important than ever to apply a good-quality waterproof woodworking adhesive to each joint before assembly, and to keep each joint firmly cramped until the adhesive is thoroughly set.

MATERIALS

Part	Quantity	Material	Length
BACK LEGS	2	100 × 75mm (4 × 3in) PAR softwood	1035mm (41in)
FRONT LEGS	2	75 × 75mm (3 × 3in) PAR softwood	430mm (17in)*
SIDE FRAME RAILS	4	75 × 50mm (3 × 2in) PAR softwood	480mm (19in)
FRONT RAIL	1	As above	1790mm (70$\frac{1}{2}$in)
LOWER BACK RAIL	1	140 × 32mm (5$\frac{1}{2}$ × 1$\frac{1}{4}$in) PAR softwood	1790mm (70$\frac{1}{2}$in)
UPPER BACK RAIL	1	75 × 50mm (3 × 2in) PAR softwood	1880mm (74in)*
BACK SLATS	32	38 × 25mm (1$\frac{1}{2}$ × 1in) PAR softwood	Distance between back rails
SEAT BOARDS	4	140 × 32mm (5$\frac{1}{2}$ × 1$\frac{1}{4}$in) PAR softwood	1865mm (73$\frac{1}{2}$in)
DOWELS (seat to lower back rail)	5	From 12mm ($\frac{1}{2}$in) hardwood dowelling	Approx. 95mm (3$\frac{3}{4}$in)
DOWELS (to join seat boards and fit back slats)	As required	From 8mm ($\frac{5}{16}$in) hardwood dowelling	Approx. 40mm (1$\frac{1}{2}$in)

* Overlength and then cut to size after fixing – see text

TOOLS

WORKBENCH (fixed or portable)

MARKING KNIFE

STEEL MEASURING TAPE

STEEL RULE

TRY SQUARE

PANEL SAW (or circular power saw)

TENON SAW (or power jigsaw)

CHISELS

MARKING GAUGE

MORTISE GAUGE

POWER DRILL

DOWEL or CENTREPOINT DRILL BIT – 8mm ($\frac{5}{16}$in)

FLAT BIT – 12mm ($\frac{1}{2}$in)

DOWELLING JIG

ONE PAIR OF SASH CRAMPS (or webbing cramp)

SMOOTHING PLANE (hand or power)

POWER ROUTER and ROUNDING OVER BIT

MALLET

ORBITAL SANDER (or hand sanding block)

GARDEN BENCH ASSEMBLY

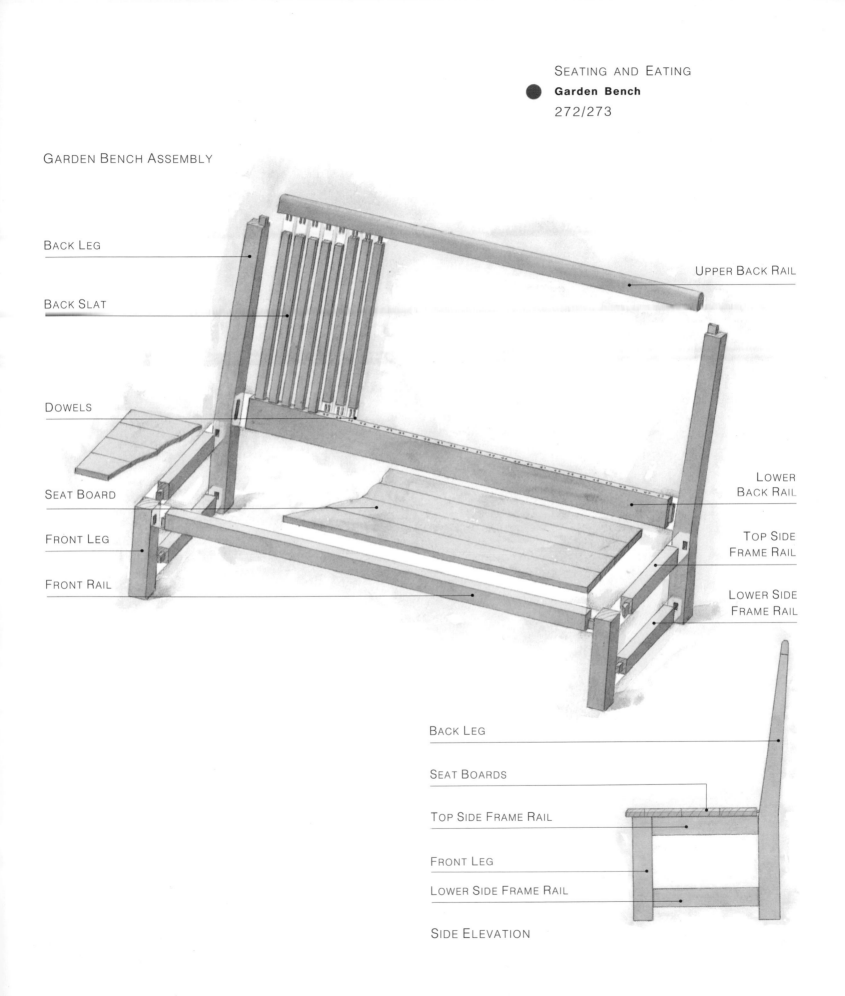

BACK LEG

BACK SLAT

DOWELS

SEAT BOARD

FRONT LEG

FRONT RAIL

UPPER BACK RAIL

LOWER BACK RAIL

TOP SIDE FRAME RAIL

LOWER SIDE FRAME RAIL

BACK LEG

SEAT BOARDS

TOP SIDE FRAME RAIL

FRONT LEG

LOWER SIDE FRAME RAIL

SIDE ELEVATION

GARDEN BENCH

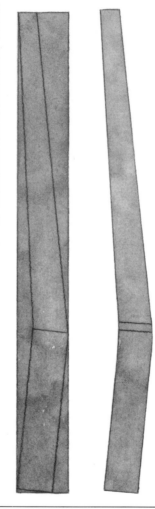

1 **Shaping the Back Legs**
**Lay front leg at an angle on back leg
and mark its position. Measure
35mm (1⅜in) in from the back at the
top and join marks with top of front
leg marks. Cut out around marked
lines, curving the shape at the back.
Mark off seat thickness parallel with
top of front leg position.**

SEAT SIDE FRAMES

SHAPING THE FRONT LEGS

Cut the front legs overlength – at
least 430mm (17in) long in total –
and measure 400mm (15¾in) up
from the bottom to mark off the
finished length. Square a line
around the leg on all faces (*see*
Techniques, page 396). Put the
front legs aside for the time being.

SHAPING THE BACK LEGS

The back legs are shaped from
100 × 75mm (4 × 3in) timber. Mark
out the legs by laying one of the
front legs on the wider face of one of
the back legs, sloping at an angle
but touching at the bottom and side
edges (fig 1). Remember that the
front leg is overlength at the top, so
align with the finished leg line. Mark
round the shape of the front leg
onto the back leg.

At the top of the back leg, measure 35mm (1⅜in) from the back
face on both sides and join these
two points to the top points of the
marked front leg position, giving the
shape for the back leg (fig 1).

With one back leg marked, cut
out around the marked lines, with
straight lines at the front face of the
leg, but rounding off the angle at the
back of the leg to produce a gentle
curve. Plane the face edges at the
front straight and square to the
sides as the joints are measured
from this edge.

Use the cut-out back leg to mark
the other one and cut it out. When
both legs are cut, mark off the seat
thickness, parallel with the top of the
front leg position, using a seat board
and a try square.

MARKING UP THE
MORTISES AND TENONS

Take one of the front legs and line
one of the side rails (wide face
against the leg) to the top marked
line (fig 2), taking into account the
excess length at the top. Mark off the

position of the bottom of the rail onto the leg. Working from this line, mark off the length of the mortise 50mm (2in) up. Square the lines round to the two inside faces *(see* **Techniques, page 396** *)*

For the bottom joint, measure 60mm (2⅜in) up from the bottom of the leg on the back face, then another 50mm (2in) up for the top of the mortise. Transfer all of these lines to the back of the other front leg using a try square. Square the lines of the top mortise round to the inside face of the second front leg.

Using a try square, transfer the length and position of the mortises from the front legs onto the front face of the back legs.

Take a 19mm (¾in) chisel and set a mortise gauge to this width with the stock set so that the mortise is central to the edge of the side rails (*not* central on the legs).

Mark off the top mortises on the front faces of the back legs, and on the two inside faces of the front legs. Measure from the *outside* edge in each case so that the front and upper side rails will be flush.

On the ends of all four side rails, mark off the tenons (fig 3) and also mark off the tenons on the ends of the front rail.

Re-set the stock on the mortise gauge so that it is central on the legs and mark off the lower mortises centrally on the inside faces of all the legs for the lower side rails.

Measure 50mm (2in) in from each end on one of the side rails and mark the shoulder of the tenon. Square round all faces. Using a try square, transfer the lines onto all the other side rails. Measure 50mm (2in) in from each end of the front rail and square round as before. To ensure a strong construction, it is important that all the lengths between the shoulders on the side rails are accurately marked. Mark the widths of the top tenon 50mm (2in) from the bottom edges of all the *top* rails so that the tenons are bare-faced to the lower edge.

The tenons are central on the two *lower* side rails, so measure 10mm (⅜in) up from the lower edge, then 50mm (2in) for the width of the mortise (fig 3).

CUTTING THE JOINTS

Cut the mortises slightly deeper than 50mm (2in) *(see* **Techniques, Mortise and Tenon Joint, page 402** *)* and then the tenons.

Dry assemble the parts to check the fit. The ends of the tenons on the front rail and the ends of the front tenons of the top side rails will all need to be cut at a 45° angle to ensure a tight fit (fig 4).

Cut off the 'horns' (protruding ends) at the tops of the front legs to leave the front legs flush with the upper side rails.

THE BACK

FITTING THE LOWER BACK RAIL

Take a chisel about 12mm (½in) wide and set a mortise gauge to exactly this width. Set the stock so the tenon will be offset to the back on the lower back rail, making a bare-faced tenon joint (fig 1, page 276). Mark the mortise on the inside faces of the back legs, working from

the front faces. Mark the bare-faced tenons on the lower back rail.

Align the lower back rail with the mark for the seat at the front so that it is square to the top front face of the back leg (fig 1, page 276). Mark off the position of the rail, and mark a 15mm (⅝in) shoulder at the top and bottom.

On the lower back rail, mark 50mm (2in) in from the ends and 15mm (⅝in) in from the edges for the shoulders. Before cutting the tenons, check that the length between the shoulders is the same as the front rail. Cut the tenons and then chisel the mortises to a depth of 50mm (2in).

FITTING THE UPPER BACK RAIL

Mark 50mm (2in) down from the top of the back leg and square round using a try square. Transfer these lines to the other leg. With the mortise gauge still set to 12mm (½in) set the stock so that it is central at this shoulder line, working from the front face (fig 2, page 276). Now mark off the tenon on both legs.

---

② **Front Leg Mortises**
Mark rail positions on leg. Mortises are central to edge of front and top side rails, central on lower side rail.

③ **Front and Side Rail Tenons**
Top **Cut bare-faced tenons for front and top side rails.** *Bottom* **Tenon is central on lower side rail.**

④ **Dry Assembly of Front Legs to Front and Side Rails**
Left **Position of cut mortises on front leg.** *Inset* **Plan view shows front rail and upper side rail flush with outside edges of front leg.** *Right* **Ends of tenons are angled on front and upper side rails.**

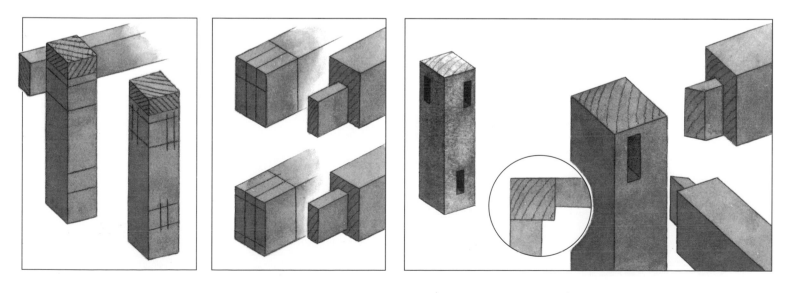

GARDEN BENCH

The upper rail should be cut over-length by 50mm (2in), but use the lower rail to mark the exact length between the shoulders and square round the upper rail at each end. From these lines mark 50mm (2in) to the outside (towards the ends).

With the mortise gauge still set for the width of the tenon, mark the mortises on the bottom edge of the rail, working from the front face (fig 2). Mark the width of each tenon to 50mm (2in) from the inside face of the legs so that the tenons are bare-faced.

Cut the mortises to 50mm (2in) deep, and cut the tenons. Dry assemble the back legs to the upper and lower rails to check the fit and cut off the 'horns' (protruding ends) flush with the outer face of the legs.

SHAPING THE UPPER RAIL

The upper rail has to be shaped at the back to follow the taper of the back legs (fig 3). Strike a line up each back leg to continue the taper onto the rail and then join up these lines by marking a line along the top edge of the upper rail.

Remove the rail and cut off the waste with a power plane or by using a hand saw. This is a long rip cut and will need care. Finish the taper by planing the surface of the upper rail smooth.

FITTING THE BACK SLATS

The width and spacing of the back slats is a matter of preference. We used 38×25mm ($1\frac{1}{2} \times 1$in) slats, spaced about 19mm ($\frac{3}{4}$in) apart.

The easiest way to fit the slats is to use two dowels top and bottom, positioned by means of a dowelling jig. We used 8mm ($\frac{5}{16}$in) dowels, 40mm ($1\frac{1}{2}$in) long. For an even stronger fixing you can use mortise and tenon joints top and bottom, but without a mortising machine it would be a very time-consuming task to make all the necessary joints.

Measure on the back leg the distance from the top of the lower rail to the underside of the upper rail, and cut the slats to this length if you will be fixing them using dowels. Cut the slats about 19mm ($\frac{3}{4}$in) longer at each end if you intend to use mortise and tenon joints.

DETAIL OF THE GARDEN BENCH
For decorative effect, the outside edges of the legs, frame rails, seat boards and so on are chamferred before final assembly.

1 **Fitting Lower Back Rail to Back Leg**
Lower back rail fits square and flush with slope of front face of back leg and will align with back edge of seat boards. Mark mortises on inside faces of back legs and cut bare-faced tenons on lower back rail.

2 **Fitting Upper Back Rail to Back Leg**
Mark mortise on ends of upper back rail (remember it is overlength) and cut out. Mark rail position on top of back legs and cut bare-faced tenons on legs. Cut excess from ends of rail to fit flush with back legs.

Mark up the ends of the slats for the two dowel holes (fig 4) and, using a dowelling jig, drill the ends of the slats to a depth of 22mm ($\frac{7}{8}$in) using an 8mm ($\frac{5}{16}$in) dowel (centre-point) drill bit.

Mark a centre line along the top edge of the lower rail and the bottom edge of the upper rail for the centre line of the dowel holes.

Work out the positions of the slats along one of these, adjusting as necessary to give an even spacing between the slats. Mark the centres of the dowel hole positions all the way along.

Cramp the two rails together and transfer the dowel centre marks to the other rail. Drill the dowel holes to a depth of 22mm ($\frac{7}{8}$in).

ASSEMBLING THE FRAME

Dry assemble the whole bench. Chamfer the edges of the front and back legs, the lower side rails, the underside of the upper side rails, the edge of the lower back rail and the underside of the front rail using a router with a chamferring bit or a power plane.

Sand all the components to smooth the faces and edges, and to clean off any pencil marks. Glue up the end frames using a gap-filling waterproof glue such as Cascamite, cramping it tightly until the glue has thoroughly dried.

At this point, an adjustment has to be made to the height of the back legs to allow the seat to angle back slightly to assist rainwater drainage. This is done by standing the end frame on a flat surface, such as the workbench, and packing the front edge of the front leg by 15mm ($\frac{5}{8}$in) using a scrap piece of timber (fig 5).

Using an offcut of the same thickness, scribe the back leg and the side and back of the front leg to the correct angle. Cut off the bottoms of the legs to these lines. Repeat for the other end frame. Glue the front rail and the lower back rail into the end frames, then glue all the dowels and slats into the lower back rail. Apply glue to the tops of the slats and to the dowels and seat-back tenons, then tap the upper back rail into place. You will need someone to help you with this.

THE SEAT

CONSTRUCTION

The seat is a solid piece formed by dowelling together a number of narrow lengths of timber. Use a dowelling jig and join to the frame with 8mm ($\frac{5}{16}$in) dowels, 40mm (1$\frac{1}{2}$in) long, spaced about 150–225mm (6–9in) apart.

After dowelling, glue the lengths together using a gap-filling waterproof wood adhesive, such as Cascamite, and hold the assembly together with sash cramps or folding wedges against a fixed batten nailed to a worktop.

When the glue has dried, sand the surface flush and position the seat on the seat bench frame, leaving a 4mm ($\frac{1}{8}$in) wide gap at the back for drainage. Mark round so that there is a 19mm ($\frac{3}{4}$in) overhang at each end and at the front, then trim the seat to this line.

Cut a 12mm ($\frac{1}{2}$in) chamfer on the top edges at the front and sides using a router with a rounding over bit or a power plane.

FIXING

Fix the seat down using zinc-plated shrinkage plates – two at each end and three along the front – and screw into the seat rails and underside of the seat.

To keep the seat rigid so it will not bow in the middle, drill through the back rail into the seat in five places using a 12mm ($\frac{1}{2}$in) flat drill bit. Drill about 50mm (2in) into the seat. Cut five lengths of 12mm ($\frac{1}{2}$in) dowel about 95mm (3$\frac{3}{4}$in) long. Use a tenon saw or the point of a nail to cut two grooves 2–4mm ($\frac{1}{16}$–$\frac{1}{8}$in) deep along the dowel lengths to allow glue and air to escape as the dowels are driven into position.

Apply waterproof adhesive to the holes and hammer the dowels into position using the mallet. After the glue has set, saw off the protruding ends flush with the seat rail.

Chamfer the bottom edges of the legs so the wood will not split if the bench is dragged on the ground. To prevent the legs rotting, fix large, metal hammer-in glides to the bottoms of the legs.

❸ Shaping Upper Back Rail
Mark sides and back of back rail to follow taper of back face of back leg. Remove waste and plane smooth.

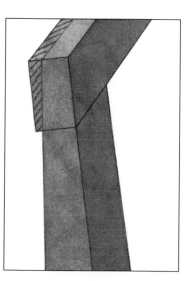

❹ Fitting the Back Slats
Mark slat and dowel positions on rails. Fit slats between back rails using two dowels each end.

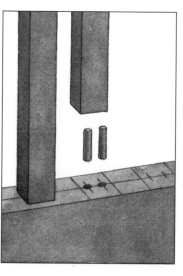

❺ Angling the Legs
Above **Stand bench frame on a flat surface and pack front leg with scrap timber. Scribe legs as necessary.**

❻ Cross-section of Seat
Below **Seat boards are butted up and joined using dowels. Longer dowels fix seat to lower back rail.**

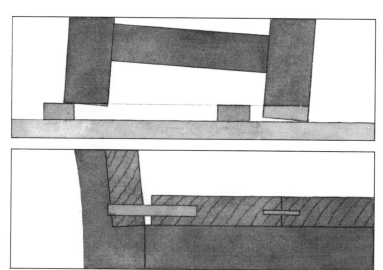

OCTAGONAL TREE SEAT

Even in the smallest garden, a tree seat makes an inviting point of interest. Any type of seating really makes a garden look furnished, but a seat which encircles a tree is particularly appealing. Children enjoy playing on, under and around the shady platform and seem to gain endless amusement sitting on opposite sides from each other or their parents.

Although this seat looks complicated, it is actually fairly simple to make.

Nevertheless, it is a time-consuming project. Because the back leans inwards, cutting the back slats could have been quite a difficult proposition. To prevent unnecessary complication, a gap has been left between the slats to accommodate any discrepancies that may occur.

Other design simplifications were made. There is a simple bold structure for the frame underneath rather than complicated mortise-and-tenon joints.

Softwood is an easy timber to work with and contributes a great deal to the ease with which a structure like this can be made. But softwood does need to be protected in some way, by treating with preservative, and then by applying a final finish of wood stain or, as in this case, paint. Depending on where in your garden the seat is positioned, you might like to choose a brighter colour: a strong blue would be very effective.

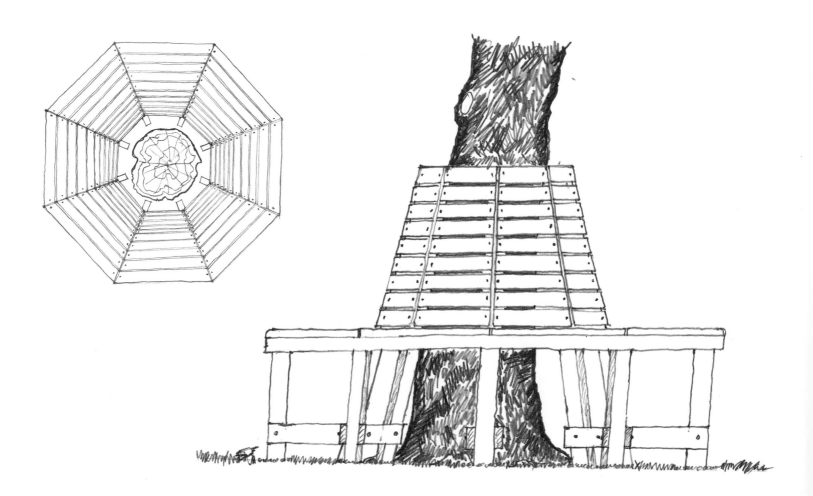

OCTAGONAL TREE SEAT

TOOLS

WORKBENCH (fixed or portable)

STEEL MEASURING TAPE

STEEL RULE

TRY SQUARE (or combination square)

SLIDING BEVEL

PROTRACTOR

CIRCULAR POWER SAW – preferably bench-mounted (or panel saw)

TENON SAW

POWER DRILL

DRILL BIT – approximately 3mm ($\frac{1}{8}$in) diameter

COUNTERSINK BIT

SCREWDRIVER

CLAW HAMMER

NAIL PUNCH

PINCERS

SMOOTHING PLANE (hand or power)

MATERIALS

Part	Quantity	Material	Length
BACK LEGS	8	75 × 50mm (3 × 2in) PAR softwood	1050mm (42in)
FRONT LEGS	8	As above	500mm (20in)
SEAT FRAME RAILS	32	75 × 25mm (3 × 1in) PAR softwood	530mm (21in)
SEAT SLATS	48	As above	As required
APRON BOARDS	8	As above	As required
BACK SLATS	72	50 × 16mm (2 × $\frac{5}{8}$in) PAR softwood	As required
APRON FIXING BATTENS	8	25 × 25mm (1 × 1in) PAR softwood	150mm (6in) shorter than apron boards

Also required: waterproof woodworking adhesive; 38mm (1$\frac{1}{2}$in) No 8 zinc-plated countersunk wood screws

The size of this eight-sided tree seat is governed by the size of the tree you wish to surround. Remember, you must leave room for the trunk to expand as the tree grows! Some trees grow faster than others: we built our seat around a small walnut tree, which is a slow-growing species, but even so we allowed an internal diameter of 600mm (24in) at the very top of the back support. Quite large tree specimens are available from good garden centres, so it could be worth planting a small 'standard' tree (that is, one with a long trunk) just as the focal point around which to build this seat.

The basic construction consists of eight separate frames on which the seat and backrest slats are fixed. The frames are of a pre-determined size, but the length of the slats is varied according to the internal diameter of the seat.

The seat is made in two sections, dry assembled to each other, so the two halves can be easily unscrewed to fix around the tree.

SEAT FRAMES

Cut the components of the seat frames to length.

Chamfer the front face of each back leg at an angle of 22$\frac{1}{2}$° from the centre line of one of the 75mm (3in) faces (fig 1). It is best to do this using a circular saw canted over at the correct angle – use a sliding bevel aligned on a protractor to set this. Finish off using a hand or power plane for a smooth finish.

1 **Chamferring the Back Leg**
Draw a line down middle of front face of each back leg. Chamfer legs at an angle of 22$\frac{1}{2}$° from this line.

2 **Making the Spacing Template**
Cut a spacing template from a scrap piece of board to the dimensions shown below. The template is used for accurate positioning of the front and back legs and the seat frame rails to make up the seat frames.

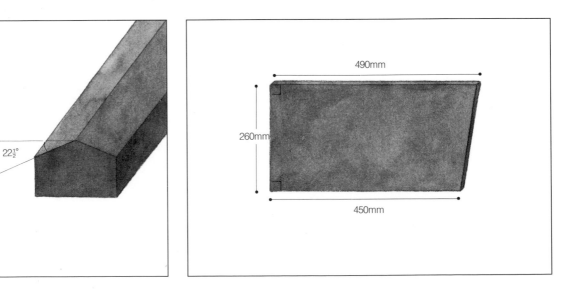

OCTAGONAL TREE SEAT ASSEMBLY

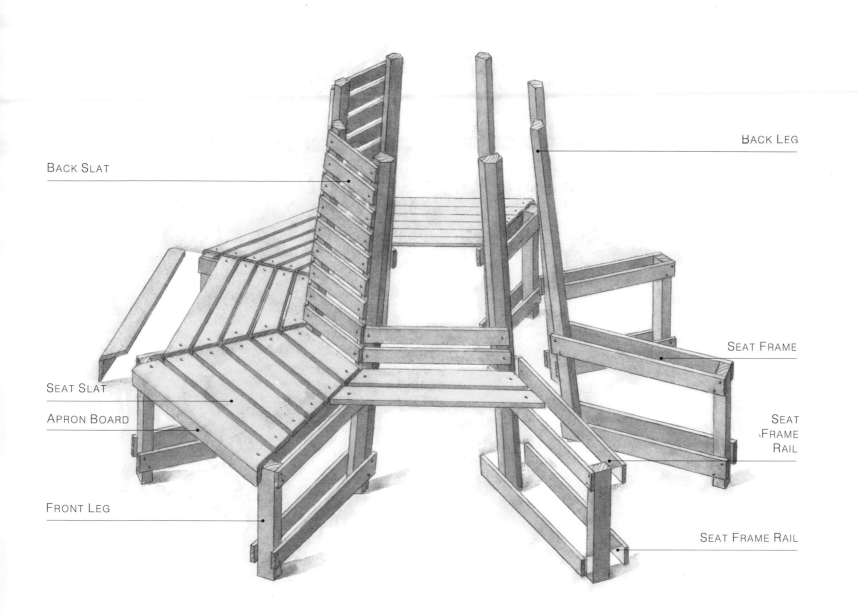

BACK SLAT

BACK LEG

SEAT SLAT

APRON BOARD

FRONT LEG

SEAT FRAME

SEAT
FRAME
RAIL

SEAT FRAME RAIL

OCTAGONAL TREE SEAT

Using a scrap of hardboard or chipboard to the shape and dimensions shown (fig 2, page 280), make up a template for fixing the seat frame rails on to the front and back legs to make up the seat frames.

Temporarily nail a batten to your workbench to give a flat surface to rest the feet of the legs against. Lay the front and back legs of one frame on the bench with two seat frame rails on top and the spacing template between them (fig 1). The back leg must be angled to align with the back of the template and the front leg should be exactly flush with the front edge of the template. The bottom of the legs should be resting against the batten nailed to the workbench.

The bottom seat frame rail is positioned so that it overlaps the front leg by 12mm ($\frac{1}{2}$in), while the top frame rail should be flush with the front and top of the front leg.

If a suitable flat workbench is not

DETAIL OF SEAT LEGS

Gravel-filled holes around the front and back legs of the seat frames make levelling easier and keep the legs off water-logged ground, reducing the risk of the wood rotting.

❷ Finished Construction of the Seat Frames
Above Glue and screw seat frame rails to legs, then trim overlap at the back so it is parallel with slope of back leg and protrudes 12mm ($\frac{1}{2}$in). *Below* Finished frame shows frame rails screwed in position to front and back legs.

❶ Making Up the Seat Frames
Lay the front and back legs of one frame on a flat surface so they are flush with template. Top frame rail rests on template and is flush with the top and front of front rail; bottom frame rail overlaps front leg by 12mm ($\frac{1}{2}$in).

12mm

available for this setting out, the pieces can be laid out on a flat floor, with the legs resting against an adjacent wall, so that the wall aligns the base of the legs.

Glue the top of the seat frame rail in place using a waterproof wood-working adhesive (such as Casca-mite), then drill pilot holes and screw it to the front and back legs using two screws at each end. Glue and screw the bottom seat frame rail to the legs in the same way.

Turn the frame over and position the other two seat frame rails in the same way, top and bottom. It is very important that these rails are exactly square to the ones on the other side so that the rails will be flush across the top where the seat slats will be fixed (fig 2).

To complete the construction of the frames, the seat frame rails are trimmed off in line with the back leg, but leaving a 12mm (½in) overlap (fig 2). Strike a line at this position, and then trim off using a panel saw or circular saw.

Repeat the construction for the remaining seven frames.

SEAT SLATS

The seat slats are cut from 75 × 25mm (3 × 1in) PAR (planed all round) softwood. The dimensions of the seat frames are pre-determined, so that the number of slats required will not vary, no matter how large the finished seat. What you will have to calculate yourself, however, is the length of each slat. This will depend upon the internal diameter of the seat, itself dependent on size of the tree trunk around which you assemble the project.

To measure up for the seat section, stand the eight frames around the tree roughly in position and spaced at the required distance from the tree, allowing for growth and depending on how large you want the diameter of the tree seat.

MAKING THE SEAT SLATS

When you are satisfied with the spacing of the seat frames, measure the distance between the centres of the back legs at seat height and calculate the average ('x' in fig 3).

This will be the length of the inside edge of the innermost seat slats (ours are 380mm [15in] long).

Mark length 'x' on to the back edge of a piece of the slat timber and draw $112\frac{1}{2}°$ angles off at either end using a sliding bevel. You can then use this slat to help draw up a full-size plan of a seat section (fig 4) which will enable you to cut the remaining five seat slats to the correct length.

To make the full-size plan, mark off the back measurement using the innermost slat as a guide for the angles. Extend the angled lines outwards, using the sliding bevel to double check that the angle is $112\frac{1}{2}°$. Returning to the seat frame, measure the distance from the centre of the back leg to the front of the frame ('y' in fig 3). On a full-size plan, mark the length 'y' on the angled lines, and add 20mm (¾in) to allow for the approximate thickness of the apron board at the front of the seat. Join up the two marks 'y plus 20mm (¾in)' at the front of the plan, parallel with the back line, to give the front edge of the seat.

You can now work out the necessary spacing for the slats. Place the innermost slat in position on the full-size plan and roughly cut five more slats, making sure that they are overlength. Bunch the slats together against the innermost slat, measure the remaining distance to the front line of the seat, and divide by five to give the amount of space to be left between each slat. If you want to increase the spacing, at this stage plane the edge of the innermost slat to reduce its width.

Using one of the slats and a spacing batten or spacing blocks cut to the width of the calculated space, draw out all six slats in position on the full-size plan. You will then be able to measure off the plan for the exact lengths of all the slats in each section of the seat.

Cut out all the slats for one seat section, but cut 2mm (about $\frac{1}{16}$in) inside each marked line in order to create a deliberate gap between the ends of the slats. You can use the slats cut for the first seat frame as templates for cutting the seat slats for the other sections.

③ Measuring up for the Seat Slats
Measure distance between centres of back legs at seat height ('x') to calculate length of innermost slat. Measure distance between centre of back leg and front of frame ('y') to calculate spacing between slats.

④ Drawing up Full-size Plan of Seat Section
Mark length 'x' and draw lines 'y plus 20mm (¾in)' either end at $112\frac{1}{2}°$ angle. Bunch six slats on plan, measure remaining distance to front and divide by five to calculate spacing. Cut spacers to size, then mark slat positions.

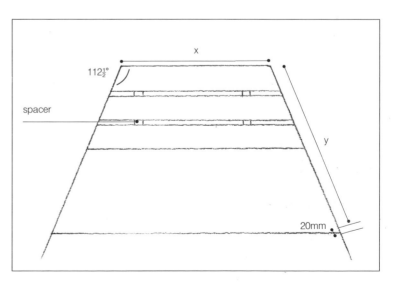

Octagonal Tree Seat

Fixing the Seat Slats

Fix the innermost slats first. Place the first slat across the back of two seat frames, spaced 2mm (about $\frac{1}{16}$in) in from the centre of the back legs, then glue and screw the slat to the top seat frame rails with one screw at each end (fig 1).

Take another seat frame and innermost slat, and space in the same way. Glue and screw in place as before.

Continue in this way for two groups of three sections each. It is very important that you only dry assemble two sections opposite one another, as you will need to remove the slats on two opposite sides of the structure in order to fix the seat frames around the tree.

To fix the subsequent slats, line up the next shortest slat with the innermost slat (fig 2). With the spacing batten (or blocks) between the slats, align one end of the new slat with a batten held against one end of the previously fixed slat. Glue and screw into the top seat frame rail at each end.

Continue with this second size slat all the way round, remembering only to dry assemble where you did before. Carry on in this fashion, one row at a time, assembling without glue those slats in the two sections that are dry assembled.

Before the frontmost slats are fitted, the apron boards must be assembled (fig 3). Cut a piece of 75 x 25mm (3 x 1in) timber to the longest length of the frontmost slat and bevel back the edges at each end so they are in line with the angles of the seat slat. Cut a 25 x 25mm (1 x 1in) fixing batten about 150mm (6in) shorter than the apron board and glue and screw it centrally in place to join the apron board to the frontmost slat. The front edge of the slat must be flush with the front face of the apron board. Repeat the process to make the other apron boards.

Round off the front edges of the frontmost slats to give a smooth finish. Glue and screw into place at the front edges of the frames, remembering not to glue the dry assembled sections.

The Back Slats

The back of each seat section is comprised of nine slats, cut from 50 x 16mm (2 x $\frac{5}{8}$in) PAR (planed all round) softwood. However, because the back legs are angled, the slats are not all the same length; instead, they get shorter as they reach the top.

Decide on the spacing of the back slats, and use scrap pieces of timber of the required thickness as spacing blocks. Lay the spacing blocks at seat level so that you start with a space, then lay the first slat, left overlength for the time being, in position. Mark off the ends in line with the centres of the back legs (fig 4). Set a sliding bevel to this angle, and cut the back slat to the marked length. Use the sliding bevel to mark off the correct angle and cut the first slats for the remaining back sections to length. Glue and screw the first back slats in place to the front of the back legs of all the seat sections, but leave the slats dry assembled in the same sections as you did before on the seat slats.

Use the spacing blocks to position the next length of slat (fig 4), mark off the ends as before, and cut to length. Repeat for the other seven slats in the row around the seat, and fix in place as before.

Continue in this way, row by row, until the seat back is completed (nine rows in our case). If the back legs protrude above the top slats they can be cut flush with the top of the slats for a neat appearance.

Dismantle the dry joints so that the seat is in two 'halves' (actually, two three-eighths).

Assembly

Take the two 'halves' of the seat to the tree and partially re-assemble it without glue so you can mark on the ground where the legs are positioned. Dismantle the seat again.

At the leg positions, dig holes for each of the 16 legs, 150mm (6in) in diameter and 150mm (6in) deep, and fill them with gravel. The gravel provides good drainage, reducing the risk of the legs rotting, and allows you to level the seat easily.

---

1 Fixing the Innermost Seat Slats
Use plan as guide but cut slats about 2mm ($\frac{1}{16}$in) short both ends. Space slat about 2mm ($\frac{1}{16}$in) in from centre of back legs, then fix between two top frame rails. Work round frames, but *dry assemble* slats on two facing sections.

2 Fixing Subsequent Slats to the Frame
Align next shortest slat with innermost slat: put the spacers or spacing battens in position, align ends of slat with innermost slat, and fix to frame rails. Continue round frame, then repeat for next size slats.

FINISHING

Before painting, it is important to treat the seat with a good-quality wood preservative which can be painted when dry – most clear and green grade preservatives fall into this category. We applied two coats, allowing each to dry thoroughly, and stood the legs in dishes of preservative for a couple of days.

Once the wood preservative is thoroughly dry (allow at least a week), the seat can be painted. We used a microporous paint which needs no primer (apart from preservative) and is intended for outdoor woodwork. The seat can be treated with a water-repellent preservative stain if a 'wood' finish is preferred.

After finishing with paint or wood stain, the seat can be finally assembled around the tree. Make sure the seat is well-bedded in the gravel and stands level on the ground. You can glue all joints at final assembly, or leave two sections of slats 'dry' to allow easy removal of the seat should the need arise.

3 **Making the Apron Board**
Above Use fixing batten to attach apron board to frontmost slat.
Below Front edge rounded over.

4 **Spacing and Fixing the Back Slats**
Back slats are initially overlength. Use spacing batten or spacing blocks to position back slat, and mark off ends of slat to line up with centres of back legs. Cut slats to length, then reposition and glue and screw in place.

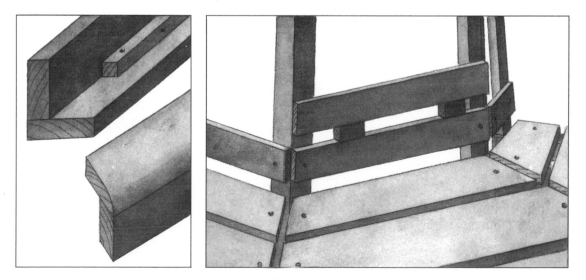

BARBECUE

Most barbecues, whether they are DIY or ready-made versions, have a number of design problems. One common fault is that they are generally too low to work at comfortably, which means the cook spends most of the time crouched awkwardly over the grill. The second problem is that grilling areas are often too small, providing food for only a limited number of people at a time.

This barbecue area corrects both of these typical defects, as well as providing a carefully considered series of spaces and surfaces for serving the food, storing fuel and keeping pans and dishes.

The generous grill area can be temporarily reduced in size if you only want to cook a small amount of food by placing bricks in the middle and confining the space in that way. The grill supports consist of several strips of angle iron cemented into place and these hold the grill tray. The entire structure is built up against a brick wall. With time, the wall will blacken with smoke, but this is not an unattractive effect. If you do not have a similar site for the barbecue, you can build a small brick wall at the back instead or leave the barbecue free-standing.

One particular advantage of this construction is the spaces it provides at either end of the grill area as well as beneath. On top, two quite extensive surfaces can be used as a place for resting pans and dishes of food in preparation. Underneath, timber can be stored. If you use the barbecue often and for long enough, the whole structure will warm up and the timber will be 'kiln-dried'.

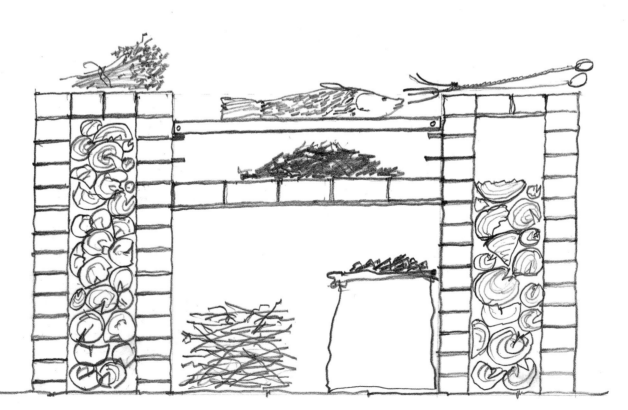

BARBECUE

Few pleasures are equal to that of sitting outside on a warm, summer's evening, eating food in the company of family and friends. If you build a barbecue, it will add a second focal point to your sitting-out area, but be careful to site it away from overhanging plants and any other vegetation that might catch fire while you are cooking.

The barbecue here is built from reclaimed bricks which match the wall against which it is built. Second-hand bricks are marginally larger than new bricks, but the dimensions here are calculated in courses rather than specific measurements, and you can use either sort of brick for building this project. The grill area is large enough to cook a substantial amount of food, but you could build the ends closer together if preferred.

The barbecue can be built against an existing wall or it can be free-standing. You can either build it on top of paving slabs, or you can lay paving slabs around the barbecue once it has been built. If you choose the latter option, you will

have to cut the paving slabs to fit, and you will also need to dig foundations before laying the first course of bricks. The foundations will need to be 150mm (6in) deep and 200mm (8in) wide around the outline of the barbecue. Lay 100mm (4in) of hardcore in the trench, ram it down, and then cover it with a 50mm (2in) layer of concrete. Check that the surface is level, and then leave the base to dry out and harden for a day or so.

As long as the paving slabs are level and are correctly laid on a firm base, however, it will be easier to build the barbecue on existing slabs. It is a good idea to protect the paving on which the barbecue is to be built with a sheet of thick, heavy-duty polythene. Simply lay the polythene sheet over the paving, build up the barbecue on top of the polythene, and then cut away the protruding sheet afterwards. The polythene will protect the surface of the paving from staining with wet cement while you are building, and will keep the brickwork at the base clean and dry.

CONSTRUCTION

Lay the bricks following the course-by-course plans (figs 1–3; see also **Techniques: Bricklaying, pages 404/5**). You will find it helpful to set out this project to ensure that the side walls are built exactly at right angles to the rear wall. A builder's square is quite easy to make from three battens with lengths in the proportion of 3:4:5. These should be nailed together to form a right-angled triangle – a useful size of square to make is a triangle with a base measuring 450mm (18in), a height of 600mm (24in) and a hypotenuse of 750mm (30in). Leave all of the battens slightly overlength, then nail or screw them together to form *exactly* these dimensions. Saw off the surplus afterwards.

Using a tight string line and the builder's square, make sure that the bricks in each course are straight and, using a spirit level, make sure that each course is built vertically.

When the seventh course is reached, bed angle irons across the

central section to support bricks forming the firebed. Do *not* lay these bricks for the time being.

Lay the eighth to eleventh courses, and on the eleventh course bed mild steel strips across the side walls to support the 'table' tops.

Spread the mortar on the strips, then lay the twelfth course. Finally, lay bedding mortar on the angle irons in the central section and lay the firebed bricks edge on.

After the mortar has dried out, drill the bricks in the eleventh and twelfth courses to take steel supports (coach screws with the heads cut off are ideal) which will support the food grill tray above the firebed. Measure the size of the central opening and get a blacksmith or steel fabricator to make a grill tray by welding an outer frame of mild steel strips, braced with mild steel strips and fitted with mild steel rods welded about 25mm (1in) apart.

To protect the bricks of the firebed from excessive heat and to keep them clean, at the same time as the grill is made you could get a steel tray made up to cover the firebed.

TOOLS

BRICKLAYER'S TROWEL

POINTING TROWEL

CLUB HAMMER

BRICK BOLSTER CHISEL

SHOVEL

BUILDER'S BUCKET

BUILDER'S SQUARE

SPIRIT LEVEL (long)

MATERIALS

BRICKS – 231 new or second-hand

MORTAR – from cement and builder's sand in the proportion 1:6

STEEL ANGLE IRONS – 4 pieces, 1016mm (40in) long

MILD STEEL STRIPS – 6 pieces, 100 × 300mm (4 × 12in)

MILD STEEL – for grill; measure finished barbecue for exact dimensions

1 *Above* **Plan View of 1st, 3rd, 5th and 7th Courses**
Lay bricks as shown; bed angle irons to support firebed on 7th course only.
Below **Plan view of 2nd, 4th and 6th Courses**
Cut three-quarter length bricks to enable courses to be staggered.

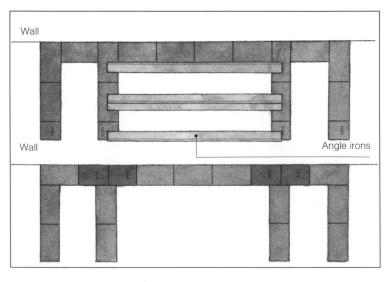

BARBECUE ASSEMBLY

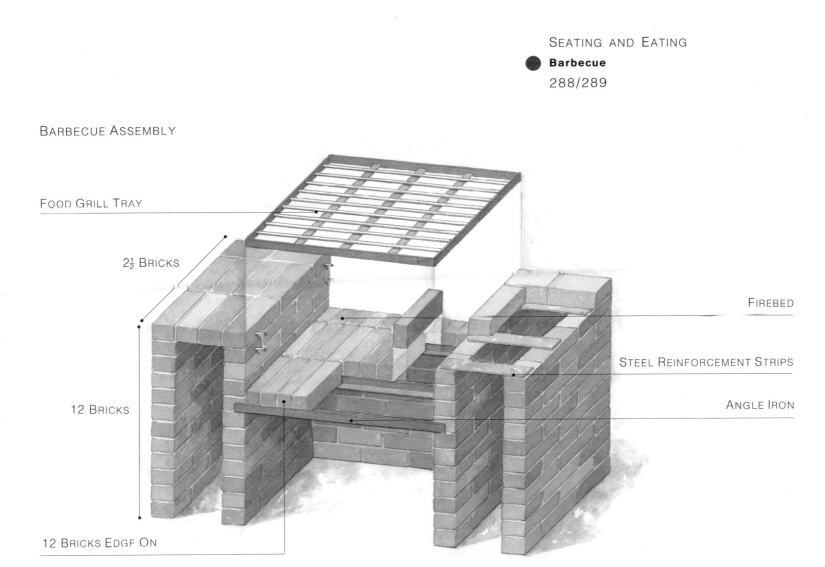

FOOD GRILL TRAY

$2\frac{1}{2}$ BRICKS

12 BRICKS

12 BRICKS EDGE ON

FIREBED

STEEL REINFORCEMENT STRIPS

ANGLE IRON

② *Above* **Plan View of 8th Course**
Two rows of 12 bricks are laid edge on above angle irons to form firebed
Below **Plan View of 9th and 11th Courses**
From 9th course, bricks only laid at ends; steel plates above 11th course.

③ *Above* **Plan View of 10th Course**
Lay six bricks each end as shown.
Below **Plan View of 12th Course**
Ten bricks each end are laid above steel strips to form top.

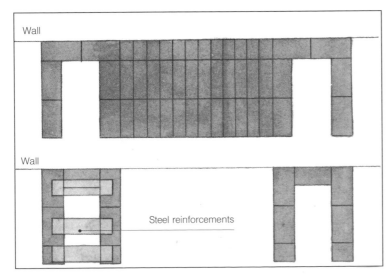

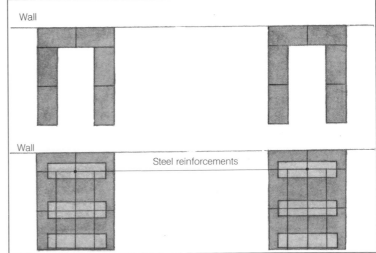

AWNING

An awning over a patio or sitting-out area gives privacy and allows you to use the area in most weather. The awning here is an optional addition to a simple pergola attached to a house wall. It rests on the pergola and can be brought out in sunny or warm showery weather, yet is simple to remove when not required.

You can make the pergola more or less any size to suit your patio or paved area. The structure is made from preservative-treated planed timber; western red cedar is ideal, but ordinary softwood treated with a water-repellent wood stain is a very serviceable alternative.

The supporting posts are made from 100 × 100mm (4 × 4in) timber of sufficient length to give headroom of at least 2.3m (7ft 6in) under the pergola structure. The posts are positioned about 2.4m (8ft) apart and are linked to the house wall by 175 × 50mm (7 × 2in) roof joists. At the front, the posts are steadied and separated at the top by a fascia board measuring 100 × 38mm (4 × 1½in) which runs the entire length of the pergola.

In the example shown, where there is a wall at the end of the terrace, there is no need to position a post and roof joist against the house wall. Instead, a length of 100 × 50mm (4 × 2in) timber is bolted to the wall so that the top of this length of timber is at the same level as the tops of the roof joists. Use expanding wall bolts to ensure a secure fixing.

On the main wall of the house, the roof joists can be supported in galvanized steel joist hangers, which are screwed and wallplugged to the house wall; the roof joists are then screwed into the joist hangers. An alternative method for supporting the roof joists is to rest them on a 100 × 50mm (4 × 2in) timber beam (called a wall plate) which is fixed horizontally to the wall, using expanding wall bolts, so that it supports the roof joists at the correct height. In this case, the roof joists can be fixed to the wall plate by nailing at an angle through the sides of the roof joists and into the top of the wall plate (see **Techniques, Skew Nailing, page 399**).

An unusual but practical feature of this pergola is the covered roof section close to the wall of the house. This provides permanent shelter and shade at the back of the seating area, and also strengthens the pergola, prevents sideways movement in high winds, and keeps rain off the house window frames.

The removable awning is made from deck chair canvas and is intended to be fitted during the warmer months of the year. It is draped across the roof joists and is held in place by tapes that loop around the roof joists. The tapes are secured by Velcro fasteners. The awning is stiffened at each end by being folded over and tacked to a 19 × 9.5mm (¾ × ⅜in) strip of hardwood or ramin.

CONSTRUCTION

Start by cutting the support posts to length. You need to take into account that the roof joists are fixed at a slight downward slope, and that you might not have a great deal of flexibility over the height at which

you can fix the joist hangers or wall plate onto the wall of your house. You also need to decide how the posts will be fixed at the bottom. The easiest method of fixing the posts is to slot them into socket-type supports which can be screwed to the surface of the patio (fig 2). Alternatively, each post can be fitted over a protruding bolt or bracket cemented into the surface of the paving. Yet another option is to chip a hole through the surface of the patio using a hammer and cold chisel so that the bottom of the post can be concreted in place.

Once the length of post has been decided, the top can be angled and the joint cut to accommodate the roof joist. Saw down to form a slot to suit the width of the roof joist – its actual width will be less than 50mm (2in). Most of the waste can be removed by sawing, and finally the joint (a form of bridle joint) can be cleaned up using a chisel.

If the roof joists are to be fixed to the house wall using joist hangers, these are fixed next. Make sure that they are level by lining them up with

❶ Detail of Top Section
The roof joists are supported by 100 × 100mm (4 × 4in) posts at the front and by the main wall of the house at the back. Shade is provided by the permanent covered section and the removable canvas awning.

❷ Socket-type Post Supports
Metal support is screwed or bolted to ground. Post slots in support and is fixed by tightening screws at side.

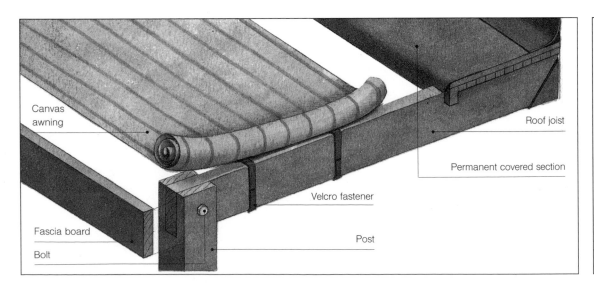

Canvas awning

Roof joist

Permanent covered section

Velcro fastener

Fascia board

Post

Bolt

a line drawn along the wall. Check that the line is horizontal using a spirit level and fix the joist hangers in place using zinc-plated screws into wallplugs. Alternatively, fix the wall plate in place using expanding wall bolts. Slot the roof joists in place between the post and joist hanger or wall plate, and fix with a bolt through the post, and by screwing through the joist hanger. Skew nail the joists if they are resting on a wall plate (fig.3). Nail the fascia board to the top of the support posts.

All that remains is to fix the permanent covered section (fig 4). Nail 38 × 12mm (1½ × ½in) cedar or stained softwood slats across the joists finishing with a 38 × 25mm (1½ × 1in) batten which is notched at intervals to accept the roof joists and is fitted vertically against the lowest slat. The top is covered with a 915mm- (36in-) deep sheet of exterior grade chipboard which is then covered with roofing felt. The roof-to-wall joint is sealed by pressing a strip of self-adhesive flashing strip firmly in place across the entire length of the joint.

❸ Fixing the Joists to the Wall
Left Joist hangers are aligned at correct height and screwed to wall; joists sit in hangers and are screwed in place. *Right* 4 × 2in (100 × 50mm) wall plate fixed horizontally to wall; joists skew nailed in place.

❹ Permanent Covered Section
Softwood slats are nailed to roof joists. Batten at front of slats is notched at intervals to accept joists. Section is then covered in exterior-grade chipboard and roofing felt. Seal roof-to-wall joint with flashing strip.

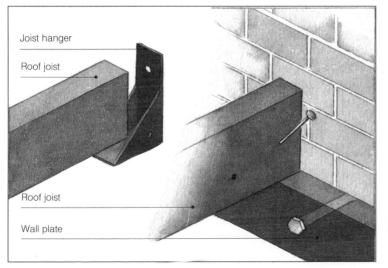

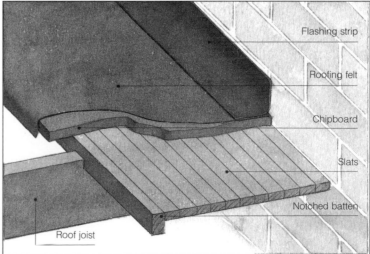

TIMBER TABLE

This sturdy garden table makes an attractive feature in any outdoor setting. The table shown is only 375mm (15in) high, but by increasing the height of the base on which it is built you can make it to any height required. If, for example, you make it about 750mm (30in) high you will be able to sit around it on garden chairs and use it as an outdoor dining table.

Apart from the brick base, the table is made entirely from solid timber. Preservative-treated quality softwood is ideal; hardwood could be used, but because of the large quantity of timber required, its cost would be prohibitively high.

The table top is made from 75 × 50mm (3 × 2in) timber, in the form of 12 square frames which become progressively larger from a central block. There is a gap of about 5mm ($\frac{1}{4}$in) between each square, which is created automatically by using 50mm (2in) wide PAR (planed all round) timber for the table top. PAR timber is sawn to its nominal width – in this case 50mm (2in) – and then each face is planed about 5mm ($\frac{1}{4}$in) so that the actual width is about 45mm (1$\frac{3}{4}$in).

CONSTRUCTION

Start by building a base from brick, stone or reconstituted stone-and-concrete blocks (see **Techniques, page 404/5**); the base should measure 560 × 560mm (22 × 22in) and it should be about 225mm (9in) high if you want to make the table as shown in the photograph. The height could be increased to as much as 600mm (24in) if an outdoor dining table is required.

The table top is fixed on two diagonal supports which are fitted to the base plinth to form an 'X'. Cut cross halving joints (see **Techniques, page 400**) at the point where the supports intersect (fig 2). For neatness, the ends of the supports are sloped as shown in the side view (fig 2). The last 300mm (12in) is sloped from the full depth of 75mm (3in) to 25mm (1in) at the end. Assemble the supports by gluing the cross halving joint with waterproof woodworking adhesive and then cramp the supports until the glue sets, checking first that the supports are exactly at right angles.

If you are unable to buy preservative pressure-treated timber, then at this stage it is wise to treat the supports with a good quality water-repellent preservative; apply a second coat of preservative 24 hours later.

The supports are fixed down to the base plinth using expanding wall bolts into holes drilled in the base plinth and recessed into the supports. Before tightening these bolts, check that the supports are absolutely level using a spirit level and put packing pieces underneath them to adjust as necessary.

FORMING THE TABLE TOP

The table top consists of concentric 'frames' which fit one inside the other down to the solid block

MATERIALS

Part	Quantity	Material	Length
PLINTH	As required	Bricks or concrete blocks	As required
TABLE-TOP SUPPORTS	2	75 × 50mm (3 × 2in) PAR timber	1700mm (67in)
TABLE-TOP FRAMES	4	75 × 50mm (3 × 2in) PAR timber	1200mm (48in)
	4	As above	1100mm (44in)
	4	As above	1000mm (40in)
	4	As above	900mm (36in)
	4	As above	800mm (32in)
	4	As above	700mm (28in)
	4	As above	600mm (24in)
	4	As above	500mm (20in)
	4	As above	400mm (16in)
	4	As above	300mm (12in)
	4	As above	200mm (8in)
	4	As above	100mm (4in)

ALSO: about 15m (48ft) of 9.5mm ($\frac{3}{8}$in) diameter hardwood dowel to be cut into 100mm (4in) lengths for joining corners; 4 expanding wall bolts for fixing down table-top supports; waterproof woodworking adhesive.

1 **Brick Plinth Base**
Table rests on brick or stone plinth built to required height. Fill middle with rubble topped with concrete.

2 **Making the Table-top Supports**
Cut cross halving joints in the supports so that they meet to form an 'X', with the supports exactly at right angles. The ends of the supports are sloped on the underside through the last 300mm (12in).

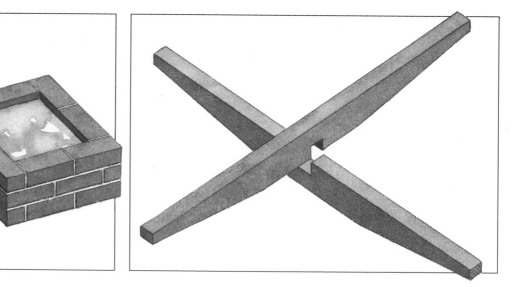

formed of four pieces in the centre. Although the timber is 75 × 50mm (3 × 2in), the 'frames' are formed just like giant picture frames, with the corners mitred at 45°. The easiest way to cut these mitres is to use a power saw with the blade tilted to a 45° angle. You can use an ordinary portable circular power saw with the timber held securely in a vice, but it will be even easier if you hire or buy a mitre cut-off saw, a radial arm saw, or a circular saw table for the purpose.

Cut the largest frame so that it gives external dimensions of 1200 × 1200mm (48 × 48in). Apply waterproof woodworking adhesive to the mating parts of each joint, then draw them together with frame cramps before drilling into the joint with a 9.5mm (⅜in) drill bit, keeping the bit at a 90° angle to the joint. Drill two holes in each joint and then drive 9.5mm (⅜in) long wooden dowels into the holes, after coating the dowels with waterproof wood-working adhesive. Before applying the adhesive, make a shallow saw cut along the length of each dowel,

which will help to ensure that not all of the glue will be driven out when the dowel is inserted. At this stage, make sure that the dowel is long enough to protrude from the hole at each end; when the adhesive has set, the ends of the dowels can be sawn off close to the sides of the frame and the surface then neatly planed smooth to give an unobtrusive fixing. Make up the remaining frames in the same way to the dimensions specified in the Materials chart (opposite).

The central block is formed by cutting four pieces of 75 × 50mm (3 × 2in) timber sections which are joined by dowels to form a square block. The frames are treated with two coats of water-repellent wood preservative to ensure longevity before being assembled on to the timber supports.

The table-top frames are fixed to the table-top supports using water-proof woodworking adhesive and dowels inserted into holes drilled vertically down into the supports and vertically up into the undersides of the table-top frames.

❸ Fixing Table-top Supports to Plinth
Use expanding wall bolts to fix the supports at each corner of the plinth. Drill the plinth to accept the wall bolts and drill 50mm (2in) deep holes to recess the bolts in the supports. Check supports are level before final fixing.

❹ Forming Table-top Frames
Cut 45° mitres at corners and fix using waterproof adhesive and dowels through the sides.

❺ Fixing Frames to Supports
Drill corresponding holes down into supports and up into corners of frames. Fix using dowel joints.

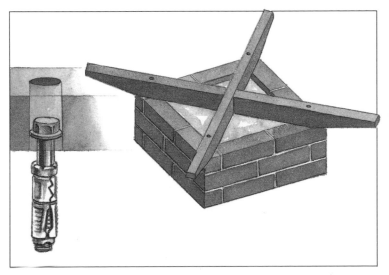

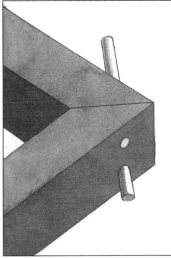

PART 6

GARDEN HOUSES

The garden house is a subject in itself. At one extreme, garden houses can be supremely romantic, providing a true retreat from the world; at the other, they can be as mundane as a shed. In between come summer houses, gazebos, pavilions, follies, greenhouses, workshops, Wendy houses, studios, offices and garden rooms. One could even include dovecotes, pigeon lofts, rabbit hutches, dog kennels and chicken coops, since animal houses so often accompany human ones. But whatever their ultimate function, there is something uniquely appealing about buildings on such a small scale. For the garden designer, they are places where wit and imagination, as much as practicality, can come into play.

Children have inspired some of the most charming versions of the garden house, while animal houses, when they are decorated rather than strictly functional, also tend to be designed to amuse and appeal to children. More than any other type of garden structure, the many varieties of garden house offer the opportunity to use bright paints, providing a much-needed splash of year-round colour in the garden.

Garden Houses

The summer house or garden retreat has a long tradition in Europe and an even longer tradition in the Far East. As a pavilion or gazebo it was essentially built to provide a platform from which to view a garden, or, in Eastern terms, to contemplate nature. However, from the eighteenth century onwards, the nature of the garden house evolved from being a viewing place to a kind of architectural attraction in the garden. Chinese pavilions, Japanese tea houses, miniature thatched cottages, classical temples and Gothick grottoes were some of the styles that were enthusiastically embraced.

As a rule, follies of this kind really need acres of parkland to act as a foil for their charms; today, however, garden houses are usually simpler in design, reflecting their essentially practical nature. Nevertheless there are many attractive 'ordinary' buildings to act as inspiration, including bathing huts, lodges and gypsy caravans. Painted wood, clapboarding, shingle and exterior-grade plywood are all good basic construction materials. Roofs can be tiled, felted or made of corrugated iron; for a truly rustic look, you could seek out a thatcher, or have the roof covered in turf. Building a garden house can be an exercise in creative salvage and recycling for those with that kind of imagination and skill.

The degree of finish depends on the ultimate use of the house: a building which must function as an annexe for overnight guests obviously needs to be completed to a higher standard of comfort than one which merely serves as a place to read a book or escape from the rain. If you are going to use the house as a studio or office, for example, you will need to lay on electricity; in other cases, having a supply of water might be a distinct advantage. Similarly, building permission may have to be sought from your local authority or government department, depending on the intended size and function of your shed or house.

Site is an important issue. A summer house or pavilion plays an obvious role in the layout of the entire garden. If you are going to sit there and admire nature, the view must be worthwhile. Paving and

HOME FROM HOME

The garden house – shed, pavilion, workshop or summer house – is innately appealing (left and far left). Part of the charm of these small-scale buildings is their forthright style and use of simple materials.

Ample garden storage is an invaluable asset (above). Wall-mounted racks are generally a good idea; hanging tools saves floor space and prevents tines and blades becoming damaged. Ceiling hooks can be used to suspend baskets and trugs.

Garden Houses

planting should be planned taking into account the site of the building as far as possible. You could arrange for a pavilion to be set at the end of a walkway to give impact to a formal design, placed on a higher level to offer a commanding view, or secreted in a sheltered corner to add a sense of mystery and surprise.

Although there is nothing mysterious or romantic about a garden shed, with a little thought it need not be the unlovely and somewhat blatant feature common to so many gardens. A garden shed which functions as a true garden room for maintenance of tools, potting up and storing seeds and bulbs is an invaluable resource in any household.

Storage is one of the main requirements. You will fill a shed very quickly with outdoor and garden equipment, so it is important to build or buy one which is big enough for your needs. The first consideration is likely to be providing an efficient system for storing garden tools, seeds, bulbs, fertilizer and so on.

In addition to tool storage, you will need floor space for big items, which may include a lawnmower, bicycles, garden furniture, awnings and umbrellas packed away during the winter, portable barbecues and large toys. You will also need somewhere to put bags of compost and charcoal, as well as a dry, high shelf for storing fertilizers and pesticides out of the reach of children and animals. Ceiling hooks can be used to accommodate baskets and trugs; shelves will take pots and seed trays. It is also useful to have somewhere cool and dark for storing bulbs or root vegetables during the summer or after the harvest.

One advantage of a well-planned storage system is that you can see at a glance if anything has not been put back. But the benefits are not merely practical. As well as providing an efficient area to work, a carefully organized garden room or shed, with its array of traditional garden tools and equipment, can be as pleasant a place in which to spend time as a kitchen.

As far as site is concerned, there is no reason why a shed needs to be in full view. You may not have all that much choice when it comes to position, but it is a good idea to place the shed out of the way, near a compost heap or bonfire site. Alternatively, you can create a utility area by positioning the shed near an existing garage, dustbin store or greenhouse and screen the view by adding trellis panels and climbing plants.

Off-the-peg sheds, which come in ready-to-assemble packs, are rarely as attractive as those you design and build yourself. But there are ways of improving the appearance of the standard shed which are especially useful if you have little choice about where the shed is positioned. Many examples look better if they are simply painted. Good quality brick paviours laid around the base, plant tubs filled with flowers and trellis with plants trained over will all help to connect the shed to its surroundings, making it look less brash and out of place.

GARDEN RETREATS

A garden house can provide a secluded spot for sitting and watching the world go by (far left, centre and far right). If you want to disguise a structure or hide an ugly shed from view, fast-growing climbers such as Russian vine (Fallopia aubertii) or mile-a-minute (Polygonum baldschuanicum) are the answer.

ANIMAL HOUSES

Coops, dovecotes, bird-houses and the like can be the excuse for wit and decorative flair to come into play. These structures provide a good opportunity to practise DIY skills.

SUMMER HOUSE

Most people could well do with the extra space that a summer house provides. And although this is the perfect place for storing tools, bulbs and seeds, or potting up and a variety of other garden chores, you need not necessarily put it to horticultural use. A DIY workshop, an artist's studio, a guest annexe, the ultimate play house – it is easy to think of a host of functions for this kind of structure to fulfil, although the use it is put to can mean that you will have to seek planning permission before you start building. It could prove invaluable as a home office or study, offering an important psychological separation of home and work for those who work at home. And it is substantial enough to serve as a pavilion on a village cricket green.

The house may appear a daunting prospect for all but the most ardent DIY enthusiast; but the skills you require are well within the average range of ability and there is no need for the kind of refinement demanded by furniture-making. There is no sophisticated jointing and there are few techniques which should not already be familiar. The cost of materials, all readily available, are roughly the same as a family holiday, which makes it fairly reasonable, unless you put a high price on your own time and labour. The major commitment is time. Working alone during the evenings and weekends, it should take about three months. Full-time, with one or two willing assistants, it might only take a couple of weeks.

As far as the design is concerned, there were a number of influences. The idea to use corrugated iron (actually profiled steel) for the roof came from the houses of the Australian outback. The shape of the roof was suggested by the roofline of the traditional cricket pavilion. In different colour combinations, the house acquires quite different aspects: green and white for a cricket pavilion; pale pastels for a seaside look; vibrant blues, greens and pinks to suggest the Caribbean.

The project is a major undertaking. We would recommend that you attempt most of the other projects in the book before tackling this one. But if the demands are high, so are the rewards. What could be more satisfying – or useful – than building your own garden house?

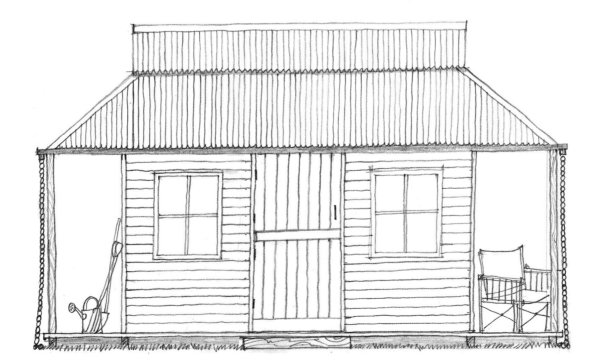

SUMMER HOUSE

A summer house, somewhere in a secluded part of the garden, is a delightful retreat to be savoured when you want to relax away from the bustle of the house. This design captures all the magic, charm and intrigue required from a garden hideaway and just invites you to explore inside. The size of the room is approximately 3.6 × 2.4m (12 × 8ft) which is a comfortable size to furnish with wicker chairs yet remain cosy and intimate. The extended roof covering over the veranda gives the impression of greater size while providing a 1000mm (39in) deep protected area on showery days when you want to sit outside. The size of the base is partly dictated by the area that can be built upon without the need of planning permission. However, check with your local authority, since the use to which you put the building will also affect the need for permission.

The red-and-blue colour scheme chosen here not only accentuates the design and materials but is fun, too. By changing the colour combinations you can substantially alter the finished look of the building; a few suggestions for alternative colours are illustrated on page 67.

The basic structure rests on a level base of concrete slabs which in turn support timber joists. The veranda is treated slatted wood, while the interior floor is exterior-grade plywood finished, in this case, with floor paint, although you could equally use carpets, tiles or boards. It would be perfectly possible to extend the walls to take in the veranda area if you require more indoor floor space. The interior walls are also clad with plywood to give the structure rigidity – between this and the outdoor boarding is a layer of insulation. The level ceiling is covered in tongued-and-grooved

boards and is also insulated. You could leave the roof structure exposed if you wanted, although you would lose a lot of heat in cold weather as a result. If you require heating, a paraffin heater or a fan heater are the best options.

The chains leading down from the guttering at the four corners of the building act in the same way as the drainpipes, conducting water down to the ground, where four soakaways are dug: a feature of traditional Japanese houses.

The illustrations below and opposite give an overall impression of the construction of the front, back and side walls and of the roof. However, in addition to the project text and illustrations, you may also need to refer to the sections on Materials and Techniques (pages 394–5 and 396–405) when further guidance is needed on individual stages of the construction.

TOOLS

PORTABLE WORKBENCH

STEEL MEASURING TAPE

STEEL RULE

TRY SQUARE or COMBINATION SQUARE

ADJUSTABLE SLIDING BEVEL

PANEL SAW (or circular saw)

POWER DRILL

DRILL BIT – 12mm ($\frac{1}{2}$in) and 3.2mm ($\frac{1}{8}$in)

SPANNER

HAMMER

NAIL PUNCH

PINCERS

CHISEL

MALLET

TIN SNIPS

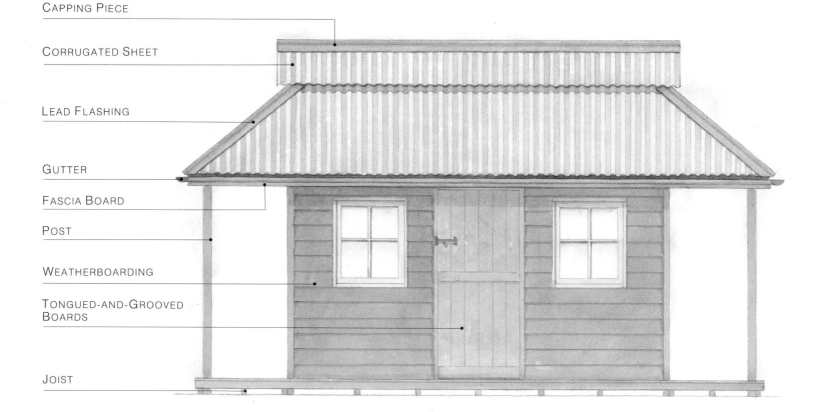

CAPPING PIECE

CORRUGATED SHEET

LEAD FLASHING

GUTTER

FASCIA BOARD

POST

WEATHERBOARDING

TONGUED-AND-GROOVED BOARDS

JOIST

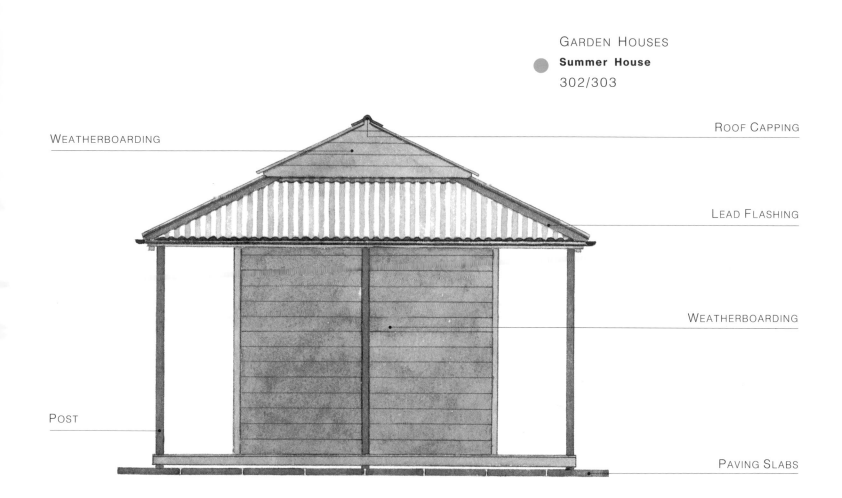

WEATHERBOARDING

POST

ROOF CAPPING

LEAD FLASHING

WEATHERBOARDING

PAVING SLABS

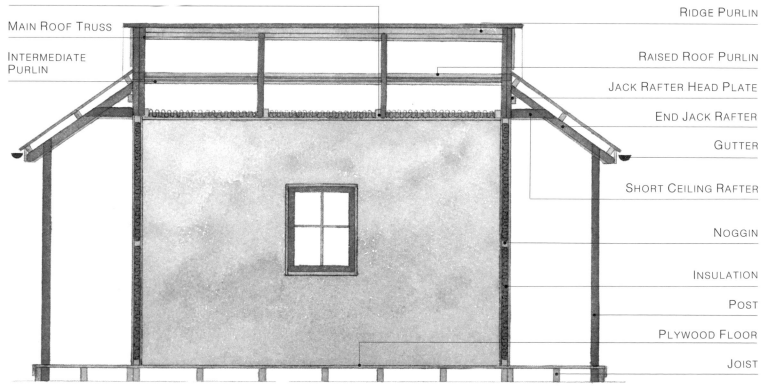

CEILING JOIST

MAIN ROOF TRUSS

INTERMEDIATE PURLIN

RIDGE PURLIN

RAISED ROOF PURLIN

JACK RAFTER HEAD PLATE

END JACK RAFTER

GUTTER

SHORT CEILING RAFTER

NOGGIN

INSULATION

POST

PLYWOOD FLOOR

JOIST

Summer House: Foundation and Base

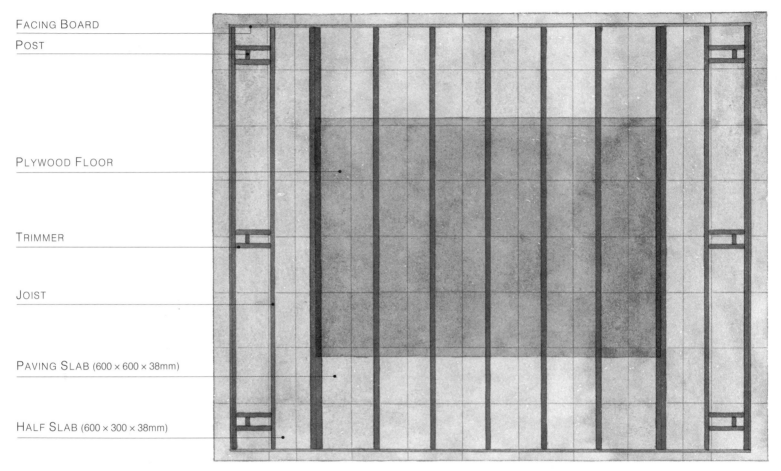

FACING BOARD

POST

PLYWOOD FLOOR

TRIMMER

JOIST

PAVING SLAB (600 × 600 × 38mm)

HALF SLAB (600 × 300 × 38mm)

BASE ASSEMBLY

1 Setting Out Position of Base

Use pegs and stringline to set out base outline. Two sizes of slabs are used –
600 × 600mm (24 × 24in) and 600 × 300mm (24 × 12in) – to ensure joists are
supported centrally while leaving a narrow border around house perimeter.

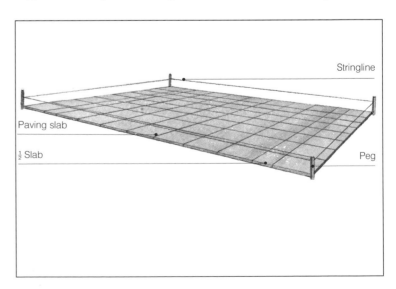

Stringline

Paving slab

½ Slab

Peg

FOUNDATION AND BASE

Set out the site to be covered by the complete base using four corner pegs and a string line (fig 1). Choose a sheltered part of the garden: this will minimize the risk of structural damage in storms and high winds. The summer house is not anchored to the ground, so you must site it with care.

Avoid sloping terrain as this would need a lot of excavation work for a level base to be laid.

The base can be laid using either paving slabs or concrete. If you choose slabs, then you will need 72 slabs measuring 600 × 600 × 38mm (24 × 24 × 1½in). You will also need 16 half-size slabs (600 × 300mm [24 × 12in]). These are required so that a narrow border remains around the walls while the joists rest centrally on the slabs (Base and Floor Assembly illustration).

The slabs should be laid on a 1:5 mix of cement to sharp sand. You need to build in a slope of 1 in 60 from front to back to ensure that rainwater drains away and does not lie alongside the joists and cause them to rot away.

Alternatively, if you use concrete you will have to dig out about 125mm (5in) of soil and lay a foundation of well-compacted hardcore covered with a 50mm (2in) layer of concrete mixed from one part cement to five parts ballast.

You will have to set up a formwork (wooden frame) of timbers to retain the concrete, again having first pegged out the site. The formwork timbers should be held in place using stakes driven into the ground. Old floorboards, or similar, are ideal as formwork. Do not forget to build in a slight fall in the formwork from front to back.

When the base is completed you can lay out the joists. Use 100 × 50mm (4 × 2in) sawn timber for the floor joists, making sure that it has been thoroughly treated with preservative. Ideally, pressure-impregnated timber should be used. There are 13 joists in all, with a double row being used to support the end walls. The outer joists support the veranda floor at each end.

Each joist should be laid on a strip of bituminous felt to serve as a damp-proof membrane and to prevent moisture seeping up through the base. Since the base has a slight fall built into it from front to back, you will need to lay small packing pieces about every 600mm (24in) under each joist to bring it level. This is important since you want to have a level floor.

Next lay the summer house floor (fig 3). This is 19mm (¾in) WBP plywood and the area is nominally 3.6 × 2.4m (12 × 8ft). The sheets should be fixed to the joists using 38mm (1½in) No 8 screws at 400mm (16in) centres around the edge. Fix the middle sheet first and then a sheet either side, cut to fit as needed. Next lay 50 × 19mm (2 × ¾in) packing strips of plywood on which the front and back walls will sit.

The end joists, which will support the veranda floor, can be removed temporarily since they will be a hazard while the summer house is being constructed.

② **Setting Out and Levelling Floor Joists**
Timber joists are laid down at 600mm (24in) centres. A double row is needed to support the end walls. Since the slabs are laid to a slight fall, packing pieces are needed below the joists to level them.

③ **Laying the Plywood Floor**
The floor is formed from 19mm (¾in) thick WBP plywood screwed to the floor joists using 38mm No 8 screws. Lay the middle panel first and then one other panel on each side.

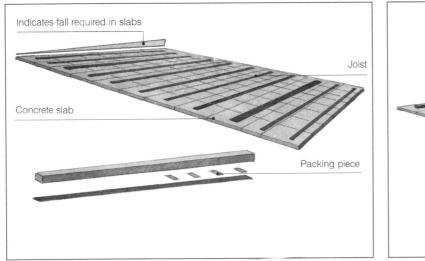

Indicates fall required in slabs

Joist

Concrete slab

Packing piece

SUMMER HOUSE: WALL ASSEMBLY

WALLS

The inner faces of the walls are made from 12mm ($\frac{1}{2}$in) WBP plywood. Cut out the pieces needed for each of the four walls. The window openings, front and back, are about 700 × 600mm ($27\frac{1}{2}$ × $23\frac{1}{2}$in) and the doorway is about 2000 × 810mm (78 × 32in). If you intend to buy the door ready-made then tailor the door opening to the required size – remember to allow for the dimensions of the door frame reveal.

Taking each wall by turn, lay out the 50 × 50mm (2 × 2in) studding at the centres shown (fig 1). Note also that the short horizontal noggins are intentionally slightly misaligned in order to stagger the screw fixings in the panels.

Lay the plywood panels on the studding with the inside surface uppermost – these will form the internal walls of the house (fig 2). Use 38mm ($1\frac{1}{2}$in) No 8 screws to fix the panels to the studs at 400mm (16in) intervals. Countersink and fill all of the screw heads.

The door and window openings are all framed with 50 × 25mm (2 × 1in) trimmers skew nailed to the studs using 50mm (2in) nails (*see* **Techniques, page 399**).

The walls are joined together using 125mm (5in) long 12mm ($\frac{1}{2}$in) diameter bolts. If you position all four walls (fig 3) using a helper and temporary supporting struts, you can drill bolt holes at the corners through adjoining vertical studs. Cramp each corner before drilling the holes and fixing the bolts, leaving a little 'play' at this stage for final adjustment of the four walls. Four bolts are needed at each corner at the approximate positions indicated (fig 1, back wall). The order of assembly is to offer up the front wall to one end wall and bolt together; then bolt the back wall to the other end wall; finally, bolt the two remaining corners together.

When all the walls have been joined and are square, the sole plates of each wall (fig 2, front wall) can be nailed to the joists using 100mm (4in) nails at approximately 400m (16in) centres.

① Assembling Framework for each Wall
The illustrations show the arrangement of the 50 × 50mm (2 × 2in) studding for each of the four walls. *Top* Front frame with allowance for the door and windows. *Middle* Rear frame with a window opening. *Below* Solid end walls.

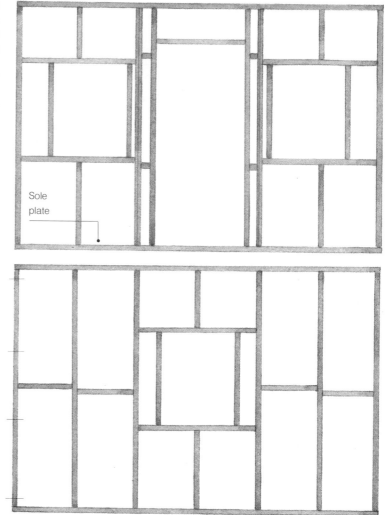

Sole plate

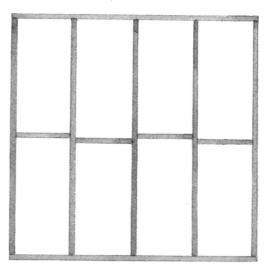

WALL FRAME ASSEMBLY

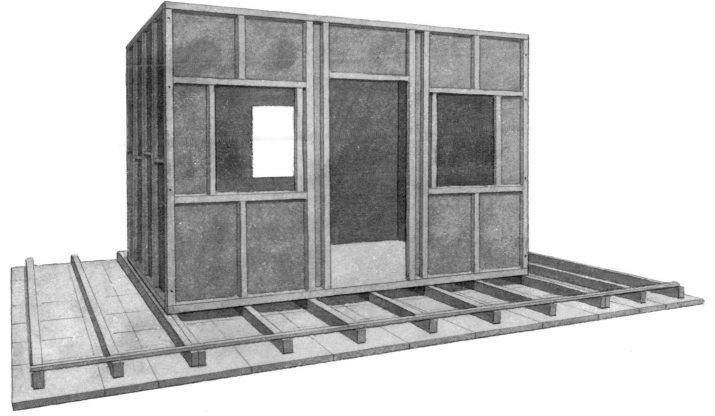

2 **Adding Inner Walls to Frames**

The inner walls are formed from 12mm ($\frac{1}{2}$in) thick plywood. The front wall is made from five pieces with cut-outs for the windows in the side sections. The sheets are fixed to the frame using 38mm No 8 screws.

3 **Joining the Four Frames Together**

Each studding framework is joined together using 125mm (5in) long bolts. Using a helper, supporting struts and cramps, keep the frames aligned at the corners. Drill holes for four bolts at each corner and bolt together.

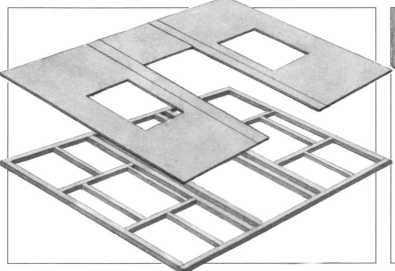

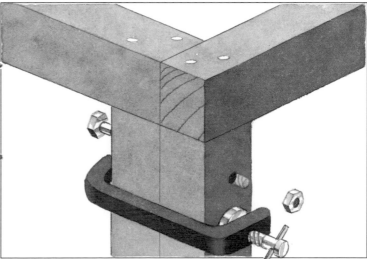

Summer House: Roof Assembly

Layout of Roof Timbers

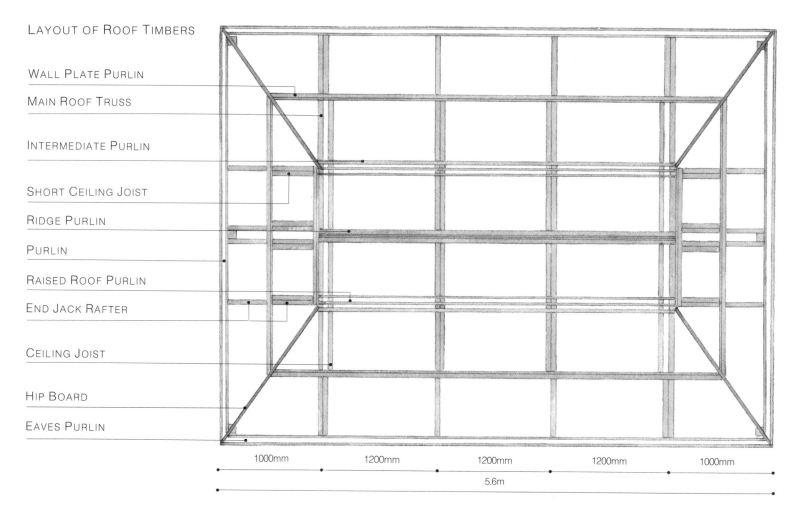

Wall Plate Purlin

Main Roof Truss

Intermediate Purlin

Short Ceiling Joist

Ridge Purlin

Purlin

Raised Roof Purlin

End Jack Rafter

Ceiling Joist

Hip Board

Eaves Purlin

1000mm   1200mm   1200mm   1200mm   1000mm

5.6m

Section across Length of Roof

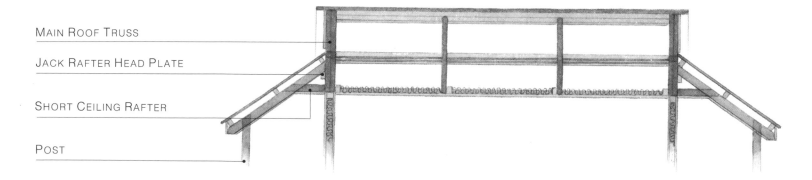

Main Roof Truss

Jack Rafter Head Plate

Short Ceiling Rafter

Post

ROOF

The striking, veranda-covering roof of this summer house is a fundamental part of its design. It consists of a pitched roof clad with sheets of corrugated steel and with a 'hip' at either end projecting out to cover the sides of the veranda. It is quite complicated, so it is strongly recommended that you spend a little while studying the plans, and then tackle the construction one step at a time as described here. The positions of the rafters and purlins will become much clearer as you start to fix the pieces together.

MAIN TRUSSES

Start by making the four main roof trusses. Each truss, a triangular-shaped frame mitred at the top, is made from two 75 × 50mm (3 × 2in) angled rafters each about 2.6m (8ft 8in) long (allowing for them being overlength), reinforced with a triangular plywood gusset at the top, and braced with a ceiling joist at the appropriate level.

The rafters are cut at an angle at the top, butted together and held at the correct angle by being nailed to a 12mm (½in) thick triangular plywood gusset. Each triangular plywood gusset is pitched at 26°, and this controls the angle of all the rafters. The rafters are prevented from spreading by the ceiling joists which are bolted to them towards the bases of the rafters.

All the main trusses are the same, except that the two end trusses have double rafters, formed by bolting pairs of rafters together using 12mm (½in) coach bolts with steel timber connectors on the bolts sandwiched between the two timbers. Similar sized bolts and steel timber connectors are used to bolt the ceiling joists to the rafters.

Ensure that the four main trusses are cut and nailed at the same angle: nail up the first truss on a flat surface, and use this truss as a template for nailing subsequent trusses.

Make all the rafters about 200mm (8in) overlength; they can then be cut to the correct length after fixing. Nail the top firrings in place.

FIXING MAIN TRUSSES

Lift the main trusses on to the walls, spacing them approximately 1200mm (48in) apart. Do not forget to position the double rafter trusses at each end. Make sure that all the trusses are square and vertical, and then nail them down to the head plates of the front and back walls, using 150mm (6in) round head nails which should be skew nailed into the head plates (see **Techniques, page 399**).

Temporarily hold the trusses in place so that they are vertical: nail long battens diagonally across the rafters to act as bracing (fig 1, below). Position the battens carefully so that there is enough room to fix the purlins at the ridge, wall plate and eaves levels.

FIXING PURLINS

Cut and fix the ridge purlins (horizontal timbers) in place. These are the same overall length as the front and back wall structure and are fixed to the firrings on either side of the apexes of the main trusses.

Cut the eaves purlins (positioned at the front and back to support the outermost edges of the pitched roof covering) 2.5m (8ft 2in) overlength to give an overhang of 1250mm (49in) at each end (fig 2). Fix in place by nailing into rafters.

Next cut the front and back wall plate purlins (the ones above the eaves purlins), approximately 650mm (25½in) overlength at each end to allow for trimming later. Nail in place on the rafters (fig 2). Remove the diagonal bracing and cut and fix the two intermediate purlins (one each side) midway between the ridge and wall plate purlins. These butt up against the ends of the firring pieces, which should now be cut to length. The intermediate purlins are about 300mm (12in) overlength each end for cutting back at an angle later.

MAKING THE RAISED ROOF SECTION

The firrings act as packing over the rafters. Fit a second purlin close to the lower end of the firring pieces to form the raised roof section.

① **Construction of Main Roof Trusses**
Each truss is formed by nailing it to a pre-cut 12mm (½in) thick plywood gusset pitched at 26°, and then braced by a ceiling joist for stability. End trusses have double raters. After positioning, rafters are braced by purlins.

② **Fixing the Purlins to the Roof Trusses**
With trusses spaced along the head plates on the walls, and held upright by temporary diagonal braces, cut and nail the ridge purlins in place. Note that eaves, wall plate and intermediate purlins are left temporarily overlength.

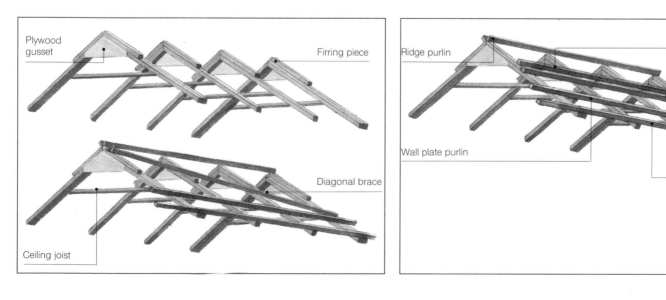

Plywood gusset

Firring piece

Ceiling joist

Diagonal brace

Ridge purlin

Raised roof purlin

Intermediate purlin

Wall plate purlin

Eaves purlin

SUMMER HOUSE: HIP ROOF ASSEMBLY

SETTING OUT HIP ROOF AT EACH END

Measure 1000mm (39in) along the top outer edge of the eaves purlin, measuring from the outer face of the outside truss. Tack a line from this point (string will do) to where the end lean-to roof meets the end truss. This should form a roof pitch at the ends of about 36°. Make up a triangle of plywood or scrap battening to this angle and use it to check the roof pitch during all stages of construction (fig 2).

Tie another string line from the top of the first eaves purlin (1000mm [39in] from the face of the end truss) to the top of the corresponding eaves purlin on the opposite side (1000mm [39in] out from the end truss). From this point, take another string line up to where the end lean-to roof meets the end truss. With these string lines in place, 1000mm (39in) out from the end truss, the general arrangement of the roof hips and pitch down to eaves level on the lean-to roofs at each end of the building will become apparent.

Cut the end jack rafters (four at each end) overlength, and also the short ceiling joists for the ends (again, four at each corner). Both are cut from 75 × 50mm (3 × 2in) sawn timber (fig 6).

Cut the jack rafter head plates (which support the jack rafters against the end trusses). Nail or bolt these to the end trusses as shown (fig 3), and after fixing trim the ends of the head plates to the slope of the main roof rafters.

Use an adjustable sliding bevel to set the angle required for the ends of the jack rafters where they butt against the end trusses, and trim the ends of the jack rafters to this angle. On the underside of each rafter cut a birdsmouth (notch) so that the rafter will sit neatly on the head plate. The eaves ends are left overlength for the time being.

Nail the four jack rafters and the four short ceiling joists in place at each end. Check that the top of the rafters are aligned and slope in line with the previously fixed string guidelines. Make sure that the undersides of the short ceiling joists

are horizontal and are in line with the undersides of the ceiling joists at the front and back of the building.

Note that in the centre of the ends there are two rafters fixed 75mm (3in) apart (fig 4). Later these will be bolted to the central veranda support post.

Cut the 150 × 25mm (6 × 1in) hip boards (rafters) overlength and hold them as close to their final position as possible so that the correct angles can be marked on the ends of the front and rear purlins which rest against the hip boards and which are now cut to length. Again, an adjustable sliding bevel is used to mark these angled cuts, which are angled in two directions to ensure that the ends of the purlins fit tightly against the hip boards when these are fixed in place.

At the top, the hip board is notched to fit over the jack rafter head plate (fig 3), and the end of the hip board is angled so that the hip board fits tightly against the main end truss. This angle needs careful marking with an adjustable sliding bevel to ensure an accurate

fit, particularly of the support notch at the top end. The top surface of each hip board should be lined up with the top of the purlins.

The hip boards can now be fitted and held in place by nailing to the ends of the front and rear purlins.

Next, cut and fasten by nailing the three 75 × 50mm (3 × 2in) purlins on the lean-to roofs at the ends of the building. They must be cut to length and angled so that they butt tightly against the hip boards at the ends, and align at the corner hips with the front and back purlins.

Cut and fit the 75 × 75mm (3 × 3in) veranda support posts in the middle of the end sections to fit between the concrete base and the twin central jack rafters. The base of each post should sit on a small piece of lead, which seals the end grain very effectively. Using timber connector plates and 12mm ($\frac{1}{2}$in) diameter coach bolts, drill and bolt to the floor joists at the base and between the twin jack rafters at the top. Leave overlength for the time being, and later trim flush, angled with the tops of the purlins.

① Cross-section of the Width Showing the Raised Roof Section
Note how the firring pieces lift the ridge and raised roof purlins to create the raised roof section. Also look at the eaves area and note how the truss ends are trimmed vertically, level with the front top edge of the eaves purlin, to give a plumb fixing for the fascia board to which the gutters are fixed.

② Trimming the Rafter Ends
Sliding bevel marks rafter ends (shown without eaves purlin). Use a template to check roof pitch.

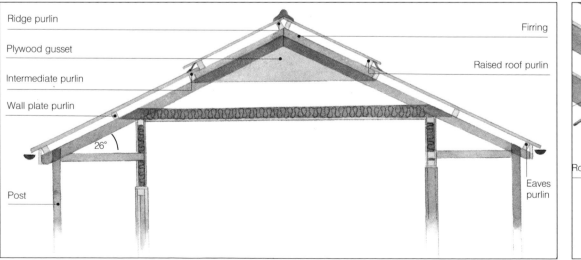

Ridge purlin
Plywood gusset
Intermediate purlin
Wall plate purlin
26°
Post
Firring
Raised roof purlin
Eaves purlin

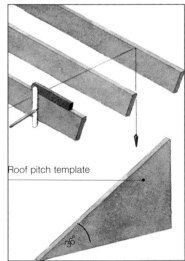

Roof pitch template
36°

HIP ROOF ASSEMBLY

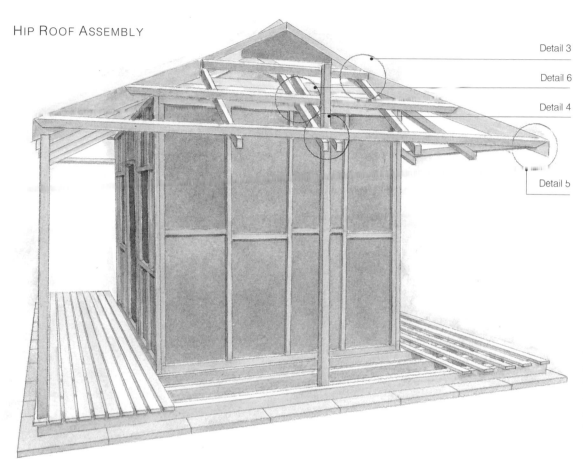

Detail 3

Detail 6

Detail 4

Detail 5

The 75 × 75mm (3 × 3in) corner veranda support posts fit between the concrete base and the top sides of the hip boards. Allow 25–30mm (1–1¼in) clearance from the eaves purlins. The undersides of the hip boards are notched to take posts, and the top ends of the posts are cut out with matching notches which allow them to be bolted to the hip boards (fig 5). Cut the post tops to the same angles as the roof pitches and to the level of the purlins.

FITTING FASCIA BOARDS

Use a sliding bevel to mark the rafter ends with a vertical line where they will be trimmed. When the fascia boards are fixed on to the rafter ends they will be upright, allowing gutters to be fitted. Trim the rafters in line with the top of the eaves purlin. The bottoms of the rafter ends are trimmed level with the bottom of the fascia boards, either before or after the fascias are fixed. Also trim the ends of the hip boards to take the fascia boards.

Cut the fascia boards from 150 × 25mm (6 × 1in) sawn timber.

---

③ Hip Board/Head Plate Join
Notch hip board to fit over jack rafter head plate. Angle board end to fit against truss. Purlins fit against hip.

④ Intermediate Veranda Support Post
Posts bolt between central jack rafters. Saw tops level with purlins.

⑤ Corner Post/Hip Board Join
Notch hip boards for corner posts, which are slotted to fit over hips. Bolt and trim tops to roof slope.

⑥ Jack Rafters/Ceiling Joists
Underside view of the jack rafters nailed to short ceiling joists. Tops of rafters must align.

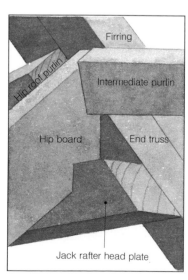

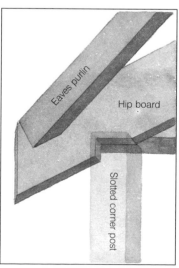

SUMMER HOUSE: ROOF AND DETAILING

FITTING CORRUGATED METAL ROOF

You can buy corrugated metal sheets cut to any size. Fix the lower sections first by nailing through the peaks of the corrugations into the purlins and screwing through the valleys using special self-sealing screws. Make sure that adjacent sheets overlap by at least two corrugations on each side of the panels.

Fix a lead flashing along the lower purlin of the raised roof sections and press the lead down on to the lower roof sheets using a roller. Apply a similar strip of flashing from the main end trusses on to the end lean-to roof sheets (fig 1). Nail 12mm (½in) feather-edge boards to the end trusses to form gable ends (*see* **Techniques, page 399**).

Finally, fix the raised-roof corrugated sheets, screwing and nailing (as above) into the firring pieces. Adjacent sheets must overlap at least two corrugations on both sides of each panel. Fit and fasten metal capping pieces to the ridge and hips of the hip roof sections.

① Lower Roof Flashing
Lay lead flashing along the lower raised roof purlin; roll the flashing on to the lower roof sheets.

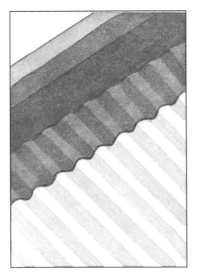

DETAILING

With the main walls constructed and the roof in place, the final detailing jobs can be completed.

Between the wall studs on all four walls, fit 50mm (2in) thick Rockwool wall batts for insulation (fig 4). The material is semi-rigid and, if necessary, can be held in place by tapping panel pins into the studs in much the same way that glass is held in a window frame.

The window and door frame reveals are then cut to length from 125 × 25mm (5 × 1in) PAR (planed all round) softwood and temporarily screwed in place (figs 2 and 3). Make up the window frames from 50 × 50mm (2 × 2in) timber screwed together, and then nail through the outsides of the frames to fix the glazing bars (these are stocked by timber merchants). Screw the frames into the reveals.

The weatherboarding can now be nailed in place on each wall, starting at the base and working upwards (fig 4). Cut the boarding to fit neatly around the window and door frames (*see* **Techniques, page 399**).

Cut and nail in place the 150 × 25mm (6 × 1in) fascia boards to the eaves and the 50 × 50mm (2 × 2in) rafter ties.

Closing battens are needed at the four corners of the summer house to close off the end grain of the weatherboards. The battens should be cut to length and fixed temporarily in place.

Having checked everything over you can now start to decorate. Remove the closing battens while the weatherboards are treated with exterior grade preservative, stain or paint, then paint the battens in a contrasting colour before nailing them back in place.

The door and window frames can now be painted, along with the roof and fascia board.

Now fix the guttering, giving it a slight fall towards each corner, where a small hole should be cut. Fix a chain through each outlet and run it down to the ground to channel rain water into a soakaway. Alternatively, you could fit a combined stopend and downpipe outlet at each corner of the guttering; however, this will mean that you will not be able to run the chains down to the ground at the exact corners of the summer house – to the detriment of the overall design.

If the external joists were temporarily removed while the project was being built then relay them now on a strip of bituminous felt and fix them to the veranda support posts as described earlier (page 62).

The 'duckboard' floor of the veranda is now formed by screwing

75 × 25mm (3 × 1in) slats to the joists leaving 19mm (¾in) spaces between them. Use 50mm (2in) long No 8 screws.

The window can now be glazed using 3mm (⅛in) glass held in place with glazing bars pinned to the frame. It is important that the glazing bars are fixed square to each other so that the glass will slot comfortably in place. Check each 'window' for square by measuring the diagonals, which should be equal. When ordering the glass, buy it 2–3mm (about ⅛in) smaller than the window opening, both in width and height, to allow for normal expansion.

If you prefer, you can buy a ready-made ledged and braced door; alternatively, you can make one using tongued-and-grooved boarding with 100 × 25mm (4 × 1in) timber for the ledges (cross rails) and braces (diagonals). The door can be full-length or a stable door as here. If you choose the latter, you simply make the two smaller doors with a lower ledge for each one. In a full-length door, only one central ledge is needed.

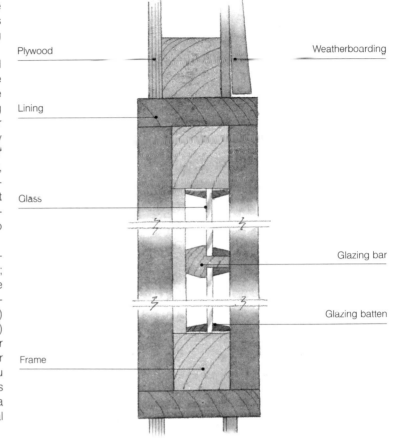

Plywood — Weatherboarding

Lining

Glass

Glazing bar

Glazing batten

Frame

② **Fixing the Door Head**
Screw door lining to the studwork, with 25 × 12mm (1 × ½in) doorstops nailed to sides and top of frame.

③ **Window Frame Assembly**
Above The top and bottom sections of the frame are fixed to the 125 × 25mm (5 × 1in) linings.

④ **Fixing Weatherboarding**
Below Exterior walls are formed from overlapping boards nailed to the studwork; work from bottom up.

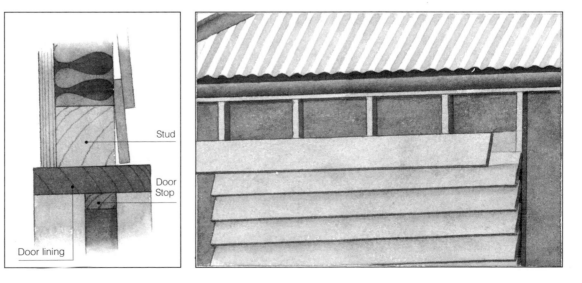

Stud

Door Stop

Door lining

SUMMER HOUSE: DETAILING

A ledged and braced door is made by simply nailing the boards to the ledges and braces. It is constructed by laying the top and bottom ledges on a flat surface and then screwing the tongued-and-grooved boards to them (*see* **Techniques, page 399**). The boards should overlap the ledges by about 25mm (1in) at either end.

The diagonal brace is then fitted by notching it into the ledges and, again, screwing through the door and into the brace. The purpose of the brace is to transmit the weight to the hinges and so prevent the door from sagging. It is important that the braces are fixed the right way round as shown (fig 1).

Use two butt hinges to hang each door. These are fixed to the end grain of the ledges. If you make a framed door then also use butt hinges: two 75mm (3in) sizes for each half of a stable door, or three for a full-length door.

Next, fit the 25×12mm ($1 \times \frac{1}{2}$in) door stops – two vertical pieces and a horizontal top piece – to the door reveal (fig 2, page 313). These stops must be positioned accurately: hold the door in place and mark the positions of the stops immediately inside its closed position. This ensures that the stops are fitted accurately. Here, they are positioned about 25mm (1in) back from the front of the door reveal.

Complete the interior by cladding the ceiling using tongued-and-grooved boards, not forgetting to insert Rockwool insulating bats between the joists (fig 2), held in place by panel pins as with the walls. The walls can be decorated according to your requirements using exterior paint, varnish stain, or microporous paint.

Finally, at each corner, dig a $300 \times 300 \times 300$mm ($12 \times 12 \times 12$in) soakaway hole and fill with shingle or pebbles (fig 3). Bed the ends of the chains into them so that they are held tautly in place.

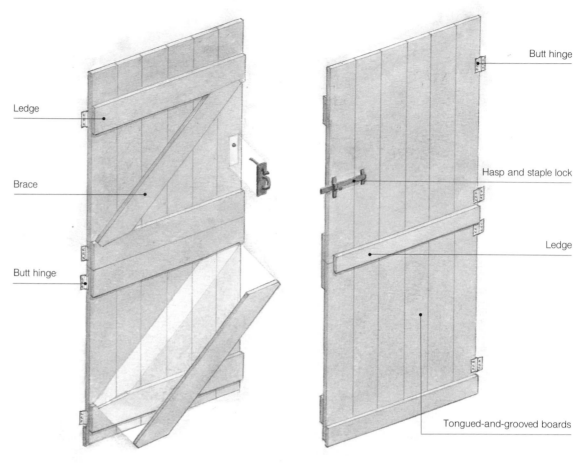

Ledge

Brace

Butt hinge

Butt hinge

Hasp and staple lock

Ledge

Tongued-and-grooved boards

1 Door Assembly
Above The ledged and braced door can either be a stable door (as shown) or a single unit.

2 Insulating the Ceiling
Clad the ceiling with tongued-and-grooved boards, and place insulating batts between the joists.

3 Making the Soakaways
A chain conducts rainwater from the gutters to a soakaway – a hole filled with shingle or pebbles.

DEN . . . GAZEBO . . . HIDEAWAY . . . CHALET . . . SHANTY . . . BOTHY . . . HUNTING BOX . . . CROFT . . . PAD . . . OUTHOUSE . . .

SHACK . . . PLAY HOUSE . . . SNUG . . . CABIN . . . SHED . . . BOLT HOLE . . . STUDIO . . . PAVILION . . . LODGE . . . RETREAT . . .

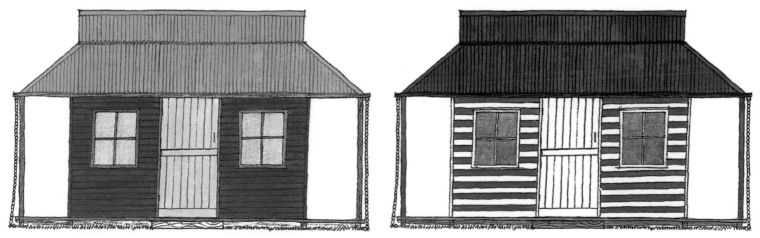

POTTING SHED . . . HUT . . . SANCTUARY . . . HIDEY-HOLE . . . CUBBYHOLE . . . HAVEN . . . GARDEN ROOM . . . .

SUMMER HOUSE

A CHANGE OF SCENERY

In a secluded part of the garden, the summer house can be used as a simple retreat. The interior is large enough to function as a tool room and potting shed (right) or as a cosy study or home office (opposite).

PLAY HOUSE

A HOME OF THEIR OWN

Whether as a private den away from their parents or as a 'real home' on a miniature scale, a play house in the garden will give children hours of fun and laughter.

A play house in the garden will attract children like bees to a honey-pot. Play houses are excellent for developing children's learning skills, encouraging them to exercise their imaginations. As they play with other children, they will develop inter-personal skills at the same time as enjoying hours of fun. Depending on the age of your children, you can decorate the interior for them, or encourage them to equip it and paint it themselves. In the latter case, make sure that they only use non-toxic paints, which should also be washable, so that the walls can be painted time and again.

By keeping internal fixtures to a minimum, the children can use the play house to represent a variety of structures: from a hospital to a shop, an adult living room to an office, or as a den away from the grown-ups.

When children finally outgrow the play house, it can be adapted without too much expenditure or alteration for use as storage space for garden equipment.

The model shown in the photo-graph is situated in the grounds of Castle Drogo, a Lutyens house near Exeter now administered by the National Trust. The play house was built *circa* 1909 as a birthday pres-ent and was transferred to its pres-ent home from a house in Sussex *circa* 1928.

Our plans show how a play house of a similar style could be constructed. For all the framework timber use 38 × 38mm ($1\frac{1}{2} \times 1\frac{1}{2}$in) PAR (planed all round) softwood, as accuracy is important. All the relevant dimensions are shown on the illustrations. Glued and nailed butt joints are used throughout.

PLAY HOUSE ASSEMBLY

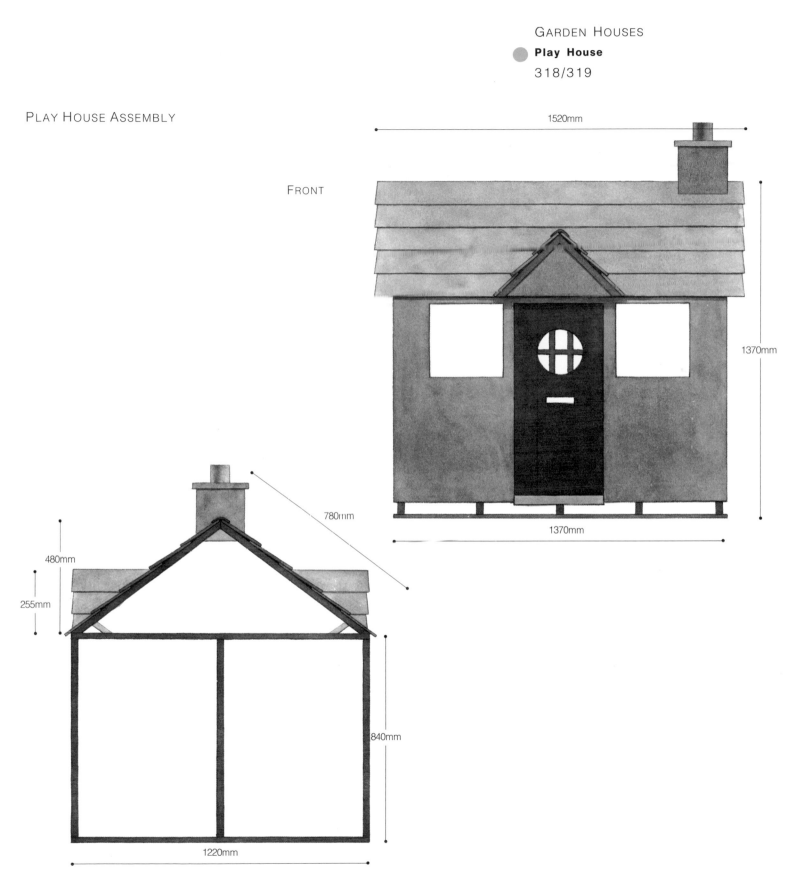

FRONT

1520mm

1370mm

1370mm

SIDE

780mm

480mm

255mm

840mm

1220mm

PLAY HOUSE

BASE

A solid, level base is essential, otherwise it will not be possible to build the house. The simplest method is to lay paving slabs on sand. To prevent damp in the soil creeping up and attacking the floor, lay a polythene membrane below the sand.

The base should be made slightly smaller than the house so that the wall cladding extends just beyond it all round. This means that rainwater running down the walls will not trickle inside the house, but will instead drip onto the ground.

The overall area of the house is 1370 × 1220mm (54 × 48in) and the base is 5mm ($\frac{1}{4}$in) less all round at 1360 × 1210mm (53$\frac{1}{2}$ × 47$\frac{1}{2}$in). The floor itself is constructed as a normal house floor with floorboards nailed at right angles to joists. For the joists, use 50 × 25mm (2 × 1in) rough sawn timber. Five joists running from front to back will be sufficient. The two end joists should be just inside the ends of the floorboards, and the other three should be spaced equally between.

The floorboards can be square edged or tongued-and-grooved. The former simply butt up to each other, while tongued-and-grooved boards interlock. You can use either 125mm (5in) or 150mm (6in) wide boards for the floor; thicknesses range from 12–32mm ($\frac{1}{2}$–1$\frac{1}{4}$in), but buy the thinnest available.

Lay the five joists on the ground, then nail one end board at right angles to each joist. Repeat for the other side. Use 50mm (2in) lost head nails and punch the heads below surface.

At this point, the floor will be held solidly in position so that you can add more boards, making sure that square edge boards butt up closely and that tongued-and-grooved boards are tightly interlocked. You will probably have to remove the last board, fixed earlier, to trim it to size before refixing it.

WALLS

Fix 19mm ($\frac{3}{4}$in) thick marine plywood over the softwood framework. The front of the house is split into two separate frameworks with the

door in the middle. The two frameworks are identical with allowance made for a window on either side. The windows can be any size provided that they look right proportionately – here, 300mm square (12in square) is about right.

The top horizontal member holds the two frames together, but until the side and back frames are added it will be flimsy. So, as a temporary support, add a strut across the doorway as shown (fig 1). This can be nailed in place and removed when the frameworks have been joined and the wall panels added.

Light through the front windows is unlikely to be sufficient: a window up to 500 × 380mm (20 × 15in) can be built into the rear wall.

The side walls are plain. Use a top and bottom horizontal member for rigidity and to strengthen each plywood wall panel.

ASSEMBLING THE WALLS

The front and back wall frames are screwed to the base using 75mm (3in) No 8 screws. This is especially vital in exposed positions where

high wind could turn the house over. The horizontal members on each side are now fixed, together with the central supports.

The plywood wall panels can now be cut to size and nailed to the frames using 38mm (1$\frac{1}{2}$in) nails, again punching the heads below the surface. When these are in place, the house will be very solid. Remember to cut the panels to extend just below the base.

ROOF

First fix the dormer roof in position. This is made from two A-shaped frames joined with a glued mitre joint and reinforced with two 38mm (1$\frac{1}{2}$in) corrugated fasteners. Plywood offcuts nailed in place strengthen the roof-to-wall joints and reinforce the mitre joint at the apex of the A-frame, while a batten the length of the side wall frames runs between them at the apex. These frames are then clad with featheredge facing boards, nailed in place with 50mm (2in) lost head nails.

Start at the bottom and work up to the ridge. The boards are nailed

① Constructing the Front Framework
Build all of the frames from 38 × 38mm (1$\frac{1}{2}$ × 1$\frac{1}{2}$in) PAR softwood. Brace the opening for the door at the front and allow for a window on either side. Dormer roof frame rests centrally on top.

② Constructing the Back Framework
The back frame is a very simple construction of glued and nailed butt joints. A central window can be fitted at the back to improve the amount of light inside the play house.

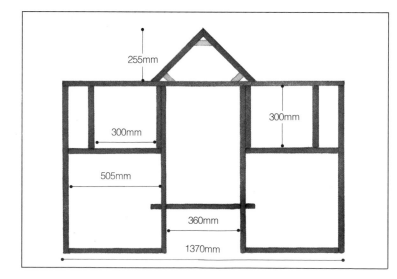

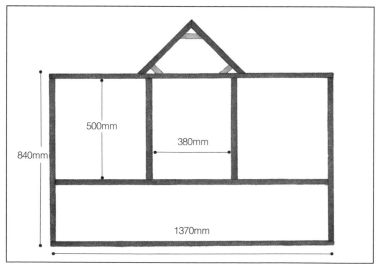

with the thinner edge uppermost so that the thicker edge of the board above overlaps it by 12mm ($\frac{1}{2}$in) (*see* **Techniques, page 399**).

At the top, you will probably have to trim the last board to fit. The ridge is sealed by fixing self-adhesive aluminium flashing tape in position. Cut the strip to the required length from the roll, peel back a little of the backing paper and position the tape on the roof. Press the tape into place with a cloth, peel back more of the backing paper and continue in this manner until the ridge is covered. Do not peel away all of the backing paper at once – the adhesive is powerful and will start to stick itself to the roof in the wrong place. Add two triangular plywood panels to enclose each end of the dormer. These are inset into the A-frames and glued in place.

When the dormer is complete it can be lifted into place and screwed and glued in place to the top of the wall frames.

The main roof is constructed similarly except that the A-frames are fixed in place and then the feather-edge boarding, cutting it to fit around the dormer as necessary.

Use plywood offcuts to strengthen the joints as before, and use triangular plywood panels inset into the A-frames and glued in place at either end.

WINDOWS

You have a choice for the windows: you can either use plain acrylic sheet, or else you can decorate it with self-adhesive lead strips as imitation leaded lights. A similar effect can be achieved with self-adhesive black tape. An alternative is to use thin battens to form small 'windows' within the main frame. For safety reasons, do not use glass.

DOOR

Construct the door from floorboards and fix two 100 × 25mm (4 × 1in) battens horizontally to serve as bracing and to prevent the door warping. Alternatively, you can use shiplap cladding smooth side out, which will give slightly better weather resistance (*see* **Materials, page 394**).

CHIMNEY

The chimney is an optional extra. Make it from plywood offcuts joined with 25mm square (1in square) plywood strips in each corner, or use plastic joint blocks. A piece of plastic pipe forms the pot.

PAINTING

Before painting, all the timber which the children will be able to touch should be very carefully smoothed by sanding it down with a power sander to remove any splinters.

Use masonry paint for the main walls and treat the door with primer, undercoat and exterior gloss. Coat the floor with an appropriate wood dye and exterior-grade varnish or a varnish stain; alternatively, it can be painted with masonry paint.

GUTTERS AND PIPES

The gutters and drainpipes are purely decorative. Use offcuts of plastic guttering – the smallest section made for sheds will do. Make the drainpipes from waste pipe held in place with pipe clips.

---

③ Constructing the Dormer Roof Frame
Re-inforce the A-shaped frames with plywood offcuts at the apex. Additional plywood offcuts strengthen the roof-to-wall joints at the front and back. A batten the length of the side walls runs between the A-frames.

④ Making the Door
Make door from floorboards braced top and bottom. Weather bar at bottom throws rain clear of the base.

⑤ Making the Chimney
This is purely decorative. Angle the plywood to sit on the apex of the roof. Add plastic pipe to form pot.

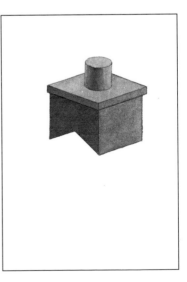

RABBIT RUN

RUN RABBIT, RUN
Pet rabbits can exercise in safety if you build a rabbit run. The dimensions can be adjusted according to the size and number of rabbits. The enclosed end section provides shelter in bad weather.

An enclosed run such as this will provide your rabbits with an area for safe daytime exercise. One section of the run is fully enclosed for occasions when the weather turns nasty. Be sure to anchor the run firmly to the ground to ensure that the rabbits cannot escape.

Treat all the timber with a good quality wood preservative that will not harm your rabbits and allow it to dry thoroughly. For the side cladding panels use 6mm ($\frac{1}{4}$in) thick marine or WBP grade exterior plywood; use the same material for the doors, but use 9mm ($\frac{3}{8}$in) thickness for the floor.

Make up four A-shaped frames using 50 × 25mm (2 × 1in) softwood and strengthen them with 25 × 25mm (1 × 1in) cross pieces. The apex of each frame needs to be mitred and this joint can be secured with a 25mm (1in) wide corrugated fastener. The other joints in the frame are secured using 38mm (1$\frac{1}{2}$in) No 8 rustless screws. Use waterproof adhesive on all joints.

Position the frames at 600mm (24in) spacings, then link them at either side with 1800mm (72in) lengths of 38 × 6mm (1$\frac{1}{2}$ × $\frac{1}{4}$in) plywood battens, top and bottom, fixed in place using 25mm (1in) No 8 screws driven into the A-frames.

Add the floor to the section that will be beneath the side cladding panels, pinning it to the two cross rails at the bottom of the A-frames with 25mm (1in) panel pins.

Use 12mm ($\frac{1}{2}$in) plastic-coated wire netting, which should be cut to finish 50mm (2in) inside the position of the plywood side panels. Use 19mm ($\frac{3}{4}$in) netting staples to secure it to the frame of the run and secure it very strongly with staples at 75mm (3in) intervals. Cut out a triangle of netting for the back frame of the run and secure it in the same way as for the sides. Pin the side panels in place on the frame, enclosing the edges of the netting. The frame battens will create a small gap between the A-frame and the side panels – add a filler piece if you want the panels flush.

The outer door should be cut out to sit snugly inside the end frame. Add small spacer blocks to bring it flush with the frame, then add a turnbutton for each corner to hold it in place. Make a turnbutton from an offcut of the 6mm ($\frac{1}{4}$in) plywood and a 25mm (1in) No 8 screw. Drill 12mm ($\frac{1}{2}$in) ventilation holes in the door and nail an offcut of wood to act as a handle.

The internal door is pinned in place inside the rabbit run to give access between the covered and uncovered sections. Drill 12mm ($\frac{1}{2}$in) ventilation holes and cut the entrance with a jigsaw or coping saw.

Add a capping of roofing felt to seal the apex of the roof. Use bitumen-based adhesive to attach it.

RABBIT RUN ASSEMBLY

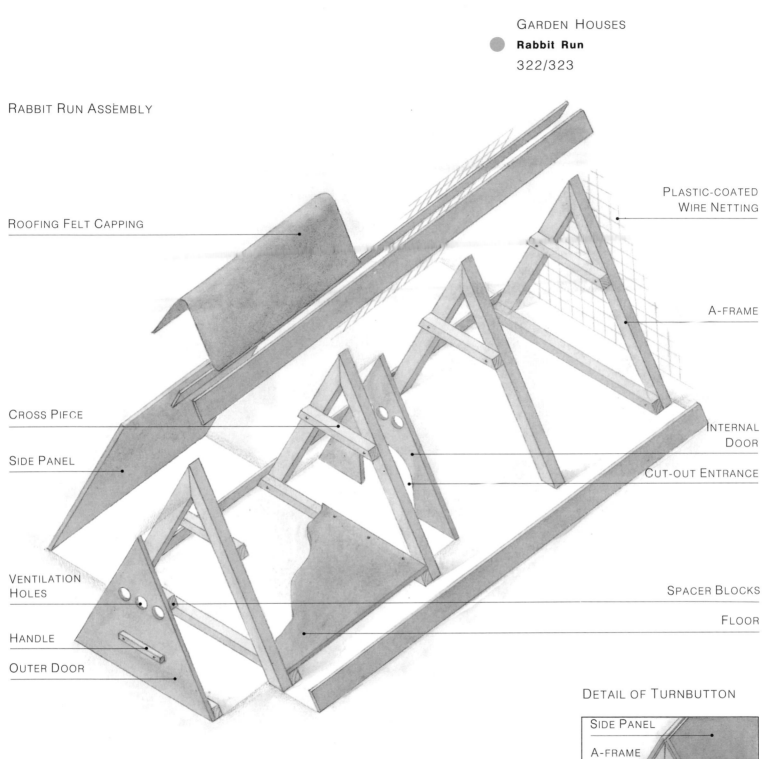

ROOFING FELT CAPPING

PLASTIC-COATED
WIRE NETTING

A-FRAME

CROSS PIECE

SIDE PANEL

INTERNAL
DOOR

CUT-OUT ENTRANCE

VENTILATION
HOLES

SPACER BLOCKS

FLOOR

HANDLE

OUTER DOOR

DETAIL OF TURNBUTTON

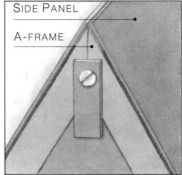

SIDE PANEL

A-FRAME

NESTING BOX

The introduction of a nesting box to your garden will help to conserve bird life and provide entertainment for the family. Given time, the birds will gain in confidence and come closer to your home.

The sizes given for this particular box (similar to the one in the photograph) are not critical so they can be altered by 25–50mm (1–2in) if preferred. The only thing that must be specific is the diameter of the entrance hole since this will govern the species of bird that will be encouraged to nest. The height that the box is sited above the ground is also important, but is generally not as critical as that of the entrance hole. A table of entrance hole diameters and above-ground heights is given opposite.

Rough-sawn timber is ideal for boxes, and a thickness of 16mm ($\frac{5}{8}$in) makes jointing easy. All joints are butted, and secured with waterproof wood adhesive and galvanized or alloy nails. Wood is a good insulator against heat and cold, it resists condensation and blends well with any environment.

First, cut out the two side pieces, each measuring 200 × 120mm (8 × 4$\frac{3}{4}$in). Next, cut a groove along the inside front edge of both pieces to serve as a channel for the door to slide in. The channels must be perfectly aligned; marking out, therefore, must be very accurate.

If you have a router then the channels can be cut out quickly and precisely using a straight-sided router bit. If you do not have a router then use a marking knife to scribe the edge of the groove. Next, use a tenon saw to cut the groove to the required depth along each edge before paring out the waste with a chisel. Work slowly and carefully until the sides and base of the channels are flat.

The back panel is a complete piece, shaped to support the roof panels. In position, it is slightly inset between the side panels.

The front is constructed from two separate pieces. The top triangular section is fixed to the roof and has a hole of the required diameter drilled through it. The hole can be drilled using either an auger bit or, if you have one, an expansive bit fitted in a wheel brace.

Should you not have a bit suitable for cutting large diameter holes then use a padsaw or jigsaw. First, drill a hole inside the outline of the hole to leave a starting position for the saw blade. Drill the hole with a normal twist drill. Cut out the shape carefully and finish by sanding the edges (see **Techniques, page 397**).

The door is cut to dimensions of 200 × 160mm (8 × 6$\frac{1}{2}$in). A rebate is taken from each side so that the door sits neatly in the side panels.

The rebate is cut easily with a router and straight-sided bit or with a tenon saw and chisel (see **Techniques, page 398**).

The roof is comprised of two panels; each panel measures 215 × 155mm (8$\frac{1}{2}$ × 6in). The roof is joined at the top using a mitre joint. The joint, as throughout, is glued but this time it is secured with a 25mm (1in) corrugated fastener, which is tapped home flush with the surface.

When all the pieces have been cut to size, treat the exterior faces and edges only with a water-based wood preservative. It is best to leave internal faces untreated to avoid any toxic risk to the birds.

To assemble the box, first join the two side panels to the floor and then add the back panel.

Make up the roof, including the triangular front section, and attach this to the lower part.

Finally, with the sliding door in the closed position, drill a hole through either side of the nesting box and into the door to a depth of 25mm (1in). Insert a 50mm (2in) galvanized steel nail into each hole to hold the door in place. The holes should be of a diameter to give the nails a tight but sliding fit.

BACK GARDEN BIRD-LIFE
A nesting box provides a safe haven for small birds and their young. By encouraging birds to nest in your garden, you will derive personal satisfaction and the enjoyment of observing wildlife close at hand.

Siting is not crucial, although a location within view of your house is obviously desirable for the family's enjoyment. Try to avoid anywhere where water is likely to cascade down, and, if your garden is exposed, position the box on the most sheltered side to avoid strong winds. Most birds prefer a direct flight line to the entrance.

If you are lucky, the box may lodge conveniently in the fork of a tree, but in most cases some form of fixing will be required. The simplest way is to secure plastic-coated garden wire to the back of the box using fencing staples, and then to wire the box to a tree trunk. With an imma-ture tree, attach the wire fairly loosely to allow for growth of the trunk. It is best not to nail or screw directly into the trunk or branch of a tree as this may damage it.

Alternatively, you can place the nesting box on top of a post. Sink a post support into the ground at the chosen site and insert a 75 × 75mm (3 × 3in) post cut to the appropriate height (see **Techniques, page 400**). Remove the sliding door from the nesting box, drill a pilot hole through the base and into the post, and screw in place.

Remember to clear out the nesting box annually, after the fledglings and their parents have flown.

NESTING BOX ASSEMBLY

SPECIES	HOLE DIAMETER	HEIGHT ABOVE GROUND
BLUE TIT	25mm (1in)	2–5m (6–15ft)
GREAT TIT	28mm (1⅛in)	2–5m (6–15ft)
COAL TIT	25mm (1in)	1m (39in)
MARSH TIT	25mm (1in)	1m (39in)
WILLOW TIT	25mm (1in)	1m (39in)
NUTHATCH	32mm (1¼in)	4–5m (12–15ft)
TREE SPARROW	32mm (1¼in)	4–5m (12–15ft)

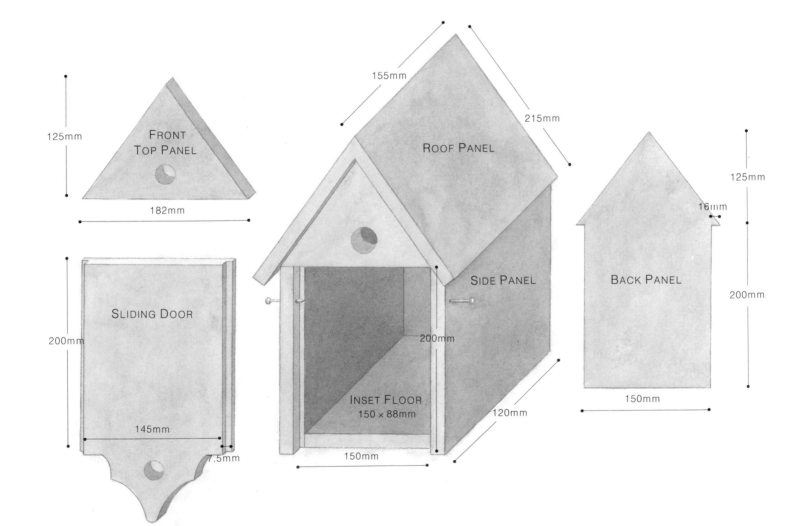

FRONT TOP PANEL — 125mm, 182mm

ROOF PANEL — 155mm, 215mm

SIDE PANEL — 200mm, 120mm

BACK PANEL — 125mm, 16mm, 200mm, 150mm

SLIDING DOOR — 200mm, 145mm, 7.5mm

INSET FLOOR 150 x 88mm — 200mm, 150mm

PART 7

PATIOS, PATHS AND PONDS

The contrast between various garden surfaces – hard and soft, paved, turfed, planted or water-filled – gives a garden its fundamental shape and design. Considerations such as where to build a patio or a flight of steps, which area to link with paths or how to edge a flowerbed are not details to be decided piecemeal but basic issues which should be resolved at the outset.

All gardens, even informal ones, need some hard surfaces. Modern gardens are generally small and demands on the space available are high. One of our most important requirements today is that the garden should function as an extension of the house, as an outdoor room, which usually means that there must be some sort of paved seating area for relaxation. And there will always be the need for paths to connect one part of the garden to another, as a practical surface for walking and tending beds, and visually to divide flowerbeds from the lawn. Wherever possible, construct hard surfaces from natural materials that weather and age, and allow plants or grass to grow in the crevices of paving and paths, softening the edges so that these areas blend harmoniously with the rest of the garden.

Patios, Paths and Ponds

Because hard surfaces are relatively expensive, fairly permanent and take time and effort to install, it is critically important to work out your ideas on paper first. This is also the stage at which to plan changes of level or to work out how to accommodate an existing slope in the form of steps or terraces. Look at the shapes – the overall pattern – that the paved areas will create. Make sure that paths do not leave useless margins of lawn or awkward-shaped flowerbeds. Plan the connections so that the paths really go somewhere, rather than meander aimlessly. Establish the basic proportion of patio to lawn so that the paving reinforces the overall design of the garden. A formal layout, for example, usually relies on a strong, symmetrical grid which can be expressed in a higher proportion of paths and paved areas. In a town garden, you may decide to dispense with a lawn altogether and work out a series of connecting paved areas and raised beds.

The range of materials suitable for hard surfacing is so great that there really is no need to rely solely on concrete. All the natural materials are much more sympathetic in the garden and they not only work well with plants but also with each other, so that you can mix materials to create interesting contrasts of texture and pattern. Bricks can be laid to create herring-bone or basketweave patterns as well as simple coursing; be sure to choose frost-proof varieties for outdoor use and avoid ugly stock bricks which never weather. Stone – including York stone, slate and granite sets – is traditional and expensive but can sometimes be reclaimed much more cheaply from building sites or builders' yards. Gravel can be rather dull; pebble paths are much more positive. Sea pebbles, in particular, set into concrete look wonderful laid in a mosaic. Treated wood is an excellent

garden material. Railway sleepers, which have a uniform thickness and are already treated against rot, can be put to a number of uses, from making steps to forming the sides of raised beds. Slices can be cut from the trunks of fallen trees, treated, and used end grain-on for paths, steps and patios. Decking, as a terrace or around the perimeter of a pond, is contemporary-looking and absorbs the heat of the sun to make a warm, comfortable surface.

Whatever material you choose will probably depend to a large extent on the amount of money you can spend, but try to form some kind of connection with the overall style of the house and the materials from which it is built. This is an important consideration, particularly for terraces or patios that immediately adjoin the house and create a relatively large surface area which has an impact on how the house is viewed.

If you cannot avoid the use of concrete, there are many ways of improving its rather dull and uniform appearance. Paviours are much better than a poured concrete slab and can be enormously improved if, instead of setting them in cement, they are laid with gaps in between. You can then fill the gaps with pebbles or plants such as creeping thyme or camomile to soften the edges. Choose paviours of a neutral shade and let colour come from lichens and mosses: you can encourage lichen to grow by treating concrete with non-pasteurized milk or houseplant food. Even if most of the paving is concrete, an edging of brick or another more harmonious material will lift it out of the ordinary.

A path makes a good edge for a flowerbed or herbaceous border, separating planted areas from lawn and making mowing easier. In the absence of a path, beds need some form of containment. Conventional edging includes brick,

Outdoor Flooring

The surfaces you choose for outdoor flooring can reinforce the overall style and design of the garden. A regular gridded pattern of smooth stone slabs suits the modern formal style of a town garden (above). Deck boarding is particularly sympathetic surrounding the perimeter of a pool, where it makes a comfortable surface for bare feet (above right). Slate tiles create a sleek paved area in a town garden (above far right). For a more informal, country setting, a sweep of large cobblestone makes an attractive paved area (below right).

PATIOS, PATHS AND PONDS

looped wire which also serves to prop up plants, and concrete bricks. Traditional terracotta edging, particularly the Victorian rope design, is also available. Less conventionally, you can make effective edging with whatever comes to hand: slivers of stone, old roofing slates or thin horizontal slats of treated hardwood nailed to posts.

Water is one of the most delightful of all the elements in garden design, providing another contrast of surface, and retaining its interest even in winter when the garden is bare. A sheet of water, reflecting the sky, has always been a feature of formal designs; surrounded by moisture-loving plants and filled with fish and lily pads, a pond can come close to fulfilling everyone's dream of having a river running through the garden. Moving water – a jet, a fountain, a cascade or a water sculpture – adds another dimension, that of sound. The tinkling noise of running water in the garden is extremely pleasant and restful.

There are also good practical reasons for incorporating water in a garden design. A pond or pool provides a supply of water at air temperature, which presents far less of a shock to young seedlings than water from a hosepipe. Even in a dry

COOL WATER

Formal pools of water can be incorporated into even the smallest town garden (right and above right), although pools designed to look like natural lakes need more space around them to be successful.

SURFACE INTEREST

A contrast of different surfaces – terracotta, stone, brick or concrete – enlivens a garden design (opposite and above opposite.).

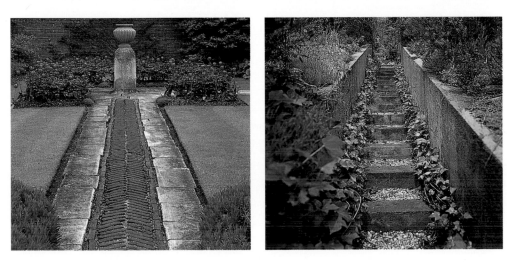

area, a pond will create its own microclimate where you can grow species such as arum lilies, irises and other plants which flourish in damp conditions. And you do not have to stock your pond with fish for it to be attractive to insects, butterflies and other wildlife.

In whatever form, water is a natural focal point in the garden. If the garden slopes, it is a simple proposition to create channels where water flows down the incline and collects in a pool, to be pumped back by an inexpensive recirculating pump. In hot countries, water in channels or running down steeped terraces has long been a means both of irrigating vegetable crops and, in courtyard gardens, of cooling the air. A still pool of water in a geometric shape is often the centrepiece of a formal garden, and formal cascades, for example, were an important feature of Italian Renaissance gardens. Sunken or raised pools in rectangular, circular, square or L-shapes are relatively easy to build from concrete block with waterproof facing, the edges softened by clumps of rushes and irises. And in a small town garden, the suggestion of water can be created very simply by the addition of a water sculpture. Water falling over large urns, slabs of stone or boulders is much more effective and attractive than a waterfall or fountain which involves a contrived, rather crudely cast garden ornament.

Informal ponds and pools, where the intention is to create as natural an effect as possible, demand a larger garden to be successful. Groups of boulders, timber decking, dense perimeter planting and perhaps a flat, low bridge can give an informal pond a Japanese quality. Water on this kind of scale demands more attention and general maintenance than a simple formal pool if it is to be convincing and appealing.

WATER SCULPTURE

The delightful sound of running water in the garden is especially restful and pleasing. A water sculpture can be made very simply and economically, requiring only a minimal outlay for a small pump and the careful installation of a power supply.

This fountain consists simply of a large ribbed terracotta pot set into a pool which is in turn sunk into the ground and overhung with a brick surround. The dimensions have been calculated using standard bricks as a module.

A black polythene pond liner is fitted inside the pool, and bricks and a tile used to make a central platform on which the pot rests. A waterproof power cable runs from the pump through a special conduit to connect with the main power supply. A word of caution: special care must be taken to ensure that there is no leaking where the cable exits from the pool. It is also vital to lay the correct conduit for the cable so that it cannot be accidentally cut when digging above it.

An earthenware pot makes the best choice for the sculpture since terracotta is easier to drill than stoneware. A copper pipe is inserted through a hole drilled in the base of the pot. When the pool is filled with water, the pump sends a jet of water up through the pipe to fill the pot and overflow down the sides.

During the winter months, the power supply should be switched off and the pot emptied to prevent the risk of it being cracked by a hard frost.

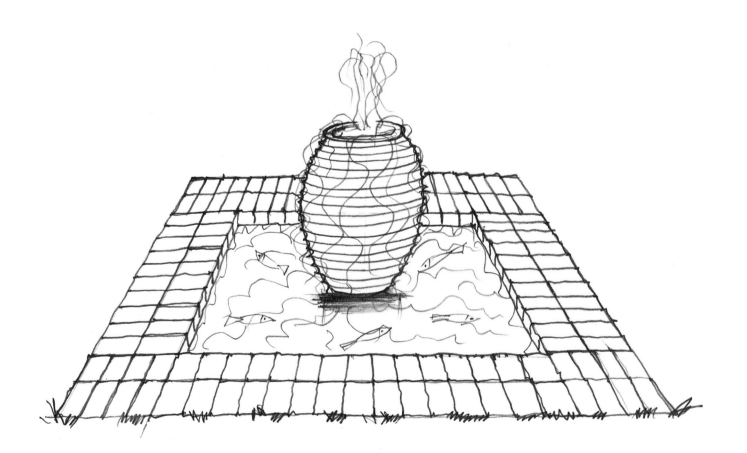

WATER SCULPTURE

The sight and sound of moving water is one of the most pleasurable experiences to be had in a garden on a hot summer's day. You need not go to the trouble and expense of installing an elaborate pond complete with waterfall, fish and plants to enjoy this in your own garden – you can build this simple yet very effective water sculpture. The size of the pool is entirely optional, as is the centrepiece. We chose a pot with ridged sides since it gives an interesting surface for the water to splash on to and run down.

A submersible pump pushes the water up and out of the pot. As the pump is electrically operated from the house supply, it makes sense to keep the water sculpture as close to the house as possible since this saves having to run the buried cable a long way. The submersible pump can be hidden beneath the pot or in a corner of the pond to be covered by pond weed or water lilies.

With any water feature in the garden, safety must be paramount: a child can drown even in shallow water. If you have children and choose to install a pool then do make sure that it is made child-proof.

BUILDING THE POOL

Choose a level site and mark out the ground using a string line and pegs or a hosepipe. This will give you a good idea of whether the position and size is satisfactory. Our pool is 1000mm (39in) square.

Dig out the hole to a depth of about 300mm (12in). The four sides should be tapered outwards slightly and the base should be flat – check this using a spirit level.

Cut out four pieces of plywood to form the sides of the pool. The top edge of the plywood should align with the level of the surrounding soil once you have cut around the edge of the pool to bed the brick or stone surround which will lie flush and overlap the edge of the pool slightly.

TOOLS

HAND SAW

SPADE

SPIRIT LEVEL

SANDING BLOCK and ABRASIVE PAPER

STEEL RULE

TROWEL (if paving laid on mortar)

CLUB HAMMER

POWER DRILL

ADJUSTABLE SPANNER

HACKSAW

SCREWDRIVER

MATERIALS

Part	Quantity	Material	Length
POT	1	Terracotta	As required
TUBE	1	12mm ($\frac{1}{2}$in) copper tubing	Height of pot
TILE	1	Terracotta	300 × 300mm (12 × 12in)
PAVING SLAB	1	Concrete	600 × 600mm (24 × 24in)
SIDES OF POOL	4	19mm ($\frac{3}{4}$in) shuttering plywood	As required

Also required: 1 submersible pump and outdoor cable; 12mm ($\frac{1}{2}$in) compression tank outlet; jubilee clip and rubber washers; PVC or butyl pond liner; sand for lining pond; bricks for supporting terracotta tile and for pool surround; sand or soil for bedding brick surround

In our case, the plywood was 220mm (8$\frac{3}{4}$in) deep. Place the plywood pieces in position and sand them carefully to remove splinters.

Bed down a paving slab in the middle. If you lay it on sand it will be simple to level. Lay a sand screed across the excavation, covering the slab by about 12mm ($\frac{1}{2}$in).

The brick or paved surround will be far more appealing if weathered, second-hand material is used. Dig out the area around the pool to the width and depth required for the bricks or slabs being used. In our case, the area was 425mm (17in) wide all round to allow for a double row of 225mm (9in) bricks overlapping the pond edge by 25mm (1in). The depth was approximately 80mm (3$\frac{1}{8}$in) to allow for the 65mm (2$\frac{1}{2}$in) brick depth plus a 15mm ($\frac{5}{8}$in) layer of fine soil or sand underneath. If you excavate to a depth so that the brick surround will be level with the lawn, mowing will be easier.

FITTING THE LINER

The length of liner should be twice the pool depth plus the overall length of the pool (including the brick surround); the width of liner should be twice the depth of the pool plus the overall width.

Lay the pond liner in place following the manufacturer's instructions. Allow the excess edges of the liner to lap up over the sides of the pond, then weight it down temporarily while the pond is being filled. The weight of the water will gradually force the liner to stretch to the shape of the plywood walls. Check with the instructions as to how long you should allow the liner to stretch until it will be smooth.

Remove the temporary bricks and trim the liner to leave about 150mm (6in) to lie below the brick surround.

Next, lay the bricks. Lay the course surrounding the edge of the pool first so that the bricks will overlap the water by 25mm (1in). It is a good idea to lay the corner bricks first and then to rest a straight-edge and spirit level across them; bring them level by adjusting the bed of sand or fine soil below and tapping each brick with the shaft of a club hammer. It is then easy to fill in the remaining bricks, levelling each one with neighbouring bricks, and filling in the gaps with sand or soil so that plants and moss can grow up in the cracks. Although reasonable alignment of the bricks is important, second-hand bricks can tend to be slightly off centre, but that gives the

surround a rustic charm. However, it is important that the surface is level so that no-one will trip. Note the brick arrangement used to turn the corners (fig 1)

PREPARING THE POT

The base of the pot sits on a 300mm square (12in square) terracotta tile, itself supported by two levelled bricks, laid edge on and spaced at the required distance (fig 2). The water level should be slightly above the tile so that the bottom of the pot is just submerged. The pump is placed below the tile.

Drill a 19mm ($\frac{3}{4}$in) diameter hole through the centre of the base of the pot to take a 12mm ($\frac{1}{2}$in) tank outlet fitting. Use a tungsten carbide drill bit at slow speed. A larger hole is needed in the tile to take the pipe from the pump; to make this, drill a series of small holes closely together in a circle. As the small holes are joined up, a larger hole will automatically be formed.

FITTING THE PUMP

Fit the compression tank outlet through the holes in the pot and tile ensuring that rubber washers are used on both sides and that the nuts are not overtightened, otherwise the pot could crack. Using a hacksaw, cut a length of copper tube to extend from inside the compression joint to the rim of the pot (fig 3).

Attach the rubber tube from the pump to the compression outlet, if necessary using a jubilee clip to secure it. If the base of the pot is too thick then there might not be sufficient thread left to attach the tube. If so, screw on an extension piece.

The pump is powered from the house electrical supply. It can be operated directly from the mains but it is safer to feed it back through a transformer situated in the house which makes the supply low voltage for safety but adequate to power a pump. The cable should be armoured for outdoor use and laid in a plastic conduit underground and fed into the pool from below the brick surround. There may be local regulations about this, so check first.

You can then switch on the power supply to the pump and enjoy the results. It is a good idea to remove the pot and store it inside during the winter as it may crack in freezing weather.

WATER SCULPTURE ASSEMBLY

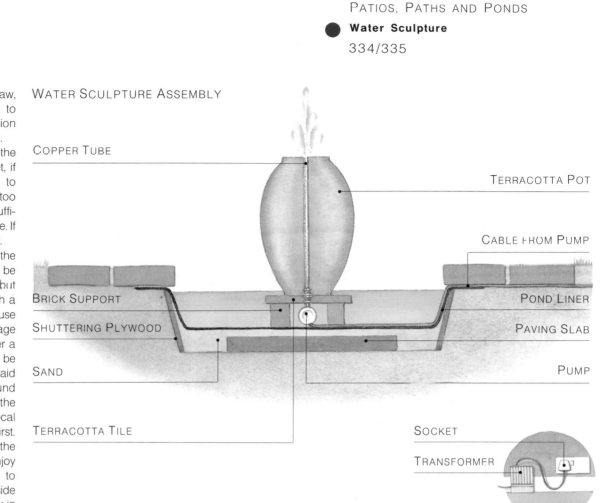

COPPER TUBE

TERRACOTTA POT

CABLE FROM PUMP

BRICK SUPPORT

POND LINER

SHUTTERING PLYWOOD

PAVING SLAB

SAND

PUMP

TERRACOTTA TILE

SOCKET

TRANSFORMER

❶ Detail of Brick Surround
At each corner of the surround the bricks are laid in pairs perpendicular to the adjoining pair.

❷ Terracotta Pot Support
Pot rests on tile supported by two bricks. Copper tube is connected to pump through holes in pot and tile.

❸ Connecting Pump to Pot
Pump pipe is connected to copper tube by compression tank outlet which feeds through pot and tile.

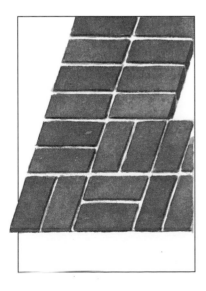

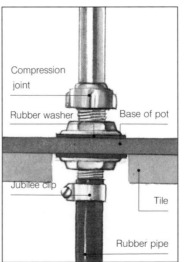

Copper tube

Tile

Pump

Cable feed

Compression joint

Rubber washer

Base of pot

Jubilee clip

Tile

Rubber pipe

JARDINIERE

This elegant, rectilinear jardinière, or plant stand, is inspired by the work of the early twentieth-century designer Josef Hoffmann (1870–1956). He was a Viennese architect, a founder member of the Wiener Werkstätte and a pioneer of functional design. His furniture displays a lack of embellishment and an interest in proportion that was developed further by designers of the Modernist Movement.

Essentially a simple structure, it is made slightly more complicated by the number of right-angled joints. The jardinière incorporates a shallow tray at the top and a shelf at the bottom to hold a collection of plant pots. It is intended for both outdoor and indoor use. The gridded design has been painted a pale 'bone' colour, but other neutral shades would be equally effective.

The idea of grouping elements together to increase their impact is as important in garden design as it is in the design of interiors. Filled with geraniums, the jardinière would brighten up a corner of a patio or seating area, while, positioned near the kitchen door, either outside or in, the stand would also make a convenient home for a collection of herbs grown in containers.

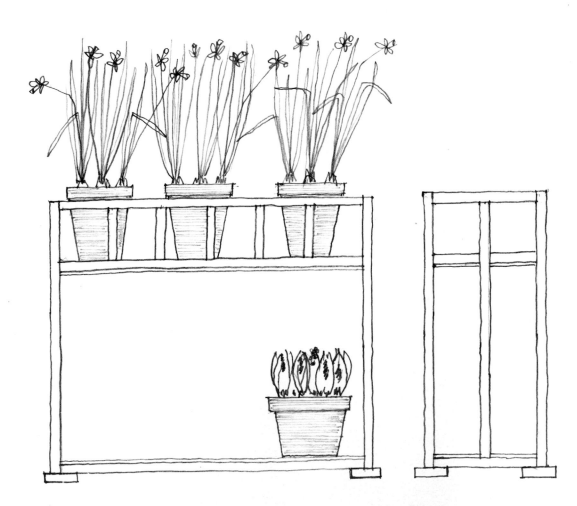

JARDINIERE

This simple stand for plants and flowers looks equally good in the garden or the conservatory. The jardinière shown here is made from PAR (planed all round) softwood and then painted. However, if you want to retain the timber finish, then be sure to make it from good-quality softwood or even hardwood, which can then be treated with a water-repellent preservative stain.

The design of the frame uses a number of wood joints, and for ease of assembly we suggest that these are dowelled together. For a stronger job, the joints could be mortised and tenoned, but unless you have a mortising machine it would be too time-consuming to attempt to construct the frame by this method.

TOOLS

WORKBENCH (fixed or portable)

MARKING KNIFE

STEEL MEASURING TAPE

STEEL RULE

TRY SQUARE

PANEL SAW (or circular power saw)

TENON SAW (or power jigsaw)

CHISEL

MARKING GAUGE

POWER DRILL

TWIST DRILL BIT – 3mm ($\frac{1}{8}$in)

DOWELLING JIG

DOWEL BIT – 10mm ($\frac{3}{8}$in)

MALLET

SCREWDRIVER

POWER SANDER (or hand sanding block)

MATERIALS

Part	Quantity	Material	Length
CORNER POSTS	4	38 × 38mm (1$\frac{1}{2}$ × 1$\frac{1}{2}$in) PAR softwood	779mm (30$\frac{5}{8}$in)
MIDDLE POSTS	2	As above	711mm (28in)
LONG RAILS	6	As above	847mm (33$\frac{3}{8}$in)
END RAILS	6	As above	237mm (9$\frac{5}{16}$in)
VERTICAL PIECES	10	As above	122mm (4$\frac{3}{4}$in)
SHELVES	2	6mm ($\frac{1}{4}$in) WBP plywood	270 × 880mm (10$\frac{5}{8}$ × 34$\frac{5}{8}$in)
FEET	4	Offcut of hardwood or softwood	90 × 90 × 30mm (3$\frac{1}{2}$ × 3$\frac{1}{2}$ × 1$\frac{1}{8}$in)

Also required: 10mm ($\frac{3}{8}$in) diameter dowelling; 50mm (2in) No 8 zinc-plated screws; panel pins

FRAME CONSTRUCTION

Cut all the components to length, following the Materials chart.

MAKING THE END FRAMES

Cut a halving joint to form the intersection of the middle post with the middle end rail (*see* **Techniques, page 400**). Mark off on the middle post where the middle end rail will cross it using one of the short vertical pieces as a spacer. The top of the cross halving joint will be this distance down from the top of the middle post.

Mark out and cut the halving joint on the middle post and the middle end rail (fig 1). Repeat for the other end frame.

Strike diagonal lines to mark the centre points for the dowel holes on the ends of all the end rails, on the ends of the middle posts and on the ends of all the short vertical pieces. Using a dowelling jig and a dowel bit (or a drill fitted with a dowel bit and held in a vertical drill stand) drill 10mm ($\frac{3}{8}$in) diameter holes centrally into the marked positions. The hole depths should be slightly over half the lengths of the dowels (ie, 22mm [$\frac{7}{8}$in] deep holes for 40mm [1$\frac{1}{2}$in] long dowels). This gives a small cavity at the end which will accommodate trapped air and glue (*see* **Techniques, Dowel joints, page 402**).

1 **Fixing Middle End Rail**
Mark position of middle end rail on middle post and cut halving joints to fix the two pieces together.

2 **Top and Bottom End Rails**
Mark dowel hole positions centrally on both ends of middle rail. Dowel to top and bottom end rails to fix.

3 **Adding Corner Posts**
Dowel posts to end rails: top end rail is flush with top of posts, bottom end rail flush with bottom of posts.

Jardiniere Assembly

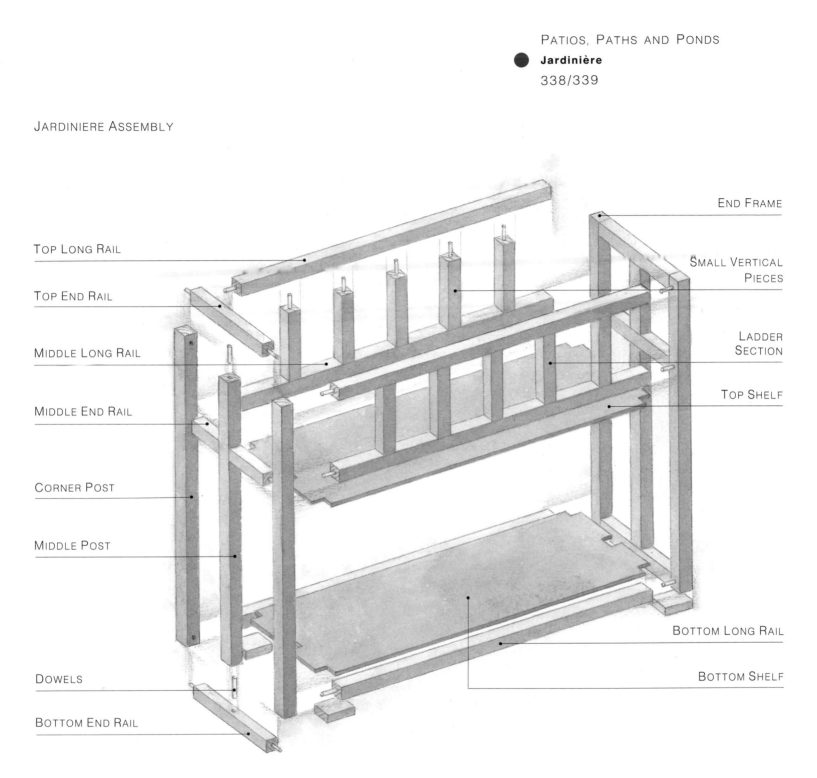

Top Long Rail

Top End Rail

Middle Long Rail

Middle End Rail

Corner Post

Middle Post

Dowels

Bottom End Rail

End Frame

Small Vertical Pieces

Ladder Section

Top Shelf

Bottom Long Rail

Bottom Shelf

JARDINIERE

Mark out the position of the top and bottom end rails on to the inside faces of the corner posts and strike diagonals again to mark the positions of the dowel holes. Drill the holes as before. Also mark out on each corner post the dowel hole positions for the middle rail, which is the same distance down as the length of a short vertical piece plus the 38mm ($1\frac{1}{2}$in) depth of the top end rail. Square round on to the other internal face of each corner post to mark the dowel hole positions to take the top, middle and bottom long rails.

Dry assemble the middle post and the middle end rail together to form a cross, and then dowel on the top and bottom end rails, again without glue (fig 2, page 338). Complete the dry assembly of the end frames by adding the corner posts (fig 3, page 338).

FRONT AND BACK FRAMES

To make up the front and back frames, which look like ladders, mark the positions of the short vertical pieces along one long rail,

and mark dowel hole centres regularly and centrally along the rail (fig 1). There is an internal spacing of 110mm ($4\frac{1}{2}$in) between each short vertical piece, and also between the end-most vertical pieces and each of the corner posts.

Use this rail as a pattern to transfer the marks on to three of the other long rails. Drill all the dowel holes to the required depth and dry assemble the ladder frame sections.

Drill the dowel holes on the inside of the corner posts, using the marks transferred from the front and back ladder frame construction.

Mark the dowel hole positions centrally on the ends of the bottom long rails, then drill the holes in them and in the bottoms of the corner posts as before.

Dowel and dry assemble each ladder frame section, together with the long bottom rails, into the corner posts of the end frames (fig 2).

Make sure that the assembly is square and fits together perfectly, dismantle in reverse order, then re-assemble, this time gluing the joints using waterproof wood adhesive.

SHELVES

The two shelves are cut so that they finish half-way across the thickness of the frame, rather than fitting flush with the outside edges of the frame rails. Notch out the corners and the central part at the ends to fit round the middle and corner posts.

Cut out the bottom shelf to fit on to the bottom rails, and glue and pin it down to the frame (fig 3).

The top shelf is glued and pinned to the underside of the middle rails.

FEET

The feet are fixed underneath each corner and protrude at the sides and ends by the same amount as the 'step' for the bottom shelf (that is, approximately 19mm [$\frac{3}{4}$in]) (fig 4). Any offcut of softwood or hardwood can be used to make them.

Apply waterproof woodworking adhesive, then screw up into the rails using two screws for each foot.

Fill any gaps using an exterior-grade cellulose filler. Finally, paint as required or apply a water-repellent wood preservative stain.

---

❶ Adding Vertical Pieces
Vertical pieces are dowelled in place at equal internal spacings between top and middle long rails.

❷ Frame Assembly
Mark dowel positions on corner posts and ends of top, middle and bottom long rails. Drill and join.

❸ Adding Bottom Shelf
Cut shelf to finish half-way across frame rails. Notch ends to fit around posts. Glue and screw in place.

❹ Adding the Feet
Cut feet from offcuts of wood. Glue and screw them up into rails so that they protrude by about 19mm ($\frac{3}{4}$in).

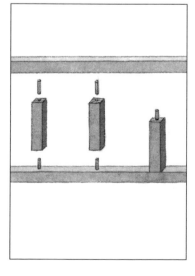

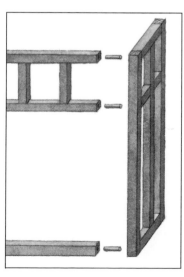

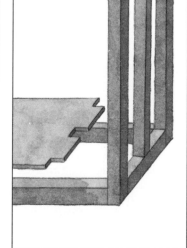

PONDS

An ornamental fish pond will enhance even the smallest garden, providing interest and pleasure with water lilies, reeds and fish mingling with dragonflies, water beetles and small frogs. Ponds are easy to install and require little maintenance.

There are various ways to build a pond, but to ensure success, the whole project needs to be carefully planned in advance, taking into account the way in which the pond will be constructed, its size, shape and location.

First, consider shape and location. The former is purely a matter of taste – a question of whether you want a formal rectangle or would prefer a more natural, curved outline. The main consideration is how you see the whole design blending with your garden, although you should avoid an over-complicated design as this will make the pond more difficult and more expensive to build. The location of the pond is critical, however. Ideally, it should receive sunlight for at least half the day to enable flowering pond plants to thrive. You should try to keep it away from overhanging trees since the shade will not be good for plants and mosquitoes will be encouraged. Deciduous trees pose a particular problem in autumn, when leaves falling into the water can have a harmful effect on pond life if they are left to rot.

A pond at the end of a long garden may sound appealing, but remember that if you want to include a waterfall, underwater lights or a fountain, you face the problem of running an electricity supply a considerable distance. Also, you may not be able to enjoy the sight of the pond from indoors.

The basic factors governing the size are the proportions of the garden and how much time and money you want to spend on the pond. You must ensure that the pond is not 'lost' in the garden, nor must it completely dominate it. Do not make a pond too small since a 'puddle' will not provide the right conditions for water, plants and fish to harmonize. The minimum surface area is really about 3.5 square metres (38 square feet). A smaller pond will not allow the water to be aerated and so it may become cloudy, in which case you would need to install a filtration system.

Water depth should not create major problems. The main hazard is with water that is too shallow, causing the pond to overheat in hot weather (leaving the fish short of oxygen) and to freeze in winter. Anything between 400–750mm (16–30in) will enable an excellent selection of plants to flourish. You should include a 225mm- (9in-) wide planting shelf, about 225mm (9in) below the water surface. The shelf should run around most, if not all, of the perimeter of the pond.

POND TYPES

Although a pond can be built using concrete to form the walls and base, few people would attempt this method nowadays since construction can be both tedious and difficult, and the pond may be prone to leaking and cracking. The two most common methods today involve using a pre-formed pond or a liner.

With a pre-formed pond, the size and shape of the pond is governed by the models available, whereas a liner allows you to create whatever shape you want. If you decide on a special shape or a very large pond, then you will have to use a liner, but otherwise both types have advantages and disadvantages when it comes to installation.

The choice of material to line a pond is between butyl rubber and PVC. Although any type of liner can be pierced by sharp objects such as stones or digging implements being thrust into the water, this is less likely to happen with the thicker, better-quality types. Even an economy-grade liner can be expected to enjoy

A POND FOR A PATIO
Not all gardens will have space for a full-sized pond. A half-barrel provides a simple solution that is easy to maintain and will have space for two or three small goldfish and for colourful water lilies.

a lifespan of ten years if it is properly installed and respected.

Colours readily available are black, stone, blue or grey. Although stone, blue and grey are more natural, many people prefer black since it is much less obtrusive in use. However, colour is not vitally important since, after a while, the base of the pond will be covered with a thin layer of mud and its sides will be creamed with algae.

A liner can be used in an above ground pond where the walls are constructed from brick or ornamental stonework. It can also be set into the ground in a level excavation made to the required depth and shape. In this case, sharp objects must be removed from the excavation and a 25mm (1in) layer of sand spread across the bottom. The liner is then placed in the excavation, the edges weighted with bricks, and water then added. The pressure of the water stretches the liner to the shape of the excavation.

Finally, paving slabs are used to make a border around the pond and to conceal the edge of the liner.

Pre-formed ponds are made from plastic or (more expensively) glass-fibre and can also be used above or below ground. In both cases, it is vital to support the sides and to ensure that the rim is exactly level.

The lesser-quality plastic ponds are neither as big nor as strong, but should certainly last for at least ten years and enable you to enjoy a wildlife pond in that time. However, if you really want a stock of outstanding fish and plants then you will need one of the better-quality models, which will last for years if it is properly installed and not damaged by sharp objects.

Whether you plan the pond to be below or above ground, it is vital that the excavation of the framework of bricks or ornamental stonework is lined with sand to provide adequate support for every nook and cranny of the pond's outline as the water exerts pressure on it.

PLANTS

Choose a mixture of types for the best effect; most are grown in plastic containers resting on the base of the pond or on the shelf.

Water lilies are a must, really, while shallow water marginals can be either tall and spikey or ground-carpeting. Deep water aquatics have their roots in containers but their leaves float on the surface, giving interest and shade to the water. Floating plants do not need soil for their roots and some only rise to the surface when flowering. Oxygenating plants, as the name suggests, supply oxygen to the pond and discourage algae. Use four or five for every square metre (yard) of water surface.

Almost inevitably, weed will build up in the pond. Pull up weeds regularly: if the size and location of the pond allow, simply reach in to the water and weed by hand; otherwise, use a rake or a long stick for any parts of the pond that are inaccessible. On no account, however, should you use a chemical algicide. Not only will it kill off the weed, leaving it to decompose in the pond, it may also contaminate your plant and fish stock.

There are many kinds of fish you can use to stock the pond apart from the ubiquitous goldfish, so read a bit about the subject and visit a good local specialist shop or a garden centre with a pond department to see what is available.

BARREL POND

Any water-tight container can be used for a small water garden and a half-barrel is one of the most popular choices. Half-barrels that previously contained beer, wine or vinegar are normally available from large garden centres.

It is important to scrub clean the inside of the barrel first using only clean water, never detergent. A clean barrel is important because otherwise the water will quickly become contaminated, posing a threat to your plants and fish. For this reason do not use a barrel that previously contained either wood preservative or oil.

When you are satisfied that the barrel is thoroughly clean, spread 75–100mm (3–4in) of clean soil in the base of the barrel – keep out weeds or vegetation which will rot and pollute the water. Add enough water to enable you to mix the soil into a slurry of mud.

Planting should be carried out in spring or early summer. Use minia-ture water lilies and some other small, less vigorous plants. Include oxygenating plants to help keep the water clear.

Next, spread a 50mm (2in) layer of pea shingle over the soil to prevent the fish stirring it up and to help prevent the plants from becoming uprooted. Then fill the barrel with water through a hosepipe with its outlet inside a polythene bag (fig 2); this prevents the jet of water disturbing the soil.

When the barrel is almost full, turn off the water and remove the bag and pipe. Allow about a week for the water to settle and the temperature to stabilize before introducing the fish – two or three small goldfish – and a few snails. The fish will discourage mosquitoes in summer, but do transfer them to a larger pond or to a fishtank indoors for the winter as the small amount of water in a barrel is almost certain to freeze over in a cold winter. In early spring, before returning the fish to the barrel, replace most or all of the water and allow it to settle and the temperature to stabilize as before.

❶ Through-section of Pond with Liner

A hole of the required dimensions is dug and lined with sand before the liner is laid in place. Include a planting shelf around the perimeter. The liner is held in place at the edges by bricks, stones or paving slabs.

❷ Making a Pond from a Half-barrel

Scrub the barrel clean and place a layer of soil at the bottom for planting. A layer of pea shingle prevents soil mixing with water. Fill pond with water through a hosepipe with its nozzle in a polythene bag.

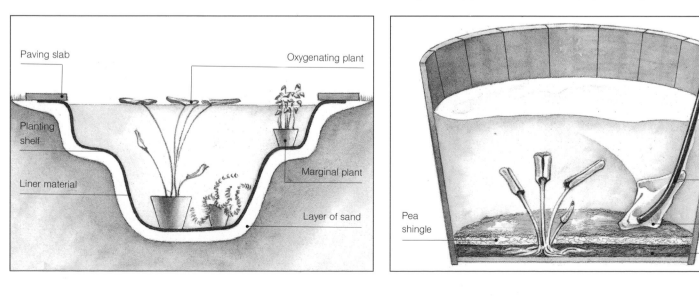

PART 8

SUPPORTS AND DIVIDERS

The opposition of closed and open space is fundamental in garden design. All gardens have boundaries, more or less secure perimeters defined by walls, fences or hedges. But often there is a need to break up space within the garden, dividing one part from another, screening the view of a utility area or vegetable garden, or making a garden 'room', an enclosed area which can create a heightened sense of 'hazard and surprise'. Simple boundaries can be made from living dividers such as hedges, through semi-transparent picket, wattle and beanstick fencing to proper garden walls of brick or stone.

Moving from a rose-covered pergola to an expanse of lawn is far more pleasing than walking along an exposed path. Framing a view with a simple arch, dissolving a boundary wall with climbers trained over a trellis, creating an arbor in a corner of the garden are all design devices which add depth and perspective to what might otherwise be flat and monotonous. By growing plants up pergolas, arbors and other dividers you have the opportunity to add light and shade: the dappled sunlight created by foliage is one of the most appealing sights in the garden.

SUPPORTS AND DIVIDERS

Trellis is indispensable. Off-the-peg square or diamond wooden mesh is available very cheaply, ready treated, in panels which can be assembled to create a variety of structures or to cover a large surface area. As an extension to a boundary fence, trellis covered with climbing plants filters the wind so that it cannot cut across the garden, and gives a degree of privacy without entirely blocking airflow and light. It is also one of the most economical ways of getting rid of eyesores – ugly sheds, bare blank walls in sour stock brick, concrete blocks, anything which cannot easily be removed can be covered with trellis and plants encouraged to grow. Climbers such as Russian vine (*Fallopia aubertii*) or mile-a-minute (*Polygonum baldschuanicum*), clematis, climbing roses, honeysuckle (*Lonicera* sp) and Virginia creeper (*Parthenocissus quinquefolia*) can materially alter the appearance of any structure. Wisteria will need a greater degree of support and ivy should be avoided at all costs: its aerial roots dig into mortar and damage brickwork. You can also use trellis to make free-standing structures to block unwelcome views.

Trellis can be put to more positive use, to create a whole range of effects. *Treillages*, intricate flat wooden frameworks, were a feature of French formal gardens, traditionally painted green and used against ecru walls. These were often arched, with tapering lines that gave a subtle sense of perspective – a simple *trompe-l'oeil* that enlivened Parisian courtyards. Less elaborate trellis still has this ability to 'dissolve' a flat, dull expanse of wall. Depending on how positive you want the trellis to be, you can stain or paint it to add interest in the winter when the leaves have fallen. Trellis helps to blend and merge the garden with the house, taking greenery up onto walls, the sides of buildings and fences.

A pergola is another type of support for plants, but one which involves some kind of canopy, either as a free-standing arch, a covered walkway or a simple framework projecting out from the side of the house. It is commonplace in Mediterranean countries to attach a plain metal framework and wiring to the house over a rear courtyard or front entrance and allow a vine to create a type of living awning. The leaves of the vine keep the sun off and deflect the heat in the summer; in the winter, the frame and the house are revealed: a cheap, effective solution and one which generates interest by changing from month to month. Plain or painted trellis can also be used overhead; the grid takes the strength out of the sun and makes a lively pattern of light and shade.

In design terms, a pergola acts as a kind of picture frame, intensifying a view. It usually demands some type of focal point – a seat or urn at the end of a walkway, for example. But it also produces a contrast of light and shade which is so attractive in a garden, and it makes an ideal support for plants, since they are freely exposed to sunlight, air and rain.

While there is something especially English about a rose-covered pergola, it is the French who excel at garden ironmongery, including that wonderful green iron which goes to make curved frameworks, such as the one which forms the laburnum avenue in Monet's garden at Giverny. There are different ways of making a pergola, but, generally, if you want the top to curve it must be made of metal, although it is possible to wire beansticks to achieve a curve. A simple version is to attach small sections of curved metal to wooden uprights. Wires for training plants can be passed through holes in the metal frame or trellis attached to the posts to support climbing roses, honeysuckle, and espaliered and cordoned fruit trees.

TRELLISWORK

Trellis is much more than just a support for plants. Trompe-l'oeil *designs add wit and interest to plain expanses of wall (opposite above and opposite centre). Trellis can also be attached to free-standing copper pipes or posts and used to support climbing roses and other plants (opposite below). For a town garden, with little horizontal growing space, trellis provides a vertical extension, acting as a support for container plants (left).*

ALL FENCED IN

Most people need some sort of way to mark boundaries, either with a neighbouring house or between different areas of the garden (overleaf). The style of fencing you choose should reflect and enhance the overall design of your garden: use white painted fencing to contrast with bright flowers, natural rustic poles for a rambling country feel, or strongly geometric panels for a look of urban chic.

SUPPORTS AND DIVIDERS

Another type of garden enclosure or room is the arbor. Essentially a seat shaded by a canopy of plants, the arbor always adds a certain mysterious, romantic quality to a garden. As well as its visual impact, there is often the added dimension of the perfume of scented flowers growing overhead. The framework itself can be as simple as you like. Trellis is a good component, but special metal arbor frameworks are also available.

There is great diversity in the materials and methods used to create boundaries in a garden. While there is no need to look for an exact match to the design of your house, some styles of fence and wall will be more appropriate than others. Metal railings, of the kind seen in public parks, are generally better in town situations; lapboarding and paddock-style timber fencing are really for the country. Avoid,

if you can, building walls in cheap stock bricks which never weather; breeze blocks and concrete posts and wire mesh fencing can also be unappetizing. An existing wall which presents this kind of eyesore can be ameliorated either by covering it with trellis or, in the case of a concrete structure, encouraging the growth of lichens and moss.

Semi-transparent boundaries can be made cheaply with trellis, using standard panels secured to posts. Today you can buy spiked steel socket-type supports which make the job of sinking posts much easier. Inspiration for other types of wooden or panel fencing can be taken from the Japanese, who excel at Mondrian-type arrangements of panels and screens using bamboo uprights and woven rush, roughly equivalent to European traditional wattle fencing.

Wall building is an art in itself. There are many intriguing and inspiring examples: stone inset with flints, shells, pebbles or bottle ends; dry stone walling; brick walls built with spaces to let air and views through; walls made of logs and driftwood. It is a good idea, if you are building a wall from scratch, to leave pockets so that plants can be grown on the vertical face. Alyssum, thrift, aubrieta, campanula and other rock plants will grow in cornices, wall pockets and on tops of dry stone walling.

Hedges are the living boundaries in a garden, easy on the eye, good at creating windbreaks and relatively simple to maintain. As far as types are concerned, there are many alternatives to the ubiquitous privet. Box (although slow-growing), beech, yew, hawthorn and hazel all make excellent and attractive hedges.

ARBORS

Structures which provide a support for climbing and trailing plants also make ideal locations for garden seats, creating a shady, scented retreat from which to view the garden. Aesthetically, an arbor also provides contrast of light and shade which is so important in giving depth and definition to a layout.

Walk-through Pergola

In a small garden, a pergola, or framework for climbing plants, makes an architectural addition which gives focus to the entire layout, especially when centrally positioned. In a larger garden, a pergola can be extended further to create a proper walkway, a semi-enclosed space to contrast with the open areas of lawn and flowerbed. This particular design can be adapted to vary the length as required, but would not really be effective if made any shorter than three units long.

The structure and the dimensions of the pergola are based around standard trellis panels, which are much cheaper than any you could make for the purpose.

The easiest way to assemble the structure is to construct the top frame first, adding the struts to make the pyramid roof afterwards. Then the position of the posts, or uprights, can be marked out on the ground where you want the pergola to go and metal shoes or spiked steel supports driven in.

The final stage is to cover the outside of the structure with trellis. When viewed from the side, the trellis wall appears to be continuous, but, because the trellis is fixed only to alternate bays, you will get glimpses of the garden as you walk through. As a plain, undressed structure with no covering of plants the pergola has its own attractions, especially when painted a strong positive colour. To support climbing plants over the roof, simply staple wire around the pyramids.

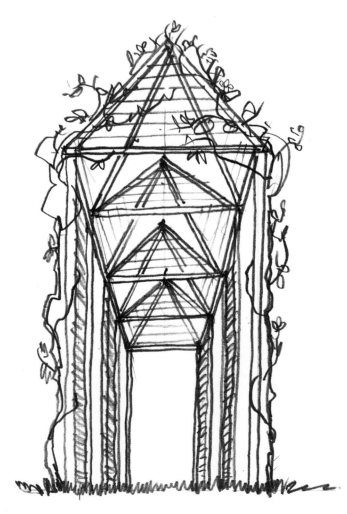

WALK-THROUGH PERGOLA

The light and airy framework of this pergola can be built over a garden path to form a covered walkway of colourful and sweetly-scented climbing plants trained over the easy-to-make, but distinctive, trellis and wire-covered framework. Good plants to use include clematis, especially the small-flowered species such as *C montana* and *C armandii*, climbing hydrangea (*H petiolaris*), sweet-scented plants such as jasmine and honeysuckle, and wisteria. The many varieties of ivy are quickly established, although they can be difficult to contain; instead, you could try ornamental grape vines, the leaves of which turn to spectacular colours in autumn.

The 'roof' is a series of simple pyramids on a timber framework which is fixed on top of fence posts held upright by hammer-in steel fence post supports. Training wires for climbing plants are stapled around the pyramids, and trellis panels are fixed at the sides between the post supports.

Trellis panels usually come in 1830mm (72in) widths, and in heights of 600mm (24in), 900mm (36in) and 1220mm (48in). For this project, the panels are turned to give a height of 1830mm (72in) and a width of 1220mm (48in).

The size of the trellis panels also determines the dimensions of the pergola – ours is 1220mm (48in) wide, and the posts are spaced 1220mm (48in) apart. It is best to keep these measurements the same so that the 'base' to each pyramid is a square, ensuring that the struts are in proportion to the main frame. The height of the posts is 2m (6ft 6in) which means that the trellising is raised off the ground by 170mm (6in). We have only fixed trellising to alternate bays, but this is simply for effect. Our pergola is four bays long, but this is variable and you can have more or fewer bays, according to your requirements.

All timber used is sawn and preservative-treated softwood, as used for fencing.

PYRAMID ROOF STRUCTURE
The series of pyramids that form the 'roof' of the pergola add visual interest and extra height to the design. Training wires are stapled around the struts, enabling plants to grow and thrive and to form a 'living ceiling'.

MATERIALS

Note: All timber is sawn and preservative-treated softwood

Part	Quantity	Material	Length
LONG RAILS	2	75 × 50mm (3 × 2in)	5.25m (17ft 3in)
CROSS RAILS	5	As above	1200mm (48in)
PYRAMID STRUTS	16	75 × 25mm (3 × 1in)	1350mm (53in)*
POSTS	10	75 × 75mm (3 × 3in)	2m (6ft 6in)
TRELLIS PANELS	8		1830mm (72in) high × 1200mm (48in)
HAMMER-IN POST SUPPORTS	10		
TRAINING WIRE	1 large coil		
SCREWS		Zinc-plated steel	50mm (2in) No 8
STAPLES		Galvanized fencing type	19mm (¾in)

* Approximate length only – measure and cut on site for accuracy

TOOLS

WORKBENCH (fixed or portable)

STEEL MEASURING TAPE

STEEL RULE

TRY SQUARE

COMBINATION SQUARE – for marking 45° angles

PANEL SAW (or circular power saw)

TENON SAW

MARKING GAUGE

POWER DRILL

DRILL BIT – approximately 3mm (⅛in) diameter to drill pilot holes for screws

SLEDGE HAMMER

CARPENTER'S HAMMER

CHISEL – about 25mm (1in)

MALLET

WALK-THROUGH PERGOLA ASSEMBLY

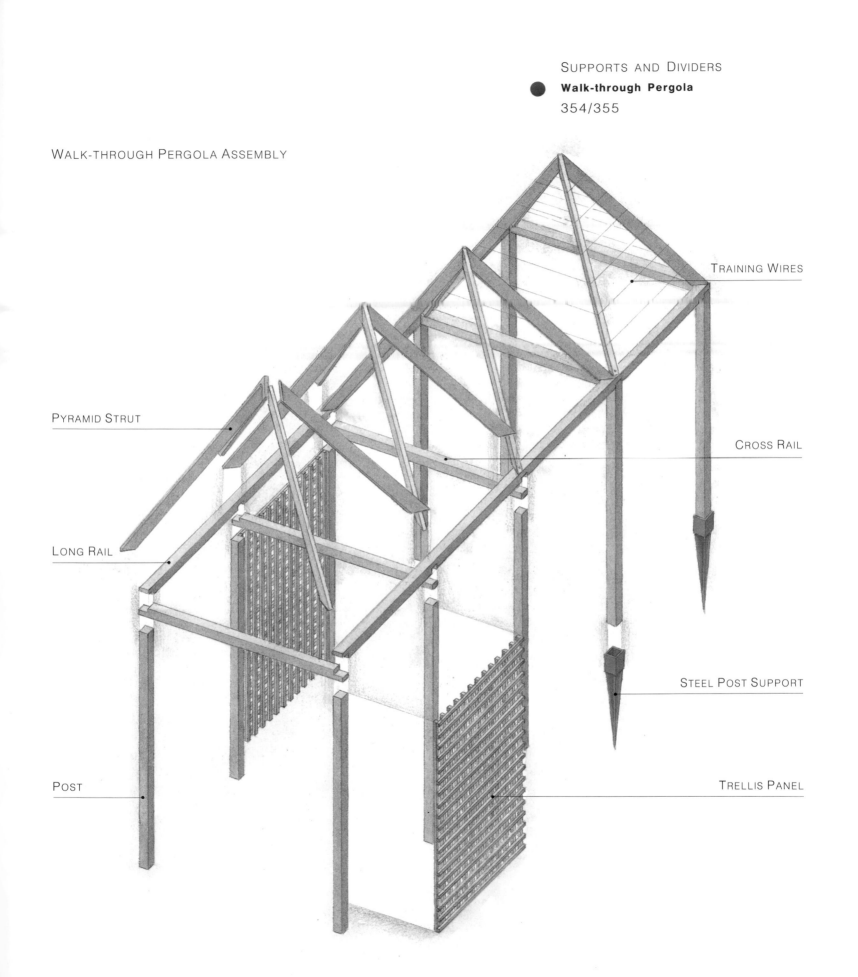

TRAINING WIRES

PYRAMID STRUT

CROSS RAIL

LONG RAIL

STEEL POST SUPPORT

POST

TRELLIS PANEL

WALK-THROUGH PERGOLA

TOP FRAME

Start by making the top frame on which the 'roof' of pyramids is fixed and which will eventually be supported on the vertical posts. The top long rails are made from 75 × 50mm (3 × 2in) sawn and preservative-treated timber, ideally in one full length (that is, if you are making the pergola to the proportions shown in the photograph, the length of four trellis panels plus the five posts of 75mm [3in] width). If it is impossible to buy timber the length required, two shorter lengths can be joined end to end with a simple lap joint or halving joint (*see* **Techniques, Wood Joints, page 400**).

Cut the cross rails to the width required, in our case 1370mm (54in) (the spacing between two posts plus the thickness of the posts).

Mark out the positions of the posts on the long rails to suit the width of the trellis panels, in our case at *internal* intervals of 1220mm (48in). Cut halving joints at the appropriate places on the long rails

and at the ends of the cross rails, so that they form corner halving joints on the cross rails at either end (fig 1) and T-halving joints on the intermediate rails (*see* **Techniques, page 400**). Form the joints so that the long rails are on top.

Screw the joints together through the cross rails from the underside.

'PYRAMID' ROOF SECTIONS

To work out the exact length of the pyramid struts, measure the diagonal of the base across the frame. Mark this length on a flat floor and strike equal length lines at 45° to this line at either end to give the point of the apex of the pyramid. This gives the lengths of the timber required for the structure forming the pyramid – the measurement should more or less correspond to the length of the cross rails.

Cut the required number of struts slightly overlength and then mitre them all at 45° at both ends in opposite directions and to the correct length required.

To assemble, hold two of the struts in a vice so the mitred faces of one end meet. Screw through from each side using 50mm (2in) No 8 zinc-plated woodscrews (fig 2).

Hold this frame upright in a workbench and lay a third strut against the joint and pilot drill through at approximately 45° into the other frame (fig 3). Repeat for the fourth pyramid strut (fig 4).

Make up the required number of pyramid structures. These are delicate, so handle them carefully.

Place each pyramid on top of the frame already made and fix down into it with a single screw at each corner (fig 5). Once fixed, this is a very strong structure. Repeat for all of the pyramids.

Staple training wires at 150mm (6in) intervals up the pyramids.

FIXING THE POSTS AND FINAL ASSEMBLY

Carry the top structure to its final position and use it to mark on the ground the positions of the fence posts. The posts are spaced at

internal intervals of 1220mm (48in) so that they coincide with the cross rail positions.

The easiest way to fix the posts is with steel post supports. These supports are simply hammered into the ground and the posts slot into sockets at the tops of the supports.

Stretch a string line along the line of the posts. This string line will help you to line up the supports and will also give some idea of levels. Push the tip of the support into the ground and use a spirit level to check that it is upright. To drive the support into the ground, a heavy hammer, such as a sledge hammer, will be required. Insert a short length of 75 × 75mm (3 × 3in) timber post into the socket to protect the support from hammer blows, or use a proprietary metal-capped driving tool which should have a tommy-bar handle allowing you to steady the socket and prevent it from twisting as it is hammered in place.

Drive the support into the ground with firm, slow blows of the hammer. At regular intervals, insert a post into the socket and use a spirit level on

1 Joining Top Frame Rails
Frame rails form corner halving joints at ends and T-halving joints (not shown) at intermediate points.

2 Joining First Two Struts
Mitre ends of struts at 45° and butt cut faces together. *Inset* Fix with screws at oblique angles.

3 Adding Remaining Struts
Hold frame in a workbench. Screw through from sides of third strut to face of joint; repeat for fourth strut.

4 Apex of Finished Pyramid
Finished joints neatly form pyramid apex. *Inset* Angled screws fix third and fourth struts to first two struts.

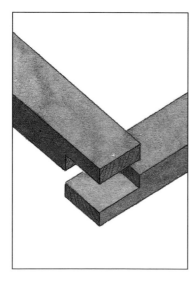

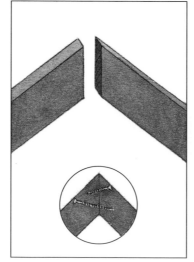

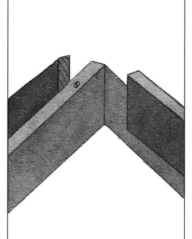

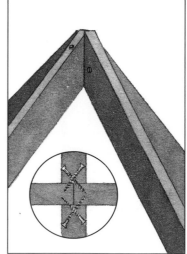

two adjacent faces to check that the spike is going in vertically. Adjustments can be made by pulling or twisting the sockets as necessary.

When the supports have been inserted the posts can be fitted. In some designs of post supports, two bolts have to be tightened to cramp the posts in position, while in others the posts are held with large screws. Double-check that the posts are upright and use a length of straight timber and a spirit level to check that the tops of the posts are level. On flat or slightly sloping ground this will be easy to achieve, but on steeply sloping ground it may be acceptable if the tops of the posts follow the slope of the ground. Use a length of string or a long batten to level the post tops which can be trimmed to an even height, if necessary, using a hand saw.

The next stage is to fix the trellising between the posts (we only fixed it to alternate bays of the pergola). Place bricks or blocks on the ground to support the trellis panels about 150mm (6in) from the ground. We used metal clips to hold

the panels of trellis in place and the clips are first nailed to the posts so that they are vertical and inset by the same amount – about 25mm (1in). The panels are then lifted into place and a check is made that the horizontal rails of the trellis panels are level. The panels are then fixed to the clips using zinc-plated screws (see **Techniques, page 400**).

If required, the trellis panels can be fixed directly to the posts. Position and level them as above, then drill through the side frames of the panels so that 75mm (3in) long galvanized fencing nails can be driven through the panels, without splitting them, and into the posts. Three fixings will be required on each side of a 1830mm (72in) high trellis panel.

You will need some help to lift the pyramid roof onto the posts. Adjust the roof so that the vertical posts coincide with the corner and cross rail joints, then nail the frame to the tops of the posts using two 100mm (4in) nails skew nailed through the top frame and into each post (see **Techniques, page 399**).

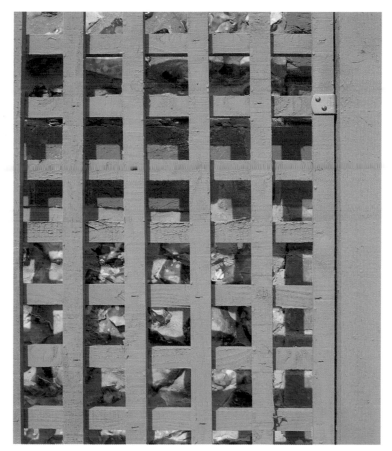

5 **Fixing Pyramids to Frame**
Screw the pyramids to the top frame using a screw through each corner and into the frame rails.

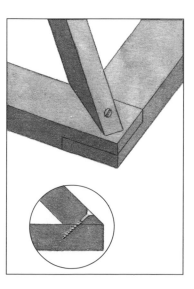

TRELLIS WITH FALSE PERSPECTIVE

Trellising has varied garden applications. This project goes a stage further and follows the French tradition of using trellis to give blank walls a sense of depth and perspective. The result, although simple to construct, is a memorable and effective exercise in *trompe-l'oeil*. You can adapt this idea to cheer up any featureless expanse of wall or disguise unsympathetic stock brick or breeze block.

Perhaps the easiest project in the book to accomplish, this false-perspective trellis could be assembled without too much trouble during the course of a single afternoon once you have established your required dimensions and perspective.

The first step is to draw up a full-size plan: you can adapt the design shown here to fit your space. A false perspective is generally more effective if you arrange it so there is a contrast with a real view. Incorporating a doorway, as here, or any other kind of opening heightens the element of 'hazard and surprise'.

The next stage is to pin together slats of timber to make the required design. Bend the nails over and hammer them flat as they go through the back so they will not pull out. If you want a curved arch, you could make the curve out of exterior-grade plywood cut with a jigsaw.

This trellis design was painted a pale grey to tone with the lichened wall. Trellis looks very effective painted, but the colours should not be too harsh and bright or the illusory effect will be lost.

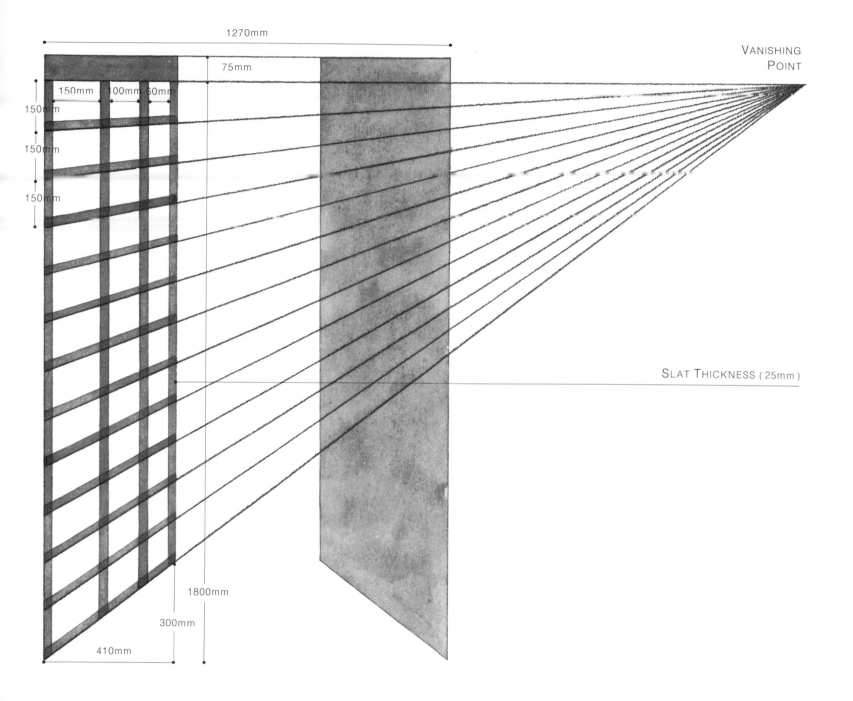

DRAWING UP A PLAN OF THE TRELLIS STRUCTURE

You will need to draw up a full-size plan to calculate the length of the slats and the degree of perspective. The overall height and width shown here are based on the dimensions of the door alongside which we built this project, and can be altered according to the space available.

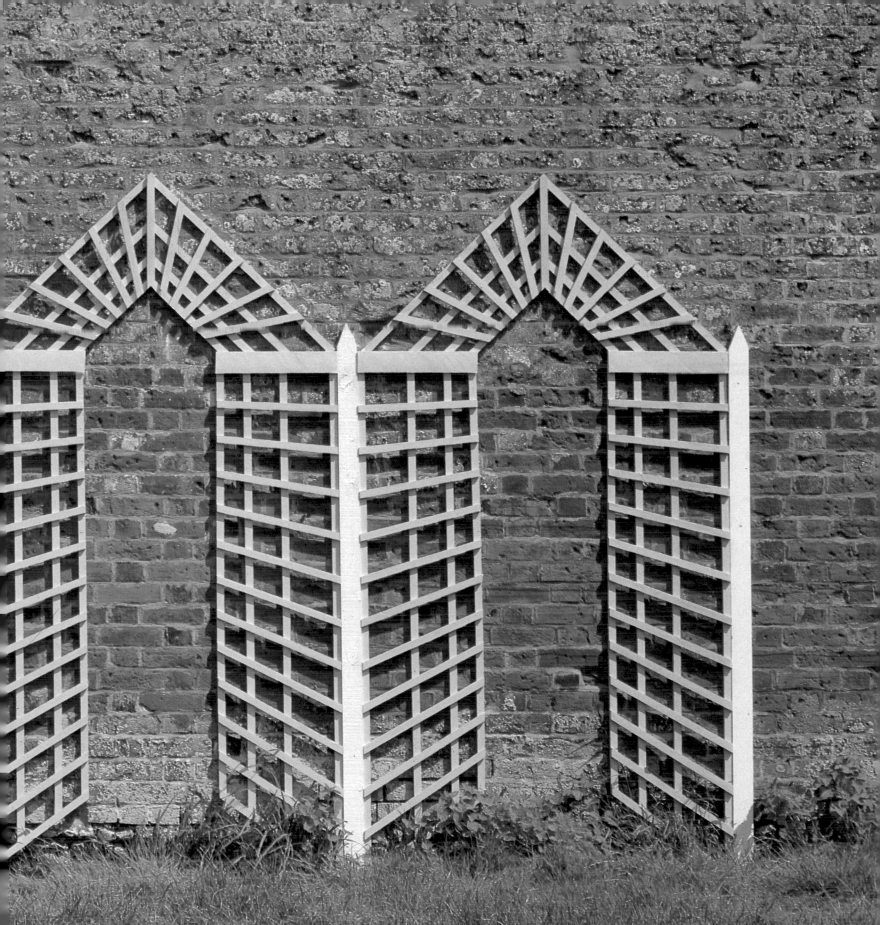

TRELLIS WITH FALSE PERSPECTIVE

This trellis is constructed so that when it is fixed against a wall, it deceives the eye into believing it is looking at a three-dimensional arch, or a series of three-dimensional arches if several are fixed side by side as shown here.

If you fit the trellis around a door or gateway, sizes are dependent on the dimensions of the door. We used three archways alongside a garden door, which has a matching trellis 'roof' above it. Our arches are separated by 75 × 25mm (3 × 1in) timber 'posts' chamferred at the top. However, the principles of construction are easy to adapt to other sizes and designs according to the size of your garden, the amount of wall space, and personal preference.

A wider batten has also been incorporated at the top to align with the top of the door frame, replacing one of the 'normal size' trellis slats, but again this is optional.

The density of the trellis and the amount of perspective incorporated is entirely down to individual taste, but the dimensions here are a good standard to work from.

Obviously, you will need a wall on which to fix the trellis. This need not be a garden boundary wall: it could be a plain wall of the house, or the wall of a garage or outbuilding.

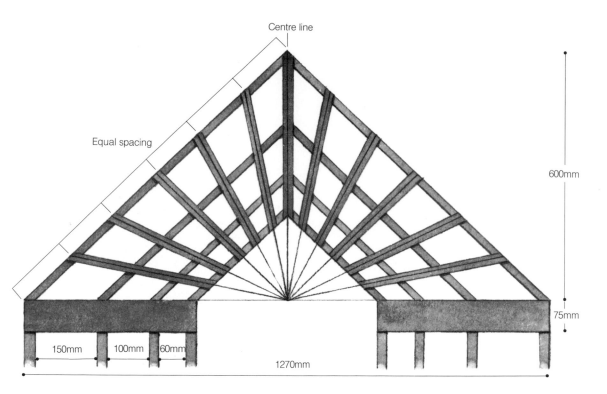

1 Drawing Up a Plan of the Roof Structure
Draw a line to trellis width. Draw a line perpendicular to centre point – top of this line represents apex. Draw in slat thickness, then two sides of triangle. Mark where vertical slats of side panels fall along base and extend lines to centre line, parallel with triangle sides. Mark five equally spaced points on each side and join to centre of base.

TOOLS

WORKBENCH (fixed or portable)

STEEL MEASURING TAPE

TRY SQUARE

TENON SAW (or power jigsaw)

HAMMER

POWER DRILL

DRILL BIT – 3mm ($\frac{1}{8}$in)

MASONRY DRILL BIT – 6mm ($\frac{1}{4}$in)

SCREWDRIVER

SPIRIT LEVEL

MATERIALS

Note: If you experience difficulty buying 25 × 12mm (1 × $\frac{1}{2}$in), you can cut your own slats by ripping down 200 × 25mm (8 × 1in) timber using a circular saw; this will give 16 slats per board if saw blade is not too thick

Part	Quantity	Material	Length
VERTICAL SLATS	8 per trellis arch	25 × 12mm (1 × $\frac{1}{2}$in) sawn softwood	1800mm (72in)*
CROSS SLATS	As required	As above	As required
ROOF SLATS	As required	As above	As required
TOP BATTEN (optional)	1 per arch	75 × 12mm (3 × $\frac{1}{2}$in) sawn softwood	1270mm (50in)**
POST	1 between each arch	75 × 25mm (3 × 1in) sawn softwood	As required

* Finished size – cut overlength and then cut to size after fixing (see text for details)

** Length given is width of each trellis arch; top battens can be cut from two shorter lengths of softwood because centre section is cut away on assembly

CONSTRUCTION

The easiest way to make this trellis is first to draw up full-size plans on a large, reasonably flat surface such as a garage floor, tables pushed together, or a flat area of concrete, such as a driveway.

You may be able to draw the plan directly on to your flat surface, but it is more likely that you will have to make the drawing on several sheets of paper which can then be taped together to produce a full-size plan. Wherever you construct the trellis, it will be necessary to have enough space for all the pieces to be laid out on this plan and nailed up in place on top of the drawing.

DRAWING UP PLANS

Using our diagrams as a guide, draw up plans for one side of the upright trellis. You need to decide on the height and spaces required. Ours is 1800mm (72in) high, with 12 equal spaces down the outer side, giving 150mm (6in) centres (actually from the base of one slat to the base of the next).

Mark off the width of this one side of trellis; ours is 410mm (16¼in) from the outside edge of the outermost vertical slat to the inside edge of the innermost vertical slat. Two more vertical slats are placed between them to give *internal* spacings of 150mm (6in), 100mm (4in), and 60mm (2½in) respectively.

The innermost vertical slat is only 1500mm (60in) long and is placed 300mm (12in) up from the ground. Join the bottom two points and continue this angled line up until it meets a horizontal line drawn across at the very top. This gives you a vanishing point where the two lines cross. All the other cross lines must converge at this point.

Use a slat to mark off the thickness of all the slats across the width and down the length of the trellis.

Draw up the 'roof' section next,

starting with the base line of the triangle. Find the centre and draw a vertical line (at exactly 90°) up, 600mm (24in) long, to give the apex of the triangle. Draw in the slat thickness over this centre line. Then draw in the outer lines of the triangle.

If you have made this drawing separate from the main trellis, mark off where the vertical slats of the main trellis will fall along the base line. Draw lines from these positions on to the roof section, parallel with the outer lines of the triangle, joining them all at the centre line.

Equally space five points along each of the upward-sloping sides of the triangle (giving six equal spaces on each side) and join these points to the centre of the base line. Start with the central one, and then space two slats on either side.

Draw in the other slat thicknesses as before, finishing the cross slats at the innermost roof slat (fig 1).

Use the drawings to measure off for the lengths of slats that will be required (remembering to multiply the number of slats in the vertical structure by two), and then multiply the total by the number of arches required. Add on a little extra to each length to allow for trimming the angles at the ends.

When the slats have been obtained, cut them all to length, again allowing a small surplus to allow for trimming at the ends.

MAKING UP ONE SIDE

Start by laying all the cross slats accurately on the drawing, and then place the vertical slats on top.

Apply a dab of waterproof wood glue at every intersection of the slats, then fix by driving a ring-shanked nail through each intersection. If you are nailing up on a workbench, a good way to hold the slats firm while nailing is to drive nails temporarily into the bench at all corners, where the slats cross each other. Make up the required number of trellis frames to this pattern.

MAKING UP OPPOSITE SIDE

Turn over the first side of trellis panel, then draw around it onto the work-surface to give a mirror image of the plan. Make up the required number of trellis frames to this pattern in the same way as before.

MAKING UP THE ROOF

The roof is made in the same way as the side panels. Position the cross slats on the plan, and then place the long parallel slats on top. Glue and nail the intersections.

FINISHING OFF

Saw the protruding ends of the slats flush with the edges of the frames.

Prepare the 'posts' and the top battens. In the latter case, the centre section will be cut out on assembly, so you could use two offcuts for these pieces, rather than a batten the full width of the trellis arch.

Ideally, you should use preserva tive-treated timber. If not, at this stage treat the whole trellis with a water-repellent preservative. The finished trellis is painted with three coats of microporous paint, or one coat of exterior undercoat and two coats of exterior gloss paint.

FIXING THE TRELLIS

If the trellis is going to support climbing plants, spacers must be inserted between it and the wall so that plants can twine behind the trellis. Otherwise, the trellis can be screwed directly to the wall.

Position a post against the wall, and use a spirit level to check it is vertical. Drill clearance holes for two screws through the post and allow the drill tip to mark the wall. Remove the post and, using a masonry bit, drill the holes to the depth required for the wallplugs. Insert the wall-plugs, then drive zinc-plated screws through the post and into the plugs. The screws should penetrate the wall by about 38mm (1½in).

Fix the adjacent side panel and, using an offcut of top batten as a spacer, fit the roof section, then the next post, then the next roof trellis, then the next post, and so on right across. After this, add the other side trellises, with lengths of top batten, if required, fixed between the top of the side panels and the undersides of the roof panels.

❷ Nailing the Trellis
Lay cross slats on plan, then position vertical slats above them. Glue and nail through intersections.

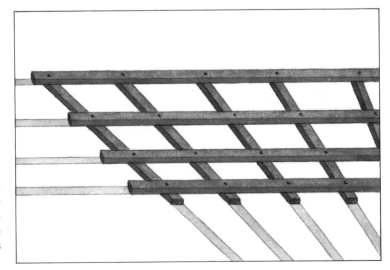

HEXAGONAL ARBOR

An arbor makes a distinctive feature in any garden, displaying climbing plants to great advantage and exposing them to optimum conditions of light and air. Arbors are often all-metal structures, but this simple but elegant framework makes use of ordinary copper tubing and plain wooden rustic posts, readily available from most DIY outlets. The construction process is fairly quick and easy to do.

The three sections of copper tubing (which have been rubbed with plumbers' flux to give them a green colour) are cut to precisely the same length and bent into shape using a curved piece of blockboard or chipboard as a former. Holes are drilled about 100mm (6in) apart along the tubes. Thin green plastic-covered wires are threaded through the holes to make a support for the plants.

As is the case with all posts that need to go into the ground, it is much easier to use spiked steel supports with sockets. The metal spikes are readily driven into the ground and the end of the post can be dropped into the shoe and held in place.

The uprights and cross rails must be treated with a preservative and the resulting dark brown makes a pleasing contrast with the greenish copper.

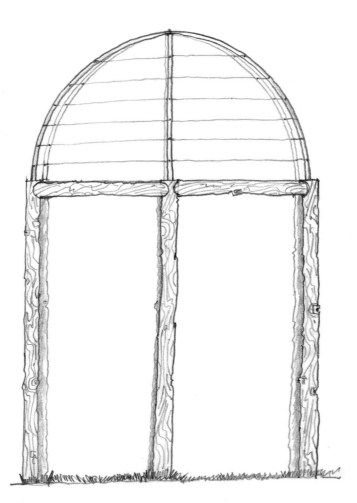

HEXAGONAL ARBOR

This arbor is made from six preservative-treated rustic poles set into the ground at equal intervals and joined by cross rails, with a dome above made from copper tubing. If you brush the tubing with plumbers' flux, a green patina will result. Garden wire is fed around the tubing as a support for climbing plants.

TIMBER FRAME

The height of the frame can be varied slightly. However, the poles should not be less than about 2m (6ft 6in) above ground, otherwise some people may hit their heads on the cross rails; and, for stability, the poles should not be much higher above ground than 2.5m (8ft).

PREPARING THE SITE

Choose a flat site and, using pegs and string lines, mark out the hexagonal shape (fig 1) for the positions. The posts are spaced at 1000mm (39in) centres, with 2m (6ft 6in) between any two opposite posts. It is essential that the post positions are accurately marked.

Dig 600mm (24in) deep holes for the posts. This can be done using a narrow spade or, if available, a post hole borer which is driven into the ground and then removed to deposit excavated earth. Fill the bottom 150mm (6in) of each hole with hardcore to ensure good drainage and prevent the post bottoms rotting.

MAKING THE FRAMEWORK

Make up six L-shapes comprising a post and a cross rail as follows.

Position two posts in neighbouring holes and wedge them vertically. Measure the internal distance between them and add 50mm (2in) to allow for shaping the ends of the cross rails. Remove the posts.

Use a jigsaw to make a curved cut in the ends of the cross rails so that they fit against the sides of the posts. Alternatively, use a hand saw to cut out V-shapes in the cross rails.

At the top of each post, draw 60° angles as a guide to aligning the cross rails (fig 2, below). Continue the lines to the opposite sides of the post as a guide for the dowel fixing positions. Cut the dowelling into 150mm (6in) lengths.

Lay one post on a flat piece of ground. Position a cross rail against the post and drill through the post and into the rail to accept the dowel (fig 3). At least 50mm (2in) of dowel should enter the rail. Fit the dowel using waterproof wood adhesive. Repeat to make five more L-shapes.

ERECTING THE FRAME

Position two posts in their holes and align the cross rail that falls between them with both posts. Use a straight edge and a spirit level to align the posts – if necessary, add or take away a little of the hardcore in the base of the hole. Drill through the 'free' post into the end of the cross rail to align with the angles marked on the top. Join the 'free' post to the cross rail with a dowel as you did before (fig 3).

Continue to join up the L-shaped sections in the same way, checking that the tops of the posts are all at the same height, and then saw off any protruding dowel ends flush with the posts.

MATERIALS

Part	Quantity	Material	Length
POSTS	6	75–100mm (3–4in) diameter treated rustic poles	2.4m (7ft 8in)
CROSS RAILS	6	50–75mm (2–3in) diameter treated rustic poles	As required
DOME BARS	3	22mm ($\frac{7}{8}$in) diameter copper tubing	As required

Also required: Approximately 2m (6ft 6in) of 12mm ($\frac{1}{2}$in) diameter hardwood dowelling

TOOLS

- WORKBENCH (fixed or portable)
- SPADE or POST HOLE BORER
- PANEL SAW
- SPIRIT LEVEL
- STEEL RULE
- JIGSAW
- POWER DRILL
- HAMMER
- SCREWDRIVER
- PLIERS
- HACKSAW
- CRAMPS
- SHOVEL

1 Drawing up a Ground Plan
Posts are spaced 1000mm (39in) apart: mark centre and strike off 1000mm (39in) lines at 60° angles.

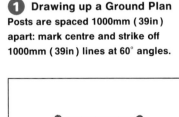

2 Shaping the Cross Rails
Angle ends of cross rails to fit around posts. Use jigsaw for smooth curve or make V-cuts with hand saw.

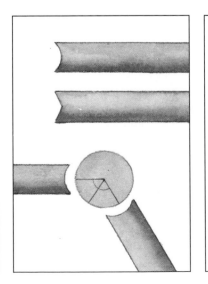

3 Fixing the Cross Rails
Drill holes through posts into cross rails. Insert dowels to fix in place. Angled screw holds dowel in place.

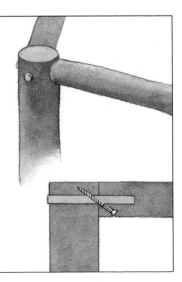

To secure the joints, use a 75mm (3in) screw inserted diagonally through each cross rail (fig 3).

Finally, tie a length of garden wire around the top of the posts, holding it in place on each post using 30mm (1½in) staples. To make the wire taut, twist the two ends together using pliers.

THE DOME

Draw a semi-circle on a large sheet of plywood or chipboard (fig 4) using a pencil and a piece of string to act as a compass. This will describe the section of the dome. When this is done, mark off at 150mm (6in) centres for the positions of holes through which training wires will later be threaded.

Use a piece of 19mm (¾in) chipboard or plywood to make a former for bending the tube to the correct shape. Trace the curve on to the former and cut it out using a jigsaw.

BENDING THE TUBE

Cut the copper tubing to length using a hacksaw. Our tubes were 3.14m (10ft 4in) long. Since the copper will need to be bent a little tighter than the arc, bring it down about 38mm (1½in) at each end.

Cramp the former to a workbench or table and start to bend the piece of tube around it. You will need someone to help you with this: each person should exert a little pressure until the tubing is bent to follow the shape of the former. If you find that the ends lose their shape then you can use a 22mm (⅞in) internal pipe bending spring.

Lay the bent tube on the original dome profile and mark off the 150mm (6in) spacings on to the tube. Drill 3mm (⅛in) diameter holes through the tubing at these marks.

Bend the other two tubes to the shape of the former and then drill the holes as before. Always mark off the spacings on the tubing against the original dome profile.

ASSEMBLING THE DOME

Mark the middle point of each tube, then hammer it flat so that you can drill a 6mm (¼in) diameter hole through each piece (fig 5). Bolt the three pieces together.

Next, drill a 25mm (1in) diameter hole, 50mm (2in) deep in the centre of the top of each post.

The dome can now be lifted on to the top of the posts and the tube ends located in the holes (fig 6). There is sufficient movement in the structure to enable the dome to be positioned.

Thread garden wire through each row of holes, tying each length securely in place.

To fix the dome to the rustic poles, drill straight through the tube horizontally above each post and slip a 50mm (2in) nail through.

Finally make up a dryish concrete mix of five parts sand to one part cement and pour it into each hole along with some small pieces of stone. Tamp it down, then shape it into a convex collar so that rain water will drain away.

HEXAGONAL ARBOR ASSEMBLY

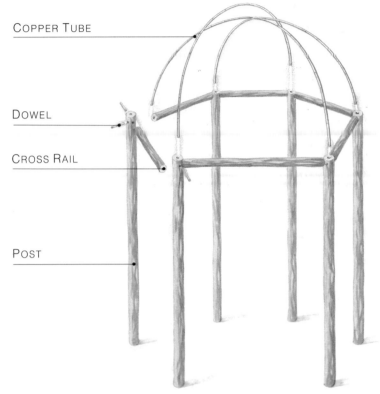

COPPER TUBE

DOWEL

CROSS RAIL

POST

4 **Dome Section and Former**
Mark off 150mm (6in) spacings on semi-circle. Transfer section of curve to plywood to make former.

5 **Fixing the Dome**
Flatten out tops of the pieces of tubing, drill a 6mm (¼in) diameter hole through them and bolt together.

6 **Fixing Dome to Posts**
Drill a hole centrally in the top of each post. Slot dome into post and drive nail through tubing.

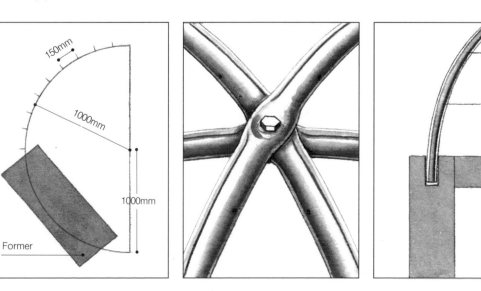

150mm

1000mm

1000mm

Former

BEANSTICK FENCE

New fencing can look rather harsh and brash and hedges, even when composed of the most quick-growing species, are unfortunately not instant solutions to the problem of garden enclosure. This beanstick fence was designed to provide a more natural-looking boundary than the standard commercial timber fencing; almost, in fact, a 'man-made hedge'. The look is reminiscent of the traditional wattle fence; another source of inspiration was the type of wonderful screens and panels seen in Japanese gardens and walkways. Here the effect is created by combining a strong rectilinear framework with the natural, random texture supplied by the beansticks.

The fence is very easy to make. The beansticks are trapped in the sawn frame, held in place in two grooves made top and bottom between the top rails and a couple of battens between the bottom rails. The sticks are cut to the same length, slotted into the groove and pushed up together.

The sticks themselves do not need to be treated, although the ends could be dipped in preservative to prolong their life. If sticks do become broken or damaged, it is easy to replace them.

This fence, formal enough for a front garden, would also be a good choice for a new house where the planting had not yet had a chance to become established. The beansticks are sufficiently firm and resilient to be animal-proof but chinks of light lend it a lively and varied effect.

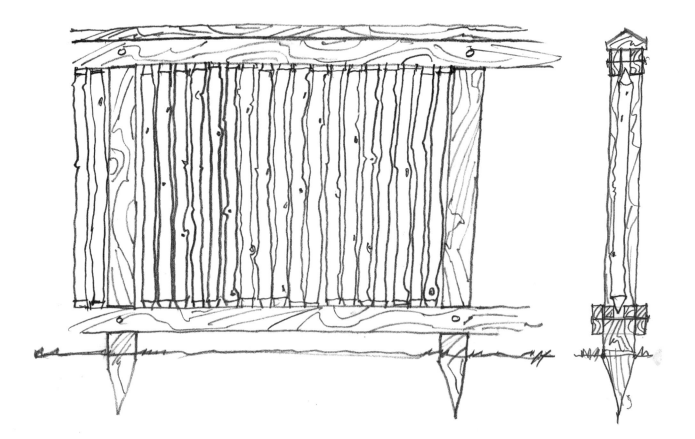

BEANSTICK FENCE

This rustic-looking fence is an ideal project if you want your boundary to look just a bit different from those of your neighbours. It is made from beansticks fixed between a framework of sawn and preservative-treated timber. This can be left in its natural state, it can be stained a darker wood colour, or it can be painted as shown in our example – microporous paint is ideal for treating the timber, being easy to apply without a primer, and easy to re-treat in future as the need arises.

It is unlikely that you will be able to buy the beansticks from a timber merchant. More likely sources are fencing suppliers and garden centres, or directly from the wood-men who cut the sticks.

Cutting is done in winter and early spring, and this is the best time to obtain the sticks. You will need large numbers for this project, and it is a good idea to buy one or two bundles of sticks to start with to see what proportion of the fence they cover. Then you will be able to put in an order to cover the full length of the fence you will be making.

The spacing of the posts depends on the length of the rails you will be using. Rails must be joined at post positions, so if you have 3m (10ft) rails, posts must be spaced 1500mm (60in) apart. For 2.4m (8ft) rails, the post spacing will be 1200mm (48in). Once this is decided, you will be able to work out how many posts (and post supports) are required.

You also need to decide on the height of the posts. Our fence is about 1000mm (40in) high, and in this case the posts are 1500mm (60in) long which allows 500mm (20in) of post to be in the ground. A good rule of thumb is to allow a minimum of 500mm (20in) of post in the ground, or one third of the fence height, whichever is the greater.

Alternatively, you can fit the posts into metal spike post supports which are simply hammered into the ground. The posts fit into sockets in the tops of the spike supports. In this case, 600mm (24in) long spikes are suitable for fences up to 1200mm (48in); for fences up to 1800mm (72in) high use 760mm (30in) long post supports.

The metal post supports are driven into the ground with a scrap of loose-fitting fence post in the socket to protect the socket from sledge hammer blows, keeping a check with a spirit level on all sides of the socket that the spike is going straight into the ground. You will also be able to heave on the spike to correct any tendency for it to go into the ground out of plumb (vertical). Stretch a horizontal string line along the line of the proposed fence to ensure the metal spikes are driven into the ground in line and to the same height.

If you do not use metal post spikes, it is possible on soft ground to sharpen the ends of the posts into spikes and simply hammer them into the ground. However, using this method it is usually difficult to get the posts absolutely in line and vertical, and it is better to take out a hole for each post using a metal post hole borer tool, which can be hired. This hand-operated tool removes a plug of soil to leave a neat circular hole about 225mm (9in) in diameter, and up to 600mm (24in) deep.

Posts can then be stood in the holes, lined up against a string line, and their heights adjusted to bring them all level by packing the holes as necessary. The posts are held upright by ramming hardcore around them, and finally topping off with a collar of concrete around the post at ground level to throw rain-water clear of the post.

PREPARING AND FIXING POSTS

If you decide to point the posts to drive them into the ground (*see* above), the joints can then be cut with the posts in position. In all other cases it is better and easier to cut the joints with the post on a bench.

Hold a side rail flush with the top of the post and mark its depth on the post. Repeat for the other side of the post, and notch out 25mm (1in) wide recesses to the depth of the rails at the top of each post (fig 1).

Position the posts by either dropping them into metal post support sockets or setting them into the ground, adjusting them to the same height. Place a long, straight batten across the post tops or post support sockets and use a spirit level to check that they are level.

If using metal post supports, screw or cramp the post bottoms into the supports. If fixing posts in holes in the ground, pack around them with hardcore and a concrete collar. Double check that all posts are in line, that they are vertical, and that the tops are level.

FIXING TOP RAILS

Fix the top rails to the posts using two coach screws each side.

If it is necessary to join two rails, cut the rails to coincide with a post position and make a spliced joint (fig 2). To maintain the strength of the fence, you should have only one spliced joint per post, staggering them from side to side.

At the fence ends, cut the rails flush with the edge of the post.

TOOLS

WORKBENCH (fixed or portable)

STEEL MEASURING TAPE

TRY SQUARE

PANEL SAW (or circular saw)

TREE-PRUNING SAW

HAMMER

DRILL (hand or power)

DRILL BIT – 6mm ($\frac{1}{4}$in)

SPANNER

SPIRIT LEVEL

CHISEL

MALLET

BILLHOOK (or axe or sharp knife)

MATERIALS

Part	Quantity	Material	Length
POSTS	As required	75 × 75mm (3 × 3in) sawn and treated softwood	As required*
RAILS	As required	75 × 25mm (3 × 1in) sawn and treated softwood	As required
BATTENS	As required	32 × 25mm (1$\frac{1}{4}$ × 1in) sawn and treated softwood	As required
CAPPING BOARD	As required	75 × 38mm (3 × 1$\frac{1}{2}$in) sawn and treated softwood	As required
BEANSTICKS	As required	Hazel, birch or chestnut	As required

* Post length will depend on the height of the fence and whether you are fixing posts into the ground or into metal spike post supports

FIXING BOTTOM RAILS

The bottom rails are screwed to the outsides of the posts about 150mm (6in) up from ground level. Fix a coach screw at one end of the rail, and use a spirit level to get the rail level before drilling and screwing at the other end into another post. Use two coach screws per post, and make spliced joints if necessary to coincide with post positions.

Measure the distance between the posts and cut pieces of roofing batten to fit snuggly between them (fig 3). Fit the battens inside the bottom rails, flush with the top edge, with the narrower edge towards the rails. Drive four zinc-plated screws through the bottom rails and into each batten. The battens create a gap about 12mm ($\frac{1}{2}$in) wide centrally between the bottom rails.

Repeat all along the fence.

If you plan to paint or stain the frame of the fence, do this now.

FITTING THE BEANSTICKS

Measure the distance from the top of the top rail to the bottom of the bottom rail, and cut all the beansticks to this length. They will tend to clog the saw teeth, so use a tree-pruning saw for this job.

Use a billhook, axe or sharp knife to sharpen one end of each of the beansticks so that they wedge into the gap between the battens.

Starting at one end, feed the sticks in through the gap at the top of the frame and wedge them into the gap at the bottom, bunching them tightly until the frame is filled.

Trim all the beansticks flush with the top of the top rails. Use a pruning saw or handsaw, and press each stick down firmly as you cut it.

Finally, nail the capping board along the top of the fence, making sure it covers the edges of the top rails. If you cannot buy a capping board, you can cut one from a length of sawn timber. Paint or stain it to match the fence frame.

BEANSTICK FENCE ASSEMBLY

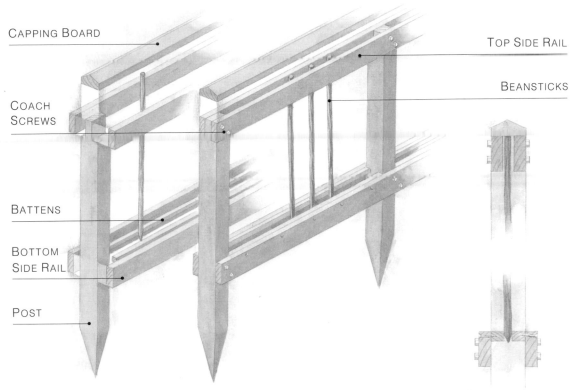

CAPPING BOARD

COACH SCREWS

BATTENS

BOTTOM SIDE RAIL

POST

TOP SIDE RAIL

BEANSTICKS

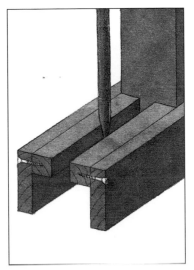

SECTION VIEW

1 **Fixing Top Rails**
Notch out 25mm (1in) recesses to depth of side rail on sides of post at top. Screw rails to post.

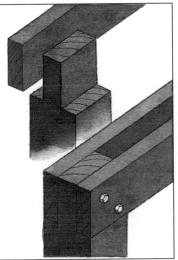

2 **Joining Lengths of Rail**
Join rails at post positions, if necessary, cutting rails at an angle to form spliced joint.

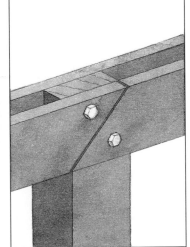

3 **Fixing Beansticks**
Sharpen one end of stick to a point and feed through top to wedge between bottom rail battens.

PART 9

CONTAINERS

Every year at Versailles, it takes the army to bring in the lemon and orange trees for the winter, hundreds of planted tubs comprising what must be the ultimate container garden. Container gardening is not usually on such a grand scale, but in every garden there is a place for at least some plants in pots, whether a pair of bay trees in formal tubs flanking an entrance, a collection of simple terracotta bowls tumbling with flowers, or cheerful hanging baskets providing a splash of summer colour.

The versatility of container gardening is one of its main advantages: you can match plants exactly to their soil requirements, and place them where they will look most effective. If the container is not too large, you can move it to a position of prominence when the plant is in bloom. Planters and window boxes are excellent DIY projects, allowing you to tailor-make your containers to suit their location exactly. If you use the same type of containers inside and out, group pots around entrances, on either side of French doors and on window sills you will create views which will help to dissolve the boundary between your house and the garden.

CONTAINERS

There are many advantages to gardening in containers. Usually, little or no weeding is required, which saves considerable maintenance time for people with only a few hours to spare. Compost and soil can be tailored to the precise needs of the plant, enabling a far greater range of species to be grown in the same location. Plants can also be arranged to suit the demands of the garden design, or to give shape to a flat landscape. You can also furnish an area with plants which might otherwise be barren, such as in the dry shade under a tree or on a roof.

Some plants positively flourish in containers. Figs, for example, like to be contained; a considerable number of other species can live undisturbed for many years in pots. Growing untidy and invasive herbs, such as mint, in containers also benefits the rest of the garden.

If containers provide a quick and easy way of creating a garden, they are also flexible enough to accommodate and express a whole range of garden styles. Containers are often associated with formal garden designs. Symmetrical arrangements of tubs, clipped box in painted wooden planters and stone urns at the end of walkways or in the centre of radiating beds are all ways of using containers to emphasize the geometry or architectural quality of a garden design.

However, containers can also be delightfully informal. Mediterranean gardens and terraces often feature large terracotta pots carefully positioned to make punctuation points in the overall design. In many Italian and Greek villages, painted and planted oil cans crowd windowsills and balconies, adding a jolt of colour to the elevations of houses. Window boxes or hanging baskets spilling over with vivid geraniums and lobelia also work well in country locations or cottage-style gardens.

POTS OF PLANTS

Container gardening is flexible and provides an instant garden for a small space. Tubs or pots flanking an entrance are a common feature of formal garden designs, but can work well combined with less structured planting (above left). A variety of species can be grown in containers; you can train climbers to grow up purpose-built trellis from a tub (above) and even grow small trees (right).

CONTAINERS

Whatever the overall style of the garden, containers should be used in a positive way. Place them to create a focal point, in the centre of planting, or arrange a series of pots asymmetrically to lead the eye on through the garden. Containers can also introduce changes of height if they are placed on top of a wall or hung from the side of a house, an important consideration if the rest of the garden is fairly flat. You can also delineate an enclosed area or patio with a row of pots or planters, or make a special feature of an entrance by flanking it with a pair of tubs.

Wherever possible, mass containers in groups for increased effect, rather than dot them about the garden where their impact will be lost. You can group pots on metal garden staging which looks very attractive positioned at either side of a door, or adopt one solution seen on a French roadside, where the entire length of a garden wall was lined in shelves, set about 45cm (18in) apart, on which were ranged dozens and dozens of planted pots.

Plants should be massed in much the same way, although filling a container with a single variety is often more effective than a careful composition of a small amount of different species. Wooden boxes simply planted with box and ivy provide a graphic line of green at the window and require little maintenance to remain attractive and flourishing.

As far as the container itself is concerned, material, size and style vary tremendously. Wherever possible, keep to natural materials – stone, wood and terracotta all look marvellous and age in a sympathetic way. Metal containers, especially when made of lead, zinc or copper, can be attractive and even rubber – in the form of old tractor tyres – can be effective, contributing textural interest. Avoid plastic: it always looks glaringly out of place in a garden; its harshness

seems to stem from the fact that, unlike everything else, it does not weather or change, and usually has no texture.

In terms of size, choose containers which are on the generous side. Small pots will be overlooked and tend to have a prissy appearance which is at odds with the robust and striking effects you should be trying to create.

Ready-made containers include a range of plain terracotta shapes from urns to shallow bowls, from traditional flowerpots to troughs. Simple reconstituted stone containers can also look good, particularly if you encourage a little weathering. Wooden planters and tubs available commercially can be customized by staining or painting them to blend in with your house or to make a vivid colour accent. Wooden containers are also, of course, a natural choice for DIY and suit a variety of different applications. A wooden tub is an excellent container home for small trees and shrubs, and half a wooden barrel is a classic. Wooden troughs or planters also make excellent raised beds, a practical and enjoyable way of gardening for older people or those with limited physical strength. Planting does not necessarily have to be at a low level in a container: a pyramid of bamboo sticks tied together and placed in a pot and planted with scarlet-flowering runner beans is a lovely sight!

One of the most appealing features of container gardening is the scope for improvisation and humour in the choice of container. In this area, more than any other, there is great opportunity for creative salvage. Everything from half-barrels to old watering cans can be used as a plant container. Old sinks, wash tubs, chimney pots and stone troughs can all be recycled to great effect, and architectural salvage yards can be a tremendous source of objects in this respect.

THE CONTAINED GARDEN

One of the most important advantages of container gardening is its ability to establish a visual connection between the house and garden. The current popularity of the conservatory bears out the common desire of people to include a sense of the outdoors in their homes. An array of the same type of containers can be used indoors and outside to create views that dissolve the boundary between house and garden.

COMPOST BIN AND PLANTER

The compost bin and planter are very similar in construction, made from rough-sawn boards fixed to posts. The simple nature of the design and lack of precision required in the finishing mean that these two structures offer a good means of practising your DIY skills and gaining the confidence to move on to more elaborate projects.

A compost bin is an invaluable asset for the gardener, providing a supply of rich organic matter which makes all the differ-ence to the way plants grow. At the same time, recycling your garden and kitchen waste is environmentally beneficial and economically sound.

The front posts of the bin are doubled up, making a slot where boards can be dropped into place as the pile builds up, or easily removed as the compost is taken out. It is worth buying 'pressure pre-served' timber – compost is both hot and wet, so the wood needs the maximum degree of protection.

The planter provides a support for young trees, many of which either blow over or suffer from 'windrock', instability of the root structure where growth stops and starts rather than proceeding at an even pace. The cross supports enable the trunk to be fixed firmly in place while the tree becomes established.

The planter is painted with a coat of black tar to preserve the wood. Coach screws are used to bolt the boards to the uprights, giving a smart finishing touch.

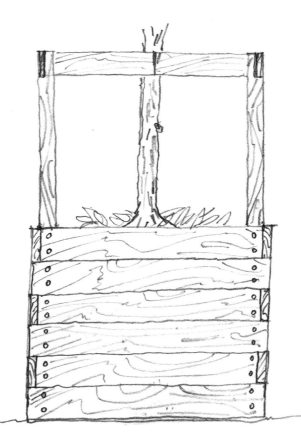

COMPOST BIN

The principle of construction for the compost bin is the same as for the planter (pages 383–385). It is made from fencing-quality sawn and preservative-treated timber which is often sold and cut in imperial as well as metric sizes.

The size of the bin can be varied to suit the site, but it should not be too large, since air will not be able to get to the centre of the heap, hindering the production of good garden compost.

Our bin is about 915mm (36in) square. The height can also be altered according to your own requirements, but you should work in multiples of 150mm (6in) plus an allowance for ventilation gaps between the boards. Our bin is about 990mm (39in) high. Bear in mind that you want a height at which it will be comfortable to tip garden waste into the bin. Also, the heap does not want to be too high or you will not be able to climb onto the heap to tread down the waste material. Opinion varies on the optimum size for the ventilation gaps; we suggest 12–19mm ($\frac{1}{2}$–$\frac{3}{4}$in).

CONSTRUCTION

Cut all of the components to the lengths specified in the Materials chart below. The posts are left long and are cut down to size after the boards have been fixed to allow for the ventilation gaps between the boards. The bin is held together with coach screws, and G-cramps are useful for holding the boards squarely in place while they are being fixed. The coach screw heads are a decorative feature of this compost bin, and it is important that they line up with each other and are the same distance in from the corners.

At the front of the bin, the only fixed board is at the bottom. The other retainer boards slot into the groove between the posts and are built up to the height required. They are therefore easily removed to gain access to the bin contents when the time comes to fork out the rotted compost.

MATERIALS

Note: All timber is sawn and preservative-treated softwood

Part	Quantity	Material	Length
'LONG' BOARDS	9	150 × 25mm (6 × 1in)	915mm (36in)
'MIDDLE' BOARDS	6	As above	890mm (35in)
'SHORT' BOARDS	4	As above	865mm (34in)
RETAINER BOARDS	6*	As above	As above
POSTS	6	50 × 50mm (2 × 2in)	1220mm (48in)
COACH SCREWS	100	Zinc-plated steel	8 × 50mm ($\frac{5}{16}$ × 2in)

* Cut 7 retainer boards if you want the boards at the front to be level with the boards at the side and back

TOOLS

WORKBENCH (fixed or portable)

STEEL MEASURING TAPE

STEEL RULE

TRY SQUARE

PANEL SAW (or circular power saw)

MARKING GAUGE

POWER DRILL

DRILL BIT – approximately 6mm ($\frac{1}{4}$in) diameter to drill pilot holes for coach screws

SPANNER

ONE PAIR OF G-CRAMPS

---

1 Fixing the First Board to the Posts
A 'short' length of board is fixed to the two posts flush and square with the ends to form the bottom row of the back of the bin. Two coach screws at each end hold it in place.

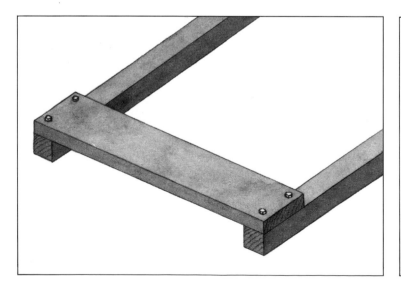

2 Adding the Side Posts and First Retainer Board
A 'long' board at both sides is screwed in place, flush with the ends of the posts. The first retainer board rests against the back of the front posts and is later screwed to the posts from behind.

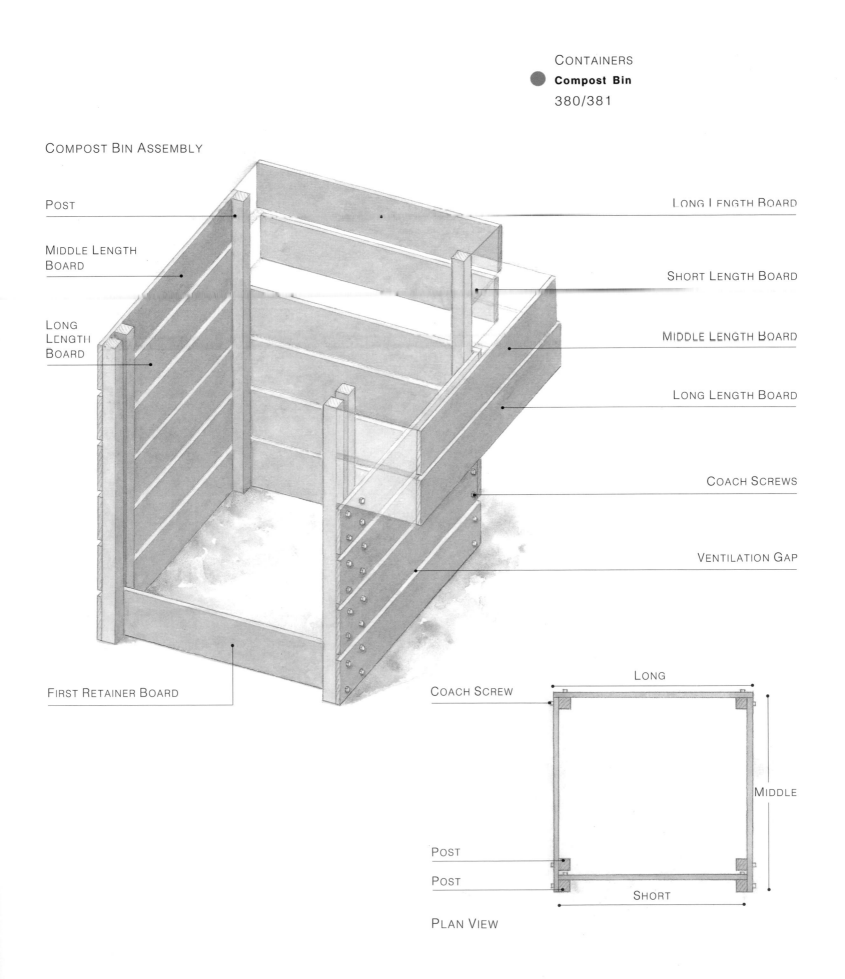

COMPOST BIN ASSEMBLY

POST

MIDDLE LENGTH BOARD

LONG LENGTH BOARD

FIRST RETAINER BOARD

LONG LENGTH BOARD

SHORT LENGTH BOARD

MIDDLE LENGTH BOARD

LONG LENGTH BOARD

COACH SCREWS

VENTILATION GAP

COACH SCREW

LONG

MIDDLE

POST

POST

SHORT

PLAN VIEW

COMPOST BIN

SQUARING THE FIRST ROW

Start to form the back of the bin by laying two of the posts on a flat surface. Then lay a 'short' length of board across them flush with the bottom ends of the posts, so the outer edges of the posts are 865mm (34in) apart (fig 1, page 380).

Check that the board is square to one of the posts, then cramp it to the post. Drill pilot holes for two coach screws and insert the screws to fix the board to the post.

Use a second board at the other end of the posts to ensure that they are square to the 'short' length of board, then double-check that the post is square to the first board using a try square. Drill pilot holes for the two coach screws to be inserted into the other end of the first board, the same distance in as the coach screws at the other end.

Stand the frame upright and place a 'long' board along the side, flush with the post, and secure it to the post with a G-cramp. Pilot drill and screw it to the post using two coach screws centred on the post.

Repeat for the other side with another 'long' length of board.

Place another post inside this board flush with the end, check that it is square at the top using another 'long' board, and screw into the post through the side board using two coach screws as before.

Take a retainer board and place it on the inside of the front posts (fig 2, page 380).

BUILDING UP THE ROWS OF BOARDS

Place spacing blocks or a spacing batten about 12–19mm ($\frac{1}{2}$–$\frac{3}{4}$in) thick on top of the back board, then lay a 'long' length of board across the top (fig 1). Check that it protrudes an equal distance beyond the outside edges of both the posts, then fix it in place with two coach screws at each end as before. For neatness, make sure that the coach screws line up with those on the board in the row below.

Repeat the process with one 'middle' length board on each side; these should both fit flush with the ends of the back board.

Continue working in this way, one row at a time so that the back boards run alternately with 'short'/ 'long' lengths, and the sides with 'long'/'middle' lengths to the height required. Ours is six boards high plus spaces.

As you work it is important to check that the structure is square by holding a spare board at the top flush with the posts each time a new board is added.

THE FRONT

With the bottom board at the front, screw through into the back of the front posts using two coach screws at each end.

Place the final two posts in position behind the coach screw heads, leaving at least a 12–19mm ($\frac{1}{2}$–$\frac{3}{4}$in) gap from the front board to create a slot in which the retainers will be a very loose fit. Hold a post in position on the side boards using a G-cramp, then mark a vertical line on the outside of the boards for the coach screw positions (fig 3).

Screw through each board into the post from the outside using two

coach screws per board. Repeat for the post on the other side.

Drop the retainer boards into the slots created by the two posts on each side, building the retainers up to the height required. If you want the retainers to finish level with the boards at the sides and back, rip cut the top one to size.

Finally, cut off the tops of the posts so that they are flush with the top edges of the boards.

Place the bin in an appropriate site away from general view. Almost all types of organic matter can be used for producing compost, although anything too bulky should be avoided because it will slow down the rate at which composting takes place. Similarly, large quantities of leaves also tend to slow the process, and are best kept to decompose separately. Farmyard manure, on the other hand, will accelerate production, and it is a good idea to add a layer of manure or proprietary compost accelerator to your bin every 125–200mm (5–8in). Your compost should be ready after six months or so.

---

1 Building Up the Rows of Boards
Use spacing blocks or a spacing batten to allow for ventilation gaps when fixing subsequent boards to the back and sides. Alternate 'short' and 'long' boards at the back, 'long' and 'middle' boards at the sides.

2 Back Corner Detail
Saw the posts so they are flush with top boards. Note that coach screws line up for a neat appearance.

3 Forming the Front Slot
A second post each side is screwed 38mm (1½in) behind front posts and retainer boards drop in place.

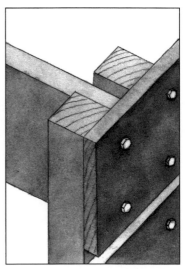

PLANTER

This planter allows you to grow trees, roses, shrubs and other flowers where normally you would not be able to, such as on a paved patio or on a concrete path or driveway. The planter is made from fencing-quality sawn and preservative-treated timber. Much of this is still sold in imperial sizes, although all suppliers will accept orders given in either imperial or metric units. Since the finished planter would be too heavy to lift, there is no need for a floor panel – the planter is placed where required, the planting compost is added and the tree or shrub is planted. There is normally room for other plants around the edge, which will enhance your display.

The size of these planters can be varied according to your specific needs – ours is 760mm (30in) square and 760mm (30in) high, which is a good size for medium-sized trees. For smaller shrubs and flowers you can make smaller planters, and if these are of a size

that will still be light enough to move when planted, then it is worth fixing a floor panel in the planter so that you can reposition it at will (see **Making a Floor Panel, page 385**).

The corner posts are extended upwards and are joined at the top by two cross pieces which form a useful tree support. The planter is held together with coach screws, and it is important that these should neatly align with each other.

POSTS – CUTTING THE TOP JOINTS

Cut the corner posts to length, and then use the clean sawn end of the post to mark out the top joint for housing the cross supports. Place the edge of a length of 75 × 25mm (3 × 1in) timber (cut from 150 × 25mm [6 × 1in]) centrally on the post end at a 45° angle and mark its position (fig 1).

Place the cross support 3mm ($\frac{1}{8}$in) down from the top of the post, ensure it is at right angles, and mark off the bottom edge. Square round on all four faces, then gauge lines down the sides of the post from those drawn at the top.

Cut down the marked lines on each side of the post with a tenon saw and use a coping saw to remove the centre section.

Repeat for other three posts.

MATERIALS

Note: All timber is sawn and preservative-treated softwood

Part	Quantity	Material	Length
'LONG' BOARDS	10	150 × 25mm (6 × 1in)	760mm (30in)
'SHORT' BOARDS	10	As above	710mm (28in)
CORNER POSTS	4	50 × 50mm (2 × 2in)	1350mm (53in)
CROSS SUPPORTS	2	150 × 25mm (6 × 1in) cut to 75 × 25mm (3 × 1in)	1220mm (48in) cut to length as required
COACH SCREWS	80	Zinc-plated steel	8 × 50mm ($\frac{5}{16}$ × 2in)

TOOLS

WORKBENCH (fixed or portable)

STEEL MEASURING TAPE

STEEL RULE

TRY SQUARE

COMBINATION SQUARE – for marking 45° angles

PANEL SAW (or circular power saw)

TENON SAW (or power jigsaw)

COPING SAW

MARKING GAUGE

POWER DRILL

DRILL BIT – approximately 6mm ($\frac{1}{4}$in) diameter to drill pilot holes for coach screws

SPANNER

ONE PAIR OF G-CRAMPS

HAMMER – if fitting floor panel

1 Marking Top Joint on Posts
Mark cross support centrally on post end at 45°. Gauge lines down post to marked position and remove centre.

2 Fixing the Second Frame to Form Main Construction
Fix 'short' boards flush with the ends of two lots of two posts. Screw 'long' boards to the sides of one frame, then place the second frame inside the 'long' boards so that the ends are square and flush.

PLANTER

MAIN CONSTRUCTION

Lay two of the corner posts on a flat surface and place a 'short' length of board across them flush with the ends so that the outer edges are 710mm (28in) apart.

Secure the board to the posts by drilling two pilot holes at one end, about 25mm (1in) from the end, and screw in two of the zinc-plated coach screws. For a neat finish try to ensure that each coach screw is the same distance from the edge.

Hold a spare board at the other end to make sure that the post is square, double check using a try square and secure the opposite end of the first board in the same way, drilling the holes the same distance in from the outside edge.

Repeat the process with the other two posts, fixing a 'short' board betweeen them at the base.

Stand one of the frames upright, and place a 'long' length of board along the side flush with the post and secure it in place using a G-cramp. Pilot hole and screw to the corner post with two coach screws centrally on the post. Repeat for the other side of the frame, using a 'long' length of board as before.

Place the other frame inside these 'long' boards, with the corner posts on the inside (fig 2, page 135). Fix the sides to the corner posts with two coach screws at each side.

BUILDING UP THE ROWS OF BOARDS

Take another 'short' length of board and place it on top of the fixed 'long' board so its ends are flush with the posts. Cramp the board to the posts using a pair of G-cramps and fix it in place with two coach screws at each end, aligning them with the screws on the board below.

Take a 'long' length of board and place it on the adjacent side so it overlaps the end of the short board (fig 1). Make sure the end is flush, then screw it into the corner post.

Continue in this way, one row at a time, so that the 'short'/'long' boards run alternately, and ends are visible on each side on alternate rows. Build to five boards high (or whatever height you have decided on). It is most important to check that the structure is square as you work: do this by holding a board at the top flush with the posts each time a board is added.

FIXING THE CROSS SUPPORTS

Measure diagonally across the corner posts at the top of the planter and add 50mm (2in) so that there will be an overhang at each end. Cut two lengths to this measurement from 75 × 25mm (3 × 1in) timber.

At the middle of these two cross supports, cut two cross halving joints (see **Techniques, page 400**) and slot together. Fit the cross supports into the slots in the corner posts and glue them in place (fig 3).

Unless you wish to colour the wood there is no need to apply a special finish, as preservative-treated timber is used for this project.

1 Building Up the Sides of the Planter
Build up the rows one at a time, fixing 'short' boards above 'long' boards and vice versa. Always check boards are square with the frame and ends are flush before screwing in place. Align screws with those on the boards below.

2 Joining the Cross Supports
Cut cross halving joints in the middle of the two cross supports so that they slot together.

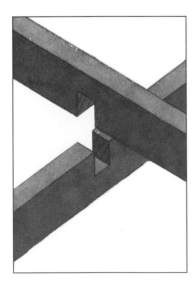

If you do want to change the colour of the wood, apply a water-repellent preservative wood stain of the desired shade. To avoid getting stain onto the coach screw heads, push lengths of plastic or rubber tubing over the heads before staining the planter.

MAKING A FLOOR PANEL

If a floor panel is required, screw 50 × 50mm (2 × 2in) battens to the inside of the planter at the base. Lay 150 × 25mm (6 × 1in) boards across the planter, resting on the battens. Space the boards so that there are narrow gaps about 3mm ($\frac{1}{8}$in) wide between them to allow drainage of excess water. To assist the base in supporting a heavy weight of soil, reinforce it with additional 50 × 50mm (2 × 2in) battens spaced about 225mm (9in) apart under the floor panel and running at right angles to it.

Move the planter to the chosen site before adding the soil and planting the tree or shrub. A layer of small stones at the bottom of the planter will assist drainage.

③ Fixing Supports to Posts
The cross supports fit into the slots cut in top of each post and protrude an equal distance. Glue in place.

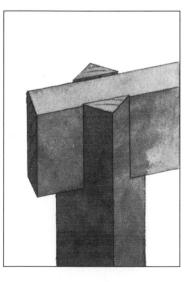

PLANTER ASSEMBLY

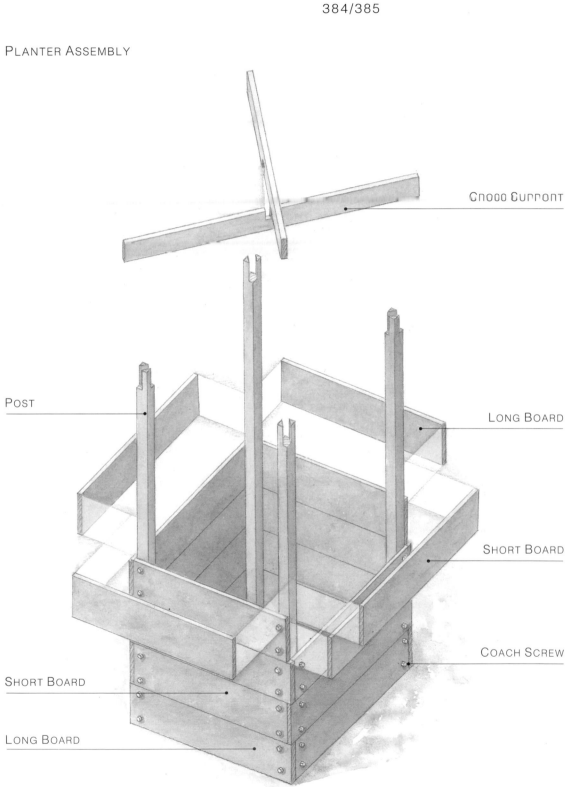

CROSS SUPPORT

LONG BOARD

POST

SHORT BOARD

COACH SCREW

SHORT BOARD

LONG BOARD

COLD FRAME

If you can't afford a greenhouse, a cold frame is the next best thing. Most important for raising seedlings or growing early vegetables, it can also be used to provide salad ingredients such as lamb's lettuce, broquette or treviso all through the winter: a year-round usage which makes it an invaluable addition to any garden. If you do have a greenhouse, a cold frame can be used to harden off bedding plants raised in the greenhouse and as a place for overwintering tender biennials.

The design of this cold frame varies little from the traditional version which is such a common garden sight. Extremely versatile and very simple to make, the wooden base is treated with exterior-grade preservative, contrasting with the crisp, white painted 'light' or glazed lid. An important feature of the design is the ability to remove the entire light so that there is free access to the area of ground covered by the cold frame, enabling it to be dug over and planted easily.

Cold frames should be sited in south-facing positions where they will receive maximum sunlight, but, because they are usually portable, the position can be varied from year to year. If there is a danger of scorching at the height of summer, the glass may need to be coated with white 'obscuring paint'.

Unlike traditional cloches or glass bell-jars, a cold frame can be made simply and economically to provide a versatile extension of the growing season.

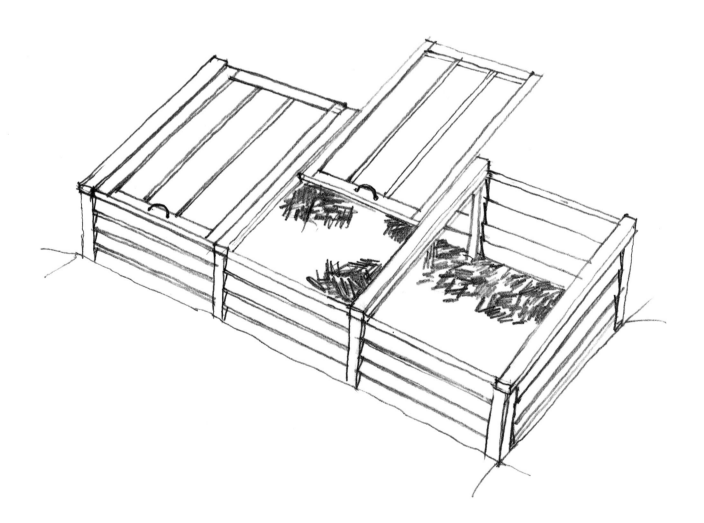

COLD FRAME

TOOLS

WORKBENCH (fixed or portable)

STEEL MEASURING TAPE

STEEL RULE

TRY SQUARE (or combination square)

PANEL SAW (or circular power saw)

TENON SAW

MARKING GAUGE

POWER DRILL

DRILL BIT – approximately 3mm ($\frac{1}{8}$in) diameter

COUNTERSINK BIT

SCREWDRIVER

CLAW HAMMER

NAIL PUNCH

PINCERS

CHISEL – about 25mm (1in)

MALLET

SASH CRAMPS (or folding wedges)

MATERIALS

Quantities are for the three-bay frame illustrated

Part	Quantity	Material	Length
FRAME STRUCTURE			
BOTTOM RAILS	4	50 × 50mm (2 × 2in) sawn and treated softwood	1220mm (48in)*
FRONT POSTS	4	As above	270mm (10$\frac{1}{2}$in)*
BACK POSTS	4	As above	400mm (16in)*
TOP RAILS	4	As above	1230mm (48$\frac{1}{2}$in)*
TOP SUPPORT BATTENS	6	25 × 25mm (1 × 1in) PAR softwood	1230mm (48$\frac{1}{2}$in)
FRONT FIXING BATTENS	6	As above	330mm (13in)*
BACK FIXING BATTENS	6	As above	460mm (18in)*
FRONT & BACK CLADDING	As required	6 × 19 × 150mm ($\frac{1}{4}$ × $\frac{3}{4}$ × 6in) feather-edge boarding	Width of glazing frame plus clearance
END CLADDING	As required	As above	1120mm (44in)
GLAZED LIGHTS			
SIDE RAILS	6	50 × 38mm (2 × 1$\frac{1}{2}$in) PAR softwood	1270mm (50in)
TOP RAILS	3	As above	800mm (31$\frac{1}{2}$in)
BOTTOM RAILS	3	75 × 25mm (3 × 1in) PAR softwood	800mm (31$\frac{1}{2}$in)
CENTRAL GLAZING BARS	3	38 × 25mm (1$\frac{1}{2}$ × 1in) PAR softwood	1270mm (50in)
GLASS SUPPORT BATTENS – LONG	12	25 × 12mm (1 × $\frac{1}{2}$in) PAR softwood	1150mm (46in)*
GLASS SUPPORT BATTENS – SHORT	6	As above	400mm (16in)*
GLASS SHEETS	18	Approx. 425 × 400mm (17 × 16in) clear glass	

Also required: 3 D-handles; metal glass clips; mastic for bedding glass; sprigs for holding glass in place; glazed light supports; hinges (optional)

* Leave overlength and then cut to size after fixing – see text

A cold frame will be appreciated by all keen gardeners, whether their speciality is flowers, fruit or vegetables. The frame will be useful for seedlings, propagation and for growing tender and/or early plants.

Our frame has been developed from the tried and tested standard cold frame that has evolved over the years. The main frame is made from sawn and preservative-treated (tanalized) softwood, put together in a series of inset 'bays' clad with feather-edge boarding fixed between the main frames. This gives the frame a distinctive style and avoids the bland appearance of a conventional cold frame. However, you may prefer to run the cladding along the whole length of the frame, which is quicker and easier.

The size of the frame from front to back and end to end is optional and can be varied as you wish according to what you want to grow. Our frame is a good average size, being 370mm (14$\frac{1}{2}$in) high at the front, 500mm (20in) high at the back and 1220mm (48in) from front to back. The beauty of this design is that you can have a single section, or make a block of two, three or more. We have built a three-section frame, and quantities in the Materials chart are for a frame of this size.

The glazed lights in our design are loose, giving flexibility in use. You have the option of sliding them back a little way for ventilation, farther back to tend for plants within the frame, or they can be lifted at the front and propped open a little way for ventilation. Alternatively, they are easy to slide off, either from the front or the back, allowing them to be removed completely. However, you could glaze the lights with sheets of clear plastic, which is also a safer option if young children play in the garden. In this case, you would fix the lights at the back with hinges; you will need a 75 × 50mm (3 × 2in) timber rail along the back, level with the support battens.

COLD FRAME ASSEMBLY

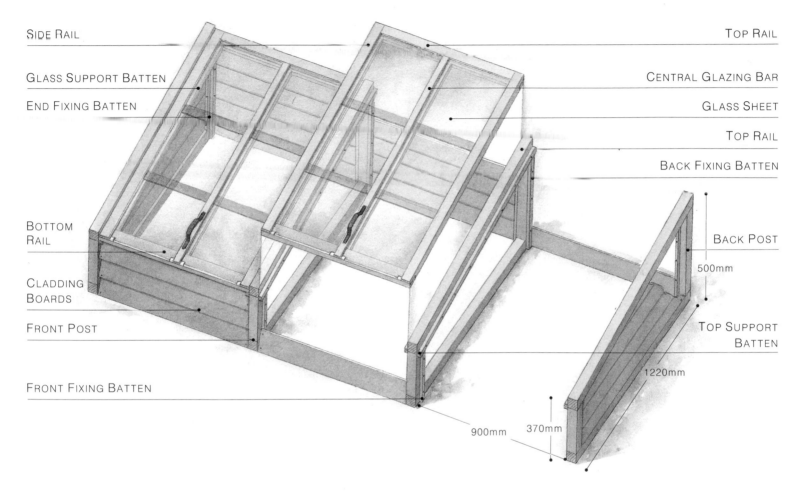

SIDE RAIL

GLASS SUPPORT BATTEN

END FIXING BATTEN

BOTTOM RAIL

CLADDING BOARDS

FRONT POST

FRONT FIXING BATTEN

TOP RAIL

CENTRAL GLAZING BAR

GLASS SHEET

TOP RAIL

BACK FIXING BATTEN

BACK POST

500mm

TOP SUPPORT BATTEN

1220mm

900mm   370mm

FRAME STRUCTURE

MAKING THE DIVIDERS

The ground frame structure is built around four dividers (if you are making a three-bay cold frame), and construction starts with these. Start by cutting out the four components of the dividers – the top and bottom rails, and the front and back posts – from 50 × 50mm (2 × 2in) sawn softwood all at least 50mm (2in) overlength.

Lay the bottom rail down and mark off its final length centrally on one side. Place the front and back posts in position alongside.

Mark off the final heights of the front and back posts, and then lay the top rail alongside these top marks (with the correct post heights on the outer edges of each) so that the correct angles to cut the tops of the posts can be marked. Cut the posts to length.

Nail up the frame by skew nailing through the bottom and top rails into the posts.

Once the frame has been finished, check it for square, then cut off the 'horns' (protruding ends) of the top and bottom rails so they are flush with the posts. Make up the required number of frames – four in our example.

SUPPORT AND FIXING BATTENS

Place an offcut of the 50 × 38mm (2 × 1½in) glazing frame side rail, 2mm (1/16in) down from the upper edge of the top rail to position the top support battens. You will need one on each side of the central dividing frames and on the inner sides of the end frames. Nail them in place, then saw the ends flush with the front and back posts.

Unless you are nailing the cladding in continuous lengths to the front and back of the dividing frames, you will need to nail fixing battens to the front and back posts.

Hold the battens in place so that the tops can be marked at the angle of the top support batten. Cut the battens to this angle, then screw them in place so that they are flush with the inside edges of the front and back posts (fig 1, page 390). Saw the ends of the battens flush with the bottom edge of the bottom rail. Fix side battens on both sides of the dividing frames, and on the inner sides of the end frames.

To support the cladding at the ends, measure internal heights of the front and back posts on the end frame. Cut battens to these lengths and fix to the inside edges of the end frames (fig 2, page 390).

COLD FRAME

GLAZED LIGHTS

Cut out all the components. Each glazed light frame will require two sides, one top rail, one bottom rail and one central glazing bar (fig 3).

Mark out all the joints as shown (fig 3). The sides are jointed to the top rail using corner halving joints (*see* **Techniques, Halving joint, page 400**). The bottom rail is lapped on to the sides so that the bottom rail is on the underside.

The glazing bar is joined to the top rail with a T-halving joint and to the bottom rail with a lap joint on the *opposite* side (the underside) so that it laps on to the bottom rail as shown (fig 3).

Letter all the joints clearly to identify them for assembly, and then cut them all out.

MAKING UP THE GLAZED LIGHT FRAMES

Glue all the joints to the top and bottom rails, starting with the central glazing bar. Use a waterproof woodworking adhesive such as Cascamite. Turn the frame over so that it can be screwed together from the underside. Use a try square to make sure that the frame is square, and hold it with cramps to keep the joints tight while drilling two pilot holes and a countersink for each of the three top joints. Screw the top joints together.

Drill and screw the bottom corner joints with three screws each. Measure to check that the central glazing bar is central on the bottom rail, then drill two holes and screw the bar to the bottom rail.

Lay the frame on a flat surface and check it is square by measuring the diagonals. Then nail on a bracing batten to keep the frame square while the glue is drying. Clean off any excess glue with a damp cloth and leave the joints to dry.

Repeat the process for the required number of frames – in this case three.

GLASS SUPPORT BATTENS

Cut four lengths of 25 × 12mm (1 × $\frac{1}{2}$in) batten to the internal length of the glazing frame and nail them so that they are flush with the underside of the frame.

Then cut two lengths to the internal widths between the side battens at the top. Nail the battens at the top between the two pairs of side battens, with the lower edge flush with the underside of the frame.

Repeat for the other frames.

CLADDING

Although we used feather-edge boarding for cladding the frame, other cladding boards could equally well be used – for example, shiplap, tongued-and-grooved, or V-jointed.

For the sides, cut the cladding to the internal dimensions of the end frames. Fix the cladding, working up from the bottom board, nailing into the fixing battens. When using feather-edge boards, the cladding boards should overlap by about 12mm ($\frac{1}{2}$in), and the nails holding the lower edge of each board should pass through the top edge of the board beneath to hold it securely. Use galvanized round head nails. When fixing the end cladding, the top boards must be shaped to the slope of the top rail.

The front and back cladding boards are cut to fit between the dividing frames so that the glazed frames, when fitted, will be a loose fit. You will need to leave enough clearance to allow for the timber to swell when it gets wet. Check that the main dividers are spaced so that there is about 2mm ($\frac{1}{16}$in) clearance between the dividers and the sides of the glazing frames so that they will slide easily.

Nail the cladding boards to the front and back fixing battens, working up from the bottom boards as before. The upper corners at each end of the top boards will have to be notched out so that the cladding boards will fit tightly around the top support battens.

If you are fixing the front and back cladding in a continuous strip, dispense with the front and back fixing battens, and nail the cladding boards directly to the front and back posts of the dividing frames. If the boards are of insufficient length to

1 **Fitting the Top Support Batten and Side Fixing Battens**
Left Detail shows spacing block held 2mm ($\frac{1}{16}$in) down from top rail to position top support batten. *Below* Top support batten runs length of top rail; side fixing battens fit flush with inside edges of front and back posts and are angled at top to fit beneath top support battens.

2 **Fixing End Battens**
Cut end panel fixing battens to internal heights of posts, and fit flush to inside edges of frame.

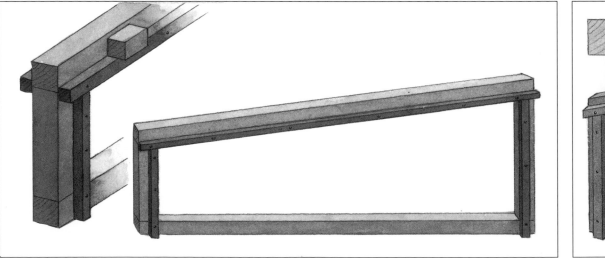

③ Making the Frames for the Glazed Lights
Top Corner halving joints fit side rails to top rail; T-halving joint fits glazing bar to top rail; lap bottom rail to underside of side rails and glazing bar.
Below Glue and screw from underside; bracing batten holds frame square.

clad the frame in continuous strips, shorter lengths of cladding boards can be used: simply butt joint them together so that the joint coincides with the mid-point of a front or back post. Stagger these joints so they do not line up with joints in boards directly above or below.

PRESERVING AND FINISHING OFF

It is most important to treat the whole of the frame assembly with at least two coats of clear or green grade wood preservative. When dry, this can then be painted with a micro-porous or exterior gloss paint, or it can be treated with a water-repellent preservative stain if a natural wood colour is required. You must not use creosote or any wood preserver that is harmful to plants.

FITTING THE GLASS, HANDLES AND HINGES

Have the glass cut to fit the glazed frames. We had ours cut in three sheets on each side, with the bottom sheet feeding first and subsequent sheets overlapping the previously fixed sheet. The bottom sheet is held by small aluminium clips, nailed to the bottom glazing frame rail and bent back over the edge of the glass to prevent it from slipping out. All the sheets are bedded into mastic on the glazing support battens. The glass sheets are held with small nails, called glazing sprigs, nailed into the side rails so that they are horizontal and hold the glass down. The bottom edges of the overlapping sheets of glass rest against two glazing sprigs which prevent the sheets from sliding down.

As an alternative to glass, the lights can be glazed with clear plastic sheeting, which is cheaper and much safer. Make sure that you buy purpose-made horticultural plastic which will encourage the plants to thrive and will also prevent premature yellowing and cracking of the plastic. Do *not* buy plastic containing an ultra-violet (UV) inhibitor as nothing will be able to grow in the cold frame.

To make it easier to lift the glazed lights for ventilation and access to the plants, screw a D-handle into the bottom end of the glazing bar.

If the glazed lights are left loose, they can be lifted at the front edge and wedged open with a wooden block for ventilation; the lights can also be slid backwards or forwards to gain access to inside the frame.

Alternatively, the glazed lights can be hinged at the back, and this is a particularly good option when the lights are glazed with plastic and are therefore lighter. In this case, cut a 75 × 50mm (3 × 2in) batten to the total length of the frame and bevel the top edge to allow the glazed light to fold back beyond 90° (so that it will rest open against a wall or fence behind the frame). With the batten level with the top support battens, screw it to the back posts. Then screw hinges into the back edges of the glazing frames, and into the top edge of the bevelled batten (*see* **Techniques, page 400**).

A simple ventilation prop can be made from a 150 × 100 × 50mm (6 × 4 × 2in) timber block with 25mm (1in) steps cut along one edge to allow variable ventilation up to 150mm (6in). Another method is to fix a swing-down prop to hold the glazed light partially open. The prop can be fixed to the underside of the central glazing bar and held out of the way in a spring tool clip when not in use.

If the frame is glazed with plastic lights and hinged at the back, fix hooks and eyes to the front edge of the frame to hold the lights firmly closed in windy conditions.

The frame should be positioned in a sunny place, and can simply be rested on the soil. Alternatively, you could place it on a partially buried row of bricks which will help to keep the timber dry. If the frame is to be permanently sited, it should be placed on a strip of damp-proof course placed on two rows of bricks over a concrete foundation. Fix the frame using expanding wall bolts inserted into the brick foundation through the bottom rails, or you could use metal strips screwed to the foundation and to the inside of the frame structure.

④ Glass Support Battens
Cut side battens to internal lengths of frame and top battens to internal length between side battens.

Tools for Preparation

Bench stop and vice A vice is fitted to the underside of a bench, the jaws level with the bench top. The jaws are lined and topped with hardwood to protect the work and any tools being used. Some vices incorporate a small steel peg (a 'dog') that can be raised above the main jaw level. This allows awkward pieces of wood to be cramped in position when used with a bench stop fixed at the opposite end of the bench.

Drill stand Enables a power drill to be used with extreme accuracy when, for example, dowel jointing. The hole will be perpendicular to the surface and its depth can be carefully controlled. The drill is lowered on to the work with a spring-loaded lever which gives good control.

Sliding bevel This is a type of square used to mark out timber at any required angle.

Marking gauge This is used to mark both widths and thicknesses with only a light scratch. The gauge comprises a handle, on which slides a stock bearing a steel marking pin which can be fixed at a precise point.

Mortise gauge Similar to a marking gauge, it has two pins, one fixed, one adjustable, to mark out both sides of a mortise at the same time.

Marking knife Used to score a thin line for a saw or chisel to follow, ensuring a precise cut.

Mitre box A simple open-topped wooden box which is used to guide saws into materials at a fixed 45° or 90° angle, to ensure an accurate cut.

Plumb bob and chalk Used to check or mark accurate vertical lines on walls. A plumb bob is simply a pointed weight attached to a long length of string. The string can be rubbed with a stick of coloured chalk to leave a line on the wall.

Portable workbench A collapsible, portable workbench is vital for woodworking. It is lightweight and can be carried to the job, where it provides sturdy support. A portable bench is like a giant vice — the worksurface comprises two sections which can be opened wide or closed tightly according to the dimensions of the work and the nature of the task.

Spirit level Used for checking that surfaces are horizontal or vertical. A 1000mm (39in) long level is the most useful all-round size. An aluminium or steel level will withstand knocks and it can be either I-girder or box-shaped in section. A 250mm (10in) 'torpedo' spirit level is useful for working in confined spaces and can be used with a straight-edge over longer surfaces.

Steel measuring tape A 3m (3yd) or 5m (5yd) long, lockable tape (metal or plastic) is best, and one with a top window in the casing makes it easier to read measurements.

Steel rule Since the rule is made of steel, the graduations are indelible and very precise. A rule graduated on both sides in metric and imperial is the most useful. The rule also serves as a precise straight-edge for marking cutting lines.

Straight-edge Can be made from a length of 50×25mm (2×1in) scrap wood. It is used in combination with a spirit level to tell whether a surface is flat and also for checking whether two points are aligned with each other.

Try square An L-shaped precision tool comprising a steel blade and stock (or handle) set at a perfect right angle to each other on both the inside and outside edges. Used for marking right angles and for checking a square.

Combination square A versatile measuring and marking tool comprising a steel rule, try square, mitre square and spirit level.

Tools for Sharpening and Cutting

Chisels Used to cut slots in wood or to pare off thin slivers. Some chisels may be used with a mallet when cutting slots. When new, a chisel's cutting edge is ground and must be honed with an oilstone to sharpen it before use.
Mortise chisel Used for cutting deep slots.
Firmer chisel For general DIY use.
Bevel-edge chisel Used for undercutting in confined spaces.
Paring chisel Has a long blade for cutting deep joints or long housings.

Dowelling jig Cramps on to a piece of work, ensuring that the drill is aligned over the centre of the dowel hole to be drilled.

Drills

Hand drill For drilling holes for screws or for making large holes, particularly in wood. It will make holes in metal and is useful where there is no power source. A handle attached to a toothed wheel is used to turn the drill in its chuck.
Power drill These range from a simple, single-speed model (which will drill holes only in soft materials) to a multi-speed drill with electric control. Most jobs call for something in between, such as a two-speed drill with hammer action.

Drill Bits

You will need a selection of drill bits in various sizes and of different types for use with a drill.

Auger bit Has a tapered, square shank that fits into a carpenter's brace. It is used to make deep holes in wood, the usual lengths being up to 250mm (10in). Diameters range from 6mm ($\frac{1}{4}$in) to 38mm ($1\frac{1}{2}$in). The tip has a screw thread to draw the bit into the wood.
Countersink bit After a hole is drilled in wood, a countersink bit is used to cut a recess for the screwhead to sit in, so ensuring that it lies below the surface. Different types are available for use with a carpenter's brace or a power drill.
Dowel bit Used to make dowel holes. The top has two cutting spurs on the side and a centre point to prevent the bit from wandering off centre.
End-mill/Hinge-sinker bit Primarily used for boring flat-bottomed holes to accept the hinge bosses on concealed hinges. End-mills are used in electric drills, ideally fitted in drill stands, and should be set to drill no deeper than 12mm ($\frac{1}{2}$in).
Flat bit Is used with a power drill. For maximum efficiency the bit must be turned at high speed from about 1000 to 2000 r.p.m. It drills into cross grain, end grain and man-made boards.
Masonry bit Has a specially hardened tungsten-carbide tip for drilling into masonry to the exact size required for a wallplug. Special percussion drill bits are available for use with a hammer drill when boring into concrete.
Twist drill bit Used with a power drill for drilling small holes in wood and metal.

Power router This portable electric tool is used to cut grooves, recesses, and many types of joints in timber, and to shape the edge of long timber battens. A range of cutting bits in different shapes and sizes is available and when fitted into the router the bits revolve at very high speed.

SAWS

Circular saw For cutting large pieces of timber or sheets of board, as well as grooves and angles. The most popular size has a diameter of 184mm (7¼in). Circular saws can be extremely dangerous and must be used carefully. The piece of work must be held securely, supported on scrap battens, and the blade depth set so that it will not cut into anything below the work. The tool should be fitted with an upper and a lower blade guard.

Coping saw Used to make curved or circular cuts. It has a narrow blade, which can be swivelled. When cutting, the blade can be angled so that the frame clears the edge of the work.

Hacksaw For cutting metal. A traditional hacksaw has a wooden handle and a solid metal frame. The blade is tensioned by a wing-nut. Modern hacksaws have a tubular frame which is adjustable for different lengths of blade.

Jigsaw More versatile than a circular saw, although not as quick or powerful. It cuts curves, intricate shapes, angles and holes in a variety of materials. The best models offer variable speeds.

Padsaw Has a narrow, tapered blade to cut holes and shapes in wood. A hole is drilled and the saw blade is inserted to make the cut.

Panel saw A hand saw used for rough cutting rather than fine carpentry. It has a flexible blade of 510–660mm (20–26in).

Tenon saw For cutting the tenon part of a mortise and tenon joint, and for other delicate work. It has a stiffened back and the blade is about 250–300mm (10–12in) long.

Rasp A coarse file, available with flat or half-round surfaces, used to shape wood.

Surforms Available in a range of lengths from approximately 150–250mm (6–10in), these rasps are useful for the initial shaping of wood. The steel blade has a pattern of alternating small teeth and holes through which waste wood passes, so that the teeth do not get clogged up.

HAND TOOLS

Abrasive paper *see* **Sanding block**

CRAMPS

For securing glued pieces of work while they are setting. There are many types of cramp, but the G-cramp is the most commonly used and is available in a wide range of jaw sizes.

G-cramp Also called a C-cramp or fast-action cramp, it is important for our projects that the jaws of the cramp open at least 200mm (8in). The timber to be held in the cramp is placed between the jaws which are then tightened by turning a thumb-screw, tommy bar or other type of handle. With a fast-action cramp, one jaw is free to slide on a bar, and after sliding this jaw up to the workpiece, final tightening is achieved by turning the handle. To protect the work, scraps of wood are placed between it and the jaws of the cramp.

Sash cramps These employ a long metal bar, and are indispensable for holding together large frameworks, although you can improvise in some cases by making a rope tourniquet. This consists of a piece of rope which is tied around the object, and a length of stick to twist the rope and so cramp the frame tightly.

Webbing cramp The webbing, like narrow seat-belt type material, is looped around the frame, pulled as tight as possible by hand, and then finally tightened by means of a screw mechanism or ratchet winder.

HAMMERS

Claw hammer The claw side of the head of the hammer is used to extract nails from a piece of work, quickly and cleanly.

Cross-pein hammer The pein is the tapered section opposite the flat hammer head, and it is used for starting off small pins and tacks.

Pin hammer A smaller version of the cross-pein; this is useful for light work.

Hand staple gun A trigger-operated tool which fires a staple straight into a surface, usually fabric, fibreboard or thin wood over a wooden batten. Its advantage over conventional pinning with a hammer is that it is used one-handed.

Mallet Most commonly used to strike mortise chisels, although if a chisel has an impact-resistant handle then a hammer may also be used. The tapered wooden head ensures square contact with the object being struck.

Nail and pin punches Used with a hammer to drive nails and pins below the surface so that they are hidden and the holes can be filled.

Orbital sander This gives a fine, smooth surface finish to wood. A gritted sanding sheet is fitted to the sander's base plate. Sheets are graded from coarse to fine, and the grade used depends on the roughness of the surface to be sanded. Orbital sanders produce a great deal of dust, so always wear a mask when using one.

Paintbrushes A set of paintbrushes for painting and varnishing should ideally comprise three sizes – 25mm (1in), 50mm (2in) and 75mm (3in). A better finish is always achieved by matching the size of the brush to the surface – a small brush for narrow surfaces, a large brush for wide areas.

PLANES

Block plane Held in the palm of the hand, it is easy to use for small work and chamfering edges. Also useful for planing end grain.

Jack plane A good all-purpose tool with a long blade used for straightening long edges.

Power plane Finishes timber to precise dimensions. A one-hand model is lightweight and can be used anywhere, whereas the heavier two-hander is intended for workbench use. A power plane will also cut bevels and rebates.

Smoothing plane A general-purpose, hand-held plane for smoothing and straightening surfaces and edges. The plane is about 250mm (10in) long and its blade 50–60mm (2–2¼in) wide. The wider the blade the better the finish on wide timber. There is a fine adjustment for depth of cut and a lever for lateral adjustment.

Sanding block and abrasive paper A sanding block is used with abrasive paper to finish and smooth flat surfaces. The block is made of cork, rubber or softwood and the abrasive paper is wrapped around it. Make sure in doing so that the paper is not wrinkled. Coarse paper is used for a rough surface and fine paper for finishing.

Screwdrivers Come in many shapes and sizes, the main differences being the type of tip (for slotted or cross-point screws), the length, and the shape of the handle, which varies from straight or fluted to bulb-shaped.

Ideally, you should have a range of screwdrivers for dealing with all sizes of screws. Ratchet models, which return the handle to its starting point, are easy to operate since your hand grip does not need to change.

Spanner A spanner is required for tightening coach-bolts, and any type that fits the head of the bolt is suitable. If the correct-size open-ended or ring spanner is not available, any type of adjustable spanner may be used.

MATERIALS

TIMBER AND BOARDS

Timber This is classified into two groups – softwoods and hardwoods. Softwoods come from evergreen trees and hardwoods from deciduous trees. Check your timber for defects before buying it. Avoid wood which is badly cracked or split, although you need not be concerned about fine, surface cracks since these can be planed, sanded or filled. Do not buy warped wood, as it will be impossible to work with. Check for warping by looking along the length of a board to see if there is any bowing or twisting.

Wood for outdoor projects must be protected from rot and insect attack. It can be bought pre-treated with preservative, but this is expensive and not always readily available. Alternatively, you can buy untreated wood and treat it, as soon as possible, with one of the finishes described here. Pay special attention to end grain and to posts which will be buried below ground – a double coating is a good idea here.

Softwood Although usually referred to as 'deal' or 'pine', it comes from many different sources. Softwood is much less expensive than hardwood and is used in general building work. It is sold in a range of standard sizes. After 1.8m (6ft), lengths rise in 300mm (12in) increments up to 6.3m (20ft 8in). Standard thicknesses are from 12mm ($\frac{1}{2}$in) up to 75mm (3in) and widths range from 25mm (1in) to 225mm (9in).

It is important to remember that standard softwood sizes refer to sawn sizes – that is, how it is sawn at a mill. Sawn timber is suitable for most of the projects in this book. However, where a smooth finish is specified, where appearance and accuracy are important, it will need to be planed. Such wood is referred to as PAR (planed all round), and, since planing takes a little off each face, it is approximately 5mm ($\frac{3}{16}$in) smaller in width and thickness than stated.

Hardwood Expensive and not as easy to obtain as softwoods, hardwoods often have to be ordered or bought from a specialist timber merchant. Many timber yards will machine hardwood to your exact specification.

Boards Mechanically made from wood and other fibres, they are versatile, relatively inexpensive, made to uniform quality and available in large sheets. You need to know the advantages of each type of board before making your choice.

Plywood Made by gluing thin wood veneers together in plies (layers) with the grain in each ply running at right angles to that of its neighbours. This gives it strength and helps prevent warping. The most common boards have three, five or seven plies. Plywood is graded for quality: A is perfect; B is average; and BB is for rough work only. Usual thicknesses of plywood are 3mm, 6mm, 12mm and 19mm ($\frac{1}{8}$in, $\frac{1}{4}$in, $\frac{1}{2}$in and $\frac{3}{4}$in). WBP (weather and boil proof) grade board must be used for exterior work.

Blockboard Made by sandwiching natural timber strips between wood veneers, the latter usually of Far Eastern redwood or plain birch. Although plain birch is a little more expensive than redwood it is of a much better quality. Blockboard is very strong, but can leave an ugly edge when sawn, making edge fixings difficult. Blockboard is graded in the same way as plywood and common thicknesses are 12mm, 19mm and 25mm ($\frac{1}{2}$in, $\frac{3}{4}$in and 1in).

Tongued-and-grooved boarding Also called match boarding, or matching, this is widely used for cladding frameworks. The boarding has a tongue on one side and a slot on the other side. The tongue fits into the slot of the adjacent board; this join expands and contracts according to temperature and humidity without cracks opening up between boards. Make sure you use exterior grade boarding for outdoor projects.

Feather-edge boards These taper from a thick edge across to a thin edge. When fixed in place, the thick edge of one board overlaps the thin edge of the next board.

ADHESIVES AND FILLERS

Adhesives Modern adhesives are strong and efficient. If they fail, it is because the wrong adhesive is being used or the manufacturer's instructions are not being followed carefully. For outdoor woodworking, you must always use either a synthetic resin adhesive that is mixed with water (this has gap-filling properties, so is useful where joints are not cut perfectly) or a two-part epoxy resin adhesive where the parts are applied separately to the surfaces being joined.

Fillers For outside work, always use an exterior grade filler which has been specially formulated to withstand the natural movement of cracks and holes caused by weather changes.

If the wood is to be painted over, use an exterior cellulose filler. This dries white and will be evident if used under any other kind of finish. When a clear finish is needed, fill cracks and holes with a proprietary wood filler or stopping. These are thick pastes and come in a range of wood colours. You can mix them together or add a wood stain if the colour you want is not available. Choose a colour slightly paler than the surrounding wood, since fillers tend to darken when the finish is applied. Some experimentation may be needed on a waste piece of matching wood.

FINISHES

The choice of finish is determined by whether the wood or board is to be hidden, painted or enhanced by a protective clear finish.

Paint A liquid gloss (oil-based) paint is suitable for wood, and is applied after undercoat. Generally, two thin coats of gloss are better than one thick coat. Non-drip gloss is an alternative. It has a jelly-like consistency and does not require an undercoat, although a second coat may be needed for a quality finish. If you intend to spray the paint, you must use a liquid gloss.

Microporous paint This is applied directly to the wood – neither primer nor undercoat is needed. The coating will not flake or blister as the special formulation allows trapped moisture to evaporate. If applied over old gloss paint, it will lose the quality that prevents flaking or blistering.

Preservative Unless timber has been pre-treated with preservative and it is not to receive an alternative decorative finish, you must use a coat of preservative. Modern water-based preservatives are harmless to plant life. They are available in clear, green and a number of natural wood colours. The preservative sinks well into the wood, preventing rot and insect attack.

Varnish For outdoor use, you must always use an exterior grade varnish – stated on the container – or a yacht varnish. It is available as a gloss, satin or matt finish, all clear. Varnish also comes in a range of colours, so that you can change the colour of the wood and protect it simultaneously. The colour does not sink into the wood, so if the surface becomes scratched or marked then its original colour will show through. A wood stain or dye can be used to change the colour of wood. It sinks into the wood, but offers no protection, so varnish is also needed.

CONCRETE

Concrete Made by mixing Portland cement and ballast (a mixture of sand and aggregates) with water. The usual mix for paths, bases and foundations is one part cement to four parts ballast. Although concrete mix is available dry-mixed in bags, it is only economically viable for small jobs. Concrete can be mixed by hand, but it is an arduous task, and it is advisable to hire a small electric mixer.

Precast concrete paving slabs These come in a range of shapes and sizes with 450mm square (18in square) being the most popular, since anything larger is difficult to handle. There is a limited range of colours, and surface finishes are smooth, patterned or textured. Thicknesses are usually 35–40mm (about $1\frac{1}{2}$in).

Bricks and **Mortar** *see* **Techniques: Brick-laying, pages 156–7**

DIVIDERS

Fences Required principally to mark boundaries and to create privacy and security. Among the most popular types are:
Vertical closeboard A solid, secure fence which can be of any height. Feather-edge boards are nailed to horizontal arris rails which, in turn, are fixed to timber or solid concrete posts.
Waney-edged panels Pre-fabricated panels made from larch or pine planks which overlap horizontally. The panels are normally 1800mm (72in) wide and 600–1800mm (24–72in) high, and are fixed to timber or concrete support posts.
Palisade Vertical timber pales (stakes) nailed to arris rails at 50mm (2in) intervals and in turn fixed to timber posts. Pales can have ornate or square tops. Heights vary, but 900mm (36in) is the most popular. Usually used for front gardens.
Ranch-style Horizontal timber rails nailed at intervals to timber posts. A two-rail fence is usually about 1000mm (39in) high; a four-rail fence is about 1300mm (51in) high.
Chain link A secure fence, 900–3600mm (36–144in) high. The metal mesh can be galvanized or plastic-coated. Posts are iron or concrete.
Plastic wire Ornamental fencing commonly used to mark a boundary or surround a fish pond or herbaceous border. The fencing can be fixed directly into the ground, but it should be fixed to posts if it is over 600mm (24in) high. It is sold in rolls and cut to the required length.

Rustic poles Hazel, birch or chestnut poles are available from garden centres. Diameters generally range from 50–125mm (2–5in). You will need the larger sizes for main uprights and bearers and the thinner ones for cross beams. The poles have bark attached; this will peel off in own time.

Trellising Square trellis is available in panel heights from 600–1220mm (24–48in) and in 1800mm (72in) long sections. The squares are each about 150mm (6in) and the trellis is made from hardwood battens. Diamond trellis comes in heights from 300–1220mm (12–48in) and lengths of 1800mm (72in).

FIXINGS

The choice of fixing depends on the size and weight of the materials being fixed.

Nails For general-purpose frame construction.
Round wire nails With large, flat, circular heads, these are used for strong joins where frames will be covered, so that the ugly appearance of the nails does not matter.
Annular ring-shank nails Used where really strong fixings are required.
Round lost-head nails or **oval brads** (*oval wire nails*) Used when the finished appearance is important.
Panel pins For fixing thin panels, these have unobtrusive heads that can be driven in flush with the wood's surface or punched below it.
Masonry nails For fixing timber battens to walls as an alternative to screws and wallplugs.

Screws All types of screws are available with conventional slotted heads or cross-point heads. The latter are the best type to use if you are inserting screws with an electric screwdriver.

For most purposes, screws with countersunk heads are ideal as the head lies flush with the surface after insertion. Round-head screws are for fixing metal fittings such as door bolts, which have punched-out rather than countersunk screw holes. Raised-countersunk head screws are used where a neat appearance is important.
Wood screws These have a length of smooth shank just below the head. This produces a strong cramping effect, but there is a possibility of the unthreaded shank splitting the wood.
Twin-thread screws Less likely to split wood than wood screws. Except for larger sizes, they are threaded along their entire length, giving an excellent grip in timber and boards.

Coach screws For heavy-duty fixings when making frameworks requiring a strong construction. The screws have square or hexagonal heads and are turned with a spanner. A washer is used to prevent the head cutting into the timber.

Wallplugs Use a masonry drill bit to drill a hole which matches the size of screw being used (a No 10 bit with a No 10 screw, for example). Insert the plug in the hole, then insert the screw through the object being fixed and into the plug.

Wall anchor bolt Similar to a wallplug, but with its own heavy-duty machine screw. You need to make a much larger hole in the wall, typically 10mm ($\frac{3}{8}$in) in diameter. The anchor sleeve expands in the hole as the bolt is tightened.

Expanding wall bolt This comprises a segmented body which expands as the bolt inside it is tightened. The body grips concrete, brick or stone securely. There are various lengths and diameters and there are also versions containing a hook or an eye. Most bolts are zinc-plated, but aluminium bronze versions are available where greater resistance to corrosion is required.

Corrugated fasteners For strengthening glued joints in frameworks. Sizes are 6–22mm ($\frac{1}{4}$–$\frac{7}{8}$in) deep and 22–30mm ($\frac{7}{8}$–$1\frac{1}{4}$in) long.

Staples A useful means for quickly anchoring plastic mesh fencing to timber posts.

Battens A general term used to describe a narrow strip of wood. The usual sizes are 25 × 25mm (1 × 1in) or 50 × 25mm (2 × 1in).

Battens can be screwed to a wall to serve as bearers for shelves or they can be fixed in a framework on a wall, with sheet material or boards mounted over them to form a new 'wall'.

Dowels Used to make framework joints or to join boards edge-to-edge or edge-to-face.

Hardwood dowels are sold in diameters ranging from 6–10mm ($\frac{1}{4}$–$\frac{3}{8}$in). Generally speaking, dowel lengths should be about one-and-a-half times the thickness of the boards being joined.

Dowels are used with adhesive and, when the joint is complete, it is important to let excess adhesive escape from the joint. Dowels with fluted (finely grooved) sides and chamfered ends will help this process. If you have plain dowels, make fine sawcuts along the length yourself.

TECHNIQUES: SAWING AND CUTTING

MEASURING AND MARKING SQUARE

Mark the cutting lines lightly with a hard pencil first, and then use a marking knife, straight–edge or try square along a steel rule to create a sharp, splinter-free line.

To mark timber square, use a try square with the stock (handle) pressed against a flat side of the timber, called the face side or face edge. Mark a line along the square, using a knife in preference to a pencil, then use the square to mark lines down the edges from the face mark. Finally square the other face side, checking that the lines join up right around the timber.

If you are measuring and marking a number of pieces of the same length, then cramp them together and mark across several of them at the same time.

SPACING BATTEN

This is simply an offcut of wood, about 19mm or 25mm square ($\frac{3}{4}$in or 1in square), which is used to ensure that any slats to be fixed across a frame are spaced an equal distance apart. To ascertain the length to cut the spacing batten, simply bunch all the slats at one end of the frame. Measure to the other end of the frame and divide by the number of spaces (which you can count while you have the slats laid side by side). The resulting measure is the length to cut the spacing batten, which is used to position each slat exactly.

BRACING

When making a frame, it is vital that it should be square, with corners at perfect right angles. You can ensure this by using one of two bracing methods.

3-4-5-method Measure three units along one rail, four units down the adjacent rail, then nail a bracing batten accurately to one of the unit marks. Pull into square so that the bracing batten measures five units at the other unit mark, forming the hypotenuse of the triangle. Saw off the batten ends flush with the frame, but do not remove the batten until the frame is fitted in place.

Try square method Nail a batten into one rail, pull into square by using a try square, and then nail the batten into the adjacent rail.

MAKING FOLDING WEDGES

Folding wedges are very useful for cramping large frames on a bench top during assembly. The wedges are always used in pairs, but more than one pair may be used to hold a large framework.

Make each pair of wedges from a piece of timber (hardwood is an ideal material for this) measuring $38 \times 38 \times 330$mm ($1\frac{1}{2} \times 1\frac{1}{2} \times 13$in). Make the wedges by sawing the timber diagonally into two pieces.

To use the wedges, a wooden batten is first nailed to the bench and the item to be cramped is placed against the batten. Another batten is nailed to the bench, parallel with the first, and about 45mm ($1\frac{3}{4}$in) away from the item. The wedges are now placed between the item and the second batten. Next, the ends of the wedges are knocked inwards with two hammers, thereby cramping the frame.

SAWING AND CUTTING

Cross-cutting to length by hand Hold the timber firmly with the cutting line (see **Measuring and Marking Square,** above) overhanging the right-hand side of the bench (if you are right-handed). With the saw blade vertical and the teeth on the waste side of the line, draw the handle back to start the cut. To prevent the saw jumping out of place, as you start hold the thumb joint of the other hand against the side of the saw blade.

Rip-cutting by hand With the timber or board supported at about knee height, start the cut as described above, then saw down the waste side of the line, exerting pressure on the down cut only. If the saw blade wanders from the line, cramp the edge of a timber batten exactly above the cutting line on the side to be retained, and saw along it.

Using a portable power saw If the cutting line is only a short distance from a straight edge, adjust

---

1 Marking Timber to Length and Square All Round
Mark across the face of the timber with a trimming knife held against a try square blade. Move knife around corners and mark sides, and finally mark other side to join up the lines.

2 Using Spacing Battens
Measure distance from bunched slats to frame end. Divide by number of spaces to get spacing batten size.

3 Making Folding Wedges
Saw wood diagonally. Nail batten to bench; wedges fit between batten and item being cramped.

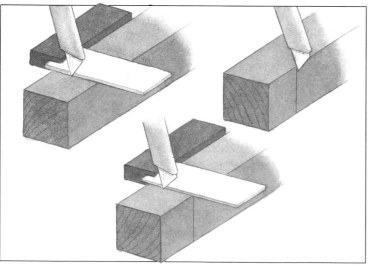

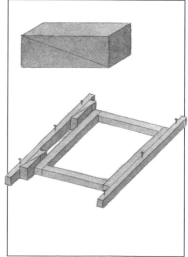

the saw's fence so that when it is run along the edge of the timber, the blade will cut on the waste side of the cutting line. If the timber is wide, or the edge is not straight, cramp a batten to the surface so that the saw blade will cut on the waste side of the line when run along the batten.

Ensuring a straight cut When cutting panels or boards using a power circular saw or jigsaw, the best way to ensure a straight cut is to cramp a guide batten to the surface of the work, parallel with the cutting line, so the edge of the saw sole plate can be run along the batten. The batten position is carefully adjusted so that the saw blade cuts on the waste side of the cutting line. Depending on which side of the cutting line the batten is cramped, when using a circular saw, it is possible the motor housing will foul the batten or G-cramps used to hold it in place. In this case, replace the batten with a wide strip of straight-edged plywood cramped to the work far enough back for the motor to clear the cramps.

4 **Cross-cutting to Length**
Hold the timber firmly. Steady the saw blade with the thumb joint as you start to saw.

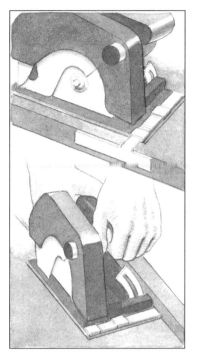

5 **Straight Power-Saw Cutting**
Top Use the rip fence of the saw if cutting near the edge. *Above* Cutting alongside the batten as a guide for obtaining a straight cut.

6 **Cutting with a Tenon Saw**
Start the cut as for a hand saw. As the cut progresses keep the blade horizontal.

CUTTING A CIRCLE

With a coping saw Mark out the circle, score the cutting line, and drill a hole about 10mm (⅜in) in diameter just on the inside of the circle. Disconnect the blade from one end of the frame, pass the blade through the hole, and re-connect it to the frame. It will be best to cramp the piece of work vertically when cutting the circle. The blade can be turned in the frame to help the frame clear the piece of work, but even so, with a coping saw you will be restricted in exactly how far you are able to reach away from the piece of work. If the circle is some way from the edge, use a padsaw to cut it.

With a padsaw A padsaw, also called a keyhole saw, has a stiff, triangular pointed saw blade attached to a simple handle. A very useful padsaw blade is available for fitting in a regular knife handle.

Because this saw has no frame, it is ideal for cutting circles and other apertures, like keyholes, anywhere in a panel.

7 **Straight Rip-cutting**
Cramp a straight batten alongside the cutting line and saw beside the batten. A wedge holds the cut open.

Preparation of the circle for cutting is the same as for a coping saw. When cutting with a padsaw, keep the blade vertical and make a series of rapid, short strokes without exerting too much pressure.

CUTTING GROOVES

By hand Start by marking out the groove with a marking knife. Hold the piece of work on a bench and, with a tenon saw, make vertical cuts just inside the marked lines to the depth of the groove. If the groove is wide, make a series of other vertical cuts in the waste wood. Now chisel out the waste, working from each side to the middle. Finally, with the flat side of the chisel downwards, pare the bottom of the groove so that it is perfectly flat.

With a router Use a straight-sided router bit set to the depth required for the groove. Ideally, the bit should be the exact width of the groove. Make the cut along the waste side of the line with a batten cramped in place to guide the base of the router.

8 **Cutting Circles by Hand**
1 Drill a small hole and cut circle using a padsaw. *2* Making cut with a coping saw.

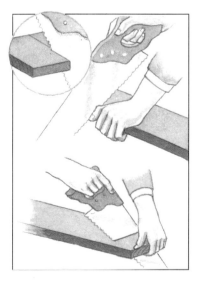

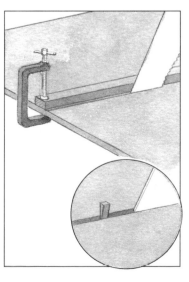

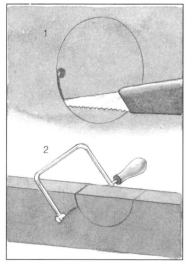

Techniques: Drilling and Fixings

Cutting Rebates

A rebate is an L-shaped step in the edge of a piece of timber.

By hand Use a marking gauge to mark the rebate width across the top face of the piece of work and down both sides. Mark the depth of the rebate across the end and sides.

Hold the timber flat and saw down on the waste side of the marked line to the depth of the rebate. Chisel out the waste one bit at a time along the end grain.

With a router It is not necessary to mark out the rebate unless you want a guide to work to. However, do practise on scrap wood to be sure of setting the router correctly.

If using a straight cutter, adjust the guide fence on the router so that the correct width is cut, then plunge and adjust the cutting depth so that the router will cut to the correct depth. When the router is correctly set up, simply hold it flat on the piece of work and move it against the direction of the cutter's rotation.

If you are using a cutter with a guide pin, simply adjust the depth of cut and then run the cutter along the edge of the wood to form the rebate. The cutter will follow irregularities in the wood, so make sure your wood is perfectly straight.

Planing

By hand Make sure that the plane blade is sharp and properly adjusted. Stand to one side of the work with feet slightly apart so you are facing the work. Plane from one end of the work to the other, starting the cut with firm pressure on the leading hand, transferring it to both hands, and finally to the rear hand as the cut is almost complete. Holding the plane at a slight angle to the direction of the grain may improve the cutting action.

With a power plane Remove loose clothing, and wear goggles and a dust mask. Cramp the work in place. Start the plane and turn the adjuster knob to set the depth. Start with a shallow cut and increase the depth if necessary.

Stand comfortably to one side of the work and, holding the plane with two hands, set it into the work at one end and pass it over the surface to the other end. When you have finished, switch off and make sure the blades stop spinning before resting the plane down with the cutting depth at zero.

Drilling

To minimize the risk of splitting timber, drill pilot and clearance holes for screws.

The **clearance hole** in the timber should be fractionally smaller in diameter than the screw shank.

The **pilot hole** to receive the screw should be about half the diameter of the clearance hole. The hole depth should be slightly less than the length of the screw.

To ensure that screwheads lie level with the surface of plywood, chipboard and hardwood use a **countersink drill bit**.

Drilling vertical holes To ensure vertical holes mount the drill in a stand. If this is not possible,

stand a try square on edge so that its stock is resting on the work alongside the drilling position, and the blade is pointing up in the air. Use this as a siting guide and line up the drill as close as possible with the square to ensure the drill is vertical. It is also helpful if an assistant can stand back and sight along the drill and square from two sides to ensure the drill is straight.

Screwing

When screwing one piece of wood to another ensure that half of the screw penetrates through the bottom piece of wood. Its thickness should not exceed one-tenth of the width of the wood into which it has to be inserted. Keep screws at a distance of five times their shank diameter from the side edge of the wood, and ten times the shank diameter from its end.

Nailing

The correct length of nail to use is two-and-a-half to three times the thickness of the timber being fixed. However, check that the nail will not

1 Chiselling a Groove
After making saw cuts at side, chisel out waste from each side. Finally pare base flat.

2 Drilling Vertical Holes
With a drill stand, not only will the drill bit be held vertical, but depth is controlled.

3 Freehand Drilling Guide
When drilling it can be helpful to stand a try square alongside the drill to ensure accuracy.

4 Drilling Depth Guide
There are various guides to control drilling depths, such as rings for drills and sticky tape.

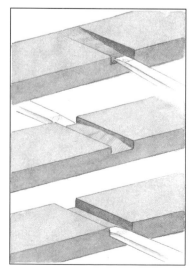

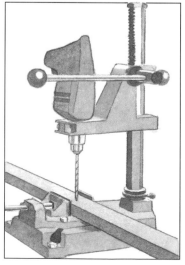

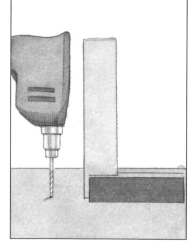

pierce right through two pieces being fixed. Wherever possible nail through the thinner piece of wood into the thicker piece.

Nails grip best if driven in at an angle ('skew nailing'). A row of nails should be driven in at opposing angles to each other. Framework joints are usually held in by skew nailing. Cramp or nail a block of wood temporarily against one side of the vertical piece to stop it sliding as the first nail is started.

To prevent wood from splitting, particularly if nailing near an edge, blunt the points of the nails by hitting them with a hammer before driving them home. Blunt nails will cut through timber fibres neatly, while pointed nails are more likely to push the fibres apart like a wedge.

FIXINGS

Solid wall The normal fixing for a solid wall is a woodscrew and plastic or fibre wallplug. Before drilling the fixing hole, check with a metal detector that there are no pipes or cables hidden below the surface. Drill the holes for the wall-

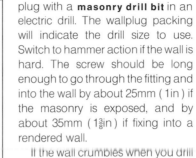

⑥ Skew Nailing for Strength
Hold the frames together in a cramp and join them by skew nailing (driving nails at an angle). The joint will not then pull apart.

plug with a **masonry drill bit** in an electric drill. The wallplug packing will indicate the drill size to use. Switch to hammer action if the wall is hard. The screw should be long enough to go through the fitting and into the wall by about 25mm (1in) if the masonry is exposed, and by about 35mm (1⅜in) if fixing into a rendered wall.

If the wall crumbles when you drill into it, mix up a cement-based plugging compound (available from DIY stores). Turn back the screw by about half a turn before the compound sets (in about five minutes). When it is hard (in about one hour) the screw is removed and a heavy fixing made.

If your drill sinks easily into the wall once it has penetrated the rendering, and a light grey dust is produced from the hole, you are fixing into lightweight building blocks. In this case, special winged wallplugs should be used.

To make a quick, light-to-medium weight fixing in a solid wall, a masonry nail can be used. Choose a length that will penetrate the

material to be fixed, and pierce an exposed masonry wall by 15mm (⅝in) or a rendered wall by about 25mm (1in). Wear goggles in case the nail snaps when you strike it; hammer it gently through the material to be fixed and into the wall.

Expanding wall bolts In rugged construction work, wall fixings are made with expanding bolts. The hole drilled in the wall must be deep enough to accept the segmented body of the bolt. Check the manufacturer's instructions for the exact diameter of the hole. The body of the bolt is placed in the hole, the bolt passed through the fixture to locate in the body, and then the nut of the bolt turned with a spanner, expanding the segmented body and causing it to grip tightly.

Fixing cladding Always fix cladding boards from the bottom upwards. Use a spirit level to check that the first board is horizontal – if it is not exactly level, the boards above will start to run out of true, making it impossible to fix them.

⑤ Drilling Holes for Screws in Timber
Drill a clearance hole in the thinner piece. Countersink this hole, then drill a pilot hole to slightly less than screw length. *Inset* To counterbore, drill to the diameter of the screw head to required depth, then as above.

⑦ Techniques for Joining Wood by Nailing
Nails should be two-and-a-half to three times the thickness of the timber being fixed. Assemble frames on bench by nailing against batten. *Inset* Blunt nail points to avoid splitting timber.

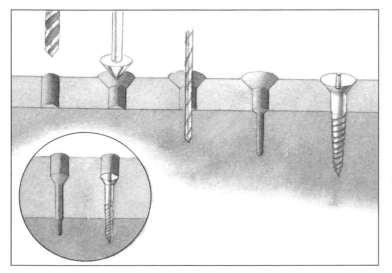

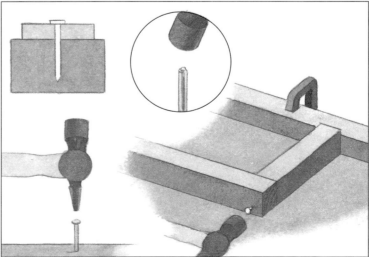

TECHNIQUES: FIXINGS AND WOOD JOINTS

Nail through the centre of the first board into each of the vertical support battens behind, using 25mm (1in) galvanized round head nails. If boards have to be joined to span the full width of the structure, then butt the edges closely and ensure that joints are always made against a vertical support batten.

If you are fixing feather-edge boards, it is important that they overlap uniformly and you will need to use a spacing block cut from a spare piece of wood. If the boards are 112mm (4½in) wide and the spacer is 100mm (4in) wide then, by aligning the spacer with the bottom edge of the previously fixed board and resting the overlapping board on top, you will get a consistent overlap of 12mm (½in). Nail through the lower edge of each board, into the top edge of the board it overlaps and through into the batten.

Tongued-and-grooved boards are fixed by driving the nail at an angle through the tongue and tapping the head below the surface. The groove of the next board slides over the tongue to conceal the nail.

Shiplap cladding is fixed in the same way except that the boards do not interlock, but simply overlap.

Fixing trellis Trellis should be fixed about 150mm (6in) clear of the ground so that it will not rot at the base. Stand the trellis on blocks of the correct height while it is being secured to timber uprights or a wall. Use a spirit level to check that the horizontal rails are true, then drill holes into the side uprights of the trellis through which galvanized nails are inserted and then driven into the posts behind. If you nail directly into the trellis there is a chance the wood will split. Three fixings either side of an 1800mm (72in) high trellis panel will suffice. Alternatively, use purpose-made clips screwed to support posts. The trellis panel slots into clips.

When fixing to a wall, use 25mm (1in) thick wood blocks behind each fixing point to keep the trellis clear. Pre-drill the holes and use about 75mm (3in) long No 8 or 10 zinc-plated screws and wallplugs to secure the trellis.

Fixing posts and poles On concrete paths and paving slabs laid on mortar you can use a steel base as a fixing point for posts. The base is a square plate with a projecting cup into which the post is located. The base is bolted in place.

Metal post spikes are driven into the earth. Again, the post fits into a square cup and is cramped in place. As the post is above ground it is far less susceptible to rotting at the base.

Posts and poles can be fixed directly into soil. In firm soil and where shorter posts are used, then well-compacted hardcore is usually adequate support. In loose soil and for longer posts and poles, a combination of stones and concrete should be used. For a post 1800mm (72in) high, at least 600mm (24in) should be buried below ground.

FITTING HINGES

Butt hinges These are conventional flapped hinges and are available in steel (commonly) or in brass, which is better for high-quality work. They are relatively simple to fix in

place, except that the hinge flaps have to be recessed into the timber using a chisel or router.

Mark out the hinge positions on the frame of the item to be hung, making sure that the hinges are not positioned so that the fixing screws will go into the end grain of cross members and be likely to pull out.

The length of the hinges is marked out first, using a marking knife, then the width of the hinge and the thickness of the flap are marked using a marking gauge. With a chisel held vertical, and a mallet, cut down around the waste side of the recess, then make a series of vertical cuts across the full width of the recess. Remove the waste by careful chiselling, then finally pare the bottom of the recess flat using the chisel held flat side downwards (fig 4).

If you are careful, you can remove the bulk of the waste from a hinge recess using a straight bit fitted in a router. The bit is set to cut to the depth of the recess required, and afterwards the corners can be finished off using a chisel.

WOOD JOINTS

Butt joint This is the simplest frame joint of all. The ends of the timbers to be joined must be cut square so that they butt together neatly. Corner and T joints can be formed, which are glued and nailed for strength. Corrugated fasteners can also be used to hold these joints, especially where the sides of the frames will be covered to hide the fasteners. When T joints are being formed from inside a frame, they can be skew nailed.

Halving joint Also known as a half-lap joint, these may be used to join wood of similar thickness at corners or to T or X joints. The joint is formed by cutting each piece to half its thickness. Use a **try square** to mark the width of the cut-outs and a **marking gauge** set to half the thick-

① Fixing Cladding
Above Nail tongue, then slot groove of next board over. *Below* Use spacing block for feather-edge boards.

② Fixing Posts
Left and top right Post spikes fix posts in place. *Below right* Post hole borer digs hole in which to fix post.

③ Fixing Trellis Panels
Panel clips are screwed to vertical support posts. Trellis panels slot into clips and are screwed in place.

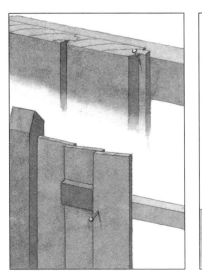

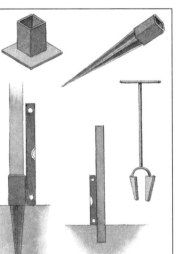

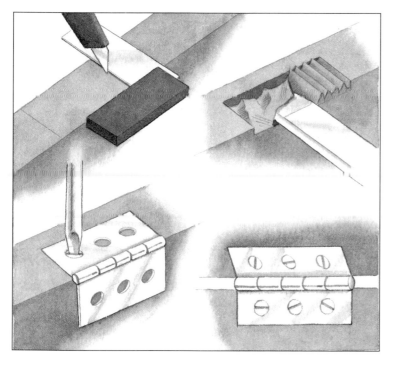

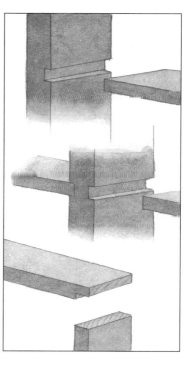

ness of the wood to mark their depth. Be sure to cross-hatch the waste wood with a pencil so that the correct side is removed. To form a corner half-lap, saw down as for making a tenon joint (*see* **page 402**). To form a 'T' or 'X' half-lap, saw down each side of the 'T' cut-out to the depth of the central gauge line, then chisel out the waste.

Housing joint Used mainly for shelving, this is basically a slot into which a shelf fits. The 'through' housing joint goes to the full width of the shelf, while a 'stopped' housing joint is taken only part of the way across the board. Chisel the waste away from each side. In the case of a stopped housing, chisel the waste from the stopped end first. If you have a router, it is easier to cut a housing joint by running the router across the board against a batten which is cramped at right angles to the board.

A rebate joint is similar to a housing joint, but positioned at the top of a piece of board; it can be cut in a similar way.

④ The Stages in Fitting a Butt Hinge
Using a try square and a trimming knife, mark out the length of hinge. With a marking gauge mark width and thickness of hinge flap. With chisel vertical, cut round outline of hinge. Make series of cuts across width of recess. Pare out the waste then check that flap lies flush. Screw the butt hinge in place.

⑤ Simple Butt Joints
Top Corner and *Below* T joints can be formed by skew nailing or by using corrugated fasteners.

⑥ Types of Halving Joints
Top A corner halving joint. *Bottom left* A T-halving joint. *Bottom right* A cross halving joint.

⑧ Types of Housing Joints
Top A through housing joint; *Middle* Through housing joints on the side of a central support; *Bottom* A corner housing joint.

⑦ Forming a Halving Joint in Timber Battens
Mark width of the cut-out. Mark half the thickness of the wood with a marking gauge. Cross hatch area to be removed. Saw down sides with a tenon saw, then chisel out the waste.

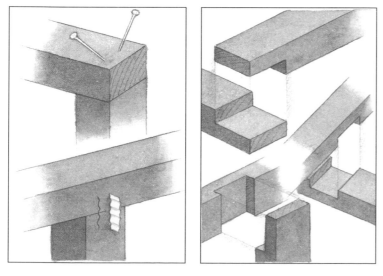

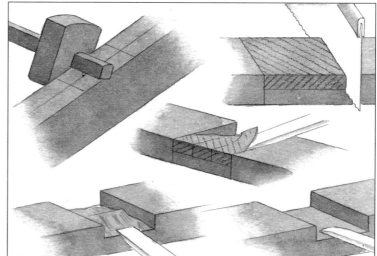

Techniques: Wood Joints

Dowel joint Dowels are a strong, simple and hidden means of joining wood together.

Use pre-cut grooved dowels with bevelled ends (*see* **Materials, page 395**). These range from 6mm ($\frac{1}{4}$in) diameter by 25mm (1in) long to 10mm ($\frac{3}{8}$in) by 50mm (2in). The dowel length should be about one-and-a-half times the thickness of the wood being jointed. When making your own dowels, their length can be twice the thickness of the wood. Cut grooves down the length of dowel to allow glue and air to escape, and chamfer the ends.

On both pieces of wood, use a marking gauge to find the centre line, and mark with a pencil. Drill the dowel holes to half the dowel length with the drill held in a **drill stand**, or aligned with a **try square** stood on end. Drill the dowel holes in one of the pieces to be joined, insert centre points in the holes, then bring the

1 Dowels to Join Panels
Right Mark dowel positions. Drill holes, insert centre points. Mark second piece.

2 Types of Dowel Joint
Dowels can join panels edge to edge and join frames at corners. They can be hidden or have ends exposed.

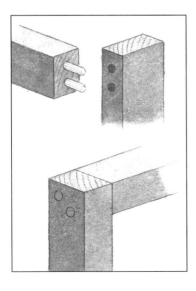

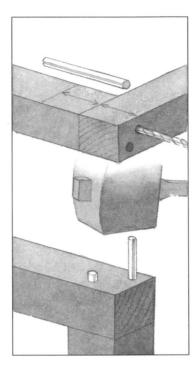

3 Making a Dowelled Frame
If edge of frame will not be seen, drill holes for dowels after making frame. Hammer dowels home; cut ends flush after glue dries.

4 Using a Dowelling Jig
If dowels are to be hidden, a dowelling jig makes it easy to drill holes that align in both pieces.

two pieces of the joint together so they are carefully aligned. The centre points will make marks in the second piece of wood where the dowel holes should be drilled. Drill the holes to half of the length of the dowels, plus a little extra for glue. Where dowels are used for location rather than strength, set the dowels three-quarters into one edge and a quarter into the other.

Put adhesive in the hole and tap dowels into the holes in the first piece with a mallet. Apply adhesive to both parts of the joint; bring the pieces together and cramp them in position until the adhesive has set.

Using a dowelling jig A dowelling jig enables accurate dowel holes to be drilled. It is cramped over the workpiece above the pre-marked hole centres. A bush of the same diameter as the drill bit is selected and fitted on the jig. The bush holds the drill vertically as the hole is made. A depth gauge ensures that the hole is the required depth. The jig is then set up on the mating piece of wood and the process repeated.

Mitre joint A simple mitre joint is glued and pinned; a stronger one is made using dowels, or by sawing oblique cuts into which wood veneers are glued. Cut the joints at 45° using a mitre box as a guide.

Mortise and tenon joint A mortise and tenon joint can be marked out with a mortise gauge. Mark out the tenon (the tongue) so that it is one-third of the thickness of the piece of wood. The mortise (the slot) is marked at the same width in the other piece. The length of the mortise should match the width of the tenon being fitted. Drill out most of the waste with a series of holes using a bit slightly smaller than the mortise width. Working from the centre, chop out the mortise with a chisel to the depth required. If making a through joint (in which the end of the tenon is visible), turn the wood over and finish chiselling out the mortise from the other side.

Hold the tenon piece upright, but sloping away from yourself, secure in a vice, and use a tenon saw carefully to cut down to the shoulder. Then swivel the wood around to point the other way, and saw down to the other side of the shoulder. Next, position the wood vertically and cut down to the shoulder. Finally, place the wood flat and saw across the shoulder to remove the waste. Repeat for the waste on the other side of the tongue. Check that the two pieces fit well before gluing and assembling the joint. For added strength, cut small additional shoulders at each end of the tenon.

Bare-faced mortise and tenon joint If the tongue of a tenon joint is offset to one side, this produces a bare-faced tenon as shown (fig 8). This produces a strong joint where narrow rails meet thicker frame rails.

A bare-faced tenon is cut in the same way as a halving joint.

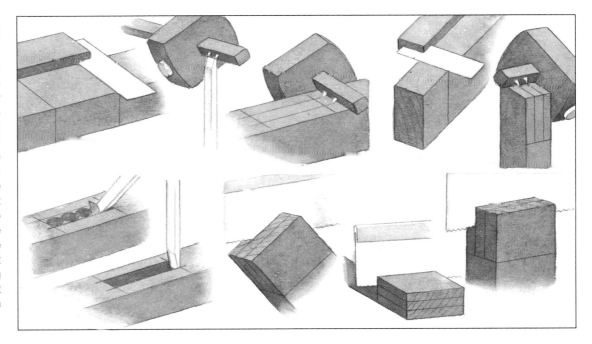

6 **Marking and Cutting a Mortise and Tenon Joint**
Mark the length of the mortise slot to match the size of the rail being joined. Set the mortise gauge to the width of the chisel being used to cut out the mortise slot. (Chisel should be about one-third the width of wood being joined.) Use the mortise gauge to mark the mortise, and also the tenon, on the rail. Drill out the mortise and complete the cut with a chisel. Use a tenon saw to cut out the tenon.

5 **Cutting Mitre Joints**
Mitres make right-angled joints. Use a mitre box to ensure a 45° angle and cut joint with a tenon saw.

7 **Mortise and Tenon Joints**
Top A common or stopped mortise and tenon joint. *Below* Through mortise and tenon joint.

8 **Making a Bare-Faced Mortise and Tenon Joint**
Tenon is offset to one side. Mark and cut as shown here.

9 **Shouldered Tenon Joint**
For enhanced strength, saw down small additional shoulders at each end of the tenon.

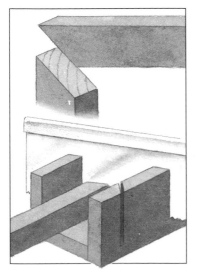

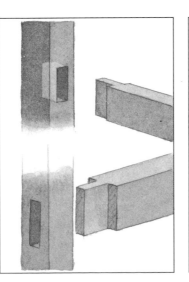

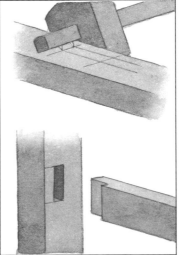

TECHNIQUES: BRICKLAYING

TOOLS

Bolster chisel and club hammer For cutting bricks.

Buckets You will need two of the same size, one for measuring mortar ingredients, the other for cement.

Builder's square Three battens in the proportions 3:4:5 nailed to form a right-angled triangle. Used to check that each course is vertical.

Gauge rod This is a 25 × 25mm (1 × 1in) batten marked off in 75mm (3in) increments. It is used to check that courses of bricks are vertical. It should be slightly longer than the intended wall height.

Laying trowel Used to spread mortar on bricks.

Mortar board For holding small amounts of mortar.

Pointing trowel Small trowel for shaping mortar joints.

Profile board Made from a piece of scrap wood about 500mm (20in) long, nailed across two battens which are driven into the ground. You will need two – one for either end of the wall. The top of each board is notched at appropriate intervals to represent the edges of the foundation strips and the wall. The notches then hold the string line taut for accurate bricklaying.

Shovels You will need two of these, one for mixing and one for lifting cement from its bag.

Spirit level For checking brickwork horizontally and vertically.

String line Needed as a guide to laying the brick courses horizontally.

Watering can For adding water to the mortar mix.

MATERIALS

Bricks Bricks are made to a uniform size of 215 × 102.5 × 65mm ($8\frac{5}{8} \times 4\frac{1}{8} \times 2\frac{5}{8}$in). Since allowance has to be made for 10mm ($\frac{3}{8}$in) thick horizontal and vertical mortar joints, they are regarded as being 225 × 112.5 × 75mm ($9 \times 4\frac{1}{2} \times 3$in).

Bricks come in many colours and textures, and it is important to choose a type that will harmonize with your garden and house. Second-hand bricks are popular for garden projects since they blend well with any environment. Builders' merchants stock a selection of bricks; local demolition sites or architectural salvage yards are good hunting grounds for second-hand bricks.

Mortar This is needed to bond the bricks together. It is made by mixing cement, soft builders' sand, and lime or plasticizer in the proportions of 1:5:1 with water. Bags of ready-mixed mortar are available, but they are really only economical for very small jobs such as repair work.

Ordinary Portland cement (sold in 50kg [110lb] bags) is usually used although white Portland cement is available if you want pale joints to match pale bricks.

Builders' sand is sold by the cubic metre (yard). Most builders' merchants will sell smaller quantities in bags – larger quantities are tipped from a lorry into a loose pile.

Lime is sold in bags, liquid plasticizer in containers.

When calculating how much to buy, a good rule of thumb is to allow one bag of cement and 0.2 cubic metres (yards) of damp sand for every 400 bricks.

Should you need to store cement before use, then keep it under cover and raised off the ground. A pile of sand will attract children and animals so cover this, too.

Mix mortar on a clean surface. In hot weather, only mix as much as you can use in an hour, since the mortar will start to stiffen. Never try to reactivate mortar by adding more water: it will crack up. On a hot day, it is worth dipping each brick in water before laying it.

First, mix the dry ingredients until the pile is a uniform grey colour. Make a crater in the top and pour in some water, then turn the pile over continuously, adding a little more water from time to time until the mix is buttery. A good test for the right consistency is to chop the mixing shovel through the pile until the ridges remain intact.

TECHNIQUES

Laying foundations Unless the brickwork is built on a firm base it will soon start to subside. Judging foundations is a matter of common sense, although always err on the side of caution if in any doubt.

Whereas a low brick planter or barbecue can be built on a sound existing patio or drive, more ambitious projects require tailor-made solid concrete foundations. For a garden wall up to 1000mm (39in) high (two brick thickness), dig a trench 500mm (20in) wide and deep, and lay a levelled bed of concrete in the trench to a depth of 230mm (9in). For a single brick thickness wall, you will need to dig a

1 Single Brick Foundation
Dig trench and lay concrete bed as indicated. Lay bricks and backfill with soil once mortar has hardened.

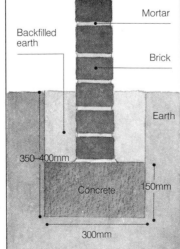

2 Laying First Two Bricks
Lay first brick using profile board as guide. Lay second brick 1500mm (60in) away; check it is level with first.

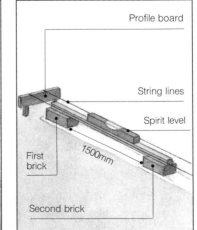

3 Laying the Second Course
Begin with a half brick to stagger courses, then continue along. Always check bricks are vertical and level.

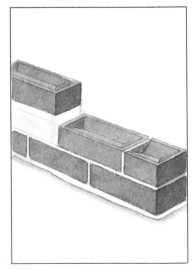

trench 300mm (12in) wide and 350–400mm (14–16in) deep, and lay a 150mm (6in) deep bed of concrete in the trench.

The concrete mix should be one part cement to four parts of ballast. Allow it to harden for four days and keep it covered with polythene in wet weather. In hot weather, cover the concrete with damp sacking, spraying it occasionally with water.

Cutting bricks To cut a brick, score a continuous line around all four faces using a bolster chisel and a club hammer. Place the brick on a pile of sand, put the blade of the chisel in the groove and tap sharply with the hammer for a clean cut.

Brickwork bonds For stability, a wall must be built in a definite bond formation such as one of the examples illustrated (fig 7). Stretcher and open bond formations are suitable for single brick thickness walls up to a height of 1000mm (39in). Piers (support columns), as indicated (fig 5), are essential at both ends and at 1800mm (72in) centres.

A double brick thickness wall requires bricks to be cut near the corners to ensure that the vertical joints are staggered.

Laying bricks Set up string lines at either side of the foundation trench as a guide to laying the first course of bricks. Make profile boards from pieces of scrap wood notched as appropriate for a single or double brick wall – the notches trap the string, pulling it taut.

Spread a layer of mortar about 1500mm (60in) long and lay the first brick in place with the indentation facing upwards. Lay a second brick 1500mm (60in) or so away. Place a spirit level on a straight-edge piece of wood spanning the two bricks and tap the higher brick down using the trowel handle until both are level.

Mortar should always be a little thicker than 10mm ($\frac{3}{8}$in) since the bricks will compress it slightly.

As each brick is laid, spread a 10mm ($\frac{3}{8}$in) layer of mortar on the end to form a vertical joint between it and the preceding brick. Use the spirit level and trowel to level each

brick. Complete the first course.

Cut a brick in half to start the second course. Build up the ends of the wall as shown (fig 4), so that you are always working three or four courses above the course being filled. The course being completed must be laid to a taut string line which should be anchored into the course above using bradpoint nails.

Check continually with the gauge rod that the courses are accurate. Also check the face of the brickwork to ensure it is plumb.

The top course of bricks (the coping course) protects the wall from the weather. On a single brick wall, stand half bricks on edge. Whole bricks on edge complete a double thickness wall.

Joint finishes It is best to finish the joints as each course of bricks is completed. The simplest joints to make are flush joints, made by scraping away excess mortar using the edge of a trowel.

Rounded joints are more decorative and are made by drawing a steel rod through the mortar.

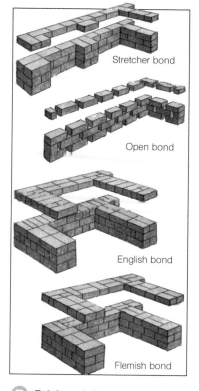

Stretcher bond

Open bond

English bond

Flemish bond

⑦ Brickwork Bonds
Each course must be laid to stagger with the course above and below. Four popular bonds are shown here.

④ Laying Additional Courses
Build up the ends of the wall first, then fill in the intervening bricks, completing one course at a time.

⑤ Forming Piers
For long walls, stagger the brick formations as shown to form piers at 1800mm (72in) centres.

⑥ Forming the Ends
Use a combination of half bricks and whole bricks to form the bonding necessary at either end of the wall.

⑧ Cutting a Brick
Score line around faces of brick. Lay it on bed of sand, insert chisel in groove, tap sharply with hammer.

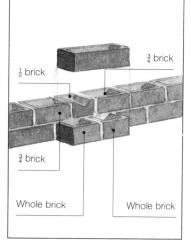
$\frac{1}{2}$ brick
$\frac{3}{4}$ brick
$\frac{3}{4}$ brick
Whole brick
Whole brick

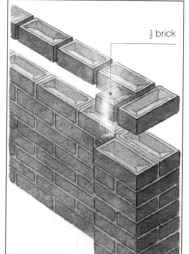
$\frac{1}{2}$ brick

INDEX

INDEX

Acknowledgments

The publisher thanks the following photographers and organizations for their kind permission to reproduce the photographs in this book:

10 left Camera Press; **10** right Michael Freeman; **11** (c) Jon Jensen; **48** left Camera Press; **48** centre Richard Bryant/Arcaid; **48** right Ken Kirkwood; **49** Simon Brown/Conran Octopus; **50** Karen Bussolini (House Beautiful Specials); **51** Aldo Ballo; **52** left Jean-Pierre Godeaut; **52** right Fritz von der Schulenburg; **53** left La Maison de Marie Claire (Sarramon/Forgeur); **53** right Pascal Chevalier/ Agence Top; **54** above Neil Lorimer/Elizabeth Whiting & Associates; **54** below left Rodney Hyett/Elizabeth Whiting & Associates; **54** below right Tim Street-Porter/ Elizabeth Whiting & Associates; **55** above Tim Street-Porter/Elizabeth Whiting & Associates; **55** below left Elizabeth Whiting & Associates; **55** below centre Lars Hallen; **55** below right Jean-Pierre Godeaut; **56–57** Jean-Paul Bonhommet; **58** above Richard Bryant/Arcaid; **58** below Tim Street-Porter/Elizabeth Whiting & Associates; **59** left Tim Street-Porter/Elizabeth Whiting & Associates; **59** right Jean-Pierre Godeaut (designer Lydia Kumel); **60** left Simon Brown/Conran Octopus; **60** right Rodney Hyett/Elizabeth Whiting & Associates; **61** Rodney Hyett/Elizabeth Whiting & Associates; **62** above designer Rudiger Mahlau (photographer Michael Scheffler); **62** below Jean-Pierre Godeaut (designer Geneviève Lethy); **63** Lars Hallen; **64** Rodney Hyett/Elizabeth Whiting & Associates; **65** Tim Street-Porter/Elizabeth Whiting & Associates; **66** above Neil Lorimer/Elizabeth Whiting & Associates; **66** below La Maison de Marie Claire (Sarramon/Forgeur); **67** Dennis Krukowski (designers Spottswood/Byron); **68** above Rodney Hyett/Elizabeth Whiting & Associates; **68** below left Andreas von Einsiedel/Elizabeth Whiting & Associates; **68** below right Simon Brown/Conran Octopus; **69** Tom Leighton/The World of Interiors; **70** left Garry Chowanetz/ Elizabeth Whiting & Associates; **70** right Jean-Paul Bonhommet; **71** left Vogue Living (Rodney Weidland); **71** right Rodney Hyett/Elizabeth Whiting & Associates; **72** Rodney Hyett/Elizabeth Whiting & Associates; **73** Lars Hallen; **74** left Tim Street-Porter/Elizabeth Whiting & Associates; **74** right Christian Sarramon; **75** above Richard Bryant/Arcaid; **75** below left James Merrell/Homes & Gardens/ Syndication International; **75** below centre Elizabeth Whiting & Associates; **75** below right Belle (Geoff Lung); **114** Rodney Hyett/Elizabeth Whiting & Associates; **115** Camera Press; **116** Pascal Chevalier/Agence Top; **117** Belle (Neil Lorimer); **118** left Derry Moore; **118** centre Camera Press; **118** right Maison Française (Jean-Pierre Godeaut); **119** Juliana Balint (photographer Paul Ryan); **120** above Rodney Hyett/Elizabeth Whiting & Associates; **120** below left Rodney Hyett/Elizabeth Whiting & Associates; **120** below right Jean-Paul Bonhommet; **121** above Trevor Richards/Homes & Gardens/Syndication International; **121** below left Rodney Hyett/Elizabeth Whiting & Associates; **121** below right Jean-Paul Bonhommet; **122** Derry Moore; **123** Michael Freeman; **124** above Tim Street-Porter/Elizabeth Whiting & Associates; **124** centre Ken Kirkwood; **124** below Richard Bryant/Arcaid; **125** Friedhelm Thomas/Elizabeth Whiting & Associates; **126** above Simon Brown/Conran Octopus; **126** below left Roland Beaufre/Agence Top (designer Anne Gayet); **126** below right Jean-Paul Bonhommet; **127** left Jean-Paul Bonhommet; **127** centre Jean-Paul Bonhommet; **127** right Karen Bussolini (designer Russota/Cama Design Associates); **128** above left Jean-Paul Bonhommet; **128** above right Richard Bryant/Arcaid; **128** below left David Montgomery/Conran Octopus (designer Tricia Guild); **128** below centre Jean-Paul Bonhommet; **128** below right Ken Kirkwood; **129** Pascal Hinous/Agence Top (designer Manual Canovas); **130** above Neil Lorimer/Elizabeth Whiting & Associates; **130** centre La Maison de Marie Claire (Chabaneix/Puech Postic); **130** below Jean-Paul Bonhommet; **131** above Rodney Hyett/Elizabeth Whiting & Associates; **131** centre Jean-Paul Bonhommet; **131** below Clive Frost/The World of Interiors; **132** left Belle (Geoff Lung); **132** centre Elizabeth Whiting & Associates; **132** right Michael Dunne/ Elizabeth Whiting & Associates; **133** left La Maison de Marie Claire (Hussenot); **133** centre Lars Hallen; **133** right Jon Bouchier/Elizabeth Whiting & Associates; **134** Juliana Balint (photographer Hannu Mannynoksa); **135** Simon Brown/ Conran Octopus; **136** left Jean-Pierre Godeaut; **136** centre Karen Bussolini (architect William Herman); **136** right Dennis Krukowski (designers Spottswood/Byron); **137** above Richard Bryant/Arcaid; **137** below left Vogue Living (Rodney Weidland); **137** below centre Maison Française (Luc de Champris); **137** below right Simon Brown/Conran Octopus (Elyane de la Rochette); **138** Elizabeth Whiting & Associates; **139** Jean-Paul Bonhommet; **140** left Woman Syndication International; **140** right Lars Dalsgaard; **141** left Fritz von der Schulenburg; **141** right Jerry Tubby/Elizabeth Whiting & Associates; **171** above Fritz von der Schulenburg (designer Mimmi O'Connell, paint finish by Peter Farlow); **171** below left Elizabeth Whiting & Associates; **171** below centre Dennis Krukowski (James Franklin Mitchell); **171** below right Chris Sanders; **172** Richard Bryant/Arcaid; **173** Clive Frost/Homes & Gardens/Syndication International; **174** Rodney Hyett/Elizabeth Whiting & Associates; **175** Simon Brown/Conran Octopus; **176** left Rodney Hyett/Elizabeth Whiting & Associates; **176** centre Fritz von der Schulenburg; **176** right Fritz von der Schulenburg; **177** Friedhelm Thomas/Elizabeth Whiting & Associates; **178** Jean-Pierre Godeaut; **179** Simon Brown/Conran Octopus; **181** above Simon Brown/Conran Octopus; **181** below left Alfredo Anghinelli/Elizabeth Whiting & Associates; **181** below centre Jean-Pierre Godeaut; **181** below right Maison Française (Jean-Pierre Godeaut); **182** above Tim Street-Porter/Elizabeth Whiting & Associates; **182** centre Ken Kirkwood (designer David Pocknell); **182** below Vogue Living (Geoff Lung); **183** left Jean-Pierre Godeaut; **183** above right Andreas von Einsiedel/ Elizabeth Whiting & Associates; **183** centre right Tim Street-Porter/Elizabeth Whiting & Associates; **183** below right Rodney Hyett/Elizabeth Whiting & Associates; **184** Karen Bussolini (designer Nelson Denny); **185** Andreas von Einsiedel/Elizabeth Whiting & Associates; **186** above Richard Bryant/Arcaid; **186** below left Neil Lorimer/Elizabeth Whiting & Associates; **186** below right Rodney Hyett/Elizabeth Whiting & Associates; **187** above Rodney Hyett/Elizabeth Whiting & Associates; **187** below left Camera Press; **187** below right Rodney Hyett/Elizabeth Whiting & Associates; **188** above Lars Hallen; **188** below Michael Crockett/Elizabeth Whiting & Associates; **189** left Camera Press; **189** above right Jean-Pierre Godeaut; **189** below right Rodney Hyett/Elizabeth Whiting & Associates; **190** left Vogue Living (George Seper); **190** centre Richard Bryant/ Arcaid; **190** right Jean-Paul Bonhommet; **191** above Richard Bryant/Arcaid; **191** below left Maison Française (Jean-Pierre Godeaut); **191** below centre Tim Street-Porter/Elizabeth Whiting & Associates; **191** below right Rodney Hyett/ Elizabeth Whiting & Associates; **192** above Simon Brown/Conran Octopus; **192** centre Vogue Living (Rodney Weidland); **192** below Wulf Brackrock/designers Titterio-Dwan for Architektur & Wohnen; **193** Gabriele Basilico/Abitare; **252–253** Fritz von der Schulenburg.

Special photography by Hugh Johnson and Simon Lee for Conran Octopus.

Hugh Johnson 1, 2, 6 right, 7 left, 8–9, 39, 46, 76–83, 106–107, 142 left, 144–145, 150, 151 above, 152–163, 167, 194–197, 209, 214–215, 223–227, 232–233, 239, 242–243.

Simon Lee 6 left, 7 right, 44, 92–101, 102–104, 112–113, 142 right, 149, 151 below, 164, 203, 212, 219–221, 228–230, 240, 247, 249.

256 left Brigitte Thomas; 256 right Gary Chowanetz/Elizabeth Whiting & Associates; 257 Lamontagne; 258 left Brigitte Thomas; 258 Jerry Harpur/Conran Octopus (designer Tim Du Val); 259 left Marijke Heuff (designer K Noordhuis); 259 above right Brigitte Thomas; 259 below right Marijke Heuff (The Coach House - Little Haseley); 260 above left Lamontagne; 260 above right Ron Sutherland/Garden Picture Library (designer Rick Eckersley); 260 centre left René Stoeltie 260 Georges Lévêque; 260 below left Brigitte Thomas; 260 centre right Georges Lévêque; 260 below left Brigitte Thomas; 260 below right Arnaud Descat/Agence Bamboo; 261 above left Bent Rej; 261 above right John Glover/Garden Picture Library; 261 centre left Lamontagne; 261 centre right Lars Hallen; 261 below left Tim Street-Porter/Elizabeth Whiting & Associates; 261 below right Georges Lévêque; 262 left Gilles de Chabaneix for Terence Conran; 262 centre Lamontagne; 262 right Gary Rogers/Garden Picture Library; 263 Brigitte Thomas; 264 Marijke Heuff (designer Mien Ruys, Dedemsvaart); 265 Georges Lévêque; 266 above left Lamontagne; 266 above right Georges Lévêque; 266 centre left Ron Sutherland/Garden Picture Library; 266 centre right Gary Rogers; 266 below left Brigitte Thomas; 266 below right Ron Sutherland/Garden Picture Library; 267 above left Brigitte Thomas; 267 above right Steven Wooster/Garden Picture Library; 267 centre left Anthony Paul/Garden Picture Library; 267 centre right Lamontagne; 267 below left Lamontagne; 267 below right Ron Sutherland/Garden Picture Library; 268 above Georges Lévêque; 268 below left Belle (Geoff Lung); 268 below right Georges Lévêque; 269 above Tim Street-Porter/Elizabeth Whiting & Associates; 269 below left Bent Rej; 269 below right Rodney Hyett/Elizabeth Whiting & Associates; 291 Neil Lorimer/Elizabeth Whiting & Associates; Lars Hallen (M-L Rosenbroijer); 294 left Andrew Payne/Garden Picture Library; 294 centre René Stoeltie; 294 right Gary Rogers/Garden Picture Library; 295 Brigitte Thomas; 296 Lamontagne; 297 left Gillian Darley/Edifice; 297 right S&O Mathews; 298 left Marijke Heuff (designer K Noordhuis); 298 centre Andrew Lawson; 298 right Brigitte Thomas; 299 above Oliver Gregory; 299 below left Andrew Lawson; 299 below right Marijke Heuff (Mr & Mrs Brinkworth); 318 Boys Syndication; 322 Marijke Heuff (Mr F Tiebout and Mr F de Greeuw); 324 Marijke Heuff (Mr & Mrs Adriaanse-Quint; 326 left Brigitte Thomas; 326 centre Lamontagne; 326 right Brigitte Thomas; 327 Ron Sutherland/Garden Picture Library; 328 Nexus Designs, Melbourne, Australia; 329 above left Christian Sarramon; 329 above right Lamontagne; 329 below Georges Lévêque; 330 above Hugh Palmer; 330 below left Ron Sutherland/Garden Picture Library (designer Murray Collins); 330 below right Lamontagne; 331 above Brigitte Thomas; 331 below left Eric Crichton; 331 below right Lamontagne; 342 Lamontagne; 344 left Joanne Pavia/Garden Picture Library; 344 centre Brigitte Thomas; 344 right Brigitte Thomas; 345 Hugh Palmer; 346 above Brigitte Thomas; 346 centre Lamontagne; 346 below Georges Lévêque; 347 High Palmer; 348 above left Georges Lévêque; 348 above right Philippa Lewis/Ediface; 348 centre left Lamontagne; 348 centre right Marijke Heuff; 348 below left Lamontagne; 348 below right Houses & Interiors; 349 above left Brigitte Thomas; 349 Philippa Lewis/Ediface; 349 centre right Gary Chowanetz/Elizabeth Whiting & Associates; 349 below left Ron Sutherland/Garden Picture Library; 349 below right Gary Chowanetz/Elizabeth Whiting & Associates; 350 left Hugh Palmer; 350 right Georges Lévêque; 351 above Brigitte Thomas; 351 below Gilles de Chabaneix for Terence Conran; 372 left Lamontagne; 372 centre Georges Lévêque; 372 right Lamontagne; 373 Georges Lévêque; 374 left Jerry Harpur/Elizabeth Whiting & Associates; 374 right Gary Rogers/Garden Picture Library; 375 Brigitte Thomas; 376 Jerry Harpur/Elizabeth Whiting Associates (designed by Clifton Nurseries); 377 above Eric Crichton; 377 below left S & O Mathews; 377 below right Georges Lévêque.

Special photography by Hugh Johnson, Simon Lee and Nadia Mackenzie for Conran Octopus.

Hugh Johnson: 1, 2, 6 right, 7 left, 8–9, 39, 46, 76–83, 106–107, 142 left, 144–145, 150, 151 above, 152–163, 167, 194–197, 209, 214–215, 223–227, 232–233, 239, 242–243

Simon Lee: 6 left, 7 right, 7 left, 8–9, 39, 46, 76–83, 106–107, 142 left, 144–145, 150, 151 above, 152–163, 167, 194–197, 209, 214–215, 223–227, 232–233, 239, 242–243

Nadia Mackenzie: 271–287, 301–317, 333–340, 354–69, 379–387.

PUBLISHER'S ACKNOWLEDGMENTS
The publishers would like to thank the following for their invaluable assistance in producing this book:

Jonathan Chidsey, Lady Caroline Conran, The Conran Studios, Julie Drake, Mike Goulding, Vana Hagarty, Gordon Hurden, Gareth Jones, Sian Jones, Wendy Jones, Harold Lee, Malcolm and Steve and all at Benchmark Woodworking Limited, Alan Rayner and the staff at Servis Filmsetting Ltd, Hickson Timber Products Ltd, Bridget Bodoano and the Conran Shop, the Administrator of Castle Drogo, Tabby Riley and Alex Willcock.

The projects in this book were specially built by SEAN SUTCLIFFE of Benchmark Woodworking Limited.

Special thanks to SIR TERENCE CONRAN for original project sketches and to PAUL BRYANT for his superb original illustrations.

The designs for the projects on pages 270-277,278-285,286-289,300-317,332-335,336-341,352-357,358-363,364-367,368-371,378-385, and 386-389 are copyright © Sir Terence Conran and may be built for personal use only.

The publisher would like to thank the following companies for supplying material for photography:

78 Franke (UK) Ltd. The Conran Shop, David Mellor Design Ltd, Divertimenti, Philips Major Appliances Ltd, The Kitchen Range, Neff (UK) Ltd, Stephen Long Antiques, W H Newson & Sons Ltd; **80** Aston-Matthews Ltd, W H Newson & Sons Ltd, David Mellor Ltd, Heal & Sons Ltd; **83** The Conran Shop, Neff (UK) Ltd; **106** The Conran Shop; **144** The Conran Shop; **159** Authentics, INC Office Equipment, The Conran Shop; **167** General Plumbing Supplies; **196** The Conran Shop, Ideal Standard Ltd, C P Hart Ltd; **209** London Architectural Salvage Company, The Conran Shop, Ideal Standard Ltd; **214** Paul Jones, Eximious Ltd, Sam Walker; **242** Gallery of Antique Costume and Textiles.